Engaging Bioethics

Engaging Bioethics: An Introduction with Case Studies draws students into this rapidly changing field, helping them to actively untangle the many issues at the intersection of medicine and moral concern. Presuming readers start with no background in philosophy, it offers balanced, philosophically based, and rigorous inquiry for undergraduates throughout the humanities and social sciences as well as for health care professionals-in-training, including students in medical school, pre-medicine, nursing, public health, and those studying to assist physicians in various capacities. Written by an author team with more than three decades of combined experience teaching bioethics, this book offers

- Flexibility to the instructor, with chapters that can be read independently and in an order that fits the course structure
- Up-to-date coverage of current controversies on topics such as vaccination, access to health care, new reproductive technologies, genetics, biomedical research on human and animal subjects, medically assisted death, abortion, medical confidentiality, and disclosure
- Attention to issues of gender, race, cultural diversity, and justice in health care
- Integration with case studies and primary sources
- Pedagogical features to help instructors and students, including
  - Chapter learning objectives
  - Text boxes and figures to explain important terms, concepts, and cases
  - End-of-chapter summaries, key words, and annotated further readings
  - Discussion cases and questions
  - Appendices on moral reasoning and the history of ethical issues at the end and beginning of life
  - An index of cases discussed in the book and extensive glossary/index
- A companion website (www.routledge.com/cw/seay) with a virtual anthology linking to key primary sources, a test bank, topics for papers, and PowerPoints for lectures and class discussion.

Gary Seay is professor of philosophy at Medgar Evers College of the City University of New York.

Susana Nuccetelli is professor of philosophy at St. Cloud State University in Minnesota.

Praise for this edition

"Seay and Nuccetelli have done an admirable job of distilling and making accessible a large body of medical information, complex case law, and philosophical ethics. Their text makes the project of developing competence and understanding in bioethics a lot less daunting, without simplifying the philosophical and scientific issues. The book is organized so that instructors can easily design a course around a subset of the topics covered, and its teaching and learning resources are outstanding. This is the best bioethics textbook I am aware of, for students and teachers alike."

Brandon Cooke, *Professor and Chair (Philosophy),*
Minnesota State University, Mankato

"This is a concise introduction to bioethics that covers a lot of ground. The chapters are sufficiently self-contained so that the text can be adapted to different course designs, and the boxes and figures throughout are helpful learning aids. Important cases are discussed but don't dominate the discussion, so the emphasis remains on the philosophical arguments and issues."

William A. Bauer, *Teaching Assistant Professor,*
North Carolina State University

"Seay and Nuccetelli offer a refreshing and bold approach to bioethics that confronts readers directly, requiring them to wrestle intimately with the most pressing issues through numerous case studies and a nuanced analysis of the core concepts and principles. The authors strike a delicate balance between accessibility and depth, with the results being a text that is eminently readable. This is not easy material, but the authors have created a text open to readers with little or no philosophical background without sacrificing the complexity found in these important discussions. They also offer an expansive and up-to-date sourcebook to find primary sources online in the companion website."

Scott O'Leary, *Assistant Professor, University of Saint Mary*

Engaging Bioethics

An Introduction with Case Studies

Gary Seay and Susana Nuccetelli

Routledge
Taylor & Francis Group

NEW YORK AND LONDON

First published 2017
by Routledge
711 Third Avenue, New York, NY 10017

and by Routledge
2 Park Square, Milton Park, Abingdon, Oxon OX14 4RN

Routledge is an imprint of the Taylor & Francis Group, an informa business

© 2017 Taylor & Francis

The right of Gary Seay and Susana Nuccetelli to be identified as the authors of this work has been asserted by them in accordance with sections 77 and 78 of the Copyright, Designs and Patents Act 1988.

All rights reserved. No part of this book may be reprinted or reproduced or utilized in any form or by any electronic, mechanical, or other means, now known or hereafter invented, including photocopying and recording, or in any information storage or retrieval system, without permission in writing from the publishers.

Trademark notice: Product or corporate names may be trademarks or registered trademarks, and are used only for identification and explanation without intent to infringe.

Library of Congress Cataloging-in-Publication Data
Names: Seay, Gary, author. | Nuccetelli, Susana, author.
Title: Engaging bioethics : an introduction with case studies / by Gary Seay and Susana Nuccetelli.
Description: New York, NY : Routledge, 2017. | Includes bibliographical references and index.
Identifiers: LCCN 2016028430 | ISBN 9780415837958 (pbk : alk. paper) | ISBN 9780415837941
   (hbk : alk. paper) | ISBN 9780203788707 (ebk)
Subjects: LCSH: Medical ethics. | Medical ethics—Case studies.
Classification: LCC R724 .S397 2017 | DDC 174.2—dc23
LC record available at https://lccn.loc.gov/2016028430

ISBN: 9780415837941 (hbk)
ISBN: 9780415837958 (pbk)
ISBN: 9780203788707 (ebk)

Typeset in Minion Pro
by Apex CoVantage, LLC

MIX
Paper from
responsible sources
FSC® C013985
www.fsc.org

Printed in the United Kingdom
by Henry Ling Limited

Contents

Detailed Contents

About the Authors

Gary Seay is professor of philosophy at Medgar Evers College of the City University of New York. With Susana Nuccetelli, he is co-editor of *Ethical Naturalism: Current Debates* (Cambridge University Press, 2012) and *Themes from G. E. Moore: New Essays in Epistemology and Ethics* (Oxford University Press, 2007). He has served on the American Philosophical Association's Committee on Philosophy and Medicine and was consulting bioethicist on the Ethics Committee of the New York Hospital Medical Center of Queens.

Susana Nuccetelli is professor of philosophy at St. Cloud State University in Minnesota. Her articles in ethics, philosophy of language, and Latin American philosophy have appeared in many edited volumes and journals. She is the author of *Latin American Thought: Philosophical Problems and Arguments* (Westview Press, 2002). With Gary Seay, she is the author of *How to Think Logically* (2e, Pearson, 2012).

Preface

Our view in writing this book represents a departure from the prevailing wisdom about how bioethics should be taught. For most of the subject's brief history, questions about pedagogy have been mostly cast in terms of two governing assumptions: first, that it is chiefly medical school students in training to be physicians, along with some undergraduate 'pre-med' majors, who take courses in bioethics, and, second, that the best way for these students to understand the central issues of the discipline is through using an anthology of original sources. But neither of these assumptions any longer applies. Students enrolled in bioethics today are as likely to be undergraduates in nursing programs or training to be physician-assistants, or physical therapists, as med school students. And there are better ways to teach these diverse kinds of students than to throw at them a massive, often expensive, collection of primary sources, culled from various journals in medicine, philosophy, and law. This textbook borrows what's best of the traditional approach—using case studies and providing references for original sources online—and combines it with a clear, student-friendly introduction to the complex subjects and arguments, including the major moral controversies of 21st-century medicine. The book should therefore be valuable to students with different backgrounds and who are approaching the ethics of medicine from numerous angles. There are, of course, already other bioethics textbooks, but, we think, none that cover so thoroughly and lucidly the major moral controversies of contemporary bioethics as this book does.

Engaging Bioethics offers flexibility to the instructor. It can be used as either a stand-alone textbook or in combination with one of the major anthologies, as its eighteen chapters, grouped in six parts, unfold in a way that allows instructors to supplement each topic with readings of original sources. A "virtual anthology" on the companion website links to key original sources, further allowing for seamless integration of primary sources. At the same time, chapters are generally self-contained units, and the topics are presented in a way that permits instructors to assign them in different sequences according to their needs. For example, instructors wishing to spend less time on theoretical issues could skip Chapters 1 and 2, and fill in the gaps on moral theory and methodology as the course unfolds. Instructors who want to devote more time to moral reasoning may assign Appendix A, while those wishing to cover some of the history of end- and beginning-of-life issues may assign Appendix B. Throughout, we have aimed at even-handedness in reconstructing facts and arguments, leaving alternative evaluations for further discussion in the classroom.

Intended for students of introductory courses in bioethics or biomedical ethics, this book assumes no background in those subjects, or in moral philosophy. We've tried to make the writing style simple and direct, with jargon kept to a minimum. Scattered throughout are special-emphasis boxes and figures in which important points are summarized to help students focus on crucial distinctions and fundamental ideas. Each chapter opens with a set of learning objectives to frame the chapter's goals and a case study to get students immediately engaged. At the end of each chapter are summaries, key words (bolded throughout on first use, and defined in a glossary at the end of the book), brief annotated lists of suggested readings, and some questions and cases for further consideration. Among these, in each chapter, is a case raising a cultural, racial, or gender issue in medicine, always listed at the end for easy reference. Pedagogical aids at the back of the book include an index of all cases, a list of major abbreviations, additional bibliographical references, and a glossary. More tools can be found at the book's companion website, with open-access resources for students and password-protected instructor's resources. Instructor's resources include a test bank of multiple-choice questions with answers, topics for papers, and PowerPoint presentations. For students and instructors alike, we have created a unique **virtual anthology**, listing original sources that are available electronically through most university libraries' subscriptions to databases. This feature includes links to most of the Suggested Readings found at the end of each chapter (marked with an asterisk in the chapter and online), as well as additional links selected from a variety of sources, including professional associations, news items, legislation, blogs, interviews, podcasts, and videos relevant to the chapter topics. Wherever possible, links are provided via multiple sources, with stable URLs and/or DOIs. This unique approach allows instructors to teach from a textbook while also supplementing with original sources without the burden of an expensive print anthology, whether they assign additional readings or use them for research papers or homework assignments.

Finally, two notes about terminology are in order. One concerns the absence of a universally accepted collective noun for all members of the medical team. For brevity, when possible we have used 'health care provider' with this comprehensive sense. The other issue concerns our eclectic way to avoid sexist language throughout. Rather than always including all pronouns (e.g., he/her, his or hers), which can become messy to read, we simply tried to balance our use of masculine and feminine pronouns or use 'they/their.'

We wish to acknowledge some contributions that have made this a much better textbook, especially those of our very patient and unfailingly helpful editors at Routledge, Andrew Beck and Alison Daltroy. Special thanks are due also to Natasha Meed and Josiah Enninga for their technical assistance and to anonymous reviewers who provided insightful guidance. There are several persons to whom we owe thanks for comments and assistance with details that helped to shape our views on various topics: Stefan Baumrin, Tony Cunningham, Jordan Curnutt, Rosamond Rhodes, Alan Seay, and Mark Timmons. Our thanks go also to our students at Medgar Evers College of the City University of New York and at St. Cloud State University, on whom we tried earlier drafts of the chapters.

Abbreviations

AMA	American Medical Association
ANH	Artificial Nutrition and Hydration
AWA	Animal Welfare Act
D&X	Intact Dilation and Extraction
DCD	Donation after Cardiac Death
FLOA	Future-Like-Ours Argument
EoL	End-of-life Measure
ER	Emergency Room
FDA	Food and Drug Administration
GP	Groningen Protocol
GSA	Good Samaritan Argument
HGP	Human Genome Project
ICU	Intensive Care Unit
QALY	Quality-Adjusted Life Years
IRB	Institutional Review Board
IVF	In-Vitro Fertilization
LST	Life-Sustaining Treatment
NICU	Neonatal Intensive Care Unit
NRT	New Reproductive Technology
PAD	Physician-Assisted Dying
PAS	Physician-Assisted Suicide
PGD	Preimplantation Genetic Diagnosis
PPACA	Patient Protection and Affordable Care Act
PVS	Permanent Vegetative State
RCT	Randomized Clinical Trials
SSA	Sex-Selective Abortion
SSS	Sliding-Scale Standard
STD	Sexually Transmitted Disease
UDD	Unified Determination of Death Act
HRC	Human Reproductive Cloning
VAE	Voluntary Active Euthanasia
VLBW	Very Low Birthweight
WHO	World Health Organization

PART I

Bioethics and Moral Theory

1 The Study of Morality

Learning Objectives

In reading this chapter you will

▶   Identify the historical roots of contemporary bioethics in the development of Western medicine and its professional ethics.

▶   Recognize descriptive and normative senses of morality.

▶   Distinguish philosophical studies of morality from those of the sciences.

▶   Place bioethics in the landscape of ethics.

THIS CHAPTER INTRODUCES **bioethics** as a practice and an area of ethics of interest to several disciplines. It does so by first looking at an early landmark case where protecting public health infringed on an individual liberty to refuse vaccination. Until the 1970s, such conflicts were resolved by appeal to accepted practice and professional codes. After briefly reviewing the history of these, the chapter looks closely at bioethics today, outlining its main branches and relations to other areas of ethics.

1.1 Rev. Jacobson's Refusal of Vaccination

The advantages of vaccination policies to prevent outbreaks of infectious disease are now widely acknowledged. Yet vaccination has not always been smooth sledding. In 1758 the American Calvinist theologian Jonathan Edwards died of a smallpox inoculation shortly after his inauguration as president of what is today Princeton University. Such casualties were not uncommon when vaccinations were first introduced. The eventual eradication of smallpox and the significant progress that has been made in reducing the threat of other serious diseases, such as polio and measles, are however among the global, public-health successes of vaccination. In the US, the moral and legal grounds of vaccination mandates by the state came to be questioned most forcefully when a smallpox epidemic spread through the Northeast in 1901, causing 773 documented cases and 97 deaths. The following year Cambridge, Massachusetts reported 2,314 infected individuals, of whom 284 died. Citing an existing statute, the city's board of health decided to enforce vaccination against smallpox for all residents, and stipulated a five-dollar fine for those who failed to comply. Among the delinquents was the Reverend Henning Jacobson, who refused the vaccine for himself and his son. He had a previous adverse reaction to it and, more important, thought the ordinance violated his right to care for his own body in the way he thought best.

The city responded by requesting payment of the fine, which prompted Jacobson to initiate legal action. The court decided that, under the police power of the state, the city's ordinance did not violate any liberty rights guaranteed by the Fourteenth Amendment. Jacobson then appealed to the US Supreme Court, which in 1905 found for the state, emphasizing the Commonwealth's power to enact and enforce laws aimed at protecting the public from communicable diseases.

■ ■ ■

This was the first ruling by the US Supreme Court concerning the scope of state power in public health law. More than a century later, vaccination continues to present moral and legal challenges worldwide. In 2009, 5-year-old *Edgar Hernandez*, soon to be known as 'patient zero', returned from school one day with symptoms consistent with 'swine flu' (the H1N1-virus infection). The virus was not to remain in his remote Mexican village. A month later, it afflicted some 1,000 individuals in all parts of the United States. By June, there were 18,000 reported cases. Five months later, the Food and Drug Administration approved the use of H1N1 vaccines, and roughly 61 million Americans were vaccinated within the first three months. Faced with a short supply of the new vaccine, the State of New York's Department of Public Health sought to protect hospital patients, who generally have greater vulnerability to infectious disease, by imposing vaccination mandates for health care providers. It considered the mandate justified by precedent from state court rulings in previous cases of mandatory rubella vaccination and annual tuberculosis testing of health care providers. *The New York Times* reported that three nurses obtained the mandate's suspension by questioning the vaccine's proven effectiveness.[1]

They thus won a legal battle but not the moral war. For as health care providers, they faced a moral conflict: on the one hand, they had the duty to promote their patients' health; on the other, the exercise of that duty interfered with their individual liberty interest to refuse vaccination or any other medical treatment. In *Jacobson v Massachusetts*, the Supreme Court emphasized that many liberty interests must be limited in pursuit of the common good because "a community has the right to protect itself against an epidemic of disease which threatens the safety of its members."

Controversies over vaccination mandates may result from differing beliefs about the facts, the law, religion, or morality. Rev. Jacobson questioned the facts—namely, whether

- Unvaccinated individuals put the public at an increased risk of contracting smallpox.
- The state had the power to enforce vaccination ordinances.
- The epidemic would spread according to natural, rather than, Divine plans.

But his deepest disagreement with the court concerned the right thing to do, from the moral perspective, when protecting public health infringes on a person's liberties. Questions of this

---

1 Anenoma Hartocollis and Sewell Chan, "Albany Judge Blocks Vaccination Rule," *New York Times*, 10/17/2009.

sort pertain to bioethics, a practice and a field of academic inquiry with roots in the development of Western medicine and the professional codes of health providers.

IMAGE 1.1
©iStockPhoto/Steve Debenport

▊ 1.2 The Evolution of Bioethics from Professional Ethics

The Hippocratic Tradition

The patient's right to refuse medical treatment, including vaccination, was generally ignored until the rise of contemporary bioethics in the 1960s and 1970s. But long before that there were concerns in medicine about other matters of moral right and wrong, especially in connection with patient welfare. From the very beginnings of Western medicine in 5th-century Greece, physicians sought to regulate their practice by moral rules. Those who embraced the teachings of Hippocrates of Kos (ca. 460–370 BCE) hoped their rules would be adopted by other physicians. In this way, persons of defective character—including quacks and dishonest schemers of all kinds—might find the calling of medicine too morally rigorous for their taste and be driven away. The rules of **Hippocratic medicine** became background assumptions that persisted through more than 20 centuries until the rise of contemporary bioethics. They chiefly concern *duties* and *decorum*. Among other things, Hippocratic doctors pledged to avoid harming their patients, to keep confidential the things revealed to them in the course of treatment, and to ask as a fee no more than what the patient could reasonably afford to pay. But they were also expected to cultivate certain traits of character or virtues. Physicians should have a demeanor of seriousness, scholarliness, dignity, and reserve. They were to be scrupulously honest and polite with their patients, striving always to bring credit to their profession and to put the patient at ease. In addition, they were to regard the practice of medicine as a 'holy' calling, and hold their mentors in great reverence.

It is striking how many of these ideals persist even today in the mystique of medicine that undoubtedly contributes to its high social status. And although some Hippocratic duties such as what appears to be a strict prohibition of both abortion and euthanasia are controversial today, others continue to carry weight in contemporary bioethics. These include that patients have an obligation to cooperate with their health care providers, and that physicians have a duty to relieve suffering and should neither try to apply curative treatment where no cure is possible nor attempt to save from death a patient who cannot be saved.

Medieval Developments

The Influence of Christianity and Maimonides

Over the centuries, a number of other ethical rules have taken hold in the practice of medicine. Some of these originated in the late Roman period and early Middle Ages owing in part to the influence of Christianity, such as the duty of medical professionals not to abandon their patients. St. Basil of Cappadocia, probably inspired by Jesus' teaching that one must care for the sick, founded the first hospital at Caesarea in 372, where nuns and monks served as health care providers. Hospitals on this model soon began to spring up all over Christendom. At the same time, the Hippocratic tradition took on a new moral imperative for physicians: the duty to care for the sick, putting the patient's interest first, even when they risked exposure to deadly disease. Later, during the high Middle Ages, this duty came to be interpreted in Italian commercial cities as a duty of health care providers not to abandon patients, even in a time of plague, without regard to risk to themselves. Not surprisingly, the compliance with this new medical duty was uneven. Some were able to muster the courage to act on it, but many did not. For nurses, such a stringent duty of care had long been taken for granted, a fact evident later in Florence Nightingale's criticism of medical professionals who care more about themselves than about their patients.

In the medieval period, however, the moral influences on Western medical ethics came not only from Christianity. Jewish scholars also made substantial contributions. Chief among them was the physician and philosopher Maimonides (1135–1204). His voluminous writings as a Talmudic scholar touch occasionally on ethics in medicine such as the duties to care for the sick and wounded and to preserve human life whenever possible. So important was the latter duty, Maimonides thought, that religious duties—even Sabbath observance—could be suspended, if necessary, to comply with it.

Thomist Ethics

Another medieval thinker with influential views on the ethics of medicine was Thomas Aquinas (1225–1274), the Italian Catholic theologian and philosopher whose writings are the foundations of what's now called 'Thomism.' Thomism sanctions an iron-clad duty of health care professionals to protect and extend human life whenever possible. In reasoning about this weightiest of moral matters, Thomists think that the intention with which an action is taken is important in assessing whether the action is morally right or wrong—something consistent with the common intuition that, for instance, an amputation, normally forbidden on moral grounds as mutilation, would be right when necessary to remove a gangrenous limb, thereby saving a life.

Thomism also refined **casuistry**, a method for deciding what to do or believe, morally, about any given case that's now preferred by some bioethicists over an alternative method that invokes general principles. Casuist decisionmaking begins by identifying the morally relevant facts of a case, drawing moral conclusions by comparing it with similar cases that have been already decided. We consider both methods in Chapter 3. For now, note that Thomist bioethics continues to be a force today.

Later Developments

Percival's *Medical Ethics*

Some new developments occurred at the very beginning of the 19th century. In 1803 an English doctor, Thomas Percival (1740–1804) of Manchester, introduced the expression 'medical ethics' in an influential book with that title. It was a large-scale treatise dealing with doctors' duties in four areas: hospitals, the law, the professional conduct of physicians in private practice, and relations with pharmacists. Physicians have those duties because they are trusted to act in the best interests of the patient. Their good reputation depends on such public trust, which must never be betrayed. It is earned through an uncompromising devotion to the patient's welfare, high scientific standards, and the benefit physicians bring to society. Doctors must also respect their patients, the poor and obscure no less than the wealthy and prominent. But they are also paternalistic toward them: the physician determines what's in the patients' best interests, and makes treatment decisions accordingly. We return to **paternalism** in Chapter 3.

Percival followed the Hippocratic tradition, not only in assuming paternalism, but also in rejecting strict veracity as a duty of physicians toward patients. A physician may deceive patients whenever she thinks that not to know the truth is in their best interest. But his contemporary, John Gregory (1724–1773), a respected Scottish physician and professor at Edinburgh, took just the opposite view, and over the next century and a half he was joined by three eminent American medical school professors who wrote on ethical questions in medicine, Benjamin Rush (1746–1813), Worthington Hooker (1806–1867), and Richard Clarke Cabot (1868–1939). All argued that doctors have a duty to tell the truth to their patients.

In contemporary bioethics, the trend to favor a strict duty of veracity has grown parallel to the rise of awareness about respect for **patient autonomy,** a medical duty also to be considered at some length in Chapter 3. Here, let's note that this duty correlates with

> A patient's right to make self-regarding decisions about medical treatment freely, without any coercive interference.

In the English-speaking world, owing partly to the human-rights movements of the 1960s and 70s, and partly to the efforts of 20th-century bioethicists, respect for patient autonomy now prevails over paternalism. Protestant theologians Joseph Fletcher (1905–1991) and Paul Ramsey (1914–1988), two especially noteworthy pioneers of bioethics, were among those who offered influential arguments for this change. The increasing acceptance of those arguments led to acceptance of the now familiar right of patients to refuse treatment, including life-saving treatment.

IMAGE 1.2
©iStockPhoto/ericsphotography

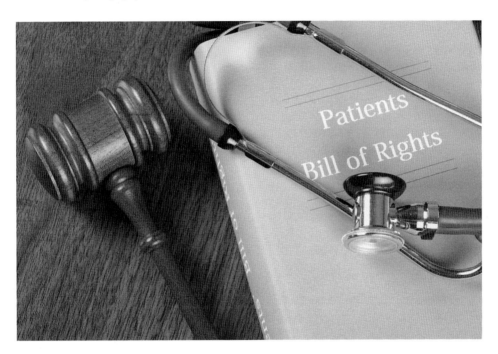

The 1847 AMA Code

This overview of professional ethics in the history of medicine would be incomplete without mentioning two more milestones, both in connection with the appearance in 1847 of the first *Code of Ethics* of the American Medical Association (AMA). One concerns the *Code*'s recognition of some significant obligations that patients owe their doctors, in addition to a long list of duties of physicians—some from the Hippocratic tradition and Percival's *Medical Ethics*, others breaking new ground. The other concerns the *Code*'s article IV, which excludes from the profession all who practice nonstandard forms of medicine outside allopathic medicine, the strictly science-based mainstream of Western medicine. Thus it became a firm rule of medical ethics that respectable doctors were to have nothing to do with folk 'healers' who practiced homeopathic and naturopathic remedies of various kinds.

This position was defended enthusiastically by Hooker, who thought that physicians therefore had a professional duty to be scientifically educated in ways appropriate to their specialties. Hooker's idea was in fact not really an innovation in bioethics, but acquired new urgency in the 20th century because of the rapid development of new technologies. It implies that health care professionals have a firm obligation to keep abreast of the most recent scholarly literature in their specialties and to know about the latest technologies for treatment. In the early 20th century, Cabot added another dimension to the needed clinical competencies: health care professionals must be not only highly proficient in the most up-to-date science of their specialties but also careful to cultivate communication with patients and cooperation of health care teams in the hospital environment so as to maximize the patient's chances of recovery.

Contemporary Bioethics

The Emergence of Biomedical Ethics

Bioethics became an independent field in the 1960s and 70s, with medical ethics as one of its main areas of concern. Among the factors contributing to this development were

- Radical changes in the deliverance of health care as hospitals became 'medical centers' and health-insurance-funded medicine became 'managed care.'
- Rapid developments in medical technology that brought unexpected ethical problems. Vastly increased technical proficiency had in many cases only created new moral quandaries.

BOX 1.1 ETHICAL RULES FOR HEALTH CARE PROVIDERS FROM THE HISTORY OF PROFESSIONAL ETHICS IN MEDICINE

| Two Types of Rules in Hippocratic Medicine | • Of duty: Avoid harming patients, keep confidential information revealed during treatment, do not ask patients for a fee they cannot reasonably afford.
• Of decorum: Cultivate seriousness, scholarliness, dignity, reserve, and other desirable traits of the health professional's character. |

| Other Ancient and Medieval Rules for Medical Caregivers | • From Christianity: Do not to abandon your patients.
• From Maimonides: Care for the sick and wounded, preserve human life whenever possible.
• From Thomism: Never act with the intention to undermine or destroy life. |

| 19th Century Rules | • From Percival's *Medical Ethics*: Earn your patients' trust through devotion to their welfare, high scientific standards, and the benefit you bring to society.
• From the first AMA *Code*: Avoid practicing nonscience-based medicine or associating with those who do. |

In the decades after World War II, medicine made spectacular advances in scientific knowledge and developed powerful new technologies for healing. With progress came increasing uncertainty about whether medicine should always do for a patient all it *could* do. Did the application of sophisticated technology and invasive surgery always serve the patient's best interests? Health care providers began to realize that the use of medicine's full armament in the service of healing might actually make some patients *worse* off—something scarcely imaginable before.

Philosophers, theologians, and legal scholars interested in such questions joined efforts with physicians, nurses, and other health care providers in seeking adequate answers. This in turn led to the birth of bioethics as an interdisciplinary field of inquiry and area of concern within which medical ethics figures prominently. Hospitals began to set up their own **ethics committees** to advise health care professionals and administrators wrestling with moral dilemmas. At the same time, centers of scholarship in the new field of bioethics began to appear. In the US, notable institutions arose at the Hastings Center in New York, at the University of Pennsylvania, at the University of Minnesota, and at Georgetown University's Kennedy Institute of Ethics, among other locations. In the late 1970s, the Kennedy Institute published an influential work in contemporary bioethics, Warren Reich's *Encyclopedia of Bioethics.* Meanwhile, Georgetown's Tom Beauchamp and the University of Virginia's James Childress brought out their path-breaking book, *Principles of Biomedical Ethics.*

Bioethics Today

While the long history of ethics in the medical profession and the newly crafted professional codes provide us with some guideposts in the bewildering forest of contemporary bioethics, they do not really explain how we're *justified* in taking one path rather than another when we face a moral quandary. Moral codes, whether ancient and revered or the most up-to-date, have no power to obligate us unless their rules are well supported by independent moral reasons. This is where bioethics comes in.

Bioethics is an interdisciplinary area of concern about moral issues that arise in (1) the practice of medicine and biomedical research, (2) public health policy, and (3) our relationships with nonhuman animals and the environment. (1) and (2) constitute the parts of bioethics known as **biomedical ethics,** which focuses on moral issues in medicine and clinical ethics, biomedical research ethics, and public health ethics.

Among other things, biomedical ethicists advocate for the rights of patients, offer guidance to the health care community about what interventions are morally obligatory, forbidden, or optional in specific moral dilemmas, and counsel health care officials on morally sound public health policies. They also grapple with theoretical questions concerning the moral reasons for and against certain medical interventions at the end of life, or at its beginning, such as euthanasia and abortion, professional duties in medicine such as truth-telling and confidentiality, and policies for the allocation of scarce medical resources such as organs and access to intensive care.

Note that, although biomedical ethics is only one part of bioethics, here we'll follow the common practice of using 'bioethics' and 'biomedical ethics' interchangeably. Either way, bioethics as a field of inquiry is interdisciplinary, because it includes elements of philosophy, medicine, theology, the social sciences, and the law. Its main tools are

- Reasoned argument and conceptual analysis (from philosophy).
- Scientifically rooted information about the facts of human physiology and the healing arts (from medicine).
- Knowledge of cultural and religious traditions (from theology and the social sciences).
- Careful consideration of legal decisions in landmark cases involving bioethical questions (from the law).

The issues and arguments of bioethics have roots of two kinds: some have emerged in the history of medicine, others as a result of contemporary reflection about moral right and wrong in the practice of medicine. The chapters to follow will take up each of these foundations in turn.

FIGURE 1.1   Bioethics as a Field of Inquiry

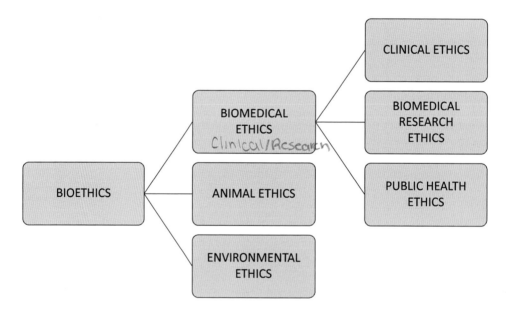

1.3 Bioethics in the Context of Ethics

Descriptive and Normative Senses of 'Morality'

Ethics or *moral philosophy* provides bioethics with a set of lenses through which to look analytically at the moral issues arising in the practice of medicine. Ethics is the philosophical study of morality, and as such, must be distinguished from **morality** itself, which consists of the rules people set to govern their relationships with each other. Thus understood, morality amounts to a code of conduct that could be based on religion, culture, loyalty to a cause, or something else. Our hominid ancestors probably had a rudimentary morality for the purpose of governing their social practices in hostile environments. Since having some such rules of conduct is sufficient for morality, we may speak of a Christian, a Maori, or even a Nazi morality. Ethics goes beyond studying which rules of conduct are accepted by a people to examine the *rightness* of any proposed rules. Thus it goes beyond merely describing facts about some peoples' rules to ask whether those are rules anyone should actually have. This is the **normative** sense. Moral rules make demands that are

- Universal—They hold generally, not just locally in a country or region or at a certain period in history.
- Objective—They do not depend on human authority or institutions.
- Authoritative—Violations are typically more serious than violation of conventional or legal demands.

The demands of morality concern a great variety of issues, from justice and individual rights to veracity, gratitude, and avoiding harm to others. A number of moral theories have been developed to attempt to settle the question of which demands, if any, take priority. The moral theories also aim at establishing what is truly praiseworthy (or blameworthy) behavior and what are good (or bad) features in persons and states of affairs. Chapter 2 examines their performance by means of a philosophical method of detachment, wherein we'll 'stand back' and consider each theory, disregarding our personal preferences.

By contrast, **descriptive ethics** is interested in accounting for facts about morality with empirical (observational) methods. For instance, the psychologists' interest in discovering whether morality is exclusive to humans, or whether people of different socioeconomic status view the morality of abortion, incest, and other issues differently, falls within **descriptive morality**—as do the studies listed in Box 1.2.

BOX 1.2 SOME AIMS OF DESCRIPTIVE ETHICS

- Developmental psychology—Explaining the acquisition and development of morality since childhood.
- Evolutionary psychology—Determining how morality has evolved in the natural history of the human species.
- Neuroscience—Establishing the brain regions' networks involved in
moral decisionmaking and the brain processes that account for individual differences in moral decisions.
- Cultural anthropology—Identifying the moral codes and taboos to be found among peoples in different cultures.

Moral philosophers are often attracted to descriptive approaches and work collaboratively with scientists interested in descriptive ethics. But **philosophical ethics** is not chiefly concerned with discovering facts about the social phenomenon of morality or formulating explanations of why individuals have certain moral beliefs or how these might vary across cultures. As we'll see next, philosophical ethics has its own concerns.

The Philosophical Study of Morality

Philosophical ethics proceeds by methods characteristic of philosophical inquiry: conceptual clarification, assessment of factual claims, and reasoned argument. We say more about these in Appendix A. For now, note that philosophical ethics has two distinct areas of concern about morality, **metaethics**, and normative ethics. Metaethics, the more theoretical of the two, is the philosophy of ethics. Within its scope are questions such as what it means to say that some action is morally right (or wrong) and that some person or condition is morally good (or bad), or exactly what moral rightness (or wrongness) and goodness (or badness) are. Thus its foundational issues include the very nature of morality, our knowledge of it, and the defining features of the language we use to make moral judgments.

Normative ethics, on the other hand, is the branch of philosophical ethics focused on how to decide when an action is right, forbidden, or optional, and a person or thing morally good or bad. In Chapter 2, we examine nine theories of **general normative ethics** purporting to account for these aspects of morality. Many of them propose one or more fundamental *rule*, *norm*, or *principle* as both action guides for **moral agents** and explanations of an action's **deontic status**—where

- A *moral agent* is anyone with the capacity to choose according to reason and to act intentionally.
- A *moral rule* is a prescription prohibiting, requiring, discouraging, encouraging, or allowing an action. All moral rules have **normative force** or go beyond merely describing facts to guide action.
- *Deontic status* concerns whether an action is obligatory, forbidden, or optional.

FIGURE 1.2   The Study of Ethics

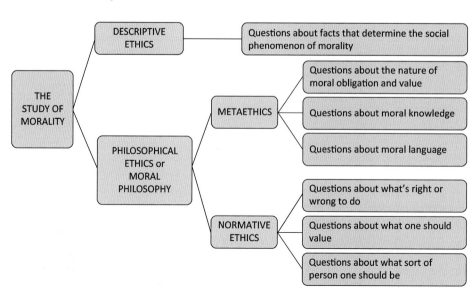

Normative Ethics

Normative ethics may be **general** or **applied,** depending on the scope of its issues. Issues of wider scope fall under general normative ethics (hereafter 'ethics') and those of narrower scope under one of the many branches of *applied* or *practical* normative ethics (hereafter 'applied ethics'). For example, whether lying is justified in cases where the expected beneficial outcome outweighs the intrinsic wrongness of the action is an issue that belongs to ethics. But whether doctors are always bound to tell the truth to their patients is an issue in bioethics, and thus falls within applied ethics. Applied ethics also comprises other currently flourishing fields such as business ethics, journalism ethics, environmental ethics, and criminal justice ethics. (For a snapshot of all these subdivisions, see Figure 1.3.)

Applied ethics has developed in close relation to ethics, whose theories can provide insight on criteria for deciding the right thing to do, as well as accounts of why some conduct, states of affairs, or persons have certain moral features. As we shall see in Chapter 3, ethical principles in medicine may be considered special instances of more general principles identified by one or another of the ethical theories—for example, that

- Medical professionals have a duty to tell the truth to their patients, follows from the more general principle that
- One ought to tell the truth.

Thus, principles in bioethics may be regarded as special instances of some of the main ethical theories' recommendations. Something similar could be said about other areas of applied ethics.

FIGURE 1.3   The Branches of Normative Ethics

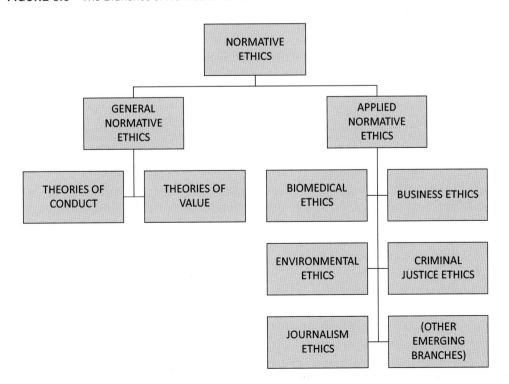

Moral Standing in Bioethics

The concept of **moral standing**, *status*, or *worth* is particularly relevant to many issues in bioethics considered in this book. It refers to the moral importance of a thing or being. In other words,

> Moral standing is the property of a thing in virtue of which it matters morally how that thing is treated.

When a thing has moral standing, there is a moral reason to treat it with a certain consideration. This may range from preventing its destruction to providing it with some benefits. In the case of persons, since they are moral agents, their standing is sometimes called 'dignity.' Often used in bioethics, this expression is rarely defined. We think of persons as beings with *full* moral standing, which includes a right to life.

On our view, there are degrees of moral standing: persons have more of it than other things, and some things have none. Furthermore, it is not only humans that may have it, but also, for example, chimpanzees and the Grand Canyon. In addition, we consider moral standing an intrinsic property of whatever has it. Things that have it must be treated with a certain deference: they are valuable for their *own sakes*. A thing with moral standing matters morally in itself, not as a means to something else, or by virtue of its relationship to other things. For example, someone may think that setting fire to a cat for fun is wrong only because it indirectly wrongs the cat-owner by depriving her of her pet, or that it wrongs those who actually ignite the cat, since their cruelty to the cat is an irrational action that makes them worse morally. If that's all there is to it, the cat lacks moral standing, and no such action can directly wrong the cat itself. But if the cat has *an independent moral importance*, the action is wrong for the cat's own sake—surely a more plausible thing to say.

On our gradualist account, cats may have moral standing but not to the same degree as **paradigm persons**, a category that includes adult human beings who are moral agents. The very young or cognitively impaired are **nonparadigm persons**. Since paradigm persons have the highest moral standing, killing them unjustly is a serious moral wrong. In the language of rights, paradigm persons have a *right to life*. The class of *persons*, in this moral sense, need not overlap with the class of human beings. Some humans may not have the full moral standing of persons, while some nonhumans may have it. Although we'll say more about this in Chapter 10, let's now consider some examples.

Humans who might not have the moral standing of persons include fetuses and neonates, permanently unconscious patients, and the severely cognitively impaired. Killing neonates is ordinarily considered wrong, independent of whether they are wanted by their parents or other adults. But not all agree. Some bioethicists think that killing a neonate is wrong only when doing so undermines the interests of its parents or potential adopters. If so, the action is not wrong for the newborn's own sake, or intrinsically, but rather for the sake of others. Supporting this challenge is an Appeal to Psychological Personhood, according to which self-consciousness, rational thought, sense of time, communication, and other psychological capacities are necessary conditions for having the full moral standing of persons. Beings that lack these, or have them only to an insignificant degree, are not persons.

Although in principle human embryos, fetuses, and newborns will come to develop such capacities, since they presently lack them, they are, according to this view, not persons—neither are humans who, owing to a genetic disorder, birth defect, injury, or advanced age, have permanently lost them, such as patients in permanent vegetative state, or the later stages of Alzheimer's disease. Thus, given the Appeal to Psychological Personhood, some humans lack the moral standing of persons, including the right to life.

On the other hand, there might be nonhuman persons. Prime candidates are the great apes (orangutans, gorillas, chimpanzees, and bonobos). The evidence now suggests that these nonhumans have some of the capacities typical of persons to a degree that qualifies them for having full moral standing. Although it may seem odd to think of a chimp as a person, it is in fact not unusual to think of some nonhumans as persons—for instance, God and angels (if they exist), and also fictional animal characters such as Peter Rabbit, Winnie the Pooh, and Donald Duck. In addition, if there are any extraterrestrials with comparable psychological capacities, they would, arguably, be nonhuman persons. That is, they would have a full moral standing that provides a strong moral reason against unjustly killing them.

On the other hand, a being's moral standing may be doubtful or fall short of providing such a strong reason against killing it. Think, for example, of insects, whose **sentience** (i.e., capacity to experience pleasure and pain) is unknown. Or consider predators like rats, whose moral standing may not provide a strong moral reason against public health programs for their eradication. Later chapters of this book reassume the discussion of personhood and moral standing. For now, note that either of these notions has a certain normative force.

1.4 Chapter Summary

This chapter began with a landmark case in public health ethics, a subdivision of biomedical ethics which, together with animal ethics and environmental ethics, makes up bioethics, one of the currently flourishing areas of applied ethics. Other subdivisions of biomedical ethics include clinical ethics and biomedical-research ethics. Although Western bioethics, especially its biomedical ethics branch, developed in the second half of the 20th century, its roots are in the history of Western medicine. We traced it to the ancient Hippocratic tradition, the rise of hospitals in the Middle Ages, the ethical concerns of some physicians in the 18th and 19th centuries, and the early ethical codes of professional associations. As practiced today, bioethics is an area of applied ethics where the interest of philosophers, physicians, theologians, jurists, and many others converge. With other branches of applied ethics, bioethics uses fundamental concepts of general normative ethics to provide moral guidance and morally evaluate medical interventions. Its crucial concepts include 'morality,' 'moral rule,' 'moral agent,' and 'moral standing.' In our view, because paradigm persons (i.e. cognitively unimpaired human adults) have full moral standing, killing a person is a serious moral wrong. But the wrongness of killing a *non*paradigm person is a matter of dispute, something to be discussed in connection with end-of-life and beginning-of-life issues (Parts III and IV). As a branch of applied normative ethics, bioethics often invokes the theories of general normative ethics considered in the next chapter. Together with metaethics, normative ethics (whether applied or general) makes up philosophical ethics. Since this approach to the study of morality uses the tools of philosophical inquiry, it must be distinguished from descriptive studies of morality as well as from morality itself.

1.5 Study Aids

Key Words

Applied/general ethics, 13
Bioethics/biomedical ethics, 2/9
Casuistry, 6
Deontic status, 12
Descriptive/philosophical ethics, 11
Ethics committee, 8
Hippocratic medicine, 4
Metaethics, 12
Moral agent, 12
Morality (descriptive or normative), 10
Moral standing, 14
Nonparadigm person, 14
Normative force, 12
Paradigm person, 14

Questions and Cases for Further Consideration

1. Which would *you* say should govern public health policy during outbreaks of infectious diseases, paternalism or respect for individual autonomy? Why?

2. *Tyler's* heroin addiction *ultimately became so debilitating that, when he turned 18, his parents pressured him to enter a rehabilitation clinic. Unfortunately, this strategy seems not to be working. Tyler refuses to participate in behavioral therapy and only grudgingly accepts the pharmacological treatment. His health care providers think that the treatment won't work unless he cooperates with it.* Did his parents fail to respect his autonomy by having him admitted to the clinic? Is it excessively paternalistic for the medical team to treat him against his will? Are they obligated to do so according to Hippocratic medicine?

3. Copper bracelets *are magnetic wrist straps that some arthritis sufferers wear in the belief that they relieve pain. No scientific evidence shows that they actually do so, as Dr. Stewart J. Richmond recently reported. But Richmond also found that some participants in his study at the University of York benefitted from the bracelets' placebo effect. He wondered whether he should tell the truth to those participants.* Would most health care providers in Percival's time have a moral dilemma here? What about now? In your view, are the pharmacists who sell these bracelets doing something immoral by promoting quackery? What might the 1847 AMA Code imply for them?[2]

4. According to medical evidence, unvaccinated individuals and their communities are at a greater risk of contracting infections. But by 2014, all 50 US states allowed vaccination exemptions for medical contraindications, 48 states allowed religious exemptions, and

---

2 Adapted from Nicholas Bakalar, "Magnets Fail to Relieve Pain," *New York Times*, 9/24/2013.

20 states allowed exemptions for religious or philosophical reasons. What might legally justify states in invoking such reasons? Which moral objections could they face? Can ignorance of a vaccination mandate justify violating it?

5. *In 2014, Kaci Hickox, a nurse returning from tending to patients during the Ebola outbreak in Sierra Leone, challenged the Governor of Maine's order to remain isolated for 21 days after exposure to the virus. Since she had no symptoms, she found the mandate lacking in scientific support.* Which moral reasons can be brought to support Hickox's challenge, and which the Governor's order? Which ones have more moral weight? Among moral principles traceable to the development of bioethics in professional ethics, which are at stake here? Might Hickox's position resemble Rev. Jacobson's?

6. *In 2012,* polio vaccination *in Pakistan was stalled by an increased local mistrust of Western powers. It was prompted by evidence that the CIA sent "vaccination teams" into Osama Bin Laden's compound to gather samples of its dwellers' DNA. Before and after the incident, legitimate vaccinators were often run out of tribal areas. To Western health officials, the locals' fear of vaccination resulted from ignorance.*[3] Were those officials' comments justified, given that Western countries commonly grant vaccination exemptions on the basis of religion, personal preference, and fear about unproven side effects? What could be said for and against granting similar exemptions to entire groups or communities? Might paternalism toward the anti-vaccinators be justified by fairness to, and the protection of, the wellbeing of global community?

Suggested Readings*

*American Medical Association, "History of AMA Ethics," Available online at http://www.ama-assn.org/ama/pub/about-ama/our-history/history-ama-ethics.page.
   Brief history of the AMA's *Code of Ethics* with links to different versions (requires library's subscription).
*American Nurses Association, "Code for Nurses with Interpretive Statements," and "Short Ethics Definitions," 2001. Available online at http://www.nursingworld.org/MainMenu Categories/EthicsStandards/CodeofEthicsforNurses/Code-of-Ethics-For-Nurses.html. Contains excerpts of the Association's code of ethics and definitions of some of the expressions used in bioethics.
*Churchill, Larry, "Narrative Awareness in Ethics Consultations: The Ethics Consultant as Story-Maker," *Hastings Center Report* 44.1, 2014: 36–40.
   Discusses the role of consultant ethics committees, drawing on the author's first-hand experience.
*College of Physicians of Philadelphia, "Ethical Issues and Vaccines," 2015. Available online at http://www.historyofvaccines.org/content/articles/ethical-issues-and-vaccines.
   Outlines the moral issues raised by vaccination, with links to its US history and some cases.
Foster, Charles, *Medical Law: A Very Short Introduction*. Oxford: Oxford University Press, 2013.
   Offers an overview of contemporary common law on key issues of bioethics.

---

3 D. McNeil Jr., "CIA Vaccine Ruse May Have Harmed the War on Polio," *New York Times*, 7/9/2012.
*   Asterisks mark readings available online. See links on the companion website.

*Gert, Bernard, "The Definition of Morality," *The Stanford Encyclopedia of Philosophy*, Edward Zalta, ed., 2011. Available online at http://plato.stanford.edu/entries/morality-definition/. Thorough overview of both descriptive and normative definitions of morality.

*Gordon, John-Stewart, "Bioethics," *Internet Encyclopedia of Philosophy*. Available online at http://www.iep.utm.edu/bioethic/.
Overview of bioethics as an academic discipline, with incursions into its history and relation to general normative ethics.

Hauser, Marc, *Moral Minds: How Nature Designed Our Universal Sense of Right and Wrong*. New York: Harper Collins, 2006.
Descriptive study of morality from the perspective of evolutionary psychology. Argues for the innateness of abstract rules prior to the acquisition of particular moralities.

*"Hippocratic Oath," ca. 425 BCE. *National Library of Medicine*. Available online at http://www.nlm.nih.gov/hmd/greek/greek_oath.html.
Offers an early version of this code, with the rules of physicians' duties expressed as religious vows.

*Jaworska, Agnieszka and Julie Tannenbaum, "The Grounds of Moral Status," *The Stanford Encyclopedia of Philosophy*, Edward Zalta, ed., 2013. Available online at http://plato.stanford.edu/entries/grounds-moral-status/.
Discusses the notions of moral status and full moral status, offering an overview of criteria for moral status based on cognitive capacities, species membership, and special relationships.

*Jonsen, Albert R., *A Short History of Medical Ethics*. New York: Oxford University Press, 2000.
Traces the evolution of bioethics from professional ethics to its flowering as an independent subject in the 1960s and 70s. (For more on this topic, see Baker and McCullough (2009), and Temkin and Temkin (1967).)

Kitcher, Philip, "Biology and Ethics," in Copp 2006, pp. 163–85.
Descriptive study of how ethics evolved among our remote ancestors in response to resource scarcity and the difficulties of social life.

*Kopelman, Loretta, "Bioethics as Public Discourse and Second-Order Discipline," *Journal of Medicine and Philosophy* 34.3, 2009: 261–73.
Argues that bioethics is also part of the public discourse, as evident in the United Nations' "Universal Declaration on Bioethics and Human Rights."

*Moreno, Jonathan D., "The End of the Great Bioethics Compromise," *Hastings Center Report* 35.1, 2005: 14–15.
Critical of the future of bioethics, in light of the dissolution of the consensus reached since its emergence in the 1970s.

*Pinker, Steven, "The Moral Instinct," *The New York Times Magazine*, 1/13/2008.
Analyzes what's distinctive about moral judgments from the descriptive perspective of cognitive psychology.

*Spike, Jeffrey, "Bioethics Now," *Philosophy Now* 55, 2006. Available online at https://philosophynow.org/issues/55/Bioethics_Now.
Introduces the main areas of bioethics within their historical contexts. Accessible by subscription only.

*Tapper, Elliot B., "Consults for Conflict: The History of Ethics Consultation," *Baylor University Medical Center Proceedings* 26.4, 2013: 417–22.
Discusses the origins and function of ethics committees from the perspective of clinical medicine.

2

Philosophical Accounts of Morality

Learning Objectives

In reading this chapter you will

▶   Consider whether culture or God could be the source of morality.

▶   Distinguish moral theories centered on a single rule of conduct or value from those centered on a plurality of them.

▶   Learn how to incorporate the insights of the main moral theories in moral deliberations in medicine and research.

▶   Evaluate the challenge that general moral principles can undermine recognition of the morally significant aspects of particular cases.

THE MORAL THEORIES explored here were proposed as alternative accounts of what one ought morally to do or believe in a situation. But a closer look at moral dilemmas in clinical practice, of the sort illustrated in this chapter, shows that, depending on the case, these theories can provide lenses through which to discover the right moral verdicts.

2.1 Baby Theresa and the Problem of Anencephalic Organ Sources

In 1992, Theresa Ann Campo Pearson, later known to the courts and the media as 'Baby Theresa,' was born in Florida with *anencephaly*. This severe congenital defect, characterized by the absence of a major portion of the brain, skull, and scalp, is untreatable and invariably fatal. When anencephaly is detected during pregnancy, approximately 95% of the women have a therapeutic abortion. Most of those who carry the pregnancy to term have a still-birth. Early detection was not an option for Laura Campo. With no medical insurance, she saw an obstetrician for the first time at week 24 of pregnancy. Theresa was born alive but dying. Her physician wanted to take her organs for transplantation to infants suffering from organ failure, to which the Campos consented. As is typical with anencephalic infants that survive birth, Theresa breathed without assistance and had heartbeat and other spontaneous functions of the brainstem. As a result, she was not legally dead according to the brain-death criteria prevalent in most countries. In the US, there is a disjunctive criterion requiring the permanent cessation of either lung and heart function, or function of the entire brain (more on this in Chapter 6). Furthermore, vital-organ donation is regulated by the so-called dead donor rule: vital human organs can be retrieved only from dead donors. Since Theresa was not dead, retrieval of her organs needed a court order. A lower court refused to provide it, citing these legal reasons. On appeal, its ruling was upheld by the Supreme Court of Florida. Theresa's organs could not be taken while she was alive. The physician and parents, prepared to pursue further appeals, were speaking on television when Theresa died.

■ ■ ■

A combination of medical and legal facts justifies the courts' decision from the perspective of the law. A deeper moral issue, however, is whether cases of this sort question that law, which this case would do if the physician's proposed action was *morally* permissible. In order to answer this question, some clarity about the facts of anencephaly, pediatric organ transplants, and human death is first needed. We'll have more to say about each of these in the chapters to come. For now, keep in mind that up to 55% of anencephalic infants are stillborn. One in 4,000 anencephalic infants is born alive, but none will ever develop consciousness (thoughts, desires, seeing, hearing, even feelings of pain and pleasure). Furthermore, they typically die within days or hours, rarely living for about one year or two.

On the other hand, in the United States alone, some 1,500 babies each year need organ transplants, which generally means pediatric size-organs are obtainable only from other babies. About half of them die waiting for organs.[1] Lawful vital organ transplants require that donors must be dead, and Theresa was not dead according to the US criterion of death. Today organ retrieval from anencephalic infants is rare even in jurisdictions where it is legal, in part because of the poor quality of anencephalic organs, the sharp reduction in the number of babies born with anencephaly (because of better knowledge of its link to low levels of folic acid during pregnancy), and the difficulties in finding matched recipients.

FIGURE 2.1   Deontic Status

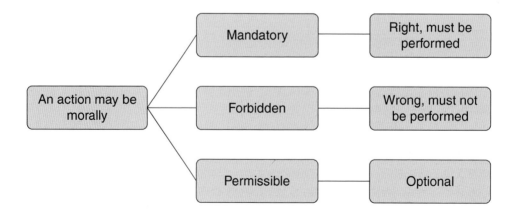

---

1 "Organ Donation Law – Should Dying Babies be Organ Donors?" *Bloomberg Law*, 2007. http://law. jrank.org/pages/8948/Organ-Donation-Law-Should-Dying-Babies-Be-Organ-Donors.html.

The moral reasons for and against the physician's proposed action were varied. *For* the action are Theresa's grim prospects, her lack of interests in need of protection, the physician's beneficence motives, and her parents' right to decide. *Against* it are respect for the value of human life and the possible bad consequences for the society of allowing organ retrieval from individuals with debilitating conditions. Thus the moral reasons on both sides include appeal to the action's consequences, the values at stake, and the agent's motives. As we'll see next, the main moral theories take into account one or more of these considerations to determine an action's **deontic status,** understood as outlined in Figure 2.1 above. This chapter takes *Baby Theresa* as a test case for evaluating the theories. But before turning to that, here are some crucial features that count toward a theory's acceptance.

1. *Explanatory power*—The theory explains why some actions are morally right (or wrong), or persons and things good (or bad) in a way that agrees with a wide range of our deeply held, reflective moral beliefs. In *Baby Theresa*, for example, the theory should explain the right action to take.
2. *Applicability*—The theory provides an adequate decision procedure, or action guide that produces moral verdicts about which we feel a high degree of confidence, especially in morally complex cases such as *Baby Theresa*.
3. *Consistency*—The theory avoids contradictions. For example, if a theory produces opposite verdicts in *Baby Theresa* and relevantly similar cases, it is inconsistent and should be rejected.

Standards (1) and (2) are a matter of degree: a theory has more of (1) when it explains a wider range of beliefs, and of (2) when it issues more adequate verdicts. (3) is *not* a matter of degree: a theory is either consistent or inconsistent.

We'll use these three standards to evaluate the moral theories that come next. Our exploration begins with two theories that identify sanction by an *authority* as what makes actions morally right or wrong and agents good or bad. Since each turns out unsatisfactory with respect to one or more standards, we'll next consider theories that ground moral notions in factors other than authority.

▌ 2.2 Authority Is the Source of Normativity

Culture as Moral Authority

Characterizing Relativism

Cultural **relativism** about morality, a common form of relativism, holds that culture is the moral authority. This may mean the weaker, **descriptive** claim that moral beliefs vary radically across cultures, or the stronger, **normative** claim that one's culture determines which actions are actually morally right (or wrong) or things good (or bad).

Given descriptive relativism, cultures may differ about the deontic status of an action and such disagreements cannot be settled by further knowledge of the facts. Infanticide, for example, counted as permissible in ancient Greece but impermissible in modern Judeo-Christian culture. Today revealing bad news to patients is thought mandatory in some

FIGURE 2.2   Two Forms of Moral Relativism

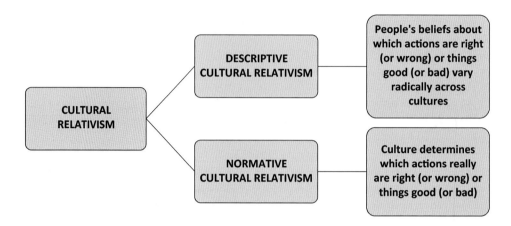

cultures and forbidden in others. For normative relativism, those disagreements suggest that an action can be *both* permissible and impermissible depending on the culture. No action is morally permissible or impermissible *period.*

Evaluating Relativism

Is descriptive relativism true? Skepticism about this invokes the universality of basic moral beliefs. Consider again disclosing to terminally ill patients bad news about their medical conditions, a physician's duty in some cultures, but not in others where next of kin, not patients themselves, should be informed. Either way, the physicians are pursuing the same thing, *what they think best for dying patients*, though they disagree about *how to accomplish that.* Thus, what descriptive relativism considers deep moral disagreements would in fact be superficial differences about how to act on universally held moral beliefs.

This objection is, however, inconclusive, because the social sciences have yet to show that there are cultural universals. So far, the evidence supports descriptive relativism, which in turn supports normative relativism as the best explanation of why different cultures have radically different moral beliefs. Even so, best explanations could still be false: think of the explanation of illness as an "imbalance of the human body's humors" that was invoked for almost 2,000 years to justify bloodletting for restoring health.

Note that, since cultures' moral beliefs might differ without this affecting what one truly ought to do, descriptive relativism's impact on bioethical decisions is limited to recommending sensitivity about cultural differences. But normative relativism (henceforth, simply 'relativism') implies that some actions that commonsense morality considers either obligatory or forbidden are both, depending on each culture's norms. Think of the mistreatment, and even torture, visited upon the mentally ill in Western countries before mental illness came to be understood as a pathology to be treated by mainstream medical psychiatry. Or consider biomedical research in the developing world conducted without the consent of its women subjects on the grounds that it was acceptable in the culture. Commonsense morality suggests that such actions are forbidden *period*, no matter where or when they happen. Those involved in them were (and, where such benighted practices persist, are) doing something morally wrong. It counts against relativism that it must deny such apparently objective truths.

Furthermore, relativism must deny the strong common intuition that there has been moral progress on these and other moral issues. In addition, it must oppose moral reforms, since it takes the moral rules of one's culture to be always right, whatever they are, just because they are the moral rules of the culture. As a result, relativism cannot adequately explain why those who fight to change unjust rules are thought to deserve praise and gratitude.

There are two more problems facing relativism. First, it is unclear whether it promotes moral tolerance, as sometimes claimed. For, if the moral rules of the relativists' culture recommend moral intolerance, then those relativists should be intolerant. And because nearly all modern, industrial societies are now highly pluralistic, the talk of "norms of a culture" has become outdated. For an Italian patient dying in the UK, *which* norms about disclosure should apply, the Italian or the British? In *Baby Theresa*, since for better or worse our society's norm opposes retrieval of transplantable organs from anencephalic babies that are alive, relativists in our society cannot even begin to consider whether the action sought by the parents and doctor called for changing that norm. For all these reasons, relativism should not be taken for granted in bioethics.

God as Moral Authority

The Divine Command (DC) Theory

According to this theory, God determines the value of actions and things, including persons. Reasons *for* the **DC theory** include common claims such as

1.   Without God's authority, there would not be morality.
2.   Nothing but God can create moral laws.
3.   Without God's authority, relativism would follow, leading to moral anarchy.

Taking a closer look, none of these supports the DC theory. Underwriting (1) is the view that God is necessary for moral rectitude. But morally upright unbelievers (even *one*) show that belief in God's authority is necessary for neither moral guidance nor moral motivation. Furthermore, it is not sufficient for moral rectitude, as shown by believers who do the right thing only out of fear of God or the desire for reward in an afterlife. In (2), the expression 'moral laws' refers to moral principles, such as that one should help others when possible or avoid lying. *Contra* (2) is the fact that, although statute laws require legislators, not all laws do—for example, the laws of logic or laws of nature. If moral principles are like these, then their provenance need not be God.

Claim (3) above, that without God as moral authority, moral relativism would follow, conflicts with the fact that many secular, moral theories avoid relativism. Here is one:

> It is universally valid that actions with overall results that benefit people are right, and those with overall results that harm them, wrong.

Although this is very simple, section 2.3 below outlines a number of plausible, secular moral theories that oppose relativism. These avoid the problems facing the DC theory, which also include its difficulties in resolving the 'Euthyphro dilemma.'

The Euthyphro dilemma

Known since antiquity, this dilemma for DC theorists suggests that their view is inconsistent. It arises because they regard God as a being with perfect rationality, goodness, omnipotence, and omniscience. But the DC theory, together with a claim about God's perfections, presents them with this choice: either

1.   God commands some actions just because they are right, and forbids others just because they are wrong; or
2.   Right actions are right just because God commands them, and wrong actions wrong just because God forbids them.

DC theorists must embrace (2), for given (1) God is not the source of normativity and the DC theory is false. But (2) entails that God is imperfect (since He would command actions for no reason, and thus lack perfect rationality) or the DC theory is false. Furthermore, then *just anything* could be morally right if God approved of it, which conflicts with God's perfect benevolence.

   As a result, at least this traditional version of the DC theory fails the standard of consistency. In fact, empirical studies (Nucci, 1986) indicate that most believers, including Christian fundamentalists, take the Euthyphro dilemma's option (1), which amounts to rejecting the DC theory. Does this mean that all moral rules in sacred texts or religious traditions fail too? No, since many moral principles widely endorsed among different religious faiths are justifiable. For example, the commonly cited Golden Rule

> Do unto others as you would have them do unto you.

This principle can be justified by appeal to some of the secular accounts considered below.

Further Problems

Given the DC theory, there must be a God, who's the moral authority, and also a way for us to know what He permits or commands. Each of these assumptions requires support, since first, God's existence is a matter of dispute. Second, to avoid skepticism about morality, there must be a way to know God's will, for example, through a sacred text. But *which* faith's sacred text serves as His vehicle? Assuming that that question can be settled, it remains a problem *which* interpretation of that text is the correct one.

2.3 Authority Is Not the Source of Normativity

Natural Law Theory

Characterizing Natural Law (NL) Theory

Systematized in the Middle Ages by Thomas Aquinas (1225–1274 CE), the official philosopher of the Catholic Church, **NL theory** locates the source of morality not in authority but in the human capacity to act according to reason. Following Aristotle (384–322 BCE), whose views we'll consider later, Aquinas thought that

1. All things have a natural tendency to develop toward realizing their own essence (i.e., their purpose, or what they are for); and
2. A being's perfection or excellence consists in its fullest development according to its kind.

Humans reach their flourishing, called also 'perfection,' 'excellence,' or 'virtue,' by achieving their natural purpose or aim, namely, a life lived in accord with what's in their rational nature. Nonhuman animals, although they also flourish when their natural development fulfills what's in their nature according to their species, lack a rational soul. Aquinas linked this idea of human flourishing to moral value and right action: "there is in every man a natural inclination to act according to reason, and this is to act according to virtue" (*Summa Theologica*, art. 3). In his view

1. Actions in accordance with reason promote human flourishing, and those against reason undermine it.
2. Actions in accordance with reason are right, and those undermining it wrong.

---

3. Therefore, actions promoting human flourishing are right and those undermining it wrong.

Human reason is thus connected to human flourishing. Conducive to such flourishing are four basic values: life, knowledge, procreation, and sociability. Actions that promote one or more of these are right, those that undermine or destroy them are wrong. Each of them is

1. Intrinsic—depends only on the internal features of the thing that has it; is sought for its own sake, not as a means to something else.
2. Basic—cannot be deduced from another value.
3. Absolute—holds without exception.
4. Indefeasible—cannot be undermined by reason or authority.
5. Self-evident—is known to be valuable just by thinking.

Life, for example, has all these features, while *health* is not basic because it is sought for the sake of life. Accordingly, the value of Baby Theresa's life has all features (1) through (5), independent of her irreversible unconsciousness or what the health care providers and public thought about it. Since taking her organs would have destroyed that value, it was morally forbidden.

NL theory is a type of moral **pluralism** contrasting with moral **monism,** the view that there is just one basic moral value or principle. Like other forms of pluralism, it needs to say what should be done when promoting some values comes at the cost of undermining others. Consider this story from the movie version of a Sinclair Lewis novel:

> *Dr. Arrowsmith* has discovered a serum that might treat bubonic plague. When plague breaks out in the West Indies, Arrowsmith's mentor urges him to conduct a clinical trial there without first obtaining the participants' consent. The serum will be given to only half of the population and a placebo to the other half. Since the treatment had proved effective on cows, the clinical trial might advance medical science while also saving some lives. Although Arrowsmith wants to advance medical knowledge, he questions the morality of the suggested trial.

The theory outlined so far appears unable to resolve Arrowsmith's dilemma. For, the intended experiment has the potential to both promote and undermine the basic values of knowledge (by advancing medicine while deceiving some participants) and life (by saving possibly many lives while losing some). To resolve such dilemmas, NL theory appeals to 'double effect.'

The Principle of Double Effect (PDE)

What should be done where an action has both good and bad effects? NL theorists have sought to resolve such dilemmas by adopting the **PDE**, which justifies violations of basic values that meet these conditions:

PDE-1. The action has at least one good and one bad effect,
PDE-2. The bad effect is not a means to obtaining the good effect,
PDE-3. The bad effect is merely foreseen and not intended by the agent, who intends only the good effect, and
PDE-4. The good effect is great enough to outweigh the bad.

In some end-of-life scenarios, a patient's habituation to pain relievers requires increasingly higher doses. Ultimately the doses are so large that they can hasten death. Such terminal sedation is justified whenever pain relief is the intended outcome and the patient's death is foreseeable but unintended. But withdrawal of artificial nutrition and hydration is not justified: it fails PDE-3, since the patient's death is intended. More generally, violations of a basic value may be indirect or direct. Indirect violations meet all the PDE conditions and are justified; direct violations do not meet those conditions and are unjustified. Now NL theorists can say

1. An action is forbidden just in case it directly violates a basic value.
2. An action is obligatory just in case it would, if not performed, directly violate a basic value.
3. An action is permissible just in case it does not directly violate a basic value (though it may *in*directly do so if justified by the PDE).

FIGURE 2.3   Permissible versus Forbidden Violation of a Basic Value

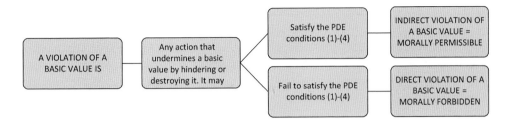

In *Baby Theresa*, the organ retrieval would promote life for some babies (good effect) by taking Theresa's own life (bad effect). Thus it fails PDE-2, since the bad effect *is a means* to obtaining the good end. The action is a direct violation of a basic value, life, and therefore forbidden. But the moral permissibility of Arrowsmith's experiment is less clear. Suppose he intends only to save lives and promote knowledge, and not the foreseeable deaths of subjects in the placebo group. Since the cause of death is the disease, the experiment appears justified by the PDE. Yet in some sense the good effect is obtained by means of the bad one. After all, placebo-controlled trials rely on the comparison of effects. So NL theory is indeterminate in certain cases, a weakness in the standard of applicability. Furthermore, contrary to the PDE, intention is not always relevant to moral accountability. Consider

R v Desmond. In 1868, an English court held an Irish Fenian guilty of murder for the deaths of some inmates killed when he dynamited a prison wall he mistakenly believed to be that of the exercise yard where his comrades would be waiting to escape. The court argued that, where an agent has full control over his action and foresees that it is likely to result in harm, he is responsible for it—even if the harm was neither intended nor a means to what the agent regarded as good.

In fact, refusals by the courts to exempt agents from blame for foreseen, adverse, direct results of their actions, whether or not they had intended them, are not uncommon.

The upshot is that the PDE is unreliable. Therefore, if NL theory is to have explanatory power and applicability, it cannot be both absolutist and pluralistic about values.

Consequentialism

For **consequentialist** theories, as for NL theory, promoting certain values matters to an action's deontic status. But while NL theory is pluralist, the consequentialist theory of concern here is monist. For it is concerned with the promotion of one type of value, understood as happiness, desire satisfaction, or welfare. In medicine, this translates into patient health benefit or wellbeing.

Characterizing Utilitarianism

For **utilitarianism**, an action's rightness depends on whether it is the one that, in a situation, either (1) directly produces the best outcome among alternatives for all affected by it, or (2)

exemplifies a moral rule whose application, over time, produces it for all affected if nearly everyone follows it. (1) characterizes *act* and (2) *rule* utilitarianism. In clinical practice, these yield that the right intervention is the one that either

1.   Produces the greatest total balance of wellbeing over harm for those involved; or
2.   Is required by a moral code made up of rules whose general application promotes the greatest balance of wellbeing over harm for those involved, compared with alternative codes.

Act utilitarianism (1) and rule utilitarianism (2) agree that the more wellbeing, the better. Yet (1) must justify actions such as lying or causing harm when they maximize wellbeing. So it cannot explain why observance of moral norms for keeping promises and helping others, or against causing harm and lying, bears on the moral assessment of an action. But (2) can explain this and the centrality of precepts in favor of some behaviors (e.g., truth-telling and medical confidentiality) and against others (e.g., manipulating and harming patients) in medicine.

Since rule utilitarians assess each action according to whether it is permitted, obligatory, or forbidden by a rule whose general adherence leads to the best outcome, they must establish first the consequences of observing that instead of an alternative rule. In *Arrowsmith*, the proposed experiment would amount to acting on a rule allowing biomedical research without the subjects' consent. Following this rule would erode people's trust in biomedical research and society's ability to benefit from it. Thus a rule proscribing research without consent would produce better health outcomes over time. The proposed experiment is wrong.

Act utilitarians may disagree. The experiment will promote the greatest balance of benefit over harm. It has the potential to produce health benefits for half the affected population, curb new epidemics, and do no harm to those in the control group. Everyone will be worse off without the experiment, including those in the experimental group. Since, given act utilitarianism, an action is right if it promotes the greatest balance of wellbeing over harm compared with alternative actions, the experiment is not only permissible but mandatory.

Note that rule utilitarians need not reject this claim. For their rules could be very complex, allowing for exceptions, much like the law, which sometimes allows for exceptions when the balance of public interest conflicts with individual interests. Their code might rule that, in any such conflict, public interests trump. Think, for example, of mandatory vaccination. Since informed consent protects the interests of individuals, and the plague in *Arrowsmith* poses a serious risk to the local population, the case may qualify as an exception to the informed consent rule. On the other hand, act utilitarianism can also look at consequences over time and thereby, in effect, agree with the rule utilitarian analysis above. So rule and act utilitarianism can coincide (and often do), depending on the particulars of the case and on how moral rules are cast. In what follows, we'll look closely at an influential form of act utilitarianism and its bioethical applications.

Classical Utilitarianism

In Jeremy Bentham's (1748–1832) and John Stuart Mill's (1806–1873) classical utilitarianism, utility is the positive outcome of an action, and this principle determines deontic status:

> **Principle of Utility** (UP): The rightness or wrongness of an action depends on its tendency to augment or diminish the happiness of those affected by it.

Given **UP,** the outcomes that matter for moral evaluation are mental states: happiness and unhappiness, understood as *pleasure and the absence of pain* and *pain and the privation of pleasure*. Thus, UP is hedonistic, because it takes pleasure ('hedone' in Greek) to be intrinsically good and pain intrinsically bad. This captures the idea that sentience, or the capacity to feel pleasure and pain, is sufficient for having interests that can be promoted or undermined. So for classical utilitarians, all sentient beings are part of the moral community which is made up of those whose interests must be taken into account for their own sake. This consideration is crucial to the utilitarian verdict in *Baby Theresa*. And, as noted in later chapters, it fuels utilitarian approaches to moral questions about the treatment of nonhuman animals and humans who are not yet conscious, or will never be again.

But are all pleasures equally valuable? On this, classical utilitarians disagree. Bentham thought only their quantity matters, while Mill took into account also their quality, arguing that intellectual pleasures are inherently superior (e.g., listening to Mozart, working out a mathematical equation, or resolving a puzzle in philosophy), in the sense that they are pleasures fitting for human beings to enjoy, preferable *in kind* to mere sensual (or physical) pleasures. In any given circumstance, it is difficult to calculate the total sum of pleasure resulting from an action. Mill's qualitative view makes it more so, for there is neither a formula to measure and compare different types of pleasure, nor 'moral experts' who can do the calculating. This creates an applicability problem that contemporary utilitarians have tried to solve by replacing the hedonistic understanding of utility with one focused on nonhedonistic values such as welfare or preference satisfaction.

The Scope of Moral Obligation

Whose welfare or preferences should count in evaluating an action? How should these be weighted? Classical utilitarianism is universalist: what matters morally is the action's consequences for *all* individuals affected by it. It is also impartialist: the interests of each individual affected by an action count the same, and no particular interest of individuals is to be favored—whether these be the disadvantaged, the political establishment, or any others. In Bentham's formulation,

> Each to count for one, no one for more than one.

For utilitarians, given their impartialism, in determining the value of an action's outcomes neither one's own wellbeing nor that of others counts more: each will sometimes be promoted and other times undermined, depending on which action, in the situation, best promotes wellbeing. Given their universalism, moral evaluation is spatially and temporally neutral: comparable interests of members of the moral community deserve equal consideration whether those members are known to us or unknown, near to us or far away in either space or time. For example, the interests of future generations and ours count equally. Tom Beauchamp and James Childress (1979/2009: 200–1) find such impartialism too demanding and incompatible with common morality, which they regard as justifying special obligations to those nearest and dearest to us.

Utilitarianism in Medicine

Act utilitarians determine an intervention's deontic status by considering whether it will produce the best outcome overall for patients, their families, health care workers, and anyone else involved. Consider intensive care, which can extend some terminally ill patients' lives but also prolong their suffering and their families' and health care providers' distress, while consuming scarce medical resources. Whether intensive care should be provided in a given case is decided on the basis of evidence about its possible beneficial effect, together with the following rules sanctioning that a medical intervention is

- Obligatory, just because it's the action that promotes the greatest balance of wellbeing over harm.
- Forbidden, just because it's the action that promotes the lesser degree of wellbeing, or greater degree of harm.
- Permissible, just because it's the action that promotes the same balance of wellbeing over harm as its alternatives.

Suppose some possible interventions would produce exactly the same balance of overall benefit and there is at least one alternative that would produce a lower balance of benefit. In that case, the caregiver must avoid that alternative and take one of the other options. When all possible options would produce only varying degrees of harm, the right action is the one that produces the least harm.

Utilitarianism's strengths include the intuitive appeal of the idea that maximizing wellbeing and minimizing harm for all affected by our actions matters morally. Simplicity in moral guidance is another plus: a single rule, the UP, determines deontic status. Furthermore, utilitarianism avoids reliance on notions that are controversial or difficult to grasp, such as human rights and the value of life—as can be seen in its verdict about *Baby Theresa*, based on whether removing Theresa's organs for transplantation would make life better or worse for all involved. Utilitarians would first note that organ retrieval was what Theresa's parents and physicians wanted. Furthermore, the shortfall of transplantable organs is particularly high for children, who are more likely than adults to die awaiting transplantation. The doctors estimated that her organs and tissues could save other infants with organ failure. This potential benefit might assuage the parents' and health care providers' distress at her untreatable condition. And these benefits would come at no harm to Theresa herself, who, doomed to a short life of irremediable unconsciousness, was unable to experience pleasure or pain. The alternative was to let her die. But by then, her organs would have become unfit for transplantation. No one would benefit. There was, however, also a chance that the procedure would undermine people's trust in transplantation programs, and more generally, in the medical profession, since the intended action involved taking organs from a donor who was not legally dead. This might have eroded respect for human life. Of these worries, utilitarians would put aside the latter as too speculative, and address the former by responding that public policy for anencephalic donations might help preserve people's trust. With such a safeguard, the proposed 'harvesting' of organs seemed the action with the greatest balance of benefits over harms.

BOX 2.1 UTILITARIAN CALCULATION IN *BABY THERESA*

The Organ Retrieval's Potential Benefits

1. Several infants saved
2. Parents' and caregivers' distress reduced
3. A new source of pediatric organs for transplants found

The Organ Retrieval's Potential Harms

1. Precedent for organ retrieval from living donors set
2. Trust in transplantation programs and the health care system eroded
3. Risk of loss of respect for the intrinsic value of human life created

Of course, none of the probable benefits might have materialized: the recipients might have rejected Theresa's organs, and anyone concerned fallen into deeper emotional distress. In this scenario, utilitarianism has recommended an intervention that was, according to its own principle, wrong. Utilitarians may still justify it, given the evidence for the likelihood of successful transplants. But the knowledge problem remains: since we cannot know with certainty all the consequences of our actions, on occasion utilitarianism recommends actions that turn out wrong given the UP.

Further Problems

For utilitarianism the impartial agent should always choose the action that produces the greatest utility, understood as pleasure, happiness, welfare, or preference satisfaction. This prescription to maximize utility produces troubling verdicts in cases such as

Orphan 1. A perfectly healthy newborn is the only survivor of a family caught in cross-fire while fleeing a war zone. Neither orphan asylums nor private citizens nearby can care for this infant. Working under extreme scarcity of resources, a physician kills the orphan to take organs for saving the lives of five infants that would otherwise die.

Since 'utility' in the medical context means *health benefit*, or more broadly, *patient wellbeing*, and *Orphan 1* maximizes overall wellbeing, act utilitarians are committed to approving of the harvesting, something that conflicts with plausible intuitions about justice and nonmaleficence. Rule utilitarians may reply that any such interventions can, in the long run, erode trust in the health care system, thus producing the most overall harm. The ideal code would have a rule proscribing them. But given their view, this proscription would have exceptions whenever the intervention cannot erode trust—for example, if the physician is acting alone and about to retire.

Furthermore, utilitarianism of either type considers obligatory actions most people would think praiseworthy but optional. Consider,

Orphan 2. A member of the medical team ventures into cross-fire to transport all infants in *Orphan 1* outside the war zone, where each then receives the care needed to live a healthy life.

Since this hero's act of putting himself in mortal danger has produced the greatest balance of wellbeing over harm for the greatest number, thereby maximizing utility, utilitarianism must say that his action was obligatory. But common sense says it was merely optional. Utilitarianism, then, seems too demanding, for it requires us to maximize good constantly and sometimes behave like heroes.

Kantian Ethics

Unlike consequentialism, **deontology** (from the Greek 'deon,' *that which is binding*, and 'logos,' *study*) denies that the promotion of valuable ends always matters morally. On occasion, agents may even be morally required to act in ways that undermine such ends. In scenarios such as *Orphan 1*, deontological theories do not share the utilitarian's confidence that the physician did the right thing in killing one child to save five. Here we examine Kantian ethics, a paradigm deontological theory that, like utilitarianism, is also monist, in that it rests on a single moral principle.

The Moral Law

In a number of complex works, Immanuel Kant (1724–1804) offered a deontological account of morality according to which neither a moral authority nor the achievement of ends persons set for themselves are essential to the rightness of actions. Rather, it is whether agents perform them out of respect for the moral law. Since it is centered on a supreme moral principle or law taken to determine the deontic status of actions for all rational beings in all circumstances, Kantian deontology is not only monist but also absolutist. The community of beings to which the moral law applies includes only *persons*, understood as beings capable of setting ends for themselves and acting according to reason. Only rational agents are persons. Since only these matter morally for their own sake, some humans do not matter morally (viz., humans who were never rational and never would be), while some nonhumans do (viz., any beings who are rational agents). Nonhuman animals, as nonpersons, are excluded from the moral community—though cruelty towards them is forbidden when it can negatively affect persons (more on this in Chapter 16).

Kant also held that, like the principles of mathematics, the moral law is the same for all persons, disregarding contingent differences in their capacity to reason. He called 'maxims' the subjective principles on which each person acts, arguing that to be permissible, the maxim implicit in a proposed action must be consistent with the moral law, understood as a **Categorical Imperative.** Main features of this principle include that it is

1. Categorical—Amounts to a requirement that's unconditional or independent of achieving certain ends;

2.   Imperative—Objectively constrains what moral agents do (i.e., any fully rational person would follow it);

3.   Universal—Has the force of a law in all circumstances.

In addition, Kant (controversially) took the moral law to admit of several equivalent formulations.

The Formula of the Universal Law (FUL)

This principle prescribes

> Act only according to a maxim by which you can at the same time will that it should be a universal law. (Kant, 1785: 421)

When understood as a universalizability test or decision procedure, the FUL determines the deontic status of actions by distinguishing underlying maxims that can be universalized from those that cannot. A maxim universalizes when no contradiction is involved in the agent's willing that it become a law for all rational agents. If the attempt to universalize a maxim leads to contradiction, the proposed action is forbidden. Otherwise, it is permissible or mandatory, depending on further tests. Suppose I intend to borrow money by falsely promising to repay. Given the FUL, my action is permissible only if I can will that all persons make deceptive promises. But in that scenario nobody would take promising seriously. Thus, a world where I can make a false promise is inconsistent with one in which all act according to my maxim. My intended action is therefore forbidden.

Now let's apply the test to the physician's intended action in *Baby Theresa*. Suppose its maxim is

1.   I may kill a dying patient to harvest her transplantable organs.

Once universalized, (1) becomes

2.   Every physician may kill dying patients to harvest their transplantable organs.

Can (1) be conceived in a world where (2) is the universal law? No, because in such a world patients would have lost trust in physicians and avoid their care. Thus the contemplated killing is forbidden. But suppose the action's maxim is instead

3.   Whenever the parents consent, I may kill anencephalic newborns to harvest their transplantable organs.

Given the facts about anencephaly and parental consent, (3) is conceivable in a world where all physicians act on it. This result undermines the universalizability test. After all, a single action might be describable in more than one way, some expressing a maxim that does universalize, others one that does not. This problem might in part be solved by choosing the maxim that most closely describes the intended action, which in our example is (3). But differences in casting a maxim may often arise. Besides, although failing the universalizability test may suggest the impermissibility of an action, it does not explain why the action is forbidden. For that, Kant offered the formulation of the Categorical Imperative, coming next.

The Formula of Humanity as an End in Itself (FH)

This principle recommends:

> **FH**: Act so that you treat humanity, in your own person as well as in that of another, always also as an end and never only as a means. (Kant, 1785: 429)

Here 'humanity' means *rational nature*, a unique quality of persons. For Kant, rational nature has supreme moral dignity, understood as absolute value or worth, and deserves respect unconditionally. The practical upshot of this doctrine is that some actions are wrong because they show disrespect for rational nature, whether in another person (lying) or in oneself (suicide). The same is true in medicine of any action that fails to acknowledge the moral autonomy of patients, including their right to decide for themselves on matters that directly affect their wellbeing. Thus there is a direct connection between the FH and respect for patient autonomy, which supports truth-telling, avoidance of coercion, and promise-keeping in nearly all circumstances, even in cases where it's most uncomfortable and difficult to do.

In *Arrowsmith*, given the FH, the experiment was forbidden because it lacked the subjects' consent, thus treating them *merely* as a means. Likewise, in *Baby Theresa*, the physician's intended action would be forbidden in the absence of parental consent, since it would amount to treating them as a mere means (to benefitting other infants). Since her parents did consent, the action's permissibility turns on any duties persons may have toward anencephalic babies, who would never be rational. These 'nonpersons' can be used as mere means, especially to fulfill an imperfect duty of beneficence toward the infants her organs could save. In Kant's conception of duties, there is some flexibility about how, and to what extent, imperfect duties are fulfilled, by contrast with the absolute demand of perfect duties, such as avoidance of lying. Furthermore, physicians might have an *indirect duty* to care for anencephalic babies because otherwise they might develop a tendency to mistreat persons. Thus, even when supplemented with the Humanity Formula, **Kantian ethics** leaves the moral verdict in this scenario undetermined. The Categorical Imperative seems to capture aspects relevant to the permissibility of actions: viz., their universalizability and respect for persons. But no single rule might be able to capture the complexity of moral decisions.

Virtue Ethics

Virtue ethics focuses on questions about morality altogether different from those at the center of the theories so far discussed. Its emphasis is on how one should live one's life. It embraces a very old tradition that associates morality with a good life, the sort of life that deserves praise and emulation. Living a good life requires developing a good character. One's character is good when one has successfully cultivated certain excellences or

---

Virtues

Intrinsically desirable traits of thought, attitude, and behavior.

One then has a firm disposition to act on them when the circumstances call for it. The virtues include honesty, courage, kindness, compassion, loyalty, and justice, among many others. Conversely, general negative character traits, called 'vices,' include dishonesty, cowardliness, unkindness, indifference, treachery, and injustice. Since each virtue amounts to an intrinsic value (and each vice to an intrinsic disvalue), virtue ethics encompasses a pluralist theory of value from which the deontic status of action can be inferred.

Virtue, Moral Motivation, and Right Conduct

Virtue has intellectual, affective, and motivational-behavioral components. A good person is not merely one who is virtuous in the sense of having taught herself to act in accordance with praiseworthy traits of character. Rather, it is one who also acts for the appropriate reason and out of the appropriate motivation and feeling. When a virtuous person shows fairness in her dealings with others, it is not only because she is inclined to act that way—or, more important, is following a rule—but because she considers fairness something good for its own sake (intellectual component), aims at it (motivational component), and is disposed to disapprove of those who do not behave similarly in the situation in question (affective component). Since a virtuous character is desirable for its own sake and not only for its tendency to produce good results, happiness is not guaranteed, and is not the aim. Happiness is rather a likely by-product of a virtuous character under propitious circumstances.

Essential to virtue ethics is the notion that the ideals embodied in the virtues set a standard for human life, a goal toward which individuals may strive, and which may be realized more completely in some lives than in others. Individuals who fully achieve the virtues are **moral exemplars,** or virtuous persons from whom we can learn how to live our lives well. We develop a virtuous character by observing how these virtuous mentors actually live and emulating them. Ultimately we begin to think, act, and feel ourselves as the virtuous person would.

Besides being instrumental in explaining moral development, the idea of a moral exemplar can also be the basis of a theory of right conduct based on virtue. Accordingly,

1. Obligatory action is the sort of action a virtuous person, when acting in character, would not fail to take in the circumstances.
2. Permissible action is the sort of action a virtuous person, when acting in character, may take.
3. Forbidden action is the sort of action a virtuous person, when acting in character, would avoid taking in the circumstances.

Virtue ethics can invoke these rules to decide the deontic status of actions.

Aristotle's Virtue Ethics

For history's most famous virtue ethicist, the Greek philosopher Aristotle, rationality is the source of virtue. Rationality distinguishes humans from other living creatures. A good person is virtuous in the sense of living most closely in accord with reason. She has a completely realized rationality, evident in her adequate moral assessments of each situation. Such assessments require 'phronesis,' also known as 'prudence,' 'discernment,' or practical wisdom (see Rossian ethics). People with practical wisdom are moral exemplars from whom one can learn how to be virtuous. The best guide to right action is simply to emulate what they would do in a given situation.

To this account of the good person, Aristotle added his **doctrine of the mean**, according to which

A virtuous person:

- Seeks always the middle way between extremes in emotions and actions.
- Regards either too much or too little of something as a vice.

Thus finding the middle way between extremes is characteristic of virtue. Courage is a virtue because the virtuous person finds in it the right degree of action in the face of danger, neither too little—as in cowardliness—nor too much—as in foolhardiness or rashness. Similarly, when it comes to enjoyment of physical pleasures, the virtuous person will follow the middle path: she'll go for moderation (the virtue) and avoid both over-indulgence and abstemiousness alike (both vices). On this view, the person of practical wisdom can find the middle way between extremes that is characteristic of virtue for many different types of human thought, action, and emotions.

Problems for Virtue Ethics

Contemporary virtue ethicists face some problems. One concerns the relativity of virtue. Moral exemplars are likely to have some moral biases that are culturally specific. Traits of character that seem self-evidently virtuous to a Norwegian may not seem so at all to a Saudi Arabian. Assumptions about human nature that are taken for granted in a small town in the Midwestern USA might seem highly dubious to Londoners or New Yorkers. In short, *who is to count as an exemplar of virtue* may vary across cultures. The virtue ethicists' burden is now to show that some crucial virtues are universal, which requires evidence from empirical studies.

A different problem arises for their view that questions about how one should live have priority over questions about how one should act. Consider the moral exemplar: why are her traits of character virtues? If it is because she is disposed to act *rightly*, then the question of how one should act is prior to that of how one should live. On the other hand, if her being virtuous does not depend on the rightness of her actions, then it is mysterious or even arbitrary why her traits of character amount to virtues. If virtue ethics is recast as a pluralistic theory of value, like Natural Law theory above, it would avoid this problem.

A further objection concerns the assumption that people can develop durable traits of character. The evidence now suggests that human behavior is largely in response to situational influences and does not manifest the pervasive behavioral consistency over time and across trait-relevant situations we would expect to find if there actually were robust character traits (Merritt et al., 2010). In reply, virtue ethics needs evidence from psychology supporting its conception of moral character.

Even if the above problems could be solved, there would remain the objection that virtue ethics provides no action guide in moral dilemmas. Given its focus on agents' enduring traits of character, are there concrete actions it could recommend to the physician and parents in *Baby Theresa*, beyond looking at what the moral exemplar would do when acting in character? That would not count as guidance since moral exemplars might disagree about the case. Some might think that health care providers who take her organs would fail to care for Theresa, and thus be disrespectful toward her. Others would judge them as *benevolent* toward infants who could be saved, as well as *respectful* of Theresa herself, because the indignity of her terribly stunted life would then be ended sooner. Virtue ethicists may insist that (1) their aim is to provide an account of moral character, not action guidance (Campbell, 2005: 48–9), or (2) no plausible theory can resolve such dilemmas. Neither reply is a happy one: (1) abandons a common expectation about moral theory; (2) amounts to a 'companion-of-guilt' argument.

Virtue Theory in Medicine and Nursing

Virtue need not, however, be narrowly construed as the sole element of an ethical theory. If an account of *virtue* is part of a broader framework, virtue theory can avoid some of the above problems and have fruitful applications. Although a comprehensive virtue theory in bioethics is still a work in progress, it is undeniable that the virtues play an important role in accounting for some responsibilities specific to the medical profession. A normative theory sensitive to the moral agents' traits of behavior, thought, and feeling seems especially well suited for the world of clinical medicine, where health care professionals have traditionally gauged their own competence as healers in terms of the effectiveness of their cultivated, professional skills. The skills that matter morally here go beyond mere technical proficiency in a specialty or health care field to comprise certain 'medical arts,' such as that of communicating with patients and winning their trust, and the art of finding the treatment or therapy that can do the most toward restoring the patient's health while also respecting his values and autonomy as a moral agent.

Arguably, good physical therapists, nurses, physicians, researchers, and hospital administrators are those who have cultivated the virtues of medical professionals in their respective fields. Prominent among their virtues is *caring*, which manifests itself in the respect and devotion some health professionals show their patients, clients, and experimental subjects. In clinical medicine, caring has traditionally been seen as a fundamentally desirable character trait of physicians, without which they could not establish the sort of relationship with patients needed to facilitate healing. In their influential *Principles of Biomedical Ethics*, Tom Beauchamp and James Childress identify caring as the "fundamental, orienting virtue" that grounds five other "focal virtues for health professionals": compassion, discernment, trustworthiness, integrity, and conscientiousness. But other important virtues of health professionals might be added, including truthfulness, reliability, calmness, benevolence, reserve, and technical proficiency in one's field.

Care Ethics

The ethics of care, or **care ethics** (Noddings, 1984; Held, 2005), shares with virtue ethics a dissatisfaction with accounts of morality centered on rules of right conduct. In addition, care ethics takes issue with the impartialism of utilitarian and Kantian theories, whereby beings with comparable interests (utilitarianism) or the capacity to act according to reason (Kantianism) should each count as one. The problem with such impartialist accounts is that they give no weight in moral assessment to the self and the special duties arising from relationships.

Care versus Justice

Care ethics agrees with feminist objections according to which the moral theories face substance and method problems. Their method problem consists in the implicit bias shown by theories proposed exclusively by men, which becomes patent in their thought experiments featuring an 'ideal' moral agent, who is fully rational and well informed, deciding what should be done. Their substance problem arises because the theories, focused entirely on evaluating actions and traits of character, ignore the moral relevance of moral attitudes to others. From the women's perspective, morality demands receptivity to the needs and wants of others, as well as recognition of this attitude by those cared for.

The development of care ethics, as a distinctive moral account, grew out of psychologist Carol Gilligan's (1982) own research on women's morality and her critique of Lawrence Kohlberg's (1971) doctrine of moral development in childhood. According to Kohlberg, moral development goes through five stages of psychological maturation, the last of which involves the acquisition of universal ethical principles. Only boys reach this stage, which allows them to adopt rationality-based standards of rightness and justice. Women's development stops at stage 3, where mutual interpersonal expectations and conformity determine moral judgment, and values such as trust and loyalty are paramount.

Gilligan reinterpreted the data, questioning the picture that mature moral deliberation involves a moral agent capable of making autonomous decisions on the basis of universal principles, and of acting freely on those decisions guided by reason alone. In her view, although it is true that women tend to remain in stage 3, progression through all five stages is not a sign of moral maturity. Rather it suggests that, unlike men, women tend to respond to moral situations by appeal to emotion as well as reason and by taking into account their relationships with others. Gilligan thus challenged the marginal moral role assigned to relationships by the moral theories without claiming that the care perspective is exclusive to women: men can, and do, adopt it.

Following Gilligan's lead, care ethicists take the child-parent relationship to be a paradigm in shaping the care perspective. Its analogue in clinical practice is the relationship between patient and health care provider. Both relationships rest on respect and trust, which require empathy with the needs of the less powerful by the more powerful. The moral theories adopt a 'justice' perspective that ignores the moral significance of emotions and relationships. Such a perspective cannot account for basic moral intuitions, such as, that moral responsibility arises primarily out of empathetic understanding of the needs of others and oneself. Fueling this failure is the justice perspective's attempt to account for morality by focusing on duties or intrinsic values. Care ethics also questions the justice perspective's main focus and conception of moral agency.

FIGURE 2.4   Care versus Justice

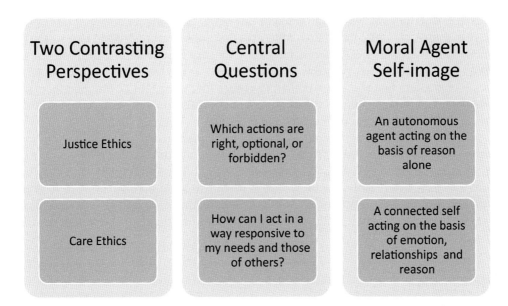

By contrast with the justice perspective, the care perspective fully acknowledges that, in a moral situation, we are conditioned by our relationships with others and perceptions of needs (theirs and our own). This is true of women and men, even though men tend to adopt the justice perspective.

Care Ethics in Clinical Medicine

Care bioethicists worry that an ethic focused on impartiality in treatment and respect for patient autonomy may well lead only to a dehumanized clinical practice characterized by the health care providers' insensitivity to individual needs of patients. Moral deliberation requires attention to the particularities of each patient and situation, fostering benign interference through empathetic relationships rather than patient autonomy. Care bioethicists argue that this approach better fits the clinical setting, where patients fear neglect and abandonment. Assuaging these fears may be more important than respect for patient autonomy. They also hold that the health care provider has responsibilities arising from her relationships with patients, and that these are consistent with her role as healer and member of a community of professionals devoted to the wellbeing of patients (Verkerk, 2005; Manning, 2012). Although meeting these responsibilities may amount to a breach of the autonomy of the less powerful, it need not amount to an infringement of respect, which care ethicists take to be essential to proper caring relationships.

Objections to Care Ethics

Care ethicists think their theory should be embraced by men as well as women to resist sexism. But its view that women's morality is more emotion- and relationship-driven than men's appears a sexist stereotype. To counter this objection, care ethicists need reasons beyond Gilligan's reassurance (2011) that they oppose "the association of care and caring with women rather than with humans, the feminization of care work, [and] the rendering of care as subsidiary to justice. . . . " Also facing care ethicists is the problem that negligent harm, discrimination, and other injustices in access to health care may require adding benevolence and justice to the list of virtues. With this amendment, care ethics looks like a version of virtue ethics, a conclusion that some care ethicists embrace (Manning, 2012). But then they must explain why care should count as the highest virtue, and also provide an account of the differences of care from virtues such as love and compassion (Veatch, 1998).

Furthermore, since care ethics rejects moral principles altogether, it is as indeterminate as virtue ethics. Consider *Baby Theresa*. Did the parents and medical team have a relationship with this baby? Theresa had no mental life at all and no possibility of ever having one. Could they have been responsive to her needs when she could hardly be said to have had needs, since she had no experiences? At the same time, they seemed to have cared for the babies who stood to benefit from Theresa's organs, even when they had no previous relationship with those infants.

Rossian Ethics

Characterizing Rossian Ethics

W. D. Ross (1877–1971) developed a pluralist theory of duty designed to accommodate plausible intuitions of the Kantian and utilitarian traditions while avoiding some of their problems. Both traditions attempt to account for right moral conduct by appeal to one exceptionless supreme principle. As a result, Ross thinks, each fails to capture the complexity of moral situations, which typically call for actions with conflicting features. Some of these are 'right-making' (a reason for performing them), others 'wrong-making' (a reason for not performing them). For example, that a medical intervention would produce the best health outcome is right-making (i.e., it counts for it), while that it is against the patient's wishes is wrong-making (i.e., it counts against it). In *Arrowsmith*, that the proposed experiment can potentially benefit humanity as a whole counts in its favor, while that it involves deceiving the experimental subjects counts against it. In these examples, some moral reasons for acting concern consequences, others respect for persons. According to Ross, the following 'self-evident' principles capture these and other reasons for action:

1. Beneficence—Increase the total amount of good.
2. Nonmaleficence—Avoid harming others.
3. Self-improvement—Strive to increase your own level of virtue and knowledge.
4. Justice—Promote a fair distribution of benefits according to merit.
5. Fidelity—Keep your promises and tell the truth.
6. Reparation—Take action to right a previous wrong you have done.
7. Gratitude—Return services to your benefactor.

Ross thought that this list of duties, though perhaps incomplete, expresses objective requirements of all moral agents. These requirements are also basic (not derivable from any other duties) and action-guiding, yet count only as **prima facie**, not **actual, duties**.

BOX 2.2 ROSSIAN DUTIES TO ACT IN A SITUATION[2]

One has a prima facie (or other-things-being-equal) duty to act morally in a situation if and only if one's action

1. Has a right-making feature, and
2. Is such that one would have an actual duty to perform it if that were the only duty or were weightier than other duties in the situation.

One has an actual (or all-things-considered) duty to act morally in a situation if and only if the action

1. Is one's sole prima facie duty, or
2. Is the prima facie duty that outweighs one's other such duties in the circumstances.

One's actual duty in a given situation can be determined only by weighing all of one's relevant prima facie duties in that case, which in turn requires identifying the right- and the wrong-making features of available actions. Thus, one's actual duties depend on one's prima facie duties in a situation. Accordingly, Rossian duties differ from Kantian duties as outlined in Figure 2.5.

Note that since **Rossian ethics** postulates seven prima facie duties, it is a pluralist deontology. Some such duties concern outcomes (1 and 2), while others concern justice and

FIGURE 2.5 Kantian and Rossian Duties

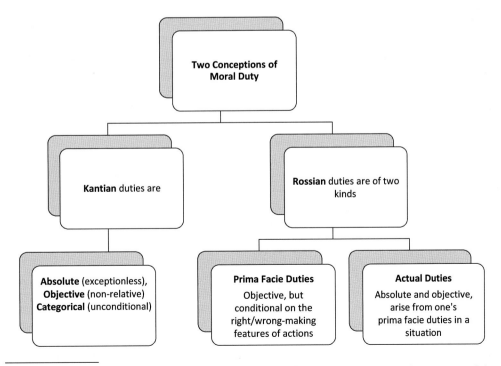

_____

2 For an action with wrong-making features, one would have an actual duty of forbearance if that were the only duty or were weightier than other duties in the situation.

respect for persons (3, 4, and the so-called duties of special obligation 5 through 7). The theory thus incorporates some consequentialist and Kantian considerations.

Problems for Rossian Ethics

This pluralist approach faces three main problems:

1.   Indeterminacy as action guide,
2.   Lack of unity in the list of prima facie duties, and
3.   Intuitionism.

Problem 1 arises because Rossian ethics amounts to a pluralism of *unranked* prima facie duties. If in each moral situation agents need to figure out the particular weight of duties, the theory fails to offer a decision procedure. Problem 2 arises because those duties amount to an 'unconnected heap'—i.e., Ross lacks unified grounds for duties, some of which are more consequentialist, other more Kantian. And problem 3 arises because of skepticism about Ross's appeal to intuition: the prima facie duties are allegedly self-evident.

In reply to 1 and 2, Rossians emphasize the complexity of moral dilemmas, which often require weighing considerations of different kinds—some consequentialist, others Kantian—and doing so in novel ways that defy any approach proposing a single principle or fixed molds. For example, although it is generally wrong to harm people in order to help others (or to keep a promise, tell the truth, express gratitude, etc.), some situations may be exceptions. In *Baby Theresa*, the physician faced a conflict between nonmaleficence (to avoid harming Theresa) and beneficence (to save other infants). Although nonmaleficence generally trumps, given the facts about Theresa's anencephaly, in this case helping other babies may be weightier, all things considered. If so, the decision by the Florida court was misguided, morally speaking. On the other hand, in *Arrowsmith* the subjects' participation in a risky experiment without their consent amounts to exploitation. Since this violates the researchers' duty of justice toward participants, here the prima facie duty of justice trumps beneficence. Arrowsmith is justified in questioning his mentor's plan.

The bottom line is that what an agent must do morally always requires discernment, what Aristotle identified as 'practical wisdom.' Discernment begins with our judgments about a situation's morally salient features. The goal is to make judgments consistent with our theory, in a process that works like this: in everyday situations, we should act in accordance with whatever prima facie duty is relevant to the situation. Where prima facie duties conflict, we must exercise practical wisdom in weighing the competing duties to determine which are the most stringent. No master principle can tell us what to do in such dilemmas. Yet there is a right, and a wrong, action. To decide which is which, we must examine the moral situation guided by our prima facie duties and use discernment.

However, as we saw in connection with the challenges facing Aristotle's theory, recent psychological studies argue against people's having a regular capacity of moral discernment. Furthermore, persons of practical wisdom may differ radically in how they perceive the same moral situation, with some for example prioritizing a duty of gratitude while others one of self-improvement. This raises the threats of relativism (contrary views about what do in a situation might both be correct) and skepticism (we can never know our moral duties). Ross attempts to avoid these threats by taking the prima facie duties to be self-evident, knowable by intuition—just as the truths of mathematics are. We'll have more to say about the problems facing such appeal to discernment and moral intuition in connection with particularism. For now, notice that this analogy between moral and mathematical knowledge is weak, for moral truths lack the general consensus of mathematical truths.

Particularism

The Rossian theory of prima facie duties shares with the main ethical traditions outlined here the assumption that general principles capture certain basic values or duties. These provide not only (1) explanations of the deontic status of actions but also (2) action guides. In Ross's theory, for example, that an action may fulfill a promise or help others are right-making features that *always* create, for *any* agent, prima facie duties to perform it. Such generalizations are offered as principles for explaining the deontic status of an action (goal 1), and deciding the right thing to do (goal 2) in a situation. Jonathan Dancy's (Singer, 1991) **particularism** denies that such *principlism* can achieve these goals.

The Particularist Critique of Principlism

Particularists argue against principlism with counterexamples. Some aim at showing that whether a feature is right- or wrong-making varies from context to context. Others aim at showing that the moral relevance of a fact to a case cannot be predicted from its previous relevance.

BOX 2.3 PARTICULARISM AND MORAL PRINCIPLES

Eliminate Principles: they fail to explain an action's rightness or wrongness.

Avoid Principles: they are not action guides in particular cases.

Given these counterexamples, generalizations such as Ross's prima facie duties appear unwarranted. Consider the Rossian prima facie duty of beneficence. *Orphan 1* above is a counterexample to this duty because it shows that increasing the total amount of good is not *always* a right-making feature. Similarly, Ancient Rome's popular enjoyment of gladiatorial combat and other gruesome entertainments are counterexamples to the utilitarian principle that producing the most overall pleasure among those concerned *always* provides a reason in favor of an action. Furthermore, what is a reason for or against an action in one case might be just the opposite in another case or not count at all. Withholding relevant information from participants is a reason *against* performing the experiment in *Arrowsmith*, but not in a blind psychological experiment where its release would undermine the outcome.

Such counterexamples fuel the following particularist argument:

1. There are no facts with stable moral valence.
2. If there are no facts with stable moral valence, then no moral principles can explain the deontic status of an action.

___

3. Therefore, no moral principles can explain the deontic status of an action.

Given this argument, moral principles are not needed and should be avoided since appeal to principles under which cases supposedly fall is of no help. But particularists are not relativists: they do think that some actions are objectively right and others wrong. What do they propose for determining the deontic status of an action? Like Aristotle, particularists appeal to moral discernment in each situation.

Moral Discernment

Unlike sense perception (e.g., seeing a tree), the kind of perception involved in **moral discernment** is more akin to the intuitive apprehension of a particular geometrical figure—as when one *sees* the circular shape of the moon in looking at the sky. This happens directly without recourse to inference from geometrical principles (Jonsen, 2000). Similarly, clarity on what ought to be done rests on developing a certain sensitivity to the morally relevant facts of each situation. Persons with that sensitivity have "the ability to listen to and appreciate a story" (Singer, 1991: 114). Thus, moral discernment consists in the intuitive recognition of what to do. It often comes from the construction of an internally coherent narrative about a case that misses no morally relevant facts. That narrative provides the insight about what to believe or do in a certain situation, and thus a reason for one's belief or action. In this process, contends Dancy,

> [O]ne is not arguing for one's way of seeing the situation. One is rather appealing to others to see it. . . . the way one sees it oneself, and the appeal consists in laying out that way as persuasively as one can. The persuasiveness here is the persuasiveness of narrative: an internal coherence in the account which compels assent. We succeed in our aim when our story sounds right. (Singer, 1991: 113)

Problems for Particularism

Some problems are metaethical and go beyond our scope. For now note, first, that since discernment varies from person to person, exclusive reliance on moral discernment may leave the deontic status of actions undetermined. This is a problem not only for particularism but also for virtue ethics and Rossian ethics. In reply, the discernment theorists can insist that, given the complexity of moral situations, there is nothing else to rely on.

Another problem is the inconclusiveness of the particularist argument against principlism. As we'll see next chapter, general principles can gradually be made more specific to account for cases, thereby reducing their vulnerability to particularist counterexamples. Or they can be recast in certain ways so that they are not absolute or become sensitive to context.

Finally, there may be prudential reasons against particularism, since arguably observing principles might make agents more likely to believe or do the right thing. Suppose a doctor can use his influence to move his wife up in a cancer-treatment waiting list. Anyone who observes strict principles of justice in health care might be less likely to engage in such special pleading.

▇ 2.4 Chapter Summary

Moral theories generally attempt to account for right conduct and provide action guides. They are not arbitrary, for they can be evaluated according to how well they achieve these goals. Accordingly, we have looked at whether each of nine moral theories meets standards of (1) explanatory power, (2) applicability, and (3) consistency. We first examined theories that appeal to culture or God as moral authority. Although normative relativism is the best explanation of descriptive relativism, it proves weak in standard (2). The Divine Command theory is instead weak in (1) and (3). These problems suggest that the source of normative notion lies elsewhere—as held by the main moral theories considered next, which may be thought of as contributing different lenses with which to look at moral situations and decide what to do or believe. Natural Law theory proposes a plausible pluralism of four basic values, but its **absolutism** about them makes some conflicts of value irresolvable, even with the Principle of Double Effect. Monist theories, among which are consequentialism and Kantian ethics, avoid such problems. We looked closely at classical utilitarianism, a type of consequentialism holding that actions that produce the most overall happiness for all concerned are mandatory and those that produce the least of it are forbidden. In medicine, utilitarians seek maximization of health benefit and wellbeing, which clearly matter in determining what should be done. But utilitarianism can value patient autonomy and, more generally, respect for persons only instrumentally, as means to maximizing happiness. Kantian ethics does value respect for persons in itself, but gives no moral weight to utilitarian considerations that also matter morally. Furthermore, its main principle, the Categorical Imperative, is too general and open to interpretation. In the end, both monist theories were shown to perform poorly in (1) and (2), which indirectly supports moral pluralism. This class of theories includes virtue, care, and Rossian ethics. Rossian ethics introduces the notion of prima facie duties, while virtue ethics centers on the traits of character that agents should cultivate in order to flourish—thus changing the main ethical question from "How should I behave?" to "What sort of person should I be?" We've interpreted care ethics as a type of virtue ethics with a distinctive focus on the self and its relationships with others. Particularism presents a challenge to principlism, but like virtue ethics and Rossian ethics, it too relies on moral discernment to determine what to do in a situation. As a result, neither of these score high on standard (2) above. Determinate verdicts in complex moral situations may, however, be beyond any theory's reach.

▋ 2.5 Study Aids

Key Words

Absolutism, 45
Actual/prima facie duty, 41
Care ethics, 38
Categorical Imperative, 32
Consequentialism, 27
Deontic status, 21
Deontology, 32
Descriptive/normative relativism, 21
Divine command (DC) theory, 23
Doctrine of the mean, 36
Kantian ethics, 34

Questions and Cases for Further Consideration

1. How might utilitarians and Kantians account for the view, common now in many Western countries, that health care providers have a moral duty to listen to patients and to try to understand their values, desires, and life plans?

2. Do virtue and care ethics have anything in common with moral particularism or relativism? Which consideration, if any, may each contribute that could help to determine an action's deontic status?

3. *During the 2014 Ebola epidemic in West Africa, the World Health Organization's (WHO) "Ethical considerations for use of unregistered interventions for Ebola virus disease (EVD)" recommended experimental drugs. Researchers proceeded with "transparency about all aspects of care, informed consent, freedom of choice, confidentiality, respect for the person, preservation of dignity, and involvement of the community."* How might care ethicists account for these conditions? How might other moral theories justify the use of drugs whose effectiveness and potential harm to humans were unknown?

4. *In* Near Death *(Frederick Wiseman's documentary), an ICU nurse tells a patient, an 83-year-old man with end-stage chronic pulmonary disease, that his lungs are in terrible shape and aren't going to get better. She bluntly tells him that although he could be put on a ventilator, this would be useless. They discuss various options for end-of-life care, and the nurse tells him: "I want to help you, but I only want to help you in the manner in which you want to be helped. I don't want to keep you alive unless you like living."* Among the rights of patients, which is the nurse addressing? Might utilitarians and Kantians each object to her tone of indifference? If so, how? If not, why not? What would Rossian theorists say about telling the truth to patients as a general rule? Would particularists agree?

5. *Michael Jackson died in 2009 of acute propofol and benzodiazepine intoxication. During the trial of Jackson's physician, the widow of the entertainer acknowledged Jackson's insistence on having the drugs to be able to sleep. Before providing them, the physician informed Jackson that they could kill him, which they did.* Might Natural Law theory

justify the physician's action? If so, how? Might Kantian theory have another justification for his acquiescence? Could these theories be combined?

6. Brazil *in 2013 was the world's largest consumer of crack-cocaine. About 1 million addicts used the drug openly in the streets of Rio and other cities. Fearing that this was harming the nation's image in advance of the 2014 soccer World Cup, the government decided to force homeless drug addicts to undergo rehabilitation. Police forcibly transported them to rehabilitation centers, where they were given compulsory rehabilitation treatment.* First, think of two reasons for and two against Brazil's measure. Then, identify the moral theories that may support those reasons. Finally, discuss what relativists would say about the fact that such paternalistic health care policies are inconceivable in the US. In your view, is theirs the best explanation of that fact?

Suggested Readings*

General
Helpful reference books include *Copp (2006), *Skorupski (2010), and *Singer (1991).
For introductions to most of the theories discussed here, see Darwall (1997), Driver (2007), Rachels (1993), Shafer-Landau (2010), and Timmons (2013).

Cultural Relativism
*Gowans, Chris, "Moral Relativism," *The Stanford Encyclopedia of Philosophy*, Edward Zalta, ed., 2015. Available online at http://plato.stanford.edu/entries/moral-relativism/. Outlines main issues and positions for and against relativism, broadly construed to include also metaethical relativism.
*Harman, Gilbert, "Moral Relativism Defended," *Philosophical Review* 84, 1975: 3–22.
Key defense of normative relativism as the hypothesis that best explains moral diversity.
Herskovits, Melville J., *Cultural Relativism: Perspectives in Cultural Pluralism*. New York: Random House, 1972.
A classic of the anthropological literature on cultural relativism and the rejection of ethnocentrism. Takes evidence for the descriptive doctrine to support normative relativism.

Divine Command Theory
*Murphy, Mark, "Theological Voluntarism," *The Stanford Encyclopedia of Philosophy*, Edward Zalta, ed., 2012. Available online at http://plato.stanford.edu/entries/voluntarism-theological/.
Distinguishes normative from metaethical forms of theological voluntarism, a set of views more commonly known as 'Divine Command Theory.' Considers these theories' options in light of criticisms such as those discussed here.
Nucci, Larry, "Children's Conceptions of Morality, Social Convention, and Religious Prescription," in C. Harding, ed., *Moral Dilemmas: Philosophical and Psychological Reconsiderations of the Development of Moral Reasoning*, pp. 137–74. Chicago: Precedent Press, 1986.
Presents the results of the psychological studies mentioned in connection with the Divine Command theory.

---

*   Asterisks mark readings available online. See links on the companion website.

Quinn, Philip, *Divine Commands and Moral Requirements.* Oxford: Oxford University Press, 1978.
   Helpful source of arguments for the Divine Command theory, as traditionally construed.
*Sinnott-Armstrong, Walter, *Morality without God?* Oxford: Oxford University Press, 2009.
   A brief but sophisticated source of objections to the claim that morality depends on God.

Natural Law Theory
*Aquinas, Thomas, *Summa Theologiae*, selection in *Thomas Aquinas: Selected Writings*, R. McInerny, ed. London: Penguin Classic, 1998.
   Original source of Aquinas's theory.
*Finnis, John. *Natural Law and Natural Rights.* Oxford: Clarendon Press, 1980.
   A contemporary version of Natural Law theory by one of its most prominent representatives.
*Murphy, Mark, "The Natural Law Tradition in Ethics," *The Stanford Encyclopedia of Philosophy*, Edward Zalta, ed., 2011. Available online at http://plato.stanford.edu/entries/natural-law-ethics/.
   A very helpful introduction to the defining features of natural law theory. Provides bibliography for the history of this theory since its medieval origins.

Consequentialism
*Bentham, Jeremy, *Introduction to the Principles of Morals and Legislation.* Buffalo, NY: Prometheus, 1988 [1789].
   Locus classicus for Bentham's hedonistic utilitarianism.
*Mill, John Stuart, *Collected Works.* John M. Robson, ed. Liberty Fund, 1963. Available online at http://oll.libertyfund.org/titles/mill-collected-works-of-john-stuart-mill-in-33-vols.
*———, *On Liberty*. 1859.
   Original source for a utilitarian defense of the instrumental value of autonomy.
*———, *Utilitarianism*. 1861.
   Original source of Mill's main utilitarian argument and his appeal to quality-of-character that's sometimes confused with rule utilitarianism.
Mulgan, Tim, *Understanding Utilitarianism.* Stocksfield: Acumen, 2007.
   Clearly written introduction to classical and contemporary utilitarianism and its critics.
Smart, J. J. C. and Bernard Williams, *Utilitarianism: For and Against.* Cambridge: Cambridge University Press, 1973.
   Smart defends the so-called average utilitarianism while Williams offers objections to utilitarianism *per se.*

Kantian Ethics
*Hill, Thomas, "Kantian Normative Ethics," in Copp 2006, pp. 480–514.
   Clear presentation of Kant's main formulas of the Categorical Imperative, with attention to their consequences for public policy, objections, and available replies.
*Johnson, Robert, "Kant's Moral Philosophy," *The Stanford Encyclopedia of Philosophy*, Edward Zalta, ed., 2008. Available online at http://plato.stanford.edu/entries/kant-moral/.
   Helpful outline of Kant's ethics. Covers several formulations of the Categorical Imperative with critical comments.

Kant, Immanuel. *Groundwork of the Metaphysic of Morals.* H. J. Paton, trans. London: Hutchinson University Library, 1948 [1785].

> One of several original sources for Kant's moral theory. The most concise and least forbidding work of this difficult thinker.

Wood, Allen, "Humanity as End in Itself," in P. Guyer, ed., *Kant's Groundwork of the Metaphysics of Morals: Critical Essays*, pp. 165–88. Lanham, MD: Rowman and Littlefield, 1998.

> Kantian defense of the Categorical Imperative's most plausible formulation, which fails by itself to support Kant's claims about suicide and other disputed issues once it's understood as a first premise in practical reasoning.

Rossian Ethics

*Dancy, Jonathan, "An Ethic of Prima Facie Duties," in Singer 1991, pp. 219–29.

McNaughton, David, "An Unconnected Heap of Duties?" *Philosophical Quarterly* 46, 1996: 433–47.

> Replies to the objections that Rossian prima facie duties are an unconnected heap, and can provide no determinate guidance.

*Ross, W.D., *The Right and the Good.* Oxford: Clarendon Press, 1930.

> *Locus classicus* for Ross's theory of prima facie duties.

*Skelton, Anthony, "William David Ross," *The Stanford Encyclopedia of Philosophy*, Edward Zalta, ed., 2012. Available online at http://plato.stanford.edu/entries/william-david-ross/.

> Overview of Ross's moral framework providing some historical context and detailed objections.

Virtue Ethics

Annas, Julia, "Virtue Ethics," in Copp 2004, pp. 515–36.

> Very helpful outline of both Aristotelian and contemporary virtue ethics.

*Aristotle, *Nicomachean Ethics.* 350 BCE.

> Original source of Aristotle's early casting of the theory.

*Copp, David, and David Sobel, "Morality and Virtue: An Assessment of Some Recent Work in Virtue Ethics," *Ethics* 114, 2004: 514–54.

> Provides a critical overview of recent virtue ethics.

Doris, John, *Lack of Character: Personality and Moral Behavior.* Cambridge: Cambridge University Press, 2002.

> Inspired by psychological situationism, casts doubts on the conception of the moral virtues invoked by virtue ethics.

*Hursthouse, Rosalind, "Virtue Ethics," *The Stanford Encyclopedia of Philosophy*, Edward Zalta, ed., 2010. Available online at http://plato.stanford.edu/entries/ethics-virtue/.

> Reviews classic virtue ethics and explores future directions.

Care Ethics

*Gilligan, Carol, *In a Different Voice: Psychological Theory and Women's Development.* Cambridge: Harvard University Press, 1982.

> Pioneering critique of the impartialism of standard moral theories from the care ethics perspective. See also interview of Gilligan in *Ethics of Care*, 6/21/2011.

Held, Virginia, ed., *Justice and Care: Essential Readings in Feminist Ethics.* Boulder: Westview Press, 1995.

> Edited volume containing essays on the relationship between justice and care.

Kohlberg, Lawrence, "Stages of Moral Development as a Basis for Moral Education," in
    C. M. Beck, B. S. Crittenden, and E. V. Sullivan, eds. *Moral Education: Interdisciplinary
    Approaches*, pp. 23–92. Toronto: University of Toronto Press, 1971.
    In line with other psychological work on the development of morality among children,
    holds that development undergoes five stages, with women reaching empathy (stage 3)
    and men reaching notions of justice and right (stage 5).
*Noddings, Nel, *Caring: A Feminine Approach to Ethics and Moral Education*. Berkeley and
    Los Angeles: University of California Press, 1984.
    Inspired by Gilligan (1982); provides the theoretical framework of care ethics.

Particularism

*Dancy, Jonathan, "Ethical Particularism and Morally Relevant Properties," *Mind* 92, 1983:
    530–47.
    Early statement of particularism in the course of a critique of Rossian ethics.
———, *Moral Reasons*, Oxford: Blackwell, 1993.
    Locus classicus for Dancy's particularism.
*———, "Moral Particularism," *The Stanford Encyclopedia of Philosophy*, Edward Zalta, ed.,
    2013. Available online at http://plato.stanford.edu/entries/moral-particularism/.
Hooker, Brad and Margaret Little, eds, *Moral Particularism*. Oxford: Clarendon Press, 2000.
    A collection of essays for and against moral particularism. Highly recommended,
    especially Hooker's critical contribution.
Lance, Mark and Margaret Little, "Particularism and Antitheory," in Copp 2006, pp. 567–95.
    Excellent critical discussion of particularism and principlism.

PART II

Theoretical and Methodological Issues in Bioethics

3

Principle-Oriented and Case-Oriented Bioethics

Learning Objectives

In reading this chapter you will

▸ Learn about a classic, principlist approach to biomedical ethics, and its grounds in common morality and some of the moral theories covered in Chapter 2.

▸ Reflect on the scope and limits of respect for autonomy, nonmaleficence, and beneficence in clinical practice and health policy.

▸ Identify instances of justified and unjustified medical paternalism.

▸ Consider casuistry's critique of principlism and its positive approach to moral decisionmaking in bioethics.

ACCORDING TO PRINCIPLISM, an influential approach to moral issues in clinical practice, health policy, and biomedical research, some general moral principles can guide action and explain why certain interventions are right, forbidden, or optional. Here we first consider the nature of principlism and some of the health care providers' obligations that its principles attempt to capture. We then turn to casuistry, an alternative approach for deciding moral cases in health care settings. We suggest that, properly understood, principlism and casuistry capture equally important aspects of the moral deliberation needed in specific cases.

3.1 Dax's Case

In 1973, Donald "Dax" Cowart, 25 and recently discharged from the Air Force, went with his father to inspect a property near their Texas home. When they returned to their car and tried to start it, a leaking gas pipeline under the ditch where it was parked caused an explosion. The father was killed, and Dax burned beyond recognition. With second- and third-degree burns over 67% of his body, he had about a 20% chance of survival, though with a severely compromised quality of life. He was blinded, seriously disfigured, and lost some use of his fingers. Any touch brought excruciating pain, but his dressings had to be changed daily. He endured treatments no longer considered appropriate, such as regular debridement and immersions in chlorinated water to thwart infections. These were so painful that he would lose consciousness. In his 232 days at Parkland Memorial Hospital in Dallas, Dax repeatedly refused treatment. But his pleas were ignored even after two psychiatrists' examinations found him competent. When he was in critical care, his mother became his proxy decision-maker, and she would not allow him to die.

Dax survived, became a millionaire through an out-of-court settlement with the gas company and graduated from law school in 1986. Yet he continued to think that he should have been allowed to die.

■ ■ ■

In Dax's case, honoring his choice conflicted with prolonging his life. His mother and health care providers were determined to achieve the latter, showing a commitment to beneficence that is morally commendable in many circumstances. After all, most patients value their lives and regard death as bad. But when it became clear, as established by two psychiatrists, that Dax had recovered a substantial capacity to make his own medical choices, including that of refusing life-prolonging treatment, his mother's and health care providers' determination arguably amounted to an unjustified restriction of **patient autonomy**, one of the central issues in this chapter.

Although Dax's case is very unusual and extreme in some respects, it exemplifies the sort of moral dilemma that may arise in medical practice and research. When faced with moral quandaries, **principlism** and **casuistry** are two alternative methods that can help professionals determine the right response. In seeking a resolution, principlists would emphasize the importance of understanding cases as instances of more general moral principles. Casuists would reason by analogy with already-decided cases, beginning with the identification of the salient moral features of the situation at hand. In our view, in light of Dax's own narrative, either method sanctions that his health care providers did wrong in ignoring his refusals of treatment. Given principlism, his health care providers wrongly prioritized their obligations of beneficence over those of respect for patient autonomy. Given casuistry, his refusal of life-prolonging treatment comes out as morally analogous to some refusals in landmark rulings that later helped to establish a patient's right to refuse even life-prolonging treatment—especially, the US Supreme Court's ruling in *Cruzan* (1990), considered in Chapter 7. We'll now examine principlism and casuistry in greater detail.

■ 3.2 Principlism

Principlism includes any moral theory that invokes general norms to account for the deontic status of actions. As we saw in Chapter 2, principlist theories in general normative ethics include utilitarianism, Kantianism, and Rossian ethics. They may be monist or pluralist; consequentialist, or deontological, or a hybrid. If pluralist, their principles may be ranked or unranked, and express absolute or prima facie obligations. Similar categories apply to principlist theories in bioethics, among which Tom Beauchamp and James Childress's **four-principles approach** (1979) figures prominently. Initially proposed for biomedical ethics, this model aims at accounting for the deontic status of interventions in clinical practice and biomedical research, while offering moral guidance to practitioners by means of (greatly simplified) principles:

1. *Nonmaleficence*—Avoid inflicting needless harm on patients.
2. *Beneficence*—Promote the patients' wellbeing.
3. *Respect for Autonomy*—Honor the competent patient's right to make self-regarding decisions.
4. *Justice*—Give each patient their due. Treat like cases alike and different cases differently.

Within this Rossian model, (1) through (4) support more specific rules of conduct. (3), for example, supports 'Do not lie to patients,' 'Keep medical information confidential,' and the like. Both principles and rules—which we hereafter do not distinguish—express prima facie obligations of health care providers and are unranked. Each is justified by being in equilibrium or balance with common morality. When in a specific case a conflict arises between some of the principles, commonsense intuitions have the upper hand. If a norm were to conflict with common morality in a particular case, balance needs to be restored by means of reflective equilibrium, a justification process that might lead to adjustments in either the norm or common morality—though any adjustment of common morality would require more support. (For more on reflective equilibrium, see Appendix A.)

Alternative principlist models invoke some other or fewer norms, depending on what they take to be the basic duties of health care providers from which more specific duties can be derived. Some rank the duties, or regard beneficence or autonomy as ideals, rather than as basic duties. Exploring these disagreements, however, is beyond the scope of this chapter. We evaluate principlism after considering some of the basic duties it commonly identifies and a casuist competitor.

Autonomy

Individual Autonomy

The Principle of Respect for Patient Autonomy (hereafter, **Respect for Autonomy**) captures a now commonly acknowledged duty in bioethics created by the right of patients and research subjects to make autonomous decisions. 'Autonomy' literally means 'self-determination' or 'self-law.' In ethics, autonomy is commonly understood as a person's right to make self-regarding choices in accordance with their own values, beliefs, and plans of life, about their medical treatment or participation in biomedical studies. Thus moral agents and their actions (choices are actions) may be said to be autonomous. The exercise of autonomy depends in part on someone's having *competence* or *capacity* to be a moral agent: that is, to act intentionally according to reason. The courts establish whether someone is *competent*, while medical professionals determine whether she has *capacity*. But like other authors, we use these interchangeably. Although competence is a matter of degree, below a certain threshold, a patient lacks it. We return to this topic in the chapter on informed consent, in connection with which we discuss intentionality, information, understanding, and voluntariness—all necessary conditions for autonomous decisionmaking.

Respect for autonomy is vindicated by the main ethical and political theories. The Kantian defense of the unconditional worth of rational agents commits to respecting a person's autonomous decisions. Like Kantians, libertarians must regard patient autonomy as valuable for its own sake, except when it may harm others. By contrast, utilitarians value it instrumentally, as a means for maximizing happiness and therefore utility for all concerned. Mill called it 'individuality,' arguing that "If a person possesses any tolerable amount of common sense and experience, his own mode of laying out his existence is the best, not because it is the best in itself, but because it is his own mode" (1859: 82). Autonomy ultimately maximizes happiness because it allows an individual to discover what kind of life is best for her. It should be restricted only when it interferes with a similar liberty of others or causes harm to them. It's as if Kantian, libertarian, and classical utilitarians were climbing the same mountain from different sides, so that they eventually reach the same summit. In the medical professions, however, it was not until the rise of bioethics, in the 1960s and 70s, that this right of patients became widely accepted.

Autonomy in Health Care

In health care today, competent patients can exercise their right to make self-regarding decisions about their treatment, including refusals of treatment, only if all conditions listed in Box 3.1 are met. Their autonomy right creates for health care providers both negative and positive duties. The former are fulfilled by noninterference, the latter by taking certain steps. Given patient autonomy, providers must abstain from any form of interference, such as pressure or coercion, but also must seek to enable patients to make autonomous decisions by, for example, disclosing to them relevant medical information in a way they can understand.

The health care providers' obligation of respect for autonomy correlates with the patients' rights

1. To form their own beliefs about acceptable and unacceptable health care in accordance with their worldview,
2. To request treatments and therapies in accordance with their plans and wishes, and
3. To refuse treatment.

For the medical team, (1) creates a duty of noninterference. Suppose a patient chooses to pursue for herself a high-risk therapy, rather than a low-risk alternative that requires surgery. Her belief that it is better not to interfere aggressively with the course of nature coheres with her worldview, and she seems competent. Given (1), the medical team must accept her decision. By contrast, (2) creates a weaker, positive duty to provide a certain treatment. Although patients may request treatments, health care providers need not honor them when they conflict with their own expert opinion, or their religious, cultural, or ethical convictions. Given their epistemic authority in assessing the risks and benefits of treatments and their right to professional integrity and autonomy, they must not provide medical treatments they judge harmful or of no benefit. We discuss this topic under "Medical Futility" in Chapter 7. Furthermore, like other professionals, they may refuse to provide certain treatments on grounds of conscience.

> ## BOX 3.1 AUTONOMOUS DECISIONMAKING REQUIRES THAT PATIENTS HAVE
>
> - Sufficient *information* about, and *understanding* of, their conditions and treatment options.
> - *Intentionality* and *mental capacity* for initiating actions for which they can give reasons.
> - *Freedom* from constraints to their ability to act freely. Constraints may be
>
> (a) *external*, such as being institutionalized, coerced, or under threats or pressure from family, insurers, or medical caregivers; and (b) *internal*, including temporary or permanent cognitive impairments caused by severe mental illness and substance abuse.

On the other hand, (3) involves not requests for, but refusals of treatment and thus creates a strong obligation for health care professionals. Such obligations are particularly difficult to honor in cases where the foreseeable result is harm to the patient—especially when the patient is refusing life support. A conflict then arises between preventing harm to the patient (beneficence) and respecting her autonomy. Consider the following case:

Elizabeth Bouvia, 26, suffered from severe quadriplegic cerebral palsy and was in constant pain from arthritis and contractures. In 1985, after a separation from her husband, she voluntarily entered the Riverside General Hospital in California as a psychiatric patient. She refused food and wanted the hospital to help her die of starvation by providing only palliative care. But the hospital initiated artificial nutrition and hydration (ANH). Ms. Bouvia then sued to obtain either a discharge from the hospital or, if she remained a patient, the withdrawal of ANH. The court found that she was competent but did not have the right to end her life with the assistance of society. But on a second appeal in 1986, a higher court ruled in her favor. By then Ms. Bouvia had accepted more aggressive pain treatment and no longer wished to die by refusing food and water. To die of natural causes, she thought, might be a better death.

For the medical team, providing ANH was in Ms. Bouvia's best interests. For the court, force-feeding her amounted to battery, and thus violated her right to bodily integrity, and ultimately to autonomy. Yet as we'll see next, a patient's autonomy can sometimes be justifiably limited.

The Limits of Autonomy

Although respect for autonomy can limit well-meaning but overreaching measures in clinical practice and biomedical research, it has its own limits. Other prima facie duties of providers may on occasion restrict agents' autonomous decisions. Common cases include restrictions necessary to prevent harm to self or others, or to maximize welfare. As argued by supporters of vaccination mandates or higher taxes on tobacco products, some measures that promote welfare at the expense of respect for autonomy seem justified. There is also general agreement that health care providers are not morally obligated to honor autonomous requests for treatment they deem harmful or medically inappropriate.

Furthermore, not all agree with the current emphasis on respect for autonomy. Tauber (2005) provides some evidence that this emphasis has contributed to dehumanizing clinical practice, given that

1. Patient autonomy is often invoked to avoid empathy—and of course, also lawsuits for medical malpractice.
2. Autonomy might be no more than an ideal. In real life, patients are too dependent on health care providers to be capable of autonomous decisionmaking.

Yet autonomy, modestly construed as a right of patients to speak for themselves and to tell health care providers what sort of care they want—or *don't* want—has now become widely accepted, at least in Western medicine. More robustly construed, autonomy runs into "The Problem of Culture" considered in Chapter 4, in connection with some appeals to cultural diversity against the Patient Self-Determination Act of 1990.

Finally, bear in mind that respect for patient autonomy does not imply that health care professionals should not try to persuade a patient to reverse an autonomous decision they foresee will have disastrous consequences. Coercion and manipulation are forbidden, but forceful attempts at friendly persuasion are permissible, and according to some, even mandatory on occasion (Maclean, 2009: 71). In addition, patients may sometimes freely defer treatment decisions to the medical team, and this is compatible with respect for autonomy.

Nonmaleficence

Most societies have moral rules against actions that cause harm to others, such as mutilation and murder. As we'll see here, the Principle of Nonmaleficence (hereafter, '**Nonmaleficence**') captures parallel prohibitions in the context of clinical practice and research. Given nonmaleficence, health care providers must abstain from any interventions that may cause uncompensated harm to patients or research subjects. Avoiding harmful interventions is a negative duty, or duty of forbearance. As explained in Chapter 18, negative duties are more easily fulfilled and generally more stringent than positive ones such as the duties of beneficence. To fulfill these, providers must take some positive steps, for example, to prevent harm or otherwise promote the wellbeing of patients or research subjects. The Principle of Beneficence (hereafter, '**Beneficence**') captures these positive duties. Although beneficence and nonmaleficence are closely related and some authors include them under a single heading, because they differ in the ways just indicated, this chapter takes up each in turn.

Harm

The sort of harm nonmaleficence recommends to avoid is commonly understood, following Feinberg's definition (1984), as *a significant setback to a person's interests*. These setbacks result, not from accidents or natural disasters, but from human actions or omissions (i.e., failures to act when action is needed). Furthermore, neither minor inconveniences nor small hurts are harms: to count as a harm, the setback to the victim's interest must be *significant*.

But frustration at the ineffectiveness of some health care systems or annoyance at some health care professionals' actions may qualify as psychological harms, depending on the degree and duration of the offense.

BOX 3.2 INSTANCES OF HARM IN MEDICINE

To Patients

- Burdensome and risky treatments with no compensating benefit, including interventions that inflict enduring pain, substantial suffering, gross disfigurement, or premature death.
- Care that causes patients to experience significant mental distress such as deep anxiety, mistrust, alienation, helplessness, loss of self-control, loneliness, and anger.

To Third Parties

- Errors in contraceptive interventions and treatments—e.g., a vasectomy that doesn't achieve sterilization.

- Failure to warn pregnant women of the dangers of drug or alcohol use in pregnancy.

To Health Care Professionals, Practices, and Institutions

- Withholding information from a lab technician regarding a patient's HIV-positive status.
- Fabricating results of medical research.
- Distorting medical records to procure benefits for one's own patients.
- Spreading false information about medical institutions.

Note that someone who has a compromised immune system and contracts a hospital-acquired infection (HAI), even when all sanitation protocols were carefully followed, is harmed without being morally *wronged*. After all, patients cannot be isolated from *every* infectious agent in the hospital environment, and this patient is abnormally sensitive. At the same time, not all wrongs are harms. Suppose a nurse on one occasion forgets to administer a patient's dose of medication as prescribed but the patient suffers no harm. Even so, she has been wronged, by being put at risk unnecessarily. She has failed to receive due care.

Another important element in the definition of 'harm' is *interests*, understood as something objective or subjective. While a patient's interests, subjectively understood, have been set back whenever her preferences have been frustrated, objectively understood they have been set back whenever she has failed to get what, as a matter of medical fact, is best for her. The objective and subjective interests of a patient may not coincide. For example, transfusing a Jehovah's Witness who refuses any blood products for religious reasons may be objectively in the patient's interest because it may be crucial to the preservation of her life. But it is not in the patient's interest from her own perspective. Whatever we say about these philosophical questions, however, it is plain that the medical team runs the risk of sometimes inflicting harm on patients. This is why the Principle of Nonmaleficence is not a platitude.

FIGURE 3.1   Nonmaleficence and Beneficence

TWO RELATED DUTIES OF HEALTH CARE PROVIDERS	
NONMALEFICENCE Recomends that they act, or omit to act, in ways that	**BENEFICENCE** Recomends that their acts and omissions promote the wellbeing of the patient by

Avoid harm to the patient	Preventing harm to the patient	Removing harm from the patient	Doing what's in the patient's best interest

The Principle of Nonmaleficence

Given this principle, health care workers must use care and apply treatments only in ways that will not cause unnecessary harm. This requires them to be up-to-date and proficient in their specialties so that, for instance, the powerful drugs they prescribe produce no seriously debilitating side effects and the surgical procedures they undertake leave the patient no worse off overall than before.

But not *all* harms can be avoided. Rather, nonmaleficence recommends that health care workers strive to avoid *needless* harm to patients. Instrumental harms are sometimes necessary to healing. When a surgeon cuts with a scalpel, this amounts to doing violence to the patient's body, to a degree that, if done by a layman in ordinary circumstances, would be unlawful as a crime of battery. The surgeon's incision on a patient under anesthesia is justified as a necessary means to a desirable end: making her whole again.

Likewise morally justified are certain instrumental harms that do *not* leave the patient whole, because they result in permanent damage or disfigurement. Where the patient's condition is bad overall, and there is no other alternative, these are justified as a means to avoiding something still worse. Thus, surgery to remove a malignant tumor in the brain might be permissible if it saves the patient's life, even if it also leaves him blind. The amputation of a foot, ordinarily an extreme measure, may nevertheless be justified when insufficient blood circulation in the lower extremities threatens the life of a patient with diabetes.

Among the noninstrumental harms proscribed by nonmaleficence are

1. Negligent harm,
2. Harm through incompetence, and
3. Malicious harm.

Only harm type (3) is intentional with a sinister motivation. Fortunately, it is rare. Consider

Beverly Allitt, a nurse known as the "Angel of Death," was sentenced by a British court in 2007 to 30 years in prison for killing four children in her care by injecting high doses of insulin. Her sentence also took into account her attempts to kill another three children, and her causing grievous bodily harm with intent to kill six others at Grantham and Kesteven hospital in Lincolnshire. Allitt allegedly suffered from Munchausen syndrome by proxy, a form of child abuse in which health care providers deliberately induce or falsely report illnesses in children with the purpose of focusing attention on themselves.

This case would illustrate malicious harm, provided Nurse Allitt knew she was perpetrating ghastly crimes. In light of the harsh sentence, the court thought she did. But it is often difficult to distinguish evil from pathology in cases of this sort.

In part for this reason, malicious harm is less common in medicine than harms type (1) or (2) above, both unjustified but nonmalicious. These harms are unintentional, though they may be foreseeable. Harm through incompetence occurs whenever health care providers intervene in areas of medicine in which they are not trained. Negligent harm results from carelessness in practice or faulty protocols. There is no malice involved, but maybe only an inclination to 'cut corners' on safety procedures which can lead to fatal errors, as in this case:

Jésica Santillán, a 17-year-old Mexican immigrant, was admitted to Duke University Hospital in 2003 for a heart-lung transplant. But, owing to carelessness, medical staff failed to notice that the donor organs came from a person with a blood type incompatible with Jésica's. Moreover, the surgeons discovered this mistake only near the end of the transplant operation when it became clear that the patient was rejecting the new organs. Tests revealed that the organ donor's blood type was A, while Jésica's was O. Jésica died shortly after a second transplant was attempted.

In 2004, Jésica's family reached a settlement with Duke. According to the hospital's website, safety improved in the nation's organ-transplant system as a result of her death. Unfortunately, medical errors attributable to flaws in hospitals' and clinics' protocols are pervasive. An early study by the Institute of Medicine of the National Academy of Sciences reported up to 98,000 deaths caused by medical error in the US in 1999. More recent studies report 440,000 yearly deaths from care in hospitals.[1]

Beneficence and Paternalism

The Principle of Beneficence

In ordinary contexts, a *beneficent* act is any act or omission aimed at helping others. 'Beneficence' is therefore related to concepts such as charity, compassion, mercy, and altruism. Associated with beneficence is *benevolence*, the virtue of those who seek benefit for others. However, common morality doesn't consider all beneficent acts obligatory. Donating an organ for transplantation or all of one's salary for famine relief fall beyond the call of duty. But responding to an elderly person's request for help in crossing a busy street or removing a stone from a bike lane that may cause a cyclist to fall seem obligatory.

In the context of medicine, beneficence expresses the medical professionals' duty to maximize patients' *welfare*—i.e., their overall physical and psychological wellbeing, of which

---

1 Marshall Allen, "How Many Die from Medical Mistakes in US Hospitals?" *Scientific American* 9/20/2013. http://www.scientificamerican.com/article/how-many-die-from-medical-mistakes-in-us-hospitals/

IMAGE 3.1
©iStockPhoto/Steve Debenport

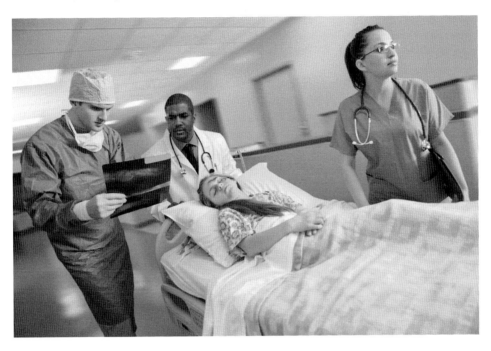

health is an important component. It comprises the duties to remove and prevent harm, and to restore the patient to physical and psychological wellbeing, to the extent possible. When that is not possible, beneficence recommends trying to bring the patient back to the nearest approximation of wellbeing, given the facts of her condition. The justification of beneficence runs along consequentialist lines. Beneficent interventions produce the best outcomes for all involved: not only patients but also families and others concerned (though the patient's interests ordinarily carry the greatest moral weight). Beneficence may, however, be constrained by other obligations stemming from justice or respect for patient autonomy. We return to this in the next section.

Rooted in beneficence are more specific duties such as to listen to the patient and attempt to understand her values, hopes, and fears, and to assume some personal risks in caring for the patient. Since at least the Middle Ages physicians were thought to have a special duty not to abandon their patients in epidemics. Doctors and nurses were expected to care for the sick, even at the risk of becoming infected themselves. Yet as often noted (e.g., Beauchamp and Childress, 2009: 198), modern medical beneficence does not strictly require health care providers to put their lives in serious danger, something reflected by professional codes that no longer require heroic sacrifices from them. Even so, a commitment to the duty of care is still very much alive in medicine. In the early days of the AIDS epidemic, many physicians and nurses met the demands of beneficence as they braved risks of accidental needle-sticks and other infectious exposure while caring for those stricken with what was then an inevitably deadly disease. In developing countries, health care professionals faced with outbreaks of Ebola, cholera, malaria, dengue fever, plague, and many other diseases continue to show such courage.

There are some types of action that would be recognized generally as *violations* of beneficence. Relative to a context, these include

- Abandonment of patients for no good reason.
- Failure to remove or prevent harm to patients, when either of these could be done.

Health care providers must not abandon their patients because of, for example, discouraging results of treatment. They must stick with them even at some risk to themselves within certain limits. When they cannot in good conscience perform a certain procedure to which the patient is entitled—for example, abortion or withdrawal of life supports—there is the option of conscientious objection. Conscientious objectors may be obliged to refer the patient to a provider willing to honor the request (more on this in Chapter 13).

Paternalism

Paternalism is the expected attitude of parents toward their children. It has two components: (1) parents restrict their child's liberty; and (2) that is for the purpose of advancing the child's best interests. Similarly, in clinical practice (1) the provider, especially the physician, limits patient autonomy by, for example, determining what treatment is best for her or withholding the truth about her condition; and (2) advancing her best interests is the reason justifying such restrictions. While adult paternalism toward children who are not yet fully competent is justified, paternalism toward competent patients and research subjects is now widely considered unacceptable in Western medicine. Until the 1960s and 70s, paternalism went hand in hand with the prevailing conception of patient welfare, which limited it to health benefits—an objective matter of fact that only the medical team was in a position to know. The team was entitled to make treatment decisions for patients according to the team's own assessment of what promoted welfare.

Critics of paternalism object that a patient's welfare depends at least partly on what he himself values and believes about what makes a life worth living and about how much benefit a treatment must offer to compensate for its burdens and risks. That some treatment option might extend life may not always be a reason to choose it. If the *quality of life* it might afford is too low to be acceptable to the patient, he can refuse it on autonomy grounds. We consider some scenarios of this sort in Chapter 7.

The courts' response to unjustified medical paternalism has been the doctrine of informed consent discussed in great detail in Chapter 5. For now, note that this doctrine sets legal limits to paternalism by sanctioning that, whatever the health care professionals might think best, they must provide patients with truthful and understandable information about possible treatment options, including nontreatment.

Another reason to be skeptical about medical paternalism is that health care professionals might make mistakes in determining which treatment option is in a patient's best interest, all things considered. Moreover, since it is the patient who will have to live with the consequences of treatment decisions, it should be the patient who makes them. There is in medicine always the possibility, albeit a remote one, that a given treatment will fail to work as reasonably expected, and instead produce only very uncomfortable side effects that are not easily remedied. If such a treatment has been imposed on a patient without her consent, it seems she has been harmed, perhaps permanently, by a procedure in whose deployment she had no say.

But in certain situations **paternalism** can be justified, whether it be **hard** or **soft**. In hard paternalism, medical providers make care decisions for the benefit of patients according to the providers' own values, but the patient has substantial autonomy: she is neither cognitively impaired nor too young to make her own decision. Hard paternalism is rarely justified. Possible exceptions include timing the disclosure of information to patients (see "Must Health Care Professionals Always Tell the Truth?" in Chapter 4) and vaccination mandates such as that in *Jacobson v Massachusetts* (Chapter 1). Here is a seemingly unjustified hard paternalist decision in health policy:

Bloomberg's Soda Ban. In September 2012, the New York City Board of Health adopted a policy proposed by Mayor Michael Bloomberg, which would have imposed a ban on the sale of large sodas and other sugary drinks at restaurants, street carts, and in movie theaters. The rationale for the proposed restriction was to help curb the epidemic of obesity, which is associated with diabetes, hypertension, and other health problems. But many New Yorkers resented the Mayor's heavy-handed interference with their own autonomous choices. "Sugar consumption might be bad for me, Mr. Mayor," they seemed to say, "but *I'll decide for myself* the size soda I buy, thank you very much." Ultimately ruled unconstitutional by the city's courts, the ban never came into effect.

Mayor Bloomberg might have intended only to promote the health of his fellow citizens. But, for critics, such public policies amount to unjustifiable interference with individual autonomy.

In soft paternalism, by contrast, the patient's autonomy is diminished to a significant degree, owing to immaturity or mental impairment (temporary or permanent). So health care professionals make a decision for her on the basis of what is in her best interests. Since the patient is *unable* to make it, soft paternalism is compatible with respect for patient autonomy. Here is a seemingly justified case of soft paternalism:

Vasectomy. In 2013 a British court ruled that doctors could perform sterilization on a mentally impaired 36-year-old man, referred to as 'D. E.,' who because of his learning disability was unable to give informed consent for the procedure. D.E. had an I.Q. of 40 and was a well adjusted man in a long-term relationship with a girlfriend, with whom he already had one child. He said, however, that he did not want another, and his relatives agreed that further offspring would likely destabilize the couple's relationship. Neither D.E. nor his girlfriend was able to understand contraception.

D. E. lacked the mental capacity to understand contraception, yet plainly desired its effects. So the court's soft paternalistic decision that sterilizing him, even without his consent, was in his true best interest seems justified.

A main problem with soft paternalism is the difficulty of determining whether, or to what degree, a patient lacks mental competence, a topic reassumed in Chapter 5. Another problem is that it can slide into hard paternalism. Assuming that smokers may be ignorant of the risks posed by tobacco, or affected by the psychological bias of overconfidence ('That cannot happen to me!'), soft paternalist advertisements about those risks seem justified. But current 'liberal paternalists' who are enthusiastic about such policies may easily slide into supporting increased taxation on cigarettes, which some regard as an unjustified restriction on autonomy (Beauchamp and Childress, 2009: 212).

Note, finally, that paternalism, when *temporary*, need not unjustifiably restrict autonomy. In an emergency, when a patient is unconscious and there is no next of kin, unilateral decisions are warranted. The ER team can assume that that patient wants to be saved. Mill in fact argues that if I see someone about to mount a dangerous footbridge, I may restrain her to find out whether she is aware of the danger. Until then, I can reasonably assume that she does not desire to fall. But note that, on the basis of Mill's view on autonomy, he is committed to rejecting both hard and soft paternalism, not because each is wrong in itself, but because—as Mill himself points out—people are the best judges of what works for them. So, respecting their choices tends to maximize happiness.

3.3 Casuistry

The bioethics approach so far considered is *principlist:* it invokes general norms that express obligations in clinical practice and biomedical research. And it does so for deciding the right intervention in each particular case. By contrast, case ethics or casuistry decides particular cases by relying heavily on the notion of moral discernment discussed in Chapter 2. Its method is rooted in ancient rhetoric and the casuist reasoning practiced during the Middle Ages and the early modern period. In contemporary bioethics, casuistry is a method for moral decisionmaking about any new case by considering its details and reasoning by analogy from previously decided cases.

Casuists deny that moral verdicts about cases follow from the application of moral principles. For them, principles are, at most, generalizations drawn from cases. Although low-level generalizations may be of help in identifying salient moral features of cases, principlism's norms are too abstract and indeterminate to account for right conduct or offer moral guidance. But a distinction should be made between radical casuists, who see no role at all for principles, and moderate casuists, who ascribe them a modest role. Among the advantages they see in casuistry are, first, that it facilitates consensus among people of different ethical persuasions (Arras, 2012). Utilitarians and Kantians, for instance, will often disagree about which principle best captures an agent's obligation in a complex case. But agreement

FIGURE 3.2 Two Senses of 'Casuistry'

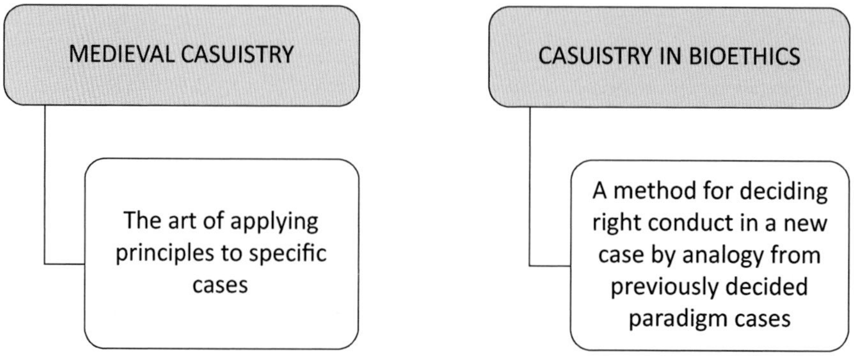

MEDIEVAL CASUISTRY

The art of applying principles to specific cases

CASUISTRY IN BIOETHICS

A method for deciding right conduct in a new case by analogy from previously decided paradigm cases is possible if they start instead by looking closely at morally significant aspects of the case. If casuistry can indeed avoid disagreements about theory, this would be a big advantage because many moral problems in medicine are time-sensitive. In addition, casuistry fits well with the already case-oriented methodology familiar to health care professionals.

How Casuistry Works

To reach justified moral conclusions about a case, casuists need to identify **paradigms** that resemble it—i.e., already-decided cases about which there is reasonable agreement. This requires that they first construct a narrative describing the case's morally salient features. Once some paradigms have been identified, casuists decide which one fits the case and decide by analogy. Consider this example:

Jehovah's Witness. A mother of seven children rejects the use of blood products during an emergency surgical procedure, thereby putting her own life at risk. She understands the risk, seems rational, and adduces religious grounds for her refusal. But she is the family's breadwinner, and the father could not properly care for the children if left on his own. (Adapted from Hanson, 2009)

Although health care providers must generally honor refusals of treatment, here respect for the mother's autonomy conflicts with protecting the welfare of her children. To find the paradigm that can help in deciding what to do, casuists would describe the case as involving:

1. A risky refusal of treatment for religious reasons by a competent patient,
2. A high risk of undermining the welfare of seven minors, and
3. A restriction on autonomy based on preventing harm to others.

They can now invoke maxims such as 'A competent patient's refusal of medical treatment should be honored,' and 'The welfare of children must not be put at risk.' These common lower-level generalizations help them classify the case and identify some related paradigms:

1. The court honored the mother's refusal, but the welfare of children was not at risk.
2. The court declined the mother's refusal to protect the welfare of dependent children.

Since paradigm 2 is clearly more analogous to *Jehovah's Witness*, casuists take this to rule *Jehovah's Witness*. Their narrative was crucial to their analogical reasoning, for it showed the moral salience of justified restrictions to autonomy.

The Top-Down/Bottom-Up Dichotomy

Casuists consider principlism a 'top-down' approach whereby decisions about cases are deduced from some accepted moral principles. While moderate casuists grant principles some roles in deciding concrete cases, radical casuists reject them altogether as obstacles to analogical reasoning. But can the salient moral features of a case be determined without generalizations? Beauchamp (1995) argues that it is only because paradigms blend facts ('The patient refused the recommended treatment') and norms ('Competent patients have a right to refuse treatment') that they can justify decisions about new cases.

Another problem with radical casuistry is its sharp distinction between

- Top-down approaches that decide cases deductively, by invoking general principles and taking particular cases to fall under them.
- Bottom-up approaches that decide cases by analogical reasoning from paradigms.

Not all casuists draw this sharp contrast. Moderate casuists incorporate in their approach low-level generalizations (the maxims). As we saw above, the four-principles approach captures prima facie duties that can be overridden in a situation and are grounded in common morality, a set of beliefs that also grounds the casuists' maxims. Furthermore, principles need not function as premises of deductively inferred verdicts about concrete cases. The justification of principles and intuitions about particular cases proceeds by reflective equilibrium, a process whereby principles and intuitions are revised when they conflict, so that they can be in equilibrium or form a coherent whole. And cases are better accounted for by gradual specification of general principles, whereby their scope is made progressively narrower until it accounts for a case and any apparent conflict is resolved. Either way, verdicts about cases need not be justified by appeal to general principles with very thin content such as 'Do no harm' or 'Promote justice.' Thus, the moderate casuist's view appears compatible with principlism.

3.4 Chapter Summary

This chapter first examined principlism, the view that some basic principles can be the point of departure in deciding what to do morally or assessing the deontic status of medical interventions. The four-principles approach takes those principles to capture duties of justice, to be examined in Part VI of this book, and of respect for autonomy, nonmaleficence, and beneficence. The nature of these, as well as their limits and possible conflicts, were examined here. In connection with beneficence, we distinguished between hard and soft paternalism. Paternalism of either type may on occasion be justified. For casuists, appeal to neither beneficence nor other general principles associated with basic duties of health care providers can help in deciding cases. But since moderate casuists recognize that low-level principles or maxims play a role, their view seems compatible with some versions of principlism.

3.5 Study Aids

Key Words

Beneficence, 57
Casuistry, 53
Four-principles approach, 53
Hard/soft paternalism, 63
Nonmaleficence, 57
Patient autonomy, 53
Paradigm case, 64
Principlism, 53
Respect for autonomy, 54

Questions and Cases for Further Consideration

1.   Is the principle of nonmaleficence equivalent to 'First, do no harm'? Explain.

2.   Consider two examples (real or imagined) of hard paternalism in clinical practice and discuss whether they can be justified.

3.   Reportedly, a disproportionate number of poor women in India undergo medically unnecessary hysterectomies because they are persuaded by doctors motivated by profit. What might principlists say about this?

4.   *Oops. In the middle of a liver transplant operation something unexpected happens. When the surgeon lifts the donor organ out of the steel basin to insert it in the abdominal cavity, he loses his grip and drops the liver on the floor! But at this point, there is no going back. They carefully retrieve the liver from the floor, rinse it off thoroughly with distilled water, and begin suturing it into place. The patient is not rejecting the new organ. Six months later, the patient is doing fine. He is grateful for what the surgical team have accomplished.* Has the patient been wronged? Should he be told about what happened during the transplant surgery? Does he have a right to this information? Is the fact that problems might develop with the new liver later on relevant? (Based on an actual case.)

5.   Vaccination. *All children entering kindergarten at the Grover Cleveland Elementary School are required to be vaccinated for polio, measles, and several other infectious diseases. This is a standard public health requirement for admission to public schools in the United States and many other countries. However, the Olmquists refuse vaccination of their daughter because they believe vaccination is forbidden in the Bible. Furthermore, they fear it contributes to autism. The principal of Grover Cleveland Elementary refuses to admit their child without the vaccinations.* Which of the moral obligations discussed in this chapter are at stake here? What reasons can be given for the principal's refusal? Does she violate her duty of respect for autonomy? Should it matter that the Olmquists are invoking their religious beliefs? How might casuists analyze this case?

6.   Alison Davis, *in a letter to the editor of the* British Medical Journal (1994) *invokes her own case of "severe spina bifida" and depression to argue that, since she had suicidal thoughts, had medical assistance in dying been legal "I would have availed myself of it." Furthermore, assisted death would reduce health care providers' motivation to help people like her. It may even "establish the view that death is in the best interests of those with incurable conditions."* Must that view always amount to unjustified paternalism? Is Davis's own position paternalistic too? Does she make a strong case against legalizing medically assisted death for nonterminally ill patients with severe disabilities? What's the role of beneficence and respect for autonomy here? Can suicidal patients ever be substantially autonomous?

Suggested Readings*

---

*Ackerman, Terrence F., "Why Doctors Should Intervene," *Hastings Center Report* 12.4, 1982: 14–17.

---

*   Asterisks mark readings available online. See links on the companion website.

Argues that, since patients are in a dependency condition, respect for autonomy cannot be understood as noninterference. Health care providers must sometimes override patients' decisions to help them recover substantial autonomy.

*Arras, John, "Theory and Bioethics," *The Stanford Encyclopedia of Philosophy*, Edward Zalta, ed., 2010. Available online at http://plato.stanford.edu/archives/sum2013/entries/theory-bioethics/.

Questions the appeal in bioethics to principles or general theories. Most of the time, these cannot help in resolving the moral puzzles that arise in clinical consultation and social policy formation. Finds also problems in casuistry and particularism.

*Beauchamp, Tom L., "Principlism and Its Alleged Competitors," *Kennedy Institute of Ethics Journal* 5.3, 1995: 181–98.

A defense of the four-principles approach as presented in Beauchamp and Childress's (1979) classic work.

*Callahan, Daniel, "Principlism and Communitarianism," *Journal of Medical Ethics* 29.5, 2003: 287–91.

Communitarian rejection of principlism, which is regarded as too individualistic and unhelpful outside the issues its principles were devised to resolve.

*Cowart, Dax and Robert Burt, "Confronting Death: Who Chooses, Who Controls? A Dialogue Between Dax Cowart and Robert Burt," *Hastings Center Report* 28.1, 1998: 14–17.

The authors agree that health providers should honor patients' valid refusals of treatment. But, for Burt, attempts at persuasion are justified—as is paternalism until health care providers can ascertain that the patient has substantial autonomy.

Goldman, Alan, *The Moral Foundations of Professional Ethics*. Lanham, MD: Rowman and Littlefield, 1980.

Rejects some main arguments for paternalism in medicine, arguing that respect for autonomy rests not only on utilitarian reasons, but, most important, on respect for persons' moral agency.

*Jonsen, Alfred, "Casuistry: An Alternative or Complement to Principles?" *Kennedy Institute of Ethics Journal* 5.3, 1995: 237–51.

Defends the moderate view of casuistry we found compatible with principlism. It contrasts with that of Jonsen and Toulmin (1988).

Maclean, Alasdair, *Autonomy, Informed Consent and Medical Law: A Relational Challenge*. Cambridge: Cambridge University Press, 2009.

Argues for the significance of respect for autonomy from the standpoint of the patient–health care professional relationship.

*Smith Iltis, Ana, "Bioethics as Methodological Case Resolution: Specification, Specified Principlism and Casuistry," *Journal of Medicine and Philosophy* 25.3, 2000: 271–84.

Introduction to an issue of this journal with important contributions to case analysis from principlist and casuist perspectives. Argues that, to be action-guiding, bioethics must move away from theory.

Tauber, Alfred I., *Patient Autonomy and the Ethics of Responsibility*. Cambridge, MA: MIT Press, 2005.

Offers a historically minded critique of the rise of respect for patient autonomy in a practice of medicine that's increasingly impersonal and cost-oriented.

4

Managing Patient Information

Learning Objectives

In reading this chapter you will

▶   Reflect on the requirement of medical confidentiality and its exceptions.

▶   Consider cases where truth-telling seems to conflict with other values in clinical practice.

▶   Distinguish some main types of deception in medicine.

▶   Evaluate main reasons for a right to remain ignorant about one's own genetic makeup.

PATIENTS AND HEALTH care providers have a special relationship that is fundamental to the goals of medicine. It is one that requires, for health care providers, maximizing health benefits for patients while upholding values such as honesty, respect for patient autonomy, beneficence, and justice for all affected parties. But on occasion upholding one of these requires sacrificing one or more of the others. For example, telling an elderly patient that they have terminal cancer appears to respect patient autonomy, but also to raise beneficence concerns, given possible harmful effects of the revelation. To complicate things more, in some cultures such revelations are expected, while in others considered shameful. What should health care providers do? Questions of this sort, involving appropriate management of patient medical information, arise in all areas of health care and social and administrative work related to medicine.

4.1 The Tarasoff Decision

According to one of the oldest ethical rules in Western medicine, health care providers have a duty not to reveal confidential medical information about their patients. But in 1976 that strict vow of silence came to be challenged. The Supreme Court of California's ruling in *Tarasoff v Regents of the University of California* upended the conventional way of thinking about **medical confidentiality.** The case concerned an incident in 1969 between two students at the University of California at Berkeley, Tatiana Tarasoff and Prosenjit Poddar. In August of that year, Poddar was in out-patient psychiatric care at the University's Cowell Memorial Hospital in Berkeley. In a therapy session, he revealed to his psychologist, Dr. Lawrence Moore, his intention to kill an unnamed young woman, easily identifiable as Tatiana Tarasoff, when she returned from her summer vacation in Brazil. After consultation with Dr. Powelson, director of the department of psychiatry at Cowell, Dr. Moore had Poddar detained by the campus police so that he could be subjected to observation in a mental hospital. But Poddar showed no evidence of irrationality and was held only briefly. Perhaps because they were well aware of the strictures of the confidentiality rule in medicine, the doctors made no effort to warn Tatiana about Poddar's threat. Two months later, Poddar stalked Tatiana and stabbed her to death.

■ ■ ■

Tatiana's parents, incensed that medical scruples about confidentiality had enabled a violent psychopath to murder their daughter, brought suit against the hospital. In their view, the doctors had failed to warn their daughter of the mortal threat from Poddar, and were thereby guilty of criminal negligence. Their case, however, was dismissed by the court on the grounds that Dr. Moore and his colleagues were protected by the rule of medical confidentiality. Unhappy with this development, the Tarasoffs appealed. Eventually the Supreme Court of California ruled that the medical staff at Cowell had indeed been negligent in their failure to protect Tatiana and that in this case the medical duty of confidentiality should have been overridden by the duty to protect a third party from impending danger. Poddar, meanwhile, was convicted of second-degree murder, a conviction that was later overturned on a technicality (the jury had not been properly instructed). The State of California decided not to pursue another trial, and Poddar was freed on the condition that he return to his native India, which he did.

In this and other cases concerning the managing of patient information by medical providers it should be kept in mind that those providers have the following obligations toward patients:

1.   Confidentiality: patient information must not be disclosed beyond what's agreed.
2.   Privacy: patients control access to their own health care information.

(1) and (2) are obligations derived from patient autonomy. As such, they may sometimes conflict with obligations of nonmaleficence, beneficence, and justice. In *Tarasoff*, (1) conflicted with the doctors' duty to prevent significant harm to Tatiana—a duty of beneficence that they could have discharged only by disclosing to the authorities Poddar's confidential information. Whether they did the right thing by honoring (1) at the cost of beneficence is a matter of dispute to be taken up below.

But not all questions about the flow of medical information involve duties of confidentiality or **privacy**. Equally essential to maintaining a patient-medical professional relationship conducive to healing is truth-telling. What are the grounds of this duty? How much medical information must be provided in cases where there is evidence that full disclosure can lead to bad health outcomes in the short run? We saw in Chapter 3 that defining goals of medicine include promoting patient health and reducing suffering whenever possible. But these goals are difficult to attain without patient cooperation. And no such cooperation would be forthcoming if patients regarded health care providers as lacking trustworthiness and honesty in their management of medical information.

4.2 Medical Confidentiality

When keeping patient information confidential puts others at risk of serious harm, there is a dilemma similar to that faced in *Tarasoff* by the therapists, which is outlined here:

FIGURE 4.1   Tarasoff-Like Dilemmas

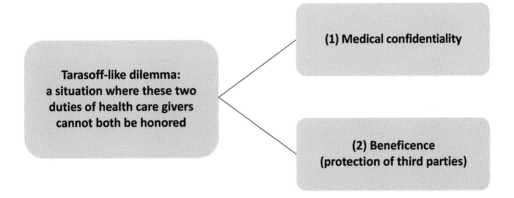

In the Tarasoff case, Dr. Moore and his colleagues took option (1) in Figure 4.1, while the California Supreme Court, in a majority opinion authored by Justice Matthew Tobriner, held that favoring that option in disregard of (2) was the wrong choice. Prioritizing medical confidentiality in the circumstances amounted to negligence. Not only did they fail to warn Tatiana (as charged by the plaintiffs), they failed to *protect* her from a foreseeable threat (the mortal danger posed by Poddar). According to the majority opinion, when psychotherapists realize a patient poses a serious risk to others, they have an obligation to "use reasonable care to protect the intended victim." Thus understood, the obligation goes beyond merely warning the victim of any potential danger. In the decades since *Tarasoff* was handed down, court rulings in most US states limited it to the duty to *protect* an individual third party when she or he is an *identifiable* potential victim.

But can psychiatrists accurately predict whether a patient will seriously harm others? Many argue that it's next-to-impossible, especially for patients who have never yet been violent. After a former marine with symptoms of mental illness went on a shooting rampage at the Washington Navy Yard in 2013, psychiatrists interviewed by *The New York Times* agreed that it was impossible to predict whether someone with a declared intention to commit violent acts would be likely to act on it.[2] Such uncertainty makes dilemmas like Dr. Moore's difficult to resolve. Furthermore, taking whatever steps are "reasonably necessary" to protect foreseeable victims of a violent patient, as ruled by the Tarasoff court, may result in a patient's detention or involuntary commitment to a mental institution, which appears unjustified on the basis of what is little more than an educated guess.

Confidentiality has long been considered a moral duty in medicine not to be taken lightly. In the "Oath of Hippocrates," we find the physician swearing to keep to himself whatever he learns about a patient during medical encounters:

---

2   Denise Grady, "Signs May Be Evident in Hindsight, but Predicting Violent Behavior Is Tough," *New York Times*, 9/19/2013.

"What I may see or hear in the course of treatment, or even outside of the treatment, in regard to the life of men, which on no account one must spread abroad, I will keep to myself, holding such things shameful to be spoken about. . . ."

Confidentiality also figures prominently in current ethical codes of professional organizations, among which the consensus is that

> In most situations, health care professionals must protect patients' privacy by keeping medical information confidential.

Thus construed, the confidentiality rule can be found, for instance, in statements such as "Patients have a right to expect that information about them will be held in confidence by their doctors," and "Confidentiality is central to trust between doctors and patients." In statements by the UK General Medical Council (2009) confidentiality is considered central to the trust between doctors and patients and a right of patients, who may expect that information about them will be held in confidence. The ethical codes of the American Medical Association, the British Medical Association, the French *Ordre National des Médecins*, the World Medical Association and other organizations contain similar statements. But these codes also recognize exceptions to confidentiality, which we'll consider later, after having a quick look at the grounds for those statements.

Philosophical Grounds

The Kantian Perspective

For Kantians, medical confidentiality is an absolute duty supported by the Categorical Imperative. First, the universalizability test suggests that, since one may (1) want information concerning one's own health care to be kept private, and (2) can consistently will that this rule become a universal law, therefore health care professionals should keep that information confidential. That is, they should manage medical information about patients much as attorneys and clergymen manage sensitive details about the lives of clients or parishioners they are trying to help, and to whom they are understood to have a duty to abstain from revealing private information. But this appeal to universalizability faces the objection that someone may instead (1) want such information to be divulged and (2) can consistently will that this rule become a universal law. So the appeal to the 'universalizability test' is inconclusive. A stronger Kantian argument for medical confidentiality invokes the 'humanity formulation' of the Categorical Imperative: health care providers have a duty to treat patients as ends in themselves, not merely as means, that's based on the requirement all moral agents have to respect the autonomy and dignity of persons. As such, patients expect that any information about their medical condition obtained in the course of treatment will be kept private. The health care provider's failure to keep a deferential vow of silence would amount to treating patients as mere means, the wrongness of which is analogous to that of breaking promises.

The Utilitarian Perspective

Given utilitarianism, medical confidentiality is a conditional duty of health care profession-als, for *if* they are to have a good chance of success in achieving the end in view (i.e., healing the patient), then they must be permitted to know crucial and often intimate details about the patient's condition. If patients believe they can trust their physician or nurse to keep medical information confidential, they'll feel more comfortable revealing private facts about themselves that may be relevant to their condition—for example, facts about their sexual practices, bodily functions, and personal habits, such as alcohol or drug use. But patients will be unlikely to reveal such information unless they can trust their health care providers to keep it confidential. The argument runs:

1. In order for medical treatments and therapies to achieve their goals, medical profes-sionals need health-related information from patients.
2. Patients will not provide that information unless it is kept confidential.

---

3. Therefore, medical professionals can achieve their goal of healing only if they observe the rule of medical confidentiality.

This argument is consistent with regarding medical confidentiality as a universal duty contingent upon the promotion of the greatest sum of wellbeing. That was the sticking

IMAGE 4.1
©iStockPhoto/Steve Debenport

point in the *Tarasoff* decision, for both the majority opinion mentioned above, and the dissenting opinion authored by Justice William P. Clark. According to the former, the greatest overall balance of wellbeing in the community requires protecting the likely victim of serious harm, which justifies breaches of medical confidentiality. Justice Clark disagreed: in the long run, such breaches will erode patients' trust in the health care system, and the community will be worse off. The mentally ill, fearing further stigmatization and even detention if their confidences were to be disclosed, will become wary of seeking treatment. In the end, Clark thinks, this would lead to an increase in violent crime in the community. Thus, as with other uncertain matters involving human behavior, in *Tarasoff* two utilitarians disagree about *which* action would maximize wellbeing. But they agree that medical confidentiality is a duty to be breached only under special circumstances.

The Virtue and Care Ethics Perspectives

For virtue ethicists, medical confidentiality is not so much a *duty* of health care providers as a practice betokening a trait of their character. Virtuous health care providers simply do not divulge medical information entrusted to them by patients, since, owing to their cultivation of certain habits of self-control, it's not in their nature to do so. Patient confidentiality is mainly associated with the virtues of loyalty, trust, respect, and care. Consistent with this view is the care-ethics approach to thinking about medical confidentiality. Care ethicists are likely to emphasize the *relational nature* of this notion. For one thing, managing medical information about a patient is a matter that concerns at least two moral agents, the health care provider and the patient. The medical encounter determines that these agents fashion a relationship of a very special kind, one that must be founded on trust and respect. Since patients expect their health care providers to protect their private information, any failure to do so would undermine trust and respect, the very foundations of the healing relationship.

The Rights-Theory Perspective

On this theory, the confidentiality rule captures a fundamental negative duty of health care providers that is associated with respect for individual privacy. Correlative with this duty is the patients' negative right of not being interfered with by the invasions of their private lives that would result from unwanted disclosure of their personal information. Like the right to make their own decisions about medical treatment, confidentiality is a negative right because it does not require the provision of assistance by others. As discussed in Chapter 18, negative rights are considered more stringent than positive rights, which do require such assistance. Privacy is very stringent: it has the status of a human right, recognized as such by the European Convention on Human Rights (ECHR), whose much-cited article 8.1 declares: "Everyone has the right to respect for his private and family life, his home and his correspondence" (European Court of Human Rights, 1953: 10).

Absolutism, Universalism, and Skepticism

Does the failure to follow the confidentiality rule *always* amount to a serious breach in what the medical team owes to patients? There are three possible positions on this question, which we may call:

1.   Absolutism—The rule must never be breached.
2.   Universalism—Although universally valid, the rule has exceptions.
3.   Skepticism—The rule is obsolete.

Since (2), confidentiality **universalism**, has already emerged in connection with *Tarasoff* and ethical codes of most professional associations, we'll here consider (1), confidentiality **absolutism**, and (3), confidentiality skepticism. Today (1) faces many criticisms. Historically, it was endorsed in Hippocratic medicine, and ratified in the AMA's 1903/1912 *Principles of Medical Ethics*, which prescribes "none of the privacies of individual or domestic life, no infirmity of disposition or flaw of character observed during medical attendance should ever be divulged by physicians except when imperatively required by laws of state" and the WMA's 1949 *International Code of Medical Ethics* which recommends "a doctor shall preserve absolute secrecy on all he knows about his patient because of the confidence entrusted in him" (cited in Gillon and Sokol, 2012). Underwriting confidentiality absolutism is the view that, over time, the greatest wellbeing for all concerned can be achieved by strict adherence to confidentiality, even in cases where it seems counterintuitive not to allow exceptions. On this view, breaches of confidentiality would erode the patient-medical professional relationship and ultimately medicine would be worse off. Kipnis (2007) provides some evidence that, when there are risks to third parties, breaches of confidentiality compromise the health care providers' trustworthiness and are less effective in enlisting patients into "therapeutic alliances" that maximize benefits for all involved.

But since there is also evidence to the contrary, absolutism conflicts with (2), a universalist view endorsed by most professional associations. Given (2), confidentiality should be honored but there are exceptions to it. Thus confidentiality universalism is consistent with the duty to disclose patients' health records in *Tarasoff*-like scenarios, something that agrees with common intuitions about the duty to report, for example, the HIV status of a patient who intends to hide it from a sexual partner, or a patient's plans to carry out a terrorist attack in a public place. Another problem is that unless medical confidentiality were the only absolute duty of health care professionals (something highly implausible), confidentiality absolutism cannot resolve conflicts with other absolute duties.

At the other extreme is (3), the skeptical view that confidentiality is no longer applicable. Skeptics such as Siegler (1982) invoke evidence from current practices in the management of patient medical records showing that far too many health care workers have access to a patient's records. The cybernetic age presents another skeptical challenge to confidentiality, since medical files are now kept in 'the cloud' which increases their vulnerability. Skeptics invoke also the many exceptions to confidentiality accepted in bioethics and the law. As shown in Box 4.1 below, these are not limited to **Tarasoff-like dilemmas**, because the law requires that health care providers report, for example, gunshot wounds, outbreaks of contagious disease, abuse (especially child abuse), and health issues that may undermine a patient's ability to operate machinery when the impairment may pose significant danger to third parties. These include drug addiction or alcoholism in a commercial airline pilot or bus driver, and epilepsy or extreme myopia in vehicle operators generally. In addition, some jurisdictions require health care providers to notify parents of teenagers when their under-age daughter is seeking an abortion. And many states require the medical team and home health providers to report physical or financial abuse of vulnerable elders.

BOX 4.1 SOME EXCEPTIONS TO MEDICAL CONFIDENTIALITY

Disclosures of patient information to third parties are justified when necessary to deliver ordinary or emergency care, or when authorized by the patient. They include information disclosed in contexts such as

- Dictating a referral letter to an employee
- Making a genetic diagnosis of a patient's relative (requires informed consent)

Morally controversial are disclosures

- To protect foreseeable victims of significant harms
- Ordered by a legal authority or statute
- For medical teaching or research
- For self-studies of health care services

Objections to skepticism about medical confidentiality are many. For one thing, it lacks support from both moral theory and the Hippocratic tradition. As we've just seen, whatever our theoretical sympathies, *most* major moral theories coincide in vindicating medical confidentiality as either a duty or a value for virtuous health care providers. Skeptics have the burden of arguing that confidentiality is not required by the health care providers' duties of beneficence and respect for autonomy. Needless to say, confidentiality breaches can result, at the very least, in great distress for the patient. They also have to argue against deeply entrenched views about the virtues of medical professionals as healers and the role of confidentiality in building trust, one of the key elements of the health care relationship.

It seems that neither confidentiality absolutism nor skepticism is supported by convincing reasons. And since, if adopted, each would come at a high cost for patients and the public, universalism, a middle-way position, appears not only more plausible but also more viable in light of existing, morally acceptable laws. For example, the US Health Insurance Portability and Accountability Act (HIPPA) requires that health care data that are personally identifiable to a patient and shared by providers be kept confidential. Data created, used, or disclosed during medical care are Protected Health Information (PHI) and fall under HIPPA. They include billing and scheduling information, results from MRI scans and blood tests, and other data personally linked to a patient. ePHI protects all individually identifiable information that is created, maintained, or transmitted electronically. By contrast, consumer health information is not thus linked and falls outside HIPPA. But the current tendency to share health data makes most patient information PHI.

4.3 Must Health Care Professionals Always Tell the Truth?

Disclosure and Deception Defined

Disclosing bad news to a patient is another vexing question concerning the management of information. Given the prevalent view in the US and other common law jurisdictions, health care providers must take reasonable steps to disclose relevant facts about their diagnoses and prognoses. Called '**disclosure**,' 'truth-telling' or 'veracity,' this obligation correlates with a positive right of patients to be sufficiently informed, in an understandable way, about their medical conditions. If patients cannot understand the information, it can hardly count as disclosed.

FIGURE 4.2   Disclosure in Clinical Practice

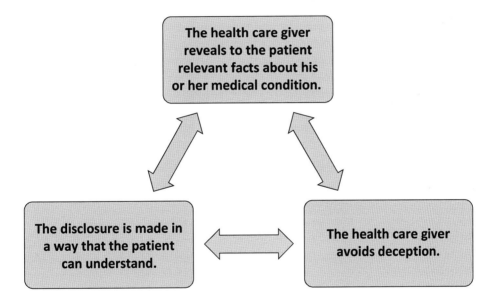

Disclosure is of course incompatible with all forms of **medical deception**. Lying occurs when a person says what she or he believes is false, with the intention to deceive, and misleading when a health care provider intentionally lets a patient believe what that provider knows is not true—as, for example, that a chronic or terminal health condition will improve, or that a treatment involves no risks when it does. Omissions such as **nondisclosure** (omitting to reveal all relevant facts about a patient's health) and **under-disclosure** (withholding some relevant facts about a patient's health while revealing others) are misleading the patient, thus counting as deception. Anything short of sufficient disclosure can harm the health care system, because it risks eroding patients' trust in providers. On these utilitarian grounds, lying is worse than misleading, because it is perceived as a more serious breach of trust. Even so, there seem to be exceptions. Here is a case where misleading might even be justified:

Mrs. Talbot has always been in good health, except for her high blood pressure. Now she and her husband are looking forward to an upcoming trip to New England to attend their daughter's law school graduation, which they expect will be a very festive occasion. But before they go, Mrs. Talbot undergoes a Pap smear by Dr. Lewis, her physician for more than 25 years. The procedure finds cervical dysplasia. Although lab reports have been delayed this week, on the very day the Talbots are to leave on their trip her report comes back pointing to abnormal cells on the surface of the cervix. While the doctor is weighing considerations for and against informing the patient immediately, Mrs. Talbot calls. "Dr. Lewis, anything I need to know before I leave?" she asks. "Oh, lab reports are delayed this week. Give me a call when you get back from your trip. We're sure to have results by then."

If Dr. Lewis discloses the truth to his patient, he will spoil her trip. Moreover, he knows that Mrs. Talbot is the sort of person who tends to have hypertension crises when told bad news. So he decides to wait and not disclose the results until the Talbots return in a few days. He will recommend further tests. Dysplasia can go away on its own, and rarely develops into cancer. A few days will probably make no difference, Dr. Lewis thinks.

Since lab reports were indeed delayed that week, Dr. Lewis did not lie but rather timed his disclosure: he omitted the truth for the time being. Because his motive was to avoid causing distress, whether his deception was justified turns on what we make of the doctor's comparative assessment of the potential harm and benefit of timing the disclosure, about which he has expert knowledge. Although his paternalistic decision deprives the patient of her right to decide whether to go on the trip, he plans a full disclosure in circumstances more conducive to her being capable of managing the news. Arguably, if Mrs. Talbot were to learn about his deception, his omission would be more easily excused than outright lying.

FIGURE 4.3   Some Failures to Disclose

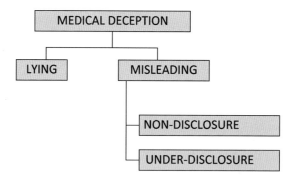

Disclosure is commonly understood as deriving from respect for patient autonomy, one of several prima facie obligations of health care providers. In some circumstances, then, disclosure may conflict with, and be overridden by, nonmaleficence, beneficence, or justice. Here is one such scenario:

Skin Cancer. A 90-year-old war veteran attaches a stigma to cancer, cannot possibly comprehend that some forms of cancer are now curable, and would become very upset if he were to learn that he in fact has skin cancer—even though it is not life-threatening. He asks his doctor whether his recent skin problem is cancer (which it is). The doctor says "No" and begins the cancer treatment (from Beauchamp and Childress, 2009: 285).

Arguably, in this case beneficence justifies the doctor's paternalistic lying. Full disclosure could cause unreasonable fear or depression in the patient, to a degree that may interfere seriously with therapeutic goals.

Evolving Attitudes toward Disclosure

Unlike medical confidentiality, whose acknowledgement by medical professionals goes back to antiquity, acknowledgment of the moral obligation of disclosure is a 20th century development. In the Hippocratic tradition, truth-telling by physicians was considered optional at best, and especially to be avoided in worst-case scenarios where the patient's prognosis was grim. In such situations, health care providers paternalistically decided that disclosure was not in the patient's best interest. As late as 1847, chapter I.1, sec. 4, of the American Medical Association's *Code* still held that a physician "should not be forward to make gloomy prognostications. . . . For, the physician should be the minister of hope and comfort to the sick. . . ."

Such paternalistic views continued through the first half of the 20th century. In the US, of a group of physicians surveyed in 1961, 88% did not regularly observe disclosure. By 1979, 98% did (Farzaneh, 2011). Today there is a much wider acceptance of a duty of disclosure among medical professionals in English-speaking countries and some other liberal democracies. But even in countries where health care professionals strive to honor respect for patient autonomy, cases where the truth is withheld from patients for paternalistic reasons are not unknown. It is, after all, one thing to give verbal assent to a rule, but another to act on it when the time comes, and it should be no surprise that delivering bad news, such as a prognosis of imminent death, is not an easy thing to do, even for health care providers of many years' experience. Being the bearer of such bad news takes a powerful emotional toll on clinicians who often must struggle within themselves to gather the strength to say what must be said (Ofri, 2012). Nurses caring for terminally ill patients develop special relationships with them, which in turn increases the moral distress when they have to choose between encouraging hope and revealing the truth.

Moral Grounds for Disclosure

Although the moral obligation of disclosure rests largely on respect for patient autonomy, it has been argued that, at least in the long run, it is in the patient's best interests. Later we'll have more to say about why disclosure is necessary for patients to be able to give valid consent. For now, keep in mind that, in the absence of adequate information, any consent to treatment a patient may give would fall short of being *informed*, and thus, of expressing an autonomous decision. Thus, deception conflicts with patient autonomy. Making autonomous decisions about medical treatment requires that patients sufficiently know, and reasonably grasp, important facts about their conditions. A patient who makes treatment decisions in ignorance of the facts does not act autonomously, since she has not been given a clear view of the options from which to choose.

Other ways in which disclosure promotes patients' best interest include that it gives them a chance to

- Avoid false hopes,
- Conclude unfinished business, and
- Put personal affairs in order.

But not all are so enthusiastic about disclosure. Mack Lipkin (1979), for example, argues that most patients, because their knowledge of human anatomy and physiology is likely to be minimal, their knowledge of medicine nil, are in no position to understand what their physicians tell them and will only be misled by the doctors' well-meaning attempt at explanation of the prognosis.

That is not, however, the prevalent view. A more typical position can be supported by different moral reasons. For natural law theorists, knowledge is a basic value that requires truth; thus, *intentional deception* in medicine is strictly forbidden. Virtue ethicists are committed to supporting disclosure because they regard veracity and honesty as fundamental traits of good character for medical professionals. Care ethicists take such traits to be essential to the trust and respect necessary for the patient-professional relationship. Kantians would especially reject lying, which shows lack of respect due to patients by failure to treat them as an end in themselves. Rossians might reject all forms of deception, adding prima facie duties of beneficence as grounds.

For utilitarians, the bad consequences of deceiving patients 'for their own good' suggest that it must *nearly always* be ruled out. Dying patients who are not told the relevant facts about their condition may not be able to put their affairs in order and make necessary arrangements for the time they have left. That can increase the total amount of suffering in the long run. Moreover, patients who are deceived may lose confidence in their health care providers once the deception comes to light. With that loss of trust, the health care system may no longer be able to treat the patient effectively. Furthermore, by contrast with poorly informed patients, those properly informed are more likely to cooperate and engage actively in medical treatment in ways that benefit them. In addition, deception may lead to misusing scarce medical resources, for patients who are not told the truth may wish to pursue treatments that are pointless, or that may not be available in their geographical area. Dialysis for patients in end-stage renal failure, for example, arguably makes this limited medical resource inaccessible for other patients in need (Pentheny O'Kelly et al., 2011). Since wasting such resources ought to be avoided, patients should be told the truth.

The Problem of Culture

The rule of disclosure faces a **culture problem** because, although many think it universally valid, its observance varies across cultures, as illustrated by these high-profile cases:

In 1989, when Japan's *Emperor Hirohito* was dying, his subjects were not told that the Emperor's illness was terminal cancer. After his death, it emerged that even the Emperor himself had not been told the truth by his doctors.

Eva Peron, Argentina's first lady in the 1940s–1950s, was told only that she suffered from a "uterine problem," when in reality it was terminal cervical cancer. She never learned that she had been subjected to a surgical procedure by an American specialist while under anesthesia and may even have undergone a lobotomy to relieve her pain (Lerner, 2011).

In Western liberal democracies, where individual autonomy enjoys high recognition, it is surprising to learn that even dignitaries as exalted as these were not considered autonomous enough to be told the truth by their doctors. But not all cultures are equally enthusiastic about patient autonomy and disclosure. The deception of Emperor Hirohito and the Japanese people needs to be understood in the context of a deep value divide that separates the individualist West and the communitarian East, something often emphasized in studies by cross-cultural psychologists (Nisbett, 2003). Given this divide, assuming the universality of those values might amount to

---

Ethical Imperialism

The attempt to impose one's own (usually, Western) ethical values or rules on others.

In cultures with a more communitarian worldview, medical decisions are made interactively between patients and family. Furthermore, it is sometimes thought that having a terminal condition is shameful, or that disclosure can shorten the patient's life by undermining hope. For example, data collected from 1/1/1999 to 6/30/2000 by the ETHICUS (End-of-Life Practices in European Intensive Care Units) study showed that, in Southern Europe, many physicians give such paternalistic reasons for disclosing bad news *only* to the patient's relatives, delegating any decisionmaking to them (Pentheny O'Kelly et al., 2011: 3839). Religious beliefs may also militate against disclosure. In Muslim culture, for example, conveying bad news to the patient shows disrespect for the belief that it is God who determines the end of life (Beyene, 1992).

What, then, should health care providers make of such different perspectives on disclosure? In our view, there are strong moral grounds for considering patient autonomy, and therefore disclosure, prima facie duties of health care providers. But they have other equally important prima facie duties such as nonmaleficence, beneficence, and justice. Autonomy needs to be balanced with these and, on occasion, can be outweighed. It is also important to keep in mind that, given patient autonomy, waivers of disclosure must be honored. We'll have more to say about this in connection with the right to ignorance below. Sensitivity to cultural and religious diversity is always recommended but need not undermine the universal value of disclosure. As discussed in Chapter 2, appeals to diversity are insufficient to support normative relativism. Furthermore, relativists about disclosure tend to reduce all reasons for it to 'preparing the patient for death,' neglecting that disclosure is necessary to protect patients from having imposed on them the 'standards of care' of their medical professionals—rather than being allowed to make their own self-regarding decisions about their care. The doctrine of informed consent was devised to protect that right (more on this in Chapter 5). The bottom line is that health care providers should devote time to learning about the patient's wishes and engaging in advance care planning. Edmund Pellegrino's early advice continues to be relevant: autonomy and beneficence can both be preserved if health care providers "get to know their patients well enough to discern when, and if, those patients wish to contravene the mores of prevailing medical culture. This requires a degree of familiarity and sensitivity . . . morally inescapable for every physician who practices in today's morally and culturally diverse world society" (1992a: 1735).

■ 4.4 Genetic Information

The rapidly changing field of genetics has made innumerable contributions to medical science, including improvements in our understanding of the pathogenesis of health conditions affecting individuals, families, and sometimes groups. Genetic testing now allows patients to acquire information about the risks for them and their future children of developing certain diseases. But that information is not always welcome. After folk-singer Woody Guthrie died of Huntington's disease in 1967, his son Arlo reportedly decided to remain ignorant about whether he carried the gene himself. (He later learned that he didn't.) Genomic testing can also reveal one's risk of developing Alzheimer's disease by showing which variant of a gene one has inherited. Variant E4 triples that risk. Some eminent researchers have chosen not to learn which variant they carry, among them James Watson, who shared the Nobel Prize with Francis Crick for discovering the structure of DNA, and Harvard psychologist Stephen Pinker (see his 2009). In some circumstances, health professionals may need to know about the genetic makeup of some patients, and this can conflict with the patient's right to remain ignorant.

Before discussing which circumstances these might be, we need some clarity about genetic knowledge, as well as about two misunderstandings of human genetics. One of these reduces all factors for health, disability, and disease to genetics; the other to environment.

Genetic Knowledge

Developments in genetics have helped to advance scientific knowledge of health, disability, and disease, while also debunking some misconceptions about their genetic components. Early in this century, genomics, the specialization within genetics and molecular biotechnology devoted to the study of the structure and function of genes, mapped the partial or entire DNA sequences of many species. A species' genome is the sum total of the DNA sequence of an organism of that species, and thus contains all the information necessary to construct and maintain the organism. A turning point in genomics occurred with the **Human Genome Project's (HGP)** mapping of the entire sequence of human DNA. The HGP, completed in 2003 by two groups of researchers working independently (one with private funds, the other with funds from the US government), revealed that the human genome contains approximately 20,000 genes, depending on how 'gene' is defined. By making all their findings available to researchers and clinicians in public databases, the HGP opened the way, at least in principle, to the identification of each gene and its function in health, disability, and disease. Before the HGP, genomics had yielded limited results, usually restricted to knowledge of congenital disorders with a clearly inherited basis, such as sickle cell anemia, Tay-Sachs disease, and cystic fibrosis. With the HGP's basic genome map, researchers saw an opportunity to advance knowledge of the genes and genetic variations and mutations that may contribute to the onset of other conditions, such as certain cancers, cardiovascular disease, and some neurodegenerative disorders. For example, in 2005 the US National Institutes of Health launched The Cancer Genome Atlas (TCGA), a multi-center research study of the genomic alterations in the tumors of ovarian, brain, and lung cancers. By 2015, TCGA was well underway and had expanded its scope to explore the genetic bases of other cancers.

Parallel to these developments were advances in genetic testing. Clinicians now hope this area of genetics will soon contribute to better treatment outcomes by revealing the most efficient therapies for a disease on the basis of gene changes. Current methods of genetic testing, however, do not always mean better therapy outcomes. In addition, the tests are commonly provided as part of a genetic consultation and involve some expense. Less costly are home-based, genetic test kits marketed online. But this option leaves users without proper direction for understanding the possible benefits and limitations of the tests, and so for making autonomous decisions about using them. Furthermore, without intervention by a genetic counselor, users are in the dark about how to interpret results. Worse, it leaves them vulnerable to the misconception we'll consider next.

Genetic Pseudo-Knowledge

Consider cancer again. Genetics in part accounts for having an increased risk of developing certain cancers, the resilience of some of them, and typical mutations in some cancer cells. As a result, screening and diagnostic tests can now be used for early detection of high risks of, for example, breast cancer in women who have inherited the gene mutations BRCA1 and BRCA2. When these mutations are present, health care professionals present the woman with possible measures aimed at prevention. Among the most radical options are elective mastectomy and hysterectomy, which involve bodily mutilation, possible psychological harms, and the risks of surgery. Each may have profound consequences for the woman's future quality of life. An informed decision then requires weighing all of these with the information provided by genetic counselors about the actual risk of having inherited the mutation.

In any case, it is important to keep in mind that, with conditions such as hereditary breast cancer, a woman's mutation for this disease, passed on to her by female ancestors, is only *one* of the factors that may contribute to the development of the disease. Other factors include age, having given birth, the full history of recent breast cancers in the family, changes in breast tissue, and even ethnic background. More generally, a weighing of all contributing factors should be done for any hereditary health condition that depends not only on genetics but also on diet, life-style, environment, etc. This requires rejecting the following pseudo-scientific assumption:

Genetic Determinism

All risk factors for hereditary diseases or disorders reduce to genetic makeup.

There is no science supporting this widespread misconception, which may have harmful consequences, such as the stigmatization of individuals at risk of genetically related illness, a common attitude justifiably feared by people at risk of genetic disease. The medical and research communities, together with the rest of society, should strive to educate the public by exposing **genetic determinism** as little more than superstition.

Likewise, there is no science supporting a contrary misconception holding that,

> **Environmental Determinism**
>
> All risk factors for allegedly hereditary diseases or disorders reduce to environment.

This generalization is false, as is shown by what is now known about exclusively hereditary conditions such as Huntington's—a rare, progressive, neurodegenerative disease that is invariably fatal if the sufferer lives long enough. Huntington's genetic basis, long suspected in medicine, was established beyond doubt in 1983 with the mapping of the disease's gene to human chromosome 4p. Later genomic discoveries paved the way for new studies ultimately designed to develop some therapies for Huntington's. At present, it can be neither cured nor prevented. When a patient has inherited this disease, some brain nerve cells will eventually stop working, usually in adulthood. This will severely impair intellectual abilities, movements, and emotions. With the onset of symptoms, a person has a life expectancy of 10 to 20 more years. The gene for the disease is present at birth, inherited from a parent. Anyone carrying it will eventually develop symptoms. Since an affected parent has a 50/50 chance of passing Huntington's on to offspring regardless of sex, patients with a family history of it can learn by genetic testing whether they carry the gene. If they do and wish to have children, a genetic counselor is equipped to explain their options.

Thus neither genetic determinism nor environmental determinism can capture the facts about the complex relations between hereditary disease, genetics, and the environment. Only genetics can, by developing branches concerned with studying those relations scientifically. Consider behavioral genetics, the branch devoted to studying behavioral variations in animals, including humans, resulting from complex interactions between genes and environment. It tells us that it is neither true that our mind is a 'blank slate' at birth (so that conditioning is the only cause of mental illness), nor that mental disorders are encoded in our genes in a straightforward way (so that it can be known by genetics whether a person will develop, for example, bipolar disorder). The truth lies in complex interactions between genes and the environment that are not yet fully understood.

Nondirective Genetic Counseling

According to the current standard, genetic counseling for patients at risk of genetic conditions should be nondirective or value-neutral. It should outline all the options available to the person, who is called the 'client,' without letting the counselor's values influence the final decision. Consider the case of a patient with a family history of Huntington's disease, who is pre-symptomatic but plans to have a child. Health care providers will likely recommend elective testing to see whether the patient has the gene that causes the disease. The patient will then be better informed to make a reproductive decision. Yet the predominant view in the genetic community is that the counselor should avoid offering any reproductive advice but instead simply present all options for having a healthy, genetically related baby. These include undergoing prenatal testing and therapeutic abortion to prevent the birth of a carrier child, or in-vitro fertilization in combination with preimplantation genetic testing to select embryos for implantation that do not carry the gene.

Note that, given **nondirective genetic counseling**, the client-genetic counselor relationship stands out as very different from that of the patient-medical team relationship. For one thing, only in the latter relationship is professional advice part of what patients generally expect. There is consensus among genetic counsellors that nondirective counseling is necessary to promote autonomous decisionmaking by clients. But some bioethicists question whether being nondirective is the right standard for genetic counseling. They also question an assumption that underlies that standard: that clients have a right to remain ignorant about important facts of their own genetic makeups.

Is There a Right to Genetic Ignorance?

Some persons at risk of genetic health conditions may wish to remain ignorant of their actual risk. This is particularly troublesome when genetic information about them can be of benefit to their relatives or to a larger group. For example, a woman from a family with a history of breast cancer may understandably say, "I don't want to be tested," or "I don't want to know the results of my test." That is, she refuses to participate in a so-called linkage study, or she might participate but prefer not to learn its results. Similarly, a person from an ethnic group with a high gene-disease association may refuse participation in a population genetics study. Or an individual with a family history for a genetic disease who is planning to become a parent may refuse genetic diagnosis, invoking a right to **genetic ignorance** (recall the *Arlo Guthrie* case). Clinicians and genetic counselors generally think that

FIGURE 4.4   Genetic Information and the Right to Genetic Ignorance

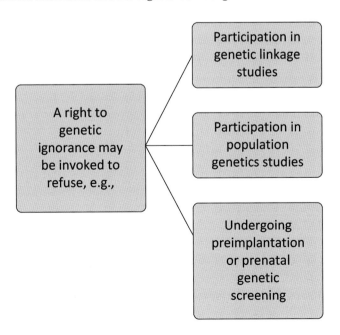

1.   Clients have a right to genetic ignorance, and
2.   Given the standard of nondirective genetic counseling, the counselor should abstain from attempting to persuade clients to undergo genetic screening when they competently refuse to do so.

In (1), the right to ignorance is regarded as a liberty that autonomous individuals have in a democratic society. Like other such liberties, this right can be limited only when its exercise may harm others (Takala, 1999). (2) rests on the consensus that nondirective genetic testing is required by respect for patient autonomy. The greatest challenge to (1) and (2) comes from cases where a patient at risk of carrying a gene with a strong disease association plans to raise a family, for an exercise of the patient's right to ignorance in those circumstances may result in the birth of a child at high risk of developing the parent's genetic condition. Refusals to participate in linkage studies fall short of posing a similar challenge, since genetic counselors can attempt to persuade those who claim the right to ignorance for participating in the study by promising that they will not disclose the genetic testing's results to them. Reasonable persuasion need not conflict with nondirective counseling.

Let's then look closely at the prospective-parent scenario. As we have seen, although genetic determinism is false, genetic factors are a component of many diseases and disabilities. Of course, one may have a natural aversion to learning that one is at risk of developing a genetic disease sometime in life. This is a difficult burden to bear and may weigh as a dark foreboding on one's enjoyment of life. But, arguably, if one is at risk of a disorder like Huntington's and plans to have a child, one has a duty to know in advance whether one carries the gene. If one has that duty, then there is no right to genetic ignorance in this scenario. The Children's Welfare Argument now charges

1.   If there is a right to genetic ignorance, then it is morally permissible for prospective parents at high risk of genetic disease to refuse genetic testing.
2.   Such refusals put their future child at risk of harm.
3.   Harming a child is morally impermissible.

---

4.   Therefore, it is morally impermissible for those prospective parents to refuse genetic testing.
5.   Therefore, there is no right to genetic ignorance.

This argument assumes that knowingly causing a child to come into existence with a severe hereditary condition amounts to harming it. But if the prospective parents had undergone genetic testing, that child might not have been born at all, so defenders of the right to ignorance find this argument unpersuasive. Among them is Tuija Takala (1999: 292), who further contends that parents have that right because "knowledge cannot be forced upon people." Having a duty to know one's genetic endowment would be contrary to human psychology, and therefore practically impossible.

The Argument from Genetic Ignorance's Foolishness is a rejoinder to this defense of the right to ignorance. It holds that prospective parents at risk of genetic conditions who claim that right will be left with the worse options of undergoing either

- In-vitro fertilization combined with preimplantation genetic diagnosis for the selective transfer of healthy embryos to the uterus, or
- Prenatal screening combined with selective abortion if the fetus carries the gene.

Each of these options is more costly, stressful, and morally problematic than preconception genetic testing of the parents. Therefore, it is foolish to refuse such testing. But this appeal offers only a prudential reason against what's regarded as a moral right to ignorance. If intended as a moral argument, it assumes that parents willing to accept the genetic lottery are doing something morally wrong. This is not evident unless it can be shown that they are harming their future children.

But given what we may call 'Kantian Patient Autonomy', prospective parents at risk of genetic disease might lack the right to genetic ignorance, and genetic counselors could accordingly be morally obliged to direct them into having genetic testing. Recall that for a Kantian, the duty of respect for patients' autonomy derives from respecting them as persons, which requires the promotion of their autonomous decisionmaking. Rosamond Rhodes (1998) argues that such prospective parents lack the right to genetic ignorance, because without genetic testing their decision to procreate lacks sufficient knowledge and fails therefore to be autonomous. Her objection aims not only at the alleged right to genetic ignorance, but also at the prevalent, nondirective standard of genetic counseling. In the scenario we are considering, however, common morality suggests that any waiver of the prospective parents' right to genetic ignorance would rest more on parental responsibilities to the future child than on the counselor's Kantian obligation of respect for their autonomy.

As a result, Rhodes' objection fails to undermine a *universal* right to genetic ignorance, which unlike an *absolute* right would have exceptions. Furthermore, as we saw above, many question generalizations about harm to future children (more on this in Chapters 14 and 15). Putting that aside, the objection fails to undermine the genetic counselors' view that they have a prima facie duty (i.e., other things being equal) to provide nondirective counseling in light of the need to avoid some moral wrongs of the early 20th-century, 'eugenic' programs. We'll consider such programs in Chapter 15.

4.5 Chapter Summary

This chapter began with the Tarasoff decision, a landmark case that introduced legal limits to the medical obligation of confidentiality, according to which patient information must not be disclosed beyond what's agreed. Our analysis of that decision led us to a closely related obligation of health care providers in the managing of patient information: respect for patient privacy, which prescribes that patients control access to their own health care information. Many bioethicists converge on the need for medical confidentiality, though their reasons differ according to their moral persuasions. Here we considered some utilitarian, Kantian, and virtue-ethics reasons.

But not all bioethicists agree about the scope of medical confidentiality: some endorse absolutism (the obligation can never be waived), others universalism (the obligation can sometimes be waived), or skepticism (in practice, the obligation can never be met). With respect to the now prevalent standard of disclosure in medicine, the bioethicists' stances also reflect their philosophical persuasions, though they may all vindicate it. Opposite to disclosure is deception, which includes lying, misleading, under-disclosure, and nondisclosure.

Our quick look at the history of disclosure in medicine showed that its recognition as a health care provider's duty is relatively recent but firm. In most common law jurisdictions, it is only under particular conditions that such duties might be waived, such as emergency situations. Standard moral theories might again agree on this, but for different reasons.

This chapter also considered how innovations in genetics raise questions about patient information. Full understanding of their significance requires the rejection of two pseudo-scientific claims: genetic determinism, the claim that all disease traits are simply encoded in our genes, and environmental determinism, the claim they are entirely a product of environmental conditions. That the truth lies somewhere in the middle is shown by evidence from genetics' studies of disorders, such as certain cancers.

Yet since conditions like Huntington's disease are genetically determined, questions arise about the prevalent, nondirective standard of genetic counseling, according to which it must be value neutral. Those questions are more pressing for prospective parents at risk of certain hereditary conditions. Given the prevalent standard, their right to genetic ignorance proscribes attempts at persuasion by genetic counselors. Against that standard and the right to genetic ignorance are objections from the Children's Welfare, Genetic Ignorance's Foolishness, and Kantian Patient Autonomy arguments—none of which can move those who take that right to be a fundamental value akin to those underlying other liberties of democratic societies.

4.6 Study Aids

Key Words

Absolutism/universalism, 75
Culture problem, 80
Disclosure/nondisclosure/under-disclosure, 77
Environmental/genetic determinism, 83
Ethical imperialism, 80
Genetic ignorance, 85
Human Genome Project (HGP), 82
Medical confidentiality, 69
Medical deception, 77
Nondirective genetic counseling, 84
Privacy, 70
Tarasoff-like dilemma, 71

Questions and Cases for Further Consideration

1. Explain which of the types of deception outlined above undermines the patient-health care professional relationship most. When, if at all, may health care providers deceive a patient?

2. The *Tarasoff* decision sanctioned that a psychotherapist must take "whatever steps are reasonably necessary under the circumstances" *to protect* third parties from significant foreseeable harms. What could such protections consist of? Why might psychotherapists object to that decision?

3. *A pilot for a major commercial airline is one of primary-care physician Dr. Burns' patients. The pilot is struggling with alcoholism, a condition that has grown worse over the years. Now he is beginning to have episodes of agitation, disorientation, and black-outs. Because of the medical confidentiality rule, Dr. Burns consults with the hospital's ethics committee about whether to inform the pilot's employer.* First, use utilitarian reasons to argue for and against honoring medical confidentiality in this case, and then decide which ones, if any, should prevail. If you were a member of the ethics committee, what guidance would you provide? (This narrative is based on an actual case.)

4. Dr. Joseph DeMasi, *a resident pursuing certification in child psychiatry at New York Medical College, began psychoanalysis himself with a psychiatrist on the faculty there, Dr. Douglas Ingram. During one of their sessions, Dr. DeMasi revealed that he was a pedophile. Dr. Ingram was stunned by this revelation, especially in view of DeMasi's intended field of specialization, which would require daily interaction with children. Mindful of medical confidentiality, Ingram neither reported DeMasi's revelation nor took steps to prevent DeMasi from completing his residency and qualifying as a child psychiatrist. Four months later, when DeMasi was in practice at Danbury Hospital in Connecticut, he molested a 10-year-old boy. The boy's parents brought suit, alleging that Dr. Ingram and New York Medical College were negligent in failing to stop DeMasi's career before he could harm children. But Ingram's attorneys countered that DeMasi had never actually announced an intention to act on his pedophile impulse. There was no identifiable potential victim to be warned.* In view of the facts, did Ingram face a Tarasoff-like dilemma? Might decisions like his be morally justified on consequentialist grounds? What difference, if any, could it have made that DeMasi never identified an intended victim? In your view, should confidentiality be breached to protect foreseeable but unknown victims?

5. Dorothy, *aged 7, was diagnosed with bone cancer and admitted to the Children's Oncology ward of a major hospital, where she is now receiving treatment. Her malignancy was caught early, so her prospects of long-term survival seem good. Even so, her parents are beside themselves with worry. They have not told Dorothy exactly what her disease is. They want to avoid frightening her unnecessarily. But one of the nurses raises a question: "What if Dorothy asks, 'Could I die from this disease?' What should we tell her? After all, children understand quite a lot, and the children on the oncology ward talk among themselves."* This case raises several moral problems. To prevent harm to Dorothy, her parents intend to keep her in the dark about her illness. Do you think that nondisclosure is likely to be in her interest over the long term? Does Dorothy have a right to medical disclosure? Should age matter for this? If the nurse were to tell Dorothy the truth without parental consent, would that be justified? (Based on Brody and Engelhardt, 1987: 349.)

6. *Carrese and Rhodes (1995) report that 86% of informants from a* Navajo Reservation *in northeast Arizona rejected medical disclosure and advance care planning. Between 1988 and*

1992, they surveyed 34 individuals, whose answers suggest that in their culture, it is believed that "bad outcomes can be avoided by not speaking of them." Dr. Stanford, whose prima-ry-care practice includes patients from the group, knows this, but is also aware that not every Navajo might agree. She wonders where her Navajo patient Thomas White stands. . . . After his episodes of lightheadedness and recent fall, she had ordered a laboratory evaluation of anemia. It revealed leukemia. But he sent his wife to receive the test results. She asked the doctor to start treatment without revealing the truth to Thomas. She would tell him that they showed anemia. (Adapted from Farzaneh, 2011.) In this situation, did Dr. Stanford have good reasons for disclosing private information to her patient's spouse? Might sensitivity to cultural differences justify her disclosure? Might it amount to 'ethical imperialism' to think that medical confidentiality and privacy are universal values? Which reasons may count for deceiving the patient as planned by his spouse? Which against it? What would a cultural relativist recommend in cases of this sort? What reasons might the doctor have to disclose the truth to the patient? What would you have done in her place?

Suggested Readings*

*Beyene, Yewoubdar, "Medical Disclosure and Refugees: Telling Bad News to Ethiopian Patients," *The Western Journal of Medicine* 157.3, 1992: 328–33.
  Argues that, in Muslim culture, disclosure is not a value. It is accepted that conveying bad news may not only undermine hope but, most important, be disrespectful to the patient's belief that it is God who determines the end of life.
Fry, Sara T., "Confidentiality in Health Care: A Decrepit Concept?" *Nursing Economics* 2.6, 1984: 413–18.
  Replies to Siegler (1982), arguing that confidentiality is a historically grounded professional obligation for health care providers. Proposes ways to handle the problem of excessive numbers of medical professionals and personnel who have access to patients' private information.
*Higgs, Roger, "Truth at the Last: A Case of Obstructed Death?" *Journal of Medical Ethics* 8.1, 1982: 48–50.
  Considers deception in terminally ill cancer patients, arguing that it can do more harm than good by encouraging misguided plans, obstructing dying, and creating patient mistrust.
Kermani, Ebrahim J. and Sanford L. Drob, "Tarasoff Decision: A Decade Later Dilemma Still Faces Psychotherapy," *American Journal of Psychotherapy* 41.2, 1987: 271–86.
  Contends that a strict interpretation of *Tarasoff* actually promotes psychotherapists' goals. Rejects absolutist arguments based on claims that predicting crimes by violent patients is impossible, that exceptions to confidentiality undermine trust, and that having a duty to warn third parties could increase their risks.
*Kipnis, Kenneth, "A Defense of Unqualified Medical Confidentiality," *American Journal of Bioethics* 6.2: 2006: 7–18.
  Argues that a no-exception confidentiality rule in medicine follows from two core values of medical professionals, trustworthiness and beneficence. Adherence to confidentiality prevents harms not only to patients but also to third parties.

---

*   Asterisks mark readings available online. See links on the companion website.

*Lipkin, Mack, "On Telling Patients the Truth," *Newsweek*, 6/4/1979. [repr. In Munson].
    Available online at https://philosophy.tamucc.edu/readings/ethics/lipkin-truth-tell-
    ing?destination=node%2F600.
    Defends the paternalistic practice of under-disclosing because telling patients the
    whole truth is practically impossible and may be harmful. Deception is justified, pro-
    vided it intends to benefit the patient.
*Pellegrino, Edmund, "Is Truth Telling to the Patient a Cultural Artifact?" *JAMA* 268.13,
    1992a: 1734–35.
    Argues that, as prima facie duties, beneficence and autonomy need not conflict in
    multicultural settings, if physicians make efforts to learn about their patients' wishes.
    Cultural diversity need not entail relativism about truth-telling.
*Pinker, Steven, "My Genome, My Self," *New York Times* 1/7/2009. Available online at
    http://www.nytimes.com/2009/01/11/magazine/11Genome-t.html.
    Objects to strong genetic and environmental determinism, arguing that behavioral
    and psychological traits are the result of subtle interactions between genetics, the
    environment, and chance.
*Rhodes, Rosamond, "Genetic Links, Family Ties, and Social Bonds: Rights and Respon-
    sibilities in the Face of Genetic Knowledge," *Journal of Medicine and Philosophy* 23.1,
    1998: 10–30.
    Appeals to Kantian autonomy for rejecting the nondirective standard of genetic coun-
    seling. Individuals at risk of genetic disease cannot make self-regarding autonomous
    decisions if there is a right to genetic ignorance.
*Siegler, Mark, "Confidentiality in Medicine: A Decrepit Concept," *The New England Jour-
    nal of Medicine* 307.24, 1982: 1518–21.
    Contends that, with the rise of hospital medicine, medical teams, and insurers, con-
    fidentiality as traditionally conceived is a thing of the past. Efforts should be directed
    toward preserving aspects of confidentiality, perhaps by separating patients' medical
    and financial records—but not in the way psychologists do it, by separating medical
    and mental information.
*Stanard, Rebecca and Richard Hazler, "Legal and Ethical Implications of HIV and the
    Duty to Warn for Counselors: When Does *Tarasoff* Apply?" *Journal of Counseling &
    Development* 73.4, 1995: 397–400.
    Invokes the principles of bioethics for a universalist view of confidentiality. In cases of
    HIV/AIDS, sometimes justice and beneficence should weigh more than loyalty. This
    should be part of the agreement with the patient.
*Takala, Tuija, "The Right to Genetic Ignorance Confirmed," *Bioethics* 13.3/4, 1999: 288–93.
    Argues that a person's right to genetic ignorance is as well established in liberal
    democracies as the patient's right to know. Analyzes main objections to the right to
    genetic ignorance, including Rhodes (1998).
*UK General Medical Council, "Confidentiality Guidance," 2009, http://www.gmc-uk.org/
    guidance/ethical_guidance/confidentiality.asp.
    Provides practical and moral guidance for appropriate handling of patient information
    in the UK.

5 Consent with Competence and Without

Learning Objectives

In reading this chapter you will

▶   Evaluate the requirements of informed consent for health care providers and researchers.

▶   Learn about alternative ways to obtain the informed consent of children and incompetent adults.

▶   Reflect on the options available when patients or their surrogates and health care providers cannot agree about medical decisions.

▶   Assess parental choice as a decisionmaking standard for children with profound mental and physical impairments.

AS MEDICAL PATERNALISM declined during the second half of the 20th century, in many Western countries awareness of patients' rights of self-determination was on the rise. Conditions soon became ripe for health care providers and researchers to embrace the emerging legal doctrine of informed consent. Our closer look at this doctrine shows it to set high standards of competence, information, and understanding—which not all agree can actually be met in practice.

5.1 *Natanson v Kline*: The Limits of Paternalistic Beneficence

Diagnosed with breast cancer, Irma Natanson of Kansas underwent a mastectomy in 1955. Following directions from her surgeon, she then sought radiation therapy with Dr. John R. Kline, head of the radiology department at St. Francis Hospital in Wichita. Her therapy aimed at destroying cancer tissue by a series of doses of radioactive cobalt applied to the site of the mastectomy and surrounding areas. Dr. Kline initiated cobalt radiation for Ms. Natanson in a "routine fashion." But the amount of radiation she received caused burns that refused to heal, and left her in pain with a persistent odor of burned flesh. In addition, she underwent more than 20 plastic surgery procedures, lost blood circulation in her left arm, and eventually required amputation of some fingers.

Ms. Natanson brought a malpractice suit against the hospital and physician, in the course of which it became clear that, although she authorized the radiation, she was not warned of possible risks. According to her statement, Dr. Kline denied any possible risks. On appeal, in 1960 the Kansas Supreme Court found for Ms. Natanson. Her lawyer had suggested she show the full extent of her injuries in a closed courtroom, which she did—thus providing the Court with direct evidence of the devastating effects of radiation on her body (Katz, 2002). At no point did the justices doubt Dr. Kline's intention. It was not to deceive, but to prevent his patient's irrational refusal of beneficial radiation. Yet, in the majority opinion, Justice J. Schroeder wrote, "Anglo-American law starts with a premise of a thorough-going self-determination. It follows that each man is considered the master of his own body, and he may, if he be of sound mind, expressly prohibit the performance of life-saving surgery or other medical treatment." The court awarded damages to Natanson to cover her continuing medical costs. She lived with serious disabilities for another 30 years. In 1989 she was diagnosed with cancer again, this time terminal.

■ ■ ■

Irma Natanson underwent cobalt radiation for breast cancer without information about its risks. Under those circumstances, whatever consent she may have given was, in the view of the Court, "ineffective." On Dr. Kline's view, the therapy's possible risks were compensated by its life-prolonging benefits, but his paternalism failed to persuade the court. He deemed irrational Natanson's possible refusal on the basis of fears about risks, even though she had given him no evidence of lacking decisionmaking **capacity**.

Like others at the time, the *Natanson* justices had to decide whether a health care provider was justified in withholding information that might jeopardize the success of a treatment. Their ruling tipped the balance toward respect for patient autonomy, which requires *informed* consent. In fact, some bioethicists have thought that autonomy and informed consent are the same concept (Katz, 1967). Be that as it may, in many countries it is today unlawful to conduct medical interventions involving risks without the patient's **informed consent**. Yet the history of this requirement is less than a century old. The very label 'informed consent' was first used in another case roughly contemporaneous with *Natanson, Slago v Leland Stanford Jr. University Board of Trustees* (1957). As you may recall from Chapter 1, patient autonomy, which provides the grounds for informed consent, is not part of the Hippocratic tradition in medicine. For one thing, it requires disclosure, which was not upheld as a duty of health care providers until the 20th century—though by that time there were some eminent advocates of the practice. By then, two main factors contributed to shaping the legal doctrine of informed consent, whose conditions are now widely embraced in clinical practice and biomedical research:

1. The public's revulsion at the abuses of experimental subjects by Nazi doctors during World War II, and
2. The increasing number of medical malpractice suits brought by patients for medical interventions performed without their full understanding and express permission.

Factor (1) made informed consent the central ethical concern of the *Nuremberg Code*. This landmark document for biomedical research responded to emerging evidence about the

IMAGE 5.1
©iStockPhoto/squaredpixels

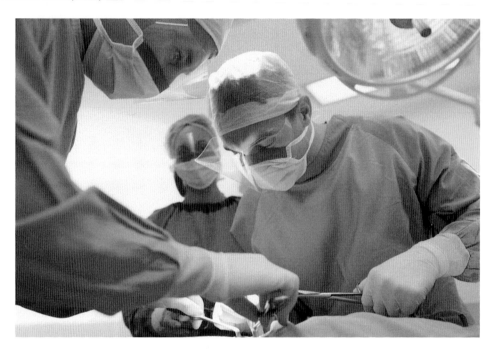

shocking mistreatment of experimental subjects by some German physicians on trial at Nuremberg after the Second World War. We discuss the *Code* in Chapter 17.

Factor (2) was prompted by bioethical reflection on those abuses together with the increasing awareness by the courts, in the 1960s and 70s, of patients' legal and moral rights. In a series of landmark cases, including *Natanson v Kline*, the US courts consistently adopted the view that interventions without patients' consent were violations of their rights to bodily integrity and an impediment to their ability to make self-regarding decisions about medical treatment. In considering such allegations, the courts developed the legal doctrine of informed consent, whose elements we consider next.

5.2 The Elements of Informed Consent

Consent

Ordinarily the word 'consent' denotes a relation between two parties: an agent who gives (or rejects) authorization to be interfered with by another agent. Consent is primarily an attitude in someone's mind. It need not be put into words. Yet in clinical practice and biomedical research, consent must be conveyed in some way, for example, words, gestures, or mouse clicks. Respect for patient autonomy requires that consent be informed. After all, an intervention recommended by medical professionals need not coincide with what the patient would want if provided with sufficient, understandable information about treatment options (including nontreatment). Collaborative decisionmaking by patients and health care providers requires respect for patient autonomy, which in turn requires that medical professionals provide sufficient, understandable information to competent patients and seek their voluntary decisions about medical treatment.

When these elements of informed consent are all present and the patient authorizes treatment, she has validly consented. If she denies authorization, she has given a **valid refusal.** Understood in this way, informed consent is a patient's right that creates the health care providers' duties outlined in Box 5.1. These duties are better conceived as prima facie, since they are not always binding. Exceptions to informed consent include emergencies and cases where a patient's choice is contrary to the public interest, to justice, or to the health care providers' own right to professional autonomy. But, for the most part, all the elements of valid consent must be honored in clinical practice. Let's take up each of them in turn.

BOX 5.1 TWO DIMENSIONS OF INFORMED CONSENT

A patient's right to

- Give or withhold authorization.
- Be sufficiently informed, in understandable language, about matters relevant to his or her decision.

A health care provider's duty to

- Obtain the patient's informed permission before acting.
- Disclose sufficient information about the patient's prognosis and treatment options, in understandable language.
- Respect patient choice, including a refusal of life supports.

Information

Note that for the patient to give *informed* consent, the medical team must disclose sufficient information about

- The patient's illness, including diagnosis and prognosis.
- Nature, foreseeable benefits, risks, and probability of success of the proposed treatment and its alternatives.

The chief argument for this duty to disclose runs:

1. Given collaborative medical decisionmaking, the medical team has the duty to obtain patients' informed consent to treatment.
2. Collaborative medical decisionmaking is the best model.

_____

3. Therefore, the medical team has the duty to obtain patients' informed consent to treatment.
4. Patients can give informed consent to treatment only if the medical team discloses sufficient information.

_____

5. Therefore, the medical team has the duty to disclose sufficient information to patients.

In Chapter 4 we saw that the medical team's duty to provide patients with information that is not only *true* but also *sufficient* is prima facie, for on occasion it might be overridden by obligations of, for example, beneficence. In *Natanson v Kline*, by omitting information about possible side effects of radiation therapy, the doctor engaged in medical deception. In common law jurisdictions, deception is now thought to undermine patient decisionmaking, and ultimately patient autonomy. Putting aside scenarios where, owing to cultural, religious, or personal preferences, patients explicitly waive their right to have relevant information, health professionals are expected to provide it. The same holds for researchers and their human subjects.

How much disclosure is necessary for informed consent? Absolute disclosure is unrealistic, since patients generally lack the medical training to understand technical details. Other constraints include the limited medical staff available for instructing patients and the time-sensitivity of certain treatments. Professional standards, patient-oriented standards, and a mix of these are alternatives for sufficient **disclosure**. Paternalistic medicine favored the use of professional standards, set by medical experts. But experts often disagree about how much to disclose. Moreover, challenges to professional standards in court require the testimony of experts who would say that accepted standards were not honored by a fellow professional in a given case. Such witnesses are difficult to find (Appelbaum et al., 1987: 42–3). Most important, *sufficient* disclosure for health care professionals might be *insufficient* for patients. Such judgments involve values. For Dr. Kline, who placed high value on eliminating Natanson's cancer, the risk of permanent damage to her upper limbs was not crucial to sufficient disclosure; for her, who could no longer play the piano after the radiation, it was.

Professional standards became unpopular with the courts after the 1960s, and were eventually replaced by patient-oriented standards and mixed standards. A milestone ruling for that change was

Canterbury v Spence. In February 1959, Jerry W. Canterbury underwent a laminectomy to correct a possible disc rupture suspected of being the cause of his severe back pain. He was recovering from surgery when, left in a bed without rails, he had a fall causing paralysis of his lower body. After four years of little recovery, Mr. Canterbury, then 19, sued the surgeon, Dr. William T. Spence, for negligent malpractice. On appeal, the issue became Spence's failure to alert the patient to a known risk of the intervention, falling out of bed. Spence argued that disclosing that risk was inappropriate, since it might have caused an adverse psychological reaction in the patient, thus undermining the success of the intervention. In 1972, the Court of Appeals of the District of Columbia ruled that patients have a right to make autonomous decisions about treatment, and that it is *this right* that "shapes the boundaries of the duty to reveal. . . ."

This 1972 ruling was influential in establishing legal precedent for patient-oriented standards of sufficient information. "Respect for the patient's right of self-determination on a particular therapy," read the leading opinion, "demands a standard set by law for physicians rather than one which physicians may or may not impose upon themselves." According to the court, physicians are required to disclose as much information as a *reasonable patient* would want to know. Left with considerable vagueness, patient-oriented standards evolved eventually into mixed patient/professional-oriented standards.

Understanding and Voluntariness

Informed consent also requires that health care providers disclose information in a way the patient can understand. As in the case of sufficient disclosure, practical constraints make this duty one of securing *sufficient* understanding that conforms to certain standards. Since patients cannot make autonomous medical choices without sufficient understanding of the disclosed information, this is an essential element of informed consent.

Another element is the voluntariness of a patient's decision, which presupposes freedom from duress, coercion, or manipulation. Any authorization granted by a patient under pressure from, say, a family member or health care provider falls short of valid consent. Suppose a patient authorizes a certain treatment only after his physician insinuates that she would not continue caring for him unless he does so. In such circumstances, the consent is invalid. Sometimes there is pressure from both health care providers and relatives—for example, when a physician enlists a close family member to get a patient's authorization for a procedure.

Competence

'**Competence**' designates a threshold of mental maturity and acuity that patients must meet to be able to make autonomous decisions about substantial matters concerning their health. Patients who meet that threshold are said to 'have capacity' or to be 'decisional.' Patients can give valid consent or refusal to treatment only when competent. Those lacking it include the unconscious, the very young, and sometimes the very old or mentally impaired.

Competence comes in degrees. Some patients are more competent than others. It may also be episodic, varying in degree at different days or times. There is evidence of episodic competence among some institutionalized elderly who may be competent enough to give informed consent to treatment in the morning but not in the evening. Meeting some agreed standard of competence is especially important when a patient refuses treatments, especially life supports.

How much mental capacity must a patient have to make a valid refusal? According to Buchanan and Brock's (1989) **sliding-scale standard (SSS)**

> The degree of competence a patient must have to validly refuse treatment is directly proportional to the gravity of the consequences of refusal.

Given the SSS, if the risk of harm involved in refusing treatment is not very great, then minimal competence is all that is needed for the patient to make a valid refusal. Consider the following scenarios:

Fred, 25, who has a slight cognitive impairment from Down syndrome, refuses antibiotics prescribed to shorten an upper-respiratory infection likely to subside on its own.

Maggie, 41, who has a similar cognitive impairment, refuses surgery for aggressive lung cancer. There is presently no evidence of metastases.

In *Fred*, given the SSS, respect for patient autonomy trumps paternalistic beneficence. Since Fred's illness is not very serious, his cognitive impairment is consistent with a valid refusal. In *Maggie*, her refusal entails a high level of risk, so a higher degree of competence is needed to be valid. SSS theorists are likely to prioritize paternalistic beneficence in her case.

SSS theorists also take into account a treatment's invasiveness in assessing the degree of competence necessary for a valid refusal. The more invasive a procedure is, the less competence needed for a valid refusal. While a high level of mental acuity is not needed to validly refuse a colonoscopy, it is needed for validly refusing a routine flu shot.

Problems for the **SSS** include that what varies in the way suggested may not be the patient's competence itself, but the *evidence* required for judging him competent. Consider for example riskiness: plausibly, the riskier a patient's refusal, the more rigorous the evidence of competence needed for accepting it as valid. From the health professional's perspective, the criterion of competence is particularly high when a patient refuses life-sustaining treatment or (in the case of mental illness) institutionalization. Even if this objection is sound, the SSS model captures a truth about 'competence:' like 'autonomy,' it is a gradient concept that definitely applies to some patients and does not apply to others. But in between, there is a penumbra where health care providers must decide case by case, guided by advance directives, when available, or any of the other decisionmaking standards considered below.

 ## 5.3 Exceptions and Doubts

Exceptions to Informed Consent

Exceptions to the requirement of informed consent include emergency situations. A cardiac arrest may give health care professionals no choice but to pursue, without the patient's consent, the resuscitation they deem in his or her best interests—unless of course the action conflicts with a known DNR order. Medical treatment without consent is justified also when a patient has autonomously waived his or her right to consent.

Therapeutic privilege is a more morally problematic exception to informed consent. Health professionals may invoke this paternalistic exception to withhold information when disclosure could be harmful to the patient. Therapeutic privilege is grounded in a model of the patient–health care professional relationship centered on beneficence. As we saw in Chapter 4, this model invokes consequentialist reasons for thinking that some disclosures to patients are bad medical practice. Prominent among these reasons is the fact that a revelation of, e.g., terminal illness may

- Put the health of some patients at risk.
- Throw some emotionally fragile patients into despair—mildly depressive patients may be made worse, and patients suffering from multiple sclerosis may experience anxiety, triggering a worsening of their symptoms.

Furthermore, deception can sometimes have health benefits. A patient who falsely believes her condition is improving may have an optimistic attitude that could actually help the healing process by, for instance, motivating her to take her medications on a regular schedule and comply with other parts of her medical treatment.

There are, however, also consequentialist *objections* to therapeutic privilege. Deception can undermine the patient–health care professional relationship and have devastating effects on patient care and the health care system as a whole. Yet the main objection to therapeutic privilege comes from a model of that relationship centered on patient autonomy. In *Natanson v Kline* and *Canterbury v Spence*, the courts invoked this model to defend the patient's right to make self-regarding decisions on important matters concerning their health—which requires sufficient disclosure.

This disagreement about therapeutic privilege reflects the tension between the health care providers' duties of beneficence and respect for autonomy. In spite of today's popularity of the autonomy model, some still think that invoking therapeutic privilege can be justified "if the physician has sufficient reason to believe that disclosure would render the patient incompetent to consent to or refuse the treatment" (Beauchamp and Childress, 2009: 84). But this argument fails to provide a limited justification to therapeutic privilege. For in neither of the envisaged situations can patients give valid consent or refusal. If the physician discloses, the patient becomes incompetent to do either; and if the physician does not disclose (i.e., invokes therapeutic privilege), the patient lacks sufficient information to do either.

Skepticism about Informed Consent

Some bioethicists are skeptical about informed consent since, as we saw, it has exceptions. Furthermore, its requirements are difficult to meet, because patients often lack the information necessary for autonomous choice, don't fully understand what is disclosed to them, or make decisions under constraints set by their own medical conditions, family members, or the health care providers. Support for these objections comes from evidence suggesting that informed consent is often a formality (see Chapter 4). In biomedical research, it appears to bias results by barring from participation people of low socioeconomic status, who lack the time or knowledge necessary to fill out consent forms (Lidz et al., 1983).

On similar grounds, for Robert Veatch (1995) informed consent is rarely achievable and should be replaced by **patient choice**, a more modest standard requiring that patients be given either

1. Details of all treatment options with a summary of benefits and risks, or
2. Information about health care providers' 'deep values' so that they can choose providers accordingly.

Yet since (1) is an element of informed consent, and (2) could be added to it, patient choice falls short of being an alternative to it. To be an alternative, it must have no other requirement. Thus construed, patient choice sets the standards too low, for (1) and (2) are useless without sufficient patient understanding or competence.

IMAGE 5.2
©iStockPhoto/rallef

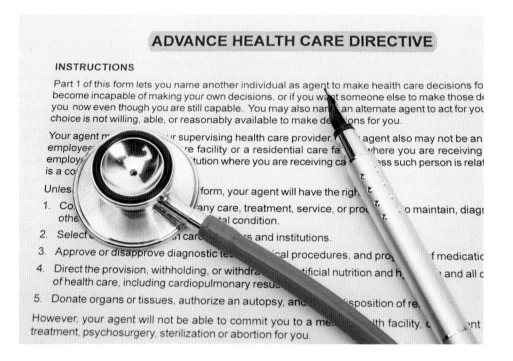

5.4 Consent in the Absence of Competence

Decisionmaking for Previously Competent Adults

Valid consents or refusals for medical interventions can also be obtained when patients lack maturity or sufficient mental competence. Here we consider standards for obtaining valid consent or refusal of treatment for previously competent adults who have lost medical decisionmaking capacity, owing to conditions such as dementia or permanent loss of consciousness. We refer to such patients as 'incompetent' or 'nondecisional' to signify that their decisionmaking capacity is below the threshold necessary for counting as autonomous.

Advance Directives

In **surrogate decisionmaking** for an incompetent adult, others make medical decisions on her behalf—usually next of kin in consultation with the attending physician. Respect for autonomy recommends that the surrogate honor what the patient would have wanted, including any refusal of treatment. An **instruction advance directive** or living will, when available, is the best way of knowing this. Such a document, composed and signed while the patient was still competent, would state her treatment preferences (including nontreatment) in case she becomes incompetent. Such instructions may also be given orally to a surrogate who will, if needed, offer testimony. Living wills are considered the gold standard in surrogate decisionmaking (Capron, 1986).

But not all jurisdictions recognize decisionmaking by living wills. Some favor the **proxy advance directive,** a medical durable power of attorney whereby a patient while competent officially designates someone else to make health care decisions on her behalf. The proxy, usually a relative, serves as her 'attorney' in the event she becomes incompetent or unable to convey her preferences. It is the responsibility of the patient to make sure the proxy is fully informed in advance about her wishes, and about the duty of the proxy faithfully to express those wishes to the patient's health care providers if the patient should become incompetent.

In the US, the Patient Self-determination Act (PSDA) of 1991 aims at promoting patient awareness of the right to have an instruction or proxy advance directive. It was passed after the Supreme Court decision in *Cruzan*, which as discussed in Chapter 7 emphasized the role of advance directives in permissible withdrawals of life supports for permanently unconscious patients. The PSDA requires that patients be given, on admission to a hospital, information outlining the state law and institutional policies governing self-determination, encouraging them to discuss end-of-life medical options with their health care providers—who in turn must be familiar with questions concerning patient self-determination. Yet having an advance directive on file does not ensure that the patient's preferences would be honored. Emergencies, for example, are exceptions to informed consent. An emergency team, even if presented with an advance directive requesting no cardiopulmonary resuscitation might still initiate it[1]. To prevent situations of this sort, some states have adopted Physician Orders for Life Sustaining Treatment (POSLT) programs, whereby patients facing death within a year can decide, in consultation with their health care providers, about which treatments they consent to, and which they refuse. A POLST form is then completed by the patient and signed by a physician, becoming a standing medical order that must be recognized by any medical team when presented. The POSLT form supplements, rather than replaces, an advance directive. Among the differences between these two approaches are

- Advance directives express decisions for future care of any person aged 18 or older and does not have the force of a medical order.
- POLST forms have the force of medical orders and can be completed by patients of any age, provided they are seriously ill.

Substituted Judgment

Advance directives of either type can be the basis of a **substituted judgment,** or decision about medical treatment made by a previously competent patient's surrogate according to an interpretation of what the patient would have wanted. When there is no advance directive, the previously competent patient's point of view is reconstructed in approximation by the surrogate, preferably the person who knows her best (e.g., her spouse, next-of-kin, or significant other). In choosing among care-alternatives, the surrogate is expected to choose not the care-alternative *he* thinks best for the patient, but the one *the patient would choose*—that is, to adopt the alternative she would want for herself in the circumstances, given her values, beliefs, and plan of life. Occasionally, the courts may appoint a guardian *ad litem* to represent the interests of an incompetent patient. Here is one such occasion:

---

1 See "Max Story," http://www.polst.org/advance-care-planning/polst-experiences/.

Claire Conroy, an 84-year-old resident of the New Jersey Parkview Nursing Home, was declared incompetent in 1979, and her nephew appointed as guardian. She experienced periodic confusion caused by organic brain syndrome. By 1982 she had developed severe dementia, inability to speak, incontinence, arteriosclerosis, diabetes, hypertension, bedsores, and a gangrenous leg. She was hospitalized twice and fed by nasogastric tube. In 1983, her nephew requested that the tube be removed. The court granted his request, but the decision was stayed pending an appeal to the New Jersey Supreme Court. That court ruled that only a rigorous determination of a patient's incompetence, together with a joint decision by the guardian, an attending physician, and a state appointed ombudsman, could justify withdrawing life supports from an incompetent patient. While the case was on appeal, Ms. Conroy died.

According to financial records, there was no inheritance or other conflict of interest behind the nephew's decision. He visited his aunt regularly and everything suggested that he believed she would not have wanted to continue living in her condition.

But the courts act on behalf of the state, whose authority to protect life includes protecting incompetent patients vulnerable to surrogates' malicious or biased end-of-life decisions. They may also intervene when surrogates and health care providers disagree about forgoing life supports for a patient. As discussed in Chapter 7 in connection with the landmark US Supreme Court decision in *Cruzan*, states have the right to set their own evidentiary standards for valid refusals by previously competent adults. Conflicts are easily resolved when the patient has an instruction advance directive. In its absence, substitute decisionmaking by next-of-kin may be morally dubious. Since end-of-life decisions rest in part on the patient's values concerning her quality of life, why think that the substitute decisionmaker would share those values? After all, kinship is an accident of birth. This might explain data suggesting that the probability that such decisionmakers are good predictors of what the patient might have wanted is mere chance (Seckler et al, 1991). Furthermore, as Kluge (2008) argues, substitute decisionmakers may not always have the patient's best interests at heart.

The Best-Interest Standard

Some of these problems for substituted judgment are avoided by the best-interest standard, sometimes viewed as its competitor. Instead of assuming that an incompetent patient should receive the medical care that she herself would have wanted, this standard assumes that she should receive the care that is in her true best interest, all things considered. The treatment decision is made by evaluating the patient's medical condition and relevant facts about her life. This has problems of its own, since treatment consent and refusals involve value judgments. Acting on the opinion of health care providers, justices might, for instance, decide that life-sustaining treatment is not in a patient's best interests. But this presupposes an evaluation of whether the patient's life is worth living. A patient with different values may consider their decision wrong or even harmful—as you may recall from *Dax's case* in Chapter 3.

American and British courts have different views about the weight of the best-interest standard for incompetent adults when an advance directive is not available. In America, it is the last resort in the absence of substituted judgment. But sometimes the best-interest standard is the only option available because there is no advance directive and no one who knows the patient well enough to exercise substituted judgment on her behalf. And on occasion, courts asked to authorize removal of life-prolonging treatment have used the patient's best

FIGURE 5.1   Medical Decisionmaking for Previously Competent Patients

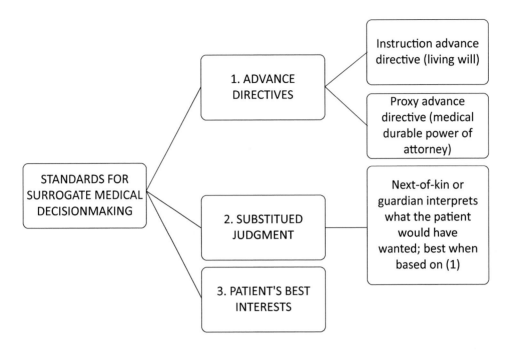

interests rather than substituted judgment by next-of-kin (as in *Conroy*). In Britain, however, the best-interest standard is the preferred approach to avoid possible conflicts of interest and selfish agendas of next-of-kin that might (sometimes unwittingly) taint a substituted judgment. In both countries, however, the courts prefer advance directives because they facilitate the previously competent patient's participation in end-of-life decisions.

Decisionmaking for Never Competent Adults

Unlike previously competent patients who might have expressed their medical preferences or completed an advance directive, some adult patients have, owing to profound cognitive impairment, never had decisional capacity. These patients pose a deeper challenge to informed consent, because substituted judgment is unachievable in their case: for reasons discussed below no one can interpret what they might have wanted. Yet in making treatment decisions for them, health care providers are constrained by the obligations to maximize wellbeing, minimize harm, respect patient autonomy and see that justice is done. Given the principles of autonomy and justice, reasonable criteria should be in place so that the never competent can, like other patients, consent to or refuse medical treatment. Furthermore, treatment decisions for them should be comparable to standard decisions for competent patients with similar clinical profiles. For example, if blood transfusions are a standard, life-prolonging procedure for competent patients with bladder cancer, then, other things being equal, justice requires them also for the never competent with bladder cancer. In addition, health care providers have a fiduciary obligation (i.e., an obligation based on trust) to intervene whenever they judge that a proxy decisionmaker's choice could harm the patient, especially if it involves forgoing life supports or administering aggressive treatments. Yet health care providers' decisions too rest not only on facts but also on values as is evident in two judgments delivered in 1981 by the same New York Court of Appeals:

Matter of Storar and *Matter of Eichner.* John Storar, whose mental age was 18 months, was institutionalized and dying of bladder cancer at age 52. Health care providers started blood transfusions as a protection against other diseases, not as a cure, since his condition was terminal. His mother, 77, who visited him every day, was his only living relation. She sought to end the life-prolonging transfusions because of the physical pain and psychological suffering they inflicted on her son, who could not understand the treatment. But the court found for the health care providers because "a parent cannot deny a child all treatment for a life-threatening condition." In *Eichner*, a 53-year-old Catholic priest, Brother Fox, had suffered anoxic brain damage as result of a cardiac arrest during a hernia operation, and this left him in a permanent vegetative state, with breathing assisted by mechanical ventilation. The same court, invoking the hopelessness of the condition, compelling evidence that Brother Fox did not want his life prolonged in that way, and common law regarding self-determination and informed consent, authorized removal of the ventilator.

These rulings seem inconsistent, since both of the cases involve refusals of life supports on behalf of patients permanently incapacitated and thus unable to make their own decisions. Yet attention to the details may help explain why the Court authorized withdrawal only in *Eichner*. First, the court was deciding on behalf of the state. Brother Fox, owing to his injury, had no prospect of ever being conscious again, and thus, of ever having interests in need of the state's protection. Storar, however, though cognitively disabled, was conscious and therefore had interests eligible for state protection.

But, most important, Brother Fox was a previously competent patient with known preferences about his medical care. Decisions in such cases are commonly made by substituted judgment, or interpretation of what he might have wanted in that situation. But Storar never had competence to consent to, or refuse, medical treatment. Nobody could interpret what he wanted. As proxy decisionmaker, his mother refused further life-prolonging treatment for him that health care providers thought medically indicated. Evidently they judged that hastening Storar's death was a harm. Given nonmaleficence, they disregarded the mother's request—which, from their perspective, might also have appeared unjust. For justice required that Storar receive treatment analogous to what any nondisabled competent patient with the same clinical profile commonly receives. Yet their perspective is based on values. Furthermore, hastening a patient's death does not always conflict with obligations of nonmaleficence (more on this in Chapter 7). Note that, from the mother's perspective, the blood transfusions did conflict with nonmaleficence, for they brought uncompensated burdens (the pain) that Storar could not understand. From her perspective, what looked unjust was the court's decision. After all, Storar was denied the right that competent patients usually have to refuse a treatment. Since his mother had a history of deciding in his best interests and reasons to support her request, the court's ruling denied to an incompetent patient a right that competent patients may usually take for granted.

Storar illustrates the difficulties involving ethical decisionmaking for never competent patients. Substitute decisionmakers cannot capture what these patients might have wanted, because that requires approximating their decisions, and they are nondecisional. So, in such cases, decisionmaking relies on the patient's-best-interest standard. Since application of this standard in part involves values, hard conflicts may arise between next-of-kin and health care providers, with occasional interventions by the courts. There is no accepted protocol to resolve such conflicts objectively in a way consistent with all principles of biomedical ethics. But all agree that, when a proxy decision seems to violate one or more principles, health care providers have the fiduciary power and obligation to intervene on behalf of these patients.

Decisionmaking for Children

Children are among the never competent. Informed consent for them, therefore, is given by substitute decisionmakers—in the US, commonly their parents. We refer to such proxy decisionmaking as '**parental choice**.' For neonates, however, their best interest is the decisionmaking standard. This section examines some problems facing parental choice and the best-interest standard. It also considers the case of *Ashley X*, a young child with profound cognitive deficits, for whom her parents requested a number of nonmedically indicated treatments that some considered morally unjustified, although they might have been in the interests of both parents and child.

Parental Choice versus Patient's Best Interests

In the 1970s and early 80s, the prevailing decisionmaking standard for neonates in the US switched from parental choice to the child's best interests. Not all agreed with that switch, which was in part prompted by some parental refusals of life-saving treatment for impaired newborns (see Chapter 9). Opposition was evident during the 1995 trial of dermatologist Gregory Messenger of Lansing, Michigan.

Baby Messenger was born by Caesarian section at 25 weeks of gestation when her mother went into premature labor as a result of pulmonary edema and hypertension. The neonatologist, Dr. Padmani Karna, predicted a 30% to 50% chance of survival for the infant, and if he survived, a 20% and 40% chance of severe impairments owing to intraventricular hemorrhage. The Messengers told Dr. Karna they did not want any heroic measures if the baby was born alive, including resuscitation. Yet she instructed the physician assistant (PA) that if Baby Messenger looked "vigorous" and "active," critical care should be initiated. The baby was born hypotonic and hypoxic, purple-blue in color, and weighing only 780g. But he had an 80 to 90 beats/min umbilical cord pulse, so the PA resuscitated, intubated, and incubated him. Upon her return to the hospital, Dr. Karna saw the baby stable in the NICU and decided to run some tests. In the meantime, the baby's father, Dr. Messenger, who saw the baby in the delivery room, asked to be alone with his son and disconnected the respirator. The infant died later in his mother's arms. Pathologists determined that the baby would have survived had he not suffered respiratory failure as a result of his father's action. In 1995 Dr. Messenger was tried for manslaughter but acquitted.

The press followed the trial closely, with the *Chicago Tribune* running the headline "Jury to Weigh Father's Guilt in Premature Baby's Death."[2] Since it was a criminal case won by the

---

2 Roger Worthington, "Jury to Weigh Father's Guilt in Premature Baby's Death." *Chicago Tribune*, 1/30/1995.

accused, it set no precedent in the law. Yet it sent a clear message: juries and the public tend to question the morality of medical interventions that conflict with the parents' reasonable choices for their medically compromised newborns. This tendency is consistent with moral theory, especially utilitarianism, given the baby's bleak prospects. But the neonatologist was not unreasonable. She followed the 'initiate and reevaluate' protocol prevailing in the US and Britain for newborns with low survival chances, whereby critical care is started at birth and withdrawal contemplated later, depending on the infant's progress.

This case suggests that the pendulum marking where the law stands on informed consent for newborns had swung too far in the early 1980s: from absolute parental choice to absolute infant's best-interests. Fueling this change was the fact that reasonable parents sometimes fail to be objective judges of their infant's best interests, and their choices can flout bioethical principles of nonmaleficence and justice. The former recommends avoidance of harm to the newborn, the latter that it receive the care that other newborns with similar life prospects receive. Other things being equal, decisions resulting in the newborn's death or impairments flout nonmaleficence; those depriving it of due care flout justice. But the best-interest standard has the problems outlined above—namely, that the medical team decides, according to their own values and notion of a life worth living, what is best for the neonate, even though it is the parents who must care for the infant after it leaves the hospital.

Moral theory offers different perspectives on who should decide. For Kant, parents have a duty to avoid decisions that harm their newborns, provided these can develop a rational nature and thus acquire the absolute moral worth of persons. So he should give primacy to the infant's best interests, on the grounds that parents are poor judges of those interests. But utilitarians, as noted in our discussion of new reproductive technologies (Chapter 14), think that, on the whole, the benefits of parental choice outweigh possible harms from making mistaken decisions, except when the neonate's life falls short of being worth living.

BOX 5.2 DECISIONMAKING FOR NEWBORNS

Prevailing Standard: The infant's best interests, when clear.

Primary Decisionmaker: The parents, unless they are incapacitated or their decision conflicts with what reasonable people think is in the infant's best interest.

Health Care Providers' Role:
(1) Developing protocols for decisions to forgo life supports, and for settling disagreements with parents.
(2) Seeking judicial review for any nonemergency parental decision seriously at odds with the provider's view of the infant's best interest.

Conflict Resolution: End-of-life decisions are reviewed by an *institutional ethics committee*. When disagreement occurs, the committee (1) verifies that the parties have up-to-date, reliable information; (2) assesses the parents' decisional capacity and understanding of treatment options; and (3) if necessary, seeks a third party's intervention (usually the courts, charged with determining the infant's best interests).

Finding a Compromise

Even if parents are poor judges of what is best for their compromised infant, since the burdens of its care after it leaves the hospital fall on them, their choices shouldn't be ignored. In 1983, the President's Commission for the Study of Ethical Problems in Medicine provided an influential framework for a compromise between parental choice and the infant's best interests. It recognized the parents as primary judges of those interests and suggested that institutional ethics committees review each decision to forgo life supports from a newborn. When disagreement arises between parents and health care providers, the committee reviews the reasons on both sides, following the steps in Box 5.2 above. Although the burden of proof is on health care providers, when they have serious doubts about a parental decision, they should seek judicial determination of a child's best interests. As we see next, that was the upshot of heated deliberation about parental choice in a case involving invasive treatment for a severely disabled child.

Decisionmaking in Ashley X

In 2004, the parents of a 6-year-old girl known as Ashley X consented to a series of medical interventions to stunt the growth of this child who had severe physical and psychological impairments. As described in their advocacy blog, the '**Ashley Treatment**' aimed at improving her quality of life and was thus in her best interests. The blog commends similar treatments for other "pillow angels"—i.e. children profoundly compromised both physically and psychologically who, lacking motor function, will never be able even to sit up or move in bed, and will always have the mental capacity of an infant. Ashley has the intellectual and developmental age of a 3-month-old. Her parents think she recognizes them "but can't be sure." She is fed through a gastrostomy tube inserted surgically when she was 5, and remains wholly dependent on others for her routine daily care. Ashley's birth was uneventful, but it was soon clear that she had sustained permanent brain damage of unknown cause. Her body was expected to grow at a standard rate, thereby presenting, from the parents' perspective, a problem for home care and some risks to Ashley's wellbeing and comfort.

The Ashley Treatment

Performed by Drs. Daniel Gunther and Douglas Diekema at Seattle Children's Hospital, the treatment has several components:

Part 1: Growth attenuation (injections of high-dose estrogen to stunt her growth, thereby keeping her body size at 9 years old)
Part 2: A hysterectomy (the surgical removal of the uterus)
Part 3: Surgical removal of breast buds
Part 4: An appendectomy (the surgical removal of the appendix)

The surgical procedures were performed in a single operation in July 2004, and continued with injections of high-dose estrogen for two and a half years until December 2006. Although no medical complications occurred, critics found the treatment at odds with nonmaleficence and justice—questioning the parents' and medical providers' appeal to beneficence. Could such procedures be actually in the best interests of these profoundly disabled children, who with parental consent are increasingly being subjected to such nonmedically indicated invasive interventions that alter their bodies permanently and substantially? For the parents, they provide a way to manage the children's disabilities. Because of their impairments, these children are not able to understand their situation and have no power to object to what is done to them. But, of course, whether they *would* be inclined to object at all if they had full knowledge of the facts is not clear.

Reasons for the Ashley Treatment

Ashley's parents offered the following consequentialist reasons for the treatment:

1.   Part 1, to keep Ashley small and light enough so that she can
      a.   Avoid bed sores
      b.   Be easily moved around the house, thus participating in family life (Ashley has two younger, healthy siblings, a sister and a brother).
2.   Part 2, to prevent
      a.   Discomforts of menstrual cramps beginning in puberty,
      b.   Uterine-related illnesses (e.g., cancer) and pregnancies.
3.   Part 3, to prevent
      a.   Discomfort resulting from large breasts when lying down or strapped in her wheelchair.
      b.   Breast cancer and also sexual abuse by caregivers.
4.   Part 4, to prevent appendicitis.

Peter Singer (2007) agrees with these reasons, holding that the treatment was in Ashley's best interests, independent of whether it also benefitted her parents: "the line between improving Ashley's life and making it easier for her parents to handle her scarcely exists, because anything that makes it possible for Ashley's parents to involve her in family life is in her interest."
    For other consequentialists, there is insufficient evidence that

•   An untested treatment's benefits can outweigh its risks.
•   Ashley's small body size and light weight can delay her institutionalization.

Against the Ashley Treatment

Appeal to Ashley's best interests may justify only Part 1, growth attenuation. The removal of breast buds, for example, carries all the risks of surgery with at most speculative benefits (3a). As for (3b), the surgery amounts to penalizing a victim and might not even deter sexual predators (Liao et al, 2007). Arthur Caplan (2007) concedes reasons (1a) and (1b) above but finds the treatment morally wrong because it attempts a medical solution for a social problem, and "a decent society" should provide resources to help families care for their disabled children. Yet support for growth attenuation is now compatible with advocacy for better social services for the disabled. The parents may agree with Caplan's argument yet reply that, given the scarce social services available, growth attenuation is justified.

Among nonconsequentialist objections to the treatment are that

1. It discriminated against a disabled child.
2. It exemplifies objectionable moral principles in medicine.
3. It is unnatural.
4. It fails to show respect for Ashley's dignity.

Given (1), the Ashley Treatment, by substantially altering Ashley's body *for no medical reason*, violated a disabled child's right to bodily integrity, which is a right of noninterference protected by the UN-endorsed *Convention on the Protection and Promotion of the Rights and Dignity of Persons with Disabilities*, whose article 17 states: "Every person with disabilities has a right to respect for his or her physical and mental integrity on an equal basis with others."

Objection (2) is Kantian in spirit. It charges that the principle underlying the doctors' express reasons for implementing the Ashley Treatment (to allow Ashley's parents to take care of her at home) cannot be right, because when universalized, it prescribes something like this:

The Ashley Treatment Principle

It is morally permissible to substantially and permanently alter the body of disabled A (Ashley) as way to help B (her parents) manage A's disability.

Maybe helping B can also benefit A indirectly. But the medical team's obligations of nonmaleficence and beneficence are owed primarily to A, the patient, not to her family. Imagine other applications of the principle, such as amputating the legs of patients with profound psychological disabilities as a way of managing them because otherwise they are too tall, or those of elderly patients with dementia who endanger themselves by wandering out of sight. Such amputations would clearly be unethical (Edwards, 2008).

Objection (3), that Ashley's treatment was 'unnatural,' is weak since even a regimen of aspirin as a blood-thinner is 'unnatural' in the sense of interfering with the course of nature. Objection (4), that the treatment undermined her dignity, fails when dignity is associated with having the moral value of persons. For persons typically have psychological capacities that Ashley lacks. She also has no prospect of developing the rational nature that Kant considers essential to persons (more on this in Chapter 10).

For Kittay and Kittay (2007), calling such disabled children "pillow angels" undermines their dignity by infantilizing them. Based on evidence from their own disabled daughter, they deny that these children always have a baby's mind. Even if their developmental age remains infantile, their new experiences will shape their preferences over time.

The upshot of these arguments for the moral justification of parental choice for the Ashley Treatments is still unclear. On the one hand, consequentialist considerations may justify part 1 of their decision. On the other, some of the objections argue for limiting parental and medical substitute decisionmakers in ways that protect the children's best interests.

To that end, the Seattle Children's Hospital now requires judicial review before authorizing an Ashley Treatment. Neither parental consent nor approval of health care providers and institutional ethics committees are sufficient safeguards alone.

5.5 Chapter Summary

The health care providers' obligation to obtain a patient's informed consent correlates with the patient's right to make self-regarding decisions about medical treatment. Two influential cases in the rise of the legal doctrine of informed consent were *Natanson v Kline* and *Canterbury v Spence*. Given that doctrine, valid consent requires that a patient's decision be based on adequate information, understanding, voluntariness, and competence. Refusals and requests of treatment have different normative force. Refusals must always be honored, while there is more flexibility in the case of requests because of the providers' own professional autonomy and expert knowledge. Exceptions allowing providers to intervene without valid consent range from therapeutic privilege to emergency situations.

When the patient lacks capacity, medical interventions may be authorized in various ways depending on whether the patient (1) has partially lost decisionmaking capacity, (2) has lost it completely, or (3) never had it. Some think that in (1), the necessary level of capacity is relative to the risks of the intervention. In situations type (2), decisionmaking rests on substituted judgment about what the patient would have wanted (best when based on an advance directive) or a determination (sometimes by the courts) of the patient's best interests. Decisionmaking for children illustrates situations type (3), where currently the best-interest standard has taken priority over parental choice. But court cases such as *Baby Messenger* suggest that parents should be primary decisionmakers unless their choice is clearly contrary to their child's best interest. But how to determine what is in a child's best interests is sometimes a difficult problem, as a parental choice in *Ashley X* illustrates. While Ashley's parents invoked her best interests to justify growth attenuation and other parts of her treatment, not all agreed. For some critics, its risks outweighed any possible benefit to Ashley; for others, it violated Ashley's rights and dignity as a disabled child.

5.6 Study Aids

Key Words

Advance directive (instruction or proxy), 100/101
Ashley Treatment, 107
Capacity, 93
Competence, 97
Disclosure, 96
Informed consent, 93
Parental choice, 105
Patient choice, 99

Questions and Cases for Further Consideration

1. The Ashley Treatment involves a nonmedically-indicated sterilization of a disabled child. What can be said for and against this aspect of the treatment? Do those reasons have moral implications?

2. Suppose health care professionals were not legally required to obtain a patient's informed consent to treatment. Would there still be reasons for obtaining it anyway?

3. There is some evidence that surrogates are poor predictors of what patients might have wanted. Does this undermine the moral justification of treatment decisions by substituted judgment?

4. Would interested parties be better off if the US allowed the medical team to make treatment decisions for nondecisional patients according to the best-interest standard? Should that standard aim at promoting what is objectively or subjectively best for the patient?

5. Consider: *Psychological studies suggest that having a disabled child affects siblings adversely. Therefore, the parents of a compromised neonate should be allowed to end its life.* What can be said against parental choice in the suggested context? Whose interests is this argument taking into account? Might degree of impairment matter?

6. *While recovering from cranial surgery in a US hospital, Ms. R, 19, developed an intracranial hemorrhage and was eventually pronounced brain dead. However, she was kept on a ventilator until the arrival of her parents from China. Her father, who had a durable power of attorney for her care, requested that she stay on ventilation for a few days more and be treated with a traditional Chinese medication for coma. An ethics committee recommended against honoring the request citing the health care providers' right of professional autonomy.* (Adapted from Applbaum et al., 2008: 2188–93.) Ms. R was dead according to the prevailing criterion of death in the US, and there was no evidence of the requested treatment's medical effectiveness. But would these reasons morally justify the committee recommendation, given that the father held a durable power of attorney for her care? Suppose that, besides his reluctance to accept the bad news, he also shared his culture's belief that such medicines clean a comatose patient's spirit before it leaves this world. Should the medical team factor in this cultural difference?

*Suggested Readings**

*Arras, John D., "The Severely Demented, Minimally Functional Patient: An Ethical Analysis," *Journal of the American Geriatrics Society* 36, 1988: 938–44.

Argues that in the case of incompetent patients, end-of-life decisions should be made by "involved and well-intentioned family members" according to the best-interest standard.

Appelbaum, Paul S., Charles W. Lidz, and Alan Meisel, *Informed Consent: Legal Theory and Clinical Practice*. Oxford: Oxford University Press, 1987.

Tracks the rise of the legal doctrine of informed consent by focusing on the landmark cases that shaped it.

Applbaum, A. I., J. C. Tilburt, M. T. Collins, and D. Wendler, "A Family's Request for Complementary Medicine after Patient Brain Death," JAMA 299.18, 2008: 2188–93.

*Brock, Dan W., "Decisionmaking Competence and Risk," *Bioethics* 5.2, 1991: 105–12.

Contra Wicclair (1991), defends the sliding-scale standard for determining appropriate levels of competence in a patient.

———, "Medical Decisions at the End of Life," in Kuhse and Singer 2012, pp. 263–73.

Proposes a model of shared decisionmaking for patients and health care providers based on promoting patient wellbeing and self-determination.

Capron, Alexander Morgan, "Historical Overview: Law and Public Perception," in Lynn 1986, pp. 11–20.

Distinguishes three levels of authority in terminal care decisions, in decreasing priority order: first, the patient's express wishes, second, substituted judgment, and third, the patient's best interests (in an objective sense).

*Eyal, Nirn "Informed Consent," *The Stanford Encyclopedia of Philosophy*, Edward Zalta, ed., 2011. Available online at http://plato.stanford.edu/entries/informed-consent/.

Thorough overview of the core elements of informed consent.

*Faden, Ruth and Beauchamp, Tom L., *A History and Theory of Informed Consent*. Oxford: Oxford University Press, 1986.

Classic account of the evolution of the doctrine of informed consent. Historically minded, but contains ethical analyses of landmark cases.

*Katz, Jay, "Informed Consent—Must It Remain a Fairy Tale?" *Journal of Contemporary Health Law and Policy* 10, 1967: 69–91.

Early rejection of paternalism while vindicating the requirement of informed consent, within a framework that favors joint patient-health care professional decisionmaking.

*Kluge, Eike-Henner W., "Incompetent Patients, Substitute Decision Making, and Quality of Life: Some Ethical Considerations," *The Medscape Journal of Medicine* 10.10, 2008: 237. Available online at http://www.ncbi.nlm.nih.gov/pmc/articles/PMC2605131/.

Criticizes five models of substitute decisionmaking for never competent patients for failing principles of justice or patient autonomy, proposing a compromise by comparing coefficients with competent patients with a similar clinical profile.

*Liao, S., Julian Savulescu, and Mark Sheehan, "The Ashley Treatment: Best Interests, Convenience, and Parental Decision-Making," *Hastings Center Report* 37.2, 2007: 16–20.

---

*   Asterisks mark readings available online. See links on the companion website.

Consequentialist objection to most parts of the Ashley Treatment, except for growth attenuation.

*Mappes, Thomas A., "Some Reflections on Advance Directives," *APA Newsletter on Philosophy and Medicine* 98.1, 1998: 106–11.

While conceding the importance of advance directives, this article explores some philosophical and practical difficulties that arise when they are used in making health care decisions for previously competent patients.

*Veatch, Robert M., "Abandoning Informed Consent," *Hastings Center Report* 25.2, 1995: 5–12.

Favors replacing informed consent with patient choice, which can be approximated by giving patients information about either all treatment options with a summary of their benefits and risks, or the health care providers' deep values.

*Wicclair, Mark R., "Patient Decision-Making Capacity and Risk," *Bioethics* 5.2, 1991: 91–104.

Rejects criteria for determining a patient's decisionmaking competence based on degrees of risk, such as the sliding-scale standard. Where risk is high, they set unattainable requirements for competence; where it is low, they result in overly weak standards of competence.

PART III

Moral Issues at the End of Life

6 Death and Dying

Learning Objectives

In reading this chapter you will

▶   Distinguish three components in the standard account of human death.

▶   Compare criteria for brain death and cardiopulmonary death.

▶   Ask whether there should be just one definition of death for all living organisms.

▶   Identify main reasons for and against Donation after Cardiac Death programs.

MODERN MEDICINE OFFERS an impressive array of new technologies and therapies developed to preserve and extend patients' lives. But some of these have also brought a blurring of the distinction between life and death. As a result, bioethics now wrestles with some crucial problems concerning what human death is and how to accurately determine when it has occurred.

6.1 Was Jahi McMath Dead?

On December 9, 2013, Jahi McMath, aged 13, underwent surgery for a tonsillectomy and removal of adenoids and uvula at Oakland Children's Hospital in California. During the procedure she suffered a brain hemorrhage with apparent hypoxia and lapsed into a coma. Two days later, Dr. Robin Shanahan, a neurologist, was called to determine whether Ms. McMath had sustained irreversible cessation of all brain function. The exam confirmed that she was unable to breathe on her own and that her brain showed neither blood-flow nor electrical activity. On December 12 the doctors pronounced Ms. McMath whole-brain dead and ordered removal of the ventilator that was keeping her breathing. Her body was discharged into the custody of the county coroner.

    Ordinarily, relatives defer to the judgments of physicians in these matters. But McMath's parents were evangelical Christians who believed that as long as her heart was beating (albeit with external support), the girl was alive. Unconvinced that their daughter was dead, they obtained a court order to move her to a rehabilitation facility and keep her on the ventilator—which they did on January 7, 2014. Medical experts deplored this development, saying that deterioration and decay of Ms. McMath's artificially ventilated body was inevitable.

Three nationally prominent bioethicists attributed the parents' zealous devotion on behalf of their daughter to a misunderstanding of the medical facts about whole-brain death, a condition from which there is no recovery. Others were also alarmed at what they perceived as a reversal of the public's acceptance of whole-brain death as death. But Nyala Winkfield, Jahi's mother, declared that her daughter was already showing signs of improvement in the new care facility. "God can overcome all things," she wrote.

■ ■ ■

Jahi McMath sustained catastrophic damage to the entire brain resulting in whole-brain death, which, together with brainstem death, is the prevailing criterion of death in most countries. Her condition attracted media attention in ways reminiscent of the cases of some brain-dead pregnant women whose hearts and lungs were kept functioning by artificial means so that their pregnancies could be carried to term. Reactions to such cases among the public vary greatly. Some accept that brain-dead patients are dead. Others deny that a human body that is breathing, fighting infections, and even carrying a pregnancy to term, albeit with assistance, could be dead. In the middle are those who take **brain death** to be a convenient fiction signaling that a patient in that condition is, as a 2001 *New Yorker* article put it, "As Good as Dead."[1] By this, author Gary Greenberg meant that the death of the entire brain has normative import: it makes permissible or even mandatory some actions otherwise impermissible—for example, disconnecting a respirator, issuing a death certificate, and, when a valid consent has been obtained, removing vital organs for transplantation, or donating the entire body for dissection in a medical school.

Public attitudes toward brain death vary. The McMaths rejected the idea that whole-brain death is death. Were they simply ignorant of the medical facts? Or did they merely share the common belief that a person is dead only with the permanent cessation of breathing and heartbeat, whether assisted or spontaneous? In *Marlise Muñoz*, a 2013 case in Texas to be discussed in Chapter 10, the parents and husband of a brain-dead woman reacted differently. Challenging the hospital's decision to keep her on life supports, they argued that 'whole-brain dead' means *dead*, demanding her removal so that they could give her a proper burial. Were they thus only seeking closure to a grim episode in their lives, or persuaded by the prevailing criterion of death? As we'll see in this chapter, health care providers' and bioethicists' attitudes toward brain death also vary. Underlying this diversity are different definitions or understandings of what death is, and criteria for establishing when death has occurred.

■ 6.2 Accounting for Human Death

Western Thought on Human Death

Definitions and criteria of death have changed through history. For Ancient Greek and Judeo-Christian cultures, death consisted of the departure of the soul from the body, something to be determined by signals such as rigor mortis and putrefaction. Through the Middle

---

1 Gary Greenberg, "As Good As Dead," *The New Yorker*, 8/13/2001.

Ages, the use of mirrors, candles, and feathers to detect absence of breath suggests an early association of death with the cessation of breathing. Shakespeare's King Lear, for example, requests a mirror to check for a sign of breath. Tests of this sort led to mistakes. One story has it that when philosopher Duns Scotus's burial vault was opened some years after his death, it revealed that he had climbed out of his coffin.

In the 17th century, the discovery of the circulation of the blood and pumping function of the heart led to associating death with the cessation of respiratory and cardiac function. Yet medical science still wasn't reliable enough to dispel fears of premature burial, which prompted the construction of coffins equipped with ventilation and alarms and fueled an extreme view that putrefaction was the only sure sign of death. With the invention of the stethoscope in 1819, the absence of heartbeat became more reliably detectable.

In the mid-20th century, several innovations in medicine revived interest in the issue of death. The introduction of the mechanical ventilator, the defibrillator, and other technologies of the intensive care unit (ICU) made it possible to maintain vital functions in patients who would otherwise have died of their illnesses or injuries. Assisted breathing and heartbeat could be provided even for whole-brain-dead individuals like Jahi MacMath. Were these patients dead or alive? By the cardiopulmonary (or heartbeat) criterion of death prevalent until then, they were alive. Denying life supports in such cases was morally and legally problematic—as was retrieving donated organs, something impermissible to do from the living. Yet life supports and organs for transplants were (and continue to be) scarce medical resources.

Awareness of these problems increased with the growth of confidence in transplants, greatly boosted in 1967 by Dr. Christiaan Barnard's successful human heart transplant. Calls for a revision of the accepted criterion of death followed. In 1968, a Harvard Medical School committee deemed the irreversible loss of function in the entire brain sufficient for death, a criterion widely hailed as an improvement. Brain-dead patients with assisted breathing and heartbeat could now be declared dead. In 1981, the President's Commission endorsed the whole-brain criterion, and in 2008, the President's Council on Bioethics provided a rationale for it: whole-brain-dead individuals lack even the minimal capacities necessary for being alive.

The Standard Account of Death

The **standard account of death** has three components: a definition, a criterion, and medical tests. Defining death is a philosophical matter. For American philosopher Thomas Nagel death is "the unequivocal and permanent end of our existence" (1979: 1). But when does one of us go out of existence? The standard account responds with the biological sciences' definition of **organismic death**:

> For all living organisms, death consists in the permanent loss of an organism's bodily integrative functions.

That is, an organism dies when it has ceased to function as a coordinated system. Death is the permanent cessation of function in the brain if this is the central coordinator of bodily

IMAGE 6.1
©iStockPhoto/Frank Ramspott

functions in humans. But if the heart and lungs are the central coordinators, then death is the permanent cessation of cardiopulmonary function.

This suggests that the criterion for determining when death has occurred is partly medical, because it requires identifying the central coordinator of bodily functions. Main candidates include cessation of function in the whole brain, the brainstem, and the heart and lungs. Whichever is selected, the resulting criterion should produce neither:

- False positives (considering dead someone who's alive), nor
- False negatives (considering alive someone who's actually dead).

Any adequate criterion of death should completely rule out diagnostic errors of either type, but false positives are more serious. A criterion yielding that someone conscious is dead has false positives. One yielding that a human body undergoing rigor mortis is alive has false negatives. Given the McMaths' view that Jahi wasn't dead, the whole-brain criterion produces false positives. Given the whole-brain criterion, **cardiopulmonary death** yields false negatives, since it considers brain-dead patients on life supports alive when they are actually dead. We'll later evaluate these implications.

Medical tests are the standard account's third element. Although checking for permanent cessation of cardiopulmonary function has proved reliable in most deaths, when a patient's heart or lungs are kept functioning artificially, brain-death criteria recommend checking neurological functions. This includes tests for deep coma, inability to breathe unassisted, and absent brainstem reflexes, such as pupillary response and cough/gag response—together with confirmatory tests of cerebral blood flow and electrical activity.

Critics of the standard account target its assumptions, to which we now turn.

FIGURE 6.1 The Standard Account of Death

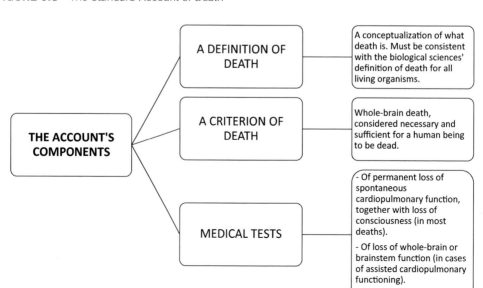

Death Is an Instantaneous Event

Processists deny this, holding that death is a lengthy process. It begins earlier in life with organ failure, developing over time and leading ultimately to irreversible loss of spontaneous heart and lung function, and ending with disintegration of the skeletal remains. Its stages include necrosis of vital organ cells, cooling, rigor mortis, dependent lividity, and putrefaction. Given processism, life and death are not exclusive categories. Furthermore, the choice of one particular stage in the dying process as a momentous event is arbitrary.

But processism conflicts with ordinary intuitions about death. Furthermore, although dying is a process, more is needed to consider death itself a process. In addition, like 'bald', 'dead' seems vague. Although losing a few hairs would not make you bald, losing indefinitely many would. Similarly, some patients may be between life and death. But at some point, they become definitely dead—or alive.

Death Can Be Defined

This assumes that there is a feature, essential to being dead, that a definition of death can capture. According to Winston Chiong (2005), there is no such feature. 'Death' is like 'game': although football, poker, and chess have some things in common, there is no essential feature all of them share, by virtue of which they are games.

But here is a counter-analogy: 'death' is like 'arthritis' and other medical/biological concepts whose precise, essential nature is ultimately established by experts. Although a nonexpert may believe he has arthritis in his thigh, medical experts now know arthritis occurs only in the joints. Similarly, experts may not yet know the essential nature of death, but from this it does not follow that it lacks one.

There Is a Single Concept of Death

A related objection by Jeff McMahan (2002, 2006) denies that 'death' has one meaning that is the same in ordinary, medical, and scientific contexts. The organismic, biological definition of 'death' fails to capture what people mean in some contexts—for instance, in saying "whosoever liveth and believeth in me shall never die," Jesus probably had in mind something other than biological death. Furthermore, some disorders argue for two concepts of death: one biological, the other personal (or psychological). Consider dicephalic twining, which results in a human organism with two heads sharing a common torso. Since we conceive of a person as essentially an embodied mind, we believe these 'twins' are two different people.

McMahan contends that biological death occurs with the irreversible loss of cardiopulmonary function, while personal death (i.e., the death of "one of us") occurs with the irreversible loss of the capacity for consciousness. Each type of death marks the point where some death-related behaviors become permissible—for example, with personal death donated organs can be procured for transplantation, even if the patient is not biologically dead. But the Jesus example is insufficient to show that there is no single concept of 'death', since it involves metaphorical language. Moreover, more needs to be said for McMahan's view that personal death produces the loss of full moral standing, a notion discussed in Chapter 1.

▇ 6.3 Cardiopulmonary Death

The Cardiopulmonary Criterion

'Cardiopulmonary death,' the prevalent criterion until the late 1960s, takes death to occur with the irreversible cessation of lung and heart function. Before the advent of mechanical ventilation and the modern ICU in the 1950s and 60s, absent circulation of oxygenated blood, the death of the brain and other organs would soon follow—together with the breakdown of cells and eventually of the whole organism. Cardiopulmonary function appeared, then, the primary integrator of a human organism's functioning as an integrated whole. That death can be easily determined by this criterion is another reason in its favor: confirmation of cardiopulmonary death requires only a physician with a stethoscope. Cardiopulmonary death also conforms to the ordinary intuition that some brain-dead patients whose respiration and heartbeat are being maintained artificially seem alive. But more than intuition was needed to keep this criterion after the above mentioned medical advances. In addition, the criterion ran into the problems considered next.

The Unilateral-Decision Problem

In the 1960s, the number of permanently unconscious patients who, previously, would have died but whose heart and lung function could now be maintained with external assistance was growing. Such patients are alive according to the heartbeat criterion, which is neutral about whether breathing and heartbeat are externally maintained. Removing them from life supports raised questions about nonmaleficence. Yet thus prolonging their lives raised questions of justice and beneficence, since it involved using a scarce medical resource for patients incapable of ever regaining consciousness.

BOX 6.1 DEAD DONOR RULE (DDR)

Patients must be dead before donated vital organs may be taken for transplantation.

The Organ-Procurement Problem

Vital organ procurement, a need that grew dramatically in the second half of the 20th century with new advances in transplantation, found an obstacle in the cardiopulmonary criterion. For the success of transplants depended in part on whether the organs were obtained from donors whose cardiovascular systems were still functioning. When a warm body cools after cardiopulmonary death, organs suffer warm ischemic damage as they continue to metabolize without sufficient oxygen, nutrients, and a way to eliminate waste. The organs of a brain-dead patient with assisted breathing and heartbeat may suffer only minimal damage. These physiological facts, combined with the evidence about severe organ shortage, created an **organ-procurement problem** for the cardiopulmonary criterion. This is because of the **dead donor rule** (see Box 6.1), which governs organ transplantation and implies that no human life may be shortened or care compromised in the service of transplantation. Retrieval of organs for transplantation follows it except when removing an organ from a living donor is safe for the donor, as in kidney transplants.

Given cardiopulmonary death and the DDR, organ retrieval from a whole-brain-dead patient on life supports is impermissible, even with consent, since the patient is not dead. This raised a practical and moral problem, since many patients who could have been saved without harm to brain-dead donors were in fact dying.

Donation after Cardiac Death

The cardiopulmonary theorists' response to this problem has been to support **donation after cardiac death (DCD)** or nonheart-beating organ donation. First implemented in the US in the 1990s, these programs of vital-organ retrieval are lawful under the **Uniform Determination of Death Act of 1980 (UDDA)**, which sanctions that a patient is dead after the irreversible loss of *either*

- Circulatory and respiratory functions, *or*
- All functions of the entire brain, including the brain stem.

Thus, the whole-brain criterion of death is an alternative to the cardiopulmonary criterion when life supports preclude a determination of death by the irreversible cessation of lung and heart functions. At the same time, it is lawful to retrieve vital organs from donors who are not whole-brain dead but can be declared dead on the grounds of having irreversibly lost autonomous cardiopulmonary function. Qualifying donors have (a) previously refused life supports, either directly or by proxy; and (b) given informed consent to the initiation of organ procurement a few minutes after a planned withdrawal of life supports. When these conditions are met, the medical team disconnects life supports, causing death by cardiac arrest. After a few minutes, vital organs are retrieved before suffering damage that would make them unsuitable for transplant. DCD was first performed in the early 1990s at the University of Pittsburgh, with a two-minute interval between cardiac arrest and organ procurement. In 2005, the Institute of Medicine set the interval at five minutes.

Problems with DCD include that it violates the DDR, since patients are not dead after a few minutes of cardiac arrest. The cessation of cardiopulmonary functions is not yet irreversible. But it *is* permanent because at that point, no attempt at resuscitation can be made (the patient or surrogate has validly refused life supports), and autonomous cardiopulmonary function will not resume spontaneously. Alternatively, cardiopulmonary theorists may respond by questioning the DDR. Still, they face the objection that, in the absence of the brain-dead criteria, the contribution of organs by DCD programs would be insignificant. The evidence suggests that if cardiopulmonary death were the only legal criterion, the scarcity of organs would increase.

6.4 Brain Death

The problems facing cardiopulmonary theorists were among the reasons for the shift toward brain-death criteria that took place in most countries during the 1970s and 80s.

Early whole-brain theorists in the US argued that, since the irreversible loss of function in the entire brain inevitably leads to loss of unassisted breathing and blood circulation, the whole-brain criterion is compatible with the cardiopulmonary criterion. But the underlying accounts differ on what function is crucial to sustaining the operation of a human organism as a cohesive whole: for one, it is brain function; for the other, lung and heart function. Clinicians welcomed both criteria as whole-brain death rapidly became the principal legal standard of death in the United States and other countries. Parallel developments in the UK led to adoption of an account focused on the loss of all function in the brainstem. Before examining either of these, we'll need to distinguish brain death from other disorders of consciousness.

Disorders of Consciousness versus Brain Death

Jahi McMath and *Baby Theresa* involved patients with permanent absence of **consciousness**. Jahi was whole-brain dead, while Baby Theresa permanently lacked higher-brain function—a condition in some respects parallel to some disorders of consciousness considered next.

The Human Brain

Anatomical studies of the human brain typically divide it into the cerebrum, cerebellum, and brainstem. Of these regions, the most primitive is the brainstem or lower brain, which controls spontaneous functions such as swallowing, heartbeat, and respiration. Its reticular activating system regulates sleep-and-wake cycles and turns consciousness on and off. But the contents of consciousness are controlled by the cerebrum or higher brain—especially by its outer shell, the cortex, sometimes called 'neocortex' because it was the last to evolve. Although much remains to be discovered about brain function, consciousness is associated with cerebral cortical and subcortical activity, on which mental capacities such as awareness, reasoning, and memory depend. When the higher brain is absent or has sustained

IMAGE 6.2
©iStockPhoto/Branchegevara

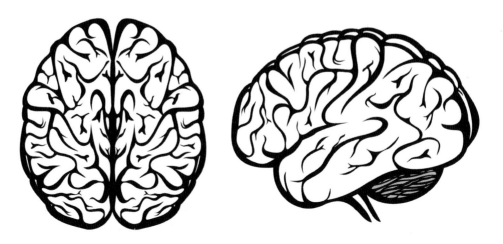

catastrophic damage, consciousness may be permanently absent, depending on the severity of the condition. Disorders of consciousness range from brain death and **permanent vegetative state (PVS)**, both characterized by the permanent absence of *all* mental activity including feelings of pain and pleasure, to the minimally conscious state (MCS) and locked-in-syndrome (LIS). MCS involves some self-awareness and the ability to follow simple commands, give gestural or verbal responses, and make purposeful movements. Patients in LIS are conscious, though brain damage has left them aware of their environment, with open eyes but total paralysis, except for, typically, eye or eyelid movements used for communication.

Other Disorders of Consciousness

Catastrophic cerebral damage may not affect the spontaneous functions of the less susceptible brainstem. Patients thus affected enter a vegetative state (VS), which may transition into MCS or PVS (roughly, after a year for traumatic injury and three months for nontraumatic injury). Some patients have lived many years in a PVS—in one reported case, 37 years.

A patient in VS lacks consciousness, a subjective state that comes in degrees and has eluded strict definition. Its two essential elements are

1. Awareness of the self and the environment in a time-ordered, organized, reflective manner.
2. Wakefulness or arousal.

The brain functions responsible for (1) are those that support attention, cognition, intentional action, and memory. During sleep or anesthesia, (2) is temporarily altered in varying degrees. For example, a sleeper with the imagery of rapid eye movement has some degree of consciousness. But someone in dreamless sleep (the so-called stage 3 slow-wave sleep) temporarily lacks it (Giacino et al., 2014: 99).

Brain-dead patients like Jahi McMath have permanently lost (1) and (2) owing to catastrophic damage to the entire brain, including the brainstem. Yet some brainstem functions can be maintained externally. By contrast, patients in VS typically retain partial or total *unassisted* brainstem functions, such as the ability to have open eyes for long periods of time, sleep/wake cycles, breathing, cough-and-gag reflex, pupillary response to light, and blood pressure. They can smile, frown, and cry, though in ways unrelated to external stimuli. None of these is considered a sign of awareness or sentience. These patients are not brain dead, though they have sustained catastrophic damage to the higher brain from which there is almost no possibility of recovery (depending on their age and the cause of damage). They are also not in a coma, which is a state of prolonged unconsciousness resulting from many conditions (head injury, stroke, brain tumor, intoxication, etc.). Although a dysfunctional brainstem may allow spontaneous breathing, comatose patients are in a sleep-like condition of unarousability with eyes closed.

We may consider patients in vegetative state not demented, but 'amented.' 'Dementia' denotes a number of brain impairments characterized by *distortions* of consciousness, not its absence. It affects consciousness's contents. For example, in Alzheimer's disease, the leading cause of dementia, there is a progressive degeneration and destruction of brain cells that disrupts memory and other mental functions while the patient still has consciousness.

Whole-Brain versus Brainstem Death

Whole-brain- and brainstem-death criteria take death to occur when the brain has permanently lost capacity for consciousness and coordination of the somatic functioning of the organism as a whole. They thus interpret, for all animals with a brain, the organismic definition of death discussed above. Accordingly, they consider brain-dead patients on life supports 'beating-heart cadavers' or 'breathing corpses.'

Although both criteria now yield the same declarations of death, they differ on the brain function that, when permanently lost, determines death. For the whole-brain criterion, it is the function of the entire brain, including the brainstem. For the brainstem criterion, it is the function of the brainstem. Someone dead by either criterion has sustained permanent loss of consciousness and spontaneous breathing. Brainstem theorists can say this because, at present, consciousness appears impossible without brainstem function. Their criterion was adopted in the United Kingdom in 1976 by the Conference of the Royal Medical Colleges and was left to stand in all subsequent revisions.

But in 2008 the US President's Council on Bioethics concluded that the consciousness of a patient with residual cortical activity and complete absence of brainstem activity is ultimately unknown. Furthermore, although today both criteria produce the same verdicts, perhaps one day patients with brain damage affecting only the brainstem could have externally maintained consciousness—something not unthinkable after the introduction of ventilators, pacemakers, and other life-prolonging technologies.

To these objections, brainstem theorists reply that *any* adequate criterion of death is open to updates in light of relevant medical advances. Furthermore, although the clinical tests for whole-brain and brainstem death are the same, confirmatory tests for the latter are simpler. Unlike whole-brain death, brainstem death does not require confirmation that *all* brain function has ceased, including cortical activity and intracranial blood flow: it requires confirmation only of the "irreversible loss of the capacity for consciousness combined with the irreversible loss of the capacity to breathe" (Pallis, 1983: 36). Moreover, the whole-brain account of death faces the problem that some brain functions continue after clinical diagnosis of death by this criterion.

To counter this objection, whole-brain theorists either advocate better checks beyond the standard clinical diagnosis of death, or contend that only some brain functions are crucial to the functioning of the organism as a whole. Those continuing after diagnosis of whole-brain death, such as neuroendocrine responses, are not.

Reasons for Brain-Death Accounts

In spite of these disagreements, whole-brain and brainstem death criteria (hereafter, simply 'brain death') share some supporting reasons and face some similar objections. The former include that, these criteria are, arguably,

1. Consistent with the scientific, organismic definition of death. The brain appears a good candidate for being the master integrator whose death brings about the permanent cessation of all coordinated functioning, including spontaneous cardiopulmonary functions.

2. Not a radical departure from tradition, since most of the time they produce the same verdicts as the cardiopulmonary criterion—except for brain-dead patients on life supports, who are not dead under the cardiopulmonary criterion.

Additional reasons are negative. For one thing, brain-death criteria avoid the organ-procurement problem (the DDR does not preclude organ retrieval from brain-dead donors on life supports) and the unilateral-decision problems facing the traditional criterion (hospitals can unilaterally decide to forgo life supports for brain-dead individuals). Recall Jahi Mac-Math: her mother needed a court order to pursue critical care for her in another facility.

BOX 6.2 BRAIN DEATH AS ORGANISMIC DEATH

For humans, death is the irreversible loss of brain function leading to the loss of coordinated function of the organism as a whole.

Reasons against Brain-Death Accounts

Neither whole-brain nor brainstem death appears to lead directly to the disintegration of somatic functioning of the human organism as a whole. If so, reason (1) above for brain death is false. Among other critics, Singer (1994) invokes cases where some somatically integrative functions continued, with external assistance, *well after brain death*. A brain-dead California woman was able to continue a pregnancy until viability. Or, consider this case:

T. K., aged 4, was pronounced whole-brain dead as a result of meningitis. His mother refused discontinuation of life support and took him home, where he received ventilation, tube feeding, and basic nursing care. After fifteen years in that condition, his brain, including the brainstem, "had been replaced by ghost-like tissues and disorganized proteinaceous fluids" (Shewmon, 1998: 136). But his body had maintained sufficient integrated functioning to allow, e.g., growth in stature, responses of the immune system, and the healing of wounds.

Confirmed cases like this are very rare but totaled about 175 at the time Alan Shewmon reported *T.K.* These brain-dead patients all retained some nonbrain-mediated somatically integrative functions for at least a week, including assimilation of nutrients, wound healing, fighting infections and foreign bodies, cardiovascular and hormonal stress responses to incisions, proportional growth in children, and successful gestation in thirteen pregnant women. To critics, these are not only counterexamples to brain accounts but show their incoherence, since such accounts are committed to these contradictory claims:

1. For *all* humans, death is the disintegration of *all* somatic functioning of a human organism as a whole, which occurs with brain death.
2. Given the data, for some humans, brain death is compatible with some somatic functioning of the organism as a whole.

Brain-death theorists might (1) accept that human death is not organismic death, or (2) hold that the integrative functions invoked by critics are not critical to being alive. If (2), the theorists must reach consensus about *which* integrating functions of an organism are essential to its continued life so that their irreversible loss determines the organism's death. The prospects for reaching it seem slim.

BOX 6.3 THE INCOHERENCE OBJECTION AGAINST THE WHOLE-BRAIN ACCOUNT OF DEATH

1. Given the whole-brain account of death, a human organism ceases to function as a coordinated whole with brain death.

2. But the irreversible cessation of all brain function is not sufficient for that.

Reply (1) is unappealing to those who think that death must be the same for all living things. Yet the irreversible loss of bodily functioning integrated by the brain seems insufficient for death, as shown by patients with locked-in-syndrome. Owing to near-total paralysis, LIS patients may have fewer bodily functions integrated by the brain than brain-dead individuals. But they are alive and conscious—something brain-death theorists often acknowledge in defining death as "the permanent cessation of all observable natural functioning of the organism as a whole, and the permanent absence of consciousness in the organism as a whole, and in any part of that organism" (Gert et al., 2006: 290).

On the other hand, since human embryos and early fetuses can also die, brain death is not necessary for human death. But suppose brain criteria are restricted to humans *with a brain*. A science-fiction scenario still suggests that brain death is not necessary for human death even then. Imagine a human being whose brain is successfully transplanted into another body, where it continues to function as usual. Arguably, biological death has occurred without brain death. Of course, at present, such 'brain transplants' are not actually possible. But they are imaginable. At this point, brain theorists might insist that, because in the imagined scenario the brain continues to have the same consciousness (memories, beliefs, desires, etc.), the human being did not die. But this response concedes that human death is not identical to biological death, a claim crucial to the higher-brain account of death.

Higher-Brain Death

The higher-brain account, so far not legally recognized in any jurisdiction, defines death as the irreversible loss of the capacity for consciousness. A person is dead under this criterion when the higher brain, the anatomical hardware essential for consciousness, is congenitally absent or irreversibly destroyed—as happens, for example, with cortical death, which involves the destruction of the cortex. The account thus avoids counting as dead people those who are temporarily unconscious because they are under anesthesia or in dreamless sleep or a reversible coma.

There is no standard neurological examination of higher-brain death. Besides checks for general nonresponsiveness consistent with absence of consciousness, confirmatory tests may include demonstrations of loss of cerebral electrical activity or blood flow. Unassisted respiration, brainstem reflexes, and other functions of the lower brain have no bearing on the determination of death according to this criterion.

BOX 6.4 HIGHER-BRAIN DEATH

1. **The Higher-Brain Definition:** Human death is the irreversible loss of the capacity for consciousness.

2. **The Higher-Brain Criterion:** The irreversible cessation of higher-brain function is necessary and sufficient for human death as defined in (1).

Although there is still much to be learned about the neurological basis of consciousness, experts generally agree that the total and irreversible destruction of the higher brain results in permanent unconsciousness.

Reasons for the Account

Of all brain functions, those responsible for consciousness support psychological capacities often associated with our being persons. For Kant, as we have seen, persons' rational nature confers on them an *absolute* moral worth. For others, self-awareness and rational decision-making are among the features that give persons full moral standing. In bioethics, these capacities ground the medical providers' duty of respect for patient autonomy. For higher-brain theorists, their account captures the intuition that, with the permanent loss of such capacities, a person is dead.

Other reasons for their account are negative. First, since it rejects the organismic definition, it avoids the above incoherence objection facing other brain-death accounts. It also avoids the unilateral-decision and the organ-procurement problems facing the cardiopulmonary account. After all, since in this criterion catastrophic damage to the higher brain is sufficient for death, forfeiting their life supports and retrieval of their donated organs are both permissible. Given this criterion, for example, organ procurement in the following case was permissible:

Dr. Shann faced a dilemma when two infants were admitted to intensive care at the Royal Children's Hospital in Melbourne, Australia. One was dying of heart failure; the other had suffered a catastrophic cerebral hemorrhage resulting in higher-brain death. Both infants were of the same blood type, so Dr. Shann thought a heart transplant seemed not only medically possible but morally mandatory, provided the parents consented. But in Australia, higher-brain-dead patients are not legally dead. Any attempt to use the heart of one of the infants to save the other would have been homicide. So, nothing was done. In a short time both infants were dead. (Adapted from Singer, 1994: 41–2.)

Note, however, that although Dr. Shann's utilitarian considerations support the higher-brain account of death, they also support abandoning the DDR.

Reasons against the Account

Critics of the higher-brain account object to its

1. Utilitarian motivations,
2. Exceptionalism about human death, and
3. Incompatibility with common intuitions about who counts as dead.

The motivations alluded to in (1) are avoiding misuse of life supports and organ procurement. As we saw, given higher-brain death, with permanent absence of consciousness, patients are dead—if not in the biological sense, at least as persons. It would then be permissible, for example, to retrieve donated organs for transplant. To higher-brain theorists, this is no objection at all: their criterion promises the most advantageous outcome for all patients, and one that harms no one. Too many people who actually die of organ failure could be saved if only there were enough transplantable organs available. Arguably, healthy hearts, livers, lungs, and kidneys are of no use to patients who are not, and never will be, conscious.

This reply, however, requires the acceptance of the criterion under challenge: opponents deny that such patients, who seem biologically alive, are in fact dead. Furthermore, if organ procurement is the rationale for the higher-brain criterion, why not instead simply abandon the DDR and say that taking organs from individuals who have permanently lost the capacity for consciousness is morally permissible whenever a valid consent has been given?

Objection (2) charges that the higher-brain account has a double standard: death for human beings is not the same as death for anything else.

A Double Standard of Death

1. Standard for humans: Irreversible loss of function of the higher brain.
2. Standard for nonhumans: Irreversible cessation of all somatically integrative functions of an organism as a whole (or something else).

Peter Singer (1994: 21–2) raises this objection to all brain-death criteria, arguing:

> Dead, *really dead*, seems to be the same for every living being. But to be 'brain dead' is something that can only happen to a being with a brain. It can't happen to a cabbage, nor to an oak, and not really to an oyster either. And though it would in theory be possible, no-one talks about 'brain death' in the case of dogs or parrots either. 'Brain death' is only for humans. Isn't it odd that for a human being to die requires a different concept of death from that which we apply to other living beings?

But this objection has no traction at all if, as discussed above, there is no single concept or essence of death.

Objection (3), the charge that higher-brain death is incompatible with permanently unconscious patients seeming alive, is weaker, since it rests on ordinary intuitions, which are often contestable. But it can be expanded to include expert opinion about who counts as dead. Consider patients with Alzheimer's disease or any other form of progressive, permanent loss of consciousness. Contrary to expert opinion, higher-brain theorists must say these patients are dying. Furthermore, no culture has ever considered these people dead, and very few health care providers would disagree, which suggests that the higher-brain criterion produces false positives.

In response, higher-brain theorists may point out that common and expert intuitions might simply have not yet caught up with the new realities brought about by advances in medical technology. The history of science affords many examples where those who challenged such intuitions were right: think of Copernicus's challenge to the geocentric view of the universe. But when mainstream beliefs are at stake, the burden of argument rests initially with the challenger—in this case, higher-brain theorists.

BOX 6.5 FOUR CRITERIA OF DEATH

Human death is determined by the permanent cessation of function in:

1. The heart and lungs—cardiopulmonary criterion.

2. The entire brain, including the brainstem—whole-brain criterion.
3. The brainstem—brainstem criterion.
4. The higher brain—higher-brain criterion.

6.5 Chapter Summary

This chapter considered the accounts of human death listed in Box 6.5. On the basis of the material covered here we cannot settle the matter of which of them is preferable. Yet given the unilateral-decision and organ-procurement problems facing the cardiopulmonary account, that account needs to be replaced or supplemented by some of the above discussed brain-death accounts—as became evident in most countries in the early 1980s. According to a standard view, any adequate account of death should have three elements: a definition and a criterion of human death, and some associated medical tests. A definition spells out what death is, while a criterion gives necessary and sufficient conditions for determining when death, thus defined, has occurred. Most cardiopulmonary- and brain-death theorists contend that their account is consistent with the sciences' organismic definition of death, but disagree in what each regards as the master integrator of bodily functions, whose permanent loss entails the death of a person. While for cardiopulmonary theorists it is heart and lung function, for whole-brain and brainstem theorists it is either the functioning of the entire brain or of the brainstem. These brain-death accounts face the incoherence objection. Higher-brain theorists avoid it by claiming instead that it is the permanent loss of consciousness (associated with the absence or destruction of the higher brain) that determines the death of a person, even if the human organism continues to function. But they seem to face the more serious of two potential problems for criteria of death: false positives, which occur when a criterion sanctions as dead a person who is alive. The other problem is created by false negatives, which occur when a criterion sanctions as alive a person who is dead.

 6.6 Study Aids

Key Words

Brain death, 117
Cardiopulmonary death, 120
Consciousness, 124
Dead donor rule (DDR), 122
Donation after cardiac death (DCD), 123
Organ-procurement problem, 122
Organismic death, 118
Permanent vegetative state (PVS), 125
Standard account of death, 118
Uniform Determination of Death Act (UDDA), 123
Unilateral-decision problem, 122

Questions and Cases for Further Consideration

1. Brain-death theorists sometimes refer to whole-brain-dead patients on life supports as 'beating-heart cadavers.' For which account of death would this express a contradictory concept? Is the expression offensive? If so, to whom? Should it be used at all?

2. If human death is whole-brain death, what implications, if any, would that have for deciding when life begins? What if death is cardiopulmonary death? Or higher-brain death?

3. *Alive in a Body Bag. In February 2014, workers at a funeral home in Lexington, Mississippi, noticed that Walter Williams was kicking inside the bag used to transport him from a hospice. On the previous evening, a hospice nurse, finding the 78-year-old unconscious and without pulse, had reported his 'passing away.' Dexter Howard, the county coroner, confirmed the absence of vital signs and pronounced him dead the following morning. According to the* Los Angeles Times[2] *the coroner interpreted what later happened as a miracle. But Mr. Williams had a pacemaker, which may have temporarily stopped working when he was examined.* One thing the major criteria of death would *not* say is that Mr. Williams was actually dead for a brief period and then revived. Why not? Such

---

2 Michael Muskal, "Mississippi Man, Kicking in Body Bag, Back from the Dead. Sort of," *Los Angeles Times*, 2/28/2014.

mistaken-for-dead incidents, though rare, may occur. Do they challenge the prevailing criteria of death? Or are they failures of nonmaleficence? Do the nurse and coroner involved in this case deserve legal or moral sanction? Explain.

4. *Crobons v Wisconsin National Life Insurance Company and Wyant. In 1982 Marvin K. Wyant took out a $100,000 life insurance policy on his business partner, Gene Crobons, which named Crobons's wife, Ann Marie, as the beneficiary. Later that year Crobons suffered a massive stroke, and on September 12 Dr. Rawal wrote in the chart, 'neuro-examination consistent with brain death.' But he postponed disconnection of life support pending results of an EEG requested by the family. On September 15, Rawal certified that Crobons died on September 14, when he was disconnected from life supports. Meanwhile, Wyant knew that the insurance policy permitted him to change the beneficiary as long as Crobons was alive, so when he learned of Crobons's stroke, Wyant did just that. On September 13 he named himself sole beneficiary. In the litigation that followed, Wyant argued that he was the legal beneficiary of the policy, since Crobons was 'only' brain dead on September 13. The brain death standard, Wyant alleged, had been enacted into law only to afford legal protection for surgeons in transplant cases, and for the purpose of insurance the cardiopulmonary standard governed. Thus Crobons died when disconnected from life support. But the Michigan courts rejected this argument, emphasizing that Michigan law stipulated brain death as the operative definition of death for all purposes in its jurisdictions.* A main issue in this litigation was exactly when Crobons died. Was it on the 12th when his doctor diagnosed brain death, or the 14th, when he was disconnected from life supports? Does the UDDA support *Wyant's* argument? Might cases of this sort call for moving toward a univocal criterion of death?

5. *Dr. Fraser Houston, a physician who, during his residency, encountered some cases of anencephaly ending in abortion, later attended at the birth of an anencephalic baby in a rural area. Before delivery, he called organ transplant centers to explore the possibility of 'harvesting' the infant's transplantable organs. At that time, organ transplantation was not advanced, and his efforts went nowhere. Today anencephalic donations are possible but rare. He still laments, "many organs from anencephalics go unused. One problem is the definition of dead donor."*[3]

    Although pediatric organs are in great shortage, given the dead donor rule, under which account of death is it morally forbidden to procure organs from anencephalic infants with spontaneous functioning of the brainstem? Why is Dr. Houston questioning the dead donor rule? Could these infants be 'donors' even when they can give no consent? What implications for organ procurement, if any, would your responses to these questions have?

6. *Ms. K, 36, has just been declared brain dead in a hospital in New York, where the law allows for "reasonable accommodation" of religious and moral objection in certifying death. Her husband has requested that she remain on life supports as long as assisted*

---

3 "Anencephaly: A Devastating Abnormality," *The Durango Herald*, 2/26/2012. http://durangoherald.com/article/20120227/COLUMNISTS16/702279991.

breathing is possible. Their religion recognizes only cardiopulmonary death as the point when the soul departs the body and the person dies. As far as he is concerned, his wife is fighting for her life. The medical team consults the hospital's ethics committee regarding the limits of "reasonable accommodation" in this case. What should the committee say? Could advice from clergy from the Ks' religion help? Should inquiries be initiated on what Ms. K would have wanted? Can the fact that she is breathing and feels warm to the touch be reconciled with her being dead? Is death in her case a matter of opinion? In a culturally and religiously diverse society like ours, what are the pros and cons in always using hospitals' protocols to override such requests?

Suggested Readings*

*Bernat, J. L., "The Whole-Brain Concept of Death Remains Optimum Public Policy," *Journal of Law, Medicine & Ethics* 34.1, 2006: 35–43.
A qualified defense of the whole-brain criterion and its rationale as adopted by the 1981 President's Commission. Objects to both higher-brain and somatic criteria of death while fully endorsing the standard, tripartite account of death.

*Chiong, Winston, "Brain Death without Definitions," *Hastings Center Report* 35.6, 2005: 20–30.
Argues that the tripartite account of death is incoherent, and that there are different types of human death. Since the concept 'death' is affected by vagueness, it resists definition in terms of necessary and sufficient conditions.

Gert, Bernard, C. M. Culver, and K. Danner Clouser, "Death," in *Bioethics: A Systematic Approach*, pp. 283–308. New York: Oxford University Press, 2006.
Defines death as the permanent loss of both whole-brain function and consciousness; also provides a useful update of the standard account of death.

*Harvard Committee, "A Definition of Irreversible Coma—Report of the Ad Hoc Committee of the Harvard Medical School to Examine the Definition of Brain Death," *Journal of the American Medical Association* 205.6, 1968: 337–40.
A turning point for the adoption in the US of the whole-brain criterion of death, understood as compatible with the cardiopulmonary criterion. Contentiously equates brain death with irreversible coma.

*McMahan, Jeff, "An Alternative to Brain Death," *Journal of Law, Medicine & Ethics* 34.1, 2006: 44–8.
Rejects the assumption in the standard account of death that there is a single concept of death. Higher-brain death, which differs from the organism's death, marks the death of the mind, when organ donation or removal of life supports becomes permissible.

*Miller, Franklin G., and Robert D. Truog, "The Dead Donor Rule and Organ Transplantation," *New England Journal of Medicine* 359.7, 2008: 674–5.
Advocates abolishing the dead donor rule because it makes the organ shortage problem more acute by not only limiting the pool of eligible donors but also delaying transplants in ways that undermine their success. Considers brain death a fiction.

---

* Asterisks mark readings available online. See links on the companion website.

*Pallis, C., "Whole-brain Death Reconsidered—Physiological Facts and Philosophy," *Journal of Medical Ethics* 9.1, 1983: 32–7.
> Argues that brain death is necessary and sufficient for human death. Brain-dead patients on respirators are unquestionably dead.

*Pellegrino, Edmund D., "Personal Statement," President's Council on Bioethics, *Controversies in the Determination of Death: A White Paper.* President's Council on Bioethics: Washington DC, 2008.
> Outlines shortcomings in main accounts of death, defending the dead donor rule on the grounds that it is wrong to harm one patient in order to benefit another.

*President's Commission for the Study of Ethical Problems in Medicine and Biomedical and Behavioral Research, *Defining Death: Medical, Legal and Ethical Issues in the Determination of Death.* Washington, DC: Government Printing Office, 1981.
> Follows the Harvard Committee (1968) lead in supporting the whole-brain criterion. Analyzes some facts about the human brain relevant to death, as opposed to the vegetative state and other disorders of consciousness.

*Singer, Peter, "Is the Sanctity of Life Ethic Terminally Ill?" *Bioethics* 9.3–4, 1995: 307–43.
> Offers standard objections to brain-death accounts, including the incoherence objection.

**Uniform Determination of Death Act*, 1980. Available online at http://pntb.org/wordpress/wp-content/uploads/Uniform-Determination-of-Death-1980_5c.pdf.
> States a disjunctive standard of death that was endorsed by the American Medical Association in 1980 and the American Bar Association in 1981.

*Veatch, Robert M., "The Definition of Death: Problems for Public Policy," *Transplantation Ethics*, pp. 53–84. Washington DC: Georgetown University Press, 2000.
> Addresses the ambiguity of 'brain death,' some central objections to whole-brain death, the reasons for higher-brain death, and the limits to tolerance of divergent criteria of death in a pluralistic society.

7 When Life Supports Are Futile or Refused

Learning Objectives

In reading this chapter you will

▶ Learn about influential court decisions in cases involving refusal of life-sustaining treatment by patients or their surrogates.

▶ Compare some seriously disabling disorders of consciousness and their impact on end-of-life medical decisions.

▶ Identify different ways treatments can be medically futile and the role patient quality of life plays in some judgments of this kind.

▶ Assess some common appeals to the Sanctity-of-Life or the ordinary-versus-extraordinary-means doctrines for deciding whether to forgo medical treatment.

RECENT ADVANCES IN medical science and technology have opened dramatic new frontiers in saving and prolonging life. Particularly relevant to this chapter are two 20th-century developments: artificial nutrition and hydration and the intensive care unit equipped with mechanical ventilators, defibrillators, and other life-prolonging technologies. But not all think the interventions requiring such technologies are always worth providing.

7.1 Was Continued Life in Tony Bland's Best Interests?

In 1993, a unanimous ruling by five justices of the House of Lords, then Britain's highest court, brought resolution to a case that was at the center of public scrutiny. Tony Bland, 22, had been crushed four years earlier in a stampede at the Hillsborough Football Stadium in Sheffield. Of the 766 Liverpool fans injured in the crowd surge, 96 subsequently died. Bland was among those who, as a result of anoxic brain damage, fell into a vegetative state that appeared to be permanent unconsciousness. Although he was able to breathe on his own, he received **life-sustaining treatment** (LST) consisting of antibiotics for infections and artificial nutrition and hydration (ANH), also known as 'clinical-assisted nutrition and hydration.' After four years in that condition, his attending physician, Dr. J. Howe, expressed an intention to withdraw all treatment. Tony's parents agreed that life had ceased to be in his interest. But the coroner and police warned that the withdrawal would amount to murder. So Dr. Howe, with the support of the Airedale NHS Trust, obtained a declaration of lawfulness from a lower court. But the Official Solicitor who had been appointed to represent Tony appealed twice. When the Court of Appeal upheld the lower court's ruling, the appeal next went to the House of Lords, where five Law Lords unanimously dismissed it, thus concurring on the lawfulness of withdrawing life supports in Mr. Bland's case. The life supports were removed, and Mr. Bland died.

BOX 7.1 LIFE-SUSTAINING TREATMENT (LST)

LST is any medical intervention that saves or prolongs life without reversing an underlying medical condition. It may consist of

- Mechanical ventilation
- Hemodialysis

- Blood products
- Antibiotics
- Vasopressors
- Intravenous fluids
- Tube feedings
- Cardiopulmonary resuscitation

■ ■ ■

Tony Bland raised complex ethical and legal issues, prompting a ruling that brought Britain into line with other **common law** jurisdictions on the lawfulness of forgoing LST for some permanently unconscious patients. But by no means did this case settle all relevant issues, as some reports later commissioned by the House of Lords show. Regulations waiving the medical team's liability for such decisions had to wait until the Mental Capacity Act of 2005,[1] which considers them permissible whenever they are in the best interests of the patient (3ff., especially paragraph 9) and the team "reasonably believes that an advance decision exists which is valid and applicable to the treatment" (16). Yet in cases of conflicting opinions among health care providers or between them and the surrogates, a declaration of lawfulness may still be needed.

Bland also drew attention to an issue fraught with controversy: the permissibility of forgoing ANH. The measure is especially emotional for the family and health care providers—and most so when the patient's wishes are unknown. Clearly, administering ANH against the patient's wishes is inconsistent with respect for patient autonomy and amounts to battery in the law, thus constituting a tort against the patient. But since Mr. Bland's wishes were unknown, critics of the measure argue

1. Artificial nutrition and hydration (ANH) is basic or comfort care.
2. Basic or comfort care is always in a patient's best interests.

_____

3. Therefore, forgoing ANH is never in a patient's best interests.

_____

1   Two previous reports commissioned by the House of Lords (1994, 2004) left unquestioned England and Wales's requirement of a prior declaration of lawfulness by a High Court judge for forgoing LST when the patient lacks competence and there is no advance directive on file.

According to these critics, administering ANH to prolong life conforms with the medical team's duties of care. Yet whether premise (1) is true remains an open question, with the courts and many health care organizations and practitioners now opposing it. The Law Lords in *Bland*, for example, accepted that ANH bears the marks of sophisticated medical intervention, and therefore differs from oral drinking and eating. Given this view, in cases like *Bland*, forgoing ANH may serve the patient's best interests rather than violate the medical team's duties of care, provided there is no malicious intent.

The Law Lords also speculated that Bland's medical condition, not the withdrawal of treatment, would be the cause of death. But critics and defenders alike reject this line of reasoning because of the difficulties in determining cause of death. What makes a moral difference, for critics, is the *intention* to cause death in forgoing life supports; for defenders, it is whether the patient has permanently lost personal interests in remaining alive. Thus, for defenders, decisions such as *Bland* are justified independently of whether the withdrawal intends or causes the patient's death.

7.2 Forgoing Life Supports

Questions about medical treatment for people whose quality of life had been severely compromised by injury or illness were once resolved by nature itself in ways that left few options to providers. The health professional's role was limited to palliation, which aims at improving a patient's quality of life by relieving the pain, symptoms, or stress caused by a serious injury or illness. But advances in medicine have changed clinical practice by providing other treatment options besides palliation—although palliation remains an option at the end of life when the goals of medical intervention change to forgoing or de-escalating the supports necessary to sustain life.

Medical advances are only one factor in the change that has swept over modern medicine. Another has been the growing emphasis on respect for patient autonomy. Over the last 50 years, patients have increasingly been brought into the very center of decisionmaking about their own medical treatment. Moreover, the circle of decisionmakers has widened to include family, other members of the health care team, and sometimes hospital ethics

FIGURE 7.1 What Counts as Forgoing Life-Sustaining Treatment (LST)?

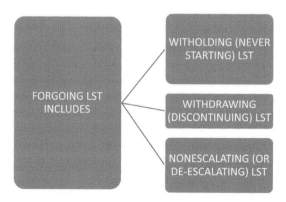

committees. These developments have led to disputes in bioethics and the law about the permissibility of forgoing LST. Litigation between patients or family members, health care providers, and the state has led to the acceptance of the patient's right to refuse treatment, including LST. When the patient has lost decisional capacity, the legal and ethical grounds for forgoing LST are less settled.

Karen Quinlan

Nearly fifteen years before Tony Bland's accident in the UK, a young New Jersey woman had made headlines across the United States with a similarly bleak prognosis. Her case led to a momentous ruling on the legal and moral permissibility of discontinuing life supports.

Karen Quinlan, 21, suffered irreversible anoxic damage to the higher brain in 1975 after ingesting barbiturates, benzodiazepines, and alcohol. As a result, she fell into a permanent vegetative state. She was placed on mechanical ventilation and given ANH by nasogastric tube. After several months in this condition, and with no real hope of recovery, her parents decided that Karen should be permitted to die. They asked that she be disconnected from the ventilator. The hospital refused, holding that withdrawal of life supports would amount to killing the patient, a view subsequently upheld by the Morris County Court. But the Supreme Court of New Jersey overturned that decision in 1976, ruling that Karen's right to privacy was grounds for withdrawing life supports. After the ventilator was disconnected, Karen proved capable of unassisted breathing and lived another nine years, though without ever regaining consciousness.

In the landscape of American law concerning end-of-life medical decisions, *Quinlan* was a harbinger of changes that were to occur in North America in the decades that followed. Although it did not settle the (still disputed) matter of whether there is a right to die, either legal or moral, it established a precedent for the right of formerly competent patients to refuse treatment, a principle grounded in the right to privacy protected by the Fourteenth Amendment to the US Constitution.

Nancy Cruzan

Quinlan was followed by *Cruzan v Director, Missouri Department of Health*, a 1990 Supreme Court decision that marked a turning point in the US as did *Bland* in the UK. At issue was the constitutionality of the state of Missouri's opposition to withdrawal of all life supports from a previously competent patient:

An auto accident in 1983 had left *Nancy Cruzan*, 25, with catastrophic higher-brain damage. Paramedics found her with no vital signs, and ultimately her condition was diagnosed as permanent vegetative state (PVS). She was able to breathe on her own but was given artificial nutrition and hydration. After Ms. Cruzan had been in PVS for four years, her parents requested the removal of ANH, for which the hospital then sought a court order. Litigation ensued, with further appeal to the Missouri Supreme Court, which refused to permit removal of life supports in the absence of "clear and convincing evidence" that withdrawal was what Nancy would herself have wanted. The only evidence available at the trial came from a roommate, according to whom Nancy, approximately a year before her accident, had said she would not want to continue living if she were permanently unconscious. But to the court this testimony was insufficiently specific to determine whether Nancy would have consented to withdrawal of ANH. On further appeal, in June 1990 the US Supreme Court upheld the Missouri verdict. By that time Ms. Cruzan had been in PVS for more than seven years. She lived another six months after the Court's decision. In the meantime, three co-workers provided evidence that confirmed the previous testimony about her wishes. In December 1990, a Missouri circuit court permitted removal of her gastrostomy tube, on the grounds that clear and convincing evidence had now been given. Twelve days later Ms. Cruzan died.

A number of factors contributed to making the US Supreme Court ruling in *Cruzan* a landmark in American jurisprudence for refusals of life supports by a formerly competent patient. For one thing, *Cruzan* was the first 'right-to-die' case decided by the highest court in the United States. In a 5-to-4 ruling, it established for the first time that

- A competent patient has a right, grounded in the 'due process' clause of the Fourteenth Amendment to the US Constitution, to refuse treatment, including life sustaining treatment (LST).
- States can set as high or as low as they deem necessary the standards of 'clear and convincing evidence' of a previously competent patient's wishes for proxy decisions about forgoing LST.
- There is no legal or moral difference between withholding and withdrawing LST.

The Supreme Court thus endorsed the state of Missouri's position while bringing attention to the importance of advance directives in verifying a previously competent patient's wish to refuse life supports. But there is nothing in its ruling requiring that advance directives be *written* in order to meet the 'clear and convincing evidence' standard that a state might set for lawful withholding or withdrawal of life supports.

The rationale for the Court's majority opinion was twofold. First, to err in keeping a patient alive is better than to err by directly causing unwanted death, which is irreversible. Second, there is no guarantee that family members will always decide correctly according to what the patient might have wanted or is in her best interests.

Nancy B

Quinlan, Cruzan, and *Bland* paved the way in the US and Britain for the legal permissibility of forgoing nonbeneficial treatment that is contrary to a formerly competent patient's or her surrogates' wishes (*Quinlan, Cruzan*) or his best interest (*Bland*). A precedent for analogous decisions in Canada, this time involving a competent patient, was set largely by this case:

Nancy B, 25, was suffering from Guillain-Barré syndrome, an irreversible neurological disorder that had left her entirely paralyzed and dependent on a ventilator. In 1992, after two and half years in this condition, she requested the removal of mechanical ventilation. Because she was mentally competent, the health care team and hospital agreed but sought clearance from the courts. Justice Dufour, of the Quebec Superior Court, affirmed the permissibility of the decision, asserting that in her case, the cause of death would be the disease, not a medically assisted suicide. Five weeks later, Nancy was given sedation to induce a coma, the ventilator was removed, and she died peacefully.

IMAGE 7.1
©iStockPhoto/Trish233

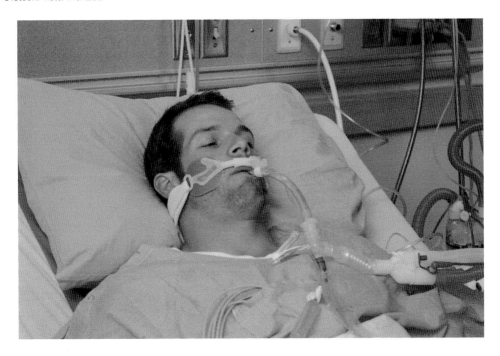

Together with cases such as *Bouvia v Superior Court* (1986) in the United States and *Ms B v NHS Hospital Trust* (2002) in Britain, *Nancy B* drew attention to the duty to honor competent patients' refusals of treatment, including life-saving treatment. When a patient or surrogate validly refuses life supports, forgoing them is now commonly mandated by law. To provide *any* refused medical treatment amounts to a tort of battery. From the moral perspective, the duty to honor valid refusals rests on respect for patient autonomy—a duty that, as we saw in Chapter 3, is supported by most ethical theories.

7.3 Medical Futility at the End of Life

What Is Medical Futility?

An intervention is medically futile just in case it is likely to produce, for the patient, either no significant benefit or no benefit at all. A judgment about the medical **futility** of an intervention for a patient at a time is strong when it rests on a sound assessment of the probability of that intervention's achieving a benefit for the patient, understood as an outcome or end. In medical decisionmaking, there is always the question of the goal or purpose for the sake of which a patient receives a certain treatment. Why is she being prescribed this procedure? Will it really contribute to her wellbeing? In other words, there is inevitably a teleological aspect (from the Greek *telos*, for 'goal' or 'end') to any treatment decision: such decisions are end-oriented. A medical intervention aims at some health outcome that is valued, and it is for the sake of that outcome that it is provided.

Associated with this teleological aspect of judgments of futility is the consequentialist notion of '**benefit**.' Although benefits are outcomes, clearly not all outcomes are benefits: some may be burdens or harms, others limited to maintaining function in a part of the patient's body without ostensibly improving his or her wellbeing as a whole. These don't amount to benefits. Treatment that merely sustains the life of a patient in PVS (as in *Bland*, *Cruzan*, and *Quinlan*) has an outcome but arguably no benefits. And so do treatments that cannot end dependence on intensive medical care or merely prolong the life of a terminally ill patient while imposing uncompensated burdens (as in *Nancy B*). That is, not all medical interventions that achieve their intended outcomes also achieve a benefit for the patient. Since 'benefit,' then, concerns outcomes of a certain type, so does 'medical futility': whether or not a treatment is futile depends on its likelihood of achieving for the patient a certain good in the circumstances (Schneiderman et al., 1990; Schneiderman and Jecker, 2011). Here it is important to distinguish medical treatment from medical care. Medical treatment may be futile. Care, whether directed at relief of suffering or at maintaining a patient's dignity, constitutes a professional moral obligation. It is something owed to patients unconditionally and cannot be futile.

Judgments of medical futility have, in addition to their consequentialist component, also a normative component, for they are intended to guide the health care provider's action: when there is a strong consensus in the medical team that a treatment is futile for a patient, that is a reason for forgoing it. And this reason is independent of any considerations of costs or rationing scarce medical resources, even when these may also recommend that decision. In *Bland*, for example, the Law Lords judged that there was no reasonable chance that medical treatments would improve Tony's condition and therefore authorized the withdrawal of treatment. Other examples of medical futility may involve cardiopulmonary resuscitation for someone who, owing to heart disease, has virtually no chance of survival, or a brain scan for a patient who has recently developed a mild headache. The scan might throw light on the cause of the headache, but so also might more low-tech means that are less costly and involve no invasive or marginally risky technologies. Since in this hypothetical case the risks of the scan outweigh any potential benefits, it should be ruled out on grounds of futility. Similar grounds are often cited to avoid unnecessary, aggressive interventions requiring admission to an ICU.

Types of Futility

Sometimes a medical intervention is denied because it is known *not* to produce in the patient the physiological effect sought. Since the medical team has expert knowledge, when they regard a certain treatment for a patient futile in this obvious sense, no further justification for their denial is needed. Such interventions are *physiologically futile*. For example, to resort to bloodletting, a medieval practice aimed at achieving 'balance' in the body humors, as treatment for a brain tumor, would be physiologically futile, since it is well known that such a treatment cannot produce a benefit for the patient. More interesting cases of futility, however, are those falling under the categories in Box 7.2.

BOX 7.2 TWO TYPES OF MEDICAL FUTILITY

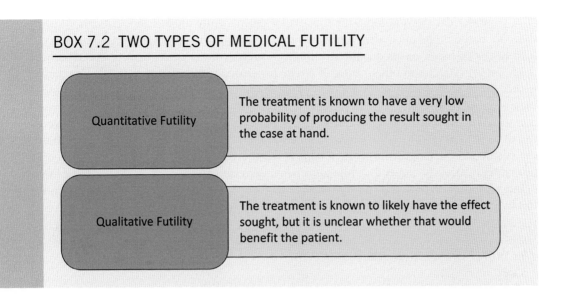

| Quantitative Futility | The treatment is known to have a very low probability of producing the result sought in the case at hand. |
| Qualitative Futility | The treatment is known to likely have the effect sought, but it is unclear whether that would benefit the patient. |

Quantitative futility involves a more objective judgment about a treatment's low probability of success and is therefore less open to challenge by patients or family than *qualitative futility*. A treatment that has a 1% (or less) chance of success (Schneiderman and Jecker, 2011: 15) is quantitatively futile. Even so, a patient or family member may request it. For example, as we'll see in Chapter 9, some parents may insist that everything be done to keep their extremely premature baby alive. They might hope that, if the child survives, any resulting deficits could be ameliorated later by therapies yet to be discovered. Or they might reject the medical team's bleak prognosis. Of course, medical predictions about a treatment's outcome, even those based on empirical studies and previous experience in clinical practice, have some degree of uncertainty. Furthermore, there is always the possibility of medical error. To make things worse for judgments of quantitative futility, low chances of success may involve odds higher than 1%. For example, a UK study in the late 2000s reports that babies born prematurely at week 24 of gestation have only a 34% chance of growing up without serious physical or mental impairment. Treatment decisions about such babies cannot be made on the basis of quantitative futility. Rather, when the baby's prospects look very grim at birth, a decision to forgo life supports is made on the basis of *qualitative futility*.

A medical treatment is qualitatively futile when it can bring the patient only an extremely poor benefit.

Although a qualitatively futile treatment may have the desired effect, its benefit to the patient is doubtful. In medicine, qualitative futility marks a threshold where 'enough is enough.' Schneiderman and Jecker (2011: 19) set that threshold this way: "If a patient lacks the capacity to appreciate the benefit of a treatment, or if the treatment fails to release a patient from total dependence on the acute hospital setting for survival, the treatment should be regarded as futile."

Consider decisions to forgo life support for permanently unconscious patients. Since these are based on its qualitative futility for those patients, they prompt more controversy than decisions based on its quantitative futility—such as when the patient is whole-brain dead. Keown (2002) and other critics of *Bland*, for example, questioned that ruling's reference to the patient's quality of life afforded by life supports. These controversies are inevitable because qualitative futility is a value-laden notion. What health care providers or the courts may consider an exceedingly poor quality of life may be a **life worth living** from the perspective of patients or relatives. The fact is that there is no training for health care providers that can ensure reliable judgments of when a life is worth living. As shown in the discussion of neonate euthanasia (Chapter 9), while some neonatologists consider not worth living the life of intensive suffering faced by newborns with severe spina bifida, other neonatologists find this judgment incompatible with evidence-based medicine.

The Moral Grounds of Medical Futility

The Biological versus Psychological Life Argument

When there is disagreement over what is best for a patient, the dispute may hinge on how best to maximize the patient's wellbeing in a compromised condition. But this challenge may arise in a vast array of different forms with different diseases, injuries, and disorders, and at all possible levels of severity. To see what is at stake, it may help to begin with a worst-case scenario. Consider the case where a patient has irreversibly lost all capacity for consciousness. The quality of life when someone becomes permanently unconscious is so poor that it is not at all clear how LST could benefit that patient. James Rachels (1986) famously defended the claim that a patient in PVS has a **biological** *but not* a **biographical life**. People in that condition lack the psychological capacities necessary for being the subject of a life, such as self-awareness and memories. Without these, the patient remains a living, human body, with no biographical life. Since the rule against hastening death, and indeed killing, applies only to persons who have a biographical life, so the argument goes, forgoing LST for a patient in PVS is therefore permissible. Jeff McMahan (2002) would agree. For him, these patients are alive only as human organisms but not as persons whose lives demand moral and legal protection. Only *minded* organisms with the capacity for consciousness qualify as persons.

In either version of the argument, these patients' exceedingly poor quality of life justifies hastening their death by forgoing futile LST. Quality of life does matter, after all, for end-of-life decisions—something acknowledged by the Law Lords in *Bland* when they deemed life no longer in Tony's interest. But the argument is vulnerable to important objections. First, from the *fact* that a patient like Tony permanently lacks consciousness, the *normative* conclusion that it is permissible to hasten his death by forgoing LST does not follow. As we saw earlier, it is not clear that judgments of value can be validly inferred from statements of fact. Moreover, not all agree with the moral decisionmaking role this argument gives to *having interests*. Among those who do agree, some think that even the dead can have residual interests that could be undermined by, for example, false claims about their past. That explains why certain behaviors toward them seem morally forbidden (Foster, 2013). In light of these criticisms, as it stands, the argument falls short of supporting its conclusion.

The Appeals to Justice and Beneficence

The health care professionals' duties of justice and beneficence provide stronger grounds for forgoing futile treatments. First, since medical resources are limited, if an intervention is foreseeably futile, then providing it amounts to wasting medical resources that could have been used to help others. And that is unjust to the patients who might have benefitted from it. Furthermore, futile interventions may give false hope to patients whose terminal condition is not yet obvious and who might thereby be deprived of a last chance to put their affairs in order. Such patients might also fall into despair when they see their hopes suddenly crushed. Another reason against futile interventions is that they might make some patients more uncomfortable or less lucid at the end of life, thereby preventing them from enjoying good moments with friends and family. Given the duty of beneficence, health care providers must prevent such harms. Therefore, justice and beneficence make obligatory the avoidance of futile interventions.

Disagreements about Futility Judgments

A patient or surrogate may disagree with the health care providers' judgment that a treatment will do no good, or its burdens outweigh the benefits. Such conflicts are less likely to arise with judgments involving quantitative futility. As discussed in Chapter 3, patients' requests for treatment lack the force of refusals. Although beneficence is a fundamental duty of health care providers, they need not provide treatment deemed futile, even life supports. This follows from their right of professional autonomy and their special epistemic (knowledge-based) authority. Owing to their professional experience and scientific expertise, their assessment of a treatment's likely benefits carries a special warrant of credibility.

Conflicts more often concern judgments about the qualitative futility of a treatment for a patient, and may involve the patient or surrogate, health care providers, and the courts. These conflicts rest not on different predictions about likely outcomes, but on differing views about whether those outcomes are valuable. As we saw in the above cases, the doctor disagreed with a guardian appointed by a lower court in *Bland*, the patient's parents with the state of Missouri in *Cruzan*, the hospital with the parents in *Quinlan*, and the patient with the hospital in *Nancy B*. While some of these parties considered life supports medically appropriate for the patient, others regarded it as (qualitatively) futile. In each of the cases, the decision would turn on an assessment of whether the treatment's outcome could be a benefit for the patient in making his or her life better overall. Such assessments are necessarily value-laden, for they depend on what the decisionmaker regards as a beneficial outcome to be sought or a harm to be avoided.

The last recourse in conflict resolution concerning futility assessments is the courts, which represent the state's interests in protecting the patient. Their rulings tend to invoke legal doctrines developed out of landmark cases such as those considered here: from *Quinlan* the principle of substituted judgment, from *Cruzan* the emphasis on patient self-determination and evidenciary standards for advance directives, and from *Bland* the best-interest standard so influential in British courts, to name but a few of the proxy decisionmaking procedures discussed in Chapter 5. Conflicts, however, are more often resolved without judicial intervention by dialogue among affected parties, input from institutional ethics committees, and reference to the health providers' policies concerning futile treatment, which increasingly try to strike a balance between consideration of health outcomes and respect for patient autonomy.

◼ 7.4 Objections and Alternatives to Medical Futility

The Sanctity-of-Life Doctrine

The **Sanctity-of-Life doctrine** embraces this claim of common morality:

> Human life in all its forms is sacred, in the sense of having value in itself, independent of any value it might have to the person whose life it is.

The doctrine may be religious or secular, depending on whether it takes God to be the source of human life's value. Either way, all Sanctity-of-Life theorists agree that human life should be respected or honored, given its sacredness.

Yet they disagree among themselves about which actions amount to disparaging or dishonoring life, as illustrated in debates about medical interventions that may damage or frustrate life at its beginning or its end. For conservative theorists, the value of life is conferred, for example, by God or by being a member of our species. Thus, frustrating or damaging a human life is always forbidden. For liberal theorists, on the other hand, the value of human life is, at least in part, contingent upon context. Although human life always commands special respect, on some occasions it is not disrespectful to damage or frustrate a life. When a mother, for example, lacks the financial resources to have another child, these theorists justify an abortion (Dworkin, 1991). We have more to say about the Sanctity-of-Life doctrine and abortion in Chapter 11. For the end-of-life scenarios of concern here, liberal theorists do not object to forgoing futile life-sustaining treatment. But conservative theorists do, whenever the intention is to cause the patient's death—though they may justify forgoing LST when medical resources are scarce and death is not intended (Finnis, 1993).

Conservative theorists do not regard futility as a reason for forgoing life supports. Furthermore, they deny any moral distinction between having psychological, or only a biological, life. For them, the life of a permanently unconscious patient has the same value as anyone else's. While a main argument for the conservative doctrine invokes the ethical tenets of the principal religious traditions, the argument for the liberal doctrine is secular. Accordingly, there are two Sanctity-of-Life conclusions about the moral permissibility of forgoing futile LST.

The Conservative Sanctity-of-Life Doctrine on Forgoing Futile LST

According to a main argument for this doctrine, human life arises through God's direction of the order of nature, which bestows on it a certain divine stamp that warrants reverence. Since life is God's gift, the intentional hastening of a patient's death is a grave moral wrong, whatever 'quality of life' a treatment might afford.

This argument assumes that it is universally accepted (1) that there is a God (2) who is the creator of human life and (3) confers on it a special value that renders morally forbidden any action that injures or destroys it. But (1) through (3) are religious beliefs that not all share. As a result, this argument for the conservative Sanctity-of-Life doctrine fails, since it rests on shaky grounds. Hence, it can be of little help in persuading people (including many religious believers) who think that in some scenarios forgoing futile LST is justified—an opinion widely held in cases such as *Bland* and *Cruzan*.

The other main argument for the conservative Sanctity-of-Life doctrine takes membership of our species to be what confers human life's sacredness—which, as we contend in Chapter 10, falls short of being a good candidate for the special value of persons. So we may conclude that the conservative Sanctity-of-Life doctrine fails to provide persuasive reasons for the moral wrongness of forgoing futile LST.

The Liberal Sanctity-of-Life Doctrine on Forgoing Futile LST

For this doctrine, such measures are permissible since:

1. Human life is sacred or valuable in itself.

---

2. Therefore, any action incompatible with the sacredness of human life is forbidden.
3. Forgoing futile LST for permanently unconscious patients is compatible with the sacredness of human life.

---

4. Therefore, forgoing futile life supports for those patients is morally permissible.

More needs to said about (1), from which (2) follows. Ronald Dworkin (1991) makes a strong case for it by invoking common morality and the law. Once (1) is accepted, (2) follows. Support for (3) comes from the facts that PVS patients have permanently lost their psychological lives, and that decisions to forgo LST are serious matters—something evident in the moral distress of relatives and health care providers as well as in the passionate controversies typical of cases reaching the courts. This suggests that forgoing futile LST need not dishonor life in some cases, and therefore, that the liberal Sanctity-of-Life doctrine is not an objection to it.

Ordinary versus Extraordinary Means

Given the ordinary-versus-extraordinary-means distinction of Catholic bioethics, endorsed by Pius XII (1957) and the Sacred Congregation for the Doctrine of the Faith (1980) among others, a medical **means** for sustaining life may count as an **ordinary** or an **extraordinary** measure depending on the case. Ordinary measures are morally mandatory, extraordinary ones optional. The upshot of this theory for life-sustaining treatment (LST) is

1. Depending on the case, LST may be an ordinary or an extraordinary measure.
2. LST is obligatory when it amounts to an ordinary measure but optional when it amounts to an extraordinary measure.

---

3. Therefore, sometimes forgoing LST is permissible.

'Extraordinary' means, also called 'heroic,' 'disproportionate,' or 'excessive,' may include medical measures as routine as cardiopulmonary resuscitation. Whether artificial nutrition and hydration (ANH) counts as ordinary or extraordinary is still an unsettled issue in Catholic bioethics, though the tendency has been to consider it ordinary nursing care that must be provided when it is effective in prolonging life and does not impose excessive burdens on the patient. Many conservative bioethicists would say that, for patients like Bland or Cruzan, ANH is an ordinary means of preserving life, similar to the provision of food and water. By contrast, the courts and many liberal bioethicists consider ANH a treatment akin to, for example, mechanical ventilation and dialysis.

The ordinary-versus-extraordinary-means distinction has been attractive to some Catholic bioethicists because it allows forgoing extraordinary measures without invoking the controversial notion of qualitative futility. Furthermore, the distinction accommodates either version of the Sanctity-of-Life doctrine discussed above—as well as the common view that forgoing LST is justified when, for example, the patient is dying or cannot tolerate ANH. Death then is said to result from the underlying illness or injury together with the medical decision to allow nature to take its course.

However, the distinction faces some challenges, beginning with an applicability problem (Brock, 2012; Kluge, 2012), given the indeterminacy about what counts as an extraordinary or ordinary measure. In some contexts mechanical ventilation may be an ordinary measure, in others extraordinary. It is a routine element of acute care when aimed at stabilizing a patient who can be expected to recover, but an extraordinary measure when used for a whole-brain-dead patient. Moreover, it is not always clear what makes a medical treatment extraordinary rather than ordinary. Is it being invasive versus noninvasive? Rare versus common? High-tech versus simple? Costly versus inexpensive?

Ordinary-versus-extraordinary-means theorists can reply that any treatment becomes extraordinary when disproportionate because it offers no reasonable hope of benefit (e.g., the patient is dying) or causes uncompensated burdens (excessive expense, pain, or other inconvenience). Yet proportionality is a matter of degree, and on occasion a treatment may be borderline, offering something between reasonable and unreasonable hope of benefit (or between being costly and inexpensive, etc.). As a result, some treatments cannot be easily sorted into the extraordinary/ordinary categories, and as result, the medical team cannot decide whether they are morally obligatory or merely optional.

FIGURE 7.2 The Ordinary-versus-Extraordinary-Means Distinction

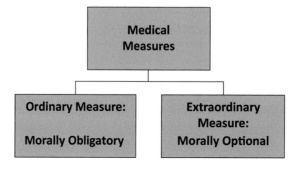

The distinction also faces the problem of drawing moral conclusions from strictly factual premises. Suppose we arbitrarily say that a medical measure is ordinary when common and extraordinary when rare. We now have to spell out which treatments count as common (those used daily?) and which as rare (those used yearly?). Even if we can settle this, why should the frequency of a treatment matter to its being morally mandatory or optional? That is, why should what is standard practice be morally obligatory and what is not be merely optional? After all, some practices, such as lying and stealing are immoral even though common. The problem is: from a strictly factual premise about a treatment's invasiveness (costs, etc.), nothing follows about its being morally optional or mandatory.

Another problem concerns consistency: the distinction requires implicit reference to a patient's quality of life, just the notion it was designed to avoid. Suppose, for example, that a certain medical intervention is predictably painful and costly. Whether it counts as an extraordinary means can be decided only on the basis of an assessment of the anticipated pain and expense against the kind of life it would enable the patient to have (Kuhse and Singer, 1985: 35–7). Therefore, the distinction presupposes that a medical intervention is

- Ordinary, just in case it will likely afford the patient an acceptable quality of life, in spite of its burdens and cost, or
- Extraordinary, just in case it will likely afford the patient a poor quality of life.

Given this objection, the distinction is either inconsistent or not an alternative to medical futility. Whether or not ordinary-versus-extraordinary-means theorists can solve these problems, the fact that they arise raises questions about its usefulness in sorting out *which* end-of-life measures are morally permissible.

BOX 7.3 THREE OBJECTIONS TO THE ORDINARY-VERSUS-EXTRAORDINARY-MEANS DOCTRINE

Problems for the Ordinary-versus-Extraordinary-Means Distinction	**The applicability problem**: there is no precise definition of 'ordinary' versus 'extraordinary' measures.
	The problem of drawing moral conclusions from strictly factual premises: that a treatment is morally optional does not follow from its being rare (or costly, etc.).
	The consistency problem: the Doctrine rests implicitly on judgments of qualitative futility, the very notion it was designed to avoid.

◼ 7.5 Chapter Summary

Contemporary technological advances have revolutionized the practice of medicine in ways that now make it possible to extend the lives of patients who would previously have died of their illnesses or injuries. But in some circumstances medical intervention may be futile, in the sense of bringing either no benefit to the patient or only minimal benefit that cannot compensate for related harms and burdens. This chapter considered some landmark cases illustrating difficult decisions on whether to forgo life supports, especially artificial nutrition and hydration. They involved patients in either PVS (*Bland, Cruzan, Quinlan*) or terminal illness (*Nancy B*), and arguments for discontinuing futile life supports. The courts generally have ruled that, when there is no malicious intent, forgoing futile life-sustaining treatment (LST) is permissible, especially where there is evidence of a valid refusal by the patient or surrogate. Disagreements may nevertheless arise within the medical team, or between them and patients or their surrogates. We also noted that as a reason for **forgoing treatment**, physiological futility is the least controversial, qualitative futility the most. This is because judgments invoking qualitative futility presuppose some value-laden assumptions about quality of life.

The strongest reasons for forgoing qualitatively futile LST invoke health care providers' obligations of justice and beneficence. At the opposite end of the spectrum is the conservative Sanctity-of-Life doctrine, with the ordinary-versus-extraordinary-means distinction in the middle, arguing that forgoing LST is justified, but only when it amounts to an extraordinary measure. Neither of these strategies to avoid invoking medical futility is persuasive. One rests on religious assumptions likely to be disputed, the other suffers from indeterminacy.

Although there is still no conclusive argument against appeals to quality of life in establishing the futility of an intervention, there is some evidence that such appeals may antagonize patients and relatives, who may feel that the patient is entitled to treatment, and suspect that the real reason for denying it is the patient's advanced age or socioeconomic status. Health care professionals should take the time to explain to the patient why a particular treatment is likely to be of no significant benefit in her condition. They should also make clear that factors such as the patient's age and the treatment's costs are irrelevant to the inappropriateness of an intervention—although they may on occasion contribute to it.

 ## 7.6 Study Aids

Key Words

Questions and Cases for Further Consideration

1.   When would administering a futile medical treatment conflict with respect for patient autonomy? What should the medical team do?

2.   Is the possibility of encouraging false hopes in patients a reason for or against invoking futility in clinical decisionmaking? Illustrate your answer with either a real or an imaginary case.

3.   *In 1995, New Zealander* James McKeown, 76, *was denied kidney dialysis. Although the decision was based on accepted guidelines for patients over 75, it also considered that he had coronary artery disease and prostate cancer. Realistically, dialysis could prolong his life for about two years. His family complained before the Human Rights Commission of age discrimination. As the media became involved, public officials insisted that the decision was based solely on health outcomes, not costs. Dialysis was eventually allowed and prolonged his life for 18 months.* Here one side regarded dialysis for Mr. McKeown as futile, the other as needed life-sustaining treatment (LST). From the hospital's perspective, dialysis for Mr. McKeown was not clinically appropriate; from that of his family, it was denied on grounds of age, not futility. What type of futility is at issue here? Can the ordinary-versus-extraordinary-means distinction help without invoking Mr. McKeown's quality of life? Which side might the conservative Sanctity-of-Life doctrine support? Since age may affect treatment outcome but also be used to discriminate against older patients, should health care providers consider age in decisions to forgo futile LST? Can facts and values be separated in such decisions? What about in decisions based on limited resources?

4.   *By 1985,* Beverly Requena *began to need ANH because of her amyotrophic lateral sclerosis, a terminal disorder of the nervous system. But the Board of Trustees of the New Jersey St. Clare's/Riverside Hospital was not prepared to honor her refusal because, in their view, food and water are basic human needs and cannot be withheld from patients in the Medical Center. This policy was an expression of the hospital's new values, assumed in the course of a merger with a Catholic institution after Ms. Requena had entered it. Although the hospital was willing to refer her to another institution, she sued and won her right to stay without receiving ANH.* What can be said for and against the hospital's contention that ANH is basic nursing care? On which grounds might the Court have filed for Beverly Requena? Should institutions be allowed not to honor refusals of treatment on the basis of conscience?

5.   Based on their experience at the Washington Home Hospice, nurses Phyllis Schmitz and Merry O'Brien (1986) wrote that ANH at the end of life often increases patient discomfort. Which principles of bioethics are consistent with their liberal view about forgoing ANH? How might they extend their argument to support Beverly Requena's request (see question 4)? What should they do if they were working at the St. Clare's/Riverside Hospital?

6.   Eluana Englaro *would, according to her father, not have wanted the ANH she was given after a car accident left her permanently unconscious at 21. In 2008, Italy's Supreme Court authorized her father to withdraw it. But no Italian health care institutions were willing to do it for fear of reprisals. Upon consultation with the Vatican, Prime Minister Silvio Berlusconi issued a decree overturning the Court's ruling. But the President of Italy, Giorgio Napolitano, refused to sign it. Eventually, a clinic in Udine came forward. In 2009, three days after her admission and seventeen years after her accident, the ANH was removed. Eluana died at 38. Her death was a momentous event in Italy. National television suspended its regular programs to broadcast discussions of it. While her doctor believed that "Eluana died 17 years ago," for Berlusconi she was murdered. Parliament hastily passed legislation requiring living wills for lawful withdrawals of life supports from permanently unconscious patients who are not dying, eventually declaring unlawful all withdrawals of ANH.*[2] Although this case compares with *Cruzan* in the involvement of third parties, can you point to any cultural differences in the way the facts unfolded? Why were the opinions so divided about when Eluana died? Might those opinions have still differed if withholding, rather than withdrawing, ANH were at stake? Is that distinction morally significant? Must there be a living-will condition on withdrawals of life supports for permanently unconscious patients? Does the duty of nonmaleficence argue for or against the father's request? Might what counts as harm vary from culture to culture?

*Suggested Readings**

Cruzan v Director, Missouri Department of Health, 497 US 261 (1990). Available online at http://www.oyez.org/cases/1989/88_1503.
> Full audio recording of the Supreme Court hearing. Particularly relevant to this chapter are Justice Scalia's reflection on whether forgoing life supports for permanently unconscious patients amounts to assisted suicide, and Justice Stevens's view that such patients no longer have personal interests.

Dresser, Rebecca S. and John A. Robertson, "Quality of Life and Non-treatment Decisions for Incompetent Patients: A Critique of the Orthodox Approach," *Law, Medicine & Health Care* 17.3, 1989: 234–44.
> Argues that courts, legislators, and physicians who are trying to help demented patients should give up trying to fit them into the model of autonomous deciders and try instead to develop ways of accurately assessing their best interests.

*Dworkin, Ronald, "The Right to Death," *The New York Review of Books*, 1/31/1991.
> Reflection on the moral standing of patients who have permanently lost consciousness. Rejects the majority opinion in *Cruzan* written by Chief Justice Rehnquist, arguing that such patients are "for all that matters dead already" (17).

---

2   Michael Day, "Italy Faces Constitutional Crisis over Coma Woman," *The Guardian*, 2/7/2009.
*   Asterisks mark readings available online. See links on the companion website.

Eberl, Jason T., "Issues at the End of Human Life: PVS Patients, Euthanasia, and Organ Donation," in *Thomistic Principles and Bioethics*, pp. 95–127. New York, Routledge: 2006.

A liberal Catholic justification of forgoing life supports for some patients, including ANH. Invokes the Principle of Double Effect and the futility of the treatment in those cases.

*Finnis, John, "'The Value of Human Life' and 'The Right to Death': Some Reflections on Cruzan and Ronald Dworkin," *Notre Dame Law School* 1.1, 1993: 559–71.

From a conservative Catholic Sanctity-of-Life doctrine, rejects the minority opinion in *Cruzan* and also Dworkin's (1991) because of the dualism implicit in holding that the person dies with the permanent loss of consciousness, even if the body remains alive.

Fisher, Anthony, "Artificial Nutrition: Why Do Unresponsive Patients Matter?" in Fisher 2012, pp. 213–347.

A conservative Catholic defense of the Sanctity-of-Life and the ordinary-versus-extraordinary-means doctrines. Counts artificial nutrition and hydration as ordinary nursing care rather than as medical treatment.

*Giacino, Joseph T., Joseph J. Fins, Steven Laureys, and Nicholas D. Schiff, "Disorders of Consciousness after Acquired Brain Injury: The State of the Science," *Nature Reviews Neurology* 10, 2014: 99–114. Available online at doi:10.1038/nrneurol.2013.279.

Outlines current medical criteria for assessing the disorders of consciousness discussed in this chapter and some difficulties in defining 'consciousness' that have implications for patient care and society's attitudes.

Keown, John, *Euthanasia, Ethics, and Public Policy: An Argument against Legalisation*. Cambridge: Cambridge University Press, 2002.

Finds unpersuasive the Law Lords' argument that withdrawal of treatment was in Bland's best interests.

*Lynn, Joanne and James F. Childress, "Must Patients Always Be Given Food and Water?" in Lynn 1986, pp. 47–60.

Describes four ways of providing ANH, arguing that none is closely related to providing food and water. Defends forgoing ANH on futility grounds and notes that ANH makes some dying patients less comfortable and is even harmful.

McMahan, Jeff, "Persistent Vegetative State and Deep Coma," in McMahan 2002, pp. 443–50.

Defends forgoing life supports for PVS patients on grounds consistent with Rachels' (1986)—namely, that these patients have permanently lost consciousness and, with it, an essential feature for having the moral standing of persons.

Pope Pius XII, "Address to the Italian Society of Anaesthesiology," 24 February, 1957.

States the Catholic Church's perspective on the moral permissibility of administering narcotics to suppress the pain and/or consciousness of terminally ill patients, where doing so carries a risk of shortening their lives.

Rachels, James, *The End of Life: Euthanasia and Morality*. Oxford: Oxford University Press, 1986.

Classic work for the view that biological human life has value only when it makes biographical life possible. Holds that a permanently unconscious patient is still a person but not "an individual who is the subject of a life." Objects to the absolutist version of the Sanctity-of-Life doctrine.

Sacred Congregation for the Doctrine of the Faith, "Declaration on Euthanasia," May 5, 1980, http://www.vatican.va/roman_curia/congregations/cfaith/documents/rc_con_cfaith_doc_19800505_euthanasia_en.html.
   States the Catholic Church's unconditional moral prohibition of any medical intervention intended to shorten or terminate a patient's life.
Schneiderman, Lawrence J. and Nancy S. Jecker, *Wrong Medicine: Doctors, Patients, and Futile Treatment*, 2nd ed. Baltimore: The Johns Hopkins University Press, 2011.
   Proposes a distinction among the types of futility discussed in this chapter, traces the notions in the history of medicine, and argues for the claim that appeals to medical futility in forgoing life supports are not only morally permissible but mandatory.
Wicclair, Mark, *Ethics and the Elderly*. Oxford: Oxford University Press, 1993.
   Argues that health care providers should avoid the evaluative notion of 'futility.' Instead, they should explain to patients why some intervention is not appropriate in the circumstances.

8

Medically Assisted Death

Learning Objectives

In reading this chapter you will

▶ Identify main end-of-life measures deliberately undertaken to hasten death.

▶ Evaluate arguments for and against the moral permissibility of such measures.

▶ Distinguish physician-assisted suicide from various forms of medical euthanasia.

▶ Learn about how these are implemented in places where one or the other is legal.

FROM THE 1970S to the present, some landmark cases in the United States, Britain, and Canada have brought attention to a widespread legal ban on **physician-assisted dying** (PAD), a category that includes medical euthanasia and physician-assisted suicide. This chapter considers moral reasons for and against these main forms of PAD, which are often implemented underground. It also looks closely at empirical data from countries where some form of PAD is legal.

8.1 Dr. Cox's Use of Euthanasia

In 1991, Dr. Nigel Cox, a consultant rheumatologist at the Royal Hampshire County Hospital in Winchester UK, administered a lethal dose of potassium chloride to end the life of a terminally ill patient who five days earlier had begun refusing all therapeutic treatment. Lillian Boyes, 70, had been his patient for thirteen years and was within hours of death. She suffered from severe rheumatoid arthritis, with internal bleeding, vasculitis, and septicemia. When her intense pain no longer responded to the strongest analgesics, she repeatedly begged Dr. Cox to end her misery. Ultimately he did so, but when the rheumatology ward sister learned about it by reading his notes, she reported it to the police. Cox was indicted for attempted murder, and during his trial Lilian Boyes's family testified on his behalf. The Winchester Crown Court found him guilty but imposed a suspended sentence—while the General Medical Council issued only a reprimand which allowed him to continue to practice medicine in Hampshire.

'Euthanasia' (from the Greek for 'good' or 'gentle death') refers to the deliberate killing of a person for that person's own good. In the context of medicine, it is usually achieved by a lethal agent administered by the physician. Dr. Cox's euthanasia sought only to spare Lilian Boyes further severe suffering. Since it was provided with her consent, it amounted to voluntary active euthanasia (**VAE**). This measure, often implemented quietly, as in the case of Dr. Cox, is unlawful in most common-law jurisdictions, but rarely leads to prosecution when unreported. According to witnesses who spoke at the trial, Lillian Boyes was suffering terribly and facing imminent death. Unable to take matters into her own hands, she repeatedly asked for Dr. Cox's assistance. Had she taken her own life with his help, hers would have been a case of **physician-assisted suicide** (PAS) whereby a patient self-administers a lethal agent prescribed by the physician. Both VAE and PAS are types of physician-assisted dying (PAD). The actual events leading to Boyes's death prompted the only conviction for 'attempted euthanasia' ever recorded in the United Kingdom—where, as in other countries, the practice often goes unreported. When discovered, the full force of the law is rarely brought to bear by the courts when there is evidence of humanitarian motives.

At present, for most medical associations, other **end-of-life measures** such as forgoing life-sustaining treatment (LST) and **terminal sedation** are instead recommended under certain circumstances. Even so, as this book goes to press, some form of medical assistance in dying is lawful in Belgium, Luxembourg, the Netherlands, Switzerland, and most recently, Canada. In the USA, Montana (2009), Oregon (1994), Vermont (2013), Washington (2008), and California (2015) allow regulated physician-assisted suicide. Euthanasia was briefly legal in Australia's Northern Territory (from July 1996 to March 1997), but no form of assisted dying is currently legal in Australia, the United Kingdom, or New Zealand.

8.2 Medical Euthanasia

Euthanasia and Other End-of-Life Measures

Physician-assisted dying is often deemed morally impermissible because euthanasia causes the patient's death and PAS contributes to causing it. By contrast, although forgoing LST and terminal sedation may hasten the patient's death, the provider's intention need only be that nature take its course and pain be relieved. In terminal sedation the patient is rendered unconscious by drugs ordinarily used for analgesia or sedation. These narcotics, administered in a large dose, can slow breathing and heart rate, thereby hastening death. Experts disagree about whether the sort of terminal sedation administered today hastens death *per se*. But the measure is sometimes combined with withdrawal of nutrition and hydration, which will of course cause it unless death is brought about by a preexisting condition.

Natural Law and Catholic bioethicists often draw a moral distinction between terminal sedation and PAD because PAD involves the *intention* to cause death. This argument, which relies on the intending-versus-merely-foreseeing-a-bad-effect distinction so central to the Principle of Double Effect, is familiar from litigation about withdrawals of LST and terminal sedation. The argument has been found persuasive by courts that justify such practices in light of the medical team's intention merely to relieve pain or to stand aside (as it were) and allow nature to take its course. Yet these measures have more in common with PAD than supporters of the argument are willing to admit.

For one thing, all of them are usually motivated by compassion for a patient who considers death in her debilitated condition more valuable than continued life. Any such patient presents a dilemma for medical professionals, given their duties to avoid and prevent harm (nonmaleficence, beneficence) and to honor patient self-determination (respect for autonomy). Furthermore, when any of these measures responds to a patient's or surrogate's request to end severe suffering or disability, it is undeniable that health care professionals *intend* to shorten the patient's life—as evident in withdrawals of nutrition and hydration for permanently unconscious patients like Tony Bland (Chapter 7).

At the same time, no interesting moral questions are raised by life-shortening measures that are self-serving for health care providers or next-of-kin in ways that amount to negligence or malice. Suppose a doctor's motive in helping a patient die is to inherit her fortune, as it seems to have been with one of the victims of the notorious Dr. Harold Shipman, a British physician convicted in 1998 of murdering about 215 patients after forging their wills so that they appeared to name him as their heir. Here there was no controversy, moral or legal. The physician's actions were a grave violation of his duties to his patients.

BOX 8.1 END-OF-LIFE MEASURES TO HASTEN OR INDUCE DEATH

Such measures include	FORGOING LIFE-SUSTAINING-TREATMENT (LST) - RESULT: May hasten death - EXPLICIT INTENT: To let nature take its course by removing technology that is delaying death	- Withholding (never initiating) LST - Withdrawing (discontinuing) LST - Nonescalating (or de-escalating) LST
	TERMINAL SEDATION - RESULT: May hasten death - EXPLICIT INTENT: To relieve pain at the end of life	Sometimes combined with withdrawal of artificial nutrition and hydration
	PHYSICIAN-ASSISTED DYING (PAD) - RESULT: May cause death - EXPLICIT INTENT: To directly induce or contribute to inducing death	Euthanasia: Physician administers lethal agent directly Physician Assisted Suicide (PAS): Patient self-administers lethal agent provided by physician

Types of Euthanasia

Euthanasia can take a number of different forms, some more open to ethical debate than others. Two classifications may help frame the debate. The categories of **passive** and **active**

euthanasia depend on whether the medical team merely lets a patient die or actively induces her death. Thus some instances of forgoing LST count as passive euthanasia, while administering a lethal drug to a patient is always active euthanasia.

Cutting across these categories is a classification based on the availability of the patient's consent, which yields the three categories listed in Box 8.2. Accordingly, passive and active **euthanasia** alike can sometimes be **voluntary**, other times **nonvoluntary** or **involuntary**, depending on whether the patient's valid consent for it has been given (voluntary), has been withheld (involuntary), or can be neither given nor withheld (nonvoluntary).

BOX 8.2 VOLUNTARY/NONVOLUNTARY/INVOLUNTARY EUTHANASIA

Euthanasia may be either	**Voluntary**–Performed with the patient's informed consent
	Nonvoluntary–The patient is unable to give or withhold informed consent (infant or patient in PVS, coma, cognitively impaired)
	Involuntary–The patient is competent to give informed consent, but has *not* done so

There is consensus that involuntary euthanasia of any kind, passive or active, is in nearly all cases morally wrong and should be prosecuted as homicide. But there is no consensus about the morality of either voluntary or nonvoluntary euthanasia. Yet, other things being equal, a decision to hasten or induce a patient's death for the patient's own benefit is less morally problematic when it is done with the patient's consent than without it. That is, voluntary euthanasia is less problematic than nonvoluntary. This is because nonvoluntary euthanasia is speculative, in the sense that the decision to hasten or actively induce death is made on the basis of a speculation by health care professionals about the patient's best interests in view of the bleak prognosis. Recall that in nonvoluntary euthanasia, the patient can neither give nor withhold valid informed consent, as for example in the euthanasia of a newborn or of a patient who is in a permanent vegetative state and has no advance directive on file. These two classifications yield the categories outlined in Figure 8.1.

Passive versus Active Euthanasia

Passive Euthanasia

Under this category fall withholdings and withdrawals of LST to hasten death for the patient's own benefit. Usually the patient requests the measure because of unrelievable, intense suffering or loss of autonomy that she finds unbearable. To count as *euthanasia*, the health care professional who administers it must (1) intend to hasten death and (2) be motivated by compassion for the patient, even when other motivations might also be at work, such as awareness of the futility of further treatment. When these requirements are not met, forgoing

FIGURE 8.1 Six Types of Medical Euthanasia

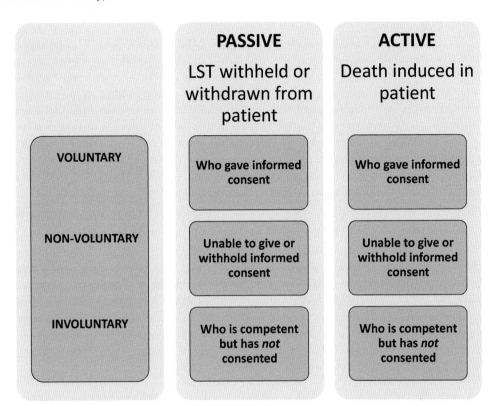

LST does not count as passive euthanasia. In *Bland* (Chapter 7), the Lord Justices argued that the withdrawal of artificial nutrition and hydration was not with the intent to cause death. Bland would die as a result of his medical condition. Now clearly, without the measure, his death would not have occurred at the time it did. Hence not everyone accepts the Justices' argument. But since the futility of treatment rather than compassion was the reason for the measure, *Bland* does not illustrate passive euthanasia. But the following example does:

Mr. Schmitz is an elderly patient suffering from lung cancer with metastasis to the brain. His pain can no longer be controlled. He also experiences seizures and needs oxygen for shortness of breath. Although he now has developed a speech impairment, he seems mostly aware of his condition. Asked by medical staff about whether to stop all therapies, including radiation, he gives consent. Sympathetic to his suffering, the medical team discontinues all treatments. Schmitz dies within two weeks.

Here the team's decision was not motivated by considerations of futility. After all, therapies that extend a patient's life are not futile when death can be regarded as a harm (as it usually can). They in fact fall under the health care providers' duty of beneficence, which includes preventing harm whenever possible. Since compassion for the patient is the measure's motivation, it counts as voluntary passive euthanasia. Medical decisions of this sort are considered permissible. Even the cautious and circumspect American Medical Association holds them to be so, while decrying active euthanasia as contrary to that for which the medical profession stands.

Yet many in medicine have now grown wary of the category 'passive euthanasia.' In Britain, two reports bearing on this issue produced by Select Committees of the House of Lords have either dismissed the category as misleading (1994), or completely ignored it (2004). And for the British Medical Association (2000) the very distinction, passive versus active euthanasia, is "ambiguous and unhelpful." Among objectors, some think that there is no distinction between active and passive euthanasia that can be grounded in a common contrast between **killing** and **letting die**. All euthanasia is active by definition, since it is an act of killing. Yet although some steps are taken in forgoing LST, the so-called pulling of the plug is not an action but an omission. Compare quitting smoking, which consists in the avoidance of smoking (an omission) even when it involves actions such as disposing of cigarettes.

Active Euthanasia

In contrast to passive euthanasia is active euthanasia, which may be voluntary, nonvoluntary, or involuntary, depending on whether the patient gives consent, is unable to do so, or withholds it. *Dr. Nigel Cox* illustrates voluntary active euthanasia (VAE), a practice illegal in most countries that nonetheless occurs unreported. The case of Tracy Latimer illustrates nonvoluntary euthanasia outside the practice of medicine. In 1993, a Canadian farmer, acting on his own assessment of what was best for his daughter in light of her poor quality of life, triggered a storm of debate by administering this type of euthanasia to her.

Tracy Latimer, a 12-year-old quadriplegic girl, was afflicted with a severe form of cerebral palsy and had the mental capacity of a 4-month-old baby. She suffered frequent seizures and increasing pain in her twisted limbs and spine as her muscles tightened with the progress of the disease. To all appearances a loving father, Robert Latimer despaired of being unable to help his daughter. When doctors called for yet another round of painful surgery for Tracy, Mr. Latimer decided she had been through enough. He put Tracy in the cab of his pickup, installed a tube from the exhaust pipe into the cab, and turned on the engine. In a short time, Tracy was dead. Latimer was convicted of second-degree murder but given a light sentence in view of the exceptional circumstances of the case. When prosecutors appealed to the Supreme Court of Canada, however, that judgment was reversed, and in 2001 Latimer was given the maximum sentence: ten years imprisonment, to be served before eligibility for parole.

Out on parole in 2011, Latimer told television journalists that he did what was needed to end his daughter's agony. In his view, he had been persecuted by malevolent judges and religious zealots. Be that as it may, it seems that further surgical procedures for Tracy would only have imposed unbearable burdens on her. But, most important, for her induced death to count as euthanasia, evidence of a compassionate motive was needed. During the trial this was provided by Latimer's wife.

Whatever we may say about the moral permissibility of nonvoluntary active euthanasia, whether the practice should become legal is another story. Even the Netherlands, Belgium, and Luxembourg, where regulated medical VAE is legal, have not legalized nonvoluntary active euthanasia.

The morality of *involuntary* active euthanasia is less controversial since it is almost never permissible. Here is an especially disturbing example:

Christine Malevre, a 33-year-old French nurse, was found guilty in 2003 of causing the deaths of seven patients, all terminally ill, at a lung hospital in a Paris suburb where she worked in 1997–98. She was also banned for life from the nursing profession. Malevre first admitted helping about 30 terminally ill patients die but later confessed to only four deaths. She testified that she had acted out of compassion for suffering patients. But the families of several of the dead denied that their relatives had asked to die.

Malevre engaged in a forbidden practice that violates the health care providers' duties of respect for persons and nonmaleficence. Yet involuntary active euthanasia may be morally permissible on grounds of necessity—for example, in this scenario:

World War I. After weeks of violent engagement with German infantry in the Battle of the Somme, British troops are pinned down in their trenches and can make no headway. One unit is completely cut off from resupply by the Medical Corps. As a result, a doctor has no medicines with which to treat a badly injured soldier who wants to live but will inevitably die in agony in the next hour. To spare him unrelievable intense suffering, the doctor administers his only remaining medical agent, a lethal dose of morphine that kills the soldier quickly and painlessly.

Situations of this sort are of course very rare. Health care providers almost never face them.

As this book is going to press, noteworthy facts about the legal status of medically assisted death include:

- The Netherlands and Luxembourg have now for some time allowed regulated VAE and PAS.
- Belgium has legislation for VAE but not for PAS.
- Switzerland and five states in the USA allow regulated forms of PAS but not VAE.
- In no English-speaking country is VAE legal, though in February 2015 Canada's Supreme Court decriminalized PAD—leaving it to the lawmakers to pass a bill, which they later did in June 2016.

▉ 8.3 Physician-Assisted Suicide

Physician-Assisted Suicide and Voluntary Active Euthanasia

The so-called right-to-die movement has had more success in decriminalizing regulated forms of PAS than VAE. The rationale for this tendency is twofold:

1. PAS is more clearly a voluntary act, at least in the sense that it is the patient who, as a competent and informed moral agent, chooses to self-administer the lethal agent.

2.   PAS involves no direct act of killing by health care professionals, who need not even be in the room when the patient self-administers the lethal agent.

Health care professionals who are willing to assist in terminations of life also regard (1) and (2) as advantages of PAS over active euthanasia, partly because they are typically wary of causing a patient's death intentionally and directly. But not all agree with this rationale or with the movement to legalize PAS.

The Objection from Justice

According to this objection, a policy of providing only PAS is unfair to patients who want assistance in dying but are unable to administer a lethal agent to themselves because they are, for example, in late stages of Alzheimer's or completely paralyzed. Consider,

Tony Nicklinson, a 58-year-old Briton afflicted with Locked-in Syndrome, wasn't terminally ill. He might have had many years of life ahead of him. But, as a reporter from the BBC put it, he was "in terminal despair." As a result of irreparable brain damage from a catastrophic stroke he suffered during a business trip, Nicklinson was totally paralyzed and mute, yet he remained conscious. He could still move his eyes, and he communicated by blinking or nodding to letters shown to him on a board. By this means, he instructed his attorneys to seek two declarations from the High Court: (1) that it would be lawful for a doctor to assist him in ending his life, and (2) that the current law for assisted death in the UK infringed on his right to a private life protected by the European Convention for Human Rights, art. 8. A panel of High Court judges rejected his request, and a few days later, on August 21, 2012, Nicklinson, who had been refusing food and water, died from untreated pneumonia. On appeal pursued by his wife, in 2014 the Supreme Court reasserted that a revision of the British ban on assisted suicide was not for the courts to make, but for Parliament.

Where only PAS is lawful, some disabled patients like Nicklinson lack the right to assisted death that other patients have. This state of affairs amounts to discrimination and is therefore unjust. Refusal of food and fluids is the only recourse available to them if they find life unacceptable. Furthermore, if ending one's life amounts to a right guaranteed by the Fourteenth Amendment to the US Constitution, as some have claimed (Dworkin et al., 1998), then US jurisdictions where only PAS is lawful violate that right.

The Objection from Nonmaleficence

This objection, if sound, supports a ban not only on PAS but also on VAE. It contends that, since death is not in a person's best interest, the health care providers' assistance in dying is forbidden by their duty of nonmaleficence. Supporters of the objection are likely to remind us of the notorious assistance in dying provided during the 1990s by *Dr. Jack Kevorkian*, a retired Michigan pathologist who made a career of helping people to die. Nicknamed "Dr. Death" by the tabloid press, Dr. Kevorkian devised suicide machines with which patients could self-administer lethal drugs or carbon monoxide. According to some accounts, at least 93 deaths were assisted by Dr. Kevorkian between 1990 and 1998. Of that number, however, it appears that only 17 deaths involved terminally ill patients. Many of Kevorkian's patients, though terrified of future mental deterioration and a foreseen death, were not even in pain. Moreover, they were often people Kevorkian barely knew, so he was hardly in a position to judge the necessity of the drastic step each was about to take. Many bioethicists, though sympathetic to the right-to-die movement, wrote him off as a public-ity-seeking crank. Kevorkian was ostracized by the medical profession, and his license to practice eventually revoked. Indicted several times on charges of assisting a suicide and other offenses, he continually eluded conviction. But his audacity ultimately brought his downfall in a notorious case:

Thomas Youk was suffering from amyotrophic lateral sclerosis (ALS), a progressive, degenerative neurological disorder. In 1998 Dr. Kevorkian videotaped himself administering voluntary active euthanasia to Youk by lethal injection. Afterwards, he allowed the tape to be broadcast on the CBS News program *60 Minutes*, daring the authorities to arrest him. The Michigan district attor-ney was all too happy to oblige him, and soon Dr. Kevorkian found himself sentenced to ten years in prison for second-degree murder. He served eight before being released on parole in 2007.

But prevention of Kevorkian-style recklessness that threatens harm to patients can perhaps be achieved without a total ban on PAS. For one thing, Kevorkian's activities were unregu-lated. Proponents of lawful PAS have no problem in condemning them while insisting that such abuses are less likely to occur if strictly regulated PAS is available when continued life has ceased to be a benefit. After looking at Oregon's model of regulated PAS, we consider another problem for the Objection from Nonmaleficence: 'suicide tourism,' a growing phe-nomenon suggesting that a total ban on PAS only encourages patients to seek it away from home, in places where regulations might make Kevorkian-style scenarios unlikely.

Oregon's Death with Dignity Act

There is a relatively recent trend in the United States toward legalizing regulated PAS. Orig-inally approved by voters by a margin of 51.31% in 1994, Measure 16, **Oregon's Death with Dignity Act,** made Oregon the first state with a statute that allows qualifying terminally ill adults to obtain prescriptions for lethal drugs. Challenged by a group of doctors and patients, a Court of Appeals ruled against the plaintiffs in 1997, and in 2006 the US Supreme Court voted 6-to-3 to uphold the statute, leaving individual states free to enact similar laws. Some did exactly that: Washington in 2008, Vermont in 2013, and California in 2015. In 2008–09, a court decision in the state of Montana had the effect of providing immunity for physicians who practiced regulated PAS, though no statute specifically legalized PAS.

In all these states, safeguards for the practice mirror those of the Oregon Death with Dignity Act, which states, among other conditions, that qualifying patients must

1. Be at least 18 years old, resident of Oregon, and able to make and communicate auton-omous decisions,
2. Have a terminal illness that, as certified by at least two doctors, will likely lead to death within six months, and
3. Make two oral and one written request for PAS to the physician.

For doctors, the Act stipulates that participation in PAS is optional. The attending physician must be licensed in the state, must inform the patient of alternatives including palliative care, and must ask the patient to notify next-of-kin. If either of the doctors evaluating an application judges the patient incompetent, they must refer her for a psychological exam. When all conditions are met, there is a 48-hour waiting period before the patient can pick up the prescribed drugs at a pharmacy. Only she can administer them.

Not all requests for PAS meeting the Act's conditions are actually granted: only approximately one out of six (Ganzini et al., 2001). Of those granted, only one out of ten actually results in suicide—which suggests that PAS in Oregon is a measure of last resort. Furthermore, although over the years more patients have made use of PAS (e.g., 38 in 2002, 21 in 2001, 27 in 1999, and 16 in 1998), there is no reason to think that the practice is expanding in a worrisome direction. Nor are there reasons to think that PAS is more requested by minorities, women, and the elderly or poor. Merrick (2005: 234) reports that in 2002, the patients whose deaths resulted from PAS, compared with those who died of other causes, were younger (69 median age), and more likely to have cancer (84%) and to be enrolled in hospice programs (92%). More men used PAS than women. Except for one patient, all others had health insurance—which suggests that financial pressure was not conditioning their decisions. According to the Oregon Department of Human Services 2003, only a few patients reported pain as a reason for requesting PAS. Main reasons were the loss of autonomy, including control over bodily functions, and decreasing ability to participate in enjoyable activities. On the whole, commentators are generally agreed that the practice of PAS in Oregon has not fallen outside of established safeguards in ways that justify concern (Okie, 2005; Merrick, 2005; Lewy, 2010; Sumner, 2011). Furthermore, the support for the practice by Oregonians suggests that it has not undermined their trust in health care professionals.

Among the objections, two concern the need for legalizing VAE too: the Appeal to Justice mentioned above, and an Objection from Failed Attempted Suicides which can cause patients great harm. If PAS is the only legal form of medical assistance in dying, physicians cannot legally help those patients. Others argue that the Oregon Act is too permissive and prone to abuses, since in the end it is for the attending physician to determine whether a case meets the safeguards, and there need be no previous relationship between physician and patient. So patients can shop around for a physician sympathetic to their request. In addition, there is no requirement that the second opinion be that of a specialist in the patient's condition (Foley and Hendin, 2002; Keown, 2002). These criticisms can be addressed by sharpening the terms of the Act. More radical are objections PAS faces together with VAE. We'll consider these after first looking at a growing phenomenon that argues for legalizing at least PAS.

Suicide Tourism

Beneficence provides another argument for PAS: namely, preventing harm to patients who travel abroad to obtain it because it is unlawful where they live. Patients from, among other jurisdictions, Britain, Australia, the USA, and until recently, Canada, engage in suicide tourism. Let's look closely at the UK phenomenon. The ban on suicide in Britain was lifted by the 1961 Suicide Act, which also made aiding and abetting a suicide unlawful. This provision, however, is not without rationale, for the state also has a duty to protect vulnerable individuals from being persuaded or coerced into committing suicide. Such crimes, though rare, do sometimes occur. For example, in 2011 detection work by a crime-aficionado and retired teacher landed William Melchert-Dinkel, a Minnesota nurse, in prison, convicted of assistance in two suicides. He apparently used the Internet for pro-suicide 'counseling' of vulnerable individuals, effectively persuading at least two to commit suicide.

Under this legislation, *any* assistance in a suicide—even from compassionate motives—amounts to secondary participation in crime punishable by up to fourteen years in prison (section 2.1). Many terminally ill patients facing much suffering or loss of autonomy consequently fear to seek assistance from friends or loved ones in terminating their lives. Anyone providing such assistance would risk prosecution—as would anyone accompanying a loved one to obtain legal PAS abroad. *The Guardian* reports that, according to data from the Director of Public Prosecutions (2009), at least 90 people in the UK did so between October 2002 and 2008, risking prosecution upon return. Two terminally ill Britons every month go to Switzerland for PAS, and 20 people commit suicide at home for reasons related to a terminal illness.[1] In 2008 the parents and a friend of 23-year-old *Daniel James* were subject to police investigation for facilitating his trip to Switzerland for an assisted suicide. In the end, prosecution was declared "not in the public interest."

Yet it is one thing to be spared prosecution and quite another to have immunity from it. Until the landmark victory considered next, patients wishing to pursue PAS abroad faced considerable uncertainty about possible prosecutorial measures against those who accompany them.

Debbie Purdy, afflicted with multiple sclerosis (MS), challenged the Director of Public Prosecutions in court to reveal prosecutorial policy in England and Wales regarding those who, with compassionate intent, facilitate a PAS abroad. She was not asking for immunity for her husband if he were to accompany her to Switzerland, but for clarification about the extent of help not liable to prosecution. In her view, prosecutorial unclarity violated her right to privacy protected by the European Convention for Human Rights, art. 8. On appeal, in 2009 the Law Lords ruled that unclarity in the application of the Suicide Act did indeed amount to an interference with respect for her privacy and family life.

Ms. Purdy's successful litigation amounted to a turning point in the UK law on assisted suicide. But when MS finally made her condition "unacceptable," she was far too weak to travel to Switzerland. She died at a hospice in Britain in 2014 from self-imposed starvation.

8.4 Physician-Assisted Dying: For and Against

Physician-Assisted Dying Is Morally Permissible

Beneficence-Based Arguments

It seems morally permissible, and even obligatory, for medical professionals to provide aid in dying—for example, when a terminally ill patient's pain is no longer controllable by analgesia and she requests it. A virtue ethics version of this Argument from Mercy invokes compassion

---

1 Mark Tran, "Assisted Suicide Campaigner Debbie Purdy Dies Aged 51," *The Guardian*, 12/29/2014.

as an essential virtue for medical professionals (Sumner, 2011). Understood as consequentialist, the argument invokes beneficence, the principle that they should always seek the best interest of their patients and keep them from uncompensated harms. Suffering is bad *as such*, especially when uncompensated by benefits. True, death is also bad. But in some cases more harm is prevented by helping a patient die quickly and painlessly than by prolonging a life of unbearable suffering. Another consequentialist argument for PAD also rests on beneficence. The Appeal to Nonabandonment reminds us of the physicians' duty not to leave their patients without medical care, which sometimes requires providing aid during the dying process.

Given these arguments, PAD may be morally defensible even in the form of nonvoluntary active euthanasia. At this point, however, a critic may object that, with modern medicine's array of analgesics and the development of highly skilled palliative care, no one need die in agony. Yet the fact remains that in some cases, pain cannot be controlled. Moreover, suffering includes other things besides pain—air-hunger, for instance, and nausea and seizures, as well as psychological syndromes less controllable than physical pain.

For other critics, the Appeal to Mercy entails that assistance in dying is a moral duty in medicine, which seems implausible. For one thing, no country or state that permits regulated assisted death has made participation by health care providers a professional duty. Providers are at liberty to participate in PAD, but not obligated to do so. Proponents of the Argument from Mercy may simply dig in their heels and hold fast to their basic position that helping qualified patients die as quickly and painlessly as possible is a professional *moral* duty, whatever the law may say.

An Autonomy-Based Argument

A different line of argument for PAD invokes the principle of autonomy to support the so-called **right to die**, understood as part of each person's right to control what happens to her own body. Given the right to die, patients should be able to control whenever possible the circumstances of their deaths, which involves the ability to choose a death that conforms to their own standard of dignity. In addition, they should be permitted to decide for themselves how much suffering is enough. This right-to-die argument runs

1. If the principle of autonomy is plausible, then patients have a right to die.
2. The principle of autonomy is plausible.

_____

3. Therefore, patients have a right to die.

This basic argument takes different forms in litigation about PAD. Here is one:

Diane Pretty, 42, feared that her motor neuron disease would cause her death by choking and asphyxia, as often happens in the final stage of that disorder. In 2001 she sought immunity from prosecution for her husband if he were to aid in her suicide, thus challenging the UK 1961 Suicide Act. Her defense rested on her right to privacy, protected by the European Convention for Human Rights, art. 8. After a defeat in the trial court and eventually also in the House of Lords, she appealed to the European Court, arguing that the British courts had abridged her human rights by refusing her request. The European Court dismissed her claim. Ten days later, in May 2002, Mrs. Pretty died by asphyxia in precisely the way she had most feared.

Diane Pretty's argument, like other right-to-die arguments, suggested that third parties are morally *permitted* to assist in someone's death under certain circumstances. But as discussed in this book's Chapter 3 and Glossary, autonomy is a negative right requiring noninterference. A patient's right to assistance in dying, if it exists, is a positive right. As such, it does not create a positive obligation of others to assist. Indeed, the courts have systematically rejected the notion that there is a duty to aid in someone's death. On the other hand, refusals of treatment are negative rights, which do create duties of noninterference, given the patient's right to privacy and bodily integrity.

The upshot is that, although competent patients have a right to make autonomous decisions about the time and manner of their deaths, relatives are under no moral obligation to provide assistance. Similarly, health care providers are at liberty to withhold assistance whenever there is a conflict with their own professional rights to autonomy and integrity. Compare capital punishment: even if some states, given their laws, can legally execute condemned prisoners, and even if physicians in those states are permitted to assist in administering the lethal injections and pronouncing the prisoner dead, they are not *obligated* to assist in either. Thus, a properly understood right-to-die argument supports the claim that PAD is morally permissible, which avoids the consequentialist arguments' problematic implication that providing it is among the physician's moral obligations.

Physician-Assisted Dying Is Morally Forbidden

A common objection to PAD rests on the Sanctity-of-Life doctrine. But from our evaluation of that doctrine in Chapter 7 we can infer that only the conservative version must forbid PAD on moral grounds. The liberal version can accommodate the patients' right to death. We have argued that the conservative Sanctity-of-Life doctrine makes controversial assumptions. Here we consider other objections to PAD.

The Appeals to Integrity and Trust

The Appeal to Integrity charges that physician-assisted dying conflicts with an essential commitment of medical professionals: the absolute ban on intentionally killing patients. Medicine, like other professions, is not merely a set of technical proficiencies but involves devotion to an ideal. For teachers, that ideal is truth and wisdom, for attorneys and jurists it is justice, and for physicians it is healing—broadly construed as to include the conservation and extension of health and life whenever possible. This ideal gives rise to duties that are specific to medicine, including the duty not to kill one's patients.

But this argument faces the objection that medicine might have more than one essential purpose: a significant part of medicine today has very little to do with healing (Seay, 2005). For example, elective plastic surgery and fertility treatments aim not at healing and the conservation of life, but at the improvement of people's quality of life as perceived by them. Furthermore, there are cases in which the duty of nonmaleficence will itself be dependent on respect for autonomy, since what counts as harm sometimes depends on what the patient values.

The Appeal to Trust invokes a devotion to healing and the avoidance of harm, together with the consequent refusal to intentionally kill, that have been the distinguishing marks of Hippocratic medicine since antiquity. The trust that patients must feel toward their physicians if healing is to be possible would be undermined by permitting assisted death. Critics, however, object that although patients generally value their lives and expect medical professionals to value them too, there are exceptions. In some end-of-life situations, patients might instead expect health care professionals to honor their autonomous choice for death with dignity or for relief of suffering through a quicker death. In any such case, although a physician is not obligated to administer a lethal agent, a willingness to do so might, in the patient's eyes, be evidence of her trustworthiness. Furthermore, the Appeal to Trust rests on a prediction about PAD's negative effects on the patient–health care professional relationship. In connection with the next argument, we consider whether that prediction corresponds with the facts from societies that allow PAD.

The Slippery-Slope Argument

Different versions of this argument against PAD contend that the practice would ultimately have very bad consequences. Among possible bad consequences are sliding into permitting involuntary euthanasia, undermining efforts to provide adequate palliative and hospice care at life's end, and discriminating against women, the elderly, the cognitively impaired, the poor, the disabled, and other vulnerable individuals. Fueling the argument is the risk of abuse that might occur if, for example, women seek assisted death in large numbers to spare their families the burden of caring for them. The argument commits a *fallacy* when the 'sliding' to a bad consequence is in fact unlikely to occur, for it provides *no good reason* to think that it will occur.

Proponents of assisted death may reply that the predicted mistakes and abuses of the practice can be minimized with proper safeguards. For PAS, Oregon's safeguards include that the patient must be afflicted with an extremely debilitating, irreversible condition, have a hopeless prognosis, and have made, consistently over time, a competent, well-informed request for assistance in dying. For euthanasia, *informed consent* or reliable ways of determining the patient's preferences is required in the Netherlands. Thus an assessment of the Slippery-Slope Argument needs to consider evidence from these jurisdictions about how the safeguards are working. Only then we can determine whether risk of abuse is a serious threat.

The Dutch Experience

In the Netherlands, for example, PAS and VAE have been legal since the 1980s—first, decriminalized by prosecutorial policies and then by the 2002 Termination of Life on Request and Assisted Suicide Review Procedures Act. Safeguards for VAE require that:

1. There are no reasonable alternatives.
2. The qualifying patient
    a. Has made a clear, voluntary, and well-considered request for assisted death,
    b. Is in a hopeless condition that causes unbearable suffering, and
    c. Is informed about that condition and prospects.
3. The euthanizing doctor
    a. Has consulted with another independent physician, and
    b. Has terminated the patient's life with due medical care and attention.

It must be noted that terminations of life without explicit request by patients have occurred, but their numbers are diminishing: 0.8% in 1990, 0.7% in 1995, 0.7% in 2001, and 0.4% in 2005 (Rietjens et al., 2009). There have also been nonvoluntary euthanasia cases. In half of these, doctors invoked patients' previous wishes and in all cases consulted the patient's family. Other areas of concern involve (1) pediatric patients and patients with mental suffering, both eligible for physician-assisted death under certain conditions, and (2) assisted deaths that are not reported as such by physicians. Not surprisingly, critics and defenders of the Dutch policy interpret the data on these problems differently. But according to recent analysis of the data (Sumner, 2011; Lewy, 2010), there appears to be no evidence that decriminalization has had negative effects on palliative and hospice care. And there is no evidence that PAD is sliding on other slippery slopes.

In Belgium, where VAE with safeguards has been legal since 2002, the evidence points to improvement in palliative and hospice care, which observers interpret as a sign that a patient's request for assistance in dying is not prompted by the lack of proper alternatives. In addition, some recent qualitative studies of physicians' responses to patients' requests for termination of life indicate that only a small number of general practitioners, on whom the practice of VAE rests in Belgium, are actually willing to administer it. In most cases, they make attempts at persuading the patient to pursue other options, including terminal sedation in extreme cases. As a result, at least so far, there seems to be no tendency to slide into expanding the scope of assisted death (Sercu et al., 2012), with the exception of the Child Euthanasia Bill signed into law in 2014. This legislation grants terminally ill children of any age who are in "great pain" the right to request euthanasia provided they also make conscious repeated requests to die, have the parents' and medical team's consent, and there is no treatment to alleviate their distress. Opinion polls showed that the bill had broad support by the public. But it was opposed by Catholic leaders and many pediatricians, who argued that it would put vulnerable children at risk. Similar legislation exists in the Netherlands for children over twelve years old.

Regarding the claim that decriminalization of assisted death would put vulnerable people at risk—such as women, the mentally impaired, the physically disabled, the poor, and ethnic and racial minorities—the evidence is inconclusive. Some argue that abuses are more likely to occur when assisted dying is left unregulated, citing the case of Dr. Kevorkian, who assisted in the deaths of many more women than men. As we saw, in Oregon, periodic studies do not point to a disproportionate number of women or other vulnerable people undergoing assisted death. Even so, potential for mistakes and abuses cannot be ruled out a priori. The possibility of these remains an open question to be settled by further empirical data.

▮ 8.5 Chapter Summary

This chapter has considered reasons for and against the moral permissibility of medically assisted dying, focusing on physician-assisted suicide and voluntary active euthanasia. We distinguished these from measures deliberately provided to hasten a patient's death. Our exploration yielded a spectrum of end-of-life measures, with terminal sedation and involuntary active euthanasia at the clearly permissible and impermissible ends. In between are controversial measures that have been defended or opposed by arguments listed in Figure 8.2. Although no conclusive reason for preferring some of these arguments over the others is available, the evidence from Oregon and other jurisdictions that allow some form of assistance in dying does not so far support the grim predictions made by opponents of physician-assisted death.

FIGURE 8.2   For and Against Physician-Assisted Dying

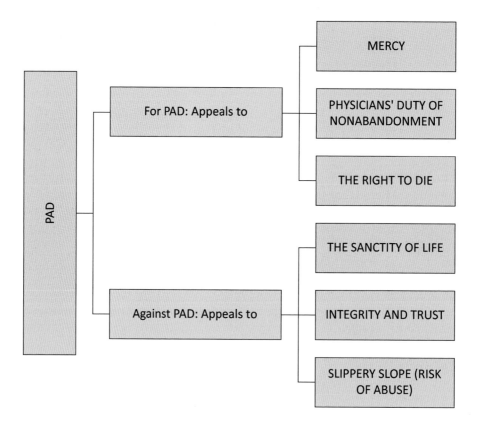

8.6 Study Aids

Key Words

Questions and Cases for Further Consideration

1. A moral and legal line between permissible and impermissible physician-assisted dying is often drawn on the basis of the cause of the patient's death and the physician's intent. Explain what might make these morally significant.

2. Is there anyone you know personally whose medical condition is such that death might be better than continued life? (a) If yes, discuss whether assisted death for that person is morally justified. If you don't know anyone with such a medical condition, discuss a hypothetical scenario. (b) In which circumstances, if any, would you consent to forgoing ANH or mechanical ventilation for someone you care about? Is it morally troublesome that the patient would die of dehydration or asphyxia? How does it compare morally if the patient dies instead by physician-assisted suicide or voluntary active euthanasia?

3. *Leo Oltzik, 88, was suffering from dementia, congestive heart failure, and kidney problems. Admitted to Long Island's Franklin Hospital in a state of agitation, he was sent to the hospice unit, where staff tried unsuccessfully to calm him. After three days, Dr. Edward Halbridge, in consultation with the family, began administering terminal sedation. Mr. Oltzik's death occurred five days later. In the end, Mrs. Oltzik regretted that the sedation, which might have hastened his death, deprived her of an opportunity to say goodbye, though it relieved her husband's pain and anxiety.* Might Leo Oltzik also have been deprived of something valuable for him? What can be said for and against substitute decisionmaking for terminal sedation? Does this end-of-life measure differ morally from physician-assisted dying? If so, how? If not, why not?[2]

4. Vacco v. Quill *is a landmark case on assisted suicide decided by the US Supreme Court in 1997, heard together with* Washington v. Glucksberg. *The plaintiffs—Dr. Timothy Quill, other physicians, and three seriously ill patients who later died—argued that a New York statute banning assisted suicide but allowing refusals of LST was inconsistent and unconstitutional. It violated the Fourteenth Amendment's Equal Protection clause by denying the right to die to patients who, owing to their condition, could not withdraw their own treatment or might need assistance in taking their lives. But the Court rejected this argument, reaffirming the distinction between legally permissible refusals and impermissible assisted suicide. For the Court, physicians, whatever their motives, may never cause, hasten, or aid in a patient's death. The New York ban was within the state's legitimate interest to protect medical ethics, prevent euthanasia, shield the disabled and terminally ill from prejudice that might encourage them to take their lives, and, above all, preserve human life.* Which principles of bioethics best account for the state's interests listed here? Might those interests, individually or jointly, outweigh a terminally ill patient's autonomy? What is your understanding of the charge of inconsistency brought by the plaintiffs against the New York ban? Does the charge have any merit?

5. Dr. Ernesto Pinzon-Reyes *admitted Rosario Gurrieri, 79, to a Florida hospital in October 1996. This doctor, recently arrived from Colombia, had treated the patient before. But*

---

2 Adapted from Anemona Hartocollis, "Hard Choice for a Comfortable Death: Sedation," *New York Times*, 12/26/2009.

now the diagnosis was terminal metastatic lung cancer. Gurrieri's pain and respiratory failure only grew worse within days. Although he was eventually sedated, his respiratory distress continued. When it was clear that death would come soon, Pinzon-Reyes gave Gurrieri a combination of drugs intended to induce death. Over the course of 30 minutes he administered 117 milligrams of morphine, 10 milligrams of Valium, and a potent dose of potassium chloride (which had neither sedative nor pain relief function). He was later indicted for first-degree murder, but eventually acquitted on the grounds that, while the potassium chloride would have stopped the heart within three to five minutes, Gurrieri died 40 minutes after the injection. Expressing their disappointment with the medical profession, some family members insisted that Pinzon-Reyes had requested neither Gurrieri's consent for euthanasia nor theirs. What type of end-of-life measure did Pinzon-Reyes administer to Gurrieri? Was his action consistent with patient autonomy? Although the courts and medical professionals in the US highly value patient autonomy, in other parts of the world, including Latin America, paternalistic beneficence often trumps. Should professionals from those parts of the world who move to practice medicine in the US be required to adopt US values? Criminal indictments of medical professionals who provide euthanasia from compassionate motives, though rare, are often brought against 'outsiders' because of their racial or ethnic backgrounds (Dr. Pinzon-Reyes) or personal and professional attitudes (Dr. Kevorkian). Might implicit bias play a role? Are such indictments just?

Suggested Readings*

*Alpers, Ann, "Criminal Act or Palliative Care? Prosecutions Involving the Care of the Dying," *Journal of Law, Medicine & Ethics* 26.4, 1998: 308–31.
Analyzes legal actions in the US against health care providers who, like Dr. Pinzon-Reyes, assist patients in dying with measures such as terminal sedation and euthanasia, expressing concerns about justice for those providers and public ignorance of palliative care.

Arras, John, "Physician-Assisted Suicide: A Tragic View," in Battin et al. 1998, pp. 279–300.
Favors the legalization of physician-assisted death on autonomy grounds, but only with appropriate safeguards and when sanctioned by legislators, not the courts.

*Brock, Dan, "Voluntary Active Euthanasia," *Hastings Center Report* 22.2, 1992: 10–22.
Takes voluntary active euthanasia to be consistent with the medical professionals' duties of beneficence and respect for patient autonomy.

*Callahan, Daniel, "When Self-Determination Runs Amok," *Hastings Center Report* 22.2, 1992: 52–5.
Invokes the killing/letting die distinction to draw a line between permissible-passive and impermissible-active euthanasia. In end-of-life measures, that distinction captures relevant moral differences in the cause of death.

*Dieterle, Jill M., "Physician-Assisted Suicide: A New Look at the Arguments," *Bioethics* 21.3, 2007: 127–39.

---

* Asterisks mark readings available online. See links on the companion website.

Brief discussion of some main objections to assisted death, classified as either consequentialist or deontological.

*Dworkin, Ronald, Thomas Nagel, Robert Nozick, John Rawls, T. M. Scanlon, and Judith J.
Thomson, "The Philosophers' Brief," *New York Review of Books* 3/27/1997, pp. 41–5.
Amici Curiae in the 1997 Supreme Court cases *Washington v. Glucksberg* and *Vacco
v. Quill.* Argues that some patients have a constitutional liberty interest in hasten-
ing their own deaths that is protected by the Due Process clause of the Fourteenth
Amendment.

*Garrard, E. and S. Wilkinson, "Passive Euthanasia," *Journal of Medical Ethics* 31.2, 2005:
64–8.
Dismisses current skepticism about the category of passive euthanasia.

Kass, Leon, "I Will Give No Deadly Drug: Why Doctors Must Not Kill," in Foley and
Hendin 2002, pp. 17–40.
Classic source for the Appeal to Integrity against physician-assisted dying.

*Lachs, John, "When Abstract Moralizing Runs Amok," *The Journal of Clinical Ethics* 5.1,
1994: 10–13.
Replies to Callahan (1992), charging that its abstract moral reasoning neglects considering the suffering of patients who request assistance in dying.

Lewy, Guenter, *Assisted Death in Europe and America: Four Regimes and Their Lessons.*
Oxford: Oxford University Press, 2010.
Very thorough coverage of the empirical data from jurisdictions where some form of
assisted death has been legal for some time.

*The Oregon Death with Dignity Act. 1994/1997. Available online at http://www.finalexit.
org/oregon_death_with_dignity_act.html.
Sets the conditions for patients to qualify for PAS in Oregon and the steps physicians
need to follow before and after writing a lethal prescription.

*Quill, Timothy E., "Death and Dignity: A Case of Individualized Decision Making," *New
England Journal of Medicine* 323.10, 1991: 691–4.
A New York physician's account of his patient's death by leukemia and of his role in
her physician-assisted suicide at the end.

*Rachels, James, "Active and Passive Euthanasia," *New England Journal of Medicine* 292.2,
1975: 78–80.
Classic source for an argument from mercy against the American Medical Association's view that passive, but not active, euthanasia can sometimes be justified. Also
questions the moral significance of the killing/letting die distinction.

Sumner, L. W., *Assisted Death: A Study in Ethics and Law.* Oxford: Oxford University Press,
2011.
Questions the alleged moral divide between permissible-passive and impermissible-
active euthanasia. The killing/letting die and the intending/foreseeing distinctions are
not helpful guides for end-of-life measures.

*Young, Robert, "Voluntary Euthanasia," *The Stanford Encyclopedia of Philosophy*, Edward
Zalta, ed., 2014. Available online at http://plato.stanford.edu/entries/euthanasia-
voluntary/.
An overview of major attempts to justify a moral distinction between passive and
active euthanasia in terms of killing versus letting die, acting versus omitting to act,
and intending versus foreseeing.

9 End-of-Life Measures for Severely Compromised Newborns

Learning Objectives

In reading this chapter you will

▶ Learn about critical care options for extremely premature or low birthweight neonates.

▶ Reflect on the moral dilemmas raised by the birth of a severely compromised infant.

▶ Evaluate legal and moral perspectives on the moral permissibility of ending the life of a severely impaired newborn.

▶ Analyze some high-profile cases where the relevant parties disagreed about what was in an infant's best interest.

THIS CHAPTER ADDRESSES moral questions concerning severely compromised newborns (infants in their first 28 days). Because of advances in antenatal diagnosis and care, there are fewer children born with severe congenital disorders. Yet infant mortality and morbidity are on the rise, owing in part to a greater incidence of low birthweight and prematurity. Newborns in these groups are at high risk of death, or of surviving with life-long severe disabilities, thus presenting parents and health care providers with difficult moral choices.

9.1 Baby Jane Doe: Parental Choice and State Duties

Keri Lynn, born in 1983 at St. Charles Hospital in Long Island, New York and known in the courts as 'Baby Jane Doe,' had the most serious type of spina bifida, excessive cerebrospinal fluid inside the skull, microcephaly, and other disabling conditions. When transferred to the neonatal intensive care unit (NICU) at the State University of New York Hospital in Stony Brook, doctors estimated that with surgery to close her spinal lesion, and a shunt inserted to drain the excess fluid in her skull, she could live to her twenties, though with severe mental impairment and high risk of meningitis, paralysis, and epilepsy. Without surgery, she could live perhaps two years. After consulting with the health care team, social workers, and a priest, her parents withheld consent for surgery but allowed antibiotics to fight infections. Two pediatricians, George Newman and Albert Butler, believe that decision was reasonable. Yet at least one physician at the hospital believed surgery was medically indicated.

Meanwhile, Lawrence Washburn, a Vermont lawyer active in the right-to-life movement, had received a confidential tip about the case, and without knowledge of the infant's medical records or consultation with her parents, sought a court order compelling the hospital to perform the surgery. When the hearing began, Judge Melvyn Tanenbaum, a former Right-to-Life Party candidate for public office, appointed attorney William Weber as guardian *ad litem* to make medical decisions for Baby Jane. Two days later, Judge Tanenbaum ruled in favor of surgery, and Weber consented. But the parents won a subsequent appeal, while quietly allowing the insertion of the shunt. Weber subsequently entered two appeals, both unsuccessful: in the first, a New York appellate court reaffirmed the parents' right to make decisions on behalf of their own child and warned third parties like Washburn to file their concerns about disabled newborns with the proper agencies instead of initiating litigation. In the second appeal, the US Supreme Court declined to hear the case, thus allowing the New York Court of Appeals' ruling to stand.

In the meantime, Washburn brought suit against the hospital in a federal district court on the grounds of discrimination against a handicapped person. But the court dismissed the charge and ordered him to pay $500, under a statute allowing fines for harassment or causing unnecessary delays and litigation costs. Keri Lynn did eventually go home with her parents. Over time her spinal lesion closed on its own. Years later, though still afflicted with serious cognitive and physical impairments, she was able to get around in a wheelchair, attended special courses for people with developmental disabilities, and enjoyed the love and affection of her parents and a circle of friends. In 2013 she celebrated her 30th birthday.

■ ■ ■

It was of course impossible to determine with certainty at birth whether the burdens of Keri Lynn's congenital disorders would outweigh the benefits of medical intervention. Dr. Newman predicted that her life would be short and that she would be unable to establish significant interaction with her environment. He was wrong on both counts. Her case came at a time of growing awareness in the US of the rights of the disabled. The tenacious struggle of the advocates of such rights contributed to increased skepticism about bold predictions of a bleak future for infants with similar physical or cognitive impairments. In addition, it contributed to the acceptance in medical practice of the right of disabled children to the same opportunities for medical treatment as other children.

Note, however, that although the parents withheld consent for Keri's surgery, since they had allowed other treatments, their decision about her care showed no evidence of either neglect or discrimination, according to the New York appellate court. The court also found no justification for having a guardian to represent her best interests. In its 1983 refusal to intervene, the US Supreme Court let stand the appellate court's ruling, thus endorsing its defense of noninterference with reasonable *parental choice*. In parallel developments, the state and federal courts responded to Washburn and Weber, as third parties, by emphasizing the right to privacy and taking parental choice to put the burden of proof on each of these challengers. That right was also invoked in two subsequent denials of access to Baby Jane's medical records by investigators from the Justice Department.

But the debate about *Baby Jane Doe* signaled a change in neonatal decisionmaking standards that was already under way in the US, one that prioritized the patient's **best interests** over parental choice. It also prepared the public for the **Baby Doe rules** sanctioned shortly afterwards.

◼ 9.2 Decisionmaking Standards for Compromised Newborns

The Baby Doe Regulations

Today in the US the infant's best interests, usually as interpreted by the parents in consultation with the medical team, is the decisionmaking standard for newborns. In the early 1980s, this standard began to replace unrestricted parental choice, in part owing to the moral controversy surrounding *Baby Jane Doe* and this case:

Indiana Baby Doe was born with Down syndrome in Bloomington in 1982. He also had a fistula allowing food to pass into his lungs and his esophagus was not open to his stomach. Without a relatively simple surgical procedure to correct these, he would die. Advised by the obstetrician, who mistakenly considered the surgery too risky and the baby's prospective quality of life very poor, the parents withheld consent to treatment, including nutrition and hydration. The family physician and a pediatrician disagreed and sought legal authorization to treat, even locating another couple willing to adopt the infant. But the Indiana Supreme Court reaffirmed the parents' right to decide. Baby Doe died of dehydration and pneumonia in six days, before the US Supreme Court could hear an appeal.

Like *Baby Jane Doe*, this case involved disagreement about the infant's prognosis and a questionable parental choice based on mistaken predictions about corrective surgery. Both cases were to have momentous consequences in the law. Indeed, the Reagan Administration responded to *Indiana Baby Doe* with its first attempt at securing the provision of *life-sustaining treatment* (LST) for medically compromised infants. In 1982, an amendment to article 504 of the Americans with Disability Act made most instances of **forgoing treatment** for infants a federal offense to be "vigorously" investigated. To this end, the federal government established a telephone hotline for anonymous reports of violations, sending teams (dubbed by critics 'Baby Doe Squads') to investigate reports. States in violation would lose eligibility for federal grants. The objective was to prevent discrimination for a preexisting disability. After all, Indiana Baby Doe, but for his Down syndrome, would have received the needed surgery.

But many health care providers found these rules intrusive and at odds with their professional autonomy. Furthermore, state courts already had the authority to intervene in decisions to forgo treatment for compromised infants when deemed discriminatory. Ultimately struck down by the US Supreme Court in 1986, the Baby Doe regulations survived in a revised form as an amendment to the Child Abuse Prevention and Treatment Act approved by Congress in 1988. They consider LST mandatory for compromised infants except when "reasonable medical judgment" determines that

1. The infant is chronically and irreversibly comatose;
2. The provision of LST would merely
   a. Prolong dying,
   b. Not be effective in ameliorating or correcting all of the infant's life-threatening conditions, or
   c. Otherwise be futile in terms of the survival of the infant; or
3. The provision of such treatment would be virtually futile in terms of the survival of the infant and the treatment itself under such circumstances would be inhumane.

The revised Baby Doe rules faced prudential and moral objections. First, they can undermine child protection by causing noncomplying states to lose federal funds for it. (But no state has ever been prosecuted for violation of these regulations.) Furthermore, they are at least in part responsible for the development of a presumption among care teams in favor of providing LST, even where it might only prolong an infant's pain and dying. Note, however, that since medical judgment about exceptions (1) through (3) allow for some flexibility, opposition to the rules by health care providers eventually waned. The American Academy of Pediatrics found them acceptable in 1994.

From the *Baby Doe Regulations to* HCA v Miller

Before the Baby Doe rules of the 1980s, infants were not considered patients in their own right but beings who belonged to their parents. The rules promoted skepticism about parents' ability to be objective interpreters of their infants' best interests and contributed to the prevalence of the best-interest standard in the courts and neonatal care. Parental choice, however, need not conflict with the best-interest standard, since arguably parents are the primary evaluators of their infant's best interests, as often recognized in bioethics and the law.

Today the compromised newborns often at the center of disputes between parents and health care providers include babies delivered prematurely or with **very low birthweight (VLBW)**. In decisions about proper level of care for these neonates, the courts have sometimes been sympathetic to parental choice. Consider:

HCA v Miller. When Karla Miller was admitted at the Woman's Hospital of Texas in 1990 in her 23rd week of pregnancy, an infection threatening her life made induced delivery necessary. If her baby survived, the risks of severe physical and cognitive impairments were high. Karla's doctor entered in the file that the Millers withheld consent for any heroic measures, including resuscitation. But according to hospital administrators, in Texas critical care must be provided to any neonate weighing more than 500g, even without parental consent. Sidney was born alive and weighed about 600g. So Dr. Otero, a neonatologist present allegedly only to evaluate its condition, responded with resuscitation and critical care—which helped the child survive, though with severe mental and physical impairments requiring long-term dependence on others for care. Because the hospital acted without their consent and contrary to their express wishes, the parents sued HCA (the hospital and its corporate entity) for battery and negligence. After a jury found for the Millers, the District Court awarded them $29,500,000 for past and future medical expenses, plus $13,500,000 in exemplary damages and $17,503,066 in prejudgment interest. But in 2000 the Texas Court of Appeals reversed that decision, invoking an exception to parental consent in life-threatening emergencies involving a child. In 2003 the Texas Supreme Court reaffirmed the reversal, also citing Texas's statute that an infant must be terminally ill for a lawful withholding of LST.

In the context of this multimillion-dollar lawsuit, the reversals of the first ruling had no substantial consequences besides freeing HCA from payment. But the District Court's decision in fact questioned whether an infant's best interest, as determined solely by health care providers, should always prevail over parental reasonable choice. Thus, regardless of its final disposition, this case discourages heroic measures for compromised newborns undertaken against parental wishes, suggesting that parents should be the primary decisionmakers. When parents of very premature or low-birthweight neonates, now a growing number, decide to forgo intensive care for their severely compromised newborns, the reason may be the bleak prospects for these infants, a topic to which we now turn.

9.3 Prematurity and Low Birthweight

Today many difficult medical decisions in the neonate nursery concern neonates of very low gestational age or birthweight (hereafter, '**preemies**' and 'VLBWs'). In 2012, 40% of all deaths worldwide among children under five involved neonates (WHO, 2012). In 2015, 270,000 such deaths were expected globally, with a great number involving preemies and VLBWs. Although these neonates now have better chances of survival with good life prospects than ever before, their future survival and quality of life depend in part on the category of prematurity and low birthweight where they fall (see Box 9.1).

When a preemie or VLBW is born, health care providers and parents often face a difficult ethical choice: must it receive critical-care, life-sustaining treatment (LST) or only palliation (i.e., care focused on relieving symptoms and optimizing the neonate's comfort)? In the past, many such newborns would die. Today critical care can sometimes save them, though often at the price of severe long-term disabilities. Decisions to provide LST are particularly difficult because of the great uncertainty about these neonates' prognoses. Given a group of preemies or VLBWs with apparently similar deficits at birth, it is uncertain which ones will die, survive with serious long-term disabilities, or grow up without major problems.

BOX 9.1 CATEGORIES OF PREMATURITY AND LOW BIRTHWEIGHT

Preemie: a neonate born at ≤ 37 weeks
- Late preterm: 34 to 37 weeks
- Moderately preterm: 32 to 34 weeks
- Very preterm: ≤ 32 weeks
- Extremely preterm: < 25 weeks

Low Birthweight: < 2,500g
- Very low birthweight (VLBW): ≤ 1,500g (3lb, 3oz)
- Extremely low birthweight: ≤ 1,000g (2lb, 20 oz)

Prematurity

Neonates born at the limit of viability (about 24 weeks of gestation) or before are not only physically small but physiologically immature. Complications from extreme prematurity are associated with short-/long-term disability, including lung and heart disease and serious brain conditions such as internal bleeding and hydrocephalus. There is also a high risk of developing cerebral palsy, cognitive and behavioral disorders, vision and hearing problems, infections, cardiovascular disease, and type 2 diabetes. Preemies who survive often need long stays in a neonate intensive care unit (NICU), where their subtle changes in vital signs can be constantly monitored and life supports provided. NICU stays of more than three months are not uncommon, generating considerable financial burdens on families and the health care system, since each day of intensive care is formidably expensive.

IMAGE 9.1
©iStockPhoto/slovegrove

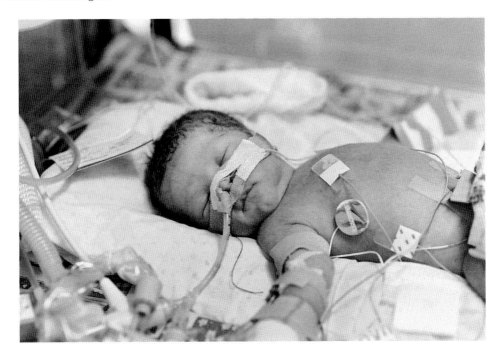

In America alone, many of the 500,000 preemies born every year do not survive. But survival rates, which depend on the stage of prematurity, are improving: up to 95% survive today, compared with 5% in the 1960s. The UK reports similar rates. Yet according to a 2006 study by the Nuffield Council on Bioethics, only 1% of infants born between 22 and 23 weeks survive. Of those born between weeks 23 and 24, only 11% survive in hospital. Some of these die after they leave it. Two thirds of survivors develop moderate to severe disability. For babies born between weeks 24 and 25, survival chances rise to 26% (Eaton, 2006). Moral questions arise as to whether health care providers should make medical decisions for infants in these groups and how much should be done to keep them alive.

Low Birthweight

Prematurity is the primary risk factor for neonates to be very low birthweight (VLBW). Other factors include pregnancies with multiples that in the US account for 50% of VLBWs, teen pregnancies, and maternal substance abuse during pregnancy. VLBWs face increased risk of death or disability owing to birth injuries and complications after birth, such as serious sickness and infections. Their potential long-term disabilities, as defined in Box 9.2 below, range from mild to severe. They often require long stays in the NICU, where they are treated for conditions such as respiratory distress syndrome, brain hemorrhages, heart disease, and intestinal problems. Other serious conditions may develop in adulthood.

BOX 9.2 INFANT DISABILITY

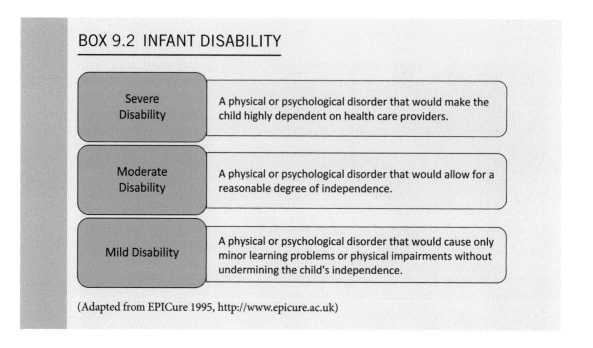

Severe Disability	A physical or psychological disorder that would make the child highly dependent on health care providers.
Moderate Disability	A physical or psychological disorder that would allow for a reasonable degree of independence.
Mild Disability	A physical or psychological disorder that would cause only minor learning problems or physical impairments without undermining the child's independence.

(Adapted from EPICure 1995, http://www.epicure.ac.uk)

The Ethical Issues

Ethical issues in the care of premature or low birthweight infants concern the great uncertainty in decisions about when, or whether, they should be resuscitated or receive life supports. For, even with recent technological advances, these neonates' future looks bleak. Accurate predictions are difficult, even after an adequate assessment of their condition at birth. Care teams have developed some protocols for ethical decisions about their care. Yet since these protocols sometimes vary in their treatment options within the same group of compromised infants, ethical questions remain. For example, the American Academy of Pediatrics recommends generally resuscitating preemies born after week 26 but not those born before week 23. In Israel, however, resuscitation and aggressive intensive care are prescribed for any preemie born alive (Gross, 2000). But then, what weight should be given to parental choice? Which protocol best captures what ought to be done, morally? As we saw in Chapter 5, disagreements on medical decisions for neonates may occur between parents and health care providers, and may require intervention by hospital ethics committees, professional mediators, and sometimes the courts. From the moral perspective, their resolution calls for reasoned argument of the sort to be considered after looking closely at the options available.

▇ 9.4 Critical Care for Severely Compromised Newborns

Medical options for a severely compromised neonate range from providing aggressive critical care at one extreme, to providing assistance in dying at the other. Each of the options may create a moral quandary that cannot be resolved by mere appeal to a medical protocol or a law regulating neonatal care. The options available to parents and health providers are:

1. Save or prolong the newborn's life—i.e., provide life-sustaining treatment (LST).
2. Hasten the newborn's death—i.e., forgo life-supportive measures in the ways outlined in Box 9.3.
3. End the newborn's life—i.e., provide **neonatal euthanasia**.

BOX 9.3 FORGOING LIFE-SUSTAINING TREATMENT (LST) FOR A NEWBORN

As with other patients whose lives can be prolonged or saved only by LST, some newborns' death can be **hastened** by:

Withholding LST—The elective nonadministration of measures necessary to save or prolong the newborn's life (e.g., do not provide resuscitation or ventilation).

Nonescalation of LST—The elective limitation of such measures (e.g., provide mask ventilation but not intubation).

Withdrawing LST—The elective discontinuation of LST already in place (e.g., terminate mechanical ventilation).

For Providing Critical Care

According to the 2006 study by the Nuffield Council on Bioethics mentioned above, 34% of preemies born at week 24 that were admitted to NICUs in the UK grew up without major disability. The rest either died or went on to develop life-long severe disabilities resulting in a permanent dependence on others for routine daily care. In Israel, every preemie born alive receives LST until it either dies or can survive without critical care. A common defense of this do-everything protocol (option 1) rests on the Sanctity-of-Life doctrine, which has the shortcomings indicated in Chapter 7. Here we consider two other reasons.

The first argument invokes the uncertainty of predictions about the future quality of life of the newborn to contend that substitute decisionmaking is impossible. Since the infant does not yet know whether continued life is, for her, better or worse than a quicker death, it makes no sense to speculate about 'what the patient would want.' Neither the medical team nor the parents can make that determination, since the patient, at this stage of life, has as yet no 'point of view.' This seems to argue for waiting until the patient can determine whether pain or disability makes her life not worth living. Furthermore, since predictions of future suffering for compromised infants are often exaggerated or based on thin evidence, critical care should be provided to all (Barry, 2010; Kon, 2008; Robertson, 1975).

Also supporting the provision of intensive care for all preemies born alive is a related Best-Option argument, which takes such measures to offer the best option compared with any competitors recommending that preemies in high risk groups be allowed to die. After all, some preemies in these groups can survive and grow up without severe impairments. And at birth, there may be no evidence that reveals their life prospects.

Against Providing Critical Care

The Appeals to Futility and Mercy

For newborns with significant risk of death or severe life-long disability, life support's burdens to the child, family, and society may outweigh any benefits. In the following case, for example, the treatment's costs and overuse of scarce medical resources seem out of proportion, given the grim prognosis:

Baby K was born in 1992 with anencephaly. Her mother insisted that heroic measures, including cardiopulmonary resuscitation, be provided. Like most US hospitals after the Baby Doe rules, Fairfax Hospital in Virginia was prepared to provide treatment for this severely disabled newborn. Ultimately Baby K became respirator-dependent and was moved to an extended-care facility, but she was readmitted to the hospital twice in respiratory crises. After the second admission, the hospital announced that further treatment would be futile and sought legal clearance for refusing to readmit Baby K. But the court ruled against this, citing family autonomy and a presumption in favor of life. On appeal, the federal court upheld the ruling, this time citing federal statutes designed to protect the right of patients to stabilizing treatment even when it is deemed futile by medical experts. Baby K lived two and a half years. At the time, each day in intensive care cost about $1,450 and her nursing $100. Private insurance and Medicaid covered these costs.[1]

Her hospital made an Appeal to Futility: in light of the facts about anencephaly, prolonging Baby K's life was of no benefit. As you may recall from Chapter 2, anencephaly is a fatal disorder characterized by unconsciousness due to the absence of parts of the brain. Intensive care for anencephalic infants amounts to a costly, uphill battle requiring scarce resources that are needed for other infants. Yet the courts gave more weight to the mother's choice in this instance (the estranged father sided with the hospital).

For dying infants with some other congenital disorders, since critical care may only prolong pain and suffering, an Appeal to Mercy contends that the harm for all involved outweighs any possible benefits. This in part accounts for the adoption of either statistical or initiate-and-reevaluate protocols for preemies. Given the statistical protocol of some Northern European countries, no preemie falling into poor-prognosis groups receives supportive measures. The problem for this protocol is that, for example, if used in the UK all preemies in the above study would have died, including the 34% that in fact grew up without major disabilities. By contrast, given the initiate-and-reevaluate protocol prevalent in the UK and the US, all neonates in that group usually receive initial life supports, with withdrawal or nonescalation considered later upon reevaluation of each infant's condition. Although this protocol allows for more individualized care and avoids the problem for the statistical protocol, in cases such as the following, it only prolongs the dying process:

Angel suffered devastating damage at birth. After a few weeks in intensive care, her parents stopped visiting, leaving all medical decisions to the medical team, the hospital, and social work-

---

1   Data from Tricia L. Romesberg, "Futile Care and the Neonate," *Medscape* 2003. http://www.med-scape.com/viewarticle/464018_4.

ers. Among these, three groups emerged which could not agree on the withdrawal of life supports, even when these interventions were clearly causing pain and discomfort to the dying girl without improving her chances of survival. She was finally allowed to die after more than two years of disagreement about what to do. (Kopelman, 2005)

Angel received medical treatment no one would want in her situation. It merely prolonged her dying. Thus, in some cases, the initiate-and-reevaluate protocol can be as burdensome for the health care system and inhumane for the patient as the do-everything protocol. The appeals to mercy and futility appear to favor the statistical protocol. But, as we consider next, not all moral theories support those appeals.

FIGURE 9.1   Intensive Care Options for Preemies

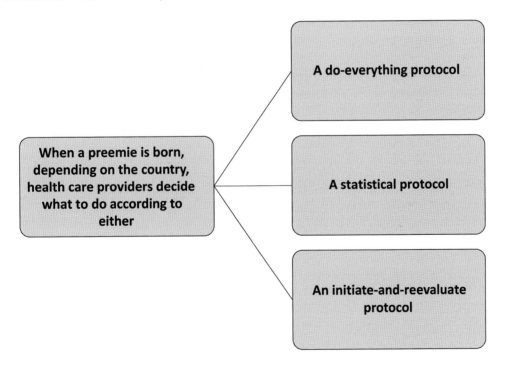

What the Moral Theories Might Say

The Appeal to Futility assumes that health care providers have obligations of justice (viz., to use medical resources fairly), nonmaleficence (viz., to avoid causing uncompensated harm), and beneficence (viz., to prevent harm whenever possible). The Appeal to Mercy focuses on their obligations of nonmaleficence and beneficence. These considerations are persuasive for utilitarians and Rossians, but less so with others. Kant himself would have rejected both appeals, since they put too much moral emphasis on pain, suffering, and burdens—which are outcomes of these decisions—while ignoring what is really important, respect for persons. What matters is not causing pain but *whether neonates can be wronged* by any such decision, which turns on whether they will develop rationality. Infants who will not, cannot be wronged. Their parents and health care providers owe them at most the indirect duty to avoid treating them in ways that might adversely affect how they treat rational beings. But with many compromised newborns, including preemies and VLBW babies, it is unclear at birth whether they will survive and grow up to be rational. As a result, Kantian ethics thus provide no clear moral guidance in these life-or-death decisions for compromised infants.

Other theorists may accept the above appeals' conclusion but support it differently. For some virtue and care ethicists, a virtuous or caring agent would see prolonging a life of very low quality as inhumane. For natural law theorists, forgoing life supports, though never mandatory, might be permissible in some cases provided (1) the intention is not to kill but to allow nature to take its course, and (2) critical care amounts to an extraordinary measure in the circumstances. In Chapter 7, we pointed out some limits of these accounts in our discussion of medical futility.

Neonatal Euthanasia

Reasons for letting a severely compromised infant die also support medically assisted neonatal euthanasia, or the deliberate ending of a newborn's life as quickly and painlessly as possible. A notable exception to the general unlawfulness of neonatal euthanasia is the Netherlands, where in 2005, after much debate about the right thing to do with newborns who are suffering badly with no realistic chance of relief, pediatricians adopted a regulation for neonatal euthanasia, the **Groningen Protocol** (GP). It was first published in the *New England Journal of Medicine*, after having been administered for seven years to some newborns with myelomeningocele (MMC), the most serious form of spina bifida. It considers euthanasia morally and legally permissible provided five conditions are met:

1.   The diagnosis and prognosis is certain,
2.   The newborn is in hopeless and unbearable suffering,
3.   There is a confirming second opinion by an independent doctor,
4.   Both parents give informed consent, and
5.   The procedure meets medical standards.

Dr. A. Verhagen and other pediatricians at Groningen developed the GP in response to a particularly painful, terminal case of neonatal epidermolysis bullosa, in which an infant's skin becomes detached from its body. Although euthanasia was then illegal, the GP was envisioned as a set of guidelines for future cases and as a way of making the administration of neonatal euthanasia more open and transparent. Its explicit goals are providing merciful assistance in dying for infants who:

- Cannot possibly survive, even with life-sustaining treatment (LST)—e.g., preemies with very undeveloped kidneys or lungs;
- Have only a small chance of survival and a virtual certainty of a very poor quality of life if they do survive—e.g., neonates with catastrophic hypoxic damage to the brain or other vital organs; and
- Though not LST-dependent, will likely have "a very poor quality of life."

These recommendations have since drawn considerable attention in the pediatric literature, largely as a proposal hotly contested on moral grounds. They have been endorsed by some physicians (mostly in the Netherlands) but emphatically rejected by others. By the time the GP was published in 2005, 22 Dutch newborns, all with MMC, had been given euthanasia on the grounds that their condition guaranteed a hopeless prognosis (Verhagen and Sauer, 2005). However, in other countries, although forgoing LST for newborns is sometimes permissible, euthanasia for them never is.

Utilitarians on Neonatal Euthanasia

End-of-Life measures (EoL) for these newborns include forgoing life supports and euthanasia. The former measures, which include withholding and withdrawing life supports, are commonly considered permissible as instances of letting die, whereby nature takes its course. But the latter measure, which amounts to actively killing them, rarely is. Utilitarians generally reject the **killing/letting die** distinction, holding that there is no moral difference between intentionally killing a compromised neonate and letting it die (Rachels, 1986; Kuhse and Singer, 1985). In fact, other things being equal, **hastening an infant's death** may be unjustified morally while actively inducing its death (neonatal euthanasia) may be justified. After all, letting it die prolongs the neonate's process of dying, causing it more pain and greater burdens for parents, health care providers, and society. A quicker killing as painless as possible is then morally preferable. Keep in mind that the reasons for either EoL are the same: futility, mercy, and the argument considered next.

The Appeal to Psychological Personhood

The fact that newborns with profound mental impairments may lack the psychological capacities necessary for being persons is a reason for the moral permissibility of neonatal euthanasia (and other EoLs). The argument is

1.   It is sometimes permissible to kill beings that are not persons.
2.   Some medically compromised infants will never be persons.

---

3.   Therefore, it is sometimes permissible to kill those newborns.

In order to avoid discriminating against disabled children, proponents of this argument need support for premise (2). Without it, the argument is reminiscent of the reasoning that sanctioned slavery, racial discrimination, even genocide. In all of these, victims were declared 'nonpersons.' But, given a standard view on personhood, having certain psychological capacities is necessary for having the moral standing of persons, even when they disagree about *which* are sufficient. The facts about infants with profound mental impairments, together with that standard view on personhood, supports premise (2). Yet it is unsettled which capacities are necessary and sufficient for personhood. And not everybody agrees with that view. As shown in Chapter 10, for other theorists it is instead membership of *Homo sapiens* that determines which beings are persons. Thus this Appeal to Psychological Personhood has no force with those who reject its premise (2).

The Analogy to Abortion for Fetal Defects

This argument contends that if abortion at the limits of viability (about 24 weeks of pregnancy) is permissible, ending the life of a compromised neonate also is. Consider neonates born at 23 weeks: they have a gestational age and life prospects similar to some fetuses aborted at 23 weeks for their defects. The only difference between them is location, which cannot make a moral difference. Yet the proposed analogy seems weak because actions that are permissible for human fetuses need not be permissible for newborns. For example, location does make a difference in the law, which (usually) counts only newborns as persons, not fetuses.

Reasons against Neonatal Euthanasia

The main objection to neonatal euthanasia runs along the lines of the above objection to forgoing life supports for preemies. It holds that medicine cannot always accurately predict the future quality of life of a severely compromised newborn. Consider infants with the most serious type of spina bifida (MMC), all eligible for euthanasia under the GP. According to critics, "MMC in and of itself is not a terminal illness when treated actively, and it is becoming evident that the majority of these patients, even those severely affected, will survive to develop into dignified adults who are satisfied with their lives. . . . The criteria outlined for patient selection in the GP are not supported by long-term quality-of-life evidence pertaining to patients with MMC" (Barry, 2010: 414). Advances in prenatal and palliative care, it seems, now afford to these patients a quality of life that is not as poor as described by neonatal euthanasia's advocates. Although focused on euthanasia for neonates with MMC, this objection generalizes. For, the first 22 patients given euthanasia under the GP all had MMC. If predictions about such patients' future quality of life are often mistaken, that would undermine justification for neonatal euthanasia.

This criticism should not be confused with the objection that legalized neonatal euthanasia is inevitably a slippery slope into lawlessness and the indiscriminate application of the procedure in inappropriate cases. The Dutch experience shows no evidence of these. On another version of this objection, neonatal euthanasia would undermine the ethics of medicine and sow distrust of health care providers. But data collected in the Netherlands (Verhagen, 2013) after the GP became accepted also fail to support this objection.

■ 9.5 Chapter Summary

This chapter focused on newborns at high risk of death or severe long-term disability. Uncertainty about what is medically best for these infants emerged as a crucial element of the moral quandaries faced by parents and health care providers. In the US, the prevailing standard for decisionmaking had long been parental choice, but with the Baby Doe regulations of the early 1980s became the infant's best interests. Even so, the presumption in favor of honoring reasonable treatment decisions made by the parents (including nontreatment) persists.

Today the groups of infants severely compromised at birth include a great number of premature and low birthweight neonates. The evidence about their grim prospects, together with the uncertainty about each infant's chances of growing up to be healthy—or to have disabilities compatible with a satisfying life—presents parents and health care providers with difficult moral choices. These include whether the medically compromised newborn should receive (1) critical care, (2) only palliative care, or (3) neonatal euthanasia. Protocols consistent with (1) and (2) are used around the world. Regulated (3) is legal only in the Netherlands since 2005. Figure 9.2 summarizes main moral arguments for and against end-of-life measures consisting in forgoing life supports or euthanasia. Main objections to the provision of critical care rely on consequentialist considerations of futility and mercy, together with the view that infants with profound cognitive impairments are not persons. Although such objections also favor (3), their strength is called into question by the uncertainty of predictions about the future quality of life of some compromised infants.

FIGURE 9.2   Arguments for and against End-of-Life Measures (EoLs) for Severely Compromised Newborns

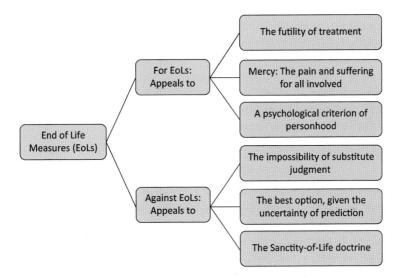

9.6 Study Aids

Key Words

Baby Doe rules, 175
Best interests, 175
End-of-life measure (EoL), 185
Forgoing treatment, 176
Groningen protocol (GP), 184
Hastening an infant's death, 185
Intensive-care protocols for preemies, 181
Killing/letting die, 185
Neonatal euthanasia, 181
Preemie, 178
Prematurity, 179
Very low birthweight (VLBW), 177

Questions and Cases for Further Consideration

1.   Some neonates with Down syndrome also have a correctible intestinal occlusion that is fatal without a relatively simple surgery. In countries with scarce medical resources the surgery might be waived as futile, but is it futile? Discuss.

2.   For the Nazis, no life of a disabled person was worth living, because it "corrupted the race." For many contemporary bioethicists, some lives of disabled persons are not worth living when they become unbearable from the person's own point of view. Can you see any relevant analogies or disanalogies between these two arguments?

3.   Sarah Thorson's *triplets were born after only 27 weeks of gestation. They were extremely small and ventilator-dependent. One of them developed a hemorrhage in his brain and lungs, a condition that often results in cerebral palsy and extreme mental impairment. Doctors rushed to his bedside. "There was a roomful of doctors around this tiny baby, trying to resuscitate him," said Mrs. Thorson. "After it was over, I looked at the neonatologist and said, 'At what point do we say enough is enough for this little boy?' The doctor snapped back, 'You don't make those decisions. We do.'"* Baby Doe rules in the US have limited parental choice but not eliminated it. Was Mrs. Thorson right in asking that question? Did the doctor give an appropriate answer? How and by whom should such treatment decisions be made?[2]

4.   Johns Hopkins Baby, *born in 1963 at Johns Hopkins University Hospital, had duodenal atresia, an intestinal blockage that could have been easily corrected by surgery. But since it also had Down syndrome, its parents, a lawyer and a nurse, denied consent for the surgery. Their rationale was that rearing a severely disabled infant could cause psychological harm to its siblings. So the hospital never sought a court order to perform the surgery, letting the baby die of starvation and dehydration in a back room. The ordeal, according to health care providers who witnessed it, lasted eleven days.* Although bioethics cases often elicit opposite reactions, here there was widespread agreement that the parents and hospital had acted wrongly. Is the killing/letting die distinction morally significant in this case? Can anything be said for the parents' decision? Can the medical team and hospital justify what happened by appeal to the decisionmaking standard for neonates prevailing at the time? What would the Baby Doe regulations have sanctioned if available then? Might the parents' social and economic status have been a factor in persuading the provider to agree with their decision?

5.   An infant is born prematurely with a high risk of either not surviving or surviving with severe physical and mental impairments. The hospital decides to provide critical care against the parents' wishes. Which of these sides, if either, would the best-interest standard support? What other interests may be relevant to the case? In your view, who should be the decisionmaker?

---

2 Adapted from G. Kolata, "Parents of Tiny Infants Find Care Choices Are Not Theirs," *New York Times*, 9/30/1991.

6.   Ryan Nguyen *was born in 1994 at Sacred Heart Hospital in Spokane, Washington, six weeks premature, with a number of severe congenital disorders. Two providers of dialysis refused to admit him, holding that treatment would only prolong his dying. An external second opinion confirmed his poor prognosis. But his parents took their inability to pay (the father was unemployed and the mother worked as a cook) to be the reason for forgoing treatment, and obtained a court injunction against it. To the hospital, further treatment was inhumane and futile, as expressed in a complaint it filed under the Baby Doe regulations. In the meantime, Ryan was transferred to the Legacy Emanuel Children's hospital in Portland, which offered to treat him. His condition began to improve, eventually rendering a kidney transplant unnecessary. Four months later he went home. Fed by tube and often treated for infections, he died at age 4. His father estimated that health care costs in his first two years of life amounted to $1.5 million.* On the basis of the facts considered here, were life supports for Ryan futile and inhumane as argued by Sacred Heart? Was it in the spirit of the Baby Doe rules to support that hospital's decision? Which of the parties in dispute, if any, was actually representing Ryan's best interests? Might the patients' low socioeconomic status be the real reason providers sometimes forgo life supports, as argued by the Nguyens?

*Suggested Readings**

Engelhardt, Tristram, "Ethical Issues in Aiding the Death of Young Children," in M. Kohl, ed., *Beneficent Euthanasia*. Buffalo, NY: Prometheus, 1975.
   Denies that young children are persons in the full moral sense, holding that, in cases where a newborn is severely disabled, the right to decide whether to treat belongs to its parents. In cases of intense suffering, allowing death and even active termination is permissible.
*Kluge, Eike-Henner W., "Severely Disabled Newborns," in Kuhse and Singer 2012, pp. 274–85.
   Overview of principal ethical questions raised by severely compromised newborns, including who should make treatment decisions and what the criteria should be.
*Kon, Alexander A., "We Cannot Accurately Predict the Extent of an Infant's Future Suffering: The Groningen Protocol Is Too Dangerous," *The American Journal of Bioethics* 8.11, 2008: 23–6.
   Argues that neonatal euthanasia might result in killing infants whose suffering will *not* be unbearable, and is thus morally wrong.
*Kopelman, Loretta M., "Rejecting the Baby Doe Rules and Defending a 'Negative' Analysis of the Best Interests Standard," *Journal of Medicine & Philosophy* 30.4, 2005: 331–52.
   Defends a negative account of the patient's best-interest standard, as what reasonable people would not find unacceptable. Argues that the Baby Doe Rules conflict with that standard.

---

*   Asterisks mark readings available online. See links on the companion website.

*Paris, J. J., M. D. Schreiber, and M. Moreland, "Parental Refusal of Medical Treatment for a Newborn," *Theoretical Medicine and Bioethics* 28.5, 2007: 427–41.
    Urges recognition of parents as primary decisionmakers for their severely impaired newborns, provided their decisions are in the infant's best interests.
*Resnik, Jack, "The Baby Doe Rules (1984)," *The Embryo Project Encyclopedia*. Available online at https://embryo.asu.edu/pages/baby-doe-rules-1984.
    Informative account of the debate about *Baby Jane Doe* and the Baby Doe rules.
*Robertson, John A., "Involuntary Euthanasia of Defective Newborns: A Legal Analysis," *Stanford Law Review* 27.2, 1975: 213–69.
    Rejects ending the lives of seriously impaired infants because of the difficulties in predicting the value life will have for them, the limits of surrogate appreciations of that, and the possibility of ameliorating any psychological harms/financial burdens such impaired infants might bring to families.
*——, "Extreme Prematurity and Parental Rights after Baby Doe," *Hastings Center Report* 34.4, 2004: 32–9.
    Reconsiders the *Baby Doe* rules in light of the increased numbers of very low gestational-age or birthweight infants. Parental decisions to forgo supportive measures when severe mental impairment is expected need not conflict with anti-discrimination rules.
*Verhagen, Eduard and Pieter Sauer, "The Groningen Protocol—Euthanasia in Severely Ill Newborns," *New England Journal of Medicine* 352.10, 2005: 959–62.
    Outlines conditions for the regulated use in the Netherlands of euthanasia for infants that are not terminally ill but have severe impairments causing unbearable pain without hope of relief.

PART IV

Moral Issues at the Beginning of Life

10 Personhood in the Abortion Debate

Learning Objectives

In reading this chapter you will

▶ Learn about the ambiguity of the word 'person.'

▶ Distinguish conditions that may be necessary and sufficient, or only sufficient for being a person.

▶ Consider why criteria of personhood matter to the debate over the moral permissibility of abortion.

▶ Reflect on why reasonable people care about that debate and avoid emotively charged language.

▶ Recognize the problems of over-inclusiveness, under-inclusiveness, and speciesism facing some criteria of personhood.

PARADIGM PERSONS LIKE you (the reader) or us (the authors of this book) have full moral standing. Killing paradigm persons is usually a grave moral wrong. By contrast, the moral standing of nonparadigm persons, which include fetuses and neonates, is an unsettled matter that bears directly on the debate over the moral permissibility of abortion. This chapter introduces the parties in that debate, looking closely at the **criteria of personhood** each may assume and the emotive language each should avoid.

10.1 Marlise Muñoz: Pregnant but Dead

In November 2013 Marlise Muñoz of Fort Worth, Texas, collapsed in her kitchen. When her husband Erick found her some time later, she was unresponsive. Mrs. Muñoz was rushed to John Peter Smith Hospital, where doctors, finding no relevant brain activity during the first two days, declared her whole-brain dead. Over the next few days, the family came to accept her death and informed the hospital of her wish not to be kept on life supports in such a condition. She and Erick had both worked as paramedics, and the subject had often come up. The situation took an unexpected turn when the hospital announced that it would *not* honor the family's request. Marlise was fourteen weeks pregnant when she was stricken by a fatal blockage in the pulmonary arteries, and a Texas statute forbids denying life support to a pregnant patient. After weeks of failed negotiations and public debate, Erick filed a lawsuit against the hospital. A Texas district judge later held that since she was legally dead, "she cannot possibly be a 'pregnant patient;'" thus the Texas statute did not apply to her. Moreover, her 22-week-old fetus was already "distinctly abnormal," perhaps owing to Mrs. Muñoz's hypoxia while she lay unconscious on the kitchen floor for what may have been about an hour before her husband found her. On January 24, 2014, Judge R. H. Wallace ordered the removal of life supports from Mrs. Muñoz by the following Monday, which the hospital did.

■ ■ ■

Erick Muñoz had won the battle, but not the war. For, to his disappointment, the ruling in his wife's case fell short of striking down the Texas statute prohibiting forgoing life supports for pregnant women with disorders of consciousness. The prohibition applies equally to women who are temporarily or even permanently unconscious. In light of Judge Wallace's ruling, brain-dead pregnant women like Marlise are exempt from the statute. But other permanently unconscious women must continue to be 'hosts' of their fetuses until a pregnancy comes to term—which is troublesome when there is an advance directive or surrogate decision against providing life supports in such circumstances.

Marlise Muñoz involves a rare but not unknown situation. Peter Singer (1994) draws attention to two similar cases of brain-dead, pregnant women on life supports. In one, a California woman died of a gunshot wound in the 1990s. Her family besought medical staff to do everything possible to bring her pregnancy to viability so that the baby could then be delivered by Caesarian section (as it ultimately was). In the other, the family of a German woman, like that of Mrs. Muñoz, opposed the hospital's intervention on behalf of the fetus. In both situations, medical technology appeared to have blurred the distinction between life and death. The moral puzzles thus created are recent ones, since it was not until the end of the 20th century that medicine had the technology necessary to sustain a brain-dead woman's vital functions until her pregnancy is carried to term. In fact, Singer takes the cases to show a pervasive confusion in modern Western societies about when a person is dead.

Be that as it may, since the women in question were dead according to the prevailing criterion of death in medicine and the law, it seems odd to say, as did some journalists, that they had a right to die, or to an abortion. It is also odd to say that the health care providers had duties of beneficence toward their fetuses, since in medicine such duties are owed to patients who are persons, and fetuses do not usually count as legal persons. But suppose what really matters is whether fetuses have the full *moral standing* of persons. If they do, this may have implications for the moral permissibility of abortion. After all, as we saw in Chapter 1, the unjustified killing of a person is a serious moral wrong. It is not surprising then that a critical issue in the debate about the moral permissibility of abortion is whether human fetuses have the property of being persons. Commonly referred to as 'personhood,' this is the property considered next.

10.2 Personhood

The Ambiguity of 'Person'

Who qualifies as a moral person depends in part on what 'person' means. Consider,

1. The bones found in the cave were of a *person*, not of a tiger.
2. No computer developed so far can compete with a *person*.
3. The prisoners should not be killed, because they are *persons*.

In (1), 'person' means *human being* in the sense of *being of the species Homo sapiens*. This concept is purely *descriptive*, not moral, since whether something is a human being is a matter of species membership, to be settled by genetic testing. (2) illustrates a more common descriptive concept of 'person,' whereby beings that have some complex psychological capacities such as the ability to reason are persons. As you can see in the capacities listed in Box 10.1, some social capacities are also considered crucial to being a person in a descriptive sense. Paradigm persons need not have all such capacities, or may have them only to some degree. But persons typically have some, and possession of a cluster of them is *sufficient* for being a person.

BOX 10.1 PSYCHOLOGICAL CAPACITIES TYPICAL OF PERSONS

A person typically

- Has preferences, conscious desires, feelings, thoughts, a sense of time, nonmomentary interests that involve a unification of desires over time, etc.
- Is able to remember its own past actions and mental states, envisage a future for itself, experience pleasure and pain, take moral considerations into account in choosing between possible actions, interact socially with others, communicate with others, and/or undergo change in a reasonably nonchaotic fashion.
- Is self-conscious, capable of rational thought, and/or capable of rational deliberation.

Yet there is disagreement about the short list of psychological or social capacities that should be in that cluster, and about to what degree a being must have them to be a person. In spite of such disagreements, it is clear that possession of some such capacities to a significant degree gives a being personhood. Furthermore, having personhood in this sense also gives a being the full moral standing discussed in Chapter 1, which implies that killing a person is (all things being equal) a grave moral wrong. In the language of rights, persons are said to have a right to life. Example (3) above, where the personhood of the prisoners is offered as a reason for the wrongness of killing them, illustrates 'person' in this moral sense.

The above examples illustrate the ambiguity of the word/concept 'person,' whose meaning may vary from sentence to sentence. In those examples, it is used to express one or more of these properties:

1. Being a human being
2. Having some psychological/social capacities typical of persons
3. Having full moral standing

The relation between these properties is a complex matter to be taken up in this chapter. For now, note that (1) through (3) are not exclusive: paradigm persons have all three at once. 'Person' in its most common, descriptive meaning refers to things that satisfy (2), which is sufficient for possession of (3). But given the conservative Sanctity-of-Life doctrine discussed in Chapter 7, beings that have (1) have (3) too, whether or not they also have (2)—for example, permanently unconscious patients and human fetuses. But not all agree. In *Marlise Muñoz*, her fetus had (1), but did it have also (3)? For those defending the hospital's decision, it did. But those sympathetic with the husband may contend that fetuses are not persons under the most common ordinary meaning of that word which is associated with possession of (2). If fetuses lack (3), allowing them to die or even inducing their death by abortion may be morally permissible.

Criteria of Personhood

Anything that is a person, then, enjoys full moral standing. Having certain psychological or social capacities is one among other criteria of personhood offered to determine *which* beings enjoy that standing. Criteria of personhood may offer *necessary and sufficient*, or only sufficient, conditions for having full moral standing. Of the two, criteria offering only sufficient conditions are more modest and therefore likely to succeed. For 'person' may be among the concepts resistant to definition by necessary and sufficient conditions. Compare 'sister': once you have determined that, to qualify for sisterhood, someone must be both a female and a sibling, you can sort out sisters and nonsisters. Neither being female nor being a sibling is sufficient in itself for being a sister, but each is necessary. And the two together are sufficient: anyone who fulfills both conditions is a sister. Sometimes, as in this case, it is a combination of two or more necessary conditions taken jointly that determines membership of a class. Other times it is one condition that is at once both necessary and sufficient. For example, being a figure with exactly three internal angles is necessary and sufficient for being a triangle.

But there is a long history of failed attempts at finding necessary and sufficient conditions for being a person. Good candidates are the two meanings of 'person' exemplified above: having certain complex psychological or social capacities, and belonging to the species *Homo sapiens*. Yet a closer look suggests that neither condition, by itself, amounts to a necessary and sufficient condition for being a person. Let's illustrate the problem by means of some candidates for the psychological capacity necessary and sufficient for personhood. If the capacity is thinking critically, then infants are not persons, and neither are adults with severe mental impairments or dementia, which conflicts with commonsense intuitions about them. Or consider having a complex language. Now humans who, because of a congenital disorder or injury, permanently lack linguistic abilities aren't persons, which is also implausible. And if the conditions are relaxed, so as to consist only in having **sentience** (the capacity to feel pain and pleasure), then lizards, mice, and cats end up being persons. The failure to identify adequate necessary and sufficient conditions of personhood favors a modest criterion offering only sufficient conditions, something we'll assume for the criteria coming next.

BOX 10.2 CRITERIA OF PERSONHOOD

Ambitious Criteria—Aim at identifying necessary and sufficient conditions for being a person, such that

- Without them no one is a person, and
- They are enough all by themselves to make something a person.

Modest Criteria—Aim at identifying the psychological capacities that are sufficient for falling under the ordinary concept 'person.'

Psychological-Property Criteria

These criteria of personhood take the possession of some psychological/social capacities to be sufficient for personhood, something consistent with the ordinary meaning of 'person.' But *which* complex psychological capacities are sufficient for being a person in that ordinary sense of 'person' and to what degree? Although so far there is no agreed upon **psychological-property criterion,** many agree with philosopher John Locke (1632–1704): self-consciousness, rational thought, a sense of time, and memory are sufficient for personhood. In his view, any being with the capacities for desiring to remain alive and for recognizing itself as itself and as the same being at different times and places is a person.

Bioethicist David DeGrazia (2007: 178–9), aware that that there is no consensus among Lockeans about a precise list of complex forms of consciousness "typical" of persons, argues that an adequate cluster of sufficient conditions for personhood includes autonomy, rationality, self-awareness, linguistic competence, sociability, and moral agency. Possession of *enough* of these is sufficient for being a person. At the same time, there are borderline cases of human beings who are neither persons nor nonpersons—for example, fetuses, anencephalic newborns, and patients in PVS or with severe dementia. But the proposed cluster determinately applies to paradigm persons, defined as "normal human beings who are beyond infancy and toddler years" (p. 178). Typical of persons is being "psychologically complex, linguistically competent, and highly social" (p. 177). If possession of such features determines personhood, it follows that any nonhumans with comparable psychological features are persons too. Thus, in this view personhood extends beyond our species to apply to, for example, extinct hominid species, fictional characters, and perhaps the Great Apes and other higher mammals.

DeGrazia thus offers a modest approach to criteria of personhood that appears unaffected by the present lack of consensus among scholars about which specific psychological capacities are sufficient for personhood, and to what degree. But its modesty comes at the price of a low performance in the problematic cases of interest to bioethics. Consider the abortion debate, in which it matters whether the human fetus has the standing of a person with a right to life. Since the fetus has none of the psychological properties deemed sufficient for personhood, the view leaves undetermined whether fetuses are persons. After all, they might acquire their personhood via a different cluster of capacities (recall that in this view the proposed capacities are only sufficient, not necessary). Furthermore, since the same could be said for individuals who permanently lack cognitive capacity, this criterion is unlikely to be of much help with the moral quandaries discussed in previous chapters in connection with brain death and disorders of consciousness.

The Human-Property Criterion

This criterion relies solely on species membership, holding that

> Mere membership of the species *Homo sapiens* is sufficient to be a person.

Since the **human-property criterion** does not invoke possession of psychological capacities as sufficient for personhood, it seems more determinate than psychological-property criteria. After all, whether a being belongs to *Homo sapiens* can be clearly established by DNA testing. But a closer look reveals some indeterminacy, since drawing clear boundaries among certain species is difficult in nature. For example, it is an unsettled matter in evolutionary biology whether the Neanderthals belonged to a distinct species *Homo genus* or were a subspecies of *Homo sapiens*. This criterion cannot, then, tell whether the Neanderthals had full moral status. And since there is now abundant evidence of their interbreeding with *Homo sapiens*, it is also indeterminate about whether the resulting offspring were persons. Even if the vagueness of 'person' may account for these complications, a problem remains. For, given the human-property criterion, humans who are ordinarily thought to lack the full moral standing of paradigm persons would have it—for example, anencephalic babies and permanently unconscious patients. Any criterion with such consequences runs into over-inclusiveness, a problem considered next.

Over-Inclusiveness, Under-Inclusiveness, and Speciesism

Criteria of personhood must avoid the shortcomings of **over-inclusiveness** and **under-inclusiveness**. Any criterion implying that some beings have a moral standing they actually lack is over-inclusive, while a criterion implying that beings lack a certain moral standing that they actually have is under-inclusive. Criteria facing either of these problems fail to be adequate. For example, a criterion taking consciousness to be necessary for personhood is under-inclusive, for it implies that someone who is under anesthesia or in dreamless sleep is not a person. Arguably, a criterion implying that young infants and cognitively impaired humans lack personhood completely is also under-inclusive because it challenges the common intuition that these individuals are (nonparadigm) persons. On the other hand, a criterion taking the capacity to feel pain and pleasure to be sufficient for personhood is over-inclusive, for it implies that *any* nonhumans are persons—including spiders, mollusks, and even mosquitoes!

A related problem facing some criteria of personhood is **speciesism:** the bias of taking species membership to determine full moral standing. The criterion that belonging to *Homo sapiens* is necessary for having full moral standing has this problem, which arises because speciesism is at once:

1. Under-inclusive, since it denies personhood to psychologically and socially complex nonhumans such as the chimpanzees just because they are not *Homo sapiens,* and
2. Over-inclusive, since it has the consequence that, for example, permanently unconscious individuals have the same moral standing as paradigm persons.

In Chapter 16, we have more to say about speciesism in connection with biomedical research on animals. For the criteria of personhood of concern here, speciesism need not be a problem facing the human-property criterion, which may be silent about the moral standing of chimps and other nonhumans. After all, it takes membership of our species to be only sufficient for personhood, which is compatible with some nonhumans acquiring the full moral standing of persons in some other way. But it does face problem (2), over-inclusiveness. Even so, Natural Law theories tend to embrace this criterion given its compatibility with their view that life, an absolute moral value, begins at conception. On the other hand, since utilitarian and Kantian theories favor psychological-property criteria of personhood, their views on whether fetuses are persons vary. Utilitarians think that sentience confers moral standing, and personhood requires the Lockean capacities mentioned above. Kant also held a psychological-property criterion of personhood, but in his view it was the capacity to develop a rational nature that confers personhood on any creature with that capacity. The upshot is a disagreement between these theories about what qualifies for personhood:

- All humans, including those in utero, given Natural Law theory.
- Any being that can develop rational nature, including fetuses, given Kant's theory.
- Any being that has certain complex psychological capacities, given utilitarianism.

FIGURE 10.1   Shortcomings for Criteria of Personhood

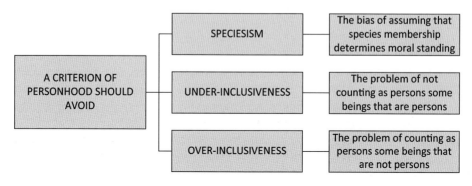

10.3 The Abortion Debate

Does the Debate Matter?

By contrast with practices commonly regarded as wrong, such as murder, rape, slavery, and child abuse, there is no consensus among reasonable people about the moral wrongness of abortion. In the United States, debates on the issue are characterized by profound disagreement at both the level of individual choice and of public policy. Fueling the disagreement are opposite views about the moral standing of human fetuses. Although you probably have your own opinion on this, you may still want to make sure that it holds up when challenged. Moreover, moral judgments are not written in stone: reasonable people often change their minds. The Spanish theologian Bartolomé de las Casas (1474–1566), an early advocate of basic human rights, was at first a supporter of the Atlantic slave trade, but later, horrified by the enormity of this traffic in human lives, publically apologized for his own endorsement of it, which he came to consider a grave moral error. Similarly, people have changed their minds in the abortion controversy. Former Vice President Al Gore and former President Bill Clinton, once opponents of abortion, now believe it is morally permissible. And Dr. Bernard Nathanson, the New York obstetrician who was a prominent abortion-rights activist, later renounced that position as he came to believe that abortion was immoral.

How to Move Ahead

Progress can be made in the **abortion debate** only by adopting a thoughtful approach to the arguments on both sides. This will require avoidance of some common obstacles in a debate that tends to arouse strong passions. There have been exaggerations and other forms of misrepresentation of rival points of view on both sides. To make matters worse, the loudest views have often rested on extreme religious or political convictions that are apt to interfere with reasoned *argument*.

Consider, for example, some emotive language used. Although our terminological choices are sometimes limited by the need to use the exact language in which a position is presented, attention should be paid to the labels for positions on each side of the debate. When defenders of abortion identify themselves as 'pro-choice,' this label suggests that the other side opposes any choice whatsoever. When they identify themselves as protecting 'abortion rights,' this assumes that abortion *is* a moral right—precisely the matter in dispute. To avoid such connotations, we refer to them as '**abortion defenders**.' For their opponents, we use '**abortion critics**,' thus rejecting the 'pro-life' label they often choose for themselves, which suggests that the other side opposes life.

In reality, many parties to this debate do not take either of the extreme positions implied by the 'pro-choice' and 'pro-life' labels. Many abortion critics do not actually oppose *all* abortion, since they usually allow some exceptions, such as to save the woman's life, or where pregnancy is the result of rape or incest. But they do oppose typical abortions, the topic of the next chapter. And abortion defenders usually don't really think that pregnant women should be free to choose just *anything at all*. Many of them would find morally objectionable an abortion for sex-selection (i.e., to try again until the fetus is of the desired sex) or an elective abortion in the eighth month of pregnancy simply to avoid inconvenience on an upcoming vacation in Aruba.

Personhood in the Abortion Debate

Opposite views about whether the fetus is a person underlie many arguments on both sides of the abortion debate. Both sides agree that

a.   Induced **abortion** (hereafter 'abortion') is the intentional killing of a human fetus.
b.   Under ordinary circumstances, the intentional killing of a person is morally wrong for that person's own sake.

Assuming (a) and (b), critics of abortion contend:

1.   The human fetus is a person.

_____

2.   Therefore abortion is morally wrong for the fetus's own sake.

Given (1), abortion is comparable to the killing of a paradigm person, a moral transgression of the most serious type. Clearly, most immoral actions are not of this sort. If Nancy breaks her promise to help Cynthia set up her new computer, or Basil falsely denies placing a bet on a horse, those are certainly moral wrongs, but they are not grave moral wrongs the way killing an innocent person ordinarily is. Furthermore, the wrongness of abortion at issue in this argument concerns the human fetus itself, independent of any wrong also done to others, such as its relatives, health care providers, or society at large. Recall the igniting-the-cat-for-fun scenario imagined in Chapter 1: many would find the action wrong for the cat's own sake. Similarly, it is often thought wrong to kill an innocent person for that person's own sake. If human fetuses are persons like you or us, killing the fetus is wrong for its own sake.

For the other side, abortion does not involve the killing of a human being with the moral status of a paradigm person. Thus, killing it wouldn't be wrong for the fetus's own sake. Assuming (a) and (b) above, the argument runs

1.   The human fetus is not a person.

_____

2.   Therefore, abortion is not morally wrong for the fetus's own sake.

These opposite arguments have conclusions supported by their premise and assumptions. Proponents of either argument agree that abortion is the intentional killing of an organism belonging to the species *Homo sapiens*. But each has a different view about what that entails for fetuses having the full moral standing of persons. The deep disagreement turns on whether the human fetus is a person, a question likely to remain open in light of the problems discussed above.

■ 10.4 Chapter Summary

Disagreement about whether fetuses are persons and the emotionally charged language often used in the abortion debate are impediments for advancing the discussion. Even if the language problem is resolved by replacing labels such as 'pro-life' and 'pro-choice' with 'abortion critic' and 'abortion defender' respectively, the other problems remain. Arguments about the moral permissibility of abortion often depend on whether human fetuses have the full moral standing of persons. If the human-property criterion of personhood is sound, since belonging to the *Homo sapiens* species would be sufficient for personhood and fetuses satisfy this human property criterion, fetuses are persons. Under normal circumstances, abortion would be morally forbidden. But this argument by abortion critics fails because it rests on an over-inclusive criterion with the implication that, for example, permanently unconscious individuals have the same moral standing as paradigm persons. On the other hand, abortion defenders may invoke certain psychological and social capacities as the grounds of personhood. Yet may they consider those capacities necessary or sufficient for personhood? If necessary, then the view is under-inclusive for it denies personhood to those who lack, for example, linguistic or critical thinking competence. If sufficient, then the view can provide no help in deciding whether fetuses are persons, since they may acquire personhood via another route. Besides under-inclusiveness and over-inclusiveness, speciesism amounts to a problem for criteria of personhood (but see discussion of humanism in Chapter 16). In the next chapter we consider how some defenders and critics of abortion have tried to support their positions without relying on controversial criteria of personhood.

 ## 10.5 Study Aids

Key Words

Abortion, 200
Abortion critic/defender, 199
Abortion debate, 199
Criteria of personhood, 192
Human-property criterion, 197
Over-inclusiveness, 197
Paradigm person, 192
Psychological-property criterion, 196
Sentience, 196
Speciesism, 198
Under-inclusiveness, 197

Questions and Cases for Further Consideration

1. Consider 'being human' as a necessary and sufficient, or merely a sufficient, condition for personhood. Discuss what each of these entails for the abortion debate.

2. Abortion critics think that the expression 'fetus' (without the precedent adjective 'human'), as used by abortion defenders to refer to the human in uterus, is biased, while abortion defenders object to the abortion critics' expression 'unborn baby' on similar grounds. What, if anything, is wrong with these expressions? Should they be avoided in the abortion debate? Can you find similarly questionable expressions in other bioethical debates?

3.   *In 1939, an immigrant named* Repouille *was charged in California with first-degree manslaughter for killing his 13-year-old son with chloroform. The boy was blind, mute, and incontinent. He had anomalous limbs and a profound mental impairment. His whole life had been spent in a tiny crib. A sympathetic jury found Repouille guilty only of manslaughter in the second degree, and an equally sympathetic judge stayed execution of his five-to-ten-year sentence. Repouille served no time.* Was the Repouille boy a person according to human-property or psychological property criteria of personhood? Which of these criteria best captures what common morality would say? What might each entail about the permissibility of the father's action? Could Natural Law theorists find that action permissible? What about utilitarian and Kantian theorists?

4.   Chantal Daigle, *a citizen of Quebec, became pregnant in 1989 as a result of her romantic relationship with Jean-Guy Tremblay, who abused her physically. After she became pregnant, she decided to end the relationship and seek an abortion. But Tremblay filed an injunction to stop her, arguing that the fetus is a person. Ultimately Canada's Supreme Court ruled that a fetus has no standing as a person in Canadian law, and that therefore men could not appeal to an alleged fetal right to life to justify injunctions to halt abortions.* Which criterion of personhood is consistent with Tremblay's position in this case? And which with Daigle's? Suppose the Court decided instead that the fetus is a legal person. Would that justify an injunction to halt her abortion? What about the fact that Ms. Daigle's pregnancy was quite advanced by the end of the trial?

5.   Duodenal atresia is a congenital, intestinal obstruction in some newborns, lethal if untreated. Survival rates with surgery are good. In a survey of 267 pediatric surgeons and 190 pediatricians (Glantz, 1983), 76.8% of the surgeons and 49.5% of the pediatricians agreed with a no-treatment decision by parents when the baby also has Down syndrome. If instead the newborn had multiple limb or cranio-facial malformation, only 62.5% of the surgeons and 47.4% of the pediatricians agreed. Interestingly, 26 participants agreed even for newborns affected only by intestinal atresia. On the other hand, for a 5- or 10-year-old victim of a car accident with similar disfigurements fewer physicians would agree to nontreatment. To some, the data suggest that, for medical professionals, newborns have little moral standing. Might the view of medical professionals matter in deciding whether newborns are persons? In your view, do neonates have that moral standing? If they don't, could they still have moral standing? Do differences in patients' age or medical condition matter for moral standing? What would the criteria of personhood considered here say about this?

6.   Ms. Erlagen, *18, was thirteen weeks pregnant when an auto accident in 1992 left her brain dead. She was kept on life supports to allow delivery by C-section at a later time. After performing an ultrasound examination at week 16, Dr. Hans-Joachim Voigt confirmed that the fetus was normal, arguing that "turning off the equipment would be homicide." A Catholic theologian interviewed by a newspaper declared that nature should be allowed take its course, while Professor Andrea Abele-Brehm decried the absence of women on the ethics committee that decided in the case, and found intolerable the use of a female corpse as a "brooding machine." The future father was unknown and Erlagen's parents opposed the hospital's decision.* Which of the above criteria of personhood is straightforwardly

compatible with the view that Ms. Erlagen was still a person? Could the Catholic theologian and Dr. Voigt have agreed with that view yet disagreed about the right course of action? How might having the perspective of women in this sort of medical decision affect the outcome, as Prof. Abele-Brehm seemed to think? Was she right in regarding the hospital's decision as disrespectful to a dead person, and more generally, to women?

Suggested Readings* 📖

*Boonin, David, *A Defense of Abortion.* Cambridge: Cambridge University Press, 2003.
> A readable book-length overview of arguments for and against the moral wrongness of abortion, including those appealing to criteria of personhood. Discusses strategies to avoid some sticking-points in the abortion debate.

DeGrazia, David, "Introduction," *Human Identity and Bioethics.* New York: Cambridge University Press, 2005, pp. 1–7.
> Proposes a psychological-property criterion of personhood along Lockean lines, which provides only sufficient conditions for personhood and is taken to capture the ordinary notion of person.

——, "Human-Animal Chimeras: Human Dignity, Moral Status, and Species Prejudice," in Gruen, Grabel and Singer 2007, pp. 168–87.
> Argues that nonhuman animals such as the Great Apes qualify for personhood, given their complex psychological capacities, and finds no grounds for fears that this would undermine human dignity.

*——, "On the Moral Status of Infants and the Cognitively Disabled: A Reply to Jaworska and Tannenbaum," *Ethics* 124.3, 2014: 543–56.
> *Contra* Jaworska and Tannenbaum's (2014) relational view of moral standing, defends the position that beings with similar cognitive capacities must have the same moral standing.

*Jaworska, Agnieszka and Julie Tannenbaum, "Person-Rearing Relationships as a Key to Higher Moral Status," *Ethics* 124.2, 2014: 242–71.
> Invokes a relational view of moral standing to argue that infants and cognitively impaired individuals have higher moral status than nonhuman animals with equal psychological capacities. After all, the former, but not the latter, can participate in person-rearing relationships.

*Kaczor, Christopher, "Does Personhood Begin at Conception?" in Kaczor 2011, pp. 91–120.
> Ascribes full moral standing to fetuses by taking membership of *Homo sapiens* to be sufficient for it, thus running into the over-inclusiveness problem.

*Tooley, Michael, "Personhood," in Kuhse and Singer 2012, pp. 129–39.
> Comprehensive discussion of criteria of personhood. Argues that fetuses and neonates lack personhood because they lack the active potentiality to have complex psychological capacities. Since without the assistance of others they could never become persons, their personhood is potential only in a passive sense.

---

* Asterisks mark readings available online. See links on the companion website.

11 Abortion in the Typical Case

Learning Objectives

In reading this chapter you will

▶ Recognize the main extreme and intermediate positions on the moral permissibility of abortion.

▶ Determine the consequences of the Sanctity-of-Life doctrine for the abortion debate.

▶ Reflect on whether abortion can compare morally to the killing paradigm persons.

▶ Consider whether abortion's permissibility may depend on the fetal gestational age.

▶ Distinguish the right to life from the right to be provided life support.

SOMETIMES A PREGNANCY is terminated for fetal defects, endangerment of the mother's life or health, and other special reasons. We leave discussion of the moral permissibility of abortion in such **hard cases** to Chapter 12. Our topic here is the moral debate over the **typical case**, which includes most actual abortions. These involve early, elective terminations of unwanted pregnancies. Neither personal belief nor public policy about abortion can be grounded on reasoned argument without a careful look at that debate.

11.1 *Roe v Wade*: A Compromise on Abortion

In 1969, when Norma McCorvey of Dallas became pregnant for the third time, abortion was illegal in Texas. Unmarried, poor, and supporting herself with menial jobs, McCorvey was determined to end the pregnancy. But Texas law offered few alternatives. McCorvey first sought a legal abortion, claiming rape, one of the exceptions then allowed. But with no police report on file, the scheme went nowhere. Having no money to travel to a state with less restrictive abortion laws, she tried to find an illegal abortion clinic in Dallas, but found them all shut down by police authorities. Ultimately she was persuaded by two public-interest attorneys, Linda Coffee and Sarah Weddington, to act as the plaintiff in a class-action lawsuit against the Texas abortion law. McCorvey agreed and, to protect her identity, was given the legal pseudonym, 'Jane Roe.' The defendant named on behalf of the State of Texas was Dallas County District Attorney Henry Wade.

The trial court found for the plaintiff, arguing that women have a legal right, grounded in the Ninth and Fourteenth Amendments to the US Constitution, to seek an abortion. Wade appealed to the Supreme Court of the United States, which in January 1973 upheld the District Court's ruling. The 1857 Texas statute prohibiting abortion was struck down. Jane Roe was vindicated, but the extensive legal implications of the decision—not to mention its political repercussions—had only begun to be understood. For McCorvey, the case had no personal consequences. Her pregnancy ended with the birth of a healthy daughter, who was given up for adoption. She had never had an abortion, never again sought one, and continued to live in obscurity until the 1980s, when she publically acknowledged her identity as 'Jane Roe.' For a time, she lent her name to abortion-defenders' political campaigns, but later converted to conservative Protestant Christianity and joined a religious movement opposing abortion on moral grounds.

■ ■ ■

Roe v Wade was a watershed event in American law that made it legal for a woman to have an abortion at any time up to viability (the last trimester of pregnancy). During the first trimester, abortion is a matter for the woman and her doctor to decide, without state interference. In the second trimester, the state may have a role, though limited to regulating abortion providers to ensure their competence and the safety of their methods and facilities. But in the last trimester, by weeks 24 to 39 of pregnancy, states could prohibit abortion outright, except where necessary to protect the life or health of the woman.

Roe also established that state laws criminalizing abortion, except to save the mother's life, are unconstitutional because they violate the Due Process Clause of the Fourteenth Amendment, which protects individual liberties, including the right to privacy. At the same time, it acknowledged that a state has a legitimate interest in regulating abortion at certain stages of pregnancy to protect the mother's health. It also argued that personhood does not legally begin until birth, because "the unborn have never been recognized in the law as persons in the whole sense." Therefore, "the word 'person,' as used in the Fourteenth Amendment (on due process and equal protection) does not include the unborn."

BOX 11.1 ABORTION IN TYPICAL AND HARD CASES

'Typical cases'—Intentional terminations of unwanted pregnancies before the 24th week. They amount to more than 90% of all abortions in the United States.

'Hard cases'—Intentional terminations of pregnancies for reasons such a rape, incest, fetal impairment, or risk to the mother's life or health.

Subsequently, other rulings have invoked *Roe*'s vindication of the state's interest in protecting life to enact legislation limiting permissible abortions, especially after viability (see gestational stages, next section). Such decisions raise important moral questions about abortion at the levels of individual choice and public policy concerning not only typical but also hard cases of abortion, as defined in Box 11.1. We consider some hard cases in the next chapter. Here our focus is the moral permissibility of abortion in typical cases. We take up major arguments for and against it after reviewing some facts about abortion.

11.2 Abortion: Some Facts

What Is Abortion?

Induced abortion, hereafter 'abortion,' is the intentional termination of a pregnancy before the fetus can live independently. In the US, *Roe* made abortion legal in typical cases, which comprise elective terminations of unwanted pregnancies occurring before week 24. Nearly all abortions in the United States (more than 90%) fall into this category. By contrast with typical cases of abortion, hard cases comprise any intentional terminations of a pregnancy because of rape, incest, fetal impairment, or risk to the mother's life or health. While elective abortions aim at terminating an unwanted pregnancy, therapeutic abortions pursue protecting the mother's life or health or terminating a pregnancy compromised by severe fetal defects. But not all terminations of pregnancies count as abortions: miscarriage (i.e., the spontaneous loss of a pregnancy before viability, about 24 weeks), preterm delivery (i.e., the loss of pregnancy after viability), and stillbirth (i.e., the delivery of a dead fetus) are unintentional and therefore fall outside that category.

Although the elective abortions of concern here are surgical, nonsurgical abortions caused by either an intra-uterine device (IUD) or RU-486 (the abortion pill) raise similar moral problems. Either of these blocks implantation of the zygote in the uterine wall, the IUD by affecting the lining of the uterus, RU-486 by interfering with the activity of progesterone, a hormone essential for continuation of pregnancy. RU-486 is an abortifacient drug (mifepristone) legal in most European countries since 1999 and in the United States since 2000. But if, as some believe, a human organism is a person from conception, then nonsurgical abortions amount to the killing of persons—which explains some opposition to RU-486 and the IUD.

BOX 11.2 HUMAN GESTATION

- At conception or fertilization, an egg (or ovum) and a sperm cell merge into a single-cell zygote. Fertilization occurs in about 23 hours, in one of the two fallopian tubes that link the egg-producing ovaries and the uterus.
- The zygote develops into a larger, multi-cell organism as its cells divide and integrate, traveling down the fallopian tube over three to five days.
- When the zygote reaches the uterus, it continues to divide, forming a hollow sphere of cells called a 'blastocyst.'

- Within approximately five days implantation occurs: the blastocyst attaches itself to the uterine wall, becoming an embryo. Identical twinning is possible within the first two weeks of gestation.
- Over the next eight weeks, the embryo gradually develops its internal organs and external features and limbs. It begins to have recognizable human form, though it remains extremely small. Between the sixth and tenth week the brain shows some electrical activity.

- At the end of the eighth week, the embryo is technically a human fetus.
- At fourteen weeks, its sex can be determined.
- At 16 to 20 weeks, quickening occurs: the woman first perceives fetal movement.
- At 23 to 24 weeks, the fetus reaches viability, when it may be able to survive outside the uterus (or womb), though babies born that early are extremely premature and often suffer severe health problems if they survive.
- A full-term delivery is now considered to occur between 39 and 40 weeks since last menstrual period.

The Practice of Abortion

In the US, some 765,651 legal abortions occurred in 2010, most of them at week 13 or earlier (Figure 11.1).[1] Between 2008 and 2011, such abortions declined 13%. Women's reasons for seeking abortions included lack of appropriate partner, financial stress, responsibilities toward other family members, the interference of childrearing with work or school, and other inabilities to care for dependents. Abortion was also correlated with social and economic status, with a greater relative incidence among women below the poverty line.

The data also suggest that the physical and mental risk of a legal abortion for the woman is minimal, especially when performed during the first trimester. It causes one death in every million abortions, if performed by week 8, one per 29,000 at weeks 16–20, and one per 11,000 at week 21 or later. Nearly half of all abortions worldwide are unsafe and occur in developing countries where abortion is illegal, with only 6% elsewhere. Unsafe abortions

FIGURE 11.1   Abortion in the US in 2010

Performed at weeks 13 or earlier (91.9%, dots), 14-20 (6.9%, lines), and 21 or later (1.2%, black)

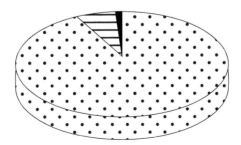

---

1   Pazol et al., 2013, available online at http://www.cdc.gov/mmwr/preview/mmwrhtml/ss6208a1.htm and Henshaw and Kost, 2008, available online at https://www.guttmacher.org/pubs/2008/09/23/TrendsWomenAbortions-wTables.pdf.

account for 13% of all maternal deaths worldwide. Every year 47,000 women die in the world from complications of such abortions.[2] If we focus on women's welfare alone, then, given the principle of beneficence, the data argue for the legal and moral permissibility of abortion. But the abortion debate is more complex. As we discuss next, it hinges also on different views about the fetus's moral standing and its right to the woman's assistance during pregnancy.

11.3 Against the Moral Permissibility of Abortion

Here we reconstruct moral objections to abortion based on either the sanctity of human life, the developmental continuity after conception, fetuses' potentiality to become paradigm persons, or the wrongness of depriving them of a future of value. These objections, if sound, would imply that typical abortions are serious moral wrongs.

The Sanctity of Life

As you may recall from Chapter 7, a plausible **Sanctity-of-Life doctrine** need not object to end-of-life measures under certain circumstances. Here we are interested in an objection to abortion that invokes that doctrine. It runs,

1. Life is sacred.
2. Abortion is the intentional termination of a life.

_____

3. Therefore, abortion is morally wrong.

Since premise (2) is uncontroversial, support for conclusion (3) hinges on (1). But this premise admits a conservative and a liberal interpretation. Of the two, it is only the conservative one that, if plausible, leads to (3).

The Conservative Sanctity-of-Life Doctrine

As discussed in Chapter 7, this version of the Sanctity-of-Life doctrine often rests on religious grounds. It takes human life to be sacred because it arises through God's direction of the order of nature, which bestows on it a certain divine stamp that warrants reverence. Life is God's gift, and its value derives from Him. As a result, abortion is a grave moral wrong, for it destroys that gift. Yet these reasons for the sacredness of human life can be an impediment to progress in the abortion debate since they presuppose that

1. God exists.
2. God confers value on human life.
3. The intentional termination of innocent human life is always seriously wrong.

_____

2 Guttmacher Institute, 2016, available online at http://www.guttmacher.org/pubs/fb_induced_ abortion.html.

Moving ahead in the abortion debate requires avoiding assumptions such as (1) and (2) since some reasonable people do question these. Furthermore, (3) is not universally accepted, even within the principal religious traditions. For example, not all Christians agree that intentionally terminating an innocent human life is always seriously wrong: for some justify terminations at the end or life, and even abortion. Their views in fact vary across faiths, and even within a single denomination. In addition, (3) is inconsistent with commonsense morality. Recall, for example, Dr. Cox, who provided euthanasia at his patient's request. His lenient sentence and the press coverage of his case suggest that many among the public consider some instances of intentional termination of an innocent human life permissible. All these suggest that the conservative Sanctity-of-Life argument above is unsound.

The Liberal Sanctity-of-Life Doctrine

For this doctrine, the sacredness of life consists of its commanding respect or being awe-inspiring. That is why its deliberate destruction is morally wrong. Or, as Ronald Dworkin puts it, it amounts to dishonoring "what ought to be honored" (1994: 74). We ordinarily believe that some things are valuable in this way: great art or the unspoiled beauty of nature, for instance. But if we are filled with awe at the power of a Rembrandt portrait or the beauty of the Rocky Mountains, and inclined therefore to say that they are valuable for their own sakes, it is plausible that we may likewise be awestruck by the phenomenon of human life. Thus,

> Life is sacred or inviolable because it is awe-inspiring.

If human life is sacred in this sense, then, since embryos and fetuses are human organisms, their lives are awe-inspiring and ought to be honored. Abortion is then a serious matter, nothing like a tonsillectomy (Dworkin, 1994: 34).

This is not to say that abortion is impermissible. The intrinsic value of fetal life, understood simply in terms of its capacity to inspire awe, might not always outweigh other reasons justifying abortion. Therefore, the liberal Sanctity-of-Life argument is compatible with the view that abortion is sometimes morally permissible.

Developmental Continuity

Among others, Pope John Paul II (1995) rests his critique of abortion on the claim that there is no significant difference early in life between each of the successive stages in a human organism's development. Thus, if a late human fetus does not have a right to life, neither does a newborn. For the same reason, if the newborn does not have it, neither does the 6-week-old infant, or the toddler, or the 6-year-old child. . . . or the mature adult. Since that is preposterous, the human organism must acquire a right to life at conception.

This **Developmental Continuity** argument trades on the vagueness of human development: there is no significant difference between, say, an 8-month-old fetus and one that is

7 months old, and between this and a 6-month-old fetus, and between that and a 5-month old fetus, and so on until we reach the zygote. The underlying reasoning here is

Since there is no significant difference in development between the human fetus at a later stage and at the stage preceding it, if it does not acquire the right to life at conception, it would never acquire it later in life.

But not all agree. For one thing, given the Appeal to Developmental Continuity, an unfertilized ovum and a nearby spermatozoon that are about to merge would have a right to life. After all, the ovum and nearby spermatozoon contain all relevant genetic materials for the future zygote. Even so, only at conception does a human organism begin to exist. The *discontinuity* between conception and what precedes it is such that the zygote, but not what precedes it, has a right to life.

A more serious problem for the Appeal to Developmental Continuity is that up until the fourteenth day of pregnancy a zygote may divide into identical twins. Until then, there is no single individual from conception that is the same bearer of a right to life as the individual that comes to have that right later. True, identical twinning is a rare phenomenon (Noonan, 1970). But since it does sometimes occur, the objection stands.

IMAGE 11.1
©iStockPhoto/koya79

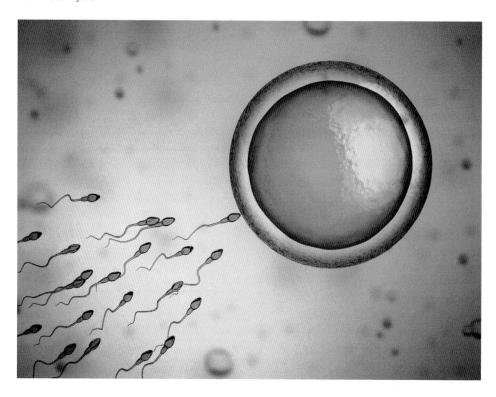

Furthermore, it is questionable that no line can be drawn marking the onset of full moral standing at a crucial point in fetal development. For Developmental Continuity theorists, such a line cannot be drawn at viability since that would make moral standing dependent on the level of technology available, which is implausible. After all, at present, survival outside the womb has been moved to roughly week 24. Soon medical advances might make survival possible at earlier stages. The problem with this reply is that, as discussed later in this chapter, there are other options besides viability for marking the onset of moral standing, including the acquisition of certain psychological capacities.

In addition, the Developmental Continuity Argument faces a slippery-slope objection: although it is true that incremental changes may make little difference between facts on a small scale, carried on to a greater extent they can result in large differences between the beginning point and end point. Light in the sky at dusk may not vary significantly from one minute to the next, but that does not mean there's no difference between day and night. Likewise, it is possible that the onset of, say, sentience marks a substantial change in the moral standing of the human fetus.

Kind Essentialism

According to Christopher Kaczor's **Kind Essentialism** (2011), fetuses share the essential properties of other *Homo sapiens* such as being oriented toward reason. As a result, like adult members of that natural kind, fetuses also have a right to life. For Kaczor, his view avoids the speciesism, under-inclusiveness and over-inclusiveness problems discussed earlier, because it considers rationality sufficient, but not necessary, for that standing. Thus, it can agree that

1. Some nonhumans may have full moral standing.
2. All humans have equal moral standing because they have the same essential properties.
3. It is morally wrong to kill permanently unconscious people because they still have those properties.
4. Spiders and worms don't have the same moral standing as humans because they belong to biological kinds that lack those essential properties.

Yet Kind Essentialism assumes that every *Homo sapiens* has a capacity for using, or disposition to use, reason. In fact, some don't have it and never will, owing to severe cognitive impairment. Among them are anencephalics and PVS patients. Furthermore, although many fetuses will develop rationality later, it is dubious that they have it in actuality. If Kaczor means that they potentially have it, then he is implicitly holding the position to be considered next.

Potentiality

Given the **Appeal to Potentiality**, the moral wrongness of abortion derives from the fetus's potential to become a person. This potentiality gives it the same moral rights actual persons have.

1. Persons have the right to life.
2. The human fetus is a potential person.

_____

3. Therefore, the human fetus has a right to life.

To critics of this argument, as famously noted by Aristotle, an acorn is potentially an oak tree only in the sense that it may, under propitious conditions, develop into an oak tree. But since it is *not* an oak tree yet, it may lack the properties of oak trees. Similarly, raisins develop out of grapes by a drying process, but their colors, shapes, and chemical and nutritional properties are different. Other counterexamples to the Potentiality Argument include: The US Vice President is a potential President.

1.   The US President has the power to veto a bill.
2.   The US Vice President is a potential president.

_____

3.   Therefore, the US Vice President has the power to veto a bill.

Clearly, premises (1) and (2) are true but conclusion (3) false. The Potentiality Argument is likewise invalid. Thus, although having a right to life is a property of paradigm persons, it need not be a property of the human fetus from conception. Even if the human fetus is potentially a person, it does not follow that it has that right.

But note that the active potentiality to be a person does carry moral implications. By contrast with passive potentiality, which requires outside causal intervention to become actuality, active potentiality does not. A being that presently lacks the complex psychological capacities typical of persons but has in itself all the elements needed for acquiring them is a potential person in the active sense—for example, an individual in dreamless sleep or temporarily unconscious. But since fetuses need the mother's assistance (her blood, hormones, nutrition, etc.) to become persons, their potentiality is passive. Objectors to the potentiality argument can now acknowledge that human fetuses have passive potentiality to become persons, while holding that only active potentiality can confer a right to life.

The Loss of a Valuable Future

Don Marquis's 1989 Future-Like-Ours Argument (FLOA)

The **Future-Like-Ours Argument** runs,

1.   The loss of the victim's valuable future is what makes killing prima facie morally wrong.
2.   A fetus usually has a valuable future.

_____

3.   Therefore, abortion is prima facie morally wrong.

Suppose (1) best explains the prima facie wrongness of killing a paradigm person. This premise, together with (2), entails that typical abortions are prima facie wrong. Since Marquis believes that fetuses generally have a valuable future in actuality, not potentially, the **FLOA** does not appear to rely on invalid reasoning of this sort:

1.   It is wrong to disobey police officers.

_____

2.   Therefore, it is wrong to disobey potential police officers.

Rather, the FLOA presupposes that, under normal circumstances, a human fetus will develop into a child and ultimately an adult who could come to value her experiences. Although the fetus cannot value its future *now*, for its future to be valuable, it is enough it could come to value it later.

At the same time, the FLOA allows for exceptions to the wrongness of killing in cases of fetuses that could not come to value their futures (e.g., severely compromised fetuses) and is consistent with the prohibition of killing those temporarily unable to value their futures (e.g., young children, infants, patients with depression or temporarily unconscious because they are sleeping, under anesthesia, etc.). In addition, the argument remains neutral about whether some nonhumans can have futures of value (Marquis, 1989: 30).

Objections to the FLOA

The FLOA assumes the numerical identity, as defined in Box 11.3, of each of us with a human embryo and fetus. Given this argument, the fetus is, from conception, the same individual that later becomes a newborn and eventually a paradigm person. But if we are essentially *minds*, an unborn human organism is one of us only after it develops certain psychological capacities, most likely after birth. And if we're essentially *biological organisms*, then it is only after two weeks of gestation, when identical twinning is no longer possible, that a human fetus is allegedly identical with a certain future adult. Otherwise, some adults would originate at conception and others after two weeks (the identical twins), which is implausible.

Another objection charges that if the FLOA were sound, then destroying skin cells would be wrong, since they could have a future of value by cloning. Contraception would too, since it precludes fertilization of embryos with a future of value. Yet Marquis can reply that skin cells or sperm and a nearby egg lack futures of values, something possible only until after conception. Be that as it may, deprivation of a valuable future is not the only factor determining the wrongness of killing. Common morality regards the death of a 20-year-old as more tragic than that of a fetus, suggesting that the victim's age and life plans have moral weight in explaining the wrongness of killing.

BOX 11.3 NUMERICAL IDENTITY

- Also called 'self-identity,' it is a relation between things that are one and the same—e.g., between Mark Twain and Samuel Clemens.

- By contrast, qualitative identity is a relation between things of the same class—e.g., between cars of the same make, model, color, etc.

Finally, Sinnott-Armstrong (1997) charges that the FLOA trades on an ambiguity in the expression "loss of something valuable." Not all losses of something valuable wrong the loser. Think of losing a prize in a fair competition: it makes no sense to say that the winner wronged you. Only the loss of goods to which you are morally entitled can wrong you. The fetuses' loss of valuable futures in abortion is morally wrong only if they already have a moral entitlement to their futures. Thus, the FLOA presupposes a certain stance on fetal moral standing, something that cannot be assumed without argument.

11.4 For the Moral Permissibility of Abortion

The positions outlined in this section argue that typical abortions are morally permissible. We group them according to the reasons they offer for that claim. Some focus on the fact that fetuses lack the psychological capacities typical of persons. Others leave the controversial issue of *fetal personhood* aside to argue that, even if fetuses are persons, abortion may still be morally permissible.

Skepticism about Fetal Personhood

Killing a paradigm person is generally a grave moral wrong for the victim's own sake. For arguments considered in this section, abortion cannot be wrong for the fetus's own sake, since fetuses lack the complex psychological capacities typical of paradigm persons. As a result, abortion is generally morally permissible except perhaps when the intentional termination of a fetus's life conflicts with the autonomous wishes of some people.

The Warren Argument

Mary Anne Warren first suggests a list of five conditions such that "any being which satisfies none of 1–5 is certainly not a person" (1973: 67):

1. Having consciousness of objects and events (whether external and/or internal to the being), and in particular the capacity to feel pain.
2. Being capable of reasoning—i.e., the *developed* capacity to solve new and relatively complex problems.
3. Being capable of self-motivated activity—i.e., activity which is relatively independent of either genetic or direct external control.
4. Having the capacity to communicate, by whatever means, messages of an indefinite variety of types, contents, and topics.
5. Possessing self-concepts and self-awareness, either individual, racial, or both.

In Warren's view, (1), (2), and maybe (3) "look like fairly good candidates for necessary conditions" of personhood, but fetuses satisfy none of the five conditions. Thus, they are not persons and lack the moral standing necessary for abortion to be morally forbidden.

Warren's view of personhood has two consequences: some beings widely accepted as persons might not be persons, and conversely, some nonhumans might be persons. Provided they satisfy her necessary and sufficient conditions, intelligent space aliens and future intelligent computers would be nonhuman persons. But human beings in utero or with profound cognitive deficits would not. For they don't satisfy those conditions. As a result, under certain circumstances, it is morally permissible to intentionally terminate the life of such human beings. Warren embraces that consequence, contending

> A man or woman whose consciousness has been permanently obliterated but who remains alive is a human being which is no longer a person; defective human beings, with no appreciable mental capacity, are not and presumably never will be people; and a fetus is a human being which is not yet a person. . . . (1973: 68)

But, as noted earlier, to say that infants or cognitively impaired individuals lack a right to life is very much at odds with common morality and runs head-on into the under-inclusiveness problem. This suggests that Warren's conditions are too demanding.

To resolve that problem, Warren (1973: 69) holds that even if infants are not persons with a right to life, killing them could still be wrong for other reasons—for example, the sentiments of affection and emotional attachment that infants typically arouse in adults, who generally care about the welfare of individual infants. In any such situation, killing the infant is an offense against the adults themselves. On this reply, then, there is ultimately a utilitarian reason—one concerning the promotion of the greatest happiness of the greatest number—that may explain why infants, though lacking a right to life, still could not be justifiably killed. But *not all infants* are lucky enough to be cared about. Notoriously, many are unwanted. Thus Warren's reply falls short of meeting the objection that would surely be raised by anyone sharing common intuitions about the wrongness of killing the cognitively disabled and unimpaired infants, even if unwanted.

The Tooley Argument

For Michael Tooley, what is necessary for having a right to life follows from what is necessary for having a right to anything. Ordinarily, when a person has a right, others have a prima facie duty not to violate it. But Tooley contends that "if an individual asks someone to destroy something to which he has a right, one does not violate his right to that thing if one proceeds to destroy it" (1972: 42). That is, an individual's moral right to something can be violated only if the individual desires that thing. Thus, my right to life can be violated only if I desire that I continue to exist. But then it is a necessary condition of my having a right to life that I'm capable of

- Desiring that I continue to exist, and
- Recognizing myself as a subject of experience.

These psychological states presuppose self-consciousness. To have awareness of myself, I must be in possession of concepts such as 'I' (oneself, the subject of the desire), 'being something that continues to exist,' and 'being a subject of experience.' Thus, a necessary condition of having a right to life is the *Self-Consciousness Requirement*:

> An organism possesses a serious right to life only if it possesses the concept of a self as a continuing subject of experiences and other mental states, and believes that it is itself a continuing entity (Tooley 1972: 45).

Given the Self-Consciousness Requirement, human fetuses and newborns lack a right to life, since clearly neither possesses such self-awareness and mental states. Yet since, given this argument, human beings with profound cognitive impairments also lack that right, Tooley also runs into the under-inclusiveness problem faced by Warren.

The Good Samaritan Argument

Unlike Warren and Tooley, Judith Thomson (1971) proposes a **Good Samaritan Argument (GSA)** for the moral permissibility of abortion that avoids the unsettled issue of fetal personhood. Given the GSA, the mother has no duty to provide the fetus with the assistance it needs to become viable even if the fetus is a person. If she chooses to do it by carrying her pregnancy to term, that would be nice, but it is not morally obligatory. It would be a Good Samaritan action: i.e., a praiseworthy but not morally required action.

The GSA

To support the GSA, Thomson offers the following thought experiment:

Plugged-In Violinist. One day you wake up in a hospital connected to a famous violinist who is unconscious. The hospital director informs you that you have been kidnapped by the Society of Music Lovers and hooked up to the violinist because he temporarily needs your kidneys to survive. After nine months he will be unplugged. You'll suffer no lasting harm.

Thomson regards this imaginary case of involuntary organ-sharing as analogous to a woman's situation during pregnancy. Surely, the violinist is a person with a right to life. Furthermore, although "you have a right to decide what happens in and to your body. . . . a person's right to life outweighs your right to decide what happens in and to your body" (Thomson, 1971: 76). Yet you are under no moral obligation to assist the violinist, since his right to life does not give him a *right* to your assistance. If you were to assist him for nine months, you would be a Good Samaritan: it would be kind of you, but not your duty. Thomson now argues:

1. Terminating a pregnancy with abortion is morally analogous to disconnecting the violinist.
2. Disconnecting the violinist is morally permissible.

    _____

3. Therefore, abortion is morally permissible.

The woman's terminating fetal assistance during pregnancy is analogous to your disconnecting the violinist because, by assumption, each of these situations features a person with a right to life who, to survive, needs assistance from someone who is under no obligation to assist. Thomson need not further argue that the mother's rights to bodily integrity and liberty are weightier that the human fetus's right to life. The same applies to your situation in *Plugged-In Violinist*. After all, a person's right to life does not create in others the duty to provide her with life support: the right to life is a negative right creating in others the duty not to be killed. But receiving assistance to survive is a positive, and therefore weaker, right. For the mother (or you), providing such support would be beyond the call of duty.

Objections to the GSA

Thomson's argument rests heavily on intuitions about *Plugged-In Violinist* and its similarity to the situation of the woman during pregnancy. But apparent dissimilarities include:

1.   A typical abortion is a *killing* of a human organism. In *Plugged-In Violinist*, the unplugging is a *letting die.*
2.   Unlike the violinist and you, the mother and her fetus are not total strangers. The duty to assist may vary accordingly.
3.   Unlike in *Plugged-In Violinist*, in pregnancy, the woman is responsible for the fetus's being in need of assistance (except in cases of rape or perhaps contraceptive failure).

Consider (1). While abortion is clearly a killing, unplugging the violinist (which Thomson regards as a killing) seems more a case of letting die. In killing someone, one takes an action that brings about the victim's death. By contrast, in letting die one refrains from taking an action that could prevent someone's death—that is, one is in a position to save the individual, but doesn't. Other things being equal, killing is often regarded as morally worse than letting die, though there is disagreement about this (especially, as we saw earlier, in connection with medically assisted death). Arguably, disconnecting the violinist would simply allow nature to take its course, so that the violinist would then die of his kidney ailment. The cause of his death would be renal failure, not your action. By contrast, in abortion the woman does more than fail to save the fetus: she deliberately and directly causes its death in the process of having it removed from her womb. (An exception would be an *extractive abortion*, in which the fetus dies as a foreseen but unintended consequence of hysterectomy, the surgical removal of the uterus.)

According to (2), by hypothesis, you and he are total strangers. As a result, the violinist's right-to-life may not include the right to use your body to survive. An unwanted pregnancy is a very different situation, since there is at least a *biological* relationship between the woman and her fetus. Parental relationships do actually involve a life-support obligation in some cases—as for instance, when parents have duties to save their children from potentially dangerous diseases, or to donate bone marrow to save a daughter or son with leukemia. Thus, what is justified in *Plugged-In Violinist* may be unjustified in an unwanted pregnancy.

(3) emphasizes another difference between *Plugged-In Violinist* and typical abortions: you have not caused the violinist's need for your life support. In a typical abortion, the unwanted pregnancy is not the result of rape or contraceptive failure. The biological parents have caused the fetus's need for life support. Since agents are ordinarily held responsible for any harm their actions cause, the GSA must assume that abortion causes no harm to the fetus. But this assumption brings the issues of fetal personhood that the GSA was supposed to avoid.

This problem, together with the noted disanalogies, weakens the GSA. At most, it offers a reason for considering abortion permissible in some *nonresponsibility situations* that are actually hard cases of abortion—for example, where the mother was raped, under-aged, or mentally impaired, and perhaps also where contraceptives failed. In none of these situations has the woman given informed consent to a sexual act resulting in a pregnancy.

▉ 11.5 Intermediate Views

For the positions we consider next, at some gestational point the fetus's moral standing is such that abortion becomes morally impermissible. But not all agree on the natural development that determines that moral standing. As a result, there are competing views about where to draw the line, and about moral permissibility of typical abortions.

Early Brain Activity

For Baruch Brody (1975), abortion becomes impermissible when the human fetus acquires whatever natural feature of human beings confers on them a right to life. That feature must be something that, when lost at death, determines the loss, at the same time, of the right to life. Brody's reasoning is:

1. The property that, when irreversibly lost at the end of life, determines the loss of the right to life is the same property that, when first acquired at the beginning of life, determines the acquisition of the right to life.
2. That property is whole-brain function.

   _____

3. Therefore, abortion becomes impermissible with the onset of whole-brain function.

Brody takes early brain activity to appear by the end of week six of gestation, though recent evidence suggests it occurs at week ten. Even thus amended, his **Early-Brain-Activity Argument**, if sound, still implies that many typical abortions are morally forbidden, since they happen after week ten.

To be sound, however, its premises need plausibility. And why think that it is whole-brain function that determines the onset or loss of the right to life? After all, as we saw in Chapter 6, there are alternatives to understanding human death exclusively as the permanent loss of whole-brain function. Furthermore, why think that a *single* natural property makes such a moral difference? There are other properties lost at death that might also be relevant to losing the right to life—for example, *consciousness*, something lost at death and ordinarily acquired in early life, but not as early as week ten of gestation. As we see next, by then there is no *organized* electrical activity in the fetus's cerebral cortex, of the kind that could support some form of consciousness.

Organized Cortical Activity

According to David Boonin, abortion is permissible in early stages of fetal development until the onset of integrated electrical activity that can be detected in the cerebral cortex "of the sort that produces recognizable EEG readings" (2003: 115). Such **organized cortical activity,** the hardware necessary for consciousness, appears by weeks 25 and 32 of gestation. Until then, abortion is permissible because the fetus lacks even the *potential* for entertaining conscious desires, such as that it continue to live. Since typical abortions occur early in pregnancy (most during the first trimester), they involve the killing of fetuses that lack such potential. But with the onset of organized cortical activity, when a fetus has the hardware to develop the desire to continue to live, abortion is generally forbidden.

Although Boonin agrees with Tooley on the moral significance of having desires of that sort, unlike Tooley he thinks that the potential to entertain them is enough for abortion to become morally impermissible. His argument does not have the consequence that abortions are *always* permissible. It also avoids the under-inclusiveness problem, because it does not entail that, for example, *neonatal euthanasia* is always morally permissible. But, as discussed above, Appeals to Potentiality are problematic. Boonin needs to say more about the moral significance of acquiring a passive potentiality for consciousness. This is the only type the fetus can acquire with the onset of organized brain activity, because it couldn't develop consciousness without the woman's assistance in carrying the pregnancy to term. Furthermore, appeals to potentiality face the invalidity objection: although having consciousness may make a moral difference, having the potential for it need not (as argued above, a Vice President is potentially a President, but lacks the President's powers and rights).

Fetal Interests

For Interests theorists, the human fetus may not have the same right to life we have. Even so, it may still have moral standing based on interests. A being with interests has a *stake* or *welfare of its own* that can be promoted or set back. Since acts or omissions by others can advance or undermine the fetus's interests, it matters morally how it is treated. There is a straightforward connection between interests and rights: rights are claims that protect interests. The right to life protects people's interest in remaining alive.

Clearly, it does not matter morally how we treat a table or a rock. Neither has an interest that can be promoted or set back by our actions, although it might matter to the table's owner or to environmentalists. In the case of a sentient creature, however, it matters morally to the creature itself how it is treated. The creature has a stake in its own wellbeing. So there is a straightforward connection between sentience, interests, and moral standing.

The interests of sentient creatures vary, since some have sophisticated mental capacities, and therefore more at stake, others only the capacity to feel pleasure and pain and therefore less at stake. Whales have more interests than mice, thus other things being equal killing a whale is more seriously wrong than killing a mouse. When human fetuses are pre-sentient, they do not have moral standing, thus typical abortions are morally permissible. But after 25 to 30 weeks of gestation, human fetuses acquire sentience, and also interests proportionate to their degree of consciousness. Their interests are not, however, comparable to those of paradigm persons, who have a richer mental life, including a concept of the self as a subject of experiences existing over time and the desire to remain alive. Therefore, a conscious human fetus might have moral standing but might not have the right to life of paradigm persons. Consequently, late abortion might also be morally permissible.

Yet Interests theorists cannot consistently assert that typical abortions are morally permissible, given their need to avoid this version of the under-inclusiveness problem: imagine aliens with interests that can be promoted or undermined, but no sentience (think of *Star Trek*'s Spock). Interests theorists cannot regard sentience as necessary for having interests. For then these beings would have no moral standing. To accommodate such scenarios, sentience need be only sufficient for having interests and therefore moral standing. Now

Interests theorists must admit that pre-sentient fetuses can have moral standing, acquired through a route other than sentience. As a result, the **Interests View** cannot rule out the moral wrongness of typical abortions.

An additional problem comes from Steinbock's (1992) imaginary case:

Pre-sentient Baby is born perfectly healthy except for a brainstem anomaly which causes it to lack consciousness (including feelings of pleasure and pain). The anomaly can be corrected with simple surgery.

Should the procedure be performed? Yes, according to common morality. But given the Interests View, since the baby lacks sentience, she has no interests that can be harmed by not performing it. Interests theorists have responded that (1) Pre-sentient Baby has potential to become sentient, and (2) such potential gives her an interest in remaining alive (DeGrazia, 2011: 30). But then we have to ascribe to the zygote a similar interest, for it also has the potential to become conscious with some external assistance.

11.6 Chapter Summary

This chapter explores a spectrum of views about the morally permissibility of typical abortions (for a roadmap, see Figure 11.2). At one extreme, since the human fetus is taken to have a right to life from conception, abortion amounts to a serious moral wrong. In support of this view are appeals to a conservative Sanctity-of-Life doctrine, Developmental Continuity, Potentiality, and Marquis's Future-Like-Ours Argument. At the other extreme are those who vindicate the moral permissibility of abortion at any time during pregnancy. Some focus on undermining the conclusion that abortion is morally forbidden because the human fetus has a right to life. Opponents of this premise argue that the fetus fails to meet some psychological conditions necessary for having a moral standing that includes a right to life, whether these be having certain cognitive and social abilities (Warren) or self-consciousness (Tooley). Also at this extreme of the spectrum is Thomson's Good Samaritan Argument (GSA), with its *Plugged-In-Violinist* counterexample designed to show that even if the fetus is a person, the woman is under no moral obligation to carry the pregnancy to term. But not all views on the morality of abortion fall in the extremes. Intermediate views claim instead that at some point in pregnancy the human fetus acquires a moral standing such that abortion becomes morally forbidden. The main question here concerns which point in fetal development is the point where abortion stops being morally permissible: if it happens with the development of early brain activity, most typical abortions are forbidden; but if it happens with the onset of organized cortical activity or sufficient interests, then they are permissible.

Although the moral permissibility of typical abortions has proved a divisive issue, this chapter suggests some promising directions for moving forward. For one thing, while the arguments in the extremes tend to rest on vulnerable premises and thus have limited scope (e.g., the GSA) or fail altogether (e.g., the Appeal to Developmental Continuity), intermediate positions face more tractable objections. Furthermore, attempts at supporting a side in this debate by relying on some psychological capacities typical of persons easily runs into either under-inclusiveness (Warren, Tooley) or over-inclusiveness (Kind Essentialism). The Interests View attempts to avoid under-inclusiveness by regarding sentience as only sufficient for moral standing. But that opens the way for critics of abortion to reassert the moral standing of pre-sentient fetuses which they may acquire just by being human organisms. In the end, no position in the abortion debate can be shown conclusive. Yet the fact that there are reasoned arguments on both sides recommends tolerant public policies, an issue we reassume in Chapters 12 and 13.

FIGURE 11.2   Arguments for and Against Typical Abortions

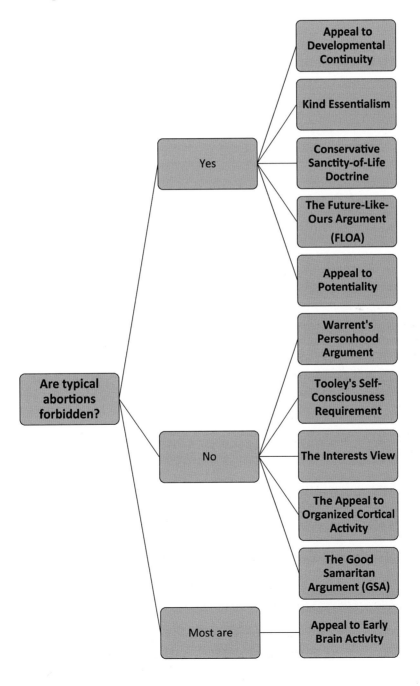

11.7 Study Aids

Key Words

Appeal to Developmental Continuity, 220
Appeal to Potentiality, 208
Early-Brain-Activity Argument, 218
Future-Like-Ours Argument (FLOA), 212
Good Samaritan Argument (GSA), 216
Interests View, 220
Kind Essentialism, 211
Organized-Cortical-Activity Argument, 218
Sanctity-of-Life doctrine, 208
Skepticism about fetal personhood, 214
Typical/hard cases of abortion, 205

Questions and Cases for Further Consideration

1.   What, if anything, is wrong with this argument: People should be left to make their own decisions on matters that concern them most. So, whether to terminate an unwanted pregnancy is a matter to be decided by the parents. Physicians, courts of law, and even society have no business with it.

2.   *In* Planned Parenthood v Casey *(1992) the US Supreme Court rejected a requirement of spousal notification for obtaining an abortion but upheld as mandatory a 24-hour waiting period for the sake of obtaining the woman's valid consent. Although* Casey *is generally consistent with* Roe v Wade, *it authorizes state regulation of abortion at early stages of pregnancy, a clear departure from* Roe. *Such regulations are permissible when "rationally related" to a legitimate state interest, and do not impose an "undue burden" on the woman's right to an abortion.* In your view, is state regulation of abortion consistent with *Roe*? Why might consent to an abortion require a mandatory 24-hour waiting period? Which cases, if any, should be exempt from state regulation?

3.   *In* Hodgson v Minnesota *(1990), the US Supreme Court upheld a Minnesota state law requiring parental notification for minors seeking abortions. The statute amounts to an exception to the medical confidentiality rule for cases in which the patient is an underage woman seeking an abortion.* What might be said for and against this legislation? Is it consistent with *Roe*? Should a minor's early abortion be held morally the same as typical abortions?

4.   *In 2012 an Argentine woman's abortion made headlines. A 32-year-old* human-trafficking victim *who had been forced into a prostitution ring was ten weeks pregnant when rescued by the police. She immediately sought an abortion on grounds of rape. But there was no evidence of rape, in the usual sense of the word, so, given Argentina's highly restrictive*

abortion laws, she had to apply to the courts for judicial permission. The judge refused to grant it, and the case was appealed. Ultimately the Supreme Court ruled her abortion legal, guaranteeing immunity from prosecution to doctors and nurses. But initially, health care providers remained reluctant to perform it. What might support the lower court's and providers' decision? If the right to life begins at conception, would it matter morally how this fetus was conceived? How might Kind Essentialism and the Good Samaritan Argument be brought to bear on the case? What would each say? Which of these would better capture what needed to be done in this case?

5. *In 2014, the Supreme Court of the United States ruled unconstitutional a Massachusetts law barring anti-abortion activists within 35 feet of abortion clinics, on the grounds that it restricted their free speech. But Chief Justice John G. Roberts Jr. held permissible a New York City ordinance making it a crime to obstruct access to an abortion provider or to follow and harass patients within 15 feet thereof. This ordinance, however, only angers New Yorkers on both sides of the abortion debate. For protesters, it infringes on their free speech. For patients and health care providers, it fails to protect them from harassment and attacks, since there is no clearly marked protest-free zone.*[3] Whose perspective, if either, seems more reasonable? Might there be alternatives that respect both protesters' and women's constitutional rights? In your view, which are the best moral grounds abortion critics may adduce to persuade women not to go into the clinic? And which may be invoked by abortion defenders seeking protective legislation?

6. *In 1998, two physicians in Western Australia were arrested for having performed, two years earlier, an abortion requested by a Māori woman who then stored her fetus in her freezer. She planned to take it to New Zealand for a proper burial in accordance with Māori tradition, so she intended the storage as only temporary. But the local constabulary in Australia took a dim view of storing an aborted human fetus in a refrigerator. The physicians who abetted it were held to be accomplices in a criminal act, along with the woman herself.* Was there anything immoral about what they did? What might either version of the Sanctity-of-Life doctrine say in this case? Should culturally or religiously motivated actions like this be illegal?

Suggested Readings*

*Boonin, David, *A Defense of Abortion*. Cambridge: Cambridge University Press, 2003.
    Comprehensive analysis of the abortion debate. Provides support for Thomson 1971.
Brody, Baruch A., *Abortion and the Sanctity of Human Life: A Philosophical View*. Cambridge: MIT Press, 1975.
    Argues that measurable brain activity is the property that confers a right to life. When acquired early in pregnancy, abortion usually becomes morally impermissible.
Dworkin, Ronald, *Life's Dominion*. New York: Vintage, 1994.

---

3 Adapted from Benjamin Muellers, "New York's Abortion Protest Law Is Praised by Justices, but Few Others," *New York Times*, 7/30/2014.
* Asterisks mark readings available online. See links on the companion website.

Defense of a liberal Sanctity-of-Life argument, holding that abortion is permissible but should be rare because of the tension between human life's inherent value and the woman's personal autonomy.

*Pope John Paul II, "The Unspeakable Crime of Abortion," *Evangelium Vitae*, 3/25/1995. Standard source for the appeal to Developmental Continuity against abortion.

*Marquis, Don, "Why Abortion Is Immoral," *Journal of Philosophy* 86.4, 1989: 183–202 (references to reprint in Dwyer and Feinberg, 1997).
Locus classicus for the Future-Like-Ours Argument.

*Noonan, John T. Jr, "An Almost Absolute Value in History," in *The Morality of Abortion: Legal and Historical Perspectives*, pp. 51–9. Cambridge: Harvard University Press, 1970.
Critique of abortion based to some extent on the Kind Essentialist assumption that fetuses have a right to life, since from conception they have the human genetic code. But see Kaczor (2011) for a book-length defense of Kind Essentialism.

*Sinnott-Armstrong, Walter, "You Can't Lose What You Ain't Never Had: A Reply to Marquis on Abortion," *Philosophical Studies* 96, 1997: 59–72.
Objects to Marquis's 1989 Future-Like-Ours Argument. Since some actions causing the loss of something valuable do not wrong the loser, more is needed for the claim that abortion is wrong for the fetus's own sake.

*Thomson, Judith J., "A Defense of Abortion," *Philosophy & Public Affairs* 1, 1971: 47–66.
Influential defense of abortion. Hinges on whether the mother has a duty to assist the fetus.

*Tooley, Michael, "Abortion and Infanticide," *Philosophy & Public Affairs* 2, 1972: 37–65 (references to reprint in Dwyer and Feinberg, 1997).
Proposes a self-consciousness requirement for having a right to life, contending that no fetuses or young infants meet it.

*Warren, Mary Anne, "On the Moral and Legal Status of Abortion," *The Monist* 57, 1973: 43–61 (references to reprint in Dwyer and Feinberg, 1997).
Argues that abortion is permissible because fetuses lack the psychological conditions necessary for personhood.

12 Abortion in the Hard Cases

Learning Objectives

In reading this chapter you will

▸ Reflect on the morality of late-term abortion and of abortion to save the mother's life or health, fetal defects, and sex selection.

▸ Learn some facts about abortion in those cases and the common moral intuitions about them that conflict with the views of abortion critics or defenders.

▸ Determine which of those cases are hard for critics and which for defenders.

▸ Evaluate the critics' and the defenders' responses to objections from those hard cases.

I N CHAPTER 11 WE examined views on both sides of the debate about the morality of abortion in the **typical case** of an unwanted pregnancy at an early stage. In this chapter we consider how abortion for other reasons or later in pregnancy, the so-called **hard cases**, challenges those views. Discussed here are late-term abortion and abortion for fetal defects, the mother's endangerment, and sex selection. While some of these are hard cases for abortion critics, others are so for abortion defenders.

■ 12.1 Sherri Finkbine's Choices

In 1962, Sherri Finkbine, the host of a children's television show in Phoenix, Arizona, was in the early stages of her fifth pregnancy when, without consulting her physician, she sought to relieve her nausea by taking a medication available over the counter in Europe. But unknown to her, its active ingredient, thalidomide, causes birth defects, such as missing limbs, blindness, deafness, and defective internal organs. When she learned about this, her doctor and a medical committee concurred that she was eligible for a therapeutic abortion, even though nearly all abortion was illegal in the US at the time. Eager to warn other women about the dangers of thalidomide, Mrs. Finkbine contacted the local newspaper and told her story, on condition of anonymity. But the paper printed a sensationalist story, revealing the name of its protagonist, and as a result, she gained national notoriety. The medical committee that had authorized her abortion, now understandably focused on following the letter of the law, rescinded its approval, and the hospital canceled her appointment for the abortion. She ultimately obtained an abortion in Sweden, on the rationale of safeguarding her mental health. The aborted fetus had only one arm and no legs, and its sex could not be determined.

■■■

Widely distributed in the late 1950s and early 1960s, thalidomide soon became implicated in birth defects ranging from mild to severe. Even today pharmaceutical companies that marketed it at the time without proper trials are held accountable by the courts. As recently as 2013, US District Judge Paul Diamond rejected a statute of limitations appeal by Grunentahl GMBH, the German company that introduced thalidomide in the US in the late 1950s. The plaintiffs, about 50 thalidomide survivors, alleged that the company either knew about the risks, or neglected to conduct proper research.[1]

The fact that Mrs. Finkbine learned about possible anomalies caused by thalidomide gave strong support to her request to terminate the pregnancy. Although it is true that patients' valid requests for medical interventions are neither legally nor morally binding in the way their refusals are, given that thalidomide's side effects were known at the time, the evidence then available supported her decision to have a **therapeutic abortion**. The health care providers first authorized it but then changed their minds in what appeared to be a response to institutional pressure. They thus failed to discharge a professional duty not to abandon or break contracts with patients. Furthermore, given the rationale for her abortion, their reversal might have caused Finkbine uncompensated psychological harm.

On the other hand, it could be argued that **fetal defects** were not recognized at the time as a legal reason for the permissibility of abortion, and that asking health care providers to break the law, in a democratic society whose legal system they accept, is an unreasonable request. Morality cannot be so demanding that it requires health care providers to break the law. Recall that before *Roe* in 1973, fetuses at all stages of gestation were protected by American law. As recently as the late 1960s, abortion was a felony in 49 states of the US, with New Jersey alone considering it a high misdemeanor. Yet even in that restrictive environment, some abortions were nonetheless held morally permissible: viz., when necessary to save the mother's life or health, or when the pregnancy resulted from rape or incest. Sherri Finkbine's case was influential in extending that list to include abortion for fetal defects. In 1967, the American Medical Association recognized abortion for any of these reasons as justifiable. Since the public and health care providers generally agree about this, abortion for those reasons are **hard cases** facing critics who think that the intentional killing of a fetus is never justifiable. A type of abortion is hard for critics or defenders when their views have difficulty explaining away some common moral intuitions about abortions of that type. Some types of abortion will present this problem to abortion critics, others to abortion defenders. Intuitions that conflict with the critics' view concern abortion in cases of rape, underage mother, severe fetal impairment, and to save the mother's life or health.

Defenders of abortion, on the other hand, find their view challenged by intuitions about, for example, abortion for sex selection or for frivolous reasons. These are hard cases

---

1 "US Judge Rejects Pharmaceutical Companies' Attempt to Dismiss Thalidomide Cases," Hagens Berman website, 9/27/2013.

FIGURE 12.1 Hard Cases of Abortion

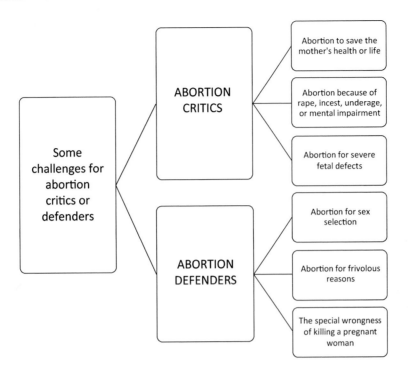

for them because their view commits them to a generally permissive stance, holding that such practices are morally acceptable, when many find them objectionable. Also, intuitions about the wrongness of killing a pregnant woman, especially in the third trimester when it often counts as two crimes, are difficult to explain away if, as some defenders maintain, abortion is permissible at any stage of gestation. Of course, it is only extreme positions on both sides of the abortion debate that face objections from hard cases. In what follows, we consider two hard cases for such critics and two for such defenders. The reader can determine why the other cases listed in Figure 12.1 are also hard.

12.2 Two Hard Cases for Abortion Critics

Abortion to Save the Mother's Life or Health

In some circumstances, a pregnancy may endanger a woman's health or even life. Consider this case:

Savita Halappanavar, a 31-year-old Indian dentist who had a practice in Ireland, was seventeen weeks pregnant when she suffered a miscarriage in October 2012. She repeatedly asked doctors at University Hospital, Galway, for an abortion, but, although they conceded that the fetus was not viable, they refused to perform one because fetal heartbeat was present. As a result of her untreated miscarriage, Mrs. Halappanavar contracted septicemia leading to multiple organ failure and died. News of her death brought an outcry from both sides in the abortion debate. Many people in Ireland called for amending the law, even when a 1992 Supreme Court ruling already allowed exceptions to the abortion ban where "a pregnant woman's life was at risk because of pregnancy, including the risk of suicide." In 2013 a new bill was signed into law by President Michael Higgins authorizing abortion whenever necessary to save the woman's life or when she is in danger of taking her own life (its most contested provision). The Catholic Church, whose doctrine is influential in Ireland, opposed the bill.

Abortion for women in this condition seems permissible, given the different moral standings of mother and fetus (Chapter 11), and the health care providers' obligations of beneficence (i.e., to prevent serious harm to the woman) and respect for autonomy (when she has made a valid request for an abortion). But particularly relevant to the case is the woman's **right to self-defense** when abortion is the only way of preventing serious harm to her. According to a principle underlying this claim, an aggressor's threat of death or serious bodily harm can justify the use of deadly force in response if there is no other way to deflect the attack. In Ms. Halappanavar's case, the 'aggressor' was the miscarried fetus.

But for critics who consider abortion an absolute wrong, the fetus is a person with a right to life, and in cases where its natural development threatens the woman's life or health, it is an **innocent threat**, so that the use of deadly force is morally forbidden. The Natural Law tradition, for example, distinguishes innocent from **guilty threats** whose propensity to cause serious harm renders them culpable and gives the targeted potential victim a moral right to defend herself in ways proportionate to the threat.

Even so, as you may recall from Chapter 2, the *Principle of Double Effect* can help Natural Law theorists to vindicate common morality's intuition that an abortion to save the mother's health or life is morally permissible. It would be so provided

- The death of the fetus is the only alternative available,
- It is not a mere means to the good end (to save the mother), and
- It is a foreseen but unintended consequence of the medical effort to save her life.

Yet as illustrated by John Finnis (1994), this reasoning fails to justify some cases of abortion to save the mother's life or health that seem morally permissible. Finnis justifies abortion for ectopic pregnancy, where the aggressor is a normal fetus that has implanted in a fallopian tube (threatening a lethal hemorrhage), provided the intention is to resolve this medical condition and there is no alternative. At the same time, for Finnis, abortion when the pregnancy poses a risk to a woman with a weak heart is impermissible, because here the termination is intended and a means to the good end. The intention is to kill the fetus to save the mother's life. He also thinks impermissible abortion to save a suicidal mother, because there are other treatment options—something not always true as a matter of medical fact. In any event, these sharply differing verdicts are a problem for Natural Law abortion critics, since no acceptable moral view should issue different moral verdicts in relevantly similar situations. Furthermore, in cases involving a pregnancy that endangers a woman's life, making a decision about the moral permissibility of an abortion should not drive parents and health care providers to double-effect reasoning and its often obscure speculation about intentions, means, and ends.

IMAGE 12.1
©iStockPhoto/Linda Epstein

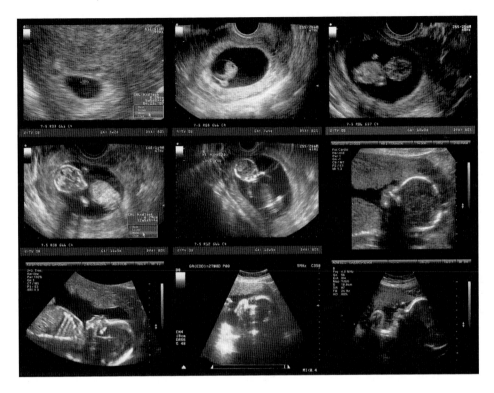

Abortion for Fetal Defects

The life prospects of neonates born with some disorders detectable during pregnancy can be very grim. But new forms of medical intervention and therapies available during pregnancy, such as corrective intrauterine surgery, have lowered the number of affected neonates. Also contributing to this tendency is progress in prenatal screening and diagnostic testing, which has increased the number of terminations of pregnancy for fetal defects. Abortions for fetal defects and to save the mother's life or health are therapeutic abortions. Before considering why abortions for fetal defects are a hard case for abortion critics, let's first have a quick look at some disorders detectable *in utero* that commonly lead to such abortions.

Some Facts about Congenital Disorders

Congenital disorders or anomalies are health impairments *present at birth*. Some produce long-term disabilities that impact not only the infants and their families, but also the health care system and society at large. They range from mild to severe. According to the World Health Organization (see also Figure 12.2), in 2014 approximately one neonate in 33 had a congenital disorder, totaling 3.2 million neonates globally. Together with conditions such as preterm complications and neonatal infections, they accounted for 2.7 million infant deaths in 2010.

Disorders such as neural tube defects and Down syndrome can now be detected during pregnancy. When this happens, the expectation often is a therapeutic abortion. In order to see why parents and health care givers then face a difficult decision, let's have a quick look at these disorders. Anencephaly and spina bifida are neural tube defects originated during the first month of gestation, when the fetus's neural tube forms and must close to allow the development of the brain and skull in the upper part, the spinal cord and vertebrae in the lower part. Anencephaly results from the neural tube's failure to close completely in the upper part. Born without portions of the brain, anencephalic babies are not only blind and deaf, but can never be conscious. If they have a working brain stem, they may retain spontaneous functions such as breathing and heartbeat, and have reflex responses to touch. Most of them are stillborn, and those born alive generally die within hours or days of birth. There is neither a treatment to improve their poor prognosis nor a known cause for the onset of the disorder during fetal development (though maternal malnourishment is thought to play a part). In spina bifida, the neural tube enveloping the spinal cord fails to close properly during the first month of fetal development. This typically causes cognitive and developmental impairments, incontinence of bowel and bladder and a number of physical disabilities, including

FIGURE 12.2   Global Neonatal Deaths in 2013

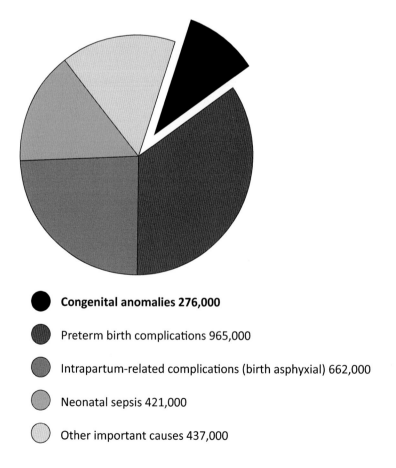

● **Congenital anomalies 276,000**

● Preterm birth complications 965,000

● Intrapartum-related complications (birth asphyxial) 662,000

● Neonatal sepsis 421,000

○ Other important causes 437,000

restrictions in mobility and paralysis of the lower limbs in varying degrees. The severity of impairments varies, with myelomeningocele presenting the most serious. According to the US National Library of Medicine, myelomeningocele affects one out of 4,000 infants in the US.[2]

Another type of congenital disorder is Down syndrome, which results from an extra chromosome or 'trisomy' for chromosome 21 (hence its alternative name, 'Trisomy 21'). It is characterized not only by mental impairment ranging from mild to severe, but also by deficits such as hearing loss, difficulties in verbal expression, and higher risks of congenital heart disorders, leukemia, and gastrointestinal anomalies. As discussed in Chapter 9, parental fears of social stigma, negative implications for the psychological development of siblings, and the burdens of caring for an infant with Down syndrome were reasons fueling some controversial decisions to forgo life-saving treatment, which in turn prompted deep changes in legal and moral reasoning about end-of-life measures for such newborns. Today Down syndrome can be detected prenatally through screening and diagnostic tests. When the condition is diagnosed, about 90% of fetuses are aborted.[3]

Abortion for Fetal Defects Is Permissible

Reasons supporting abortion for fetal defects are generally utilitarian. Consider a scenario in which a routine prenatal screening of a pregnant woman reveals that her fetus may have severe impairments—something later confirmed by diagnostic tests. The future infant will be blind and deaf, as well as quadriplegic and in pain whenever touched. It will also almost certainly have severe mental impairment. Utilitarian considerations suggest that bringing such an impaired individual into the world would increase the total amount of pain, both physical and psychological, and since a world with *less pain* is a *better* world, it would follow that the abortion is not only permissible but mandatory. Caring and fairness towards the future disabled child and its family support the same conclusion, for it would be unfair for the infant herself to have to endure a life of only suffering—as it would be also for those who would have to bear most of the burden of her care.

Fueling these arguments is the view that severe impairments are harms for those who have them and for their families, held by disabled persons and their parents who have acted as plaintiffs in lawsuits known as **wrongful-birth** or **wrongful-life actions** against health care providers. In a wrongful-birth action, the plaintiffs, usually the parents and/or child, allege that the birth of an impaired child could have been prevented by avoiding conception or terminating a pregnancy, had the providers not been negligent. Such negligence may consist of a failure to inform prospective parents about their likelihood of having an impaired child, or to conduct proper prenatal screening and testing. Either way, the result is an injurious deprivation of parental choice, as exemplified by this case.

In *Berman v Allan* two obstetricians faced legal charges for neglecting to inform Ms. Berman about the availability of screening and diagnostic tests for Down syndrome, which her baby had. The court awarded the Bermans compensation under the tort of wrongful birth, whereby the

---

2   US National Library of Medicine. "Myelomeningocele," 11/3/2015. https://medlineplus.gov/ency/article/001558.htm.

3   Mark L. Schrad, "Does Down Syndrome Justify Abortion," *New York Times*, 9/4/2015.

injury is the parents' deprivation of a choice. But it rejected the Bermans' wrongful-life action filed on behalf of their child. In an action of this sort, the injury consists, not in interfering with parental choice, but in enabling a severely disabled child to come into existence.

Here the court found the physicians culpable for wrongful birth but rejected the Bermans' contention that the case involved wrongful life. In wrongful-life litigation, the cause of action is the tort that, due to medical malpractice, a child was born into a life of suffering rather than not having being born at all. Such lawsuits are generally dismissed because the courts don't wish to engage in speculative philosophical assessments of whether a child's nonexistence is better than her existence with a very low quality of life.

Abortion for Fetal Defects Is Forbidden

Critics of abortion may insist on the wrongness of the practice for fetal defects, because of the uncertainty of judgments about the quality of life of a future child when fetal defects are detected during pregnancy. Consider myelomeningocele, the most severe type of spina bifida. Anecdotal and survey evidence from adults with myelomeningocele suggests that these patients' quality of life is not always as poor as some think (Davis, 1983; Barry, 2010).

Similar reasons can be offered against abortion for Down syndrome. In 2014, Richard Dawkins, a celebrated evolutionary biologist at Oxford, endorsed such abortions in his Twitter response to a woman who wondered what to do if she were to learn that her fetus had Down syndrome. "Abort it and try again," tweeted Dawkins. "It would be immoral to bring it into the world if you have the choice. . . ." But to BBC journalist Caroline White, whose son has Down syndrome, Dawkins's remarks were offensive. She argued that Dawkins's view was probably formed at a "time when disabled people and people with Down's were labeled and then hidden away, never given the chance to integrate, reach their full potential or form meaningful relationships with their wider community." White invokes anecdotal evidence from her son against such prejudicial assumptions about the quality of life of people with Down syndrome. More generally, the strategy can be used against the utilitarian argument for abortion for fetal defects based on the poor quality of life of people with certain disabilities. But since both sides make quality-of-life judgments, their arguments seem inconclusive.

An argument against abortion for fetal defects that avoids such judgments is Christopher Kaczor's (2011: 180). It notes that no one would seriously argue that a 6-year-old child should be killed because he is partially paralyzed. But then, given that the development of a human being is continuous from conception, it follows that killing a 6-month-old fetus with the same disability—indeed *any* disabled fetus—is equally wrong. However, what is permissible for a 6-month-old fetus need not be permissible in the same way for a 6-year-old child. As noted in Chapter 11, that children develop out of fetuses does not entail that what applies to children applies equally to fetuses. After all, children and fetuses need not have comparable psychological capacities and interests. Those who take these considerations to bear on moral standing can insist that, although it is morally wrong to kill a 6-year-old child because he is partially paralyzed, it might not be morally wrong to abort a 6-month-old fetus because it has a congenital disorder. Therefore, this argument too fails to provide conclusive reasons against common-morality's intuition that abortion for fetal defects is morally permissible.

12.3 Two Hard Cases for Abortion Defenders

Abortion for Sex Selection

Now that the sex of a fetus can be discovered by prenatal testing, parental decisions to terminate a pregnancy are sometimes affected by the desire for a child of a certain sex. Fetuses of
the 'wrong' sex are simply aborted. The practice falls into the category of

---

Sex-selective abortion (SSA)

Any elective abortion used as a method of birth control to produce an offspring of the
desired sex.

Since SSA is a post-conception method, it raises special moral issues for abortion defenders. Some of these issues also affect preconception methods discussed in Chapter 14. They
involve feminist concerns about medical interventions that in practice favor the birth of male
children, given the data from both developed and developing countries (especially in China,
Armenia, and Azerbaijan).

The SSA problem for defenders of abortion arises for those who think that, in the first
two trimesters of pregnancy, abortion is morally permissible *for whatever reason*. When the
destruction of a fetus because of its sex occurs during that period, they must find it justified
whatever the parents' motivation. But common morality has it that SSA's motivation renders
the practice morally wrong. Thus, these abortion defenders must either explain away that
intuition or change their views on abortion.

To explain away the intuition they may either:

1. Deny that SSA is morally wrong by justifying the practice in certain contexts, for exam-
    ple, when the family already has two female children and wants a boy this time.
2. Hold that SSA is wrong, but for reasons that have nothing to do with abortion.

We have more to say about (1) in connection with our discussion of procreative freedom in
Chapter 14. Our concern here is (2), which takes SSA's wrongness to derive from some bad
consequences likely to result from the practice. One such consequence is sex ratio imbalance,
already a problem in countries where SSA systematically pursues male offspring. In China
today there are approximately 121 boys to every 100 girls. If this trend continues, that could
be a harmful development, since men will find it more difficult to find mates of the opposite
sex, and prostitution and human trafficking rates may then rise significantly. Another harmful consequence of SSA is that, since the aborted fetuses in some countries are nearly always
female, SSA might implicitly devalue women. The abortion defender can invoke these bad
outcomes to concur on the wrongness of SSA, even if the aborted fetuses are not persons and
have only minimal moral standing or none at all.

Given these replies, one could be a defender of abortion and yet argue that SSA amounts
to sexism or throws the ratio of women to men in a society out of balance in a potentially
harmful way. But such imbalance and prejudice could be corrected through public policy.

Furthermore, they merely suggest that SSA is prudentially wrong, without addressing its moral aspect. Abortion defenders still need to explain away the intuition that SSA seems morally wrong given the motivation behind the practice.

Late-Term Abortion

If moral standing increases with fetal development, the loss of a developed fetus is worse than the loss of an early fetus or an embryo. The onset of consciousness is a turning point that occurs between weeks 25 and 32 of gestation, when an electroencephalograph can detect organized electrical activity in the cerebral cortex. Owing in part to this fact about human development, and also to the rising influence of religious conservatism in public policy, many have called for strict state regulation of abortion after week 20, with some possible exceptions for woman endangerment or fetal defects. But it is not these exceptions that raise a **late-term abortion** problem for abortion defenders. Rather, it is the moral permissibility of late-term abortions sought for reasons substantially similar to those offered on behalf of abortion in the typical case. Let's now consider two main objections.

The Moral Irrelevance of Location

This argument runs:

1. A 25-week-old fetus is viable (i.e., can live outside the womb).
2. The intentional killing of a newborn of comparable gestational age is morally wrong.
3. Other things being equal, it is morally irrelevant whether a human organism is inside or outside the womb.

---

4. Therefore, the intentional killing a viable fetus is morally wrong.

Abortion defenders can reply by distinguishing permissible from forbidden abortions according to gestational age. They may insist that with the development of the brain hardware needed for consciousness, abortion becomes morally impermissible. They may also point to the mother's weightier moral standing and rights, compared to those of the fetus. On this reply, a 25-five-week old human organism, whether in utero or already born, has some moral standing, so that arbitrarily killing it is wrong—except when its continued life conflicts with the mother's higher moral standing, which includes rights to liberty, self-defense, and ownership of her own body. Yet if the moral standing of late fetuses is such that it includes the right to life, this could trump those rights of the mother—a topic we reassume in Chapter 13.

Abortion defenders may also simply bite the bullet, and argue that the intentional killing of a 25-week-old human organism, inside or outside the utero, is morally permissible. Among those who have argued in this way are proponents of psychological conditions for *personhood* such as having the capacity for self-awareness over time and the desire to continue to exist. Fetuses and newborns have neither of these. But not everyone accepts criteria of that sort. In addition, among those who do accept them, some regard this reply to the Moral-Irrelevance-of-Location Argument as an uphill battle, for it challenges well-entrenched legal and commonsense intuitions about the wrongness of unjustified killings of late fetuses and newborns. According to the law and common morality, for example, a homicide of a woman in late pregnancy may count as a crime with two victims.

The Late-Term-Abortion Problem

For some, it is the nature of abortion procedures used after the first trimester of gestation that makes such abortions wrong. One of these, dilation and evacuation (D&E) causes the fetus to become dismembered. The other, intact dilation and extraction (D&X), consists in the extraction of the entire fetus through the birth canal by first dilating the cervix and 'collapsing' the skull because it is too big to pass through. For reasons discussed in Chapter 13, the US Congress's Partial Birth Abortion Ban Act of 2003 made D&X illegal. Of concern here is a *Late-Term-Abortion Problem* for abortion defenders, who seem committed to justifying procedures some consider inhumane. In reply, abortion defenders may note that if there is a problem, it is not for late-term abortions but only for the *available procedures*. Moreover, not all abortion defenders are committed to approving of late-term abortion. Those who regard gestational age as relevant to the permissibility of abortion are not. And arguably, D&E and D&X appear gruesome and inhumane only when described by laypersons—as would many other commonly accepted medical interventions when so described.

 ## 12.4 Chapter Summary

Many positions on each side of the abortion debate are quite extreme. As discussed in Chapter 11, for some, abortion is always impermissible, for others, always permissible. When a position is as extreme as these, it has problems in accommodating common morality's intuitions about some 'hard' cases of abortion: the position's verdict stands in sharp contrast to what most people think. This chapter analyzes two hard cases for extreme positions on each side, together with possible replies. Although none of these is conclusive enough to persuade all parties in this debate, some replies are stronger than others, as shown by the replies to the late-term-abortion problem. The weakest replies are by those who dig in their heels and stick to their extreme positions, unmoved by their inability to resolve the conflict with people's intuitions, the hard cases. According to a Gallup poll,[4] in 2011 83% of Americans favored the legality of abortion when the woman's life is endangered, 82% when the woman's physical health is endangered, and 61% when the woman's mental health is endangered. Similar numbers were given for abortion when the pregnancy was caused by rape or incest. On the other hand, 72% of Americans were against the legal availability of late-term abortions. Of course, as noted earlier, the pervasiveness of an intuition does not prove it reasonable. But it does put the burden of argument on those who challenge it until they provide persuasive reasons for their view.

 ## 12.5 Study Aids

Key Words

---

4 Gallup. "Abortion," 2011. http://www.gallup.com/poll/1576/abortion.aspx.

Questions and Cases for Further Consideration

1. Kuhse and Singer (1985: 136) contend that there is nothing morally wrong with abortion when prenatal tests reveal fetal defects. Furthermore, there is nothing wrong in ending the life of a compromised infant at birth, since in neither case is a person killed. That is, in neither case has the life of a person begun. How might an opponent reply to this argument? In your view, who is right?

2. If abortion for certain fetal disorders is permissible, would this justify euthanasia for newborns with similar disorders?

3. Suppose you are summoned to jury duty in a wrongful-life action. The plaintiff alleges his life is not worth having at all, owing to a severe genetic disorder for which he holds the defendants, his parents, accountable. How would you go about deciding whether his life, rather than his nonexistence, is better? Whose perspectives need to be considered? Yours, his, or both? Are these questions that could be settled by the courts?

4. *In the US, about two thirds of the states now have 'fetal homicide' laws, which criminalize killing a fetus as a form of murder. When Laci Peterson was killed in California in 2002, she was seven and a half months pregnant. Her husband Scott Peterson, later convicted of her murder, was found guilty, not only of first-degree murder for killing Laci, but also of second-degree murder for the death of her fetus, a male she had already named Connor.* Here the fetus had been killed as a result of violence against the mother, which counted as a crime with two victims. What may be said for and against the court's judgment in this matter? Can abortion defenders account for common-morality's intuition that killing a pregnant woman is worse than killing a person who's not pregnant? Might an appeal to fetal interests help?

5. Dr. S *admits a miscarrying pregnant woman to the Catholic hospital where he works. Her 19-week-old fetus has no chance of survival. She has consented to an abortion to save her life. But the hospital ethics committee refuses to allow it because an ultrasound detects fetal heartbeat. When she develops sepsis, with a 106-degree fever and profuse bleeding, it is clear that abortion is her only chance. Dr. S performs it, and later resigns his post. Against all odds, the woman survives. She leaves the ICU after ten days but has permanent injuries.* (Adapted from Sepper, 2012.) What would critics and defenders of abortion say about the morality of the doctor's action in this case? Was this a case of conflicting duties for him? What should care givers do when their views on abortion are incompatible with institutional policy?

6. *In* Curlender v Bio-Science Laboratories *(1980), the California Court of Appeals decided unanimously that a wrongful-life action could be brought under common law tort principles. The plaintiff, a guardian ad litem on behalf of Sahuna Tamar Curlender, charged that two medical laboratories and a physician failed to predict the infant's Tay-Sachs disease in the genetic testing of the parents. Tay-Sachs is an inheritable disorder characterized by progressive destruction of nerve cells in the brain and spinal cord, leading to severe physical and mental impairment and, in the most serious cases, an early death. This infant's death was expected by age four. Dismissing appeals to the sanctity of life as irrelevant, the court emphasized that in light of current genetic knowledge, society's welfare demands attention to genetic testing. Because of the laboratory's negligence on this, the plaintiff was born. As a person with rights, she could recover damages for her short existence marked by pain and suffering as well as for pecuniary losses caused by the care required in her condition. Sup-*porters of this court's decision find it justified on the grounds of justice and deterrence. How would those arguments run? What aspects of this case, if any, might explain how life itself could be an injury? Since the defendants *did not* cause the plaintiff's disorder, why should they be held accountable for it? If it was caused by the parents, should the plaintiff sue *them* instead? What can be said for and against a system where children can sue their parents for having brought them into existence? Who might qualify for initiating such litigation?

Suggested Readings*

*Annas, George J., "The Supreme Court and Abortion Rights," *The New England Journal of Medicine* 365.21, 2007: 2201–7.
    Examines the 1992 *Casey* decision in the context of the Supreme Court's overall trend since *Roe* of restricting access to abortion. Includes some discussion of late-term abortion.
*Davis, Alison, "Right to Life of the Handicapped," *Journal of Medical Ethics* 9, 1983: 181.
    Its argument that physician-assisted death devalues the lives of disabled people can be extended to abortion for fetal defects.
Finnis, John, "Abortion and Health Care Ethics," in R. Gillon ed., *Principles of Health Care Ethics*, pp. 547–607. Chichester: John Wiley, 1994.
    Defense of Natural Law thinking about hard cases of abortion. Invokes the Principle of Double Effect to justify some abortions to save the mother's life.
*Kaczor, Christopher, "Moral Absolutism and Ectopic Pregnancy," *The Journal of Medicine and Philosophy* 26.1, 2001: 61–74.
    After acknowledging the problem that abortion for the mother's endangerment poses to Natural Law theory, argues that the Principle of Double Effect justifies three of four procedures for abortion in ectopic pregnancy.
*———, "Is Abortion Permissible in Hard Cases?" in Kaczor 2011, pp. 177–214.
    Argues that abortion for fetal defects is as morally impermissible as killing disabled children.

---

*   Asterisks mark readings available online. See links on the companion website.

Kuhse, Helga and Peter Singer, *Should the Baby Live? The Problem of Handicapped Infants.* Oxford: Oxford University Press, 1985.

Vindicates the permissibility of abortion for fetal defects and of euthanasia for disabled newborns, holding that such decisions should be left to the parents. Offers a utilitarian defense of these claims, together with standard appeals to the psychological capacities typical of persons that fetuses and newborns lack.

*Purdy, Laura M., "Are Pregnant Women Fetal Containers?" *Bioethics* 4.4, 1990: 273–91.

Offers an extreme abortion-defender position, contending that since a fetus is a part of a woman's body, she has the right to decide what happens to it. Objects to harmful treatment of pregnant women grounded in the mistaken belief that fetuses are morally independent entities.

*Steinbock, Bonnie, "Sex Selection: Not Obviously Wrong," *Hastings Center Report* 32.1, 2002: 23–8.

Argues that sex selection is not inherently sexist, and that its moral permissibility depends on the parents' motives and on the social consequences of the practice.

*———, "Fetal Sentience and Women's Rights," *Hastings Center Report* 41.6, 2011: 49.

Takes sentience to be a better criterion for fetal moral standing than viability. But since abortions for the mother's endangerment is always permissible, it is wrong for states to forbid such abortion after week 20.

13 Conflicts of Rights at Life's Beginning

Learning Objectives

In reading this chapter you will

▶ Consider how to resolve the ethical dilemma that arises when a pregnant woman's life-style or medical choice is likely to produce fetal harm.

▶ Learn about US and UK regulations on abortion.

▶ Reflect on the morality of some US laws restricting public funding for abortions and certain procedures for late-term abortions.

▶ Recognize main options for medical professionals who object on moral or religious grounds to dispensing legal reproductive services.

CONFLICTS OF INTEREST or rights during pregnancy may involve not only the mother and fetus, but also the state and health care providers. One such conflict arises when a woman's life-style or medical choice during pregnancy may cause fetal harm. As discussed in this chapter, although the state may seek to restrain and even punish her, some moral and prudential reasons favor noninterference. Among them is the woman's right to liberty and privacy that also sets limits to other restrictions by the state or providers.

13.1 Deborah Zimmerman: Alcohol Abuse During Pregnancy

Deborah Zimmerman, a 35-year-old waitress in Racine, Wisconsin, had a drinking problem. But neither she nor the people who knew her were prepared for what would happen on a cold afternoon in March 1996. Shortly before 2:00 p.m., she drove to her favorite tavern and waited in the parking lot for the bar to open. Once inside, Ms. Zimmerman began getting progressively intoxicated. She was nearly nine months pregnant.

Sometime later that afternoon, Ms. Zimmerman's mother took her to a hospital, where doctors ordered an emergency Caesarian section. Once in the ER, obstetrics staff insisted on attaching a fetal monitor, but Ms. Zimmerman refused. "I'm just going to go home and keep drinking and drink myself to death, and I'm going to kill this thing because I don't want it anyways," she told the staff. Later that evening Ms. Zimmerman gave birth to a girl who bore symptoms typical of fetal alcohol syndrome: low birthweight, sluggish movements, and a forehead flatter than normal. Her blood alcohol level was 0.199, more than twice the minimum for legal intoxication in Wisconsin. Newborns with this syndrome usually have permanent neurological damage resulting in serious mental impairment.

When the Racine County district attorney's office learned these facts, Deborah Zimmerman was taken into custody and charged with attempted murder. Her case drew the attention of legal scholars and advocacy groups nationwide on both sides of the abortion controversy. Ms. Zimmerman's attorneys asked that the charges be dismissed because intentional fetal harm (which they thought doubtful in this case) differs from attempting to kill a person. The trial court rejected their argument, as did a circuit court review, but their decision was ultimately reversed on appeal in 1999. Zimmerman's was not a case of attempted homicide, the appellate court ruled, because the law does not recognize a fetus as a person.

■ ■ ■

Although the state's claim against Ms. Zimmerman was eventually dismissed, of concern to us in this chapter are the important moral and public policy issues that remain. Are restraint and punishment permissible, or even obligatory, when a pregnant woman is addicted to substances that may cause fetal harm, such as alcohol, crack, and tobacco? While **beneficence** recommends taking steps to prevent fetal harm, respect for the mother's autonomy as a person conflicts with any measure that limits her freedom. Furthermore, suppose both the woman and fetus have strong interests in need of protection. Call them 'rights.' Each may have a right of noninterference: the fetus with its development, the woman with her liberty and privacy. Whose rights should take priority when there is conflict, the fetus's or the mother's? Although some policy makers consider fetal development weightier, advocates of women's reproductive rights remind them that while there is a plurality of views about the moral standing of the fetus, no one denies the mother's *personhood.*

In addition to Zimmerman-like scenarios, fetal and maternal rights can come into conflict when a pregnant woman refuses life-saving treatment, something she is entitled to do as an autonomous patient (a matter we considered in Chapter 3). But such refusals clearly conflict with fetal development. To complicate the picture, the state and health care providers have duties and rights of their own, which may come into conflict with each other or with those of a pregnant woman. Providers are expected to assist women with their lawful requests for intervention that fall within their reproductive rights, such as abortion and contraception. Yet some providers object to dispensing these types of service on religious or moral grounds. On the other hand, the state's interest in protecting life may conflict with respect for women's choices of life-style or medical treatment during pregnancy, a topic we take up next.

■ 13.2 Maternal-Fetal Conflicts

Some Facts about Fetal Harm

Although the long-term effects of prenatal drug use (nicotine, alcohol, and controlled substances) vary, it has long been associated with fetal harm. Many women who abuse

IMAGE 13.1
©iStockPhoto/Skip O'Donnell

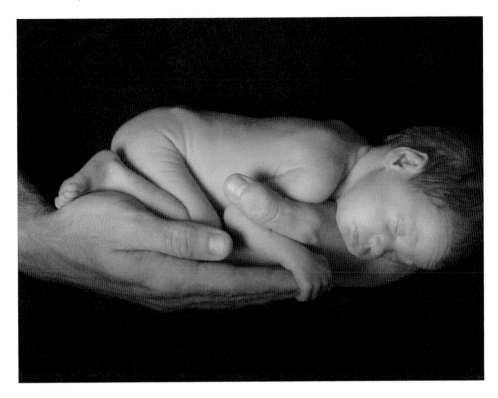

drugs during pregnancy may have little access to medical information about fetal harm. Others know, but either will not or cannot overcome the power of their addictions. Such was apparently the case for Deborah Zimmerman, whose binge alcohol use harmed her fetus, and ultimately the infant it became. As mentioned above, babies born with fetal alcohol syndrome often have low birthweight, sluggish responses, and a flattened forehead that indicate neurological damage. They may suffer mental and physical impairment for life. Statistics show that alcohol abuse during pregnancy is a leading cause of preventable child retardation in the US.[1] There is also evidence that smoking during pregnancy prevents the fetus from getting nourishment and increases the risk of premature birth or fetal death. More generally, the evidence overwhelmingly suggests that prenatal drug use can bring a disastrous prospect for the newborn, sometimes with no medical amelioration possible later in life.

---

1   US National Library of Medicine. "Pregnancy and Substance Abuse," 12/2/2016. https://medlineplus. gov/pregnancyandsubstanceabuse.html.

BOX 13.1 SUBSTANCE USE IN PREGNANCY

Based on data averaged across 2012 and 2013, the Substance Abuse and Mental Health Services Administration's "Results from the 2012 National Survey on Drug Use and Health"[2] reports that among pregnant women aged 15 to 44

- 15.9% (one in six) had smoked cigarettes in the past month

- 5.4% are current illicit drug users
- An annual average of 8.5% reported current alcohol use, 2.7% reported binge drinking, and 0.3% reported heavy drinking

Maternal Obligations and Rights

In light of the data about **fetal harm**, some utilitarians believe that society should do everything in its power to discourage pregnant women from substance abuse. Kantians may concur, since becoming pregnant creates an obligation on the part of the woman *not to do* things that may harm a being that can later be rational and therefore have moral standing. For virtue ethicists, a positive trait of character in a woman who deliberately decides to carry a pregnancy to term is caring for her fetus, which implies doing everything possible to deliver a healthy newborn. All these theorists concur that a pregnant woman should:

1. Refrain from activities experts judge harmful to the fetus.
2. Refrain from substance abuse.
3. Undergo any reasonable, medically indicated treatment to protect fetal health.

Given current expert opinion, a pregnant woman who undertakes scuba diving or roller-coaster riding fails to meet (1). Ms. Zimmerman failed to meet (2). Such violations involve life-style decisions often responsible for fetal harm. On occasion fetal harm may, however, result from the woman's rejection of (3)—as happened in this case:

St George's Healthcare NHS Trust v S. In 1998, Ms. S planned to have a natural birth. But she was diagnosed with pre-eclampsia, a potentially fatal condition for mother and fetus that required admission to a hospital with immediate induction of birth. Ms. S refused. Although there was no evidence of mental impairment, she was arrested under the British Mental Health Act of 1983 and, with a court overriding her consent, admitted to a hospital where her baby was delivered by Caesarean section. Later, the Court of Appeal ruled that her autonomy had been violated, noting that "while pregnancy increases the personal responsibilities of a woman, it does not diminish her entitlement to decide whether or not to undergo medical treatment. . . ."

This verdict reaffirmed the legal right of expectant mothers to refuse life-saving treatment, reminding health care providers and public officials of their obligation to honor refusals

---

2 See more at http://www.samhsa.gov/data/sites/default/files/NSDUHresultsPDFWHTML2013/Web/NSDUHresults2013.htm.

grounded in patient autonomy. The case thus played an important role in reasserting the full moral standing of pregnant patients at a time when public opinion and health care policy were beginning to ascribe to the state a responsibility in protecting fetal life. Also on autonomy grounds, in *Ferguson v City of Charleston* (2001) the US Supreme Court declared unconstitutional the practice of secretly testing pregnant women during prenatal exams for evidence of drug use. Prevalent in some states during the 1980s and 90s, such testing led to punitive measures against women who tested positive, sometimes stipulating mandatory rehabilitation or years of imprisonment.

Refusing life-style changes or medical treatments may be not only a liberty right of the mother but also a property right grounded in her ownership of her own body. The reasoning here is that a woman's body 'belongs to' her, and she is the only one who has a say in what is done with or to it. No one can justifiably use it or alter it without her consent. When she is pregnant, the fetus is part of her body. She is thus morally justified in refusing indicated medical treatment or life-style changes. Since the person most burdened by the rigors of pregnancy and childbirth is the woman herself, this Ownership-of-One's-Body Argument seems strong. But on scrutiny, it is odd to say that one's body, or any part of it, such as a developing human organism within it, is one's 'property.' Property can be bought and sold, rented, inherited, and used as collateral on loans, among other things. That is not exactly the relationship in which one stands to one's body.

Furthermore, even if a woman's body is indisputably hers, what, if anything, follows from *that* about what she may justifiably do to it? It is far from clear that, if one is the indisputable owner of something, one always has the right to do whatever one wants with it. Suppose Bob, a rich art collector, cuts a special deal with the government of France and buys Leonardo's *Mona Lisa*. Does that give him the legitimate moral right to destroy it when he gets tired of looking at it? Does he even have the right to alter it? No, if the painting is valuable for its own sake. He has a duty of stewardship to preserve it for posterity. In the same way, even if a woman's body and the fetus developing within it are indisputably hers, it is not clear that that 'ownership' status gives her the right to do just anything to the fetus, including kill it. To get off the ground, this argument needs convincing reasons for thinking that the human fetus either lacks moral standing or has it only to a degree that can be outweighed by a woman's right to ownership of her own body.

A Dilemma for Public Policy

It is one thing to say that any woman who decides to go through with a pregnancy must make necessary life-style changes or undergo medically indicated treatment, but quite another to say that these should be legally enforced. If such obligations were also legal duties, a pregnant woman could justifiably be coerced against her will, partly because she is pregnant. But in the name of whom—or what—may society do this? In many countries no one is a legal person before birth, and as we saw in Chapter 10, human fetuses are not among the paradigm persons who have a moral right to life. Thus, there seem to be no solid grounds for society to *compel* a woman to stop drinking or using drugs, to *punish* her if she refuses, or to *force* her to have surgery or other invasive treatment for the benefit of her fetus. Furthermore, the state's treatment of parents who elect not to save or prolong their children's lives by, for example, donating a kidney or bone marrow, ordinarily involves no punishment—which seems inconsistent with the state's reactions to **fetal abuse** cases.

Another argument against limiting a pregnant woman's autonomy in life-style scenarios of fetal abuse is consequentialist. Alexander Capron (1998) contends that society should not undertake any coercive or punitive action to that effect, citing practical grounds rather than the lack of legal personhood in the fetus or a woman's right to refuse treatment. On Capron's view, there is a **Disincentive Problem** here, since pregnant addicts should receive treatment, but

> Restraining and punishing expectant mothers for their alcohol or illicit drugs would be a disincentive for them to seek treatment.

Capron suggests that laws designed to protect the human fetus from harm by the mother would just make matters worse for all concerned, including the newborns, because the women, fearful of punishment or institutionalization, would avoid seeking treatment for their addictions. The evidence is that punished women came to regret their trust in the system, which shows that a Disincentive Problem does arise. But Capron's contention depends on the long-term consequences of restrictive policies for fetal abuse, which are unknown. Deontological considerations favor restraint and punishment for pregnant drug users: failure to do so is *unfair to the person* whose future existence might be harmed by the mother's behavior. Thus it seems that whether legal action is warranted in response to fetal abuse is a dilemma for public policy with no obvious solution. There are reasons

- Against society's interference with the mother—namely,
    - Her liberty rights.
    - Capron's least-bad outcome argument.
- For society's interference with the mother—namely,
    - The future newborn's right not to be harmed during pregnancy.
    - Obligations of justice owed to this affected party.

Since it is unclear which of these reasons are weightier, fetal abuse continues to be a public policy dilemma.

▮ 13.3 Maternal Rights and the State's Obligations

Moral questions about abortion arise not only for individuals but also for the state. They concern chiefly (a) whether the state's duty to protect vulnerable persons extends to life *in utero*, and (b) if so, how far should the state go? Suppose (a) is answered 'Yes.' Then the state may impose some restrictions, even a total ban, on abortion. But the latter measure would conflict with current public opinion in the US, which shows only a substantial minority favoring a ban on abortion in all circumstances. The majority, including a good number of abortion critics, is against it. A 2014 Gallup poll[3] shows, for example, that 47% of Americans define themselves as pro-choice and 46% as pro-life; but on the issue of whether abortion should be

---

3 For a summary of recent Gallup polls, see Gallup. "Abortion," 2014. http://www.gallup.com/poll/ 1576/abortion.aspx and Lydia Saad, "US Still Split on Abortion," 2014. http://www.gallup.com/ poll/170249/split-abortion-pro-choice-pro-life.aspx.

legal 50% are for "legal under certain circumstances," 28% for "always legal," and only 21% for "illegal in all circumstances"—with 2% for "no opinion."

Thus, a reasonable, pluralistic approach would keep in place the policies prevailing in common law jurisdictions. In what follows we'll examine briefly a sample of such policies.

Abortion Policy in the UK

In England, Scotland, and Wales, the Abortion Act of 1967 (amended by the 1990 Human Fertilization and Embryology Act) sanctions abortion permissible, provided two medical practitioners certify that one of these conditions applies:

1. The pregnancy does not exceed week 24, and continuation would involve a risk greater than termination for the physical or mental health of the mother, or of any existing children in her family.
2. Termination is needed to prevent serious injury to the mother's health (physical or mental).
3. Continuation would involve greater risk to the mother's life than termination.
4. There is serious risk of severe mental or physical impairment to the newborn.

Of the four conditions, (2) is the least speculative and (1) is vague enough to make typical abortions, in practice, available to all women. Some, however, find the two-health-practitioners requirement excessively punctilious, unnecessary, and paternalistic.

This regulation does not apply to Northern Ireland, where abortions are permitted only for fetal defects or serious risks to the mother's health or life. Since 'serious' here does not mean 'grave' but merely 'genuine,' in the sense of 'nonfake,' Hewson (2001) argues that the law in Northern Ireland is in fact more liberal than the 1967 Act. In practice, however, medical professionals there are unwilling to perform abortions, and women travel to England or Scotland at their own expense to obtain them.

Abortion Policy in the US

In the United States, the Supreme Court's (1992) ruling in *Casey* reframed the abortion debate, since although it reaffirmed *Roe's* crucial holding that there is a right to abortion before viability, it also opened the door to restrictions by establishing that the state has an interest in protecting not only the mother's constitutional rights but also fetal life.

Thus the state has the power to regulate abortion after viability, as well as an interest in protecting the health of the mother and the life of the fetus. At the same time, *Casey* adopted the standard of 'undue burden' that invalidates regulation by individual states whose "purpose or effect is to place a substantial obstacle in the path of a woman seeking an abortion before the fetus attains viability." Under 'undue burden' falls spousal involvement in abortion, but it does not include either a 24-hour waiting period for women before having an abortion or parental involvement for teenage mothers. Among the reasons for leaving the latter out is promoting a woman's informed consent by

- Preventing hasty or ill-considered decisions, and
- Allowing for reflection and possibly parental counseling in the case of minors.

IMAGE 13.2
©iStockPhoto/cosinart

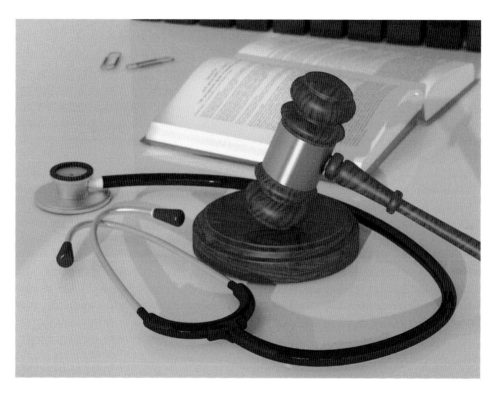

In practice, the undue-burden standard means that the state has the power to regulate abortion unless it can show that a particular regulation imposes an unreasonable or unnecessary burden on women. The Court attempted to justify this departure from the trimester framework in *Roe* by saying that a precedent is not an "inexorable command."

In sum, the US allows a state's restrictions on abortion, provided they fall short of a total ban and are generally consistent with *Roe v Wade.* After *Casey,* the number of such restrictions on abortion has been on the rise. In what follows, we'll take up two such restrictions enacted by Congress.

Banning 'Partial-Birth Abortion'

Enacted by Congress in 2003, the **Partial Birth Abortion Ban Act** made illegal *Intact Dilation and Extraction* (D&X), a procedure developed as an improvement over previous methods for *late-term abortions.* D&X consists in the extraction of the entire fetus through the birth canal by first dilating the cervix and 'collapsing' the skull because it is too big to pass through. Legislators dubbed the procedure 'partial-birth abortion,' a term later adopted by US Supreme Court but rarely used by obstetricians—perhaps because D&X is also the procedure of choice for removing fetuses that die of miscarriage or feticide.

However called, the ban on D&X was supported by some abortion critics on moral grounds. Their efforts ultimately bore fruit after some unsuccessful litigation at the outset. In

Stenberg v Carhart (2000), the Supreme Court struck down Nebraska's ban on D&X. But in 2007, the same court upheld Congress's (2003) ban in another landmark case:

Gonzales v Carhart. In this action, Dr. Leroy Carhart and some colleagues argued that Congress's Act banning D&X was, first, void due to its vagueness, since it would ban also a procedure called 'dilation and evacuation' (D&E) in addition to the less common D&X. Second, since D&E is the most common method of second trimester abortion, the Act would ban most late-term abortions, thus placing an unconstitutional "undue burden" on women's right to abortion. Third, by allowing no exception for abortions necessary to protect the mother's health, the Act was unconstitutional under the Supreme Court's decision in *Stenberg v Carhart*. But in 2007, with a 5–4 vote, the Supreme Court rejected the plaintiffs' three charges.

Dr. Carhart and colleagues probably also regarded the Act as a significant, government-imposed restriction on health care providers' professional discretion in medical decisions. But the case centered on their charges that the Court's majority opinion rejected. For them, the ban applies only to D&X under the most reasonable interpretation, so there was no vagueness. Moreover, D&X is never medically necessary, not even to protect the mother's life or health. In addition, D&X is not the only possible late-term abortion procedure.

But many are critical of these empirical claims. The plaintiffs disputed the claim that there are always alternative procedures, so that D&X is never necessary. Although the Court acknowledged this disagreement among the experts, it neglected to take it into account in its majority decision. As a result, it failed to produce a compelling verdict.

Restricting Public Funding for Abortion

Let's now consider a US policy that has been supported on the grounds that the public should not have to pay for abortion, and criticized on the grounds that it discriminates against poor women by imposing an undue burden on them. In the United States, the government provides health care for the poor and the disabled through Medicaid. In 1976 Illinois Congressman Henry Hyde proposed an amendment to the annual appropriations bill forbidding the use of federal tax dollars to pay for abortions, except in cases of rape, incest, or threat to the woman's life. The **Hyde Amendment**, as it became known, was adopted by Congress and became law in 1976. As a result, institutions using federal resources, such as Medicaid, may not subsidize abortions, either in typical cases or in some hard cases such as to protect the mother's health.

States may, and many do, subsidize abortions with their own funds. But they are not required to do so—a provision that withstood a 1980 challenge in

Harris v McRae. In response to a challenge to the Hyde Amendment, the US Supreme Court in 1980 upheld its constitutionality by invoking the 'due process' clause of the Fourteenth Amendment. It ruled that there is no state obligation to cover the shortfall in federal funding for abortion mandated by the Hyde Amendment.

A similar policy was reflected in the bill signed by President Obama after the 2009–10 debate over health care reform in the United States, which includes a provision stipulating that when abortions are covered by private insurance plans sold through state-based exchanges, they must separate federal and private money. According to this bill, the insured must make separate payments for abortion coverage (except in cases of rape, incest, or threat to the woman's life), and at least one plan offered in each state must exclude abortion coverage. The upshot of this trend in public policy is that, in the United States, no federal funds can be used for elective abortion in typical cases, and also in some hard cases, including therapeutic ones. As might have been expected, defenders as well as critics of abortion have offered their reasons for and against the Hyde restriction on Medicaid funding, and to this we turn next.

For the Hyde Amendment

An obvious consequentialist reason for the Hyde Amendment is that it saves taxpayers' money. But this empirical claim conflicts with evidence suggesting that the total cost for prenatal care, delivery services, and welfare benefits for a woman who carries an unwanted pregnancy to term amounts to four or five times the cost of paying for an abortion through Medicaid (Dadlez and Andrews, 2010: 179).

Another reason for such restrictions on public funding of abortion appeals to fairness to individuals. "That women have the right to terminate pregnancy does not mean the public has to pay for abortion," writes DeGrazia (2012: 51). In his view, since there is a substantial minority of abortion critics who desire to avoid 'dirty hands,' it is unfair to use their tax money for something they oppose. DeGrazia's argument, however, faces inevitable counterexamples. After all, in a democratic society, citizens have not only a legal but a moral duty to fund the apparatus of government through taxes, even in situations where they do not endorse and may even oppose the causes being pursued with their tax dollars. Many Americans today are strongly opposed on moral grounds to their states' use of capital punishment for certain crimes. Yet it is not unfair to them that their tax dollars are used to fund executions, since they are willing to live in a liberal democracy and accept having to provide funding for implementing their government's democratically reached decisions. By analogy, the use of federal funding for abortions seems fair to those who think typical abortions should be illegal.

Against the Hyde Amendment

Arguably, this restriction on public funding of abortion involves an inconsistency, because birth control *is* covered by Medicaid while abortion is not. In reply, supporters of this restriction may dig in their heels by invoking a moral difference between contraception and abortion that justifies different public policies. A stronger objection invokes social justice, contending

1.   Medicaid serves a sizable number of women who lack the resources to pay for an abortion.

2.   Therefore, in practice, the ban on using federal money to fund abortions amounts to a ban on abortion for a large segment of the population.

3. Therefore, a large segment of the population is being denied the legal right explicitly affirmed in *Roe v Wade*.

---

4. Therefore, US law on access to abortion, as currently construed, is inconsistent.

The charge here is that, given the Hyde Amendment, only women who are fairly well-off can actually exercise the right accorded them by *Roe*. Furthermore, since the population that cannot afford private abortions comprises many members of racial and ethnic minorities, the restriction in effect discriminates against minorities and women of low socioeconomic status.

In reply to this challenge, supporters of the Hyde Amendment argue

1. The restriction simply omits enabling abortion.
2. Failing to enable something is not the same as forbidding it.

---

3. Therefore, the restriction does not amount to a ban on abortion.

---

4. Therefore, the restriction is consistent with *Roe v Wade*.

The rationale for crucial premise (2) may be seen by analogy. The fact that the government does not fund private schools does not amount to a proscription on private education. People have the right to it if they desire it, although the government is not obliged to fund it. Yet this analogy fails because there is *no* comparable social injustice involved in banning public funding of private education.

13.4 Maternal Rights and Conscientious Objectors

Women/Health Care Providers Conflicts

Where abortion and contraception are legal, a question may still arise of whether physicians, nurses, pharmacists, and other health care providers may legitimately refuse, on moral or religious grounds, to provide these treatments to women who autonomously choose them. Some health care providers believe that, although typical abortions are legal, they should, for a variety of reasons, not provide them—for example, because human life is intrinsically valuable. Thus, they may abstain, on grounds of conscience, from participating in abortion. For similar reasons, some pharmacists have refused to fill prescriptions for Plan B, the morning-after contraceptive. Either health care professionals, institutions, or corporations may have a **conscientious objection** to providing certain medical services or products. Our main concern here is conscientious objection to abortion.

Not just any firmly held beliefs can count as *conscientious* grounds of such refusals. Some beliefs might instead afford only prudential grounds—as, for example, if a physician or nurse believes she is likely to encounter physical violence from protestors outside the clinic, and on that basis declines to participate in abortions delivered there. And parents who refuse to allow their children to have routine vaccinations because they believe that they cause autism are invoking a (mistaken) belief about cause and effect, not conscience.

- An objection is grounded in conscience just in case it is based on the objector's deeply held moral or religious beliefs.
- Whether religious or secular in content, these beliefs embody the objector's defining commitments in life and are essential to her identity and moral integrity.

When there is an appeal to conscience, understood in this way, those who make it are conscientious objectors, a protected group in democratic societies.

The Duties of Conscientious Objectors

Conscientious objection to abortion or contraception raises these moral questions:

1. Do health care providers have a moral right to such conscientious objection?
2. If they do, are there duties they owe to the patients whose reproductive decisions they refuse to honor?

Among professional organizations, the American College of Obstetricians and Gynecologists (2007) answers 'Yes' to both questions, while some abortion critics answer 'Yes' to (1), 'No' to (2). In their view, answering both questions in the affirmative is morally inconsistent. For suppose the conscientious objector has a

---

Duty of Referral

The health care providers' obligation to refer patients to any professional known to provide the services to which the patient is legally entitled.

For **conscience absolutists,** there is no duty of referral. If a health care professional refuses to provide a service she considers morally wrong, she could not in good conscience assist the patient in finding another professional willing to provide it. A physician who equates abortion with murder cannot assist a woman in obtaining one by giving her a referral. That would be inconsistent. There is no room for compromise.

Even in countries where abortion is legal in certain circumstances, absolutist conscientious objectors refuse to make such referrals. In Poland, for example, where most abortions are strictly prohibited, women may yet legally have an abortion for rape or incest, or when the life of the mother is at risk. But consider:

Polish Girl. In 2012 a 14-year-old Polish girl who was pregnant as result of rape was repeatedly denied abortion at hospitals, first in her village of Lublin, then in Warsaw. Only after she had traveled more than 500 kilometers to the northern city of Gdansk and the national Ministry of Health had intervened in her case did she find physicians willing to perform the procedure. Later, the European Court of Human Rights found that there had been numerous breaches of the girl's civil rights as a Polish citizen.[4]

---

4 Adapted from "Polish Rape Victim 'Should have had Abortion Access,'" *BBC,* 10/30/2012.

Other medical professionals may also take the dictates of conscience to be exceptionless moral imperatives. That seems to have been the view of some North Carolina pharmacists who in 2015 "were destroying prescriptions, giving patients speeches on morality, and stalling the patient beyond the point where contraception would be effective" (Tanne, 2005: 983).

But not all agree with such conscience absolutism. According to **conscience skepticism,** the fiduciary responsibility of health care professionals to their patients and to society at large always rules out a conscience-based refusal to dispense abortion or contraception. And according to **conscience universalism,** a mid-way position, although conscientious objection is a provisional, or other-things-being-equal, right of health care providers, it has exceptions. On occasion it may be outweighed by the provider's obligation to patients. Both of these views imply that health care providers claiming conscientious objection do have a duty to refer based on professional obligations.

For, given the principles of *nonmaleficence, beneficence*, and *patient autonomy*, health care providers must avoid causing uncompensated harm to patients, seek their best interests, and respect their competent choices. As a result, they must refer patients to a practitioner willing to provide a lawful service they themselves question on moral grounds. Respect for the lawful choices of competent patients may also imply that the conscientious objectors to abortion must make sure that their patients who seek abortion or store customers who seek the morning-after pill are fully informed about such procedures and products and about how to obtain them.

Furthermore, beneficence also demands that health care providers stick to their patients. Once care has been initiated, doctors and nurses have, within reasonable limits, a special duty to see to it that their patients are treated. A failure to refer in the circumstances under consideration amounts to abandoning the patient. In addition, beneficence includes the obligation to put the patient's interest first. A woman who cannot obtain a legal abortion in a timely manner may suffer undue burdens, especially when she must travel long distances to obtain the service—and even harms, for example by seeking an illegal abortion, that may

FIGURE 13.1   Three Views on Conscientious Objection

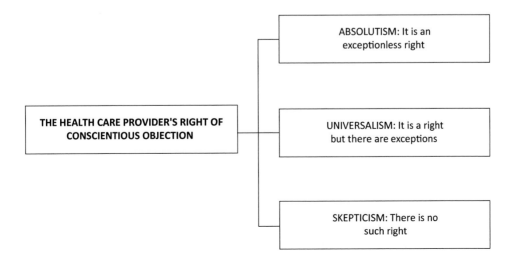

put her future fertility, health, and even life in jeopardy. According to the United Nations,[5] unsafe abortions cause 50,000 deaths per year globally, and more than 21 million women undergo them. Given these data, because health care providers are licensed by the state, they have a fiduciary responsibility to promote public health and the wellbeing of their patients or customers, and therefore have the duty to refer. In addition, conscientious objectors to abortion or emergency contraception must declare themselves, early on, as objectors, so that their institutions and patients will know what to expect from them.

The Referral Problem

For conscience absolutists, a conscientious objector to abortion or contraception has a duty *not* to refer, something supported by scenarios of this sort:

Ritual Mutilation. In some traditional African societies, it is customary to subject adolescent girls to genital cutting, as a rite of passage thought to render them marriageable. Suppose a Western doctor working in Africa refuses, on conscience grounds, to perform a genital mutilation requested by the mother of a 12-year-old girl. Must he help her locate a physician who will perform the procedure?

Capital Punishment. Suppose you are a physician employed by the state penitentiary who is assigned to care for condemned prisoners on death row. On the day before a scheduled execution, the warden asks you to be in attendance to officially verify the prisoner's death, and you refuse to do so, as a matter of conscience (you're opposed to capital punishment on moral grounds). Are you then obliged to find another doctor who will take your place and do what you believe to be immoral?

Adapted from Christopher Kaczor (2011:192–3), these scenarios suggests that the physician has no duty to refer. An absolutist about conscientious objection, Kaczor contends that the same holds for health care professionals faced with a request for abortion or contraceptives.

But Kaczor neglects a significant difference between these scenarios and conscientious objection to abortion and contraception. For there is consensus among informed, reasonable people, in both the West and Africa, that female genital cutting is a harm to a person, the young woman subjected to it. And although many such people disagree as to the justification of capital punishment, they do agree that it is a harm to a person, at the very least, the condemned. But there is no similar consensus about whether abortion is a harm to a *person*. As we saw in previous chapters, there are many different arguments about whether the human fetus has moral standing and, if so, from what point in pregnancy. The controversy remains very much alive. Since there is no real agreement among informed, reasonable people about this question, the analogy between conscientious objection to abortion and contraceptives and *Ritual Mutilation* or *Capital Punishment* fails. A prudent course would be to acknowledge that there is a plurality of reasonable views about abortion and contraception. Absolutist conscientious objectors have no clear title to the moral high ground from which they reject the compromise implied in making referrals and providing information essential to the patient's autonomous choices.

---

5   Mishra et al., "Abortion Policies and Reproductive Health Around the World," 2014. http://www. un.org/en/development/desa/population/publications/pdf/policy/AbortionPoliciesReproductive Health.pdf.

13.5 Chapter Summary

In this chapter we consider some moral conflicts at the beginning of life. They involve a pregnant woman, the child she would likely have if she carries the pregnancy to term, and the state or medical providers. One such conflict arises when a woman's life-style (e.g., drug abuse) or refusal of medical treatment during pregnancy may cause fetal harm. Public policies designed to restrain and even punish her rest on beneficence toward the fetus, but by limiting her freedom they violate respect for her autonomy as a person. Appeals to the moral standing of the fetus and mother cannot resolve this conflict, given the unsettled dispute about fetal personhood. Capron's disincentive problem offers a solution focused on the negative consequences of state policies recommending restriction and punishment.

However, as shown in our brief summary of abortion policy in the UK and US, states have reasons of their own to regulate reproduction. Invoking their duty to protect life, they have sometimes introduced regulations that conflict with women's reproductive rights. Particularly controversial have been the US Congress's Partial Birth Abortion Ban Act of 2003, which banned the late-term abortion procedure known as 'D&X,' and the Hyde Amendment, which restricts state funding for abortion. At the same time, health care providers' own convictions may conflict with women's reproductive rights. For, given the principles of bioethics, a provider who has the expertise, credentials, and means to assist his patient with her lawful request of abortion or contraception has an obligation to do so. When dispensing these types of service conflicts with his religious or moral convictions, those principles suggest that the duty to refer is among the duties he still owes to that patient.

13.6 Study Aids

Key Words

Beneficence, 240
Conscience absolutism, 250
Conscience skepticism, 251
Conscience universalism/Conscientious objection, 251
Disincentive Problem, 244
Duty of referral, 250
Fetal abuse/harm, 243/242
Hyde Amendment, 247
Partial Birth Abortion Ban Act, 246

Questions and Cases for Further Consideration

1. Some favor, others oppose legally restraining or compelling pregnant addicts to accept treatment. First, provide the reason you consider best on each side, and then discuss which of these alternatives, if either, has more weight.

2.   Why did the plaintiffs in *Gonzales v Carhart* think that the Partial Birth Abortion Ban of 2003 was unconstitutional? What can be said for and against that US Supreme Court ruling?

3.   Evaluate this argument: *The Hyde Amendment's intent is not to discriminate against indigent women, but to avoid using taxpayers' money to pay for abortions. Therefore the Hyde Amendment does not discriminate against indigent women.*

4.   *In 1992,* Cornelia Whitner *consumed crack cocaine during the third trimester of pregnancy, and her baby later tested positive for cocaine metabolites. Although the persistent effects of prenatal cocaine exposure are unclear, she was charged with violation of South Carolina's child abuse law. Whitner initially pleaded guilty and was sentenced to eight years in prison, but later she requested a rehearing, which was supported by the South Carolina Medical Association. In 1997, the South Carolina Supreme Court upheld her conviction on the grounds that a viable fetus is a child in South Carolina law. In the end, Whitner's conviction was annulled, but only after she had served eighteen months in jail. Her supporters argued that, given the medical evidence, alcohol poses a greater risk to viable fetuses than illegal drugs.* In your view, what is the role of such evidence in cases of this sort? Might knowledge of when Ms. Whitner's addiction developed be relevant to a just verdict? Should considerations of what she morally deserves matter? What about considerations of fetal welfare and of the effectiveness of imprisonment as deterrence? Are all of these compatible?

5.   Angela Carder, *at 25 weeks into her pregnancy, had a recurrence of cancer, this time terminal. She decided, for the sake of her fetus, to receive only palliation and give birth by C-section at week 28. But her health deteriorated rapidly, together with that of her fetus, which by week 26 had only a 50% chance of survival. At that point, the George Washington University Hospital in Washington, DC, obtained a court order for a C-section, which was issued on the grounds that, owing to her heavy sedation, her consent could not be obtained. The baby was delivered and lived two and a half hours. Carder died two days later. In 1990, an appellate court ruled that Carder's consent should have been sought, and had its validity been doubtful, the trial court should have made a determination by way of substituted judgment.* In this case, her refusal of life-prolonging treatment did not save the fetus. Whose rights, if any, might the hospital and trial court have prioritized in deciding for the C-section without the mother's consent? What about the appellate court? Does an appeal to rights help in evaluating the health care providers' decision? How might it be analyzed by appeal to obligations of beneficence and respect for patient autonomy?

6.   Neil T. Noesen *was the weekend pharmacist at the K-mart in Menomonie, Wisconsin. On a Saturday in 2002, a student at the University of Wisconsin requested a refill of a prescription for contraceptive pills on file at that pharmacy. Noesen, acting on the basis of his religious beliefs, not only refused to dispense them but also refused to inform the customer where she might obtain them. Since she needed to reassume the cycle of pills on the following day, she approached a Wal-Mart pharmacist, who was willing to dispense them. Yet Noesen did not authorize the transfer of her prescription. Ultimately, his superior at*

the K-mart, who had been unaware of Noesen's conscience-based objection to contraceptives, dispensed the pills one day after the student was supposed to resume taking them. The Wisconsin Pharmacy Examining Board later issued a reprimand for Noesen. Suppose Noesen's conscientious objection was legitimate. How should it be assessed, given his duty to prevent unnecessary burdens on the customer? In what circumstances could such a decision actually cause harm? Which moral reason might support it and which criticize it? Was the Wisconsin Pharmacy Examining Board's reaction fair?

Suggested Readings*

*American College of Obstetricians and Gynecologists, "The Limits of Conscientious Refusal in Reproductive Medicine," Committee on Ethics No. 385, 2007. Available online at http://www.acog.org/Resources-And-Publications/Committee-Opinions/Committee-on-Ethics/The-Limits-of-Conscientious-Refusal-in-Reproductive-Medicine.
    Argues that conscientious objection to reproductive treatments to which patients are lawfully entitled, when genuine, create in the objector the duty to practice near professionals who provide them, or make referrals, and even dispense them in emergency situations.

*Annas, George J., "Medical Judgment in Court and in Congress," *Human Rights* 34.4, 2007: 2–7.
    Objects to the US Supreme Court decision in *Gonzales v Carhart* on the grounds that neither lawmakers' nor the courts' decision should leave health care providers only with options that may harm their patients.

Brody, Baruch, "Is Abortion a Religious Issue? Religious, Moral, and Sociological Issues: Some Basic Distinctions," *Hastings Center Report* 8.4, 1978: 13.
    Favors the Hyde Amendment on the grounds that it lets the woman's interest prevail sometimes (e.g., in mother's endangerment or rape) and other times the abortion's critics (in the typical cases).

*Capron, Alexander, "Punishing Mothers," *Hastings Center Report* 28.1, 1998: 31–3.
    A consequentialist perspective on fetal abuse, taking the Disincentive Problem as a practical reason against punitive or coercive measures toward pregnant alcoholics and substance users.

*Dadlez, Eva M. and W. L. Andrews, "Federally Funded Elective Abortion: They Can Run, but They Can't Hyde," *International Journal of Applied Philosophy* 2, 2010: 168–84.
    Contends that the Hyde Amendment discriminates against poor and minority women.

*"Gonzales v Carhart," OYEZ: Chicago-Kent College of Law at Illinois Tech. Available online at http://www.oyez.org/cases/2000–2009/2006/2006_05_380.
    Summarizes the facts of this landmark decision and features audio links to two of the Supreme Court's deliberations on the constitutionality of Congress's Partial Birth Abortion Ban Act of 2003.

*Hewson, Barbara, "Reproductive Autonomy and the Ethics of Abortion," *Journal of Medical Ethics* 27 supp. 2, 2001: ii10–ii14.

---

*   Asterisks mark readings available online. See links on the companion website.

Outlines the UK's regulations on abortion, with some attention to maternal-fetal conflicts created in Ireland and the US by emergent public policies increasingly focused
on the rights of the fetus.

*Minkoff, Howard and Lynn M. Pattow, "The Rights of 'Unborn Children' and the Value of
Pregnant Women," *Hastings Center Report* 36.2, 2006: 26–8.
Contends that recent legislation in the US has radically changed the legal status of
fetuses, in effect granting them personhood, a development that undermines women's
rights.

*Robertson, John and Joseph D. Schulman, "Pregnancy and Prenatal Harm to Offspring:
The Case for Mothers with PKU," *Hastings Center Report* 17.4, 1987: 23–32.
Argues that a pregnant woman is responsible for harms to the fetus as a result of her
drug or alcohol use. Restraint, if necessary to protect future children, and legal penalties, if the newborn has defects caused by maternal alcoholism or substance abuse, are
both justified.

*Wicclair, Mark R., *Conscientious Objection in Health Care: An Ethical Analysis*. Cambridge:
Cambridge University Press, 2011.
Thorough discussion of conscientious objection in medical practice, featuring inter-
esting real-life cases of conscientious objection to abortion and contraception.

PART V

The Biotechnological Revolution

14 New Reproductive Technologies

Learning Objectives

In reading this chapter you will

▶ Reflect on how assisted reproductive technologies have revolutionized human conception.

▶ Learn about the moral issues raised by in-vitro fertilization, egg donation, surrogacy, and postmenopausal motherhood.

▶ Consider whether reproductive freedom justifies reproductive technologies whose burdens might outweigh their benefits.

▶ Evaluate reasons for and against thinking that the new reproductive technologies undermine women's interests.

RECENT ADVANCES IN medical knowledge and biotechnology have opened new frontiers, not only at the end of life but also at its beginning. Of particular interest in this chapter is the late-20th-century development of new reproductive technologies, which have extended the limits of procreation in unimagined ways. Yet they are also characterized by a moral tension between matters of reproductive freedom, justice, and the protection of human life.

14.1 Nadya Suleman's Octuplets

In 2008, *Nadya Suleman*, 33, already had six babies conceived by **in-vitro fertilization** (IVF). IVF is a treatment to achieve conception by creating embryos *in vitro*—i.e., in a lab's petri dish. The embryos are then transferred to the womb in the hope that some will implant and the pregnancy be carried to term. Since Suleman wanted more children, she asked Dr. Michael Kamrava to assist her again by transferring twelve embryos she had in storage. She later gave birth to octuplets. Now a mother of fourteen, she was an unemployed, mentally unstable single mom living with her own mother in a small house on which the mortgage was about to be foreclosed. Unable to pay even her basic living expenses, much less her astronomical medical bills or the cost of supporting fourteen children, Ms. Suleman quickly became a sensation in the tabloid press, which dubbed her the 'Octomom.'

In 2011, the Medical Board of California found that, although the evidence fell short of proving Dr. Kamrava "a maverick or deviant physician, oblivious to standards of care in IVF practices," it certainly demonstrated that "he did not exercise sound judgment in the transfer of 12 embryos to patient N.S." Ultimately, the Board suspended his license for five years. During the hearing, it emerged that Suleman still had 29 frozen embryos in storage.

■■■

BOX 14.1 THE PHASES OF IN-VITRO FERTILIZATION TREATMENT

An IVF round standardly consists of:

1. **Superovulation induction**—The woman receives fertility drugs to stimulate her production of eggs beyond the usual one per month.
2. **Egg retrieval, insemination, and fertilization**—Her eggs are retrieved and combined with sperm in a laboratory dish. Fertilization may occur a few hours later if the sperm enters the eggs. When it occurs, within five days the embryos will have several, actively-dividing cells.

3. **Embryo transfer for implantation**—After three to five days of development, some embryos are transferred to the woman's womb with the expectation that at least one or two will implant and eventually produce a live birth. Factors such as the woman's age and responses to previous IVF cycles determine how many embryos are transferred.
4. **Storage**—Remaining embryos are generally cryopreserved (frozen in liquid nitrogen) for later pregnancies or donation (to other women or research).

For the Board investigating Dr. Kamrava, the birth of Nadya Suleman's octuplets pointed to medical negligence in the use of IVF, a **new reproductive technology (NRT)** described in Box 14.1. IVF was introduced to treat infertility, characterized as the inability to conceive after a year or more of unprotected intercourse. It involves fertilization outside the woman's body. Kamrava transferred into Suleman's womb embryos for implantation in a number that doubled what most US guidelines recommended for a woman of her age and fertility record. Pregnancies with multiple embryos can cause miscarriage, stillbirth, premature labor, low birthweight, and congenital disorders. The mother is also at risk of complications and even death. But prospective parents are generally ignorant of such risks, which may be beyond parents' grasp owing to their eagerness to conceive. Without full understanding, prospective parents cannot give informed consent, which raises doubts about whether fertility clinics are fulfilling their obligation of respect for patient autonomy.

Dr. Kamrava invoked precisely that obligation when he told the Board that, in transferring an excessive number of embryos, he was only deferring to Suleman's wishes. In fact, if there is a right to reproductive freedom, Kamrava had a duty not to interfere with her decision. But he had no duty to provide the requested treatment. And it is unclear that Suleman understood the risks involved. If she did not, denying her request would have been an instance of soft paternalism justifiable by his duty to avoid unnecessary risks to the patient. In addition, as we saw in Chapter 3, health care providers' professional autonomy and integrity require them to refuse any patient request seriously at odds with what is medically indicated.

An IVF cycle's probability of resulting in a pregnancy increases according to the number of transferred embryos: using more embryos carries a higher risk of multiple births. Multiples such as Suleman's octuplets call attention to some of the ethical challenges facing reproductive innovations. When a woman pregnant with multiples declines a therapeutic abortion known as 'fetal reduction' (as Kamrava claimed Suleman did), if her babies are born alive, their chances of having severe, long-term disabilities due to prematurity and low birthweight are high. In addition, such births are exorbitantly expensive per se, without counting the babies' often necessary stay in a neonatal intensive care unit (NICU). These financial burdens commonly fall on society. Some wonder whether scarce medical resources should be used for treating infertility, which is not a disease.

14.2 The Simple Cases

The Simple Case of In-Vitro Fertilization

Some Facts about IVF

Louise Brown, the first IVF or 'test-tube' baby, was born in the UK in 1978 under the care of Cambridge doctors Patrick Steptoe and Robert Edwards. By the mid 1980s, the UK parliament made attempts at regulating this increasingly popular reproductive intervention. It commissioned the Warnock report in 1984, issued the Code of Practice of the Human Fertilisation and Embryology Act in 1990, and founded the Human Fertilisation and Embryology Authority. Updated periodically, the Code of Practice aims at protecting the welfare of future children by mandatory screening of prospective parents. By contrast with the UK, where IVF treatments are regulated and often funded by the NHS, in the US they are unregulated by the federal government and mostly privately financed, at prices driven by the market. This thriving, multimillion-dollar business that accounted for the birth of about 1 million infants since its beginning in the 1980s to 2011 is run by fertility clinics (Calandrillo and Deliganis, 2015). Two associations of physicians who provide IVF (and therefore have a stake in it) act as self-regulators.

As shown by the data in Box 14.2, IVF is still a costly, invasive, and ineffective way to procreate compared to unassisted conception. Since it is mostly privately financed, the relatively small pool of patients who can afford this reproductive assistance chooses providers on the basis of their success rates. Providers compete and are under pressure to boost success rates, which explains familiar failures in their obligations of informed consent and beneficence—such as the transfering of excessive numbers of embryos to the uterus in the hope that at least one will implant and develop to term.

BOX 14.2 IVF'S ORIGINS AND OTHER FACTS

- IVF technology originated in veterinary science, producing the first live birth (of a rabbit) in 1959. Since the 1870s, its goal was using lower-quality animals as gestational carriers for IVF embryos of higher-quality animals. Experimentation on humans began in the 1970s.

- In the 1980s, IVF ceased to require surgical retrieval of eggs by laparoscopy. Owing to advances in ultrasound technology, eggs could now be retrieved with a cheaper, quicker, and less invasive procedure: transvaginal ultrasound aspiration. It thus left surgical competitors behind.
- In the US, Elizabeth Jordan Carr became the first US 'test-tube baby' in 1981.
- By the 2000s, after almost 25 years of use, IVF's success rate of live births per initiated cycle was approximately 28% (Greif and Merz, 2007).
- In 2011, 451 fertility clinics reported 163,039 IVF cycles resulting in 47,818 live births and 61,610 neonates. In 2013, although the numbers were slightly higher (467 clinics, 54,323 live births, and 163,209 neonates), IVF continued to account for only 1.5% of all births.
- By 2015, IVF was still funded mostly out-of-pocket. A round cost between $10,000 and $20,000.[1]

The Simple Case

IVF treatments were originally intended for what Singer and Wells (1983) called 'the simple case': married, infertile, heterosexual couples wishing to have genetically related children. However 'simple' those cases may be, they raise a host of moral questions, given people's rights to procreative freedom, the wellbeing of offspring thus conceived, and justice for all involved. Moreover, fertilization outside the woman's body without sexual intercourse by itself represents a radical change in human reproduction that conflicts with the tenets of some cultural and religious traditions. And there are unresolved matters about ownership of the IVF embryos and their moral standing that bear on what is morally permissible to do with them. Other NRTs present related moral questions that we consider in due course. Next, we examine the Problem of Multiples facing both IVF technology and fertility therapy.

Fertility Therapy

Fertility therapy is an older, cheaper, and more low-tech treatment for infertility that uses ovulation-induction drugs to stimulate production of eggs beyond the usual one per month. It requires careful monitoring of the woman's ovulation and compliance with the medical advice of avoiding sexual intercourse or using IVF to limit the number of transferred embryos if the treatment results in too many eggs. If these options fail, fetal reduction is recommended. However, the woman may ignore these recommendations, making herself and her fetuses vulnerable to the risks mentioned above. The **Problem of Multiples** then arises, for there is tension between protecting the welfare (i.e., wellbeing) of the offspring, her right to make her own reproductive decisions, and justice for all involved—including society, which, as shown below, must bear huge delivery costs.

Note also that when fertility treatment leads to pregnancies with multiples, if the woman decides to carry them all to term and she does give birth to apparently healthy neonates, she

---

1   CDC. "ART Success Rates: Latest Data, 2013," http://www.cdc.gov/art/artdata/index.html.

is likely to attract public attention. A decade before Nadya Suleman became front-page news, another birth of multiples was greeted differently by the media:

> In 1997, the *McCaugheys* of Iowa, whose first child's birth had been a result of fertility treatments, again sought fertility drugs. But this time the therapy resulted in a pregnancy with septuplets, all of which the McCaugheys decided to carry to term. Although the media proclaimed the birth of the seven babies "a miracle," not all saw a cause for celebration. For many health care professionals and bioethicists, their case involved an irresponsible use of fertility treatment (and journalism). Although exactly how Bobbi McCaughey ended up with septuplets remains unclear, it is known that she and her husband ruled out selective abortion on evangelical Christian grounds. They trusted God and left the outcome to Him.

As with Suleman's octuplets, here too the medical team respected parental choice while failing to protect the mother and her future children from serious risks. Yet the media dealt quite differently with the two cases. Far from producing "a miracle," Suleman's train-wreck life won her only notoriety. Perhaps reporters were just echoing their readers' growing awareness of the moral reasons to which we now turn.

The Problem of Multiples

Reasons for and against the moral permissibility of new reproductive technologies (NRTs) need not be focused on the Problem of Multiples. We discuss later in this chapter some that do not. Here our focus is the morality of IVF and fertility therapy, given the Problem of Multiples associated with these medical interventions. The arguments of concern invoke the welfare, in the sense of 'wellbeing,' of offspring and justice for all involved.

Arguments from Justice

The Just-Distribution-of-Health-Care-Costs Objection charges that multiple births amount to a great burden on the health care system. In the US, by 2015 the standard delivery costs in uncomplicated pregnancies ranged from $21,000 for a singleton, to $105,000 for twins and $400,000 for multiples. Twins increase costs five times compared to a singleton, and triplets or more increase them twenty-fold. While costs for singletons are mother-related, they are infant-related for multiples, who often require long stays in the NICU (Calandrillo and Deliganis, 2015). Given these data, the objection is

1. Some NRTs impose unnecessary delivery and pediatric care costs on the health care system.
2. That is unfair to others in society.
3. Unfair interventions are generally morally wrong.

_____

4. Therefore, those NRTs are generally morally wrong.

Proponents of this objection further regard adoption as an alternative for infertile individuals wishing to have children. Adoption avoids misuse of scarce medical resources and benefits orphans, infertile individuals, and society as a whole.

But this claim is met by Mary Anne Warren's (1988) appeal to a Just-Distribution-of-Adoption's-Burdens Argument, which grants the Problem of Multiples but contends:

1.   At present, there is a shortage of healthy children for adoption.
2.   Without fertility therapy and IVF, infertile individuals would have to adopt children with special needs.
3.   It is unfair to put that burden only on them.

_____

4.   Therefore, fertility therapy and IVF are morally justified.

Premise (3) rests on a plausible intuition about justice: society's benefits and burdens, including the burden of rearing children with special needs, should be distributed failrly among all members. (2) is based on evidence, while (1) seems true with this qualification: in the US, it's not *adoptable babies* that are in short supply, but healthy white infants. There is no shortage of older children and infants of color or disabled. However, that there is a shortage of children for adoption overall, both domestically and internationally, is well documented. Some ascribe it to the widespread view that orphans should remain within their families and communities.[2] Be that as it may, when thus qualified the Just-Distribution-of-Adoption's-Burdens Argument succeeds in undermining the Just-Distribution-of-Health-Care-Costs Objection to the morality of IFV and feritility therapy. For other arguments supporting the permissibility of these and other NRTs, see "Other Moral Controversies" below. To succeed, however, Warren's argument needs to show that the benefits of these NRTs outweigh any possible harms to the children, a topic considered next.

The Welfare Objection

Obligations of justice are not the only ones relevant to the morality of NRTs. Beneficence to the offspring also matters, given the positive correlation between multiple births and extreme *prematurity* and *low birthweight*. As discussed in Chapter 9, for newborns these conditions mean a high risk of death or survival with severe mental and physical impairments. The Welfare Objection contends

1.   Some NRTs are linked to an uncompensated high risk of neonatal death or severe disability.
2.   Providing interventions with risks of that sort is morally wrong.

_____

3.   Therefore, providing those NRTs is morally wrong.

It must be noted in reply that, following adequate medical guidelines, NRTs need not result in pregnancies facing such increased risks. Even so, given the issues of regulation and funding of IVF treatments discussed above, premise (1) is true. Besides, recent studies also show a positive correlation between IVF and congenital disorders, especially when combined with

_____

2   See Alan Greenblatt, "Fewer Babies Available for Adoption by US Parents," *NPR*, 11/17/2011; Wendy Koch, "USA Faces Critical Adoption Shortage," *USA Today*, 1/10/2013; and Dean Schabner, "Why It Costs More to Adopt a White Baby?" *ABC News*, 3/8/2016.

IMAGE 14.1
©iStockPhoto/koya79

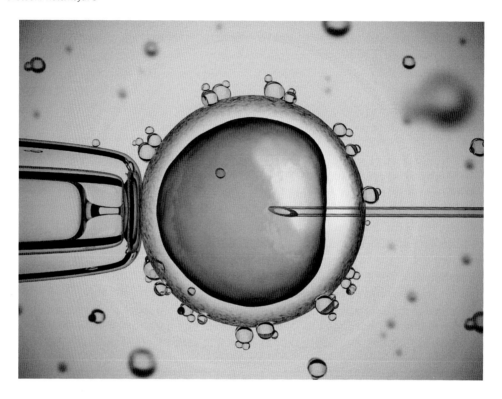

intracytoplasmic sperm injection (ICSI). In ICSI, sperm that would naturally fail to fertilize an egg is injected directly into it. Originally introduced to treat male infertility, ICSI has become a standard part of IVF treatments because it boosts their chances of producing embryos. But it does so at an increased risk of causing congenital disorders linked to the use of sperm that nature would have discarded.

The Nonidentity Problem

The main reply to the **Welfare Objection** is the so-called **Nonidentity Problem**. This is the problem that without some NRTs, many children with impairments, whose lives are worth living, would not have existed. When 'harm' is defined as a setback to someone's interests, and a given NRT used to assist a child's conception has caused her an impairment compatible with her having a life worth living, questions arise as to whether the NRT has harmed her. For how could it be in the child's interests not to exist? Clearly, without the NRT that child would not exist, and existing albeit with impairments seems better than not existing at all.

We revisit the Nonidentity Problem in Chapter 15. For now, note that not all think it arises. Cynthia Cohen (1996), for example, charges that it confuses prenatal nonexistence (i.e., to have never been born) with postnatal nonexistence (death). Prenatal nonexistence is neither bad nor good, since unlike nonexistence after death, it involves no loss of life's goods.

In our view, the perspective of the impaired offspring matters in evaluating the strengths of the Welfare Objecion and its Nonidentity-Problem reply. Clearly, some severely disabled people do regard their own existence as a harm even when their lives seem above the line of not-worth-living. This is shown by *wrongful-life* actions where plaintiffs typically contend that enabling them to come into existence was an injury. The alleged tort is that a child was born *at all* into a life of suffering which the plaintiff perceives as worse than prenatal nonexistence. Wrongful-life actions are generally dismissed because the courts wish to avoid speculative assessments concerning whether a plaintiff's nonexistence would have been better than her existence with a very low quality of life. Yet if vulnerability to harm is considered from the subjective perspective, then since from the plaintiffs' perspective, causing their existence was a harm, then their cases support the Welfare Objection: impaired children with worth-living lives can sometimes be harmed by being brought into existence.

BOX 14.3 NEW REPRODUCTIVE TECHNOLOGIES (NRTS)

Assisted Reproductive Technologies (ARTs): any NRT that handles both eggs and sperm outside the body.[3]

- In-vitro fertilization (IVF)—fertilization by combination of eggs with sperm in a lab dish.
- Intracytoplasmic sperm injection (ICSI)—injection of a single sperm into an egg to induce fertilization.

Not in the ART category, as defined above:

- Egg donation—the use of a woman's eggs for creating embryos on behalf of one or more intended parents.

- Surrogacy—arrangement whereby a woman carries a pregnancy on behalf of the intended parents. A surrogate may be the egg donor.
- Intrauterine insemination—assisted placement of semen into a woman's uterus for fertilization.
- Fertility therapy—fertility drug regime to induce egg production.

14.3 The Complex Cases

Since the 1980s, social changes and the development of new reproductive interventions have made NRTs available to same sex couples, single reproducers, and postmenopausal (beyond reproductive age) women. Human reproduction assisted by NRTs may involve IVF combined with the use of donated sperm or eggs and surrogate mothers. The expansion of NRTs added ethical challenges to the Problem of Multiples discussed above.

---

3 CDC. "What is Assisted Reproductive Technology?" 11/14/2014. http://www.cdc.gov/art/whatis. html.

Egg Donation, Gestational Surrogacy, and Postmenopausal Motherhood

IVF was initially used to treat a common type of female infertility that is caused by a fallopian tube blockage preventing the passage of the egg to the sperm or the fertilized egg to the womb. But when the woman's eggs cause infertility, becoming pregnant may then require 'donor' eggs—which in fact are commonly bought by the **intended** (called also 'social' or 'rearing') **parents** from an egg-broker agency. When there is no sperm provided by a male partner that could fertilize the woman's eggs, fertilization requires donor sperm, usually bought from a sperm bank. In a scenario where the intended parents use donor eggs and sperm, they are not genetically related to the embryos thus created.

Advances in procreative medicine have also made possible the transfer of IVF embryos into the womb of a surrogate. If implantation occurs, she is the gestational carrier of the embryos. If she provides her own eggs and the pregnancy produces at least one live birth, she is the infant's **genetic mother**. Surrogates that are only gestational carriers are usually sought when the intended mother is fertile but carrying a pregnancy to term poses a risk to her health. If she uses the services of a surrogate to conceive, she is the infant's intended and genetic mother, but the surrogate is its **gestational mother** (see Box 14.4).

BOX 14.4 THREE TYPES OF MOTHERHOOD

- The intended, rearing, or social mother—the woman on behalf of whom the child is conceived.

- The gestational carrier or host—the birth mother.
- The genetic or biological mother—the egg donor.

This and other reproductive scenarios now familiar require procreative interventions that not long ago belonged to the domain of fiction. They include **egg donation** and gestational **surrogacy**, reproductive interventions whereby, respectively,

- A woman's eggs are fertilized *in utero* or *in vitro* to create embryos for someone else.
- A so-called gestational mother provides her uterus for carrying a pregnancy to term on behalf of another woman, the intended mother.

With these interventions, the pool of people who may benefit from IVF technology has extended far beyond the simple case to include gay, lesbian, and transgender couples, single individuals, and postmenopausal women. These include women in their 50s and above who wish to bear a child but can no longer use their eggs for fertilization. Traditionally, they were thought to have passed gestational age. Yet today a postmenopausal woman's uterus can be 'primed' with hormone drugs before transferring to her womb for implantation IVF embryos resulting from donor eggs. Since the 1990s, the number of **postmenopausal pregnancies** has been on the rise, owing in part to advances in cryopreservation of eggs. Although there is some controversy about their chances for successful live births, the evidence suggests that postmenopausal pregnancies do increase the risks of prematurity and low birthweight. They also produce more Caesarean deliveries and maternal complications, such as gestational diabetes and pregnancy-induced hypertension.

For these reasons, countries such as the Netherlands forbid the use of commercial donor eggs after 45. In the US, fertility clinics have an age limit of 50 to 55 and often deny postmenopausal women IVF treatments because of their lower success rates. As discussed below, major moral worries about postmenopausal pregnancies concern the conflict between women's reproductive freedom and beneficence to future children, and the fact that restrictions of NRTs on the basis of age might involve discrimination (Parks, 1999). India allows IVF for any woman who can afford it privately, a policy that became world news when Rajo Devi, 70, gave birth to a girl in 2008. Rajo died eighteen months later from complications of the Caesarean delivery.

Some Facts about Egg Donors and Gestational Carriers

Egg donors are a scarce resource highly prized. Mature eggs and oocytes (the female reproductive cell in the process of developing into an egg) are sought not only for IVF treatments but also for stem cell research. Although some women donate the eggs remaining from IVF rounds altruistically to other women who need them, such donations are insufficient to satisfy current demand. The scarcity of donor eggs in the market is unsurprising in light of the time investment and health risks facing donors. Initially, the woman must pass a battery of mental and physical screenings. Then, she must undergo hormone therapy designed to produce superovulation, and finally, a surgical extraction of the eggs. The risks of complications from the hormone therapy include ovarian hyperstimulation syndrome, which affects 6% of the women and produces varying degrees of discomfort and harm. Heart failure, though rare, has been reported (Gruen, 2007). According to the American Society for Reproductive Medicine (2000), without any such complications, an egg donor spends about 56 hours in the clinic per cycle. Because of demand, egg sale is now a booming market, entirely unregulated in the US. Egg-broker agencies report that potential buyers often look for features in donors that suggest racial and social discrimination (blond hair, blue eyes, tall stature, high SAT scores).

Gestational carriers are also scarce, given the burdens, including physical and mental risks, involved in carrying a pregnancy to term. This market, increasingly global, shows a trend toward 'surrogacy tourism' whereby individuals and couples from the West turn to clinics in the developing world to find surrogates for their embryos at a fee lower than what they would pay in their own countries. Reportedly, the dire financial situations in developing countries sometimes force surrogates into abusive agreements.

Moral Controversies

The above arguments about fertility therapy and the simple case of IVF also bear on the morality of other NRTs. While beneficence and reproductive freedom support their permissibility, the ways they alter human reproduction, handle early life, or treat the women involved argue against it. Here we look closely at the reasons on both sides of this controversy, with an eye to identifying those that pass scrutiny and may be held by reasonable people.

The Benefits Argument

According to this utilitarian argument, NRTs in both simple and complex cases are morally justified since their benefits outweigh their burdens overall. The benefits at issue concern people who, due to involuntary infertility or other reason, are not able to have children without such assistance. Once this argument's implicit *principle of utility* is accepted, its soundness depends on evidence about the total balance of NRTs' benefits over burdens for all involved, including prospective parents and children and society as a whole. To defend it, utilitarians may invoke IVF's improved record of success since 1978 and contend that, for other NRTs too, their benefits over time will outweigh costs or risks to women and offspring (Singer and Wells, 1983). In their view, what is needed is not a moral ban but proper regulation to avoid abuses. Yet the Benefits Argument is inconclusive, given the difficulty of calculating benefits over burdens in the long run. For example, should the welfare of orphans be considered? What about credible predictions of future overpopulation and food scarcity?

The Procreative Freedom Appeal

Access to NRTs would also be a moral right given John Robertson's libertarian appeal to procreative freedom (1994: 24). It runs,

1.   Decisions that are essential to one's identity and dignity, and to the meaning of one's life, enjoy presumptive primacy.
2.   Procreative decisions are so essential.

_____

3.   Therefore, procreative decisions enjoy presumptive primacy.

Procreative freedom enjoys "presumptive primacy" because people should be at liberty to make self-regarding reproductive decisions unless there are stronger reasons to the contrary. Harm to others would count as such an overriding reason. Given the presumptive primacy of **procreative freedom**, individuals requesting NRTs to have children may morally do so provided the technologies will not harm others. While for libertarians procreative decisions can be limited only by harm to others, for utilitarians the limits are set by overall balance of benefits versus burdens. As noted in Chapter 15, some utilitarians also value procreative freedom, defined as a persons' right to decide for themselves whether to have or not to have children. By contrast with libertarians who value it in itself, utilitarians endorse J. S. Mill's view that individual liberty (including procreative freedom) is valuable as a means to happiness.

Whether consequentialist or libertarian, the Procreative Freedom Appeal is consistent with opposition to NRTs with substantial burdens. Neither interpretation entails an obligation of health care providers to honor requests for such reproductive assistance. But does procreative freedom have presumptive primacy? Dissenters include conservative moral theologians who consistently oppose not only NRTs but also contraception and abortion, and feminist theorists who regard NRTs as contrary to women's interests and dignity. We take up their objections in turn, beginning by conservative objections that assume:

1.   Any NRT that assists in achieving conception through the conjugal or sexual act of husband and wife is morally permissible.
2.   Any NRT that replaces that way of conception is morally forbidden.

The Unnaturalness Objection

Following the Sacred Congregation for the Doctrine of the Faith's *Donum Vitae* (*The Gift of Life*, 1987), conservative Catholic theologians such as John Haas (1998) and William May (2003) object to any NRTs that are incompatible with human conception according to God's plans for nature. In their view, given (1) and (2) above, Nadya Suleman's IVF was forbidden while the McCaugheys' fertility treatment was permissible, even though both NRTs face the Problem of Multiples. Note that condition (2) is quite demanding, since it makes most NRTs morally forbidden. What should infertile people wishing to have children do? May's advice is to accept their fate and adopt if they are a married couple.

The *Unnaturalness Objection* to most NRTs draws a bright moral line between natural and unnatural NRTs, based on whether they accord with God's plans for nature or do not. But the existence of such a bright line is questionable, even within religiously grounded bioethics. For surely IVF is too expensive and risky to become a standard way to conceive. But 'nonstandard' does not mean 'unnatural' in the sense of 'contrary to God's plan for nature.' In fact, the meaning of 'natural' as invoked in this objection is unclear. It cannot be *what occurs in nature*, without technical or institutional intervention, since *natural* reproduction does not require the married couple's sexual act. Suppose it is *whatever avoids interference with God's plans for nature*. Then, as we saw in connection with the Sanctity-of-Life doctrine in Chapter 11, that definition presupposes some religious beliefs. As a result, it is likely to be divisive since it involves beliefs that not everyone shares about God and His role in the natural order. But put this problem aside. Why think that some NRTs do interfere with God's plans? It cannot be because they are innovations. Otherwise *all* scientific progress would interfere with God's plan and be impermissible.

On the other hand, suppose the traditional family manifests the natural order because departures from it can result in psychological harm to the children. In surrogacy, for example, learning that a social parent is not also a genetic parent might be psychologically stressful for the offspring. If the parents keep secrecy instead, that might erode trust within the family. Under this interpretation, the Unnaturalness Objection becomes a version of the Children's Welfare argument discussed above, which has the advantage of recognizing the Problem of Multiples equally facing scenarios such as *the McCaugheys* and *Nadya Suleman*.

Embryo Mishandling

The objection to NRTs from Embryo Mishandling targets specifically IVF treatments because they typically:

1. Produce far more embryos than would be safe to transfer to the uterus.
2. Let some embryos die (those at high risk of carrying impairments).
3. Store the remaining embryos (in the US, indefinitely), to be used later by the intended parents or donated to other parents or researchers.

The objector finds all three morally problematic. IVF treatments involve (1) because creating one embryo at a time would undermine their already low success rates. But (1) leads to the problem of what to do with any remaining embryos. And how defective must a gene be to morally justify (2)? (3) requires freezing the embryos, which thereby enter a state of suspended animation (neither alive nor dead). Is that morally permissible? Transferring *all* embryos to the uterus would avoid (2) and (3), and is sometimes defended on religious grounds. But it risks pregnancies with multiples.

IVF enthusiasts reply that, at only a 30% survival chance, most embryos are naturally aborted in *un*assisted conception, and "no one suggests that natural conception is, for this reason, wrong, or that it *would* be wrong if the probability of surviving were significantly lower than it is" (McMahan, 2007: 34). Yet unlike IVF, these natural abortions may be justi-fied by *double effect*, as an unintended side effect of procreation.

A different line of reply first acknowledges that the objection would succeed if embryos had the moral standing of, for example, *paradigm persons* like us. It would then be imper-missible to create more embryos than needed, destroy some, and freeze others indefinitely. But having paradigm-person standing requires certain psychological capacities that a 5- or 6-day-old embryo clearly lacks. This perhaps explains why society has generally accepted IVF. In any event, the controversy now turns on the moral standing of embryos, an unsettled issue discussed in Chapter 10.

The Feminist Critique

Some feminists charge that NRTs

1. Undermine women's dignity and power.
2. Exploit and commodify women.

Either (1) or (2) is a reason for the moral wrongness of NRTs. Support for (1) comes from the fact that these technologies, developed and administered mostly by men, give them control over conception and birth. Men have a history of negligence in the medical care of women. Traditionally, assistance in natural conception was in the hands of midwives, but in the 19th century male doctors gradually replaced midwives. Childbirth became a 'medical condition' to be treated in hospitals, with a consequent rise in mortality and morbidity rates, owing in part to iatrogenic infections acquired in the new setting (Warren, 1988). In addition to endangering women in this way, the medicalization of pregnancy and childbirth disempow-ered women by giving control of their childbearing to men. NRTs extended this disempow-ering to the fertility clinic. Furthermore, IVF's origin in veterinary science adds injury to women's dignity.

In addition, reproduction is now a high-profit business where women's eggs, wombs, and indeed reproductive capacity are traded as commodities. The fertility clinic encourages pregnancies 'by catalog order,' whereby mostly white, well-off prospective parents select donors and surrogates according to values that reflect societal biases. Egg donation and sur-rogacy are particularly problematic because they commonly involve selling eggs and renting wombs respectively, thus introducing market values into pregnancy and childbirth. Since women are treated as mere means, NRTs undermine their interests as a group (Anderson, 1990; Raymond, 1989).

Moreover, women seeking NRTs cannot give informed consent because of the pres-sure of

---

Natalism

The prejudice that people should procreate

Natalism, a widespread societal expectation that is particularly demanding for women, conflicts with procreative freedom. If natalism determines decisions to seek assistance with NRT, consent to it lacks voluntariness. Consent is undermined too when women enter surrogacy and egg donation contracts because of their financial needs. Donors and surrogates may also suffer exploitaition by more wealthy individuals seeking their services.

But not all agree with this feminist critique. To Mary Anne Warren (1988), NRTs can boost women's reproductive autonomy, thus advancing their interests. But it should be regulated to require, for example, quotas of female medical professionals at fertility clinics. To Lori Gruen (2007), commodification is compatible with respect for women's dignity. By contrast with buying organs, payment for eggs (or wombs) compares to compensation for athletic or scientific achievements—neither of which undermines the athletes' or scientists' dignity. Furthermore, whether surrogates and egg donors are exploited depends on proper regulation of contracts and the meaning of 'exploitation.' As ordinarily understood, 'exploitation' need not apply to these women any more than to wage laborers. This reply, however, ignores the difficulties in regulating a trade marked by global economic inequality between the surrogates and egg donors in the developing world and the more wealthy Western individuals seeking their services.

14.4 Chapter Summary

This chapter first presented two cases illustrating the problem of pregnancies with multiples, which are at a higher risk of causing harm to the mother and children, and of increasing exponentially the costs of delivery. An objection from harm to children charges that such results are morally unacceptable, while one from justice focuses on another aspect of reproductive technologies resulting in the birth of multiples: the cost of delivery and neonatal critical care, usually borne by society.

From a utilitarian perspective, however, it has also been argued that reproductive innovations' benefits for many individuals wishing to have children outweigh their burdens, including risks of harm and cost. NRT enthusiasts make an appeal to justice of their own: without these technologies, the burden of adopting children, most of whom have special needs, would fall on infertile individuals wishing to raise children. Furthermore, there is a presumption in favor of individual autonomy in self-regarding procreative decisions, provided they do not harm others. Given procreative freedom, NRTs are morally permissible. But according to the feminist critique, NRTs might undermine the interests of future children, egg donors, surrogates, and women as a group. Yet there remains considerable disagreement among feminists about whether NRTs have these consequences. For a roadmap to main arguments for and against the moral permissibility of these reproductive innovations, see Figure 14.1.

FIGURE 14.1   Main Moral Arguments for and against NRTs

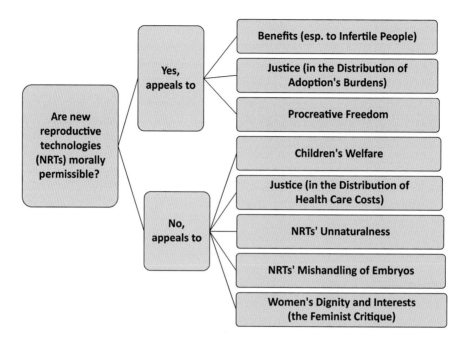

14.5 Study Aids

Key Words

Egg donation, 266
Fertility therapy, 261
Genetic/gestational/intended motherhood, 266
In-vitro fertilization (IVF), 258
Natalism, 271
New reproductive technology (NRT), 259
Nonidentity Problem, 264
Postmenopausal pregnancy, 265
Problem of Multiples, 261
Procreative freedom, 268
Surrogacy, 266

Questions and Cases for Further Consideration

1.   How do NRTs change the traditional family? Might concerns about the genetic integrity of families count in evaluating the change? What about the predicted scarcity of food, globally? All things considered, is the change for better or worse?

2. NRTs, usually privately funded, have significant costs. Does this social aspect of IVF amount to discrimination against involuntarily infertile women of low socioeconomic status? If so, should this reproductive technology be banned?

3. In 2011, a mother's registry in the US yielded 150 offspring conceived by sperm from the same donor, identified to families only by a number. For an individual donor, begetting 50 offspring is not uncommon. Eggs from the same donor may also be used in multiple pregnancies. As a result, accidental incest is a real possibility. Does this amount to a problem? If so, what kind of problem? Could it be solved?

4. Some bioethicists propose that health care providers be asked to screen and select the candidates for NRTs, as adoption agencies do. What eligibility requirements may avoid *Nadya-Suleman* scenarios? Should they include the ability to pay for childbirth and neonatal care, background checks, or advance consent to fetal reduction?

5. *In the Matter of Baby M (1988) is a landmark case in which the New Jersey Supreme Court reversed a lower court decision holding that surrogacy contracts are enforceable. Chief Justice Wilentz wrote, "There are, in a civilized society, some things that money cannot buy." In his view, a surrogate's parental rights cannot be terminated by payment. The surrogate at issue was Mary Beth Whitehead. She had agreed to artificial insemination and gestational surrogacy on behalf of William Stern, the biological father. His wife Elizabeth was to adopt the baby after birth. The Sterns were wealthy. Like many surrogates in the US, Ms. Whitehead lived modestly but was not poor. After the birth, however, she forfeited the $10,000 she would have earned and was planning to use for her two children's education. She and her husband had decided to keep the girl. The Court granted visitation rights to her and rearing rights to the Sterns. It thus recognized qualified parental rights for surrogates.* Questions to consider here include: a) Should the decision have been different? What if Whitehead was only the girl's gestational mother? b) Was the traditional, single concept of motherhood at stake in this case? c) Whose interests should matter in decisions about surrogacy? d) Might surrogacy benefit from the model of adoption which forbids payment to biological parents? e) Were the Sterns exploiting or treating Whitehead like an incubator?

6. *Rajo Devi Lohan and her husband, modest farmers from Baddhu Patti, India, wanted to have a child. They went through financial hardship to pay for an IVF treatment and Rajo gave birth at age 70. Eighteen months later, Rajo was dying from complications of the Caesarean section. Too weak to lift her daughter but happy to be a mother, Rajo told reporters her doctor never mentioned the risks of giving birth at her age. Dr. Anurag Bishnoi argued that the treatment was right, because now "she does not have to face the stigma of being barren." He also boasted that with his assistance, a 66-year-old woman just gave birth to triplets. For Rajo, dying did not matter "because I lived long enough to become a mother."[4]* Questions to consider here include: a) How might such use of NRTs benefit or harm older parents and their offspring? b) Might children becoming orphans

---

4 Meena Hartenstein, "'World's Oldest Mother' Is Dying just 18 Months after Giving Birth at Age 70," *New York Daily News*, 6/14/2010.

matter to its permissibility? c) Given that older men do not commonly face criticism for fathering children, is it sexist or ageist to think that Rajo and her physician did wrong? d) How did Rajo and Bishnoi react to the natalism in their culture? e) What might be evidence of natalism in your culture? f) Is natalism a culturally determined bias? What about procreative freedom? g) Which factors, if any, should determine when a woman is too old to have a baby?

Suggested Readings*

*Anderson, Elizabeth. "Is Women's Labor a Commodity?" *Philosophy & Public Affairs* 19.1, 1990: 71–92.
  Argues for a ban on commercial surrogacy on the grounds that it commodifies women and children.
Calandrillo, S. P. and C. V. Deliganis, "In Vitro Fertilization and the Law: How Legal and Regulatory Neglect Compromised a Medical Breakthrough," *Arizona Law Review* 57.2, 2015: 311–42.
  Good source of recent data on the use of IVF technology. Argues for pursuing federal oversight in the US.
*Cohen, Cynthia, "Give Me Children or I Shall Die!" *Hastings Center Report* 26.2, 1996: 19–27.
  Questions the metaphysical basis for thinking that, with some exceptions, it is always better to exist with disability than not to exist at all.
*Cohen, Jessica, "Grade A: The Market for a Yale Woman's Eggs," *The Atlantic* 290.5, 2002: 74–7.
  Provides evidence for the feminist critique of egg donation in the US, suggesting that the market is driven by social biases, commercial interests, and disregard for the autonomy and welfare of donors.
Greif, K. F. and Jon F. Merz, *Current Controversies in the Biological Sciences: Case Studies of Policy Challenges from New Technologies*. Cambridge: MIT Press, 2007.
  Highlights main facts and statistics about NRTs, as well as problems with the self-regulation system prevalent in the US.
Gruen, L., "Oocytes for Sale?" *Metaphilosophy* 38, 2–3, 2007: 285–308.
  Argues that neither the commodification nor the exploitation of donors is a problem for properly regulated sales of women's eggs, which may help overcome the scarcity of oocytes for stem cell research.
*Haas, John M., "Begotten Not Made: A Catholic View of Reproductive Technology," *US Conference of Catholic Bishops*, 1998. Available online at http://www.usccb.org/issues-and-action/human-life-and-dignity/reproductive-technology/begotten-not-made-a-catholic-view-of-reproductive-technology.cfm.
  Conservative Catholic objection to NRTs that replace, rather than assist, human conception through the conjugal act.
*Lizza, John P., "Potentiality and Human Embryos," *Bioethics* 21.7, 2007: 379–85.

---

* Asterisks mark readings available online. See links on the companion website.

Contends that, unlike other embryos, IVF embryos lack the potentiality to become a person.

*McMahan, Jeff, "Killing Embryos for Stem Cell Research," *Metaphilosophy* 38.2/3, 2007: 170–89.

Invokes the mindlessness of early embryos to justify how they are handled in IVF.

*May, William E., "Begetting vs. Making Babies," in Lund-Molfese, N. C., and M. L. Kelly, eds., *Human Dignity and Reproductive Technology*, pp. 81–92. Lanham: University Press of America, 2003. Available online at http://www.christendom-awake.org/pages/may/begetting.htm.

Illustrates the conservative Catholic objection that NRT conception is unnatural.

*Minkoff, H. and J. Ecker, "The California Octuplets and the Duties of Reproductive Endocrinologists," *American Journal of Obstetrics and Gynecology* 201.1, 2009: 15e1–15e3.

Argues that neither the burden to society nor parental eligibility for IVF should concern fertility specialists. But the need to avoid transferring too many embryos should.

*Murray, Thomas H., "What Are Families For? Getting to an Ethics of Reproductive Technology," *Hastings Center Report* 32.3, 2002: 41–5.

Contra the standard focus on procreative freedom in assessing the moral permissibility of NRTs, proposes to focus on the family relationships needed for the flourishing of children.

*Parks, Jennifer, "On the Use of IVF by Post-Menopausal Women," *Hypatia* 14.1, 1999: 77–96.

Argues that if IVF technology is morally permissible, there is no good reason for denying postmenopausal women access to it. To think otherwise amounts to discrimination on the basis of age.

*President's Council on Bioethics, *Reproduction and Responsibility: The Regulation of New Biotechnologies*. Washington, DC, 2004.

Examines the moral issues facing NRTs and recommends public policies for IVF, the screening and selection of embryos, egg donation, and surrogacy.

*Raymond, Janice, "Reproductive Technologies, Radical Feminism, and Socialist Liberalism," *Journal of Reproductive and Genetic Engineering* 2.2, 1989: 133–42.

Objects to "liberal" feminist views of NRTs on the grounds that these undermine the interests of women as a group.

*Robertson, John A., *Children of Choice: Freedom and the New Reproductive Technologies*. Princeton, NJ: Princeton University Press, 1994.

Defends the presumptive primacy of procreative liberty on the basis of the importance of procreative decisions for personal identity, dignity, and the meaning of one's life.

*Sacred Congregation for the Doctrine of the Faith, *Donum Vitae*, Vatican, 1987. Available online at http://www.vatican.va/roman_curia/congregations/cfaith/documents/rc_con_cfaith_doc_19870222_respect-for-human-life_en.html.

Objects to NRTs that replace the conjugal act. But once an NRT produces embryos, these are human beings with full rights. Also titled "Instruction of Respect for Human Life in Its Origin and on the Dignity of Procreation: Replies to Certain Questions of the Day."

*Singer, Peter and Dianne Wells, "In Vitro Fertilisation: The Major Issues," *Journal of Medical Ethics* 9.4, 1983: 192–5.

Defends the moral permissibility of IVF in the simple case by responding to standard objections. But its discussion of complex cases is dated, since it considers only altruistic egg donation and surrogacy.

Steinbock, Bonnie, "Payment for Egg Donation and Surrogacy," *Mount Sinai Journal of Medicine* 71.4, 2004: 255–65.

Distinguishes compensation to surrogates from payment for desired traits, arguing that only the former is morally justified.

———, "A Philosopher Looks at Assisted Reproduction," *Journal of Assisted Reproduction and Genetics* 12.8, 1995: 543–51.

Good outline of standard moral arguments against NRTs. Invokes parental responsibility and justice, not harm to future children, to explain the wrongness of knowingly using treatments that increase the risk of neonatal disability.

*Warren, Mary Anne, "IVF and Women's Interests: An Analysis of Feminist Concerns," *Bioethics* 2.1, 1988: 37–57.

Argues that the new reproductive technologies promote women's reproductive autonomy and are therefore in their interests.

15 Human Genetic Engineering

Learning Objectives

In reading this chapter you will

▶   Reflect on how genetic innovations in medicine create new moral challenges.

▶   Analyze main reasons for and against the use of genetics for the selection of in-vitro fertilized embryos before transfer for implantation.

▶   Distinguish optimist and pessimist positions on the morality of using cloning for human reproduction.

▶   Learn about the moral issues facing the possibility of human genetic enhancement.

O F GROWING CONCERN to bioethics are some recent innovations in genetics and biotechnology that seem, from a moral perspective, a two-edged sword. Their implementation in diagnosing genetic disorders strikes us as beneficial, while raising worries about the possibility of causing harm to present or future people. As we'll see in this chapter, their use in human reproduction creates moral problems of its own, especially in connection with prospective human cloning and the altering of genes for human enhancement.

15.1 Designing *Deaf Baby*

Sharon Duchesneau and Candy McCullough, a deaf couple in their 30s from Bethesda, Maryland, had already begun building a family when in 2002 they sought reproductive assistance in order to conceive a deaf child. With their first child, they were denied a chance to select for implantation only embryos with the trait of deafness that they wanted. So they sought in-vitro fertilization with sperm from a friend who had five generations of deafness in his family. They eventually succeeded in having Jehanne, a deaf girl they intended to bring up in the deaf community and culture. In their view, deafness is not a disability but a linguistic trait and cultural identity to be embraced with pride, something akin to being Black, East Asian, or Hispanic.

Like many in the deaf community, Duchesneau and McCullough cherished the use of sign language and the complex culture around it, which they wanted to share with their children. Furthermore, they thought they would be better parents to a deaf child. At seven months through the pregnancy, Ms. Duchesneau told reporters: "It would be nice to have a deaf child who is the same as us. I think that would be a wonderful experience. You know, if we can have that chance, why not take it? A hearing baby would be a blessing. A deaf baby would be a special blessing."[1] Since deafness is one of the many traits that recent reproductive technologies allow to select before implantation, she regarded as a prejudice the health care providers' refusal to help them select embryos with deafness. As it happens, their son, Gauvin, was born with partial hearing in his right ear. The couple declined medical advice to fit him with a hearing aid so he could develop comprehension of speech. They have also declined that advice for Jehanne. In their view, it should be up to the children to make that choice when they get older.

■ ■ ■

Duchesneau and McCullough decided to enlist a deaf sperm donor because they were denied **PGD**, the procedure outlined in Box 15.1. Although PGD was introduced to detect and discard embryos with certain genetic disorders linked to sex, it soon became available for selecting embryos for nonsex-related medical conditions. In 2003, French doctors learned how to diagnose dwarfism with PGD. They soon discovered that some couples were requesting PGD for the transferring of embryos with the dwarfism trait. PGD might also be used to select for the presence of traits such as sex, blindness, and some mental impairments. Yet, as in the deaf couple's case, most clinics refused to provide it for designing a disabled baby. Of 190 clinics surveyed in 2006 by Johns Hopkins University, 3% reported the use of PGD for selecting embryos with a disability trait.[2]

BOX 15.1 PREIMPLANTATION GENETIC DIAGNOSIS (PGD)

- PGD, combined with in-vitro fertilization (IVF), is used on one or two cells of a 3-day-old embryo, which by then has between five and ten cells.
- The cells are screened for single-gene defects or for genetic mutations linked to heritable disorders.

- Embryos with disease traits are discarded, the others transferred for implantation to the woman's womb, stored for later use in reproduction, or donated for research.
- The first birth from a PGD-selected embryo occurred in 1990; by 2002 there were about 1,000 according to the PGD International Society.

1   David Teather, "Lesbian Couple Have a Deaf Baby by Choice," *The Guardian*, 4/7/2002.
2   Darshak M. Sanghavi, "Wanting Babies Like Themselves, Some Parents Choose Genetic Defects," *New York Times*, 12/5/2006.

Why might many think such use morally wrong? Dena Davis (1997) provides an Autonomy Argument:

1. Designing a disabled child imposes on her the parents' conception of a good life.
2. Limiting her choices violates her right to an open future.
3. Violating a child's right to an open future is morally wrong.

---

4. Therefore, designing a disabled child is morally wrong.

Davis thinks that such decisions narrow the scope of the future child's choices when she grows up, thus violating her right to an 'open future.' Among her disadvantages later in life will be fewer options in career, marriage, and other life goals. The Duchesneau and McCullough's decision illustrates premise (1) because it imposed the couple's conception of deaf culture on their offspring. For Davis, their rationale was analogous to that of parents who decide to deprive their children of an education or life-saving treatment on the basis of their religious or life-style preferences. If those decisions undermine the children's wellbeing, they would be wrong on nonmaleficence grounds. But for Davis they primarily violate respect for autonomy by treating children as mere means to their parents' goals. Her objection is independent of whether deafness is a disability or a cultural identity. Yet it entails that "deliberately creating a deaf child is a moral harm" (Davis, 1997: 9).

BOX 15.2 UTILITARIANS AND REPRODUCTIVE FREEDOM

Reproductive freedom falls within J. S. Mill's defense of liberty by arguing that it allows individuals to discover what kind of life is best for them, thus promoting utility for all concerned.

However, some utilitarians reject the Autonomy Argument because of its incompatibility with *procreative freedom*, which they value for the reasons outlined in Box 15.2. As you may recall from Chapter 14, libertarians also value it but not as means to something else. In either view, parents are at liberty to design a disabled child unless her disability is such that her life is not worth living. Since deafness is compatible with having a life worth living, it is morally permissible to design a deaf child. Here utilitarians and libertarians invoke their own intuitions about Derek Parfit's (1987) Nonidentity Problem. Greatly simplified, this is the problem of whether parents have wronged their offspring by conceiving them with disabilities compatible with a life worth living. For these utilitarians and libertarians, a child with a worth-living life cannot be harmed by being brought into existence because had the parents made a different procreative choice, that child would not exist. Fueling their intuitions are

1. Genetic essentialism—Different genetic origins necessarily result in different persons. In the deaf couple case, a different procreative decision would have produced either no child or a different child.

2. Person-affecting harm—In designing a disabled child, what matters is harm to the child or to others.

3. Reproductive freedom—Making self-regarding reproductive decisions is valuable either by itself (libertarian view) or as a means to the best life (utilitarian view).

For example, Julian Savulescu (2002) acknowledges that the deaf couple's decision resulted in the birth of a disabled child. But since her life is worth living, it did not harm that child: "Couples should be free to request and obtain genetic testing provided there are sufficient resources and their choices do not harm the child produced or other people, even if this deliberately brings a child into the world with what most people judge to be worse than average prospects." As Jonathan Glover puts it (2006: 57), how could the couple owe to that child that she was never born? Thus, a crucial part of the utilitarian/libertarian argument is:

1. Designing a disabled child is morally wrong only if the child's life is not worth living.
2. The deaf child's life *is* worth living.

_____

3. Therefore, her parents' choice was morally permissible.

Premise (2) is uncontroversial. But (1) is vulnerable, even after accepting the value of reproductive freedom and the failure of state-mandated policies restricting such freedom (see "The Early Eugenics" below). Dan Brock (1995), for example, is committed to offer this *Wrongful-Disability Objection*: even if the deaf couple did not harm the child, they failed to bring about the best state of affairs—something morally wrong for utilitarianism. They thus produced a nonperson-affecting harm that outweighs the value of procreative freedom.

Of these three arguments about the morality of such parental choices, only one finds them permissible. But all three need further assessment since they rest on controversial moral principles or calculations and conceptions of the benefits and harms brought about by those choices. Although such assessment goes beyond our purpose here, an informed view on the matter requires a broader look at the uses of genetics in human reproduction.

■ 15.2 Some Moral Controversies in Reprogenetics

Crucial to current developments in reprogenetics, a combination of new reproductive technologies with genetic methods, was the introduction of *in-vitro fertilization* (IVF) in the early 1980s. Such combination made possible the development of preimplantation genetic diagnosis (PGD), originally designed to detect the presence of genetic medical conditions in IVF embryos before their transfer to the woman's uterus, especially when parents are at high risk for genetic disease. But as we saw, the use of PGD has expanded considerably beyond its original purpose. Furthermore, genetics may make possible **human reproductive cloning** (HRC), to which many object on the moral grounds discussed in this section. Triggering their fear is the belief that these reproductive interventions amount to a new eugenics morally analogous to the much condemned, old eugenics of the early 20th century.

Preimplantation Genetic Diagnosis

Determining an embryo's sex was initially part of the screening for specific sex-linked disorders such as hemophilia or Duchenne muscular dystrophy, but some parents now request PGD for selecting their offspring's sex. Selecting embryos for the absence of disease traits falls under preventive medicine and is therefore less morally problematic than selecting for the presence of nonmedical traits, such as sex or eye color. As in the practice of using PGD for designing a disabled baby, there are reasons for and against using PGD for selecting embryos with certain nonmedical traits. For one thing, there is the above considered utilitarian/libertarian argument, based on procreative freedom. Furthermore, given the following utilitarian principle, PGD to select for medical and nonmedical traits is not only morally permissible but obligatory:

Procreative Beneficence

"[Reproducers] should select the child, of the possible children they could have, who is expected to have the best life, or at least as good a life as the others, based on the relevant, available information." (Savulescu, 2001: 415)

Since PGD maximizes the possibility of conceiving children with the best chances of having the best life, **Procreative Beneficence** makes PGD selection prima facie obligatory. But Julian Savulescu faces the problems of

1. Defining 'best life.'
2. Recommending the use of PGD to select embryos for the presence of traits such as race and sex.

In response to (1), he defines 'best life' as that of a child with traits that can bring her as many social advantages as possible. So his view is a type of perfectionism that runs into problem (2): it is well known that in our society, being of a certain race or sex is an advantage. Procreative Beneficence condones such biases. Here Savulescu responds that it is society that is responsible for eliminating those biases.

Some utilitarians similarly justify PGD for creating a **savior sibling**—i.e., a child conceived to save an existing sibling affected by a disease of the blood or immune system. The savior sibling may, for example, be the source of hematopoietic stem cells from the umbilical cord or bone marrow to save, or ameliorate, the condition of the other child. The birth of a savior sibling is particularly crucial in situations where no compatible cells are available for a transplant that is needed to save a child affected with Fanconi anemia, who faces the prospect of premature death unless she receives blood from the umbilical cord of a perfect match. With PGD, embryos that are a good genetic match can be selected for implantation. For critics of the practice, procreative freedom and beneficence are not enough to justify the wrongness of treating the savior as a mere means to save its sibling. For defenders, evidence would be needed that the practice can harm the savior, or that it precludes wanting and loving her for her own sake.

On the other hand, the wrongness of sex selection for nonmedical reasons (family 'balancing' or personal and cultural preferences) is often cited against PGD. But as shown in Box 15.3, PGD is not the only procedure available today for increasing the chances of having a child of a specific sex.

BOX 15.3 CURRENT PROCEDURES FOR SEX SELECTION

Sperm Sorting	Preimplantation Genetic Diagnosis (PGD)	Sex-Selective Abortion
• The sex selection occurs before conception • First, X (female) and Y (male) sperm cells are separated • Next, a sample of sperm most likely to produce an embryo of the desired sex is used in IVF or intrauterine insemination	• The sex selection occurs before implantation • First, the sex of IVF embryos is identified • Next, embryos of the desired sex are transferred to the uterus for implantation	• The sex selection occurs before birth • First, a sonogram reveals a fetus's sex • Next, if it is not the desired sex, an abortion is performed

Of these three procedures, the least morally controversial is sperm sorting (because the selection is done before conception), and the most controversial is sex-selective abortion (because it is done after the embryo has implanted). All three are costly and face some of the moral objections to sex selection discussed in Chapter 12. Since PGD for sex selection faces similar objections and they were shown inconclusive, the moral wrongness of the practice remains unsettled (though it is illegal in Canada and the United Kingdom). In addition, the moral wrongness of sex selection would not undermine PGD in general but only when applied to sex selection.

Another objection to PGD, the **Expressivist Argument,** contends that in allowing parents to discard IVF embryos with disability traits, the use of PGD implicitly devalues the lives of disabled people. It thus discriminates or expresses disrespect toward the ways of life of the disabled and treats them as something to be rejected or held in contempt. Those ways of life deserve respect, just as other ways of human life do.

The Expressivist Argument, if sound, justifies banning on moral grounds not only PGD but also abortion for fetal defects and end-of-life measures for impaired neonates. The best reason for its premise is that such procedures express a bias analogous to sexism, racism, and homophobia. This analogy does not object to *all* new reproductive technologies (or to *all* abortions). But it does imply that parents and providers who use PGD or prenatal screening for genetic disability are acting wrongly. That seems an overreaction, given how severe genetic diseases and disorders can be. For one thing, given society's limitations, not every parent can care for a child with special needs. It seems that those who cannot do it are under no obligation to do it. After all, many ethicists agree that morality cannot be so demanding that saintly or heroic action is an obligation.

Furthermore, as we saw in Chapter 12, *wrongful-life* litigation suggests that some severe congenital impairments may render a life not worth living, as judged by the person whose life it is. In light of these replies, the Expressivist Argument seems compelling only in the sometimes-denounced scenarios where the parents have refused PGD because they can care for a baby with special needs, but the clinic, concerned with its IVF success rates, insists on implementing it. Other critiques of PGD range from the Embryo-Mishandling Objection discussed in Chapter 14 to the Hubristic-Motivation Appeal considered below.

Human Reproductive Cloning

Some Facts

More than 100 years ago, scientists first demonstrated that simple organisms could be replicated by embryo-twinning at early stages of development. [3] In 1958, John Gurdon performed the first successful transfer of a tadpole's intestinal cell nucleus into an enucleated frog egg, creating a clone or genetic replica of that tadpole. Known as 'somatic cell nuclear transfer,' this cloning technique proceeds by injecting the DNA of a donor cell, or fusing the entire cell, into an enucleated egg. Any resulting embryo is immediately implanted into a gestational carrier, in the hope that it will result in a live-born clone. In 1996, UK scientists Ian Wilmut and Keith Campbell transferred the nucleus of an adult sheep's udder cell to an empty egg to produce the first mammal cloned from an adult somatic cell. After 277 attempts that led to the creation of 27 sheep embryos and only 13 implantations, Dolly the Sheep was the only clone to survive. Success rates in animal cloning are disappointing, with primates posing the greatest technical challenges. But in 2013 scientists created human embryonic stem cells from a baby for the purpose of studying its rare genetic disorder. The difficulties facing such therapeutic cloning became evident during the 2004–05 scandal involving a South Korean scientist suspected of faking his data.

To date, there is no evidence that human reproductive cloning (HRC) has actually been done, despite isolated claims to the contrary. Although it is unlikely to happen soon, the fact that it may become scientifically possible has already raised moral and legal controversy. If animal reproductive cloning were to be perfected so that HRC could be tried without considerable risk of harm, should it be done?

The Morality of HRC

For **bioliberals**, who are enthusiastic about the use of genetics and biotechnology on humans, HRC is just another new reproductive technology. Its permissibility when it reaches adequate levels of safety follows from its benefits and the value of procreative freedom. Unlike

---

3 See Genetic Science Learning Center, "The History of Cloning," 12/13/2016. http://learn.genetics. utah.edu/content/cloning/clonezone/ and NIH National Human Genome Research Institute, "Cloning," 4/4/2014. https://www.genome.gov/25020028#al-6.

critics who reduce HRC's possible 'benefits' to creating a *mini-me* or replicating a celebrity, bioliberals hypothesize that HRC might benefit individuals pursuing the creation of

- A genetic replica of a dying child.
- A savior sibling for a sick child affected by some nonhereditary condition.
- Genetically related children (for those who lack a partner, are in a same-sex relationship, or cannot conceive owing to male infertility).

For bioliberals, the same arguments justifying new reproductive technologies in these scenarios also justify HRC, which should be tried when it reaches adequate levels of safety (Pence, 1998).

Bioconservatives, who are pessimistic about the use of genetics and biotechnology on humans, reject that claim: HRC crosses a moral line that should not be crossed. At present, **bioconservatism** is the prevailing official view in public policy, as can be inferred from widespread bans and moratoria on HRC. The strongest objection to it concerns preventing harm to the clone, which currently would be at high risk. This suggests that researchers should not attempt clinical trials *now*. But suppose cloning technology develops to a point where the risk becomes low. Then what? Some bioconservatives would still object, on the grounds of

1. People's reactive attitudes toward HRC,
2. Slippery-slope scenarios, and
3. HRC's hubristic motivation.

Leon Kass (2002) makes all three objections. Aware that even if pervasive, reactive attitudes such as repugnance depend on intuitions not everyone shares, Kass contends that they are enough to put the burden of argument on bioliberals. Yet since bioliberals can appeal to HRC's benefits and procreative freedom, (1) has limited impact. To succeed, bioconservatives need compelling reasons for (2) and (3). The slippery slopes in (2) consist of futuristic scenarios where the parent-child relationship is severed because of factors such as the asexual mode of conception involved in HRC and the confused family links between clones and cell donors. But pessimistic predictions about psychological harm to children born to, or growing up in, nontraditional families were made before, in connection with complex cases of assisted reproduction. Since such predictions failed to be borne out by the evidence, more is needed to support this slippery slope argument against HRC.

Fueling (3), the **Hubristic Motivation** charge, are worries about the rationale of using genetics to control reproduction, and ultimately, nature. For HRC, the worries may hinge on its unnaturalness as a means for reproduction. In Chapter 14, a similar objection to the new reproductive technologies was met with the bioliberal reply that it cannot be consistently maintained. After all, unnaturalness also applies to vaccination, fighting epidemics, even taking aspirin. But the worries might be that like PGD, HRC is old eugenics in disguise, or expresses a Promethean aspiration to make reproduction fit our desires. We take up each of these objections to reprogenetics in turn.

Early Eugenics

Before the development of contemporary genetic engineering, early eugenicists attempted to manipulate the genome indirectly, by means of controlled breeding and selection of offspring. **Genetic engineering**, sometimes called 'modern eugenics,' opened a road for the direct manipulation of an organism's gene (or genes) in order to alter it in a controlled way. The resulting genetically modified organism has or lacks some targeted genetic traits.

Genetic engineering for humans may be either

1. **Positive**—aimed at enhancing genetic makeup, or
2. **Negative**—aimed at treating or preventing genetic disorders.

The implementation of (1) and (2) during human reproduction raise moral issues. In particular, positive genetic engineering amounts to a new **eugenics** in which genetic engineering technology is put at the service of human enhancement. A host of concerns about (1) stem from the catastrophic moral failure of early eugenics programs. In fact, the word 'eugenics' (literally 'good origins') acquired its bad reputation in the early 20th century, when it came to designate reproductive policies mandated by the state for the creation of 'better' humans. The early eugenicists hoped to produce better humans by 'controlled breeding' aimed at selecting individuals with the 'best' genes.

Their programs, imbued with end-of-the-century optimism and pseudo-science, spread rapidly in the US, reaching their peak in the early 1920s. Similar programs were in place in Canada, Denmark, Finland, Sweden, Norway, and Germany. All traded on existing racial prejudices against 'inferior' races and disabled people, many of whom were forcibly prevented from reproducing and often confined to institutions. In the US, after World War I a number of pro-eugenics societies, active in most states, advocated preventing the reproduction of people with 'heritable degenerative' traits such as epilepsy, alcoholism, or poverty. Their agenda influenced laws justifying restrictions on marriage and involuntary sterilization. Indiana enacted a sterilization law in 1907. By 1931, 30 states had eugenic laws and about 12,000 sterilizations had been performed, half of them in California. In 1924, the US Congress passed the Immigration Act, and President Coolidge signed it into law, remarking that "America should be kept American. . . ." In his view, a national origins quota was needed for immigrants from groups considered undesirable such as Southern Europeans and Asians.

The National Socialist movement that came to power in Germany in 1933 took the early eugenics program to an extreme. For Nazi doctors and political leaders, eugenics was the tool for achieving a racially homogenous, 'superior,' 'Aryan' society. It required discrimination, exclusion, and ultimately the elimination of those deemed unfit for that society, which included Germans judged 'congenitally' sick, asocial, or homosexual as well as Communists, Jews, and people from other ethnic groups such as the Roma and Slavs of all nationalities. Murdering mentally impaired individuals was part of Nazi eugenics. In a single institution that is now a museum, 40,000 of them were killed.

As the eugenics agenda was evolving into a program of mass extermination in the hands of the Nazis, it was withering in North America under internal criticism, in part for its pseudo-scientific basis and its coercive character. Geneticists now believe that early eugenicists misunderstood Darwin and Mendelian laws of heredity. But Michael Sandel (2004) suspects that they never put eugenics to rest. Their eugenicist pursuits continued to operate

IMAGE 15.1
©iStockPhoto/RTImages

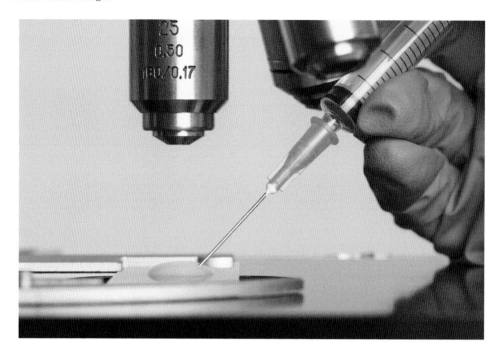

FIGURE 15.1 Early and Modern Eugenics

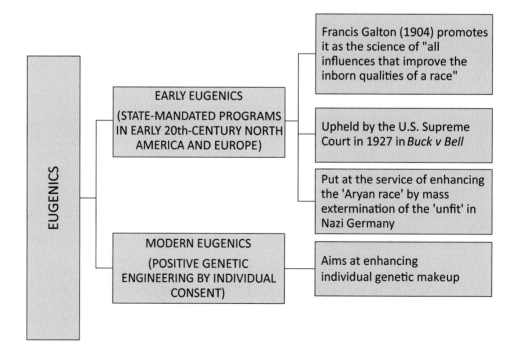

privately, not by coercive state policies, but embedded in the rationale for implementing genetic technology in order to gain control over reproduction for no medical reasons, such as in some uses of the technology we consider next.

15.3 Human Genetic Enhancement

The Posthuman Scenario

Positive genetic engineering has already shown promising results in experiments on nonhuman mammals. Studies on mice, for example, have shown that their memory and learning abilities can be greatly enhanced through genetic alterations. Similar alterations might one day be feasible in humans. As with human cloning, the prospect of **human genetic enhancement (HGE)** is exciting for bioliberals and alarming for bioconservatives. HEG may involve inter-species genetic transfer, the so-called chimeras produced by hybrid human-animal embryos, or the eugenic selection of traits for offspring by means of PGD and in-vitro fertilization—which may one day permit choosing embryos for nondisease traits such as hair or eye color, complexion, athletic ability, intelligence, and even personality. Gene editing and other technological innovations might make possible the creation of genetic sequences and protein structures associated with powers and immunities no human being has ever had. Individuals so engineered will be **posthumans** since their physical or mental capacity will be improved to a level beyond what humans can achieve without HGE.

Posthuman

Any individual genetically modified to have capacities, powers, or immunities well beyond human standard endowment.

For enthusiasts, it is only a matter of time until genetics makes the posthuman scenario possible. That would, however, require genetic knowledge well beyond that available today, since posthumans will be endowed with features beyond the average for present-day humans, such as being more long-lived, disease-resistant, intelligent, good looking, and emotionally stable, or having enhanced athletic abilities, heightened acuity for aesthetic appreciation, and greater moral discernment.

Defining 'Enhancement'

A genetic enhancement need not be so ambitious as to provide powers and immunities no human being has ever had. It may merely provide or augment a trait deemed advantageous or pleasing within a family or larger group. Such modifications count as enhancements whenever they aim at improving average capacity for the sake of providing such positional goods. They go beyond genetic therapy—i.e., modifications for treating or preventing disease.

Unlike genetic enhancement, therapeutic genetic modifications are often considered morally permissible.

But the alleged moral distinction between genetic enhancement and therapy is affected by vagueness and relativity, as can be seen when applied to genetic modification of human intelligence. According to the IQ scale, average intelligence falls between the 90 and 109 scores. Given the enhancement-versus-treatment distinction, raising someone's IQ score from 69 (mentally impaired) to 109 (normal intelligence) counts as morally permissible treatment, but raising it to 110 (the lower limit of superior intelligence) is morally impermissible enhancement. How could one IQ point make such a big moral difference? Here the problem is vagueness. Now let's consider the relativity problem, which arises because the moral permissibility of raising someone's IQ by, say, 40 points would vary from person to person. If a person's initial IQ score is 69, raising it to 109 is permissible therapy. But if it is 100, raising it to 140 is impermissible enhancement. Therefore, the moral permissibility of augmenting intelligence by exactly 40 IQ points varies from person to person. Proponents of the distinction will need a clear conceptualization of 'average capacity' to handle these problems.

A further complication arises because there might be moral differences among different types of human enhancement. Not all enhancements need be genetic. For example, athletic performance can also be enhanced by training (weight lifting), equipment (e.g., running shoes, special swimming suits), and drugs (doping). Although not all such enhancements face moral objections, genetic ones often do. In addition, Kamm (2005) classifies enhancements as 'ex ante' or 'ex post,' depending on whether they occur before or after the enhanced child exists. Ex ante changes are strictly genetic, while ex post changes also include drugs, training, and equipment. Let's now look closely at the moral controversy involving ex ante enhancements, the so-called **designer babies**.

Designer Babies

Advances in genetic engineering might one day make it possible to create designer babies. The scope of powers and capacities eligible for such genetic enhancements is quite wide. They may involve

- Physical appearance—e.g., eye color, complexion, hair color.
- Artistic abilities—e.g., musicality, appreciation of the visual arts.
- Psychology—e.g., intelligence, optimism, emotional stability.
- Morality—e.g., character, motivation to act morally, moral discernment.
- Health condition—e.g., life span, disease resistance.

Conversely, parents might want genetic alterations for their children to eliminate negative traits such as violence or depression. At present, of course, genetic knowledge enables enhancements of neither type, a situation that is likely to prevail for at least the immediate future. Consider, for instance, intelligence, whose genetic basis is still largely unknown. It is unlikely that intelligence involves a single gene that will soon be discovered by behavioral geneticists, or that it will be amenable to risk-free enhancement. As noted by cognitive psychologist Stephen Pinker (2003), gene editing aimed at enhancing intelligence might involve risks of causing retardation that no parent will want to take. But let's assume that one day such enhancements become both affordable and medically safe. Should they be an option?

Bioliberalism about HGE

Recasting the question as 'Should we take that opportunity?' bioliberals answer, 'Yes.' Savulescu (2001) endorses this answer with a so-called Perfectionist Argument for genetic enhancements contending that the parents have a prima facie obligation to enhance their offspring as much as possible, a conclusion that follows from the above discussed principle of Procreative Beneficence, according to which parents should select, among possible children, the child with the best chance to have the best life (given the available information). To support this argument, Savulescu invokes intuitions about these cases:

Rubella. A woman contracts rubella. If she conceives now, the baby's chances of severe mental impairment, blindness, and deafness are high. If she waits three months, she will conceive a different but healthy child.

Asthma. A couple have two IVF embryos, one with no abnormalities, the other showing a predisposition to develop asthma.

Procreative Beneficence captures common intuitions about *Rubella* (viz., that she should wait three months) and *Asthma* (viz., that they select embryo A). Yet perfectionists face some problems, since they are committed to the selection of offspring for trivial reasons. Consider

Pizza. A woman might give birth to either child A or child B. A has a slightly higher chance of enjoying pizza compared to child B. Other things are equal.

The intuition here is that there is no parental duty to select child A. But, given the Perfectionist Argument, there is. Thus, perfectionism is not always in agreement with intuition. Furthermore, its appeal to cases such as *Asthma* oversimplifies what will be involved in selecting the best child. Genetic knowledge is likely to yield more complex choices than child-with-asthma-versus-healthy-child, since it might reveal that child A will develop an early, intractable form of cancer while child B an also intractable mental illness. If such choices become the norm, the Perfectionist Argument will be silent most of the time. In addition, perfectionism might have ill effects for society, since as discussed in connection with PGD, it might justify selecting children for objectionable reasons such as skin color or sex. It might also produce an unjust social order where enhancement will be accessible only for the wealthy. Perfectionists can meet some of these objections by invoking public policy.

Yet, taken together, the objections suggest that perfectionism is too strong, especially compared with *libertarianism*, which makes the weaker claim that enhancing children is morally permissible. Consistent with their appeal to Procreative Freedom, libertarians think that parents have a right to choose their children, provided their choice does not harm the children or others. Another less ambitious alternative to perfectionism is sufficientarianism, which holds that the parental duty to enhance need not aim at perfection, but only at reaching a sufficient level whereby the child could achieve sufficient positional goods (Kamm,

2005: 10). In the sufficientarian view, 'best' becomes 'decent', so that parents have the prima facie obligation to select the child who has a decent chance of having a sufficiently decent life. Sufficientarianism accommodates the intuitions that in *Pizza*, the parents have no duty to select child A, while in *Rubella* they have the duty to wait. What the view would say about *Asthma* depends on what a 'sufficiently decent' life is, something that needs clarification.

Modest Bioconservatism about HGE

Bioconservatives can be modest or extreme, depending on whether they prescribe only caution about HGEs or forbid it altogether. Modest bioconservatives see nothing intrinsically wrong with HGE but they accept this general rationale for the genetic engineering of any organism:

Precautionary Principle

No positive (nontherapeutic) genetic engineering should be attempted without sound evidence that its potential benefits can outweigh bad outcomes.

Given this principle, researchers should simply steer clear of attempting any HGE until there is solid evidence of its safety. Current gene therapy on humans illustrates the potential risk of gene manipulation, about which we'll have more to say later. And as noted earlier, gene editing to enhance intelligence might carry the risk of causing retardation. More generally, genetic modifications that alter the course of natural selection might destroy the human race.

Bioliberals reject such 'alarmist' predictions, charging that the **Precautionary Principle** has paralyzing effects (Glover, 2006). If followed consistently, it would result in the starvation of the developing world. For it will not allow for genetically modified crops, which are the only hope for meeting the demands of an overpopulated planet. However, by distinguishing levels of risk, modest bioconservatives can hold some genetic modifications permissible while also allowing that HGE is still too risky as a general policy, and therefore morally forbidden. Modest bioconservatives also reject the extreme bioconservative claim that HEG is wrong *per se*.

Extreme Bioconservatism

These bioconservative arguments aim at substantiating HGE's intrinsic wrongness. For the Social Justice argument, were HGE to become an accepted practice, it would deepen economic and social injustice. It may even lead to a bifurcation of the human race into two sub-species, the enhanced posthumans (descendants of those who could afford to get enhanced) and the unenhanced underclass (everybody else). In reply, bioliberals note that this frightening, Brave-New-World scenario is just one of the possible outcomes. After all, it cannot be ruled out that public policies might be in place to ensure more egalitarian distribution of HGE, or a prioritarian distribution according to need. Besides, we already have, in the industrial democracies of the developed world, a two-tiered social-class system (much of it rooted in genetics, owing to people's preference to marry within their social class) where most benefits and burdens are distributed unevenly along class lines.

The Eugenics objection to HGE charges that it is an enterprise rooted largely in normative judgments, a slippery foundation if ever there was one. Different people will have different views about what traits should be selected for enhancement, reduction, or elimination. Considering the historical abuses of early eugenics reviewed above, who should determine which traits fall in what category? Furthermore, we may set out to change human nature for the better, but are we really confident that we know what we should change it to? Suppose everybody will agree that a tendency toward unprovoked, aggressive violence is not a desirable human trait, for instance, or that an inclination toward cooperation is desirable. Even so, there will also be countless human traits held desirable by some and condemned by others. How tall, aggressive, tolerant, or risk-averse should one be?

On the other hand, some bioconservatives predict a Human Diversity problem facing HGE. According to this objection, the aggregate effects of individual choices will be bad because they will diminish human diversity or eliminate it altogether. Most parents will select similar enhancements for their offspring, something supported by evidence from egg- and sperm-donor sales. As a result, most children will have similar traits: blond, tall, etc.

The Eugenics objection and the Human Diversity problem are *slippery-slope* arguments making empirical predictions that could turn out to be false. We need to wait and see. Their predictions might never materialize or be correctible by public policy. But other extreme bioconservatives do not make such predictions. For example, Michael Sandel's "deepest objection" focuses entirely on the wrongness of designer babies, and more generally of HGE, given the underlying hubristic attitude HGE expresses. According to this Hubristic Motivation Charge, its wrongness

> . . . lies less in the perfection it seeks than the human disposition it expresses and promotes. The problem is not that parents usurp the autonomy of a child they design. The problem is in the hubris of the designing parents, in their drive to master the mystery of birth . . . it would disfigure the relation between parent and child, and deprive the parent of the humility and enlarged human sympathies that an openness to the unbidden can cultivate. (Sandel, 2004: 57)

Enhancements made to satisfy the parents' own aesthetic or social preferences about their children's eye color or athletic ability seem wrong on a number of counts. For one thing, these are shallow values, and even outright social prejudices. Furthermore, such enhancements may treat children as mere instruments for their parents' enjoyment and thus commodify them. And by eliminating the element of chance in the natural lottery, they may also undermine the parent-child relationship.

To these criticisms, Sandel adds HGE's underlying hubristic motivation. It expresses a disposition toward mastering or controlling reproduction, one of the mysteries of nature with which we should not interfere. For him, mastery stands in contrast to "openness to the unbidden," which requires acceptance of nature's gifts and provides the basis for societal values such as humility, responsibility, and solidarity. Openness to the unbidden requires a balance between the "acceptance" and the "transforming" love parents owe to their children. One amounts to unconditional love, the other allows for seeking some enhancements short of genetic ones. Permissible enhancements are achieved through education, training, and equipment. For example, enhancing speed through the use of proper running shoes is morally permissible, but designing a baby with fast-twitch muscle fiber is not. Both actions enhance speed, a natural gift, and may result in exactly the same speed increase. What makes one permissible and the other not? Maybe that HGEs are more permanent. But this cannot be so, since many offspring alterations short of genetic enhancement also result in permanent, heritable changes. Environmental factors such as education and training can cause permanent alterations in a person's neurophysiology that will be passed on to succeeding generations. Since Sandel considers these transformations permissible, consistency requires ruling out the permanence of HGE as the reason for its impermissibility. But Sandel provides no principle for consistently distinguishing between permissible and impermissible enhancements.

Furthermore, note that agents' motivation may be hubristic or otherwise bad without this implying that their actions thus motivated are wrong. In the early 1900s, at the end of the Spanish-American War, Walter Reed and his medical staff performed experiments in Cuba that established yellow fever as a mosquito-borne illness. They exposed themselves and others to mosquito bites to test this hypothesis. Deemed a scientific success, their experiments prompted mosquito-control measures that greatly reduced the incidence of yellow fever. Traditionally, the team's motivation was associated with honor and bravery. But historians of medicine now believe that it included a great deal of professional and occupational self-interest, together with monetary compensation (Mehra, 2009). Plainly, this assessment of the investigators' attitude changes how we should evaluate their moral character, but not the value of their experiments to potential victims of yellow fever, and thus, to society.

15.4 Chapter Summary

This chapter first looked at arguments for and against the moral permissibility of parental decisions to use preimplantation genetic diagnosis (PGD) to select for the presence of certain disability traits in IVF embryos. The Autonomy Argument finds these contrary to a child's right to an open future. Reasons for the moral permissibility of such decisions invoke procreative freedom and genetic essentialism. In the deaf couple case, some libertarians and utilitarians contend that a different parental procreative decision would have produced either no child or another child. Since the deaf child's life is worth living, the couple's choice was permissible. A sticking point for utilitarians is whether all harms are person-affecting. If not, then designing disabled children is wrong when it brings about a less-than-optimal state of affairs.

For PGD critics, its use in selecting embryos for nonmedical traits such as sex (in the absence of risk for sex-related genetic disease) expresses a hubristic attitude analogous to that expressed by early eugenicists. This attitude fuels also human reproductive cloning (HRC) and human genetic enhancement (HGE). HRC defenders argue that it'll be just another new reproductive technology, justifiable by its potential benefits. Critics invoke public reaction to HRC, concerns about its potential harm (to clones, families, or society), and/or the underlying hubristic disposition toward controlling nature that HRC expresses. Since each of these objections can be met but the evidence from animal cloning suggests HRC is presently unsafe, experimentation (if any) should proceed only with proper oversight.

Like HRC, HGE involves speculative scenarios which might one day become real. While bioconservatives consider impermissible the enhancement of physical and mental capacities, for bioliberals it is permissible and even mandatory. In both camps, there are extreme and modest positions, with only the modest ones surviving criticism. In fact modest bioliberalism (sufficientarianism) can be combined with modest conservatism (the precautionary principle) to contend that HGEs aiming at improvement, not perfection, are morally permissible but should not be administered until they become safe. Here is a roadmap of these positions.

FIGURE 15.2   Main Arguments for and against the Moral Permissibility of HGE

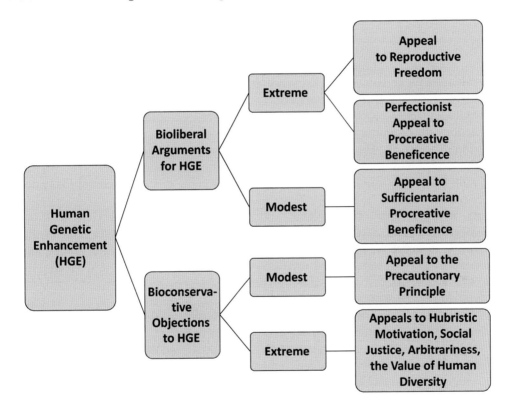

15.5 Study Aids

Key Words

Bioconservatism, 284
Bioliberalism, 283
Designer babies, 288
Eugenics, 284
Expressivist Argument, 282

Questions and Cases for Further Consideration

1. In some wrongful-life actions, a disabled person or legal guardian sues medical providers (or parents) who failed to prevent her from coming into a life of severe genetic impairment. Since the providers are not the cause of the impairment, life itself, as opposed to nonexistence, becomes the injury. Some common law jurisdictions reject such legal actions on the grounds that they imply disrespect for both a human life that has come into existence and the right to life of disabled persons. How are these views related to the Expressivist Argument? Do such lawsuits provide reasons to reject libertarian and utilitarian justifications of the use of PGD for designing disabled children? Explain.

2. In a congressional hearing about human reproductive cloning (HRC), Thomas Murray reports that a scientist took a letter by a father determined to clone his dead son as evidence for allowing research on HRC.[4] Is that a good reason for the moral permissibility of HRC? What would be other reasons for, and objections to, HRC? Which, if any, is in your view the strongest?

3. Suppose human-gorilla hybrids become genetically possible. These chimeras will have all the properties of humans except for an enhanced strength. Should humans be so enhanced? What would Procreative Beneficence and the Precautionary Principle advise? Are these two principles compatible? Which of the two better approximates what you would say? Why?

4. Where does the early eugenics fall within the distinction between positive and negative genetic engineering? Why was that practice morally wrong?

5. Molly Nash, *the first offspring of Lisa and Jack, was born with Fanconi anemia. Without a bone marrow donor transplant from a perfect HLA-match donor, she would die. Her chances of survival were expected to increase if the donor was a sibling. The Nashes decided to have another child, something they wanted to do anyway. They used PGD to screen for single-gene disorders, combined with IVF and a technique called 'HLA matching,' that*

---

4   Thomas Murray, "Even if It Worked, Cloning Wouldn't Bring Her Back," *Washington Post*, 4/8/2001.

allows selection of embryos for implantation that are HLA matches of an existing sick child without carrying the disease gene. Lisa underwent four IVF cycles, eventually giving birth to Adam in 2000. A transfusion of his umbilical cord blood cells a month later saved Molly's life. She still suffers Fanconi anemia but not bone marrow failure. Questions to consider here include: a) Was the Nashs' decision morally permissible? b) Does it make a moral difference that they intended to have more than one child? c) How would you respond to reporter Lisa Belkin's claim[5] that embryo selection for HLA match may lead to selection for intelligence or eye color?

6.   *Former US President Jimmy Carter, in a 2014 interview on* The Late Show with David Letterman, *deplored that* "160 million girls are now missing from the face of the earth because they were murdered at birth by their parents or either selectively aborted when their parents found out that the fetus was a girl." *As a result,* "in China and India and South Korea and some other countries, young men can't find brides to marry, so they buy brides, and that increases the amount of slavery that exists on earth." He concluded that a war on women is now under way—without mentioning that in developed countries PGD and sperm sorting are used for sex selection. Questions to consider here include: a) What could he say to argue that there is a moral difference between these and the sex-selective abortions and infanticide of the developing world? b) Since sex selection is also practiced in developed countries, do positions like Carter's indicate a double moral standard or cultural bias? c) Was it permissible for Carter, a Westerner, to evaluate morally the practices of nonWestern cultures?

Suggested Readings*

Brock, Dan W., "The Non-Identity Problem and Genetic Harms: The Case of Wrongful Handicaps," *Bioethics* 9.3/4, 1995: 269–75.
     Considers selection for genetic disabilities as "wrongful handicaps." Although they do not harm the child, they fail to bring about the best state of affairs.
*———, "Cloning Human Beings: An Assessment of the Ethical Issues Pro and Con," *Testimony to the National Bioethics Advisory Commission.* Washington DC, 2007. Available online at https://bioethicsarchive.georgetown.edu/nbac/pubs/cloning2/cc5.pdf.
     Given reproductive freedom and the absence of convincing reasons for HRC's wrongness, this form of reproduction is permissible but should be monitored.
*Chadwick, Ruth F., "Cloning," *Philosophy* 57.220, 1982: 201–9.
     Replies to main objections to human cloning, defending it for its potential good consequences in the treatment of genetic disease.
*Comstock, Gary, "Are the Policy Implications of the Precautionary Principle Coherent?" *Agbioworld*, 2000. Available online at http://www.agbioworld.org/newsletter_wm/index.php?caseid=archive&newsid=134.
     Challenges the precautionary principle for genetically modified foods in a way that can be extended to human genetic enhancement.

---

5   Lisa Belkin, "The Made-to-Order Savior," *The New York Times Magazine*, 1/7/2001.
*   Asterisks mark readings available online. See links on the companion website.

*Davis, Dena S., "Genetic Dilemmas and the Child's Right to an Open Future," *Hastings Center Report* 27.2, 1997: 7–15.
> Offers the Autonomy Argument for the moral impermissibility of designing a disabled child.

*Elsner, Daniel, "Just Another Reproductive Technology? The Ethics of Human Reproductive Cloning as an Experimental Medical Procedure," *Journal of Medical Ethics* 32.10, 2006: 596–600.
> Given reproductive freedom, human reproductive cloning is as morally permissible as IVF. Proposes a model to balance reproductive freedom with safety concerns.

Glover, Jonathan, *Choosing Children: The Ethical Dilemmas of Genetic Intervention*. Oxford: Clarendon Press, 2006.
> Offers a libertarian defense of reproductive genetic engineering, including the use of PGD and prenatal genetic screening, for designing a disabled child.

*Kamm, Francis M., "Is There a Problem with Enhancement?" *The American Journal of Bioethics* 5.3, 2005: 5–14.
> Considers that Sandel's (2004) argument against human enhancement fails—among other reasons, for its inability to distinguish permissible from impermissible enhancements of natural gifts.

*Kass, Leon R., "The Wisdom of Repugnance," *The New Republic*, 6/2/1997, pp. 17–26.
> Invokes common reactive attitudes, slippery-slope scenarios, and an underlying hubristic motivation against human reproductive cloning.

*Parens, Erik and Adrienne Asch, "The Disability Rights Critique of Prenatal Genetic Testing: Reflections and Recommendations," Special Supplement, *Hastings Center Report* 29.5, 1999: S1–S22.
> Outlines the expressivist argument against prenatal (and thus, preimplantation) screening to prevent the birth of babies with disabilities.

*Roberts, M. A., "The Nonidentity Problem," *The Stanford Encyclopedia of Philosophy*, Edward Zalta, ed., 2015. Available online at http://plato.stanford.edu/archives/win2015/entries/nonidentity-problem/.
> Comprehensive survey of main reasons for thinking that the nonidentity problem arises and attempts at resolving it.

*Robertson, John A., "Preconception Gender Selection," *American Journal of Bioethics* 1.1, 2001: 2–9.
> Argues for a moral distinction between pre-conception and post-conception sex selection. Sex selection in nondisease cases is justified in light of the parents' procreative freedom together with the lack of evidence about its harmful consequences.

*———, "Extending Preimplantation Genetic Diagnosis: Medical and Non-Medical Uses," *Journal of Medical Ethics* 29.4, 2003: 213–16.
> Finds uses of PGD to select for nondisease traits justified and invulnerable to common criticisms.

*Robertson, John A., Jeffrey P. Kahn, and John E. Wagner, "Conception to Obtain Hematopoietic Stem Cells," *Hasting Center Report* 32.3, 2002: 34–40.
> Considers morally justified the conception of a child to serve as a hematopoietic stem cell donor for another child, since transplantation of such cells is the treatment of choice and there are more patients in need than compatible donors. But emphasizes the importance of protecting savior siblings' rights and welfare.

*Sandel, Michael J., "The Case against Perfection: What's Wrong with Designer Children, Bionic Athletes, and Genetic Engineering," *The Atlantic Monthly* 293.3, 2004: 51–62.
Rejects genetic enhancement for its underlying hubristic attitude. But genetic therapy and some enhancements by education, training, or equipment are permissible.

*Savulescu, Julian, "Procreative Beneficence: Why We Should Select the Best Children," *Bioethics* 15.5/6, 2001: 413–26.
Locus classicus for the perfectionist defense of designer babies.

*———, "Deaf Lesbians, 'Designer Disability,' and the Future of Medicine," *British Medical Journal* 325.7367, 2002: 771–3.
Reproductive freedom and genetic essentialism justify decisions to design disabled children, provided their lives are worth living.

PART VI

Medicine and Society

16 Biomedical Research on Animals

Learning Objectives

In reading this chapter you will

▶   Distinguish abolitionism and anti-abolitionism about animal experimentation.

▶   Reflect on whether the benefits of such research can morally justify harming animals.

▶   Evaluate reasons for and against ascribing moral rights to animals.

▶   Consider whether comparable human and animal interests should count morally the same.

▶   Learn about speciesism and its alleged similarity to racism and sexism.

THIS CHAPTER LOOKS closely at some ethical problems facing biomedical research on animals. Here 'animal' is used with its ordinary reference, which excludes humans. As we shall see, although there is consensus about the need to prevent inhumane treatment of lab animals, disagreements arise over the moral permissibility of using them in invasive experiments that reasonable people would condemn if performed on humans. Those disagreements ultimately rest on incompatible views about the moral standing of both animals and humans.

16.1 Dr. Gennarelli's Head-Injury Study

Funded by the US National Institutes of Health (NIH) for more than a decade, Dr. Thomas Gennarelli's study at the University of Pennsylvania's Medical School made headlines in 1984, not for a scientific breakthrough, but for its abusive treatment of animals. Baboons were subjected to head blows intended to reproduce traumatic brain injuries like those caused by accidents in humans. Semiconscious baboons were first strapped to a machine with their heads cemented inside a helmet. Then a hydraulic piston delivered a forceful blow or twist to their heads that rendered them comatose, paralyzed, and sometimes dead. Survivors were kept for about two months to study their brain injuries and then euthanized. During the experiment, researchers smoked, listened to music, laughed, and made jokes about the injured animals. They also videotaped the scenes. In 1984, Animal Liberation

Front (ALF) activists broke into the lab and stole the tapes, which the People for the Ethical Treatment of Animals (PETA) later edited for a 26-minute film, *Unnecessary Fuss*. The activists publicly accused Gennarelli of animal cruelty, demanding the withdrawal of NIH funding. But the NIH, arguing that the lab provided humane care for the baboons, instead renewed its funding. Criticism continued to mount, culminating in 1985 with the four-day occupation by animal activists of an NIH building in Washington. Eventually, NIH funding ended and the lab closed. In September 2000, Vance Lehmkuhl[1] reported that, upon further investigation, the university was fined $4,000 for failure to comply with the Animal Welfare Act of 1966 (AWA). The headline read "Video Killed the Baboon Lab." It was referring to *Unnecessary Fuss*, the film that first antagonized the medical community but was later shown in NIH training sessions for investigators (mandated by Congress in 1985). The *Head Injury Study*, which Gennarelli resumed elsewhere using guinea pigs, appeared to have made no contribution to medicine.

■■■

By and large, the biomedical community continued to support the status quo in animal experimentation, even after further revelations by animal rights activists of ethical lapses in other labs that used animal subjects. In one raid at the University of California Riverside in 1985, the ALF stole 260 animals. Among them was a baby monkey whose eyelids had been sutured shut for the purpose of sensory-deprivation research. Many other raids and violent incidents occurred. Some involved the burning of labs, destruction of data, and defacement of walls with slogans such as "Nowhere Is Safe" and "We Shall Return." The Association of American Medical Colleges estimated that, between 1985 and 1990, such actions cost $3.5 million and 15,000 staff hours (Orlans, 1993).

Opposition to animal research was, however, nothing new in the West, where significant social movements emerged in the 19th century out of concern about the welfare of research animals. Prominent among them was the so-called antivivisectionist movement that led to Britain's Cruelty to Animals Act of 1879. Antivivisectionists sought, mainly but not exclusively, the provision of anesthesia to animal subjects during invasive research. Their agenda influenced subsequent opposition to **vivisection**, understood as research on animals that is

- Nontherapeutic for the animal subjects,
- Performed for the benefit of (mostly) humans, the environment, or other animals, and
- Likely to cause stress, discomfort, pain, and even death in the subjects.

Hereafter, animal 'experimentation' or 'research' refers to vivisection thus understood, regardless of its purpose (e.g., scientific knowledge, testing, or education), means (i.e., interventions of the sort listed in Figure 16.1), and types of animal subject (i.e., rats, mice, cats, dogs, primates, or other nonhuman animals).

Largely dormant during the first half of the 20th century, the moral issues facing animal experimentation regained public scrutiny in the 1960s and 70s. Among the factors that

---

1 Vance Lehmkuhl, "Video Killed the Baboon Lab," *My City Paper*, 9/7/2000.

FIGURE 16.1   Animal Experimentation

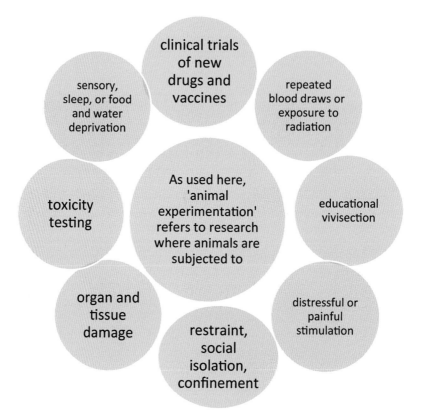

brought them back was renewed awareness about racial and sexual discrimination, environmental threats, and the biological and psychological commonalities between higher animals and humans. The publication of Peter Singer's *Animal Liberation* (1975) was a turning point in bringing those moral issues to public attention. Singer followed Bentham's utilitarian views to their logical conclusion on animal experimentation: animals that have **sentience** (the capacity to feel pain and pleasure) also have interests that deserve equal consideration when they are comparable to human interests. Supporters of this conclusion joined forces with advocates of animal rights in mounting a radical challenge to the received view on animal experimentation. Their views, if sound, would undermine the use of animals not only in research but also in farming and consumer products, which in fact account for most animal deaths. According to The Hastings Center,[2] in the US in 2010, 26 million animals were used in experimentation. Animals killed for food that year amounted to 9 billion.

2 The Hastings Center. "Animals Used in Research in the US," 2010. http://animalresearch.the-hastingscenter.org/facts-sheets/animals-used-in-research-in-the-united-states.

16.2 The Animal Experimentation Debate

Abolitionism and Its Rivals

The mainstream view in the biomedical community favors maintaining the status quo. Since it considers animal experimentation morally permissible, it is **anti-abolitionist**—where

---

Abolitionism advocates either eliminating or radically reducing animal experimentation.

But anti-abolitionism commonly rejects 'anything goes' in animal experimentation, holding that researchers should do everything possible to minimize stress, suffering, and death of animal subjects. This includes providing them with proper anesthesia, analgesics, and care and living conditions. Anti-abolitionism can thus condemn ethical lapses, such as those that occurred in Dr. Gennarelli's lab, while opposing drastic reduction or elimination of animal research.

Abolitionism challenges that view by advocating drastic changes to the status quo. It can be extreme or reformist, depending on whether it claims that animal experimentation

- Is always morally wrong and should be eliminated, or
- Is commonly wrong, with few exceptions.

To support either claim, abolitionism generally invokes obligations to animals that are grounded in their *moral standing*, which confers on them either rights that always trump, or interests that should be protected. Alternatively, abolitionism may invoke obligations based on the value animals have for us. Furthermore, abolitionism may be global or local. The former calls for elimination or drastic reduction of experimentation on animals of any kind, the latter only on animals of certain kinds—for example, the great apes. Let's now consider these parties' reasons for and against maintaining the status quo. But first, check the roadmap to these positions in Figure 16.2.

The Benefits Argument

With contemporary advances in the study of animal minds, very few would today attempt to substantiate anti-abolitionism by claiming that animals are like machines, unable to feel pain, as once claimed by philosopher René Descartes (1596–1650). Anti-abolitionism's principal support stems from the Benefits Argument, which as stated below relies heavily on animal experimentation's potential to benefit humans and occasionally animals. For anti-abolitionism, its benefits outweigh its burdens to animals.

The biomedical community leans heavily towards anti-abolitionism, chiefly because of the successes in animal research. Consider organ transplantation, an intervention that has benefited millions around the world. Cornea transplants, for example, were tried on rabbits since the early 1900s. Kidney transplants were tried on dogs, rabbits, and mice in the 1950s

FIGURE 16.2   Abolitionism and Its Rivals

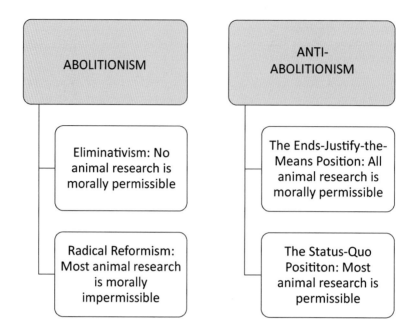

and 60s. For all transplants, the body's rejection of the organ was eventually overcome by experiments that actively induced immunosuppression in animals.

Although animal experimentation also made possible trials of vaccines, drugs, equipment, and therapies, its instrumental value has not always been straightforward. Consider

The Silver Spring Monkey Experiments. In 1981, Alex Pacheco, 23, infiltrated the Institutes for Behavioral Research in Silver Spring, Maryland, as an undergraduate volunteer from George Washington University. Later to become leader of PETA, Pacheco sought to expose Dr. Edward Taub, who was cutting long-tail macaques' sensory nerves to limbs to create nonuse limbs similar to those produced in humans by spinal cord injury or stroke. Taub kept the monkeys in filthy conditions, with open wounds and missing fingers. Further investigation found "grossly unsanitary" conditions and deficient veterinary care in his lab.

After Pacheco's revelations, although Taub managed to persuade the research community that he was a victim of ignorance and zealotry, not only did he lose NIH funding but a lower court found him guilty of six counts of animal cruelty. Eventually, the Maryland Court of Appeals overturned that conviction, a decision upheld by the US Supreme Court.

Globally, stroke is a leading cause of disabilities in adults (World Stroke Organization, http://www.worldstrokecampaign.org/learn/facts-and-figures.html). Taub's research aimed at benefitting them with the development of appropriate therapies for nonuse limbs. He hypothesized that the part of the cortex corresponding to any limb left unresponsive after a stroke or spinal injury can eventually rewire under certain conditions and some limb use be restored. In 1990, this was confirmed by neuroscientists who euthanized dying monkeys from Taub's lab that had regained use of the affected limbs. PETA had opposed their study, but in the end it proved beneficial for therapy development.

Anti-abolitionists can condemn Taub's treatment of the animals on some of the moral grounds considered below, while still endorsing this Benefits Argument:

1. Animal experimentation is crucial to medical progress.
2. Medical progress is right.

_____

3. Therefore, animal experimentation is right.

Given (1) and (2), animal experimentation is right in the sense of being morally permissible and even mandatory. But both premises are open to challenge. As we see next, abolitionists especially question (1).

Doubts about the Benefits of Animal Research

For the Benefits Argument to support anti-abolitionism, 'crucial' in premise (1) should mean 'necessary'. But on this reading, (1) seems false. For one thing, with modern computer and imaging technologies, many biomedical hypotheses can now be tested without animal experimentation. Furthermore, scientific data suggest that lab animals fail as models of human psychology or physiology. Reliance on them may in fact delay progress or cause harm to humans. For years, chimps were given the HIV virus in the hope that they would develop AIDS and could be used to try new therapies. It is now known that this rarely happens

IMAGE 16.1
©iStockPhoto/Nikola Nastasic

(Kazez, 2014). Similarly, in the early days of research on tobacco's link to lung disease, scientists exposed mice to cigarette smoke and waited in vain for results. Their studies in fact delayed educational campaigns against smoking that could have saved many lives, because evidence about the link was already available through epidemiological studies (Regan, 2005). Furthermore, because of physiological differences, interventions safe for animals might not be so for humans. For many general-knowledge studies, questions arise as to what potential benefit they could bring to either humans or animals. David DeGrazia (2002) points to a seventeen-year long, cat-sex study, conducted at New York's American Museum of Natural History beginning in 1960, which resulted in the mutilation of many cats in pursuit of knowledge that could benefit neither humans nor animals.

In light of skepticism about the necessity of animal experimentation for medical progress, the Benefits Argument fails to support the status quo. But suppose se did. It would still face problems of rights (the ends don't always justify the means) and of how to assess benefits and harms across the species. After all, when what might benefit humans can also cause harm to animals, whose interests should count more? These problems concern the moral standing of animals, which is at the root of the animal-experimentation debate.

16.3 Animal Moral Standing

For the Moral Standing of Animals

Suppose it's unequivocally true that experiments on animals contribute to advances in medicine and pharmacology that have benefitted humans and, to some extent, animals. Yet the Benefits Argument may still fail to support the moral permissibility of animal research if the two views to be considered next are plausible. Although they are usually counted as animal-rights views, only one of them invokes rights. The other invokes equal consideration of comparable interests. Accordingly, there are *rights* views and *welfare* views of animal moral standing. In addition, each could be either categorical or gradualist, where

- The categorical views find a property of animals that is necessary and sufficient for having moral standing (e.g., sentience).
- The gradualist views find a property of animals that confers moral status depending on how much of it a species of animals has (e.g., intelligence, social bonds, etc.).

The Hierarchical View

If animal have moral rights, such rights would likely include liberty and bodily integrity. These would give us strong duties of forbearance toward them with important implications for animal research. But what could be the basis of such rights? Beyond sentience, animals appear to lack the rich intellectual, social, and moral capacities of humans. According to the **Hierarchical View** of moral standing, respect for animal life is mandated only for animals with some such capacities. For example, the more intelligent an animal is, the more reasonable it is to say that it has a right to life. For 'higher' animals, such as cats, dolphins, and chimps it seems more reasonable to say it than for 'lower' ones such as insects or mollusks. On R. G. Frey's (2005) Hierarchical View, it is not intelligence *per se* but having moral agency that gives persons and animals different moral standings. In fact, there are a number of proposed hierarchies where humans invariably come out with higher moral standing—all of which are compatible with maintaining the status quo about animal experimentation. All of them face the challenge posed by the Argument from Marginal Cases. For in the Hierarchical View, what justifies animal experimentation is the lower moral standing animals have, compared with persons, as a result of their diminished capacities. Individuals with profound mental impairments create a problem for this view, since these humans' cognitive capacities can be below those of some animals. Other marginal cases are the too young or senile. The Argument from Marginal Cases charges that the Hierarchical View cannot explain why using such nonparadigm persons for risky research is forbidden while using animals with superior cognitive capacities is permissible.

The Animal-Rights View

The **animal-rights view** proposed by Tom Regan (1983, 2005) regards the Argument from Marginal Cases as a devastating objection to all anti-abolitionists. Among Regan's positive theses are that

- All animals have moral standing, and they have it categorically as opposed to in degrees, and
- Animal research should be not merely radically reduced but eliminated altogether.

Regan argues for these theses by drawing a moral distinction between being alive in a mere biological sense, and having a life, in the sense of being the subject of conscious experience, which includes sentience and many other complex psychological capacities. According to Regan, animals are not merely alive in the biological sense, but are subjects of a life. This confers on them rights to life and bodily integrity that trump any other moral consideration, just as it does for the individuals at issue in the Argument from Marginal Cases. What animals have in common with them is sentience and their inability to consent to biomedical research. Regan's strong animal-rights view amounts to an eliminativist type of abolitionism. He takes evolutionary biology to support it, especially Darwin's contention that the difference between humans and the higher animals is only one of degree, not kind—which agrees with recent discoveries in animal psychology and genetics. But these discoveries are equally consistent with the Hierarchical View as well as with the position to which we now turn.

The Animal-Welfare View

For utilitarianism, calculations of benefits over burdens are what matter most in determining the moral permissibility of animal experimentation, and these should be based on empirical evidence. For Bentham, when an action affects a sentient being, its moral permissibility depends on the maximization of pleasure over pain for all concerned. For Singer, such calculations do not favor anti-abolitionism, given the ubiquity of nonbeneficial research on animals. Furthermore, a central question is whether the comparable interests of animals and humans count morally the same. He thinks that moral standing hinges on sentience. Sentience is necessary and sufficient for a being's having interests that may be promoted or undermined by the actions of others. All sentient beings categorically have moral standing because they have an interest in avoiding suffering. But some of them also have other interests grounded in their complex psychological capacities that include beliefs, self-awareness over time, reasoning, memory, and communication. In calculating the morality of an action, interests vary according to psychological capacity, with beings possessing more complex capacities having more at stake than those with simpler ones. But, from the moral perspective, comparable interests should receive equal consideration: they should count the same, irrespective of species boundaries. Accordingly, the moral assessment of actions varies, given that, for example, a gorilla has interests not comparable to those of a rat or a fish.

"As long as a sentient being is conscious," writes Singer, "it has an interest in experiencing as much pleasure and as little pain as possible. Sentience suffices to place a being within the sphere of equal consideration of interests; but it does not mean that the being has a personal interest in continuing to live" (1979: 102). *Persons* do have such an interest, but most animals are not persons. Yet this does not mean that it's morally permissible to torture or kill them. The permissibility of painlessly killing an animal depends on the interests at stake in each situation. Where the interests of, say, a chicken and a paradigm person are in conflict, if the person has no other way of remaining alive than by painlessly killing the chicken, she may do so, since she has interests not comparable to those of the chicken. When there is an alternative way to remain alive that does not involve the killing of a sentient being, then the killing is impermissible. Thus, this **animal-welfare view** amounts to radical-reformist abolitionism about animal experimentation: given the evidence, most of it has burdens that outweigh any benefits and is morally forbidden.

On the **equal-consideration-of-interests** account, beings *of whatever species* that have the psychological capacities typical of paradigm persons have the full moral standing of persons that ordinarily renders their killing a serious moral wrong. But some intelligent animals might be more properly acknowledged as persons than marginal individuals of the species *Homo sapiens*. For instance, chimps may count as persons, while neonates and humans with profound mental impairments may not. For, a clever chimp has more interests than any such humans, and what matters for full moral standing is psychological capacity, not species membership (Singer, 1979: 97; 2009: 568).

These claims conflict with common morality's belief that such humans have higher moral standing than chimps. For Singer, however, this cannot undermine his views because common morality is often shaped by taboos and prejudices. Yet, historically, discrediting such taboos and prejudices took persuasive arguments. Singer would need similarly strong arguments to debunk common morality about the comparative moral standing of nonparadigm persons and chimps.

Note that Singer's association of interests with psychological capacity need not imply that persons of extraordinary intellectual capacity (e.g., Isaac Newton or Albert Einstein) have more interests than other, more mentally average persons. The possession of a certain level of cognitive capacity may be all that is necessary for a being to have the interests of paradigm persons. Psychological capacity beyond that threshold need not add moral standing. Compare, for instance, the minimum speed limit for driving on a superhighway: say, 40 mph. Although driving at that speed is legal, any increase in speed does not make the driving *more legal*.

Speciesism versus Humanism

Speciesism Critics

Singer and others have argued that, like membership of a sex or race, membership of *Homo sapiens* does not grant preferential moral standing. **Speciesism**, the belief that it does, is a prejudice akin to sexism and racism. Singer (2003) defines it as "the idea that it is justifiable to give preference to beings simply on the grounds that they are members of the species *Homo sapiens. . . .*" He rejects this idea because species membership, as a biological fact, does not determine moral standing. Yet given that other facts such as having certain psychological capacities do determine it, when some nonparadigm persons lack those capacities while some animals have them, moral standing should be ascribed accordingly. For Singer (2009), it is worse to kill a gorilla with a 70 IQ score than a severely retarded human with a 25 IQ score, because the gorilla's interests are not comparable to the human's. Although both may desire to remain alive, the gorilla has other interests arising from its complex mental states and intentions, including memories, reasoning, and awareness of itself as a continuing subject of experience over time.

Given this critique of speciesism, any being with psychological capacities similar to ours has similar interests and therefore similar moral standing. Think of *Star Trek's* Mr. Spock, half human, half Vulcan. If he were real, he would have the moral standing of persons. But the severely mentally impaired human or the human neonate would not.

The Humanist Response

Humanism holds that species membership can determine moral standing. It rejects Singer's charge that speciesism is a bias as arbitrary and benighted as sexism or racism since, although race and sex are irrelevant to moral consideration, species need not be. Consider the category 'race.' Science has demonstrated that it neither is a well defined biological category nor captures any interesting differences in psychological capacity. By contrast, science continues to use 'species' as the fundamental taxonomic unit of biological classification in spite of some controversy about how to define it or whether it captures a real category in nature (Ereshefsky, 2010).

There is a long humanist tradition that invokes ordinary intuitions to distinguish duties to humans and to animals, as they arise in scenarios of this sort:

Burning Lab. A biological research lab is in flames, posing serious risk to the lives of workers and the chimps and rats that are their experimental subjects. The humanist intuition here is that firefighters at the scene should save the humans first, the chimps next, and the rats last.

But this humanist reply to speciesism's critics misses the point, since critics such as Singer can justify the firefighters' action by comparing the interests of lab workers, chimps, and rats.

Yet the humanists' intuitions also arise in examples of this sort:

Farmer. A farmer provides special care for a rabbit—better food, portion size, health monitoring, etc.—because that will enable the animal to compete in the upcoming State Fair. But given her limited means, she must lower the quality of food for the other animals. The humanist intuition here is that her actions are not ***unjust*** to the other animals.

Farmer suggests that we owe duties of justice only to humans, a view early urged by humanist Michel de Montaigne (1533–1592). To animals, he thought, we owe humane care or duties of humanity, which include "graciousness and benignity."

Furthermore, when assessing how a life is going morally, membership of *Homo sapiens* can be shown to matter. As noted by Stephen J. Gould (1982), while moral judgment applies to human action, it does not to animal behavior. A cat plays with the sentient mouse before killing it. A wasp paralyzes possibly sentient caterpillars to make them live longer while it feeds on them slowly, beginning with the caterpillars' nonvital parts and ending with the parts whose loss will be fatal. In the meantime, the creature is alive but paralyzed. If a human assassin treated her victim in either of these ways, surely her life is not going well morally. This suggests that species boundaries have some bearing on the moral evaluation of actions—but only indirectly, via the fact that paradigm persons typically have some psychological capacities animals totally lack or lack to a significant degree. *Homo sapiens* may acquire a moral dimension by denoting beings that typically have those capacities.

Skepticism about Animals' Moral Standing

All arguments in this section purport to show that animals have either minimal moral standing or none. As such, they have important implications for the permissibility of animal research. For when combined with the Benefits Argument, they support anti-abolitionism. So there is a lot at stake in these arguments.

The Correlativity Argument

Animal experimentation would be forbidden if, as argued by animal rights activists, animals have the rights to freedom and bodily integrity. The Correlativity Argument contends that they lack such rights. When presented in recent litigation in the US to free some great apes from captivity, the argument has persuaded the courts to rule against the plaintiff's claim that a chimpanzee, for example, has a right to freedom. Unlike legal persons, the argument goes, a chimp has no legal duties. Lacking duties, it can't have rights either.

A parallel argument for moral rights contends

1.   Only beings with moral duties can have moral rights.
2.   Animals lack moral duties.

---

3.   Therefore, animals lack moral rights.

Of these premises, (1) is debatable, since it can be shown that having rights does not always correlate with having duties. Consider infants or the permanently and severely retarded. Common morality and the law both agree that although such nonparadigm persons lack moral duties, they have rights. Thus, using them for risky experiments would be a serious moral wrong. Besides appeals to common morality and the law, this line of reply can claim to provide the best explanation of why such experiments would be serious moral wrongs: namely, that they violate the rights of nonparadigm persons. Therefore, beings with no moral duties can nonetheless have moral rights. It follows that the *Correlativity Argument* is unsound. Like nonparadigm persons, animals too could be within the moral community, which is the community of beings that count morally.

The Slippery-Slope Argument

Since antiquity, rationality has often been considered necessary for membership of the moral community. Following Aristotle, Aquinas took rationality, what distinguishes humans from animals, to determine such membership: it is only rational beings that have natural rights, the precursors of today's human rights. Among contemporary theorists, contractarian Peter Carruthers (1992) also identifies rationality as necessary for counting morally. In his view, morality arises out of an implicit contract established by rational beings to protect their interests. Nonrational animals are excluded from that contract, and therefore, from the moral community. But these rationality-centered views of the moral community need to explain why cruelty toward animals and individuals with profound cognitive impairments seems morally wrong. With varying details, rationality-centered approaches have answered this question by invoking our **indirect duty** to avoid such acts of cruelty. The duty is 'indirect' because we really owe it to humankind, not to the animals or severely cognitive impaired individuals. Unlike paradigm persons, neither of these have moral standing.

But what is the argument? Immanuel Kant submits that

> If a man shoots his dog because the animal is no longer capable of service, he does not fail in his duty to the dog, *for the dog cannot judge*, but his act is inhuman and damages in himself that humanity which it is his duty to show towards mankind. *If he is not to stifle his human feelings, he must practice kindness towards animals, for he who is cruel to animals becomes hard also in his dealings with men.* (Kant 1963/1775–80: 240, our emphasis)

Kant's reason for denying moral standing to animals is that they "cannot judge." Nevertheless, he endorses a Slippery-Slope Argument for the conclusion that it is wrong to treat animals inhumanely. It runs,

1. We have a direct duty to be kind to persons.
2. Cruelty toward animals leads to unkindness towards persons.

---

3. Therefore, we have an indirect duty to animals to treat them humanely.

That is, persons should avoid mistreating animals for humanity's sake, not for the sake of the animals themselves. But this is consistent with anti-abolitionism about animal experimentation. As Kant himself claims: "Vivisectionists who use living animals for their experiments, certainly act cruelly, although *their aim is praiseworthy, and they can justify their cruelty, since animals must be regarded as man's instruments*; but any such cruelty for sport cannot be justified" (1963/1775–80: 240–1, our emphasis).

BOX 16.1 KANTIAN DIRECT AND INDIRECT DUTIES

Direct duties—duties owed to any being with moral standing, which is a being for which it matters morally and for its own sake how it is treated.

Indirect duties—duties owed to beings without moral standing strictly because of how the action would affect beings with moral standing—e.g., the person performing the action.

Neo-Kantians vary in what they make of this Slippery-Slope Argument. Call 'orthodox' the neo-Kantians who accept it, and 'reformist' those who reject it for some animals. Orthodox neo-Kantians hold that nonrational animals lack moral standing. As persons, we have **direct duties** to other rational creatures, and usually have indirect duties toward nonrational creatures. Avoiding cruelty towards a person's animal is a direct duty we owe to that person. We also have a direct duty to ourselves to develop our natural talents, which presupposes avoiding bad traits of character. But to those that have never been, and will never be, rational agents, including animals, we have only indirect duties prescribing that we may not torture, kill, or otherwise mistreat them for "sport." But as Kant notes, a main reason for our indirect duty of kindness toward animals is that such actions might incline us toward similar unkindness toward persons, and thus it is to "humanity" (in the person of others or ourselves) that we owe such avoidance. Yet nonrational creatures have no moral standing, so treating them as mere means is permissible.

Problems for this neo-Kantian orthodoxy include that it must justify an agent's action when, for example, she mistreats some animals in order to let off steam in her own violent inclinations, thereby enabling her to be kinder to persons. This agent would have no duty to refrain from, for example, setting fire to a cat for fun. But given common morality, the agent acts wrongly, not merely for humanity's sake, but chiefly for the cat's. Moreover, since like Kant, orthodox neo-Kantians are anti-abolitionist, they face the challenge of the above Argument from Marginal Cases: they must explain why it forbids risky research on individuals who have permanently lost cognitive capacity while considering it permissible on animals of equal or greater capacity.

Reformist neo-Kantians depart from this orthodoxy by ascribing some moral standing to the animals we now know to have at least "fragments" of rationality. With advances in animal science, few today would deny some rationality to higher mammals and perhaps other animals. For example, the great apes' cognitive abilities have been established in animal science for some time, at least since the discovery that chimps and gorillas can learn to use human language—chiefly, American Sign Language—to communicate. Among reformists, Allen Wood (O'Neill and Wood, 1998) acknowledges this fact. He contends that, once updated to reflect current scientific knowledge of animal psychology, Kant's account can grant moral standing to any animal with "fragments" of rationality. But it must abandon the requirement that only persons (with full rationality) qualify as ends in themselves. Thus Wood can be abolitionist about animal experimentation involving subjects with some rationality. These should not be treated as instruments. Yet even if (let's say) dolphins, whales and the great apes fall into this category, what about rodents and birds? Wood must say that, having no moral standing, they can be treated as mere instruments. Since these constitute the vast majority of research animals, reformist neo-Kantians also fail to account for the intuition that how we treat these animals matters morally for their own sakes.

Animal Law

Although, as we have seen, whether animals have moral rights or standing remains unsettled, there is consensus on the need for standards for humane treatment of research animals. An early attempt at setting standards was William Russell and Rex Burch's (1959) 'three Rs':

- *Reduction* of numbers of animal subjects.
- *Refinement* of techniques to reduce suffering.
- *Replacement* of live animals whenever possible.

Many countries have regulations for animal research consistent with the three Rs. In the US, the above-mentioned (Laboratory) AWA is the principal source of federal regulations for animal dealers and laboratories. Although initially enacted in 1966 to stop the trade in stolen domestic pets that were being sold to labs, this legislation was increasingly amended. It now contains standards for the protection of many species of animals in a wide variety of activities besides research. As shown in Gennarelli's head-injury study, the AWA can be used against labs that fail to meet such standards for their animals. But mice, rats, and birds were exempted from AWA protection in the 2002 amendment made as part of an Agricultural Appropriation Bill (Curnutt, 2001). The Chimpanzee Health Improvement, Maintenance, and Protection (CHIMP) Act of 2000 provides some protections to chimpanzees used in research, animals that cannot be euthanized except for humane reasons and must be retired in a chimp sanctuary. Critics of the status quo contend that CHIMP does not go far enough compared with protections in countries where animal experimentation on all great apes is banned—for example, the UK, where experimentation on other animals is regulated by the Animal Scientific Procedures Act of 1986, which requires authorization based on harm/benefit assessments. Since 2009, the European Union has banned cosmetics testing on animals.

16.4 Chapter Summary

This chapter began with a close look at factors that contributed to public awareness in the 1970s and 80s of the moral issues raised by animal experimentation. Abolitionism advocates either its elimination or radical reduction. Either way, abolitionism's scope may be local (i.e., research on certain animals) or global (i.e., research on any animals). Reasons for abolitionism concern the welfare of animals and their rights to life and bodily integrity. Although anti-abolitionism considers animal experimentation morally permissible and even mandatory, it need not favor 'anything goes'. The main reason for anti-abolitionism is the Benefits Argument. Objections to this argument include the Argument from Marginal Cases and that the actual benefits of using animals in biomedical research are far from established empirically.

Even if some of the empirical questions raised by the use of animals in medical research could be settled, the positions at stake are incompatible because they rest on contrary views about the moral standing of animals. For a summary of these, see Figure 16.3.

FIGURE 16.3 Moral Standing and Animal Research

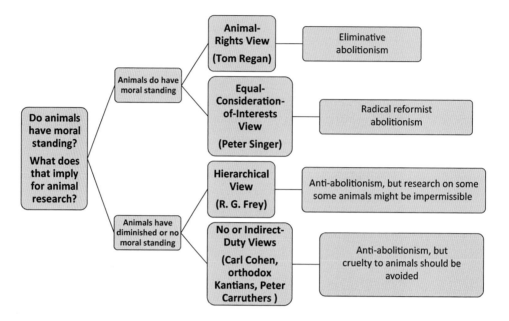

The main problems facing the views in Figure 16.3 is, for abolitionists, to make a good case against the Benefits Argument, and to show that sentience has the moral significance they take it to have. For anti-abolitionists, it is to respond to the Argument from Marginal Cases in a way that accommodates common intuitions about the moral impermissibility of doing research on less rational individuals for the benefit of paradigm persons. In spite of these deep disagreements, increasing regulation of animal research suggests a slow but steady moral progress on the treatment of animals.

16.5 Study Aids

Key Words

Abolitionism/anti-abolitionism, 303
Animal-rights view, 307
Animal-welfare view, 308
Direct/indirect duty, 311/312
Equal consideration of interests, 308
Hierarchical View, 306
Humanism, 309
Sentience, 302
Speciesism, 309
Vivisection, 301

Questions and Cases for Further Consideration

1. What is Singer's critique of speciesism? Is this critique compatible with thinking that humans have a special dignity or moral worth just because they are humans? Are you for or against speciesism? Why?

2. Could Kantians consistently oppose the use of animals in biomedical research on the grounds that pain is bad? If so, what would be the argument? Does the indirect-duty view rule out cruelty to animals?

3. Given Frey's hierarchical view, what would it take for spiders, mollusks, and bees to have moral standing? What might he argue about the moral permissibility of biomedical research on newborns and on animals of similar cognitive capacities?

4. Every year, millions of animals worldwide suffer pain, and even permanent injury or death, in the course of biomedical research. Among them are primates, birds, rodents, cats, and dogs. In light of this fact, must classical utilitarians be abolitionists?

5. *In the early 2010s,* Stephen Wise, *an attorney from* The Nonhuman Rights Project *filed several writs of* habeas corpus *in New York on behalf of captive chimpanzees. Normally these are filed on behalf of persons who are held in jail without trial or otherwise unlawfully. But Wise held that chimps share with humans sufficiently complex psychological capacities, so that they have similar fundamental rights. Therefore, he argued, chimps and other psychologically sophisticated mammals should be considered persons in the law, as corporations are. With one exception in 2015 involving a lab chimp held at the State University of New York, judges quickly dismissed Wise's actions. According to a common reply by attorneys for those wishing to keep the animals, because chimps have no legal duties, they have no legal rights.* Wise was not seeking complete freedom for these nonhumans but only their removal from cages and release in one of the eight primate sanctuaries in North America. To support his actions, he presented evidence about primate psychology from scientists who study them. Questions to consider here include: a) What might that evidence have consisted of? b) Is the common reply by the defense convincing? c) What other objections might Mr. Wise have encountered and how might he respond? d) What would be the consequences of his views for zoos or animal farming? (See Gorman 2013a and 2013b for more on Wise's actions).

6. *Wayne State University was sued in 2013 by Dr. John Pippin of the Physicians Committee for Responsible Medicine for a dog study designed to replicate cardiovascular conditions such as heart failure and high blood pressure. Pippin charged that the research "is not just cruel . . . it's unnecessary, wasteful and does not contribute to the advance of human health." About 21 dogs underwent invasive surgery to insert mechanical devices in their body cavities and to attach wires to their hearts and blood vessels for the purpose of later monitoring them during forced exercise on treadmills, experiments with drugs, and*

induced obstruction of blood flow to the kidneys. Many dogs did not survive surgery, but one that did, 2-year-old Betty, came out with nine tubes and wires. Like other survivors, she underwent all such experiments before being euthanized. A speaker for Wayne State defended the researchers, who have received up to $16 million in federal funds for their experiments. He stressed that it is irresponsible to oppose research on such important health issues, given that contemporary advances in medicine have been made possible by research on animals.[3] Suppose the facts about the dogs in the study are as described by Dr. Pippin. Questions to consider here include: a) Why might he be *irresponsible* as claimed by Wayne State? How might he respond to this charge? b) What if, as Pippin maintained, the study had no bearing on human health? How persuasive would the university's appeal to the past benefits of animal research for humans then be? c) Would it make a moral difference if the research was on rats rather than dogs?

Suggested Readings*

*Brennan, Andrew, "Humanism, Racism and Speciesism," *Worldviews: Global Religions, Culture & Ecology* 7.3, 2003: 274–302.
    Argues that speciesism is not comparable to racism, a prejudice justified by neither scientific nor folk reasons. By contrast, the long humanist tradition considers species boundaries morally relevant for reasons invulnerable to the speciesism objection.
Carruthers, Peter, *The Animals Issue: Moral Theory in Practice*. Cambridge: Cambridge University Press, 1992.
    Responds to the Argument from Marginal Cases with a contractualist denial that we have duties to animals. Animals are excluded from the social contract. In setting fair moral rules for themselves, the contractors must ignore many facts about themselves such as race or sex, but cannot ignore that they are humans because at stake is human morality.
*Cohen, Carl, "The Case for the Use of Animals in Biomedical Research," *New England Journal of Medicine* 315.2, 1986: 865–70.
    Offers an argument for the use of animals in research based on its benefits and the fact that animals cannot have moral rights.
Curnutt, J., *Animals and the Law: A Sourcebook*. Santa Barbara: ABC-CLIO, 2001.
    Comprehensive survey of animal law in the US.
DeGrazia, David, *Animal Rights: A Very Short Introduction*. Oxford: Oxford University Press, 2002.
    Very readable outline of main positions in the debate about animal rights. Particularly relevant to the topics here are the chapters on the moral status of animals and animal experimentation.

---

3   Charlie Langton, "Lawsuit Brewing against Wayne State over 'Painful' Heart Experiments on Dogs," *CBS Detroit*, 2013. http://detroit.cbslocal.com/2013/11/14/lawsuit-brewing-against-wayne-state-over-painful-heart-experiments-on-dogs/.
*   Asterisks mark readings available online. See links on the companion website.

———, "Human-Animal Chimeras: Human Dignity, Moral Status, and Species Prejudice,"
in Gruen, Grabel, and Singer 2007, pp. 168–87.
   In the course of discussing the moral permissibility of human-animal hybrids, distinguishes the equal-consideration-of-interests view of animal moral standing from what
   we have here called the 'Hierarchical View.' Draws from these some consequences for
   animal experimentation on the great apes.
Frey, R. G., "Animals," in H. La Follette, ed., *Oxford Handbook of Practical Ethics*, pp. 166–
87. New York: Oxford University Press, 2003.
   Anti-abolitionist exam of criteria of moral standing in the context of animal experimentation. Contends that only sentient beings who are subjects of experience can
   have moral standing, and that some nonhumans have more moral standing than some
   humans.
———, "Animals and Their Medical Use," in Cohen and Wellman 2005, pp. 91–103.
   Rejects both abolitionism and the anything-goes view about animal experimentation,
   defending a gradualist view of moral standing. Animals' moral standing rests on their
   having sentience. Humans have, in addition, moral agency, which gives their lives
   higher quality and value—a difference considered relevant to the permissibility of
   animal research.
*Gruen, Lori, "The Moral Status of Animals," *The Stanford Encyclopedia of Philosophy*,
Edward Zalta, ed., 2003/2010. Available online at http://plato.stanford.edu/entries/
moral-animal/.
   Offers a helpful outline of the major views about the moral status of animals. Good
   critical outline of Kant's position on animal cruelty.
*Harrison, Peter, "Do Animals Feel Pain?" *Philosophy* 66.255, 1991: 25–40.
   Rejects three main reasons for thinking that animals are sentient, thus challenging a
   common assumption since Bentham, offering some arguments for the view than only
   humans can suffer.
*Hettinger, Edwin C., "The Responsible Use of Animals in Biomedical Research," *Between
the Species* 5.3, 1989: 123–31.
   Rejects Cohen's (1986) argument, especially his view that only moral agents have
   rights and his pessimism about alternatives to animal research.
*Kant, Immanuel, "Duties towards Animals and Spirits," in *Lectures on Ethics*, pp. 239–41.
New York: Harper & Row, 1963 [1775–80].
   Clear statement of Kant's view that duties to animals are really duties to humankind.
Kazez, Jean, "We Should Prohibit the Use of Chimpanzees and Other Great Apes in Biomedical Research," in Caplan and Arp 2014, pp. 271–80.
   Offers a 'value-to-us' argument for a total ban on using chimps, our closest evolution-
   ary and genetic relatives, in animal research. Whether or not they have rights or moral
   standing, we value them as we value art, nature, and historical monuments.
*de Montaigne, Michel, "Of Cruelty," *Essays of Michel de Montaigne*, vol. 4, 1580. Available
online at http://oll.libertyfund.org/titles/1745.
   Locus classicus for the humanist view that membership to our species makes a moral
   difference.
Norcross, Alastair, "Animal Experimentation," in Steinbock 2007, pp. 648–67.
   Good overview of main objections facing the equal-consideration-of-interest view
   for a radical reduction in animal experimentation. Contends there are no good

reasons for considering animals' interests of less moral significance than human interests.

*O'Neill, Onora and Allen W. Wood, "Kant on Duties Regarding Nonrational Nature," *Proceedings of the Aristotelian Society* 72. supp. 1, 1998: 211–28.

Wood thinks that Kantians should acknowledge the moral standing of some animals by changing Kant's Formula of Humanity as an End in Itself, so that it can count some apparently rational animals as ends in themselves. O'Neill rejects Wood's modification, sticking to Kant's Formula but defending his doctrine of indirect duties to animals, which affords protection of their welfare but grants them no animal rights.

*Orlans, F. Barbara, *In the Name of Science: Issues in Responsible Animal Experimentation*. New York: Oxford University Press, 1993.

Well-informed coverage of animal-rights activism, including historical details of the baboon head-injury studies and the Silver Spring monkey experiments.

Regan, Tom, "Empty Cages: Animals Rights and Vivisection," in Cohen and Wellman 2005, pp. 77–90.

An update of Regan's (1983) classic book on animal rights. After questioning the Benefits Argument's premises, Regan argues for abolitionism about animal experimentation because, like the nonparadigm humans of Argument from Marginal Cases, animals too have the rights to bodily integrity and life. Their consciousness, confirmed by evolutionary theory, is the source of these rights.

Singer, Peter, *Practical Ethics*. Cambridge: Cambridge University Press, 1979.

Together with *Animal Liberation*, a *locus classicus* for Singer's view on the moral standing of animals. Holds that sentience is what confers moral standing to both humans and animals, but avoids claiming rights for either. Animals with higher psychological capacities have more interests than humans with profound mental impairments.

*——, "Animal Liberation at 30," *New York Review of Books* 50.8, 2003: 23–6.

Reasserts the author's critique of speciesism, suggesting that the reason why no plausible defense of speciesism has appeared over the past 30 years is that no such defense is credible.

*——, "Speciesism and Moral Status," *Metaphilosophy* 40.3/4, 2009: 567–81.

Regards speciesism as a prejudice. Although all sentient beings have equal moral standing, their interests vary according to their forms of consciousness. The result is a "graduated view that applies to animals as well as to humans."

*De Waal, Frans, "Moral Behavior in Animals," *TED Talk*, 2011. Available online at http://www.ted.com/talks/frans_de_waal_do_animals_have_morals?language=en.

Provides some evidence that certain higher mammals are capable of not only reasoning but also rudimentary morality.

Williams, Bernard, "The Human Prejudice," in J. Schaler ed., *Peter Singer under Fire*, pp. 77–96. Chicago: Open Court, 2009.

Denies that speciesism is a self-serving prejudice. Rather, it concerns who we are ethically and how we understand our practices. If aliens smarter than us decide to eliminate us to improve this part of the universe, speciesism's critics like Singer would have to take the aliens' side, which Williams considers wrong because they are not "one of us."

17

Biomedical Research on Humans

Learning Objectives

In reading this chapter you will

▶ Reflect on the rationale for testing new medical interventions on human subjects.

▶ Learn about moral dilemmas that arise for investigators when research subjects are put at risk of harm for the potential benefit of others.

▶ Consider the moral grounds and relevance of informed consent as a condition for enrolling human subjects in a clinical trial.

▶ Become aware that biomedical research may sometimes breach obligations of justice and respect for human subjects as persons, and see how this may happen.

BIOMEDICAL RESEARCH AIMS at promoting medical progress with the acquisition of new knowledge and the discovery of potentially beneficial interventions. It is often impossible to know whether certain interventions amount to improvements over available treatments without trying them on humans. However, since trials can cause harm to participants, who ordinarily do not benefit from them, when is it acceptable to risk harming a few to benefit others—probably future generations? Here we consider this question, together with matters concerning experimental subjects' autonomy, and fairness in the distribution of biomedical research benefits and burdens.

17.1 The Tuskegee Untreated-Syphilis Study

Tuskegee, Alabama, is the county seat of Macon County. In 1932, during the Great Depression, it was one of the poorest counties in the United States, with a population largely of African American sharecropper farmers. It was also a county with one of the highest rates of syphilis, with approximately one third of the male Black population affected. In that year, the US Public Health Service enlisted researchers for a study of the natural etiology of syphilis, a very familiar but insufficiently understood sexually transmitted disease (STD) that, if left untreated, can result in blindness, dementia, or death. The subjects were African American men from Macon County, 399 with untreated syphilis and 201 without syphilis. The two cohorts were simply observed, over a period of 40 years, with no syphilis treatment administered to the infected men, even after the advent of penicillin. By 1948, this antibiotic was considered effective against syphilis. But the Tuskegee study's subjects were kept ignorant, not only of their STD, but also of the availability of penicillin. They were told they had "bad blood," for which they were being treated, when in fact the study's only objective was to learn about the progress of untreated syphilis.

Data from the study circulated openly in medical journals, yet aroused no ethical concerns until 1972, when journalist Jean Heller exposed it in the Associated Press. By then, at least 28 research subjects had died of untreated syphilis.

■ ■ ■

The *Tuskegee syphilis study*, openly conducted and federally funded for four decades, had ethical lapses on fundamental rules of biomedical research involving humans. True, in the early 1930s, the high incidence of syphilis, predominantly among men, made the disease a serious public health problem. So understanding its progression was an essential goal if effective treatments were to be developed. Furthermore, the Tuskegee subjects might not have been made worse off as a result of the study. Penicillin would probably not have helped most of them owing to the latent stage of their syphilis. But there is dispute about this (Pence, 2008: 189). Even so, the study failed to show respect for them as persons and to treat them fairly. They were treated as little more than guinea pigs, or mere means to the investigators' ends. They were deliberately misled about the nature of their illness and about treatments for it when they became available, and thus never given a chance to validly consent to participation. Although it was not until the late 1940s, during the Nuremberg trials after World War II, that US prosecutors held obtaining research subjects' consent to be an ethical requirement for biomedical research, the Tuskegee scientists did not think it also applied to their study. They were by then more interested in protecting the collated medical data than in the ethics of the study.

Furthermore, questions arise about whether the subjects, even if informed, could have *voluntarily* consented to participation. Medical care was something difficult to come by for most people in the Great Depression, and even more so for the Tuskegee subjects, all selected from a historically disenfranchised racial group with little access to the health care system. This, together with their low socioeconomic status, left them little choice but to accept free medical care—a fact often noted by critics of the study charging that it amounted to racial discrimination, a topic we resume below. For now note that all enrolled subjects belonged to a **vulnerable population**, a somewhat vague category in biomedical research that refers to

Any group of people whose members, owing to their comparative disadvantage, are susceptible to undue influence or coercion for enrolling in a biomedical study. They include

- ○ People from racial or ethnic minorities.
- ○ Under-aged, mentally impaired, or institutionalized people (e.g., in prison, the army, or a nursing home).
- ○ People who have low socioeconomic status.

The Tuskegee study imposed the burdens of learning about the etiology of syphilis on African Americans in the rural South, at the time a vulnerable population victimized in countless ways. It thus amounted to an injustice, since other racial groups with an incidence of syphilis would reap the study's benefits without sharing any of its burdens.

But these conclusions about the Tuskegee syphilis study or any other experimentation on humans that violates fundamental ethical principles need not encourage skepticism about biomedical research on humans. For one thing, clarity on the ethical issues at stake in it should lead to proper external controls and regulations for effectively avoiding ethical lapses. Moreover, medical professionals and society have the duty of preventing harm whenever possible, and this might justify, if not require, conducting biomedical research of the types illustrated in this chapter. Some such studies aim at identifying the nature and causes of diseases and other health conditions affecting a population; others aim at determining whether potentially new drugs or medical interventions might represent an advance in medical care that should be adopted in clinical practice. Testing a medical intervention in controlled studies before making it more widely available for use may reveal it to be of no therapeutic value, or even harmful: bloodletting (opening a vein as way to treat illness) and insulin shock therapy (repeated administration of insulin to induce coma as a psychiatric treatment) are cases in point. Clinical trials were also necessary in the development of the polio vaccine, antibiotics, and other crucial advances in modern medicine.

17.2 Ethical Issues in Research on Human Subjects

Early Ethical Guidelines

The Tuskegee syphilis study's ethical lapses occurred at a time of evolving awareness of the standards that must be met for research on humans to be ethically permissible. A turning point came immediately after the end of the Second World War with the War Crimes Tribunals at Nuremberg, Germany, 1945–1949. High-ranking Nazi leaders, taken into custody at the war's end, were brought before a court convened by the victorious Allied Powers (Britain, the United States, and the Soviet Union) to account for war-related atrocities and crimes against humanity. Among the defendants in the so-called Doctors' Trial of 1946 were twenty physicians and three administrators charged with conspiracy, war crimes, crimes against humanity, and membership of a criminal organization. The testimony of survivors and other evidence pointed to their having conducted ghastly "medical experiments" on civilians and prisoners of war. Some of these were carried out in pursuit of the Nazi doctrine of a "superior race" and its eugenics program discussed in Chapter 15. Others were designed to help the German war effort, testing the resistance of the human body to altitude, cold, and other hazards soldiers might encounter in combat. In pursuit of these goals, nonconsenting humans were subjected to unimaginable suffering and almost invariably to death. They were Jews, Gypsies, and Slavs of many nationalities, as well as Communists, homosexuals, and the disabled, among others.

The Nuremberg Code

The Doctors' Trial made necessary a set of ethical standards for biomedical research on humans against which to judge the defendants. Six articles were quickly fashioned and later extended to ten in what is known as the 'Nuremberg Code' of 1947. Armed with this code, the prosecutor argued that the defendants' research on humans had violated the basic obligations expected of medical professionals. His case rested mostly on violations of the Hippocratic Oath's do-no-harm provision, pointing out that the defendants had experimented on human subjects in harmful ways they would not have used on animals, which were protected under a German law of 1933. (As in Chapter 16, 'animals' in this chapter excludes humans.)

The Nuremberg Code's opening article does not, however, concern biomedical researchers' duties of beneficence and nonmaleficence. It focuses instead on another type of moral duty flouted in the Nazis' medical experiments: respect for human subjects as persons. The doctors' violation of this principle drew widespread moral outrage. Article 1 emphasizes that ethical experimentation on human subjects requires that their participation be only by their own free choice, made with full knowledge and comprehension of associated risks, and without any force, fraud, deceit, or coercion. Experimental subjects must understand the purpose, duration, risks, and scope of the research.

This article rests on the idea that there is a strong analogy between the requirement of informed consent in the context of clinical ethics and in that of research ethics, which is grounded in the principle that individuals deserve to be treated as autonomous agents capable of making their own self-regarding decisions about participating in a scientific study. Consent in either context needs to meet similar standards of information, voluntariness, and understanding. But there are counterexamples (or 'hard cases') to considering informed consent essential to acceptable research. On the one hand, if it is *necessary*, then there is a problem for research where a subject's autonomy is diminished by being immature, incapacitated, or part of a group that may be coerced or unduly influenced to join a study. Institutionalized individuals, such as prisoners, raise a special dilemma because in their case researchers must either

- Allow prisoners to 'volunteer' for research activities, since it may be unfair to them to invoke their compromised autonomy in excluding them, or
- Acknowledge that their institutionalization reduces their ability to make voluntary decisions, and thus protect them (as required in the case of other individuals with diminished autonomy).

Even if this dilemma can be resolved by careful analysis of each research project, there are other counterexamples to the necessity of subjects' informed consent for permissible research. For, given this requirement, no permissible studies can be conducted in emergency situations or on children, elderly patients with Alzheimer's, and other vulnerable subjects. But this seems too restrictive, owing to the perils of, for example, using on children medications that have not been tested in children. At present, about 70% of such medications fall in that category (Wendler, 2012). In addition, informed consent need not be *sufficient* for ethically permissible research, since people sometimes consent to actions that are wrong, such as torture or slavery.

Later codes and guidelines for research ethics have incorporated additional recommendations to avoid these problems—in particular, the one to be considered next.

The Declaration of Helsinki

The World Medical Association's Declaration of Helsinki followed in 1964. Unlike the Nuremberg Code, it offered a qualified view of the centrality of informed consent in any morally permissible research involving human subjects. It looks at this standard in greater detail and was amended several times to address issues left out by the Nuremberg Code such as

- The ethics of **therapeutic (clinical) research** whereby physicians conduct a trial in the context of treating a patient, and
- The requirements for **proxy consent** in cases where the research subject cannot give consent because she lacks capacity.

About therapeutic research, the Helsinki Declaration stipulates that

> Physicians who combine medical research with medical care should involve their patients in research only to the extent that this is justified by its potential preventive, diagnostic, or therapeutic value and if the physician has good reason to believe that participation in the research study will not adversely affect the health of the patients who serve as research subjects (art. 14).

Where proxy consent may be needed, the Helsinki Declaration states

> For a potential research subject who is incapable of giving informed consent, the physician must seek informed consent from the legally authorized representative. These individuals must not be included in a research study that has no likelihood of benefit for them unless it is intended to promote the health of the group represented by the potential subject, the research cannot instead be performed with persons capable of providing informed consent, and the research entails only minimal risk and minimal burden (art. 28).

However, where proxy consent to a study has been given, conducting it would nevertheless be unethical if the subject herself refused to participate.

Like the Nuremberg Code, the Helsinki Declaration acknowledges researchers' obligations of beneficence, broadly construed as including the injunctions to do no harm to human subjects (nonmaleficence) and to promote their wellbeing (beneficence). Strictly interpreted, nonmaleficence requires refraining from any study that might harm its subjects, no matter what its benefit to society. But this is paradoxical, for unless there is proper medical or pharmaceutical testing, harmful medical methods may continue to be used. The Helsinki Declaration proposes to solve the paradox by the careful balancing of each study's expected benefits and possible risks:

> All medical research involving human subjects must be preceded by careful assessment of predictable risks and burdens to the individuals and groups involved in the research in comparison with foreseeable benefits to them and to other individuals or groups affected by the condition under investigation. . . . (art. 17)

The Declaration thus addresses the long-standing problem that biomedical researchers owe duties of beneficence not only to human subjects but also to society. These might on occasion pull in opposite directions.

FIGURE 17.1 Clinical Trials

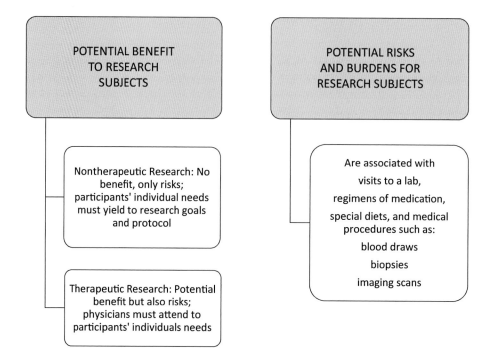

Balancing Benefits and Risks

Recognizing that the protection of subjects is a paramount consideration, the Helsinki Declaration sought to resolve any such conflicts by promoting the formation of independent research *ethics review committees*, charged with the assessment of whether to begin, continue, or stop a study when the probability or severity of risks is high.

In the US, those committees are called **institutional review boards** (IRBs) and were first mandated in 1976 by the Food and Drug Administration (FDA) for approval of any drug or device developed in research using institutionalized subjects. In 1981 the FDA extended the requirement for approvals of studies on any human subjects. Other federal agencies involved in biomedical research followed suit, requiring IRB assessment designed to protected human subjects by balancing a study's benefits and risks.

BOX 17.1 SAFETY PHASES IN PHARMACOLOGICAL RESEARCH

Preclinical phase: drug tested on animals.

Phase 1: drug tested on a small group of generally healthy human subjects.
Phase 2: drug tested on a limited number of patients with the condition for which it is being developed.

Phase 3: clinical trial (drug tested on a larger group of subjects and compared with similar medications).
Phase 4: optional post-marketing study.

In *pharmacological research*, this means minimizing the risks of an investigational drug to human subjects by requiring a number of safety phases. First, there is a preclinical phase in which a drug is tested on animals. If these tests are successful, researchers move on to phase 1, in which the drug is tested on a small group of generally healthy human subjects or patient volunteers under controlled conditions (of diet, rest, exercise, etc.), with the aim of determining whether it is safe for human subjects. If the drug is tolerated by humans, phase 2 follows, where the drug is tested on a limited number of patients with the condition for which it is being developed. This phase is focused chiefly on the drug's level of effectiveness and further safety issues. Next comes phase 3, also known as a clinical trial, in which tests are run on a larger group of subjects to check for possible side effects and compare the drug with other, similar medications currently on the market, while also continuing to check the drug for safety and efficacy and to determine best dosage schedules. Once the drug is finally approved for use, there may also be a phase 4, the post-marketing study.

These rules for clinical trials of drugs are among the extensive safety protocols that have grown out of the Nuremberg Code and the Declaration of Helsinki and current guidelines for the protection of human subjects. The early codes were influential attempts at establishing conditions for ethically permissible biomedical studies on human subjects. Since the objectives and techniques of biomedical research are always evolving, those conditions may vary accordingly, requiring revisions to the guidelines, as shown by the numerous refinements of the Helsinki Declaration. Although neither the Nuremberg nor the Helsinki codes have ever had the force of binding international law, both have been fruitful models for national biomedical research policy developed worldwide, often as a reaction to ethical lapses in actual human experimentation.

What Researchers Owe to Subjects

In the US, guidelines and federal regulation of biomedical research developed in part as a response to ethical lapses such as those in the Tuskegee syphilis study. In 1974, Congress passed the National Research Act, which mandated the creation of a National Commission for the Protection of Human Subjects of Biomedical and Behavioral Research (1974–1978). Made up of bioethicists, jurists, scientists, and physicians, the eleven members of this commission developed, among other guidelines, the 1979 Belmont Report, which offers an ethical framework for biomedical research based on the principles of respect for persons, beneficence (broadly construed as to include nonmaleficence), and justice. These principles recommend that investigators and independent reviewers evaluate a research project morally on the basis of

1. Valid informed consent from research subjects or their representatives.
2. Proper balancing of anticipated benefits with risk of harm to the subjects, done before enrolling them in a study.
3. A fair distribution of the research's benefits and burdens among the human subjects, whether as individuals or as members of a social, sexual, ethnic, or racial group.

BOX 17.2 THERAPEUTIC AND NONTHERAPEUTIC RESEARCH

- Therapeutic research is any biomedical study with potential health benefits for the research subjects—e.g., an experimental cancer intervention tested on cancer patients.
- Nontherapeutic research is any biomedical study of potential health or wellbeing benefits for individuals other than the research subjects, usually future generations.
- No biomedical research that aims only at generalizable knowledge counts as therapeutic.

Respect for Persons and Beneficence

(1) above is an obligation of respect for persons but need not be construed in the Nuremberg Code's absolutist way. Yet informed consent is not sufficient for the ethical acceptability of a biomedical study, because subjects might consent to interventions that are still morally unacceptable. Furthermore, consider **nontherapeutic studies,** defined as in Box 17.2. The evidence suggests that research subjects systematically fail to grasp that they do not stand to obtain a health or wellbeing benefit from such studies, or that their enrollment in a randomized study is done by a computer program, based entirely on chance. [1]

Yet without their understanding of these, there is no informed consent, at least as conceived in clinical medicine. But significant differences between the patient-health care professional and the subject-investigator relationship may determine less demanding obligations of respect for the subjects' autonomy by researchers.

They might also justify some degree of *soft paternalism*. For if research subjects cannot usually fulfill the requirements of informed consent, investigators have a duty to protect them from risks of serious harm (more about this in randomized clinical trials below). Furthermore, the following Benefits Argument provides grounds for using humans as models in biomedical research:

1. Progress in the biomedical sciences benefits society as a whole.
2. Such progress greatly depends on biomedical research on humans.

---

3. Therefore, biomedical research on humans benefits society as a whole.

Progress in the biomedical sciences is associated with advances in the prevention of harm and the promotion of health benefits. Proponents of this argument assume not only that progress is good but that the more of it, the better. But Jonas (1969) questions that maximizing view of progress: since biomedical advances already satisfy reasonable expectations, it is morally wrong to use humans for finding a cure for, say, baldness or arthritis. At this stage of medical development, nonmaleficence recommends avoiding risk of harm to research subjects. Yet this objection is weak, for society can reap more substantial benefits from research on humans than a cure for baldness or arthritis. Think of Ebola or cystic fibrosis.

---

1 See for instance Featherstone and Donovan (2002), Snowdon et al. (1997), and Wendler (2009, 2012).

In any case, the Benefits Argument provides only one reason for the morality of using humans as research subjects. Clearly, benefits and burdens should be considered, but so should justice and respect for participants.

Justice

Distributive justice, or fairness in the distribution of research's benefits and burdens among all members of society, is the notion of justice that matters most for the topic at hand. Standardly invoked in the context of social practices such as punishment and taxation, justice thus construed provides another argument for the morality of research on humans. This Justice Argument runs,

1. Humankind has benefitted from biomedical research on humans.
2. It is unjust to past generations that research's burdens should fall only on them, and to future generations that they be deprived of possible research benefits.
3. (2) would be the case if there is no moral duty to promote and even participate in biomedical research.

---

4. Therefore, there is a moral duty to promote and even participate in biomedical research.

This argument appeals to the unfairness of placing research's burdens inter-generationally. Its strength in part hinges on whether we have duties to past and future generations. However this difficult question is resolved, plausibly research's burdens and benefits must be distributed fairly among all segments of society, and among different generations.

BOX 17.3 TWO REQUIREMENTS OF JUSTICE

Given justice, the burdens of research should:

1. Be shared among societies, and
2. Not fall arbitrarily on any group of individuals or nations.

But in research ethics, questions of justice and exploitation arise more often intra-generationally. They may involve individuals or their communities. Exploitation is a form of injustice that typically occurs when some of these bear all the burdens of research without reaping its benefits as they deserve—as happens, for example, in studies in the developing world of potentially beneficial new treatments that will not be available to the nations providing the human subjects. In the developed world, during the early 19th and 20th centuries, research was often exploitative, with most of its burdens falling on the poor and the institutionalized, and its benefits on the privileged. As we saw, the notorious Tuskegee syphilis study illustrates a historical injustice of similar kind. Although syphilis was of course not exclusive to poor African Americans, the investigators selected subjects from only that disadvantaged racial minority, thereby flouting their obligations to distribute the study's possible benefits and burdens fairly in the society as a whole. More generally, selecting human subjects for a study on the basis of their vulnerability imposes on them and their communities an unfair distribution of research's burdens. Subjects should instead be enrolled on the basis of their relevance to the study's goals.

Research and Underrepresented Groups

When studying health conditions that typically affect only a segment of society such as sickle cell anemia, a disease that affects predominantly people of African ancestry, investigators do not violate their obligations of justice if they include more participants from this population. Similarly, in the early days of the HIV/AIDS epidemic, in the 1980s, activists argued for increased participation in research of groups traditionally stigmatized and discriminated (especially, gays, sex workers, and intravenous drug users). In their view, justice and benefi- cence trumped adverse results such as further stigma and discrimination.

Beneficence is an important consideration in therapeutic research, where the subjects themselves might benefit from the medical intervention or drug being studied. Thanks to advocacy campaigns for the rights of traditionally marginalized social, ethnic, racial, and gender-orientation groups, there is now more awareness that members of these populations deserve equal access to potentially beneficial therapeutic research.

Furthermore, justice demands careful selection, not only of human subjects during the trial phase, but also of the study's objective, especially for publicly funded research on new medical therapies or devices. Among groups traditionally marginalized in research, and thus treated unfairly, are women and members of the LGBT community. Comparatively, the study of disorders commonly afflicting women, such as osteoporosis and breast cancer, has been neglected. Feminist activism has denounced the disproportionate number of studies focused on men's health rather than women's. It also had a role in reforms leading to the mandatory inclusion of women as research subjects in studies of medical conditions not limited to men. Historically, the Food and Drug Administration (FDA) tended to approve, for use by both sexes, drugs that had been tested exclusively on men, as well as to fund studies on women only when those studies were devoted to reproductive health (Crasnow et al., 2015). And when focused on women, publicly funded studies had made heterosexual assumptions, thus failing to count sexual orientation as a variable relevant to lesbian women's health (Terry, 1999: 324–42).

Another area of pressing ethical concerns in biomedical research involves mentally disabled subjects. Problems include not only difficulties in obtaining informed consent by subjects or appropriate surrogates, but also the high risk of harm for these vulnerable subjects. Particularly problematic are the so-called washout/relapse protocols that consist in sudden medication withdrawal during 'washout' to prepare the subject for the trial of a new drug, and the characteristic relapse of previous symptoms that typically occurs before or during the trial. When subjects go untreated for some time, the relapse might include onset of psychosis, becoming delusional, and even suffering physical harm. The data point to suicides, increased criminal or bizarre behavior, and deaths during relapse (Shamoo and O'Sullivan, 2005).

17.3 Research Using Human Biological Material

The Case of Henrietta Lacks

In 1951, *Henrietta Lacks*, 31, was dying of cancer at Johns Hopkins University Hospital in Baltimore. A sample of her tumor cells, collected during a biopsy, got into the hands of Dr. George Otto Gay, who noticed the cells' ability to survive in the lab. Labelled 'HeLa cells,' they were grown and stored for use in research around the world without Ms. Lacks's knowledge or consent.

BOX 17.4 CHRONOLOGY OF THE SAGA OF HENRIETTA LACKS

1951—HeLa cells collected from a biopsy of Lacks's tumor without informed consent.

1971—Journal names Henrietta Lacks as the source of the HeLa cells line.

1973—Descendants contacted for the first time for blood sample in study of HeLa genes. No consent was requested.

2013—HeLa genome published online without family knowledge. Descendants later agreed to restricted access to genome data.

In 1973 investigators contacted Ms. Lacks's relatives, who by then included her grandchildren, for the first time. They requested their blood samples for a comparative study of HeLa genes, but not their consent. Forty years later, in March 2013, the relatives learned that the European Molecular Biology Laboratory had posted online genetic information about the HeLa cells. They also discovered that the US National Institutes of Health was about to publish in the journal *Nature* a parallel genetic study. Negotiations ensued, culminating later that year in an agreement about how to manage genetic data from the HeLa cells. The descendants, who had privacy concerns, were asked for their consent for the first time 62 years after Ms. Lacks's cells were first stored. By then, her saga had drawn media attention as a result of Rebecca Skloot's 2010 best-seller, *The Immortal Life of Henrietta Lacks*. Henrietta Lacks was a working-class woman of color living in the Baltimore area. Her relatives were employed mostly as tobacco farmers in Southern Virginia. When interviewed by the press, they found it ironic that while laboratories have made so much money out of selling their ancestor's cells, they could not even afford medical insurance.

Ms. Lacks's Descendants

Apparently, Ms. Lacks's descendants were not concerned with compensation for the use of the HeLa cells. Instead they wanted recognition of Henrietta's contribution to medical research and decisionmaking for the management of genetic information that might be detrimental to them. The research on those cells had yielded genetic information about them that they wished to keep private. It is not uncommon for people to fear stigmatization as a result of genetic studies' revealing heritable health conditions. Patients sometimes refuse to learn about their genetic makeup because they believe screening results could cause **genetic discrimination**—i.e., affect them socially or lower their eligibility for employment or health insurance. Even if such fears are unjustified, a medical professional's failure to honor the requirements of informed consent and privacy in genetic studies amounts to a serious breach of respect for the autonomy of those who might be affected by their findings. The studies of the HeLa cells that were undertaken before the 2013 agreement are open to this moral criticism.

On the other hand, assuming that the researchers cannot be morally obligated to do what cannot be done, an Appeal to Ignorance contends that

1.   The HeLa cells studies began in the 1950s.
2.   At that time, many researchers did not know about the requirement of informed consent.

---

3.   Therefore, those researchers were justified in studying the HeLa cells without informed consent.

Ignorance might excuse researchers when there was no widespread awareness about informed consent and privacy, but not after the Nuremberg Code of 1947. Thus the Appeal to Ignorance fails to justify, for instance, the mapping of the HeLa genes by investigators who in 1974 collected blood from relatives without proper consent. Furthermore, until 2013 Johns Hopkins researchers thought no such consent was necessary, since they took for granted their ownership of the cell line and data gathered from it.

Stronger grounds for the moral permissibility of the HeLa studies come from this version of the Benefits Argument:

1.   Answering the hard questions about the etiology of many serious diseases requires studies of biological materials from patients who can no longer give informed consent.
2.   Answering those questions promotes the greatest balance of benefits over burdens.

---

3.   Therefore, studies on biological materials from patients who can no longer give informed consent are morally permissible.

If sound, this argument would justify studies on biological material from patients who, like Ms. Lacks, have died or might have lost capacity to consent. After all, studies of the HeLa cells helped to produce medical breakthroughs ranging from the polio vaccine to an explanation of Ms. Lacks's cervical cancer's resilience through the discovery of the DNA of a human papillomavirus embedded in her genome. This was an important step in developing medical interventions to reduce the incidence of cervical cancer, which is receding in the US but still affects many women. According to the Centers for Disease Control and Prevention, in just one year, 2012, it affected 12,042 women, causing 4,074 deaths.

But consequences may also count against the above argument, since a widespread failure to fulfill obligations of respect for the autonomy of research subjects or their proxies is likely to undermine trust, and ultimately, biomedical research. All things considered, better outcomes can be achieved from the practice of obtaining participants' informed consent whenever possible for research using their biological materials. As shown in clinical practice, health outcomes are generally boosted in the long run when medical professionals build sufficient trust with patients.

17.4 Epidemiological and Clinical Research

Epidemiological Research

Epidemiology aims at identifying the nature and causes of diseases and other health disorders in a population. Investigators working in this discipline face specific ethical issues. They are standardly interested in establishing a health condition's (1) distribution, prevalence, or incidence, and (2) relevant determinants, including individual or environmental factors. To this end, they conduct surveillance and descriptive studies (goal 1) and analytical studies (goal 2). Either way, their results are essential to decisions about public health, the branch of biomedical science concerned with the control of causes and risk factors for the spread of disease and poor health in a population. Concern with public health goes back at least to Hippocrates, who emphasized the role of environmental factors in human disease and death. In the 19th century, a turning point in **epidemiological studies** came with movements toward better sanitation, housing, and nutrition. Today many epidemiological studies continue this tradition by linking the higher incidence of certain conditions to populations identified by factors such as socioeconomic status, race, or ethnicity (e.g., diabetes and obesity). By finding that, for example, low social and economic status or racial discrimination correlate positively with health disparities, studies may help to raise awareness about social injustices.

But if epidemiological research is to succeed, it needs access to private information about a large number of people who have not given, or could not give, informed consent. Investigators must often access large banks of data about patients, many of whom may be dead. In chronic disease epidemiology, for example, some landmark studies of this sort, conducted independently by British and American investigators in the 1950s, led to the identification of smokers' significantly higher risk of lung cancer compared to nonsmokers. They began with official mortality statistics, pathologists' reports, and physicians' reports of their patients with lung cancer. Although a great deal of their information was protected by rules of privacy and confidentiality, obtaining the subjects' consent was either impractical (because of the passage of time) or impossible (because the subjects were dead). The ethical question before them was: do the studies' potential benefits to public health outweigh obligations of respect for former patients whose data were essential to its success? Retrospectively, given a Benefits Argument, their decision to waive obligations of confidentiality, informed consent, and privacy seems justified. But since there is no general rule here, investigators and IRBs need to balance conflicting obligations case by case.

IMAGE 17.1
©iStockPhoto/luchschen

Epidemiological studies requiring access to biological sample banks, such as serum, sex hormone, cancer cell, or urine banks, raise similar ethical issues, since the biological samples to be used may have been collected many years earlier. If consent was given at all, it might have been for other purposes. Proxy consent may be unavailable or impractical. And as in the case of Henrietta Lacks, questions also arise about the ownership of the biological materials in biological banks.

Randomized Clinical Trials

The Clinician-Investigator's Dilemma

In biomedical research, **randomized clinical trials** (RCTs) are a prime instrument for measuring the outcome of a potentially new medical intervention, drug, or device and comparing it with current methods. However, in RCTs the researchers' roles as investigators and clinicians come apart in morally problematic ways. For an RCT's reliability depends in part on the randomized allocation (i.e., by chance alone) of research subjects in either

- An experimental group, where they receive the treatment that is being tested, or
- A control group, where they receive either a standard treatment, a placebo (the so-called sugar pill), or no treatment.

The control group provides the standard of comparison. In order to avoid biasing the data, RCTs' subjects are informed about the randomization but not about their allocation. Even so, the data systematically show that most subjects fail to understand the randomization process. Their false belief that participation in the study will bring them health benefits conflicts with their ability to give informed consent. This problem also affects the prime type of RCT known as *double-blind RCT*, where the allocation of subjects is masked to the researchers as well for the purpose of avoiding

---

Research Biases

Patterns of error in the design, evaluation, or reporting of clinical trials.

Now what is best for a study might not be best for the participants, as emphasized in the **RCT dilemma** (Hellman and Hellman, 1991): since investigators in clinical trials are medical professionals, they should look after the wellbeing of the subjects (sometimes their own patients). But when working in an RCT, they allocate the subjects at random, in ways indifferent to the subjects' best interests. Suppose investigators are initially truly uncertain about whether the experimental or the control group will do better. When that uncertainty diminishes with progress in the trial, investigators should give all subjects the intervention that is working best. Alternatively, they should discontinue the more risky intervention. But that amounts to discontinuing the trial, and losing the data so far obtained. The investigators in the Tuskegee syphilis study faced that dilemma with the advent of penicillin in the mid-1940s. Because administering it to the subjects would have implied losing data gathered since the early 1930s, they decided not to do it, thus resolving the RCT dilemma in a morally objectionable way.

The dilemma would disappear if informed consent were sufficient to morally justify RCTs. But subjects sometimes consent to morally unacceptable interventions, something well known in forensic medicine. Moreover, as noted above, they have problems to grasp randomization. Yet if the relationships of subject-investigator and patient-clinician were significantly different, as sometimes argued, then informed consent without full understanding might be enough to dissolve the RCT dilemma.

Uncertainty and Biases

The double-blind RCT is considered biomedical research's most useful tool. The double-blind feature (not achievable in all RCTs since interventions such as surgery are usually obvious to subjects) is done by a coding system unknown to researchers and subjects. The goal is full uncertainty or *equipoise*: investigators should be truly ignorant about which of the observed groups will do better.

BOX 17.5 WHEN RESEARCH GOES WRONG

Undermining an investigator's character may be

- **Errors** such as tainted samples and mistaken statistics; and/or
- **Misconduct** such as
  - Data massaging: includes image manipulations, exclusion of unusually high or low data points, and presenting an experiment as having found data the investigator already had.
  - Plagiarism: using without acknowledgment someone else's work.
  - Republication: using the same article, usually masked with small changes.
  - Falsification of data: reporting bogus data.

But a number of biases may preclude compliance with the equipoise principle. Some originate in the investigators' eagerness to obtain results that confirm their hypotheses. Such biases undermine the investigators' moral character. After all, as health care professionals, they are morally obligated to do no harm to research subjects. A benevolent investigator who has good reasons for thinking that the experimental group will do better than the control group would not put the latter at unnecessary risk. Yet not all investigators have this virtue. In pursuit of career goals, profit, prestige, etc., investigators may commit errors or outright misconduct of the sort outlined in Box 17.5. Some fields of specialization appear especially prone to them. Anesthesiology and psychology are high on the list.[2]

Clinical Trials of Me-Too Drugs

Trials of me-too drugs draw attention to some of the ethical problems of industry-sponsored research. Any of these drugs is structurally similar to, and essentially duplicates, the action of an existing drug or 'prototype.' For example, in 2009, Pitavastatin became the eighth statin used for lowering cholesterol in the US. The FDA approved it for sale about 25 years after its approval of the prototype, Lovastatin. Trials of me-too drugs are usually funded by pharmaceutical companies that hope to turn a profit from their sale. But a number of benefits to society have also been cited to justify putting subjects at risk of harm in developing me-too drugs. Pharmaceutical companies sometimes tout them as more effective, for certain patients, than the prototypes. But arguably, whenever that is the case, the drug in question may not be a 'me-too' after all. Supporters also adduce that, by stimulating competition, me-toos bring prices down, thus reducing the overall cost of pharmaceuticals, an important consideration in light of health care's cost. There is controversy, however, about this empirical claim.

Against research on me-toos, it has been argued that, since they do not add any therapeutic value, they amount to a waste of resources that could be better used for innovative drugs. But the strongest objection comes from the need of balancing benefits and risks: if an effective prototype already exists, it seems morally unjustified to risk the safety of subjects for the interests of pharmaceutical companies.

---

2 Benedict Carey, "Science under Scrutiny," *New York Times*, 6/16/2015.

17.5 Gene Therapy

Gene therapy aims at treating or preventing genetic disease. It falls within negative *genetic engineering* and consists in either germline therapy or somatic therapy. In germline therapy, a gene needed to treat or prevent disease is inserted into the DNA of a reproductive cell (egg or sperm), with any offspring inheriting the change. Since this type of gene therapy alters the germline, it changes the natural lottery in unknown ways, and seems more morally problematic than somatic gene therapy.

Here we are concerned with this less morally troubling type of gene therapy, also called 'gene transfer,' that aims at correcting genetic conditions by targeting only some of the patient's somatic cells. Since these are not reproductive cells, therapeutic changes are not inherited by offspring. Gene therapy aims at replacing or repairing the cells whose damaged versions of a gene cause a certain disease. To accomplish this, it delivers one or more genes with a normal copy. Research has revealed that genetically modified viruses are the best vehicles or 'vectors' for carrying a gene engineered to compensate for the abnormal one or to create a protein that is lacking. They enter the patient's body by either injection or inhalation. Genetic disorders caused by mutation of a single gene are prime candidates for gene therapy, which has been attempted on patients with disabling conditions, such as Severe Combined Immune Deficiency (SCID), hereditary blindness, and hemophilia. Although the first trial for SCID resulted in three of the ten patients developing leukemia, researchers have also reported some encouraging results. For example, gene therapy for cystic fibrosis, a hereditary, degenerative lung disease, invariably fatal, with average life expectancy of about 41 for those afflicted. The hope is to arrest deterioration of the lungs by introducing healthy genes that take over the function of defective ones. Patients in a 2015 clinical trial of gene therapy for cystic fibrosis reported modest but tangible improvements in their conditions.[3] The aim was plainly therapeutic: the alleviation, to the extent possible, of their ailment.

FIGURE 17.2   Somatic Gene Therapy in the Context of Human Genetic Engineering

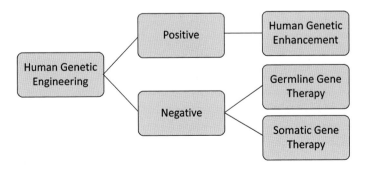

---

3   Pallab Ghosh, "Gene Therapy Stabilises Lungs of Cystic Fibrosis Patient," *BBC*, 3/7/2015. Available online at http://www.bbc.com/news/science-environment-32932922.

Therapy or Research?

These results, together with the fact that, for many genetic disorders, there are no pharmacological treatments, support a Benefits Argument for the biomedical community's moral obligation to pursue trials of gene transfer and make tested therapies available to patients.

Another argument for this duty invokes justice for persons with genetic disorders (Glover, 2006). The Justice Argument runs

1. At present, gene transfer offers the only hope for correcting some genetic disorders.
2. Genetic disorders randomly affect members of society.
3. Not to pursue gene transfer is unfair to those affected by genetic disease.

---

4. Therefore, there is strong reason to pursue gene transfer.

The encouraging results of some gene transfer trials support premise (1). Since premise (2) is now indisputable, distributive justice in health care supports (3), from which (4) follows.

But there is also a strong reason to be leery of medical interventions that are essentially experimental, potentially harmful, and may have no direct therapeutic value to participants in trials. Researchers in gene therapies are aware that, while their experiments have had some notable successes (mostly in the lab, with animal models such as rats), their benefits to humans have so far been rather limited. It may thus be preferable to speak of 'human gene transfer research.' Of course, whatever we call it, persons stricken with fatal genetic diseases are often desperate for a cure, and may place great hope in genetic transfer interventions that researchers know to be longshots. This may lead them to consent to experimental therapies carrying risks of serious harm, even death. Worst-case scenarios are incidents such as the one to be considered next, where an experimental subject was enrolled in a study, but the physician/experimenter neglected to inform him about the risks or to be certain that he understood that the 'therapy' would provide no benefit for him.

The Jesse Gelsinger Case

In 1999, *Jesse Gelsinger* was 17 years old and afflicted with a hereditary liver disorder, ornithine transcarbamylase deficiency (OTC), in which the liver is unable to remove from the blood the excessive ammonia generated in normal metabolism. Unlike most OTC patients who die in childhood, Jesse had managed to survive into adolescence through a regimen of drugs and dietary restrictions and was relatively healthy, though he knew his disorder would ultimately be fatal. Jesse also knew that there were researchers at the University of Pennsylvania conducting studies of gene therapy that might help some patients with OTC. Hoping to contribute to medical advances that could help others and perhaps benefit himself, he volunteered as a research subject. Penn researchers later claimed that they informed Mr. Gelsinger that he stood to gain nothing himself from participating as a research subject, but could only—perhaps—help future children with OTC. Jesse was just the type of subject Penn researcher Dr. James Wilson was looking for: an adult OTC patient still relatively healthy on whom gene therapy might produce significant data. The therapy, so far untested, consisted of injections of an adenovirus containing copies of the gene absent in persons afflicted with OTC.

Wilson's clinical trial, however, did not end well for Jesse. Within four days after initiating the injections, he was dead, his veins and arteries hopelessly clogged with thickened, clotted blood. The Gelsinger family, in their subsequent wrongful-death litigation against Penn, alleged that Dr. Wilson had known that the adenovirus used had harmed other OTC patients and had failed to explain to Jesse in clear, simple language the level of risk involved. Ultimately the Gelsingers settled out of court for damages in amounts undisclosed.

This case illustrates the moral dilemma facing gene therapy. For one thing, Dr. Wilson should have been wary of Jesse's ability to understand the level of risk involved—especially in light of his poor prognosis and his enthusiasm for volunteering in this clinical trial. Arguably, patients in his condition may not be able to give fully informed consent to participation in a study that they are bound to perceive as in some way beneficial to themselves. Yet gene therapy for these patients is an experimental procedure that has worked in animal models. Without studies on humans, it will remain unknown whether the lives of many patients with this genetic disorder can be extended. Dr. Wilson elected to resolve this dilemma by what appears a negligent calculation of risks to Jesse, the subject, versus benefits to society. Besides obvious flaws in obtaining the subject's informed consent and in calculating risks, his study lacked experimental neutrality: Dr. Wilson was the owner of the pharmaceutical company, Genovo, that owned the patents on the adenovirus used in the experiment, and thus stood to profit from pressing ahead with the trials.

Still, the above arguments from beneficence and justice support uses of human gene transfer that meet ethical standards for experimental therapies. Evidence from recent uses for conditions such as hemophilia, inherited blindness, and cystic fibrosis suggests this kind of therapy might ultimately help many individuals with serious genetic disorders. At the same time, while the good intentions of altruistic individuals like Jesse Gelsinger are admirable, the advances in medicine they make possible should not have to come at the cost of their lives.

◼ 17.6 Research in Developing Countries

Biomedical research on human subjects conducted in the developing world raises moral issues concerning the obligations of respect for persons, nonmaleficence/beneficence, and justice. Justice, an obligation of health care providers and researchers that we discuss in Chapter 18, is particularly important since the global disease burden falls largely on developing countries. Evaluations of the moral permissibility of RCTs in these countries need to consider

1. Local ways to approach issues of individual and public health, which may be culturally specific, and
2. The local scarcity of medical and financial resources.

These two factors, in combination, often make it difficult for local governments to ensure even minimal health care for the population, let alone to contain the spread of deadly diseases such as cholera, dengue, malaria, and Ebola. Lasting solutions would require, not only that effective therapies be found, but that they could be realistically implemented in the target regions. Western researchers and their funding agencies often cite these as reasons in favor of conducting research in developing countries.

But the burdens of any research that is expected to have a global impact should not fall disproportionately on the vulnerable, local communities. Furthermore, owing to their extreme poverty, community members might be in no position to give informed consent, or even benefit from the research. As the Helsinki Declaration states,

> Medical research with a vulnerable group is only justified if the research is responsive to the health needs or priorities of this group and the research cannot be carried out in a nonvulnerable group. In addition, this group should stand to benefit from the knowledge, practices or interventions that result from the research. (art. 20)

With this in mind, we now turn to some controversial studies in the developing world conducted by Western investigators in the 1990s.

The AZT Trials in Sub-Saharan Africa

Some Facts about the AIDs Pandemic

In the early 1990s, global health experts predicted that by the end of that decade the AIDS pandemic would affect 33.4 million people worldwide.[4] Most of its burdens would fall on the developing world. In Africa, it would amount to a plague drastically reducing life expectancy and even causing depopulation. Globally, 91% of all AIDS deaths would occur in the sub-Saharan region, which comprised 34 nations whose resources would be insufficient to respond. While HIV treatments available in the developed world involved annual costs of about $15,000 per person, some sub-Saharan countries could afford no more than $5 to $10 per person.

The AZT Trials

A crucial factor in controlling the pandemic was reducing the chance of 'vertical transmission' of the virus from infected pregnant women to their babies. Unless something was done about this, one in four or five mothers would infect her baby. At the time, approximately 800 HIV-infected babies were being born in sub-Saharan Africa every day. In developed countries, treating infected pregnant women with a long course of zidovudine (AZT), the so-called 076 regimen, reduced vertical transmission by 68% (with no breastfeeding). But the therapy involved high costs and lengthy treatment, including intravenous injection during delivery. The 076 regimen was not a realistic option in sub-Saharan Africa, where women often had no prenatal care at all until close to delivery and the treatment would be unaffordable for most patients. In 1994, the World Health Organization convened a meeting of experts to assess the global implications of the 076 regimen. Participants agreed that a short course of AZT might also effectively reduce vertical transmission of HIV and set out to test this hypothesis by means of multi-site, placebo-controlled trials conducted in both sub-Saharan

---

4   The data here is from Harvard School of Public Health, "The Debate over AZT Clinical Trials," 9/1/1991. Available online at http://www.hks.harvard.edu/case/azt/ethics/case_2–0.html.

Africa and the southern Asia-Pacific region. US researchers conducted nine such studies sponsored by the National Institutes of Health (NIH) and the Centers for Disease Control (CDC). Eight of them involved comparing the results of a treatment with a placebo group.

In these studies, HIV-infected mothers were given the drug for two days before delivery, and their infants for two days after birth. Women in the placebo-control group received the care ordinarily provided in their countries, which amounted to no treatment to reduce the chance of vertical transmission. In 1998, the CDC made public provisional results confirming that the short course of AZT does reduce vertical transmission of HIV significantly.

Cultural Imperialism versus Relativism

By 1997, some bioethicists had already raised ethical objections to the AZT studies in Africa, most notably for placing some of the infected women in a placebo arm. They could instead have received the long course of AZT without jeopardizing the trial. In an editorial in the *New England Journal of Medicine* Marcia Angell (1997) also criticized the investigators, who appeared to have flouted not only their obligations of respect for persons (by treating the women as mere means) and beneficence (by failing to prevent the infection in babies born to the women in the placebo group), but also their obligations of justice. Comparisons with the Tuskegee syphilis study were inevitable, though now the injustice was global since it involved investigators from the developed world conducting their trials on vulnerable people from the developing world. Their trials were regarded as unjust on at least two counts:

- Standard of care—The studies showed a double standard, since in the United States using pregnant women in placebo-controlled trials when an effective therapy exists is considered unethical.
- Distribution of research's benefits and burdens—The studies imposed an undue burden of biomedical research on developing nations, where most of the global disease burden falls. They were also the least likely to benefit from that trial, given local corruption and cultural differences in childbirth. Furthermore, participants came exclusively from vulnerable, historically and racially oppressed communities.

NIH and CDC staff rejected these criticisms, emphasizing the studies' beneficent goals. After all, they were designed to help reduce HIV-vertical transmission, an important element for controlling HIV/AIDS in one of the most affected regions of the world. They argued that in that region, the choice was not between the long and the short courses of AZT (which could have been tested with the so-called equivalence studies), but between the short course and *nothing* (which required investigators to use placebo groups).

The debate took a new twist when health officials in the countries where the studies were conducted voiced their defense. They charged Western critics with

---

Ethical Imperialism

A bias in thinking that one's own standards of care are valid universally

In the local health officials' view, the problem with **ethical imperialism** is its failure to recognize that different world regions may have different standards of care. Furthermore, *some* studies were better than none, since that way at least some African women would be getting AZT, and the short therapy could realistically be implemented in the future for other women.

For critics, however, when any such conflict between beneficence and justice arises, justice trumps, as shown by the widespread condemnation of the Tuskegee syphilis study. In addition, critics were quick to note that the response by African health officials failed to distinguish between believing that some standard of care is valid and the standard's actually being valid. If so, the charge of ethical imperialism implicitly assumes ethical relativism, since it can succeed only if what is ethical or unethical to do could vary from culture to culture. Because biomedical research without the participants' informed consent was once believed to be ethical, that did not make it so.

Moral Lessons from the AZT Trials

The debate over the permissibility of the AZT trials in Africa drew attention to some moral problems facing international biomedical research. For one thing, utilitarian considerations about any study's potential benefits are not enough, since beneficial research can nonetheless go wrong in a number of ways. These include, besides the issues considered already, the danger of exploiting experimental subjects in risky trials whose potential benefits may apply only to the developed world, and of leaving vulnerable subjects helpless, without long-term treatment, once the trials have concluded. Antidotes against such wrongs can be found in the major codes for ethical research covered here, beginning with the Nuremberg Code's requirement of informed consent (art. 1), and the Helsinki Declaration's proviso for the ethical use of control groups, which stipulates that "patients who receive an intervention less effective than the best proven one, placebo, or no intervention will not be subject to additional risks of serious or irreversible harm as a result. . . ." (art. 33). In addition, the International Ethical Guidelines for Biomedical Research Involving Human Subjects (CIOMS/WHO, 2002, http://www.cioms.ch/publications/layout_guide2002.pdf) recommends that the health needs and priorities of developing countries be taken into account (Guideline 8) and proscribes the use of vulnerable subjects for research that can be conducted in the developed world (Guideline 15). Finally, researchers in the US also have the moral obligation to follow existing federal regulations for protecting research subjects, which prescribe that IRBs evaluate research proposals. Investigators and reviewers should take measures to protect subjects in the face of possible local corruption and keep in mind the three principles for ethical research outlined in the Belmont Report: respect for persons, beneficence, and justice.

◼ 17.7 Chapter Summary

Biomedical research on human subjects is crucial to medical progress, because computer and animal models fall short of providing data that can readily be extrapolated to humans. The knowledge thus acquired can produce beneficial medical interventions. This Benefits Argument provides the strongest moral reason for research on humans. The types of research featured in this chapter, from epidemiological to gene transfer research, make clear that beneficence is just one of the reasons to be considered, together with justice and respect for the subjects as persons. Justice requires a balanced distribution of research's benefits and burdens in society. As a result, studies that place undue burdens on vulnerable groups or individuals are morally forbidden. But justice also requires us to make participation in research available to those groups and individuals—especially in the case of therapeutic research, where participants might benefit from it, by contrast with nontherapeutic research.

A crucial obligation of respect for research subjects is informed consent, which the Nuremberg Code considered an absolute requirement but the Helsinki Declarations qualified to allow for proxy consent. Questions about informed consent in research ethics include: Can it be obtained from vulnerable populations? What about subjects who erroneously believe a study might benefit them? Is it enough to morally justify investigators in not pursuing the subjects' best interests in a randomized clinical trial? The RCT dilemma arises because investigators' moral duties as health care professionals dedicated to healing may conflict with their duties as scientists dedicated to acquiring generalizable medical knowledge. As an RCT progresses, investigators acquire evidence that one of the treatments is more beneficial (or less harmful) than the others. At that point, their duties as health care professionals and as investigators come apart. For some, obtaining the subjects' informed consent solves this dilemma. In our view, the latter solution is not sufficient by itself, since people sometimes consent to actions that are immoral, and subjects often fail to grasp randomization.

Concerns about the welfare of subjects also argue against research in gene therapy, a form of genetic engineering aimed at treating genetic disease. Moral arguments for gene therapy appeal to its benefits as well as justice for those who, through the natural lottery, have inherited genetic disorders. Given these conflicting reasons, investigators and IRBs should make sure that research initiatives conform to existing guidelines and regulations for ethical biomedical research on human subjects.

Finally, in 1994 a group of US researchers, funded by leading US federal agencies and acting on a plan coordinated by WHO, conducted some clinical trials in sub-Saharan Africa that generated heated debates about justice, informed consent, and beneficence in global biomedical research. At stake was a new regimen of zidovudine (AZT), shorter than the one proved effective in the US. Scientists hypothesized that this too might reduce the risk of mother-to-child transmission of HIV. The long course was expensive and required a complex regimen of perinatal care in pregnancy and during delivery incompatible with local custom. These factors made its implementation impractical in developing countries, where grinding poverty and reluctance to seek early care in pregnancy are the norm for most women in rural villages. But according to critics, since an effective treatment existed, use of placebo groups in these trials was reminiscent of the Tuskegee syphilis study.

17.8 Study Aids

Key Words

Questions and Cases for Further Consideration

1. What factors in the Tuskegee syphilis study were crucial to the subjects' inability to give informed consent? What criteria might have determined their enrollment?

2. How do the Nuremberg Code and the Declaration of Helsinki differ on the issue of informed consent? What problems might face each guideline on this?

3. When do beneficence and respect for persons come into conflict in epidemiological research?

4. *According to a REVEAL Study sponsored by Harvard Medical School,[5] subjects with a genetic mutation for early Alzheimer's disease were five times more likely to buy long-term care insurance than the others. Insurance companies might use such genetic information to request higher premiums or deny coverage. For that reason, 4.5% of 220 surveyed general internists in another survey admitted to "hiding or disguising" patient genetic information in electronic records.[6] Is it reasonable to think that insurance companies can learn? Should they have a right to genetic information? What might be the perils of those internists' strategy? May other risks result from having one's DNA sequenced?*

5. *In 2003, Dan Markingson joined Dr. Stephen Olson's clinical trial of Seroquel, an anti-psychotic medication, at the University of Minnesota. Acutely psychotic and suicidal, Dan was enrolled only over his mother's objections. He had previously been found incompetent to make medical decisions for himself. Apparently, Olson told him that if he did not consent to participation in the clinical trial, he would be committed to a mental hospital. The doctor and collaborators in the study were being compensated by AstraZeneca, Seroquel's manufacturer. Several weeks into the study in 2004, Dan cut his own throat. The University's IRB responded to public complaints and a lawsuit by Dan's mother by hiring an external consultant who told them he had received payments from AstraZeneca. He concluded that nothing wrong had been done. But in 2015, the state's Legislative Auditor found the study in serious breach of basic principles of research ethics. The Auditor found that, in this botched university/industry-sponsored drug trial, researchers and the IRB acted wrongly. Questions that arise from the outline here include: a) Who should give consent for such a study? b) Are there elements that speak of coercion? b) What about conflicts of interest? c) Suppose that, as critics suggest, this is not an isolated case. What would that say about research on psychotropic drugs conducted on people with mental disorders?*

---

5 Genomes2People. "The REVEAL Study," http://www.genomes2people.org/reveal.
6 Kira Peikoff, "Fearing Punishment for Bad Genes," *New York Times*, 4/7/2014.

6. *The 1946–1948 Guatemala STD inoculation study was funded by the US National Institutes of Health and the Pan American Sanitary Bureau, and administered by several Guatemalan ministries. It aimed at collecting data on gonorrhea, chancroid, and syphilis. Scientists at the United States Public Health Service deliberately infected some 1,500 Guatemalan sex workers, prisoners, soldiers, and mental hospital patients with syphilis, neither informing the study's subjects about its nature nor seeking their consent (which by contrast they sought in parallel experiments conducted in Indiana). Most infected subjects received treatment, though whether it was complete, effective, or included the sex workers is unclear. The study remained unknown until 2010, when Prof. Susan Reverby of Wellesley College accidentally found the files while researching the Tuskegee study. Apparently, researchers and sponsors were aware of its ethical lapses.* For Reverby, the moral failure showed by researchers in this and the Tuskegee study explain the public's skepticism about biomedical research. But questions remain. They include: a) Do such studies' ethical lapses justify skepticism about biomedical research? b) What exactly were those ethical lapses? c) Could the doing/allowing distinction make a moral difference between the two studies? d) Might racism count in explaining what went wrong in each? If so, how? If not, why not?

Suggested Readings*

*Angell, Marcia, "The Ethics of Clinical Research in the Third World," *New England Journal of Medicine* 337.12, 1997: 847–49.
    Charges that the AZT trials in sub-Saharan Africa had ethical lapses analogous to those of the Tuskegee syphilis study.
*Brody, Baruch, "Ethical Issues in Clinical Trials in Developing Countries," *Statistics in Medicine* 21.19, 2002: 2853–8.
    Denies that the AZT trials in Africa were unjust or its participants coerced.
Cash, R., D. Wikler, A. Saxena, and A. Capron, eds., *Casebook on Ethical Issues in International Health Research*. Geneva: WHO, 2009.
    Structured for class discussion, outlines some landmark studies in the developing world involving ethical problems.
*Crasnow, Sharon, Alison Wylie, Wenda K. Bauchspies, and Elizabeth Potter, "Feminist Perspectives on Science," *The Stanford Encyclopedia of Philosophy*, Edward Zalta, ed., 2015. Available online at http://plato.stanford.edu/entries/feminist-science/.
    Outlines the goals and achievements of feminist advocacy in biomedical research.
*Elliot, Carl, "The Deadly Corruption of Clinical Trials," *Mother Jones*, Oct. 2010. Available online at http://www.motherjones.com/environment/2010/09/dan-markingson-drug-trial-astrazeneca.
    Detailed account of the facts and ethical lapses surrounding Dan Markingson's suicide while participating in a psychotic drug trial.
*———, "University of Minnesota Blasted for Deadly Clinical Trial," *Mother Jones*, Apr. 2015. Available online at http://www.motherjones.com/environment/2015/04/dan-markingson-university-minnesota-clinical-trials-astrazeneca.
    Sequel to Elliot (2010). See also his blog at http://www.madinamerica.com/author/celliott/.

---

* Asterisks mark readings available online. See links on the companion website.

*Glantz, L. H., G. J. Annas, M. A. Grodin, and W. K. Mariner, "Research in Developing Countries: Taking 'Benefit' Seriously," *Hastings Center Report* 28.6, 1998: 38–42.
  Argues that trials such as the AZT studies in Africa must establish in advance funding that can allow participants and their communities to benefit from expected results.
*Hellman, Samuel and Deborah S. Hellman, "Of Mice but Not Men: Problems of the Randomized Clinical Trial," *New England Journal of Medicine* 324.22, 1991: 1585–9.
  Takes randomized clinical trials using human subjects to raise a dilemma for researchers, given their conflicting obligations as clinicians and as investigators.
*Jonas, Hans, "Philosophical Reflections on Experimenting with Human Subjects," *Daedalus* 98.2, 1969: 219–47.
  Argues that since the present state of medical knowledge is adequate, there is no justification for putting subjects at risk in new research.
*Kolehmainen, Sophia M., "The Dangerous Promise of Gene Therapy," *Actionbioscience*, 2000. Available online at http://www.actionbioscience.org/biotechnology/kolehmainen.html.
  Argues that clinical trials in gene therapy are not intrinsically wrong but need extensive and effective regulation to ensure its subjects' safety.
*Marquis, Don, "How to Resolve an Ethical Dilemma Concerning Randomized Clinical Trials," *New England Journal of Medicine* 341.9, 1999: 691–4.
  Attempts to dissolve Hellman and Hellman's (1991) dilemma by invoking informed consent and differentiating the patient-clinician and subject-investigator relationships.
*National Commission for the Protection of Human Subjects of Biomedical and Behavioral Research, "Belmont Report: Guidelines for the Protection of Human Subjects of Biomedical and Behavioral Research." *US Department of Health & Human Services*, 1979. Available online at http://www.hhs.gov/ohrp/humansubjects/guidance/belmont.html.
  Offers an ethical framework for biomedical research based on respect for persons, beneficence, and justice.
*"Nuremberg Code," 1947. Available online at http://www.hhs.gov/ohrp/archive/nurcode.html.
  Early expression of an absolute requirement of informed consent in research ethics.
*Reverby, Susan M., "Ethical Failures and History Lessons: The US Public Health Service Research Studies in Tuskegee and Guatemala," *Public Health Reviews* 34.1, 2012: 1–18.
  Argues that the Tuskegee and Guatemala studies' moral failures explain public skepticism about biomedical research.
Terry, Jennifer, "Agendas for Lesbian Health: Countering the Ills of Homophobia," in A. E. Clarke and V. Olesen, *Revisioning Women, Health and Healing: Feminist, Cultural and Technoscience Perspectives*, pp. 324–40. New York: Routledge, 1999.
  Contends that biomedical research on women fails to consider sexual orientation.
*Wendler, David, "The Ethics of Clinical Research," *The Stanford Encyclopedia of Philosophy*, Edward Zalta, ed., 2012. Available online at http://plato.stanford.edu/entries/clinical-research/.
  Analyzes main ethical issues in clinical research, outlining the history of abuses and guidelines.
*World Medical Association, "Declaration of Helsinki: Ethical Principles for Medical Research Involving Human Subjects," 1964, rev. 2013. Available online at http://www.wma.net/en/30publications/10policies/b3/.
  Landmark guidelines addressing major ethical aspects of biomedical research, including a qualification of the Nuremberg Code's absolute requirement of informed consent and several recommendations for the protection of subjects.

18 Justice in Health Care

Learning Objectives

In reading this chapter you will

▶ Distinguish rationing limited resources from medical futility.

▶ Learn what justice includes and why it is often granted special moral weight.

▶ Reflect on how the value of life and health should impact allocation of limited health care resources.

▶ Consider some opposing views on the fairness of health care coverage for all.

MEDICINE IS INCREASINGLY making possible new but expensive life-extending interventions for which there is great demand but also limited availability. This chapter addresses questions of fairness in the distribution of these and other health care services. They concern justice in setting priorities among competing health care programs and patient claims of need, as well as in devising policies for health care coverage. As shown here, they thus fall within the domain of distributive justice, whose demands have special moral weight.

18.1 *Shortland v Northland Health*: Rationing Is Not Futility

By June 1997, Mr. Rau Williams, a New Zealander of Māori descent who had suffered for some time with kidney disease, reached end-stage renal failure. At 63 and with type 2 diabetes, he was also showing early signs of dementia. He needed a kidney transplant, but obtaining the organ in New Zealand at that time required a wait of up to seven years. In the meantime, he could receive renal replacement therapy (dialysis), a treatment that takes over the kidneys' function of cleansing the blood. According to his personal physician, even if Mr. Williams did not live long enough for the transplant, the therapy would improve his quality of life. He enjoyed seeing his relatives and showed a desire to live.

Yet with early dementia, he lacked the ability to cooperate with the therapy, something required by the health authority's guidelines. Citing those guidelines and clinical criteria, the medical team at Northland Health decided he was ineligible for the publicly funded End Stage Renal Failure Programme (ESRFP). Already on dialysis as a temporary expedient, Mr. Williams was scheduled to have his therapy withdrawn, which meant his life was rapidly coming to an end. Mr. Shortland, a spokesperson for Williams, immediately filed for judicial review. But in *Shortland v Northland Health*, the New Zealand Court of Appeal found for Northland Health, holding that its decisions were in Williams's best interest and based exclusively on clinical criteria. Like Northland Health, the Court described Williams's case as one of futility, for it agreed that kidney dialysis for him was "clinically inappropriate." Since the law allowed for unilateral decisionmaking by providers in futility cases, neither ethics review by an institutional board nor informed consent by Mr. Williams's proxy was necessary.[1]

Northland Health discontinued renal replacement therapy for Rau Williams on September 17, 1997. He died of kidney failure on October 10, shortly before the court hearing. A 1999 investigation by the Health and Disability Commissioner found that "Northland Health made its decision without fully recognising the importance of the process for Mr. Williams and his whanau [family], without giving sufficient weight to the fact that the clinical decision was a life decision, and without sufficient support and recognition to cultural and spiritual needs."[2]

■ ■ ■

In *Shortland v Northland Health*, the judgment that dialysis for Mr. Williams was "clinically inappropriate" was a judgment of *medical futility* based on the medical team's assessment of his quality of life. As we saw in Chapter 7, judgments of that sort are open to challenge by those who make a different assessment of the patient's quality of life, even if they accord with the health authority's or managed-care company's regulations—in this case, the New Zealand health authority. Of course, like organ transplantation and heart surgery, renal replacement therapy is a costly medical intervention of known effectiveness in postponing the death of many patients suffering from life-threatening conditions. There is sound evidence, however, that the lives of many more people can be saved when limited health funds are devoted not to rescue seriously ill patients but, for example, to prevent disease.

Recent advances in medicine have made possible developments in rescue treatments that have outrun advances in the health care systems' capacity to fund them. But it is a fact that not *all* patients in need of such treatments can presently have them. As a result, the health care authority or managed-care system issues guidelines for distribution based on a number of criteria to be discussed in this chapter. The criteria fueling the guidelines applied to Mr. Williams likely included factors such as the patient's general condition, as well as the treatment's cost-effectiveness and likely benefits. According to his family, the medical team took account of his age and the costs of additional nursing help because, owing to his mental impairment, Mr. Williams could cooperate with neither of the two types of available dialysis.

In their view, discontinuing the therapy for him was unjust. If it was, the source of the injustice might have been in the health authority's guidelines, their application, or both. The questions concerning justice in his case would vary accordingly. Might a different decision by Northland Health have condemned other patients as well? Did it matter that Mr. Williams belonged to a traditionally marginalized, vulnerable population within New Zealand? Who should be given priority for kidney dialysis? Did Northland Health apply the guidelines

1 Court of Appeal Report for 1997, https://www.courtsofnz.govt.nz/from/judicial-reports/docu
   ments/CourtofAppealReport1997.PDF.
2 Report on Opinion, Case 97HDC8872, p. 17, http://www.hdc.org.nz/media/2402/97HDC8872.pdf.

consistently to all patients with relevantly similar needs? By focusing exclusively on clinical judgment and eligibility criteria according to guidelines, the Court missed the opportunity to ask such questions. It thereby showed a familiar attitude in the courts: that of avoiding interference with clinical judgment and the legislators' allocation policies (Foster, 2013: 91).

Mr. Williams's relatives, on the other hand, would have none of that. They took issue with the fairness of Northland Health's decision. In their view, it arbitrarily deprived Rau of his right to life as recognized by local and international human rights charters. But in examining this argument, the Court determined that Northland Health's decision did honor

---

The International Covenant on Civil and Political Rights of 1966, UN, Art. 6.1

Every human being has the inherent right to life. This right shall be protected by law. No one shall be arbitrarily deprived of his life.

After all, Northland Health supplied Mr. Williams the "necessaries of life," meaning it supplied due care (although in his case that excluded death-postponing treatment), thus preventing harm to the patient whose death would result from kidney failure. With this response, the Court dodged the charge of injustice, confining the issue to medical futility and beneficence. Yet Mr. Williams might in fact have been deprived of a right, even if that was not his right to life. For, as we consider next, the moral issues facing policies for access to health care and **priority setting** for limited health care resources do not reduce to considerations of futility and beneficence. They primarily involve **justice.**

18.2 Allocation of Health Care Resources

Justice demands that persons be treated rightly, as they deserve, according to what is owed or due to them. The concept of *justice* is linked to concepts that have strong normative force such as *human rights* and *fairness*. In clinical practice, decisions involving justice are made daily. If two patients in their mid-60s are waiting in an emergency room with difficulty breathing, and their respective levels of discomfort appear roughly equal, but one arrived 20 minutes before the other, justice would seem to require that the earlier arrival be seen first. However, very often medical providers must strike a balance between considerations of justice and other moral obligations.

For example, a conflict between justice and beneficence may occasionally lead them to err in favor of beneficence, as in this case:

Organ Donor Scandal. In January 2013, the former lead transplant surgeon at Goettingen's University Hospital in Germany was brought to trial on charges of attempted manslaughter. Dr. Aiman O. had apparently faked reports of 38 patients with liver problems presented to the European organ procurement agency. By exaggerating their conditions, he managed to get them donated organs more quickly than eleven other patients who were in greater need. He was also accused of having performed three unnecessary liver transplants for misinformed patients who later died. The prosecution suspected a financial motive. Although Dr. O was eventually

IMAGE 18.1
©iStockPhoto/uchar

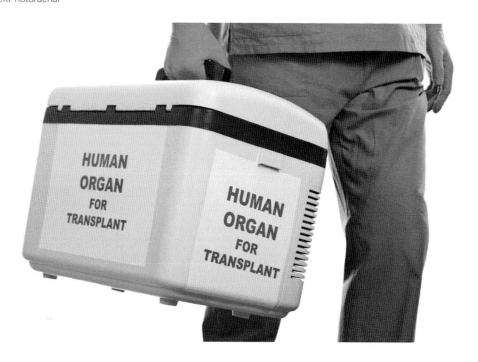

acquitted, the media blamed irregularities of this sort for the sharp reduction of organ donors in Germany in 2012. [3]

Let's assume that Dr. O was guilty of having manipulated the organ-donor priority list. The action would be morally unjustified as violation of nonmaleficence alone, since it put eleven patients at an unnecessary risk of harm, thereby making them worse off. But suppose it had no chance of producing bad results and exclusively aimed at promoting the other patients' wellbeing. Even so, it was unjust since thereby eleven patients were arbitrarily subjected to a longer wait for a life-saving intervention that was owed to them. Any act or omission that arbitrarily deprives patients of what they deserve constitutes an injustice, whether or not it produces benefits—a conclusion supported by a widespread conviction about the primacy of justice. According to this conviction, justice has special normative force: it is the weightiest of all moral demands. Justice trumps other moral obligations and interests. Although care ethics disagrees, moral philosophers of other persuasions support this conviction (see Box 18.1). Contemporary theorists who defend a strong version of the primacy of justice would contend, for example, that

> If the happiness of the world could be advanced by unjust means alone, not happiness but justice would properly prevail. And when justice issues in certain individual rights, even the general welfare cannot override them (Sandel, 1982: 2).

3 See *Deutsche Welle*, "German Doctor Cleared of Transplant Scandal Charges," 4/27/2015. http://www.dw.com/en/german-doctor-cleared-of-transplant-scandal-charges/a-18430971.

There are, of course, weaker versions of the conviction holding that justice has primacy most of the time. Either way, why might justice have such special normative force? Here moral theories part company: for utilitarians, because it contributes more to the maximization of social utility (Mill, 1861); for deontologists, because the moral law itself is about what is right, independent of whether it promotes some good end.

BOX 18.1 THE SPECIAL MORAL WEIGHT OF JUSTICE

Aristotle, ca. 350 BCE—Justice is the highest social virtue.

Locke, 1689—Justice issues in individual 'natural' rights.

Mill, 1861—Justice is the chief part of all morality, implies not only what is right but what someone else can claim from us as a matter of right.

Sandel, 1982—Justice is the grounds for the moral law.

Justice may be defined as what is morally fitting for individuals or groups in some circumstance. Different people typically have different deserts depending on factors such as their individual merits, what they have done or failed to do, and their relationships with others. Questions of justice may arise through comparison of what is owed to different individuals or groups, or involve what is morally owed to a person *as such*, independent of her relationships with others, but in connection with an ideal standard of desert against which an action is evaluated. The former questions are comparative, the latter noncomparative. Judgments of fairness in health care, our concern here, are essentially comparative and thus fall within social justice. They presuppose interpersonal comparisons of claims of health care needs, which are implicit in assessing, for example, whether it is fair to save patient A in a situation where, given available resources, that would doom patient B.

Distributive Justice

How to decide fairly between competing claims of health care needs when resources are limited is a question of social **distributive justice.**

> Distributive justice is the part of social justice concerned with what is fair in the allocation of benefits and burdens in society between individuals or groups.

In a society, the benefits up for distribution include services (health care, education, sport facilities) and material goods (food, shelter, land). Among burdens illustrated in previous chapters are participation in risky biomedical research. Other burdens include the care for people with special needs (the very young, the very elderly, and the disabled), taxation, and service in the army. Injustice in the distribution of goods calls for their redistribution. It may affect individuals, families, or entire groups and be pervasive locally (in a city, county, state, country) or globally (across world regions).

Various principles of distributive justice determine what counts as a just distribution of benefits and burdens. If the basis for having such principles is prudential (i.e., self-interest), then those principles may not apply when resources are either so superabundant that everyone who needs them can have them, or so scarce that people have to fight for them just to survive. But they would regulate distribution of extremely scarce resources if, as many believe, distributive justice's grounds are moral, not merely prudential. And they clearly apply to the health care resources of concern here, which are moderately limited. They comprise the resources necessary for preventive care (like vaccines and cancer screening) as well as clinical care, including the care of the uninsured and the under-insured that in the US is expected of hospital ERs. They apply also to biomedical research (see Chapter 17), support for the disabled, occupational health and safety, vaccination, environmental sanitation, food and drug protection, and many other areas of public health—where they may sanction, for example, that officials must distribute the burdens of sewage treatment plants and issue relocation mandates for any factories that are contaminating a populated area. They may also compel officials to make sure that the most disadvantaged members of their community have access to potable water and to immunizations for their children. Since the rationale in all such cases is removal or prevention of harm, the dictates of these principles often overlap with beneficence. But as argued above, justice is weightier.

Principles and Theories of Distributive Justice

The foundational demand of distributive justice is captured by a seemingly simple principle,

---

Formal Principle of Distributive Justice

Treat the like cases alike, and the unlike cases differently.

Given this principle, justice requires a consistently impartial evaluation of relevant analogies and dis-analogies between cases. It does not require us to treat all cases the same. If patients A and B both have cogent claims for a heart transplant, but *only* A is placed on the organ-donor priority list, the decision is unjust unless the patients' conditions can be shown to be in some way relevantly different—for example, if A, 33, can reap more benefit that B, who is 70 and in declining health. To accommodate such relevant differences, the **formal principle of justice** should be taken to recommend:

1.   Treat alike (as equals) persons who are alike (equal) in relevant respects, and
2.   Treat unalike (unequally) persons who are unalike (unequal) in relevant respects, and in direct proportion to the differences (inequalities) between them.

This formal principle is still so 'content-thin' that it does not go beyond prescribing impartiality in the treatment of individuals or groups. It offers no help in determining the likeness or difference we should be looking for. In the case of Mr. Williams, he was like other patients who were on dialysis, given their irreversible renal failure, and also unlike them in factors such as age and mental acuity.

BOX 18.2 SOME MATERIAL PRINCIPLES OF JUSTICE

1. Give to each person an equal share.
2. Give to each person according to his or her acquisitions in a free market.
3. Give to each person according to his or her individual needs.
4. Give to each person according to his or her effort.
5. Give to each person according to his or her contribution to society.
6. Give to each person according to his or her merit.

Which respects are relevant for distinguishing fair and unfair treatment? To answer this we need a **material principle of justice**—i.e., one with substantive content. A number of such principles are in the offing. They differ in what each takes to be the likeness or difference relevant to a fair distribution. Among the candidates are individual need, individual effort, and whatever is in everyone's advantage, or whatever is determined by the free market (see Box 18.2). Although some of these principles may be combined, they are usually interpreted as being exclusive, so that a just distribution is one that gives to each person according to the proposed principle *and nothing else*. When more broadly construed, however, some of the material principles are compatible. For example, in a two-tiered health care system, principles (1), (2), and (3) in Box 18.2 are compatible. This system can have a first layer providing equal access to a "decent minimum" of health care services for all according to their needs, and a second layer where less basic health care services are available according to the patient's ability to pay.[4]

Underwriting these material principles are theories of social justice of different types. We'll have a quick look at two paradigms among such theories, **liberal** and **libertarian justice**, which make incompatible claims about what is a fair, equitable, and appropriate distribution of benefits and burdens in a society.

---

4 Likewise, Feinberg (1973: 117) argues that in a just economic order, principles of equality based on need, contribution, and effort are compatible. For although in conditions of scarcity the imperative will be to address basic needs, so as to bring every person up to a certain level of equality, once the level of production increases so that there is economic abundance, principles of contribution and effort also come into play, and it is in terms of all these principles that a person's deserts would be determined.

Liberal Justice

Utilitarian and Rawlsian theories illustrate two liberal conceptions of social justice. As we have seen in Chapter 2, for utilitarians the right intervention in health care is the one that maximizes beneficial results *for all concerned*—that is, the one that promotes aggregate welfare. Liberal egalitarians in the tradition of John Rawls (1971) reject this conception of justice. In their view, justice is best understood as fairness—that is, it is not aggregate welfare, but the equality of persons with claims of needs that grounds fairness in the distribution of health care. Correct principles of justice are those that work to the advantage of all, and especially of the worst-off. Thus social justice determines what is owed to people distributively. Those are the principles that rational, self-interested people, the so-called contractors, would come to adopt by agreement if they were bargaining under ideal fair conditions of choice about what their society's basic structure ought to be. Such conditions do not obtain in practice, of course, but can be simulated by imagining that the contractors are deciding behind a "veil of ignorance." By this, Rawls means choosing under complete ignorance of their differences in race, sex, age, socioeconomic status, religion, and conception of the good life. For Rawls, the contractors would agree on two principles of justice—one, the Equal Liberty Principle, stipulates that each person in the society is entitled to the most extensive possible basic liberty compatible with a like liberty for all. The other, the *Difference Principle*, sanctions that the only justified inequalities in the society are those that work to the advantage of its least-advantaged members.

The Difference Principle

Social and economic inequalities are to be arranged so that they are

1. To the greatest benefit of the least-advantaged, and
2. Attached to offices and positions open to all under conditions of fair equality of opportunity.

Given these principles of liberal egalitarian justice, a fair distribution of benefits in society, including income and opportunity, cannot be determined by calculations of aggregate welfare as held by liberal utilitarians. At the same time, unlike the theory of justice to be discussed next, a fair distribution cannot be that determined by market forces.

Libertarian Justice

This theory of justice is familiar from the libertarian defense of a free-market economy, as well as from its opposition to redistribution of income and redistribution of opportunity in modern democratic societies and government interference beyond the protection of individual rights to life, liberty, and property. In this theory, a just distribution is one that results from the acquisition and exchange of property under free-market conditions whereby all parties to the transactions participate voluntarily. A free-market economy is the only arrangement compatible with people's right to exercise their talents and reap their rewards accordingly. Thinkers in the libertarian tradition (Locke, 1689; Nozick, 1974) link social justice to individual freedoms and ascribe to the state the primary duty of protecting them. In their view, self-ownership provides the grounds of social justice: each person owns herself, her labor, and its legitimate products, unless she freely chooses otherwise. Self-ownership accounts for individual rights understood as liberties—for example, to labor and to acquire, keep, and exchange one's property.

But libertarianism does not defend absolute freedom, because one's freedom is limited by the rights of others. So one may not trespass in, or take, someone else's legitimate property, or engage them in nonconsensual activities. Hence the libertarians' proscriptions of practices violating liberty rights overlap with many intuitions of common morality—for example, against nonconsensual physical contact, unprovoked killing, theft, and human trafficking. All of these violate the individual rights that libertarians regard as demanded by justice.

By contrast, having a low socioeconomic status or being in ill health through no fault of one's own does not violate any individual right. Although they are unfortunate conditions, neither of these amounts to an injustice. For, as discussed below, libertarians deny individual rights to be provided with a minimum level of income or health care or with anything else one might need as a result of bad luck in the economic or natural lotteries. The bottom line is: helping others in need may be praiseworthy as charity, but is not a demand of justice.

Priority Setting

As the population ages and biomedical research makes available interventions that expand the scope of clinical medicine, health care providers and public health officials face tougher decisions concerning the allocation of limited resources—whether these concern

1. Microallocation—The distribution of a medical treatment among individual patients with competing claims of need, or
2. Macroallocation—The distribution of overall funding among competing health care programs.

Decision type (1) may involve the distribution of a scarce life-saving or prolonging treatment such as kidney dialysis, an organ transplant, or intensive care. As illustrated by cases like *Shortland* above, when they do involve any of these **rescue interventions,** they are open to moral and legal challenges. But decisions type (2) are no less vulnerable, for they raise a number of justice questions. If it is fair to rescue from death the few who need, say, expensive open-heart surgery, when the health care system will then have no more funds left to support less costly treatments, such as cholesterol-lowering drugs and wellness programs to improve the overall health of the population, which are more effective in terms of lives saved in the long run? And should rescue interventions take priority over life-enhancement interventions such as hip replacement and fertility treatment? Should prevention have priority over treatment or research? Or primary care over critical care?

In light of current cost and availability of health care resources, answers to these hard questions require policies of **rationing,** where

> As standardly used, 'rationing' refers to any arrangement that limits people's access to certain goods or services.

In an extreme libertarian conception of justice, a fair rationing of health care resources should not differ substantially from the price-based rationing of commodities in the free market. That is, costly interventions should be rationed by ability to pay. Thus the libertarian model opposes regulatory policies of rationing: it is the free market that determines which patients can have certain interventions and which cannot. Although the US was one of the few developed countries that came close to realizing this model, health care reforms that culminated in the Affordable Care Act of 2010 now place the country close to the hybrid model considered below.

Libertarian rationing is rejected by those who defend a liberal position on distributive justice. The utilitarian endorsement of any particular rationing model is contingent upon its capacity to maximize welfare for all concerned, something seemingly unattainable by libertarian rationing. Rawlsians would rule this model out unconditionally, owing to (1) its failure to treat patients in need as equals and (2) its failure to support health care policies for rationing that can benefit of the worst-off in society. A contrasting model of rationing relies on government decree. Successfully implemented in communist countries such as Cuba, this model uses government mandates to limit people's access to scarce treatments that are much in demand, though some access to them might still be possible. The justice of this model depends on the underlying distributive principle, which may recommend distribution according to needs, costs, benefits, and other criteria.

A combination of regulated and unregulated rationing produces hybrid models such as one in which public policy limits access to certain expensive interventions while ensuring access to a decent minimum level of health care for all. This model is a hybrid because it allows the play of market forces and government order. Public policy guarantees access to some basic services without penalizing the purchase of additional health care by those who can afford to pay for it. A number of developed countries that offer universal access to basic health care also rely on hybrid models of rationing. Some versions of this hybrid model are illustrated below.

Measuring Health Benefits and Costs with QALYs

One of the goals of health policy is to ensure that limited resources are distributed fairly and efficiently. Efficiency in turn requires a measurement of health benefits and costs. Among the several methods of measurement devised by health care economists is Alan Williams's (1985) **quality-adjusted life years** (QALYs). Widely adopted in health- and cost-effectiveness analyses, QALYs are considered helpful in priority setting across health care programs, as well as in decisions concerning (a) what treatment some patients should receive when options with different costs are available and (b) which group of patients should not receive certain costly treatments. Given the moral significance of such decisions, let's briefly examine the basic idea in QALY measurement. The measure begins with an assessment of

FIGURE 18.1   QALY Measurement

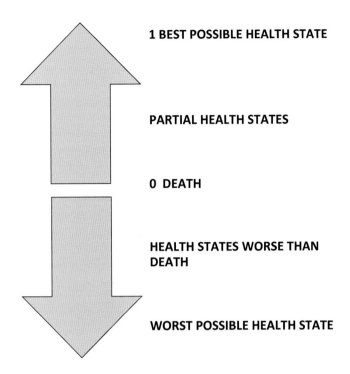

1 BEST POSSIBLE HEALTH STATE

PARTIAL HEALTH STATES

0 DEATH

HEALTH STATES WORSE THAN
DEATH

WORST POSSIBLE HEALTH STATE

the patient's "health states" (quality of life and life expectancy) *with* and *without* the treatment. A year of healthy life expectancy is worth 1 QALY, one of unhealthy life expectancy less than 1 QALY, and death 0 QALY. Health states that are worse than being dead generate negative QALYs. A simple calculation proceeds as follows:

A. Treatment: 4 years of life expectancy at partial quality of life 0.6 = 2.4 points
B. No treatment: Less than 1 year of life expectancy at partial quality of life 0.6 = 0.4 point
C. Comparative value of the treatment: 2 QALYs (the difference between 2.4 and 0.4)
D. Cost per QALY: If the treatment costs $10,000, each QALY costs $5,000

The approach is "quality adjusted" because the value of a year of unhealthy life expectancy is less than 1, with its precise QALY score depending on valuations of expected health states per year. These are performed according to factors such as pain or discomfort, mental conditions (anxiety, depression), and abilities to wash or dress or perform usual activities.

The QALY approach is welfarist, since it relies on a principle of justice along the lines of "To each according to what maximizes aggregate health benefits relative to costs." Knowing the costs per QALY of treatment options and programs can bring cost- and benefits-efficiency in resource allocation by guiding health officials in directing limited funds among competing interventions. Data show, for example, that anti-smoking campaigns, hip replacement, and cholesterol-lowering drugs generate more QALYs than liver transplants, kidney-dialysis, and surgery to remove brain tumors. As illustrated by the following chart, these interventions also differ in terms of cost per QALY:

Intervention	Cost per QALY (1990 £)
Campaign to stop smoking	270
Hip replacement	1,180
Cholesterol testing and treatment (adults aged 40–69)	1,480
Kidney transplantation (cadaver)	4,710
Home kidney-dialysis	17,260
Hospital kidney-dialysis	21,970
Neurosurgery for malignant intracranial tumors	197,780

By the QALY approach alone, then, funds should be directed to the programs at the top the list. Those should be given priority since in Williams's view "an efficient health care activity is one where the cost per QALY is as low as it can be. . . . A high priority health care activity is one where the cost-per-QALY is low, and a low priority activity is one where cost-per-QALY is high." More generally, given this approach, priority should be given to

1. The health programs that generate more QALYs (in macroallocation)
2. To patients who might respond to an intervention with higher QALY scores (in microallocation)

When (1) conflicts with current practice, health care funds should be re-directed from higher-cost-per-QALY to lower-cost-per-QALY interventions. This means, for example, that a life-enhancing intervention such as hip replacement should take priority over a rescue intervention such as kidney dialysis. Given (2), allocation priority is to be given to patients who are younger or have a life-style more conducive to states of health. Between any two patients A and B who are competing for a rescuing intervention, if all things are equal except for patient B's having a pre-existing, unrelated condition (say, rheumatoid arthritis in the knee), A has priority over B—even when B's pain makes no difference for her recovery chances.

Objections to the QALY Approach

A number of reasons suggest that measurements of cost-effectiveness and quality of life such as QALYs should not be either the sole consideration in priority setting, or a consideration at all. First, as suggested by Alex Berenson's (2007) examples, comparisons on such bases are not as simple as may appear.[5] Suppose a blind person's health states generate 0.75 point in the QALY scale. A treatment that restores full vision raises her quality of life to 1 and generates 0.25 QALYs. If she lives 30 more years, the treatment generates 7.5 QALYs. In cost per QALY, this treatment is equivalent to keeping ten patients on dialysis for a year. The QALY approach alone cannot give a satisfactory answer about which intervention should be funded, given that it is insensitive to differences between life-saving or enhancing interventions, which

---

5 "Pinning Down the Money Value of a Person's Life," New York Times, 6/11/2007.

critics of the approach find morally significant. John Harris's Double Jeopardy Argument exploits this weakness of the approach:

> QALYs dictate that because an individual is unfortunate, because she has once become a victim of disaster, we are required to visit upon her a second and perhaps graver misfortune. The first disaster leaves her with a poor quality of life and QALYs then require that in virtue of this she be ruled out as a candidate for life saving treatment, or at best, that she be given little or no chance of benefiting from what little amelioration her condition admits of. Her first disaster leaves her with a poor quality of life and when she presents herself for help, along come QALYs and finish her off! (Harris, 1987: 120)

In Harris's view, QALYs fail to take into account that the life of each individual has the same value, which does not mean that all persons should be treated the same. But it does mean that they deserve equal concern and respect—something Harris supports by analogy with the criminal justice system, which gives equal consideration to all persons by providing fair trials to all.

Furthermore, because the QALY approach requires decisionmakers to focus exclusively on people's life expectancy and quality of life, it unfairly discriminates against certain groups. Since interventions for younger patients would ordinarily generate more QALYs because of their longer life expectancy, QALYs are ageist. In addition, it fails to consider the social lottery.

BOX 18.3 SOCIAL DETERMINANTS OF HEALTH

Social determinants of health are factors that contribute to health inequalities, such as psychological or physical stress (resulting in smoking, alcoholism, drug abuse), environmental conditions, working conditions, medical services, nutrition, and shelter—all factors whose consequences for a population's health are known to vary according to race, ethnicity, gender, geography, and socioeconomic status.

Given these **social determinants of health**, vulnerable populations such as African Americans, the Māori of New Zealand, and transgender people in most cultures may simply be at a disadvantage when in need of a scarce medical resource, owing to their likelihood of having socially determined partial states of health. So the approach is racist and sexist.

But the QALY approach is not without responses. The charge of ageism fails to consider the Fair Innings Argument, according to which invoking a patient's age is morally justified, since

1. Older patients have already lived more years than younger patients.
2. Having lived longer is relevant to the fairness of prioritizing younger patients' need of rescuing interventions.

3. Therefore, when older and younger patients compete for any such intervention, it is fair to prioritize younger patients' needs.

It is a medical fact that elderly patients often do not do as well as younger ones in recovering from invasive and risky procedures such as a coronary bypass operation. But the issue at stake here is mainly moral. Since (1) is obviously true, can a case be made for premise (2)? Arguably, each person is entitled in life to a certain number of chances for success or failure in achieving fulfillment. As a person ages, she uses up her chances. A rescue intervention for a younger patient would have a greater chance of creating more 'innings of play' during which the patient can realize her chances. Moreover, a common-morality's intuition has it that death early in life is more tragic than at the end of life. But these reasons assume that a person is the same through time, and that is a metaphysical assumption that has not gone without challenge. It is, however, a topic that falls beyond our scope here.

Distributive Justice in Organ Transplants

That sensitivity to justice is a crucial consideration in resource allocation can be seen in scenarios where disputes arise over the fair distribution of transplantable organs. A successful heart transplant may add years to the life of a patient dying of congestive heart failure, but donor hearts are in short supply. There are many more needy candidates for transplant than there are donor hearts to go around. This creates a justice-based moral dilemma on two levels: first, there is the question, how do we devise a just system for the distribution of donor organs, and what standards should be used, within that system, to determine fairly who gets on the waiting list for a transplant? And, second, how do we make just decisions about *which* among these candidates actually gets a new organ?

This is where a particularly vexing moral conundrum surfaces: because a transplant may be literally the gift of life, it amounts to bestowing on an individual a prize beyond measure. But not all in need can be candidates, and the stewardship of such a valuable resource is the health care providers' responsibility. How might they make inter-personal comparisons to justify giving the heart to Mr. Smith rather than to Ms. Jones? Several nonexclusive criteria have been proposed. Here we first consider taking into account a person's moral worth. According to this criterion, a relevant factor in deciding about a patient's candidacy for an organ is whether she *deserves* it. Other criteria may focus on a person's social and economic worth, including family role or the lack of such relationship, her past contributions to the community, potential for future contributions, and relative likelihood of success (Rescher, 1969). Although we do not explore these other criteria here, like moral worth they raise the question: should the medical team be involved in this sort of judgment at all?

The Responsibility Argument

A main argument for considering moral worth a factor in deciding about a person's candidacy for an organ invokes a moral difference between being in need of a scarce medical resource as a result of bad luck (through no fault of the patient) or of a choice (a life-style or addiction known to cause it), holding that it is only needs of the bad-luck type that morally justify the use of that resource. According to this Responsibility Argument,

1. There is a significant moral difference between suffering organ failure as a result of bad luck and suffering it as result of a choice.
2. Only patients suffering from organ failure as a result of bad luck should be candidates for transplantation.

---

3. Therefore, patients suffering from organ failure as result of a choice should not be candidates for transplantation.

Some ordinary moral intuitions about the unfairness of using health care funds for needs created by choice support this argument. Few would subscribe to using such public funds for the removal of skin tattoos or for elective cosmetic surgery. With organs, the choice side of the distinction applies to patients who have damaged their own lungs and hearts through years of smoking, lost their livers to alcoholic cirrhosis, and the like. Given the Responsibility Argument, as a matter of moral desert, these patients should be excluded from priority lists for organs.

As reconstructed above, the argument is backward-looking: it focuses on how patients got to be in need of organs, claiming that some did so through fault of their own. But there is a consequentialist version that is forward-looking: it claims that the exclusion of such patients from transplant programs might act as a deterrent to smoking and to drug and alcohol abuse. Treating them as equals with 'bad-luck' patients in need of organs as a result of congenital conditions or injury would be a disincentive to those at risk of addiction.

Either version of the Responsibility Argument, however, should be distinguished from a Medical Argument according to which, since patients with certain addictions cannot benefit from organ transplants, they should be excluded from organ waiting lists. Consider, for example, patients with alcoholic cirrhosis. Although initially transplanted patients with alcoholic liver disease have the same chance to benefit from a new liver as patients with nonalcoholic cirrhosis, that's not the case if the alcoholics resume excessive drinking after the transplant. Given those patients' psychological and social vulnerabilities, a valuable organ might go to waste. The data on recidivism suggest that 20% of such patients resume drinking, and one-third of those return to heavy drinking (Lim and Keeffe, 2004). In light of the data, the Medical Argument can conclude that medical teams should screen any patients with alcoholic liver disease carefully before accepting them as candidates for liver transplantation. Most US liver transplant programs already use a six-month abstinence period as a predictor of relapse for alcoholic patients. When relapse occurs, the patient is excluded from the organ list on grounds of medical futility.

Objections to the Responsibility Argument

What about the Responsibility Argument above? As outlined there, it fails for a combination of reasons. First, there is no consensus among experts about whether, or to what degree, addictions such as alcoholism, drug abuse, and cigarette smoking are voluntary, or about how to assess degree of voluntariness. If free will plays either little or no role, the moral distinction between bad luck and choice collapses, and so does at least the backward-looking version of the argument. The forward-looking version assumes that exclusion of patients who have knowingly engaged in risky behavior can be a deterrent, and that this morally justifies waiving rescue interventions for them. But, as with capital punishment's much-disputed claim of deterrence to murder, it is uncertain whether exclusion from organ waiting lists would have a like effect on addiction. And even if it did, humanitarian reasons of the sort invoked by John Harris above seem to morally require rescuing the patient—though, given limited resources, this is controversial (see for instance Hope, 2001).

Furthermore, if moral accountability were a pre-condition to enter waiting lists for transplants, then, to be consistent, similar conditions should be placed on all other patients whose disorders or injuries were owing to their own carelessness or life-style—the sedentary, the helmetless cyclist, the frequent consumer of double cheeseburgers. There are humanitarian reasons for not doing that. When some patients with a condition resulting from 'what they have done to themselves' are competing with others for access to the same limited resource, it is contrary to current practice to count their moral character as relevant to deciding what should be done. In practice, it would be next to impossible to agree on what these patients 'deserve.' But, most important, an evaluation of a patient's moral worthiness for a transplant on the basis of her past behavior seems beyond what the medical team can be justified in doing morally. Rather, as with the allocation of other rescue interventions, once transplantation has been found clinically appropriate for some patients, decisionmaking about competing demands should be guided by fairness, beneficence, and equal respect for the value of life.

18.3 Access to Health Care

Health Inequalities and Inequities

Another main concern of distributive justice in society is health coverage, a crucial factor in people's health and longevity. Of course, access to health care is far from being the only factor that influences these. Gender, race, ethnicity, genetics, geography, socioeconomic status, and other social determinants of health also play a role. But health care, or the lack of it, is an especially significant factor, one that derives its value from the special value of life and health. Compared with the value of other goods, life's value is more basic than, say, paid leave and education—which plainly are of no use to the dead. And health seems especially valuable because some level of it is necessary for having a decent opportunity to pursue one's goals in life. A child with partial deafness who is not fitted with a hearing aid would not be able to develop comprehension of oral language, something that might limit her opportunities to pursue certain jobs later in life. People with untreated liver or kidney failure are not merely at a disadvantage in the activities they enjoy but face premature death.

BOX 18.4 HEALTH INEQUITY

A health inequity is an unjust health inequality

The special value of life and health determines that inequities in the distribution of morbidity and mortality amount to serious moral wrongs. As defined in Box 18.4, not all inequalities are inequities: only those that amount to an injustice are. Arguably, that in most countries women live longer than men on average is an inequality without being an inequity. After all, such longevity is not a controllable factor. But longevity does not mean having better health. In "10 Facts about Women's Health"[6] the World Health Organization summarizes sound data suggesting that the global burden of ill health falls mostly on women. Controllable factors concerning unequal access to information, health care, and basic health practices have led to a higher incidence of women suffering from physical and sexual violence, sexually transmitted disease (STD), HIV/AIDS, malaria, and pulmonary disease. In 2009, bioethicist Ruth Macklin gathered data showing that

- Reproductive and sexual ill health accounted for 20% of the global burden of ill health for women compared with 14% for men.
- A total of half a million women, 99% of whom were from developing countries, die every year of preventable causes.
- In developing countries, the total disease burden of STD and HIV/AIDS was 8.9% for women and 1.5% for men.

Consistent with these data, other surveys point to striking differences in the distribution of morbidity and mortality, not only between genders but also between developed and developing regions of the world. Examples of factors causing such gender inequities include female genital cutting, men's refusal to have protected sex, women's vulnerability to violence, restrictions on abortion and contraception, and poor health care infrastructures, especially for assisting women during pregnancy and childbirth. For many, these inequalities constitute inequities because they all originate in economic, social, or cultural factors that are controllable.

But not all agree that these and other differences in the distribution of health and longevity, whether globally or locally, amount in fact to inequities. There is debate in which both parties accept the special value of life and health but disagree on the so-called right to health care. Those who vindicate a right of that sort (however construed) urge a redistribution of health care resources. Others consistently deny that there is a right to health care, even for people living in affluent societies that can afford it.

The Right to Health Care

In *Shortland*, the family argued that Northland Health arbitrarily deprived Mr. Williams of his right to life. If true, they committed a serious moral injustice, since under most conceptions,

> A *right* is an entitlement that creates in others a strong duty to protect some interest of the right-holder.

---

6   *World Health Organization.* "10 Facts About Women's Health," 5/2011. http://www.who.int/features/factfiles/women/en/.

In slavery, for example, the victims are deprived of self-ownership, and equal opportunity, to which they are entitled. Although the concept of a 'human right' is modern, rights have roots in Roman jurisprudence and were incorporated into ethics in the Middle Ages by way of *Natural Law theory*. In the 17th and 18th centuries, natural rights (the predecessors of current human rights) became important in people's thinking about how law and civil society should be ordered. Having a right to something came to be equated with having a strong claim to it that other people were obliged to respect. Prominent among these rights were the *moral rights* to life, property, and liberty. Since the state and positive law were assigned the function of protecting these rights, they became *legal rights* codified in documents such as the American *Bill of Rights* and the French *Declaration of the Rights of Man*.

But moral rights are not the same as legal rights. While the former are thought to have universal authority, the latter are a more geographically local product of legislative enactment, civil decree, or **case law**. Legal rights require no grounding in moral rights, nor moral in legal. Rather, the two types may be seen as different kinds of rights in systems parallel to each other but each substantially independent, thereby allowing the system of moral rights to serve as a basis for questioning existing conventions of legal rights or, alternatively, providing them with a rational defense. Consider the American *eugenics* movement of the 1920s and 30s. It surely violated the moral rights of those sterilized as "mental defectives"— whose alleged hereditary deficiencies made them "unfit to breed." But this practice violated no legal rights. "Three generations of imbeciles are enough," wrote Supreme Court Justice Oliver Wendell Holmes, Jr., in *Buck v Bell* (1927) to justify a Virginia law authorizing eugenic sterilization. Yet in the 1940s and 50s, a growing consensus that such laws actually violated moral rights was the driving force behind legal decisions that ultimately struck them down.

Forced sterilization was unjust because it violated the victims' bodily integrity and autonomy rights. Like freedom of speech or religion, these are **negative rights**: i.e., rights to be left alone or not to be interfered with. By contrast, **positive rights** are entitlements to be provided with something—for example, health care or an education. According to the so-called **correlativity thesis**, someone's rights of either kind engender correlative duties in others. If Mr. Jones has a negative right to express his political opinion, others have a duty of forbearance toward him (i.e., of not interfering with his free expression). If Ms. Smith has a positive right to health care, others have a duty to provide her with health care—for example, the government by levying a tax and instituting a system of universal access to health care. Negative rights are generally held to be more stringent than positive rights, because the duties they create in others are more easily fulfilled: they may be discharged just by refraining from acting—that is, by doing nothing.

The correlativity thesis plays a role in many bioethical issues. For example, patients are now thought to have not only a right to confidentiality on the part of their health care providers, but also the right to refuse treatment. Both are negative rights that entail duties of forbearance on the part of health care professionals: under ordinary circumstances, they must refrain from revealing patient information to third parties as well as from interventions unauthorized by the patient. Certain positive rights also create correlative duties on the part of either health care professionals or, more generally, society. Among the former is the patients' right to be told relevant known facts about their health and treatment options. Among the latter is the right to health care.

IMAGE 18.2
©iStockPhoto/vinnstock

Universal Coverage

Some Facts about Access to Health Care

If there is a right to health care, then society must provide universal access to it—which means there should be access to at least some 'decent minimum' or basic level of medical care for all. Many countries, including some in the developing world, offer universal access. They include most European countries, Australia, Canada, Cuba, Japan, New Zealand, South Africa, and Taiwan. Their approaches to financing and organizing their health care systems make up two groups. Countries such as Australia, Britain, and Canada have in place a **single-payer system** of care administered by a health authority and funded by taxes. In a single-payer system, the government acts as a single health insurer but the delivery of care can be private or a mix of private and public. Proponents of single-payer systems mention among the systems' virtues their good performance in lowering health care costs (by reducing waste and administrative expenses, and by establishing control on skyrocketing health care costs) and providing health care services.

Other countries such as Germany, the Netherlands, and Switzerland have in place mandated **multi-payer systems**. These are multi-plan systems that rely on insurers working under government regulations and require all residents to have a health care plan, whether provided by employers or individually purchased from private or government agencies. Residents are required to declare their coverage status, and those without coverage must pay a fine. For employers, the systems may impose a 'play-or-pay' mandate requiring that employers either offer health insurance to their employees ('play') or pay a tax or premium to help subsidize coverage for people without employers' insurance ('pay').

In contrast to these systems, the US long stood alone among developed nations in failing to ensure universal health care access for its legal residents. Only recently did it conform to the emerging standard among industrialized nations and adopt a multi-payer system. This was achieved in 2010 with the enactment of the **Patient Protection and Affordable Care Act** (PPACA), known informally as 'Obamacare' because it was advocated and signed into law by President Barack Obama. Initially, some of its opponents charged that the Act was unconstitutional. But in 2012 that objection was largely put to rest by a decision of the US Supreme Court.

The public debate over health care reform in the US continued beyond 2010. Some still regard the PPACA as too radical; others as not radical enough. Among other provisions, the PPACA

1. Contains an individual mandate requiring every resident to either have health insurance or pay a special tax.
2. Establishes exchanges where insurance, in part subsidized, can be purchased.
3. Expands Medicaid, an existing insurance program for economically low income and disabled residents that is funded from both federal and state sources.
4. Has provisions for insurers to
    ○ Remove annual and lifetime caps on coverage,
    ○ Offer coverage to all, eliminating discrimination on the basis of age, sex, or pre-existing conditions, and
    ○ Remove some co-pays on services such as preventive screening and reduce other co-pays.
5. Extends family coverage for children until their mid-20s.
6. Requires that employers either 'play or pay'.
7. Offers tax credits to small businesses that provide coverage.

These provisions have significantly expanded the number of people with health coverage in the United States. By 2014, the available data showed that Obamacare was on its way toward achieving this goal. The number of uninsured in America had fallen about 5%, according to the RAND Corporation, the Commonwealth Fund, the Gallup Poll, and the Urban Institute.[7] Some estimate that provisions (2) and (3) alone will result in extending coverage to about 32 million people, a considerable number given that in 2010 there were 50 million uninsured in the US (Daniels, 2013). Unauthorized immigrants, who amount to approximately 12 million people at present, are left out of the PPACA—as are these immigrants in any other multi-payer or single-payer system. Regarding health care spending, it actually increased under Obamacare. But the real test for what happens on that score is long-term results, since spending might go up anyway if more people are receiving medical care.

It should be borne in mind that the US had long lacked a unified health care system offering basic care for all. Instead, it had a mixed system of insurance through employment

---

7   "Is the Affordable Care Act Working? – Special Report," *New York Times*, 10/26/2014.

(which covered about half of the population), numerous private insurance plans (covering about 7% of the people), and these national single-payer systems:

- Medicare—A federal program initially organized to provide insurance for people 65 years old and older.
- Medicaid—A state program with federal matching funds organized to provide insurance for the poor and the cognitively or physically disabled.
- CHIP—A state Children's Health Insurance Program providing coverage for children in families that earn too much to qualify for Medicaid.
- TRICARE and CHAMPVA—Programs of the Departments of Defense and Veterans Administration providing coverage for eligible service personnel who are on active duty (TRICARE) or veterans (CHAMPVA) and their families.
- EMTALA—The Emergency Medical Treatment and Active Labor Act, requiring that medical institutions offering emergency services stabilize and treat anyone who comes to an emergency department, regardless of insurance status or ability to pay.

The EMTALA has now in fact become the operative health care system for the under-insured and the uninsured in the US, including unauthorized immigrants. During the debate over health care reform in the US, some thought that a single-payer system growing out of Medicare might offer greater health care benefits and cost-containment than the patchy framework represented by Obamacare—which combines a multi-payer system with the already available single-payer systems listed above. To substantiate their proposal, they often invoked the higher cost-effectiveness of health care in Canada compared to that in the US. Before Obamacare, for two decades the average per capita cost of health care annually was less than $2,000 in Canada but $6,280 in the US.[8] All authorized residents had access to care in Canada, while the US left about 50 million uncovered. Average life-span was 80 years in Canada and 77 in the US. Canada also had one of the lowest infant mortality rates among developed countries, and unlike the US made available affordable long-term care in nursing homes for almost everyone.

But there were many unsettled issues concerning the role of the private sector, the level of taxation required to sustain a unified system, and cultural and historical differences— together with deep disagreements about the fairness of universal access to health care, a topic to which we now turn.

The Universal Access Argument

If there is a right to health care, then society has a duty to provide universal access to it. Thus, those who uphold that right are committed to this Universal Access Argument:

1. If there is a right to health care, then society must provide a decent minimum of health care for all.

---

8   Data from Pence (2008), Daniels (2008, 2013), and Geyman (2014). Gina Kolata ("Knotty Challenges in Health Care Costs," *New York Times*, 3/6/2012) also notes that, in 2012, annual health care cost per capita was $8,000 in the US and about $4,000 in most European countries.

2.   There is a right to health care.

_____

3.   Therefore, society must provide a decent minimum of health care for all.

A right to health care would be a *positive* right that would create in others a duty to provide access to at least a decent minimum or basic level of health care for all. This duty may be defeated or overridden by (a) more stringent moral obligations, such as other obligations of justice or respect for persons, and (b) practical considerations concerning society's means, whether financial or technical. With these qualifications, premise (1) seems true. The soundness of the Universal Access Argument now depends on premise (2), the claim that there is a right to health care. Before considering this premise, note that one may agree with this argument's conclusion for reasons other than the existence of a right to health care.

BOX 18.5 DANIELS'S ACCOUNT

- Is fueled by Rawls's theory of justice as fairness, in particular, by its principle recommending policies that distribute primary goods equally to the self-advancement of all.
- Considers that the good at issue in health care is health, a condition for persons to have equality of opportunity to pursue their life plans.

- Grants a special moral importance to universal access to health care because of health care's potential to restore or approximate health, a precondition for fair equality of opportunity.
- Defines 'health' narrowly as *species normal functioning*.

The Fair Equality of Opportunity Account

Is there such a right? Yes, given Norman Daniels's (1981, 2013) **Fair Equality of Opportunity Account**, which extends Rawls's principles of justice to health care. According to Rawls, when bargaining behind the veil of ignorance about the projected society's basic structure, the contractors would choose to distribute some primary social goods fairly for the self-advancement of all individuals. Among the sets of such goods is "freedom of movement and choice of occupations against a background of diverse opportunities." Daniels regards health care as derivative from this set of goods because of the special value of health. People who have, as a result of injury or disease, lost species normal functioning are deprived of a fair equality of opportunity for self-advancement (Daniels, 1981). When their ill-health conditions result from controllable social and medical factors, the inequality of opportunity they suffer amounts to an inequity. They have a right to be provided with available services to attend to their health care needs, but not to their preferences. Health needs call for services to maintain, restore, or provide functional equivalents of species normal functioning—as required to have a fair share of opportunity for pursuing what Rawls calls "individual conceptions of the good." Physical and mental impairments reduce individual opportunity relative to what's normal range of opportunity for members of the species. An Appeal to Fair Equality of Opportunity now yields this argument for a qualified right to health care:

1.   If justice in health care requires protecting fair equality of opportunity, then there should be universal access to health care.
2.   Given Daniels's account, justice in health care does require protecting fair equality of opportunity.

_____

3.   Therefore, given Daniels's account there should be universal access to health care.

This suggests that, given the Fair Equality of Opportunity Account, there is a right to health care grounded in the principle of Fair Equality of Opportunity. This right may, however, be overridden when society lacks the appropriate resources (Daniels, 1981). But affluent nations such as the US do have the means, and therefore, the prima facie obligation, to promote fairness of opportunity by taking the steps necessary for prevention and treatment of disease.

The Extreme Libertarian Account

But not all agree. Libertarian bioethicist H. Tristram Engelhardt, Jr., for example, bluntly declares that "a basic human secular moral right to health care dos not exist—not even to a 'decent minimum of health care'" (1996: 336). After all, in order to fund equal access to health care, the government would need to use its coercive power for collecting and redistributing the financial resources that would be needed. That would violate people's negative rights to liberty and property. For one thing, the government would (1) coercively take their property through taxation and (2) regulate a health care system, thereby limiting individual free choice in health care. It would therefore be an unjust arrangement for libertarians, who advocate a free-market system of health care where services are delivered according to ability to pay, through the private, voluntary purchase of insurance by individuals or groups. In fact libertarians often emphasize the difference between negative and positive rights, doubting the very existence of the latter and arguing that only the former have correlative duties because they are fulfilled by doing nothing. But as pointed out by John Arras (2015), such claims are misleading, since it is not exactly true that rights of forbearance are easier to fulfill. At the very least, they require governments to keep criminal law systems, revenue services, police departments, military forces, and other protective branches.

Other libertarian objections to universal access focus on its failure in securing (1) consumer choice, (2) quality care, and (3) cost containment. But objection (1) faces the problem that a two-tier system makes universal access to a decent minimum compatible with private financing of an extra level of health care. (2) and (3) are empirical claims that seem unconfirmed by data, such as annual averages of costs per capita in Canada and the US.

The Pluralist Account

There may be grounds for access to a decent minimum of care even if there is no right to health care—i.e., even if premise (2) in the Universal Access Argument is false. Allen E. Buchanan (1984), for example, takes this position. On his Pluralistic Account, invoking the right to health care provides flimsy grounds for universal access to a decent minimum of care. This is because human rights themselves constitute a contested category in political theory. The Pluralistic Account holds instead that three types of reason jointly support access to a decent minimum. They are:

- Special individual and group rights—concerning the compensatory rights of victims of past wrong-doing. Historic injustice creates a duty of reparation to make fair restitution to victims. In the US, the grievances of racial and ethnic minorities and other underrepresented groups justify the provision of a decent minimum of care as a fair restitution.
- Prudential considerations—concerning some desirable consequences of universal access such as its potential to boost the labor force's productivity and defense personnel's fitness.
- Duties of nonmaleficence and beneficence—concerning avoidance and prevention of harm, often cited as humanitarian reasons for access to a decent minimum of health care.

The Upshot

The Pluralist Account regards the claim to a decent minimum of care as supported by a variety of considerations, ranging from special rights of compensatory justice to duties of harm avoidance and prevention. Both liberal egalitarians and libertarians can object that such a 'forced beneficence' account falls short of justifying that claim: it is unclear how demanding beneficence in health care could be. For Engelhardt's Extreme Libertarian Account, if the best-off decide to fund a decent minimum of care for the worst-off, that would be praiseworthy as charity. But they have no moral duty to do so.

For Daniels's Fair Equality of Opportunity Account, the fundamental basis of the claim for a decent minimum of care is fairness in the distribution of social goods and services. Justice and beneficence may both support that claim, but as discussed above, justice has greater moral weight. When they come apart, justice prevails. This account can countenance a right to health care contingent upon the availability of resources, and therefore defeasible. Other traditions such as Natural Law theory would construe that right as absolute because health is linked to life, a basic value. Each of these accounts conflicts, however, with the Extreme Libertarian Account, whose theory of justice commits to finding universal coverage, even for a decent minimum of care, unjust. This divide cannot be bridged, for it stems from disagreement about fundamental principles of justice.

18.4 Chapter Summary

Shortland v Northland Health, the leading case in this chapter, illustrates many of the justice issues reviewed here. First, it draws attention to the fact that medical decisions based on rationing need not coincide with decisions based on medical futility. Given the evidence from the case, Northland Health's denial of renal dialysis for Mr. Williams was based on rationing, not futility. Furthermore, if as determined by the court it properly applied allocation guidelines accepted in New Zealand, it did not violate the patient's *legal* rights. But it might have violated his *moral* right to health care. Unlike the right to life, which is a negative right requiring noninterference with a person's continued existence, a positive right to health care requires that right-holders be provided with health care. If Mr. Williams had that right, that created a correlative duty to be provided with health care. But did he have a right to be provided renal dialysis replacement therapy, a moderately scarce resource? Yes, provided New Zealand could afford it for all patients in relevantly similar conditions, given the formal principle of justice, and not doing so would amount to inequitable discrimination on the basis of age or mental disability.

If there is a right to health care, a qualified conclusion of the Universal Access Argument follows: society should provide at least a decent minimum of health care for all if they can afford it. Daniels's Fair Equality of Opportunity Account is committed to that argument, while Buchanan's Pluralist Account is committed to its conclusion only because it supports it with reasons other than fairness in distributive justice. Engelhardt's Extreme Libertarian Account rejects both the Universal Access Argument and its conclusion, since it takes liberty rights based on self-ownership to be the only legitimate ones.

Suppose society has a duty to provide a decent minimum of health care. Ethical and practical questions would still remain open. Some concern which of the two systems of coverage outlined here, the single- or the multi-payer insurer, is best for fulfilling that duty in terms of goals such as freedom of choice, delivery of quality care, and cost containment. Other questions arise with priority setting and rationing, which are both unavoidable. Public health officials and health care providers find the QALY approach to these useful. But since the approach seeks to maximize health benefits and minimize costs, QALYs face moral objections when implemented as the sole consideration in priority setting and rationing. A particularly difficult allocation decision concerns the fair distribution of organs. In evaluating a patient's candidacy for a transplant, other criteria besides medical ones have been proposed. A Responsibility Argument contends that patients whose self-destructive behavior has led to the need for a transplant be excluded from organ priority lists. But the versions of that argument considered here face strong humanitarian and consistency objections.

▮ 18.5 Study Aids

Key Words

Case law, 362
Correlativity thesis, 362
Distributive justice, 349
Fair Equality of Opportunity Account, 366
Formal/material principle of justice, 351
Justice, 347
Liberal justice, 352
Libertarian justice, 352
Negative/positive right, 362
Patient Protection and Affordable Care Act (PPACA), 364

Questions and Cases for Further Consideration

1. How might beneficence and justice come into conflict in clinical drug trials in the developing world?

2. *Two Patients, One Bed. There is only one bed vacant in an intensive care unit, and there are two patients with claims of need for occupying it. One health care provider thinks the bed should go to the patient who can be most benefitted by critical care, which in this situation means the one who is sicker. Another argues that the sicker patient is more likely to die, or live with a very low quality of life, while the less sick might fully recover.* What should be done? Might the QALY approach help? Explain what you take to be the morally fitting arrangement in the circumstances.

3. R v Cambridge District Health Authority (ex p B). *In 1995, a 10 year-old British girl, known in court as 'B,' suffered a relapse of acute myeloid leukemia. She had already undergone two courses of chemotherapy and a bone marrow transplant. Further treatment, her doctors believed, had a 20% chance of success and uncompensated burdens. Moreover, if the chemotherapy was successful, B would have to undergo another costly bone marrow transplant. The health authority decided against funding, citing both medical futility and costs. But B's father persuaded the High Court to review that decision. The Court of Appeal, however, allowed an appeal by the DHA. In the end, an anonymous donor funded the treatment.* Unlike *Shortland* above, in this case medical futility and rationing seem to have coincided. In your view, was the Court of Appeal's weighing of costs against benefits and burdens consistent with justice? Should the court have been more willing to interfere with the health authority's decision? According to medical law expert Charles Foster, noninterference is a generalized tendency motivated by the courts' desire to avoid being "swamped by patients and their relatives scrabbling for the money" (2013: 94). If Foster is correct, are the courts breaching a moral right of patients? Whose responsibility is it, ultimately, to make rescuing decisions when resources are limited?

4. *At 27 weeks of pregnancy,* Venita Davis's *sonogram revealed a huge encephalocele, or sack, on the back of the fetus's head. With nearly all of the brain in that sack, the fetus had no functioning brain tissue beyond a rudimentary brainstem. After a failed abortion, she gave birth to a severely disabled and unresponsive baby, Portia. Two years later, Portia remained paralyzed, unconscious, and neurologically devastated. Fed by nasogastric tube, she had recurring seizures and received ICU care, which was formidably expensive. The costs were paid by Medicare.* (Adapted from *The New York Times*, 10/6/1993.) Keeping Portia in the ICU condemns others to death or disability. She consumes resources that

could be used to rescue those salvageable patients. But terminations of treatment in cases like hers usually invoke futility, not costs. Questions here include: a) Are health care providers being dishonest? b) Would it be unjustified discrimination if Medicare were to deny funding for providing intensive care to patients like Portia? c) Might her congenital impairment amount to an injustice of the natural lottery? d) What would libertarians say?

5.   *In 1995 Mickey Mantle, the great New York Yankees baseball star, was in a Dallas hospital dying of liver failure. Mantle's liver was riddled with lesions of a particularly aggressive cancer but was also shutting down because of hepatitis and alcoholic cirrhosis, the result of many years of hard drinking with his buddies. He needed a transplant, so his name was placed on the North Texas waiting list for a donor organ, a standard procedure that, in that geographical region at the time, would have led him to a transplant in approximately 183 days. But Mantle clearly didn't have that long to wait. Stories had already appeared in the press about the Yankee slugger's plight, generating interest among his many devoted fans. After only two days, a compatible donor organ was found. Mantle immediately underwent transplant surgery. The transplant was initially as success, but soon the cancer returned, with metastases consuming the new liver. Mantle died two months after the transplant.* This case raises some critical ethical issues. First, Mantle's liver deterioration was partly the result of alcoholic cirrhosis, and thus to some extent a problem of his own making. But then, did he *deserve* a transplant? Doesn't our responsible stewardship of this scarce medical resource require that we provide it only to those who've fallen ill not through any fault of their own? Secondly, although the Dallas doctors denied that Mantle was able to jump the queue, many assumed that he did. If so, shouldn't he have had to wait his turn the same as anyone else? Third, sound data[9] show that the burdens of ill health from drinking "fall disproportionally on the unemployed, manual workers, and those on poorer incomes." Does justice demand more flexible guidelines for the allocation of organs to society's worst-off?

6.   Gender Reassignment Surgery. *In 2014, Devin Payne decided it was time to change her name and pursue hormone therapy and gender reassignment surgery. Uninsured, she could not afford any possible complications from the surgery. Fortunately, when Obamacare was signed into law, 'gender identity disorder' could no longer be invoked as a pre-existing condition in denying health coverage to transsexuals. Payne was able to buy subsidized private insurance and did so, then sought the surgery. Eventually, she got the insurer to pay for most expenses. In her view, insurers should be required to pay because transsexuals seeking surgery are a small group and denials carry high risks of mental illness.*[10] Although anti-discrimination regulations enacted after Obamacare bans gender discrimination in medical practice, it falls short of requiring coverage for sex reassignment surgery. As result, insurers may justify denials by invoking

9   Institute of Alcohol Studies. "Socioeconomic groups' relationship with Alcohol," 2013. http:// www.ias.org.uk/Alcohol-knowledge-centre/Socioeconomic-groups/Factsheets/Socioeconomic-groups-relationship-with-alcohol.aspx.

10 Adapted from Anna Gorman, "Obamacare Now Pays for Gender Reassignment," *The Daily Beast,* 8/25/2014.

allocation decisions to fund other interventions such as renal dialysis. But single-payers systems like Medicaid and Medicare now regard sex reassignment surgery as medically necessary. Among the questions that this case raises are: a) Should the intervention fall into this category? b) Is coverage of gender reassignment surgery a fair allocation of public money, given some taxpayers' objections to it on moral or religious grounds? c) Does the need for funds for rescue interventions justify insurers' denials? What about denials to discourage gender change? d) Are denials on either grounds unjustified discrimination?

Suggested Readings*

*Arras, John D., 'The Right to Health Care," in Arras et al. 2015, pp. 3–15.
    Excellent outline of theories of justice in health care. Emphasizes role of the social determinants and defends the positive right to health care from the critique by extreme libertarians.
*Buchanan, Allen E., "The Right to a Decent Minimum of Health Care," *Philosophy & Public Affairs* 13.1, 1984: 55–78.
    Opposes any attempted defense of access to a decent basic minimum of health care that may invoke a right to health care as a matter of fairness, such as Daniels's Fair Equality of Opportunity Account. For Buchanan, a pluralistic account invoking some special rights, prudential reasons, and moral obligations better captures the grounds of universal access.
*Cappelen, Alexander W. and Ole Frithjof Norheim, "Responsibility in Health Care: A Liberal Egalitarian Approach," *Journal of Medical Ethics* 31.8, 2005: 476–80.
    After analyzing reasons for and against the Responsibility Argument holding individuals accountable for their choices leading to a need of scarce resources such as organs, contends liberal egalitarianism offers the most effective version of that argument.
*Cohen, Carl, Martin Benjamin, and the Ethics and Social Impact Committee of the Transplant and Health Policy Center, Ann Arbor, Michigan, "Alcoholics and Liver Transplantation," *JAMA* 265, 1991: 1299–1301.
    Evaluates the Moral Responsibility Argument and the Medical Argument underlying unwillingness to consider patients with alcoholic cirrhosis of the liver as candidates for transplantation, arguing that they both fail.
*Daniels, Norman, "Health-Care Needs and Distributive Justice," *Philosophy and Public Affairs* 10.2, 1981: 146–79.
    Early exposition of Daniels's Fair Equality of Opportunity Account of the right to a decent minimum level of health care, that is contingent upon availability of resources. Within this right fall any health care services necessary for maintaining, restoring, or providing functional equivalents of health, where 'health' should be construed narrowly in terms of species normal functioning.

---

* Asterisks mark readings available online. See links on the companion website.

*———, "Justice and Access to Health Care," *The Stanford Encyclopedia of Philosophy*, Edward Zalta, ed., 2008/2013. Available online at http://plato.stanford.edu/entries/ justice-healthcareaccess/.
Updates the Fair Equality of Opportunity Account for universal access to health care, paying some attention to Obamacare's provisions and early consequences.

*———, "Fair Equality of Opportunity and Decent Minimums: A Reply to Buchanan," *Philosophy & Public Affairs* 14.1, 1985: 106–10. Available online at http://www.jstor. org/stable/2265240.
Argues that Buchanan's (1984) objections to the Fair Equality of Opportunity Account rest on a misunderstanding of Daniels (1981).

*Deber, Raisa, "Health Care Reform: Lessons from Canada," *American Journal of Public Health* 93.1, 2003: 20–4.
Provides data about access, quality, and reception of Canada's single-payer health care system, arguing that this system has advantages with regard to containing health care costs, delivering quality care, and allowing for some flexibility through provincial (i.e., sub-national) systems.

*Engelhardt, H. Tristram, Jr., "Rights to Health Care, Social Justice, and Fairness in Health Care Allocations: Frustrations in the Face of Finitude," in *Foundations of Bioethics*, 2nd ed. New York: Oxford University Press, 1996.
Contra those who think that there is a right to health care, even a decent minimum of healthcare coverage, argues that such a right would conflict with the negative right to liberty, and therefore, with justice. As a health care policy, universal access is incompatible with the goals of freedom of choice and cost containment.

Geyman, John, "The United States Should Adopt Universal Healthcare," in Caplan and Arp 2014, pp. 303–13.
Defends a unified, single-payer health care system for the US by appeal to evidence from nations that have already experimented with such systems for some time.

*Harris, John, "QALYfying the Value of Life," *Journal of Medical Ethics* 13.3, 1987: 117–23.
Objects to Williams's (1985) Quality-Adjusted-Life-Year approach to measure the benefits and costs of medical interventions and programs for the purpose of priority setting and resource allocation. Finds the QALYs' assumptions about quality of life and insensitivity to the value of life incompatible with the duty to postpone a patient's death when treatments exist.

*Hope, Tony, "Rationing and Life-saving Treatments: Should Identifiable Patients Have Higher Priorities?" *Journal of Medical Ethics* 27.3, 2001: 179–85.
Rejects six reasons for thinking that the duty to rescue identifiable dying patients should take priority over preventive care in the allocation of funding, arguing that the rule of rescuing should not be used for that purpose.

*Macklin, Ruth, "Global Inequalities in Women's Health: Who Is Responsible for Doing What?" *Philosophical Topics: Global Gender Issues* 37.2, 2009: 93–108.
Argues that the US, by enacting bans on the use of its health care relief funds for NGOs involved in financing abortion and contraception, has contributed to global gender injustice. It therefore has duties of compensatory justice toward the nations affected by those bans.

*Rescher, Nicholas, "The Allocation of Exotic Medical Lifesaving Therapy," *Ethics* 79.3, 1969: 173–86.

Classic source for the view that a patient's role as a family member (or the lack of such relationship) and her past contributions to society and potential for future contributions should count in decisions about how to allocate limited medical resources such as organs.

*Williams, Alan, "The Value of QALYs," *Health and Social Service Journal* 8, 1985: 3–5. Proposes QALYs as a type of measurement that can maximize efficiency in priority setting and allocation of funds among health care interventions and programs.

*———, "Response: QALYfying the Value of Life," *Journal of Medical Ethics* 13.3, 1987: 123. Outlines the author's and Harris's differences about the QALY approach, arguing that they reduce to a disagreement of fundamental principles about how the health care system should work.

The Tools of Ethical Inquiry

▪ Moral Judgment

The principal tool of bioethics is moral argument, a type of reasoning aimed at supporting a moral judgment. Here 'judgment' refers to any thoughts or sentences representing things as being in a certain way. Thus, 'Northland Health is a health care provider' is a judgment ascribing the general concept *being a health care provider* to the specific concept *Northland Health*. Identifying moral judgments requires being able to distinguish, first, which judgments are normative and which merely descriptive, and second, which normative judgments concern moral issues and which do not.

Normative versus Descriptive Judgment

Normative Force

While some judgments have normative force, others simply make a factual claim. We call the latter judgments 'descriptive' and the former 'normative.' Examples of descriptive judgments include:

1. Northland Health is a health care provider.
2. A 65-year-old patient is a senior.
3. Mr. Williams was denied kidney-dialysis.

(1), (2), and (3) make factual claims whose truth, in each case, depends on the way things are or were. By contrast, normative judgments go beyond merely describing the facts: they are meant to guide action, because they have the force of evaluations, permissions, proscriptions, recommendations, etc. Here are some examples of moral normative judgments in the context of medicine, with the concepts providing their normative force highlighted:

4. Health care providers *must* respect patients.
5. Patients have a *right* to refuse treatment.
6. This medical team was *honest* with the patient.
7. Karl Brandt, a Nazi doctor tried at Nuremberg, was *evil.*
8. Melinda *deserves* credit for her supportive attitude toward patients.

Judgments (4) through (8) have normative force because each provides a reason for acting or believing in a certain way. Suppose

9. It is *wrong* to provide medically-assisted suicide.

Given (9), medically assisted suicide should not be provided. And given (10), distractive medicine should be avoided:

10.   Distractive medicine can cause *harm* to patients.

Notice that (4), (5), (9), and (10) are *general* normative judgments, and (6), (7), and (8) are *specific*. Unlike general judgments, specific judgments make normative claims about particular actions, persons, or situations. Figure A.1 offers examples of moral normative judgments in other contexts, dividing them according to whether they express a prescription or an evaluation—a topic we consider next.

Prescriptions and Evaluations

Prescriptions are normative judgments of conduct that typically present an action as being either permissible, mandatory, or forbidden. By contrast, evaluations are appraisals of things, including persons, practices, and policies. While all normative judgments may feature normative concepts, these may be absent in prescriptions whose normative function is performed by the imperative mood. Prescriptive concepts may express obligation (e.g., 'right,' 'must,' and 'ought' and their negative counterparts, 'wrong,' 'mustn't,' and 'ought not') for mandatory actions, or permission (e.g., 'permissible,' 'justified,' and 'may,' and negative expressions such as 'not forbidden' and 'not impermissible') for optional actions. Value is signaled by words such as 'good,' 'just,' 'and 'honest' and their negative counterparts 'bad,' 'unjust,' and 'deceptive.'

FIGURE A.1   Some Normative Moral Judgments

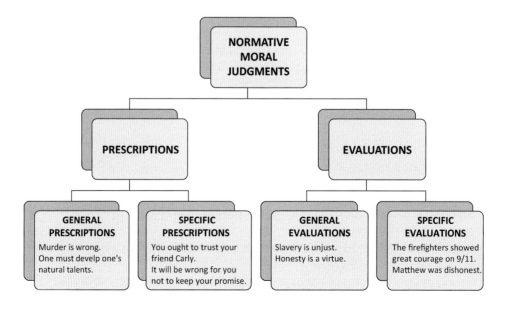

FIGURE A.2   Prescriptions and Evaluations

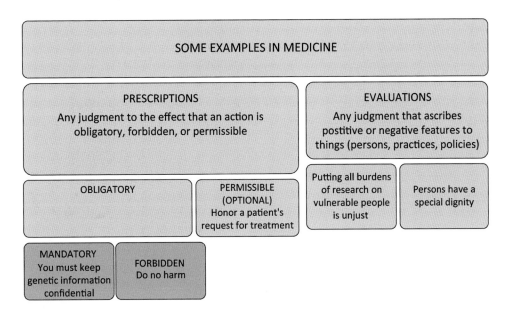

Moral Judgment Characterized

Like other normative judgments, moral judgments consist of either prescriptions or evalu-ations. Moral prescriptions express the deontic status of actions, practices, or policies—i.e., whether they are optional, mandatory, or forbidden. Such statuses are signaled by normative words such as 'right,' 'permissible,' 'wrong,' 'must,' 'may,' 'mustn't,' and the like. Moral evalu-ations can be expressed by many evaluative words ('just,' 'bad,' 'deserves,' 'cruel,' etc.). Moral judgments of either type may be prospective or retrospective. We may, for example, wonder prospectively about our duties to future generations, or retrospectively about the wrongness of paternalism in Hippocratic medicine. A moral judgment provides a reason for action or belief that is distinct from those provided by judgments of other sorts. These include

- Conventional judgments, which involve custom or etiquette ('You cannot swim without a swimming suit,' 'The bride's father must pay for her wedding')
- Prudential judgments, which involve self-interest ('You ought to be especially nice to your rich Aunt Gertrude,' 'Don't cheat your business associates if you don't want them to cheat you')
- Legal judgments, which cite or express the law, as a reason to do or forbear from some action ('No parking at any time,' 'The law stipulates that adults must file an income tax return')

Moral reasons are more authoritative or weighty than any of these. They concern deeply held prescriptions of conduct and evaluations of traits of character. To say 'Racial segregation in

FIGURE A.3   Normative Moral Judgment

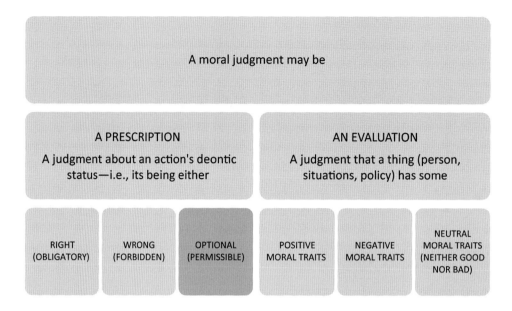

the American South was wrong' or 'Nazi medicine violated human rights' is to provide the strongest possible reason against such practices, one that overrides the fact that Jim Crow laws and Nazi statutes made them legal.

Moral prescriptions concern the deontic status of actions. As action guides, they provide reasons for action or forbearance. Consider

11. Extend a patient's life whenever possible.
12. Keep patient information confidential.

Here the imperative mood expresses the deontic status of moral obligation. (11) provides a reason for performing certain medical procedures, (12) for not revealing sensitive patient information to third parties.

Moral Argument

Decisions about what one morally must do or believe are more securely grounded when based on reasoned argument than when based on mere intuition. In an argument, a conclusion (or main claim) is supposed to follow from one or more reasons, called 'premises,' offered to support it. A moral argument is an argument with a moral judgment as its conclusion. Like other types of argument, moral ones must have premises that accurately represent any facts. They must also comply with the standards of deductive or inductive reasoning as the case may be.

Deductive and Inductive Reasoning

An argument consists of a premise or premises and a conclusion. In a deductive argument the premises are offered as guaranteeing the conclusion's truth, while in an inductive argument they merely provide *some* support for it. With a valid deductive argument, to accept its premises while denying its conclusion is to say something contradictory—it makes no logical sense. By the definition of validity, if the premises of a deductive argument are true, its conclusion cannot be false. In the following deductive argument, for example, if (1) and (2) are true, (3) cannot be false:

1. Infants cannot give consent to medical treatment.
2. The new patient is an infant.

---

3. Therefore, the new patient cannot give consent to medical treatment.

By contrast, the conclusion of an inductive argument with true premises can be false, as illustrated by this argument:

1. Most extremely premature babies have long-lasting health impairments.
2. Tommy was born extremely prematurely at 25 weeks.

---

3. Therefore, Tommy will have some long-lasting health impairments.

Standards for evaluating deductive and inductive arguments differ, with validity and soundness applying only to deductive arguments. A deductive argument is valid when its premises, if true, guarantee the truth of the conclusion. It is sound when it is valid *and* all premises are actually true.
    On the other hand,

An inductive argument is strong if and only if it has

A. True premises and
B. A reliable form (if its premises were true, it would be reasonable to accept its conclusion).

Keep in mind that strong inductive arguments may still have false conclusions, something that cannot happen with sound deductive arguments. To question the conclusion of either type of argument, you should check whether it has true premises, and a form that is deductively valid or inductively reliable. To determine whether an argument is deductive or inductive, ask yourself, Could the conclusion be false and all premises true? If Yes, then it's inductive. If No, then it's deductive.

Concepts and Facts

Neither deductive soundness nor inductive strength alone can produce persuasive moral arguments. Also needed are (1) avoidance of the so-called *fallacies*, which are common patterns of error; (2) conceptual clarity; and (3) accurate representation of the facts. Conceptual clarity is especially important, since concepts such as 'person,' 'death,' 'deception,' and 'consent' are vague (they neither definitely apply nor fail to apply to certain borderline cases), or ambiguous (they have more than one meaning). For example, as Chapter 10 makes clear, 'person' suffers from both problems.

Inaccurate representation of the facts also undermines an argument. A false, or even dubious, premise makes the argument unsound if deductive and weak if inductive. Either type of shortcoming defeats the argument. In bioethics, accuracy about the facts matters greatly. An argument against abortion may claim that fetuses can feel pain, but such an assertion must be backed up by evidence from prenatal development. An objection to medical euthanasia may claim that this practice, if legalized, would result in a mass killing of vulnerable patients. Yet again, supporting evidence is needed, in this case from societies where euthanasia has been legal for some time. In sum, the accuracy of descriptive premises must be checked before any conclusion from them can be accepted.

Moral Principles, Commonsense Morality, and Reflective Equilibrium

In this book, what we called 'principles,' 'norms,' or 'rules' are moral prescriptions that have varying degrees of generality. Of maximum generality are, for instance, the principles that

A. An action is right to take if and only if it produces, for all those affected by it, more overall happiness or less overall unhappiness than some alternative action.
B. An action is right to take if and only if it is fair to persons, in the sense that it respects them as one would oneself want to be respected.

Falling under these principles is *any action whatsoever*, so their scope is quite wide. Let's consider how one of them functions in the following argument:

1. Principle (A).
2. In some cases, helping terminally ill patients to die more quickly is the action that produces, for all those affected by it, more overall happiness and less overall pain than some alternative action would.

_____

3. Therefore, in those cases, helping terminally ill patients to die more quickly is right.

Here conclusion (3), separated by a horizontal line, is supported by moral principle (A), and factual premise (2).

But moral arguments may also feature principles of less generality. For example,

1. Deceiving a patient about her health is wrong. ← MORAL PRINCIPLE
2. Dr. Lee told a cancer patient that she doesn't have cancer. ← FACTUAL PREMISE

_____

3. Therefore, Dr. Lee did something wrong. ← SPECIFIC MORAL CONCLUSION

Moral principles held as absolute (i.e., exceptionless) are often open to challenge by counter-example. A counterexample is a real-life or imagined scenario that disproves them. A scenario where a caregiver must tell a lie to a patient to save her life is a counterexample to premise (1) above. Similarly, suppose one were inclined to think that loyalty is always preferable to disloyalty. Loyalty to Hitler would be a counterexample to that principle. But counterexamples fall short of undermining moral principles that express obligations which can be overridden in a situation. For example, one prescribing that deceiving patients about their health is *usually* wrong.

However construed, principles may on occasion conflict with common morality, the set of moral intuitions entrenched in our culture, such as that killing for fun is wrong and that helping vulnerable people is right. Ideally, justified principles are in reflective equilibrium with those intuitions. Such equilibrium is reached when principles and ordinary intuitions are in balance, a condition achieved through a process of mutual adjustment whereby the intuitions about cases that accord with a principle are considered to support it, and those that conflict, to undermine it. When conflict occurs, then, assuming those seeking justification by reflective equilibrium are reasoning under suitable conditions (they are calm, unbiased, etc.), they must either modify the principle to accommodate the conflicting intuition or reject the intuition altogether.

Of these options, rejecting ordinary intuitions requires more argument, because those intuitions are the default position in moral deliberation. Whoever challenges them has, at least initially, the burden of proof. For example, reasonable people believe that the Earth has existed for more than five minutes. If someone challenges this intuition, the burden of arguing is on the challenger, who must offer reasons strong enough to debunk that common belief. In bioethics, a principle recommending infanticide carries the burden of proof, because it contradicts the ordinary intuition that infanticide is forbidden. But the argumentative advantage of this intuition can be overridden by stronger countervailing reasons, if available.

Missing Premises and Extended Arguments

Some of an argument's premises may be implicit or missing. This happens frequently when an argument rests on a principle that seems too obvious to need stating. Consider,

1. Euthanasia involves the intentional killing of an innocent person.

   _____

2. Therefore, euthanasia is always wrong.

This argument has a missing premise to the effect that

0. The intentional killing of an innocent person is always wrong.

Making (0) explicit reveals the argument's unsoundness because (0) is unacceptable to those who regard euthanasia as mercy killing. Since controversial premises render deductive arguments unsound, and inductive ones weak, argument evaluation requires stating any missing premises.

Furthermore, arguments may be extended—i.e., they may draw more than one conclusion. Consider an argument about abortion loosely inspired by Hare (1993): someone argues that since he is happy to be alive, his mother did the right thing in not having an abortion when she was pregnant with the fetus that later became him. From this, he concludes that abortion is morally wrong. Besides having several missing premises, stated below as (0) and (0'), this argument is extended, since it goes like this:

0.   Something is mandatory if and only if it produces more overall happiness than some alternative actions would.
1.   I'm (for the most part) happy to be alive.

_____

2.   Therefore, my mother had the obligation of avoiding an abortion when she was pregnant with the fetus that later became me.
0'.   If having an abortion would have been wrong for my mother, then having an abortion is wrong for any other similarly situated woman (i.e., where the person who comes into being if the pregnancy is brought to term would be likely to be happy to be alive, as I am).

_____

3.   Therefore, abortion is wrong.

Factual premise (1) is beyond debate, since, under normal circumstances, people generally know whether they are, for the most part, happy about something. But because missing premises (0) and (0') are debatable, this argument is unsound. As you can see, it is essential to make an argument's premises explicit, especially when they are moral principles. The arguments considered here, though greatly simplified, are fairly typical of the sort to be met with in bioethics, since many of them rely on principles derived from moral theories such as those outlined in Chapter 2.

Check Your Understanding

I.   Which of the following judgments are normative and which descriptive?
 1.   Euthanasia should be permitted in some cases of terminal illness.
     SAMPLE ANSWER: Normative judgment
 2.   Health care providers ought to tell their patients the truth.
 3.   End-of-life decisions can be quite complex.
 4.   Misrepresenting medical records is dishonest.
 5.   Chimpanzees' IQs can be higher than the IQs of people with severe mental deficits.
 6.   The human fetus has a right to life.
 7.   In abortion, the fetus dies.
 8.   Telemedicine aims at improving a patient's clinical health status.
 9.   Some US citizens lack fair access to health care.
 10. Unequal access to health care is unjust.
II. Which of the following judgments are conventional, legal, prudential, moral, or a combination of some of these?
 1.   A healthy life-style recommends drinking eight glasses of water a day.
     SAMPLE ANSWER: Prudential judgment

2. Paternalism in medicine is wrong.
3. Depriving patients of their right to life violates the United Nations' charter.
4. Psychiatrists should not reveal patient information to third parties.
5. According to our guidelines, this neonate does not qualify for critical care.
6. Seeing more patients is good for earning extra money.
7. Doctor Kevorkian's 'mercy' killings were evil.
8. Physicians should address patients by their last name.
9. People have a right to procreative freedom.
10. According to the Supreme Court, the fetus should not be considered a person.

III. What's the missing premise in the following arguments?

1. Punishing people for crimes they have committed increases happiness in the world. Therefore, punishing people for crimes they have committed is always morally right.

   SAMPLE ANSWER: Whatever increases happiness in the world is morally right.

2. Chimpanzees are highly intelligent. Therefore, chimpanzees are persons.
3. Global warming is causing tornados throughout the world. Therefore we ought to take steps to reduce global warming.
4. O'Brien doesn't care about his patients. Therefore O'Brien is a bad nurse.
5. Antibiotics may become ineffective in the near future. Therefore, we ought to campaign against overuse.
6. New York City has many hospitals. Therefore, this US city serves many vulnerable patients.

Appendix B

Evolving Attitudes toward Ending or Preventing Human Life

▉ Abortion, Infanticide, and Contraception

In 2010, readers of *The Independent* learned of an archaeological site in England where scholars were excavating a Roman villa that had apparently served as a brothel. Archaeologists had discovered on the site some 97 skeletons of neonates, a shocking discovery for modern Britons, but not, it seems, offensive by Roman standards.[1] The intentional termination of early human life was common practice throughout most of the Greco-Roman world. Whether as infanticide or abortion, it was an accepted method of birth control. But Western attitudes toward them have varied greatly over the past 2,000 years.[2] In ancient Greece, impaired or unwanted infants were often abandoned in a crossroads or the precincts of a temple, and abortion was readily available from midwives and physicians.

Yet one school of medical practitioners, the Hippocratic physicians, refused as part of their professional code of ethics to perform abortion. With the rise of Christianity in late antiquity, this stricture seems to have fit well with the Judeo-Christian reverence for human life—which may, in turn, have helped to cement the dominance of Hippocratic medicine in the expanding Christian world.

Meanwhile, Roman law banned abortions after quickening, when the pregnant woman first detects fetal movement, as did English common law through the Middle Ages. This prohibition reflected an ignorance of human physiology, since an abortion performed before quickening was believed to be merely a procedure enabling a woman to return to her menstrual cycle. Before quickening, abortion was morally permissible, requiring the father's consent for fetuses conceived in wedlock. Abortions performed after quickening, however, were condemned in unsparing terms and, when perpetrators were discovered, sometimes prosecuted as homicides.

In the 17th and 18th centuries, some discoveries would ultimately correct prevalent misconceptions about fetal development. Among the earliest scientific achievements through use of the microscope was the discovery by Antonie van Leeuwenhoek (1632–1723) of sperm cells in seminal fluid. That led to a sea-change in prevailing views about the beginnings of human life. It came to be widely understood that development was continuous from conception through birth, and this contributed to more restrictive laws governing access to abortion. One by one, the European nations enacted laws criminalizing abortion—France in 1792 (reinforced by the Napoleonic Code of 1810), Britain in 1803, and most of the rest

---

1 Paul Vallely, "Better an Abortion than a Mass Grave?" *The Independent*, 6/26/2010. http://www.independent.co.uk/voices/commentators/paul-vallely-better-an-abortion-than-a-mass-grave-2011500.html.

2 A brief guide to the European history of abortion, infanticide, and contraception is Riddle (2001). For a book-length treatment, see McLaren (1990).

of Europe between 1852 and 1889. As early as 1837, abortion had already been defined as 'eliminating pregnancy at any period,' so that quickening was no longer held to be morally significant. In 1851 Pope Pius IX added the force of canon law to that definition, declaring anyone who procured an abortion to be subject to excommunication.

The restrictive trend in European attitudes toward abortion led to similar attitudes and policies in America. At the beginning of the 19th century, no US state had laws in force governing abortion. Yet by 1900 all states had laws in effect prohibiting the use of drugs or instruments to procure an abortion. The only permitted exception was abortion to save the life of the mother. The traditional doctrine that had held quickening to be the point when abortion became impermissible was replaced by the more restrictive view that held the point to be conception.

During the second half of the 20th century, however, trends shifted again. In the United States there began a gradual liberalization of statutes governing abortion, with exceptions added to permit abortion when pregnancies resulted from rape or when the fetus was severely impaired. In the second half of the century two landmark US Supreme Court decisions brought further liberalization. *Griswold v Connecticut* (1965) struck down a state law prohibiting use of contraceptives, arguing that the law interfered with a person's legitimate exercise of her autonomy by infringing the right to privacy. Of course, more access to contraceptives may reduce the frequency of abortion. *Roe v Wade* (1973) struck down a Texas law of 1857 banning abortion, in effect legalizing it throughout the United States by removing all prohibitions on abortion in the first trimester of pregnancy. It also stipulated that states may regulate abortion in the second trimester by imposing and enforcing standards of safety and medical competence for abortion providers, and may even prohibit abortion altogether in the third trimester of pregnancy for all cases except where necessary to protect the mother's life or health. *Roe* also ruled on a debate concerning whether fetuses have the rights of persons, reaffirming the conventional view that, in the law, they do not.

After *Roe*, the United States came to have a *privacy model*, according to which the question of whether to have an early abortion is a matter to be decided solely by the patient and her physician, with no government involvement. In 1991, Canada likewise came to embrace this model, in part as a byproduct of a legislative attempt to reform Canada's Criminal Code governing abortion.[3] After more than 20 years of public debate about the legalization of abortion, the nation was divided. A deadlock in a vote in the Senate led to a *de facto* lifting of all legal restrictions.

In the United Kingdom, the 1861 Offences against the Person Act and the 1919 Infant Preservation Act prohibited abortion except when the mother's health was in danger, with this exception broadened in 1938 to include risk of mental distress. By mid-century, continuing liberalization of British attitudes toward abortion (except in Northern Ireland) led ultimately to the 1967 Abortion Act, which marked a switch to the present *permission model*, in which a local medical committee must vote to approve or deny a request for an abortion. The Act made abortion legal in Britain up to the 24th week of pregnancy, with no time limit in cases where the mother's health is at risk or the fetus has abnormalities. Owing partly to the influence of British law, some other countries such as Zambia and Australia have similar laws governing abortion.

---

3   Allen (2004) provides an overview of this and other abortion models globally. For the abortion model in Canada, see Roy, Williams, and Baylis (2004).

On the continent of Europe today, the permission model is also widely accepted. Surgical abortion is legally allowed, provided a local panel of physicians reviews the case and certifies that some conditions are met. But Portugal, Ireland, Malta, and Poland ban abortions outright, except for pregnancies that threaten the mother's life, result from rape, or show fetal abnormality. Prohibition is also the prevailing model in many countries in Latin America, Central Asia, and sub-Saharan Africa. By contrast, the People's Republic of China, consistent with its 1979 one-child-per-family policy recently relaxed, encourages abortion and birth control. This policy has resulted in an increased use of abortion for sex-selection, a practice not uncommon in other parts of Asia, such as Pakistan and India, where traditional culture favors male children.

A relatively new option for early abortions (up to 49 days) avoids surgery altogether by means of an abortifacient drug. Legal in most European countries since 1999 and in the United States since 2000, the 'abortion pill' RU-486 (mifepristone) interferes with the activity of progesterone, a hormone essential for continuation of pregnancy, blocking implantation of the zygote in the uterine wall. But if, as many believe, the right to life begins at conception, then abortions induced by RU-486 would raise the same moral problem as surgical ones. In fact, RU-486 has run into fierce opposition in the United States from anti-abortion activists. Similar resistance has surfaced in Canada and Australia.

Meanwhile, an emergency contraceptive, the 'morning-after pill' (Levonorgestrel), has become available in the US over-the-counter for most women. Also known as 'Plan B,' it prevents fertilization by inhibiting ovulation and thickening cervical mucus. According to data released by the National Center for Health Statistics in 2013, the percentage of sexually active American women who have used this method rose to 11% between 2006 and 2010, compared to 4% in 2002—with one in four women between the ages of 20 and 24 having used it at some point. But the morning-after pill is likely to remain a matter of dispute, since some mistakenly take it to be an abortifacient. Others object to contraceptives generally. And there is opposition, on fairness grounds, to a new US health care law requiring employers' coverage for contraception.

Euthanasia and Suicide

In antiquity, the Greeks and Romans generally approved of infanticide for disabled children, but on the topic of euthanasia and suicide for adults, some had reservations. Hippocratic physicians rejected both, even at the patient's request. Plato and Aristotle generally disparaged suicide as a cowardly way out of one's troubles, yet allowed that it could be justified in some circumstances. Stoic philosophers Epictetus and Seneca thought that if life became so physically compromised that it was more burden than benefit, suicide was acceptable.

Opposition to euthanasia and suicide grew with the rise of Christianity, a faith committed to the sanctity of human life and, at first, to strict pacifism. For early Christians, as for Jews, human life in any form was a gift from God—something to be valued and guarded. As a result, suicide was a mortal sin akin to murder, capital punishment, and participation in war. Euthanasia, seen as a variation of suicide, was similarly condemned. With the establishment of Christianity as the official religion of the Roman Empire under Theodosius I in the late 4th century, however, some changes were required. Since the state's use of deadly force was necessary to maintain public order and repel foreign invaders, Christian moral theology was revised accordingly to permit killing in 'just wars' and capital punishment. But other prohibitions against taking human life persisted in the West through the Middle Ages and into early modern times.

In the 16th through the 18th centuries, Western society remained officially committed to the Judeo-Christian conception of the sacredness of human life, effectively ruling out euthanasia as an option while harshly condemning suicide. People who committed suicide were denied Christian burial. Their corpses were exposed, and their property confiscated to force their families into poverty. Even a philosopher as subtle as John Locke, though he would probably have thought such penalties too harsh, endorsed the view that human life was the property of God, and thus not an alienable possession that individuals could reject. For different reasons, other secular philosophers also regarded suicide as morally wrong. For Kant, it amounted to treating humanity (one's own) as only a means rather than an end in itself, thereby violating the Moral Law.

Among early dissenters might be counted Sir Thomas More, whose *Utopia* (1516) imagines an ideal society in which euthanasia would be an option for the dying. But as a devout Catholic, it is unlikely that More himself accepted suicide (Dowbiggin, 2005). A more straightforward dissent is to be found in the writings of Francis Bacon, who defended medical euthanasia as an option in helping dying patients have an easier and more comfortable death. Later, some thinkers of the Enlightenment—among them Bentham, Montesquieu, Voltaire, and Hume—argued forcefully for the liberty to take one's own life. But their arguments appear to have had little effect on public opinion, which continued through to the end of the 19th century to condemn suicide and euthanasia. Many physicians of course considered it a professional duty to ease a dying patient's pain at the bedside, and to this end administered opiates as pain relievers, but most thought it impermissible to use these narcotics to hasten death.

Even so, by the late 19th century and the early 20th century unpublicized uses of medical euthanasia involved some well known figures. In 1886 the French biologist *Louis Pasteur* was sent six Russians bitten by a rabid wolf. The men's physician, aware that Pasteur had recently developed an anti-bacterial serum, hoped his patients could be saved by it. But the serum failed to work, and the men suffered terribly for days as they slipped toward an inevitable death. At last they begged Pasteur for euthanasia. Pasteur considered the request and, after consulting with the director of the hospital and its pharmacist, ultimately decided to grant it. The pharmacist prepared lethal pills. Pasteur then administered them to the five remaining patients (one having already died), and waited as each of the men expired. "In the silence that followed the deaths," writes historian Philippe Letellier (2003), "all present wept with horror."

It is also known that *Sigmund Freud*, the Viennese founder of psychoanalysis, was given euthanasia on his deathbed. A regular cigar smoker, Freud lived for sixteen years with a diagnosis of oral cancer, ultimately enduring disfigurement and terrible pain in 34 surgical procedures. By 1939, Freud judged that he had suffered enough, and asked his physician, Max Schur, to help him have a quick and easy death. Schur reluctantly obliged, and Freud was given heavy sedation by morphine to induce death. Two days later, on September 23, 1939, Freud died.

As with the other types of intentional termination of human life considered above, Western views about the moral permissibility of physician-assisted death have varied considerably. But this need not be seen as justifying relativism about assisted death, for not all such views may be equally well supported. Surely, a relativist stance is premature until the analysis of arguments for and against the moral permissibility of assisted death has been clearly made out. For that analysis, see Parts III and IV of this book.

Glossary/Index[1]

Abolitionism/anti-abolitionism. Opposing views on the morality of animal experimentation. For abolitionism, it is morally wrong and should be either eliminated or radically reduced. For anti-abolitionism, it is morally permissible (usually, under conditions that minimize animal suffering and death). Chapter 16; 303–306.

Abortion. As a medical procedure, the elective termination of a pregnancy, generally by surgical means. See also HARD/TYPICAL CASES OF ABORTION. Chapter 10, 13; Appendix B; 193 ff., 386–388.

Abortion critic. Anyone who objects to ABORTION on moral grounds. Chapter 10; 200 ff.

Abortion debate. The controversy over the moral permissibility of ABORTION. See also ABORTION CRITIC/DEFENDER. Chapter 10; 199–201.

Abortion defender. Anyone who argues for the moral permissibility of ABORTION. Chapter 10; 200 ff.

Absolutism. Any view taking some MORAL JUDGMENTS to be exceptionless. It contrasts with UNIVERSALISM and SKEPTICISM about those judgments. Chapter 2; 27, 32.

Actual/prima facie duty. See ROSSIAN ETHICS.

Advance directive. Directions concerning medical care issued by a person while still competent in case she becomes incompetent. It may provide instructions about her treatment preferences or designate a proxy decisionmaker. Chapter 5; 100–103.

Animal-rights view. The doctrine that animals have RIGHTS, for example, to life and bodily integrity. Chapter 16; 307.

Animal-welfare view. The doctrine that animals' sentience confers on them interests, and thus MORAL STANDING. See also EQUAL CONSIDERATION OF INTERESTS. Chapter 16; 307–308.

Appeal to Developmental Continuity. ARGUMENT to the effect that ABORTION is morally forbidden because there is no significant difference between a human organism's developmental stages early in life. Chapter 11; 208, 209–211, 220–221.

Appeal to Potentiality . Argument to the effect that ABORTION is morally wrong because of fetuses' potential to become PERSONS. Chapter 11; 208, 211–212.

Applied ethics. See APPLIED/GENERAL ETHICS.

---

1 The chapter and page numbers listed here are only to the most salient references in the text. Terms that are cross-referenced appear in all caps.

Applied/general ethics. The two subdivisions of NORMATIVE ETHICS. General ethics is concerned with questions of moral character and right and wrong conduct as they arise in any area of human activity. Applied ethics focuses on such questions as they arise in specific areas of human activity – e.g., medicine, business, and the environment. Chapter 1; 12–13.

Ashley Treatment. Growth attenuation and other morally controversial interventions designed to allow home care for children with severe physical and psychological impairments. Chapter 5; 105, 107–110.

Baby Doe rules. US regulations to ensure the provision of LIFE-SUSTAINING TREATMENT to all infants, including those severely disabled. Approved by Congress in a revised form in 1988, they allow for exceptions only when reasonable medical judgment determines that the infant is irreversibly comatose, or that the treatment would be FUTILE or merely prolong dying. Chapter 9; 175–177, 182,175.

Balancing. See REFLECTIVE EQUILIBRIUM.

Beneficence. The health care professionals' POSITIVE DUTY to take steps to promote the patient's or research subject's wellbeing. See also PRINCIPLISM and ROSSIAN ETHICS. Chapter 2, 3; 34, 40 ff., 53, 54 ff.

Benefit. In medicine, any outcome of a treatment that improves patient wellbeing. Chapter 7; 142 ff.

Best interests. A decisionmaking standard based on what is objectively best for the patient. See also SUBSTITUTED JUDGMENT and ADVANCE DIRECTIVE. Chapter 5, 9; 102–105, 175.

Bioconservatism. The view that HUMAN GENETIC ENHANCEMENT is morally forbidden. Chapter 15; 284, 290–291.

Bioethics. An interdisciplinary area of concern about moral issues that arise in the practice of medicine and biomedical research, public health policy, and our relationship with nonhuman animals and the environment. See also APPLIED ETHICS. Chapter 1; 4 ff.

Bioliberalism. The view that HUMAN GENETIC ENHANCEMENT is morally permissible and even mandatory. Chapter 15; 287–290.

Biological/biographical life. A distinction between the MORAL STANDING of PERSONS and that of NONPARADIGM PERSONS such as the permanently unconscious, who lack psychological (i.e., biographical) life. Chapter 7; 144–145.

Biomedical ethics. The part of BIOETHICS devoted to clinical ethics, biomedical research, and public heath ethics. Chapter 1; 7–9.

Brain death. A set of criteria according to which human death occurs with the permanent loss of consciousness and of function in either the brainstem (brainstem death), the entire brain (whole-brain death), or the higher brain (higher-brain death). See also STANDARD ACCOUNT OF DEATH and CARDIOPULMONARY DEATH. Chapter 6; 116–177, 120–ff.

Burden of proof. In a deliberation or debate, one side's turn to offer a convincing ARGUMENT. Chapter 5, 9; 107, 175.

Capacity. See COMPETENCE.

Cardiopulmonary death. Criterion of human death that takes it to occur with the permanent loss of function in the heart and lungs. If the sole criterion for determining death, it faces the UNILATERAL-DECISION and the ORGAN-PROCUREMENT PROBLEMS. See also BRAIN DEATH and UNIFORM DETERMINATION OF DEATH ACT. Chapter 6; 118, 120–123.

Care ethics. A feminist challenge to traditional moral theories that emphasizes the moral significance of human relationships and the VIRTUE of care. Chapter 2; 38–40.

Case law. See COMMON LAW.

Casuistry. A type of moral analysis of cases wherein each is evaluated by first identifying its morally relevant features and then comparing it with an analogous PARADIGM case already decided. Whether it can be combined with PRINCIPLISM is a matter of dispute. Chapter 1, 3; 6, 52–53, 64–66.

Categorical Imperative. The MORAL RULE of KANTIAN ETHICS. Of Kant's versions, the Humanity-as-End-in-Itself Formula is the most significant in bioethics. Chapter 2; 32–34.

Common law . Precedent law, initially developed from English court decisions and custom, and distinguished from civil or codified law enacted by statute. The basis of the US legal system except in Louisiana. Chapter 4, 7; 77, 87 ff., 137 ff.

Common morality. The set of moral beliefs and rules of conduct embedded in our culture. See also MORALITY. Chapter 2, 3; Appendix A; 30, 52 ff., 381.

Competence. A threshold of mental maturity and acuity that patients must meet to be able to give INFORMED CONSENT. See also SLIDING SCALE. Chapter 3, 5; 54, 63, 97–98.

Congenital disorder. Physical, cognitive, or behavioral anomaly present at birth. Chapter 9, 10. 12; 174–182, 189, 196, 229–231.

Conscience absolutism. The view that, in CONSCIENTIOUS OBJECTION, there is no DUTY OF REFERRAL. It contrasts with CONSCIENCE SKEPTICISM and UNIVERSALISM. Chapter 13; 250–251.

Conscience skepticism. The view that health care providers ought not to morally invoke CONSCIENTIOUS OBJECTION to dispensing lawful treatments. It contrasts with CONSCIENCE ABSOLUTISM and UNIVERSALISM. See also CONSCIENTIOUS OBJECTION and DUTY OF REFERRAL. Chapter 13; 251–252.

Conscience universalism. The view that CONSCIENTIOUS OBJECTION is a provisional right of health care providers that obligations to patients can sometimes override. It contrasts with CONSCIENCE ABSOLUTISM and SKEPTICISM. See also DUTY OF REFERRAL. Chapter 13; 251.

Conscientious objection. In health care, the RIGHT to refuse dispensation of a service to patients or clients because of a conflict with the health care provider's deeply held moral or religious beliefs. See also CONSCIENCE ABSOLUTISM, SKEPTICISM, and UNIVERSALISM. Chapter 13; 249–253.

Consciousness. In medicine, a subjective state wherein a patient has wakefulness or arousal and awareness of the self and the environment in a time-ordered manner. See also PERMANENT VEGETATIVE STATE. Chapter 6; 124–125.

Consequentialism. A set of moral theories that take the value of outcomes to determine an action's DEONTIC STATUS. May be MONIST or PLURALIST. See also UTILITARIANISM and DEONTOLOGY. Chapter 2; 27–32, 42 ff.

Correlativity thesis. The view that someone's rights engender duties in others. Chapter 18; 362.

Criteria of personhood. A condition or set of conditions considered necessary and sufficient, or merely sufficient, for being a PERSON. See also HUMAN-PROPERTY CRITERION and PSYCHOLOGICAL-PROPERTY CRITERION. Chapter 10; 195–199.

Culture problem. The problem of taking some culturally dependent MORAL RULES or values to be universally valid. Chapter 4; 80.

Dead donor rule. The rule that patients must be dead before their donated vital organs can be taken for transplantation. See also ORGAN-PROCUREMENT PROBLEM. Chapter 2, 6; 20, 122–123.

Deductive/inductive argument. An argument is a logical relation between one or more reasons (the premises and the claim (the conclusion) they purport to support. If deductive, its premises purport to guarantee the truth of its conclusion, if inductive, only to give some reasons for it. Appendix A; 379.

Deontic status. Typically, the property of any action that is morally obligatory, optional, or forbidden for an agent in a situation. Chapter 1, 2; 12, 20 ff.

Deontology. The view that acting out of duty, rather than the promotion of valuable ends, determines an action's DEONTIC STATUS. See also KANTIAN ETHICS and CONSEQUENTIALISM. Chapter 2; 32–34.

Descriptive/philosophical ethics. The study of MORALITY. It is descriptive ethics when devoted to facts about morality and philosophical when focused on the evaluation of conduct and moral character. See also APPLIED/GENERAL NORMATIVE ETHICS. Chapter 1; 10–11.

Descriptive/normative relativism. The view that moral right and wrong are relative, for example, to culture. Descriptive relativism notes that some moral beliefs vary radically among human societies. Normative relativism adds the claim that some radically different moral beliefs can all be correct. Chapter 2; 21–23.

Designer babies. Infants whose genetic makeups have been manipulated to endow them with traits deemed advantageous or pleasing within a family or larger group. Not yet a scientifically feasible scenario. See also PROCREATIVE BENEFICENCE and HUMAN GENETIC ENHANCEMENT. Chapter 15; 288–292.

Direct/indirect duty. A duty is direct if owed to a being with MORAL STANDING, and indirect if owed to a being that lacks moral standing because fulfilling it would affect another being with moral standing. Chapter 2, 9, 16; 34, 184, 311–313.

Ethical imperialism. The attempt to impose one's own culturally determined ethical values or rules on people from other cultures. Chapter 17; 340 ff.

Ethics committee. Interdisciplinary body charged with advising hospital health care professionals and administrators about cases and policies that raise moral issues. See also INSTITUTIONAL REVIEW BOARD. Chapter 1, 5; 8, 106–107.

Eugenics. The genetic manipulation of organisms to improve their makeups—in modern eugenics, by individual choice of GENETIC ENGINEERING; in early eugenics, by state-mandated policies of sterilization and elimination of people with traits deemed 'undesirable.' Chapter 15; 280, 284–287.

Euthanasia. Type of PHYSICIAN-ASSISTED DYING consisting in the intentional killing of a patient for her own good—for example, to spare her severe suffering or loss of autonomy at life's end. See also PASSIVE/ACTIVE EUTHANAISA and VOLUNTARY/NONVOLUNTARY/INVOLUNTARY EUTHANASIA. Chapter 8; 156–163.

Evaluation. NORMATIVE JUDGMENT ascribing morally positive or negative features to things, including persons, situations, practices, and policies. Appendix A; 377–378.

Expressivist Argument. Objection to PREIMPLANTATION GENETIC DIAGNOSIS on the grounds that it allows the selection for fertilization of embryos without genetic disease, thereby implicitly devaluing the lives of disabled people. Chapter 15; 282–283.

Extended argument. ARGUMENT with more than one conclusion. Appendix A; 381–382.

Fair Equality of Opportunity Account. Normal Daniels's application of Rawls's principles of JUSTICE to health care. See also LIBERAL JUSTICE. Chapter 18; 366–368.

Fertility therapy. A NEW REPRODUCTIVE TECHNOLOGY that uses ovulation-induction drugs to stimulate production of eggs beyond the usual one per month. Chapter 14; 261–263, 265 ff.

Fetal abuse. See FETAL HARM.

Fetal defect. Anomaly in fetal development associated with early death or CONGENITAL DISORDERS. Chapter 12; 225–232.

Fetal harm. Injury to the fetus caused by the mother's life-style (e.g., drug or alcohol use) or medical choices during pregnancy (e.g., a refusal of medically indicated treatment). Chapter 13; 239 ff.

Forgoing treatment. The deliberate withholding, withdrawing, or nonescalating of medical treatment, especially LIFE-SUSTAINING TREATMENT. Chapter 7; 136–148.

Formal/material principle of justice. The formal principle of JUSTICE requires an impartial evaluation of cases, recommending to treat the like cases alike, and the unlike cases differently. What similarities and differences between cases are relevant is the content of material principles of justice. See also DISTRIBUTIVE JUSTICE. Chapter 18; 350–351.

Four-principles approach. A type of PRINCIPLISM that regards RESPECT FOR AUTONOMY, NONMALEFICENCE, BENEFICENCE, and JUSTICE as basic PRIMA FACIE DUTIES of health care providers. Chapter 3; 53–63.

Futility. The property of an intervention that can produce either no benefits for the patient or exceedingly poor ones. Chapter 7; 142–145.

Future-Like-Ours Argument. Don Marquis's attempt to substantiate the claim that ABORTION is morally impermissible because it deprives the fetus of a future of value. Chapter 11; 212–214.

Gene therapy. Negative GENETIC ENGINEERING aiming at treating or preventing genetic disease. In somatic gene therapy, genetic alterations are not inherited by offspring; in germline therapy they are. Chapter 17; 290, 335–337.

General ethics. See APPLIED/GENERAL ETHICS.

Genetic Determinism. The view that all risk factors for diseases and disorders reduce to genetic endowment. See also ENVIRONMENTAL DETERMINISM. Chapter 4; 83–85, 88.

Genetic discrimination. A bias against people with a genetic predisposition to congenital disease which may affect them socially or lower their eligibility for employment or health insurance. See also GENETIC IGNORANCE. Chapter 17; 330.

Genetic engineering. The direct manipulation of an organism's genes to alter them in a controlled way. It is negative when it aims at treating or preventing a genetic disorder, and positive when it seeks GENETIC ENHANCEMENT. Chapter 15; 277 ff.

Genetic ignorance. The right to refuse knowledge of one's own genetic makeup. Chapter 4; 84–87.

Genetic/gestational/intended motherhood. Terms introduced to designate, respectively, the egg donor who is the biological mother of an offspring, the carrier or birth mother, and the woman on behalf of whom the child is conceived. See also SURROGACY and NEW REPRODUCTIVE TECHNOLOGIES. Chapter 14; 266–267.

Good Samaritan Argument. Judith Thomson's attempt to substantiate the claim that ABORTION is morally permissible even if the fetus is a PERSON with a right to life. Chapter 11; 216–217.

Groningen protocol. Dutch regulation for NEONATAL EUTHANASIA. Used since 2005, this regulation includes safeguards such as certainty about the infant's compromised condition, parental consent, and a confirming second opinion. Chapter 9; 184–185.

Hard cases of abortion. ABORTION for special reasons such as SEX SELECTION, rape, FETAL DEFECTS, and endangerment of the mother's life or health. See also TYPICAL CASE OF ABORTION. Chapter 11, 12; 205, 225–235.

Hard/soft paternalism. In clinical practice, the view that medical professionals should make decisions for the patient according to their own understanding of her best interests. Paternalism is hard when the patient has substantial COMPETENCE, and soft when she has diminished competence. Chapter 3; 63–64.

Hastening death. The deliberate shortening of a patient's life by withdrawing, withholding, or nonescalating LIFE-SUSTAINING TREATMENT. Chapter 7, 8, 9; 145, 156–157, 181 ff.

Hierarchical View. The doctrine that animals' MORAL STANDING varies according to their degree of psychological capacity. Only the more intelligent animals are likely to have a right to life. See also ANIMAL-WELFARE and ANIMAL–RIGHTS VIEWS. Chapter 16; 306–307.

Hippocratic medicine. The practice of medicine according to ancient ethical rules ascribed to Hippocrates of Kos. Chapter 1, 4; Appendix A, B; 4 ff., 75–76, 78, 167, 377, 386–388.

Hubristic Motivation. An objection to HUMAN GENETIC ENHANCEMENT based on a smug disposition of 'mastering' birth that such enhancement allegedly expresses. See also DESIGNER BABIES. Chapter 15; 284, 291–292.

Human genetic enhancement. Also known as 'positive GENETIC ENGINEERING,' the manipulation of an organism's genes to enhance its genetic makeup. Chapter 15; 287 ff.

Human Genome Project. The mapping of the entire sequence of human DNA, completed in 2003. Chapter 4; 82.

Human-property criterion. THE CRITERION OF PERSONHOOD that membership of *Homo sapiens* is sufficient for being a PERSON. Chapter 10; 197.

Human reproductive cloning . Not yet attempted for human reproduction, the creation of a human clone that may one day proceed by either injecting the DNA of a donor cell, or fusing the entire cell into an enucleated egg. See also SURROGACY and IN-VITRO FERTILIZA-TION. Chapter 15; 280, 283–284.

Humanism. The view that, unlike sexism or racism, SPECIESISM is morally justified. Chapter 16; 309–310.

Hyde Amendment. A US 1976 law mandating that institutions may not use federal resources, such as Medicaid, for ABORTION except in cases of rape, incest, or threat to the woman's life. Chapter 13; 247–249.

Inductive argument. See DEDUCTIVE/INDUCTIVE ARGUMENT. Appendix A; 379.

Inductive reliability. A virtue of any INDUCTIVE ARGUMENT whose form is such that, if its premises are true, its conclusion is likely to be true. Appendix A; 379.

Inductive strength. The virtue of any INDUCTIVE ARGUMENT with true premises and INDUCTIVE RELIABILITY. Appendix A; 379.

Informed consent. A patient's autonomous authorization for biomedical interventions or research. See also PATIENT AUTONOMY. Chapter 2, 3, 5; 28, 62, 92 ff.

Innocent/guilty threat. Objection to the claim that women's RIGHT TO SELF-DEFENSE justifies ABORTION. It contends that, unlike guilty threats, the fetus in a life-endangering pregnancy is an innocent threat. Chapter 12; 228.

Institutional review board. In biomedical research involving human subjects, body of ethicists and expert reviewers charged with oversight. It aims at ensuring a study's conformity with established regulations and ethical guidelines concerning the protection and respect owed to subjects. See also ETHICS COMMITTEE. Chapter 17; 324.

Intensive-care protocol for preemies. Regulation enacted to determine which PREEMIES receive critical care, including resuscitation, and which don't. It may be a do-everything, a statistical, or an initiate-and-reevaluate protocol. See also HASTENING DEATH and NEO-NATAL EUTHANASIA. Chapter 9; 181–184.

Interest. A stake that can be advanced or set back. See also INTERESTS VIEW. Chapter 11; 219.

Interests View. The doctrine that abortion is morally permissible until the point of development where fetuses acquire the capacity for SENTIENCE. At that point, they acquire some MORAL STANDING because they have INTERESTS. Chapter 11; 219–220.

In-vitro fertilization. A treatment to assist conception by creating embryos in a lab's petri dish. See also NEW REPRODUCTIVE TECHNOLOGIES. Chapter 14; 258–261, 265.

Justice. The duty to treat persons rightly, as they deserve, according to what is owed or due to them. See also DISTRIBUTIVE JUSTICE. Chapter 18; 345 ff.

Kantian ethics. MONIST DEONTOLOGY taking the moral law or CATEGORICAL IMPERATIVE to determine right conduct for any rational being. Chapter 2; 32–34.

Killing/letting die. A proposed moral distinction between letting a patient die by allowing nature to take its course, which is permissible, and actively killing her, which is not. See also END-OF-LIFE MEASURE. Chapter 8, 9; 160, 185.

Kind Essentialism. The view that fetuses, like other members of the natural kind *Homo sapiens*, have some essential property, such as the potential for being rational, which renders ABORTION morally forbidden. Chapter 11; 211.

Late-term abortion. ABORTION after week 24. Chapter 12; 234–235.

Life-sustaining treatment. Any life-saving or -prolonging medical intervention. Chapter 7; 136–142, 147–148.

Liberal justice. A set of theories of social JUSTICE best illustrated by utilitarian justice and John Rawls's egalitarian conception of justice as fairness. They respectively take the just action to be the one that maximizes the welfare of all concerned, or the one that distributes social goods fairly for the self-advancement of all individuals, especially of the worst-off in society. See also LIBERTARIAN JUSTICE. Chapter 18; 352.

Libertarian justice. A set of theories of social JUSTICE taking the just action to be the one that results from the acquisition and exchange of property under free-market conditions whereby all parties to the transactions participate voluntarily. See also LIBERAL JUSTICE. Chapter 18; 352.

Life worth living. A life of a quality above the threshold of being acceptable to the person whose life it is. Chapter 7, 14; 144, 264–265.

Medical confidentiality. The rule that patient information must not be disclosed beyond what's agreed. See also PRIVACY and RESPECT FOR AUTONOMY. Chapter 4; 71 ff.

Medical deception. A health care provider's failure of DISCLOSURE by lying (i.e., presenting as true what the caregiver considers false), misleading (i.e., letting the patient believe what the caregiver knows is false), NONDISCLOSURE, or UNDER-DISCLOSURE. Chapter 4; 77–78.

Metaethics . The philosophy of ETHICS. Chapter 1; 12, 15.

Missing premise. An ARGUMENT's implicit premise that must be made explicit in argument evaluation. Appendix A; 381–382.

Monism. Unlike PLURALISM, any moral theory grounding the rightness of actions in a single value or rule of conduct. Chapter 2; 26, 27, 32, 46.

Moral agent. Anyone with the capacity to reason and act intentionally. See also PERSON. Chapter 1; 12, 14–15.

Moral discernment. An intuitive apprehension of the morally relevant features of a case. Chapter 2; 42–43, 44.

Moral exemplar . In VIRTUE ETHICS, a virtuous person whose character one should emulate to learn how to live one's life well. Chapter 2; 35–37.

Moral judgment. A NORMATIVE JUDGMENT concerning what to do or believe morally. Appendix A; 377–378.

Moral norm . See MORAL RULE.

Moral rule. Called also 'principle' and 'norm,' a PRESCRIPTION with the NORMATIVE FORCE of either prohibiting, requiring, discouraging, encouraging, or allowing a certain act or omission. Appendix A; 380.

Moral skepticism. In applied ethics, a view questioning the validity of certain moral values or rules. In general normative ethics, a view that challenges the universality of moral values or rules, and is llustrated in this book by RELATIVISM. To be contrasted with ABSOLUTISM and UNIVERSALISM. Chapter 2, 4, 5, 11, 16; 22, 75–76, 99, 214–215, 310–312

Moral standing. The intrinsic moral importance of a thing, sometimes called 'moral status,' 'moral worth,' and 'dignity' (for humans). See also PERSON and NONPARADIGM PERSON. Chapter 1, 16; 14, 306 ff.

Morality. In a descriptive sense, the set of rules of right conduct accepted by an individual or group, usually for the purpose of governing social practices. In a normative sense, rules of conduct distinguished from mere conventional rules by their being more universal, objective, and authoritative. See also COMMON MORALITY. Chapter 1; 10 ff.

Natalism. The prejudice that people should procreate. See also PROCREATIVE FREEDOM. Chapter 14; 271.

Natural law theory. Moral theory based on four absolute values: life, knowledge, procreation, and sociability. Appeals to the PRINCIPLE OF DOUBLE EFFECT for resolving conflicts among those values. Chapter 2; 25–27.

Negative/positive right. The RIGHTS of noninterference with the right-holder are negative; the rights to be provided with something are positive. See also CORRELATIVITY THESIS. Chapter 4, 8, 18; 74, 77, 167, 362 ff.

Neonatal euthanasia. EUTHANASIA of a newborn. See also GRONINGEN PROTOCOL. Chapter 9; 181, 184–186.

New reproductive technology. A set of medical interventions designed to assist reproduction. See also EGG DONATION, IN-VITRO FERTILIZATION, SURROGACY, and FERTILITY THERAPY. Chapter 14; 259 ff.

Nondirective genetic counseling. Genetic counseling that aims at being value neutral. See also GENETIC DISCRIMINATION and GENETIC IGNORANCE. Chapter 4; 84, 89.

Nondisclosure. A health care provider's failure of DISCLOSURE consisting in omitting to reveal to patients known facts relevant to their conditions. See also UNDER-DISCLOSURE. Chapter 4; 77–78, 87.

Nonidentity Problem. The problem of determining whether a person has been harmed by being born disabled as a result of a pregnancy knowingly associated with a high rate of disability, even when she has a LIFE WORTH LIVING. Chapter 14, 15; 264–265, 279–280.

Nonmaleficence. The health care provider's duty to avoid inflicting needless harm on patients, a basic principle of the FOUR-PRINCIPLES APPROACH. Chapter 3; 54 ff.

Nonparadigm person. Any individual whose MORAL STANDING as a PERSON is open to question because she is either too young or too cognitively impaired. Chapter 1; 14–15.

Normative force. The aspect of an expression that makes it a PRESCRIPTION or an EVALUATION. It may be MORAL, legal, prudential, or conventional, among other types. See also NORMATIVE JUDGMENT. Chapter 1; 12, 15.

Normative judgment. Judgment that goes beyond merely describing facts owing to its having NORMATIVE FORCE. Appendix A; 375–376.

Ordinary/extraordinary means. A distinction designed to justify FORGOING TREATMENTS that amount to extraordinary or disproportionate measures but not those that amount to ordinary or proportionate measures. See also LIFE-SUSTAINING TREATMENT. Chapter 7; 148–150.

Oregon's Death with Dignity Act. A 1997 Oregon law permitting PHYSICIAN-ASSISTED SUICIDE for terminally ill, eligible adults. See also EUTHANASIA and PHYSICIAN-ASSISTED DYING. Chapter 8; 163–164.

Organ-procurement problem. A problem until THE UNIFORM DETERMINATION OF DEATH ACT of 1980 for procuring organs from donors who were BRAIN DEAD but not dead according to the prevailing CARDIOPULMONARY-DEATH criterion. See also DEAD DONOR RULE. Chapter 6; 122–123, 127, 129, 131.

Organismic death. The biological sciences' definition of death that takes it to consist, for any living organism, in the permanent loss of its bodily integrative functions. Chapter 6; 118–119, 127–128.

Organized-Cortical-Activity Argument. David Boonin's attempt to substantiate the claim that abortion becomes morally impermissible with the fetal development of organized cortical activity. Chapter 11; 218–219.

Over-inclusiveness. A view counting as PERSONS any beings that fail to qualify as such. See also CRITERION OF PERSONHOOD and UNDER-INCLUSIVENESS. Chapter 10, 11; 197–198, 201, 211, 220.

Paradigm case. In CASUISTRY, an already decided case about which there is consensus. Chapter 3; 64.

Paradigm person. See PERSON and NONPARADIGM PERSON.

Parental choice. Decisionmaking standards for children based on what their parents want. Chapter 5; 105 ff.

Partial Birth Abortion Ban Act. Legislation passed by the US Congress in 2003 banning the late-term abortion procedure known as 'D&X.' Chapter 12, 13; 235, 246–247, 253.

Particularism. A challenge to traditional moral theories that invoke general PRINCIPLES of right conduct. Holds that, unlike general principles, MORAL DISCERNMENT can explain an action's DEONTIC STATUS and be action guiding. Chapter 2; 43–44, 45.

Passive/active euthanasia. EUTHANASIA is passive when health care providers remove death-postponing treatments, and active when they directly and intentionally induce a patient's death. Chapter 8; 156, 158–163, 166, 169.

Patient autonomy. A patient's right to make self-regarding decisions about medical treatment without interference by others. It correlates with the health care providers' duty of RESPECT FOR AUTONOMY. Chapter 3; 53–57, 62 ff.

Patient choice. Robert Veatch's alternative to INFORMED CONSENT. It requires that patients be informed of either all treatment options with a summary of benefits and risks, or the caregivers' deep values. Chapter 5; 95, 99.

Patient Protection and Affordable Care Act . Known informally as 'Obamacare,' the 2010 health care reform advocated and signed into law by President Barack Obama whereby the US adopted a MULTI-PAYER SYSTEM of health coverage. See also SINGLE-PAYER SYSTEM. Chapter 18; 364–365.

Permanent vegetative state. A disorder of CONSCIOUSNESS consisting in the lack of awareness that becomes permanent after a year for traumatic injury and after three months for nontraumatic injury. Chapter 6, 7; 125, 139 ff.

Person. Any being with full MORAL STANDING. Killing a person is commonly a serious moral wrong. See also CRITERIA OF PERSONHOOD. Chapter 1, 10; 14, 194 ff.

Physician-assisted dying. END-OF-LIFE MEASURE consisting of either PHYSICIAN-ASSISTED SUICIDE or EUTHANASIA. Chapter 8; 155 ff.

Physician-assisted suicide. Type of PHYSICIAN-ASSISTED DYING wherein the patient self-administers a lethal agent prescribed by the physician. See also OREGON'S DEATH WITH DIGNITY ACT. Chapter 8; 156–57, 161–164.

Pluralism. Unlike monism, any moral theory grounding the rightness of actions in more than one value or rule of conduct. Chapter 2; 26, 42, 45.

Posthuman. Hypothetical descendants of humans with genetically enhanced powers or capabilities. See also HUMAN GENETIC ENHANCEMENT. Chapter 15; 287 ff.

Postmenopausal pregnancy. Pregnancies by women in their 50s and older who wish to bear a child but can no longer use their eggs for fertilization. Pregnancy is achieved by means of NEW REPRODUCTIVE TECHNOLOGIES, such as EGG DONATION and IN-VITRO FERTILIZATION. Chapter 14; 265–267.

Precautionary principle. The injunction that GENETIC ENGINEERING of organisms should not be attempted without sound evidence that its potential benefits can outweigh bad outcomes. It is particularly concerned with the positive (i.e., nontherapeutic) genetic engineering of organisms that can be passed on to offspring. Chapter 15; 290.

Preemie. A neonate at risk of death or severe disability by being born at week 32 of gestation or earlier. Chapter 9; 178 ff.

Preimplantation genetic diagnosis. A procedure originally designed to detect genetic anomalies in embryos created by IN-VITRO FERTILIZATION before their transfer to the woman's uterus. Chapter 15; 278, 280–283.

Prematurity. The condition of PREEMIES. Chapter 9; 178 ff.

Prescription. NORMATIVE JUDGMENT recommending actions or policies as obligatory, forbidden, or optional. See also DEONTIC STATUS. Appendix A; 376.

Principle . See MORAL RULE.

Principle of double effect. The rule that an action violating NATURAL LAW THEORY's basic values is justified provided its good effect is great enough to outweigh the bad effect and the latter is only foreseen and neither intended nor a means to the good effect. Chapter 2; 26–27.

Principle of utility. A rule taking an action's DEONTIC STATUS to depend on whether it maximizes or diminishes the total balance of happiness over suffering. Chapter 2; 29.

Principlism. In BIOETHICS, any approach recommending some general moral principles as action guides and explanations of the DEONTIC STATUS of medical interventions. See also the FOUR-PRINCIPLES APPROACH. Chapter 3; 53–64.

Priority setting. Health policy determining the distribution of a medical treatment among patients with competing claims of need or the distribution of funding among competing health care programs. Chapter 18; 347, 349 ff.

Privacy. The rule that patients control access to their own health care information. See also MEDICAL CONFIDENTIALITY. Chapter 4; 70, 72.

Problem of Multiples. An objection to some NEW REPRODUCTIVE TECHNOLOGIES based on the high rates of multiple births associated with them. See also IN-VITRO FERTILIZATION and FERTILITY THERAPY. Chapter 14; 261–264.

Procreative Beneficence. The principle that parents should select the child that, given the available information, could have either the best life or at least a life as good as that of any other possible child. See also DESIGNER BABIES and HUMAN GENETIC ENHANCEMENT. Chapter 15; 289–290, 293,

Procreative freedom. People's RIGHT to make, or INTEREST in making, self-regarding reproductive decisions, including avoiding reproduction. Chapter 14; 261, 268, 271.

Proxy consent. Surrogate INFORMED CONSENT. Chapter 5, 17; 101 ff., 323, 332, 341.

Psychological-property criterion. Any CRITERION OF PERSONHOOD holding that possession of one or more psychological capacities typical of PERSONS is sufficient to be a PERSON. Chapter 10; 196–198.

Quality-adjusted life year (QALY). A measure of a person's or group's state of health that adjusts life expectancy to reflect quality of life. A year of perfect health yields 1 QALY, a year of partial health yields less than 1 QALY, and death yields 0 QALY. Chapter18; 355–358.

Randomized clinical trial. Trial (e.g., of a new drug) that allocates subjects by chance alone in either an experimental or a control group. See also RANDOMIZED-CLINICAL-TRIAL DILEMMA. Chapter 17; 326, 332 ff.

Randomized-clinical-trial dilemma. A puzzle for investigators who in a clinical trial should both act in the subjects' best interests (as medical professionals) and disregard their interests (as investigators). Chapter 17; 332 ff.

Rationing. Any arrangement that limits people's access to certain goods or services. Chapter 18; 345, 353 ff.

Relativism. See DESCRIPTIVE/NORMATIVE RELATIVISM.

Reflective equilibrium. A type of justification seeking to bring moral principles and intuitions about cases into accord by revising either the principles or the intuitions when conflict arises. See also COMMON MORALITY. Appendix A; 380–381.

Research bias. A pattern of error in the design, evaluation, or report of a biomedical study. Chapter 17; 333–334.

Rescue intervention. Any medical intervention to save or prolong a person's life, thereby postponing death. Chapter 18; 353, 356, 358, 360.

Respect for Autonomy. In clinical practice, the health care provider's duty to honor patient self-determination. As a NEGATIVE DUTY, it requires noninterference with the competent patient's self-regarding, medical decisions. As a POSITIVE DUTY, it requires taking steps to facilitate such decisions. See also PATIENT AUTONOMY. Chapter 3; 54–57.

Right. A strong moral claim that others must honor. See also CORRELATIVITY THESIS and NEGATIVE/POSITIVE RIGHT. Chapter 18; 347, 349, 352–353, 362 ff.

Right to die. A contested RIGHT of patients to control the circumstances of their death whenever possible. See also PATIENT AUTONOMY. Chapter 8; 166.

Right to self-defense. Often invoked by ABORTION DEFENDERS in life-endangering pregnancies, a person's RIGHT to use deadly force in response to an aggressor's threat of death or serious bodily harm, especially when there is no other way to deflect the attack. See also INNOCENT/GUILTY THREAT. Chapter 12; 228, 234.

Rossian ethics. Pluralist DEONTOLOGY of prima facie DUTIES. These are other-things-being-equal duties. A prima facie duty becomes an agent's actual duty in a situation where it either is her sole prima facie duty or outweighs other of her prima facie duties. Chapter 2; 40–41.

Terminal sedation. END-OF-LIFE MEASURE consisting of sedation to unconsciousness until the patient dies. It may hasten death, especially when combined with forgoing artificial nutrition and hydration. Chapter 8; 156–157, 169.

Therapeutic abortion. Any ABORTION for fetal defects, endangerment of the mother's life or health, or to prevent the birth of a child conceived as a result of rape or incest. Chapter 11, 12; 206, 226 ff.

Therapeutic privilege. An exception to INFORMED CONSENT and DISCLOSURE allowing health care professionals to withhold information they think harmful to the patient. Chapter 5; 98–99.

Therapeutic/nontherapeutic research. Therapeutic research is that having the potential to bring health benefits to participants, while nontherapeutic research may bring health benefits only to individuals other than the subjects. Chapter 17; 326.

Typical cases of abortion. ABORTION before week 24 for no such special reasons. See also HARD CASES OF ABORTION. Chapter 11; 205 ff.

Under-disclosure. A failure of DISCLOSURE by withholding some relevant facts about a patient's health while revealing others. See also NONDISCLOSURE and MEDICAL DECEPTION. Chapter 4; 77–78.

Under-inclusiveness. Any view that fails to count as PERSONS some beings that are persons. See also CRITERION OF PERSONHOOD and OVER-INCLUSIVENESS. Chapter 10; 197–1998.

Uniform Determination of Death Act. US legislation of 1980 sanctioning a disjunctive criterion of death according to which a patient is dead after the irreversible loss of function in either the heart and lungs or the entire brain. Chapter 6; 123.

Unilateral-decision problem. A problem most felt in the 1960s and 70s when health care providers could not legally discontinue LIFE-SUSTAINING TREATMENT for BRAIN-DEAD patients, who were not dead according to the prevailing CARDIOPULMONARY DEATH standard. See also ORGAN-PROCUREMENT PROBLEM. Chapter 6; 122, 127.

Universalism. Any view regarding some moral rule or value as valid universally, though with possible exceptions. It contrasts with ABSOLUTISM and MORAL SKEPTICISM about those rules or values. Chapter 4; 75–76.

Utilitarianism. A set of consequentialist theories taking the right action to be one that either directly produces the best outcome among alternatives for all affected by it (act utilitarianism), or exemplifies a moral rule whose application, over time, produces it for all affected if nearly everyone follows it (rule utilitarianism). See also PRINCIPLE OF UTILITY. Chapter 2; 27–32, 38, 45.

Valid refusal. A patient's refusal of treatment meeting all requirements of INFORMED CONSENT. Chapter 5; 95.

Validity. The good-making feature of a DEDUCTIVE ARGUMENT whose premises necessitate its conclusion, in the sense that if the premises are true, the conclusion cannot be false. See also SOUNDNESS. Appendix A; 379.

Veracity. Truth-telling. See also DISCLOSURE. Chapter 2, 4; 23, 77–78.

Very low birthweight. Neonate weighing 1,500 grams (3lb, 3oz) or less. Chapter 9; 179–180.

Vice. By contrast with VIRTUE, a bad trait of character. See also VIRTUE ETHICS and DOCTRINE OF THE MEAN. Chapter 2; 35.

Virtue. By contrast with VICE, a good trait of character. See also VIRTUE ETHICS and DOCTRINE OF THE MEAN. Chapter 2; 35 ff.

Virtue ethics. As early developed by Aristotle, a pluralist theory focused on the moral character needed for achieving a good life. Chapter 2; 34–37.

Vivisection. Risky or painful research on animals for the benefit, mostly, of humans, the environment, or animals other than the research subjects. Chapter 16; 301, 311.

Voluntary/nonvoluntary/involuntary euthanasia. Euthanasia is voluntary when the patient has consented to it, nonvoluntary when the patient lacks competence either to give or to withhold consent, and involuntary when the patient is competent but has not given consent. Chapter 8; 157–161.

Vulnerable population. Any group of people whose members, owing to their comparative disadvantage, are susceptible to undue influence or coercion in making medical decisions or enrolling in biomedical research. Chapter 17; 320–321; 341.

Wrongful-birth/wrongful-life action. Litigation sometimes brought against health care providers by a disabled person or guardian alleging that her birth with a disability (wrongful birth) or the fact that she was born *at all* into a life of suffering (wrongful life) could have been prevented by proper medical care and advice before or during pregnancy. Chapter 12; 231–232.

Index of Cases

Additional References[1]

Airedale NHS Trust v Bland, 1 All ER 821 (1993).

Allen, A. L., "Abortion: Legal and Regulatory Issues," in Post 2004, pp. 18–28.

Allen, M., "How Many Die from Medical Mistakes in US Hospitals?" *Scientific American*, 9/20/2013. Available online at http://www.scientificamerican.com/article/how-many-die-from-medical-mistakes-in-us-hospitals/.

American College of Obstetricians and Gynecologists, "The Limits of Conscientious Refusal in Reproductive Medicine," Committee on Ethics No. 385, 2007. Available online at http://www.acog.org/Resources-And-Publications/Committee-Opinions/Committee-on-Ethics/The-Limits-of-Conscientious-Refusal-in-Reproductive-Medicine.

———, Code of Ethics, Opinion 2.201, "Sedation to Unconsciousness in End-of-Life Care." Available online at http://www.ama-assn.org/ama/pub/physician-resources/medical-ethics/code-medical-ethics/opinion2201.page.

American Medical Association, *Code of Medical Ethics: Current Opinions with Annotations*, 2012–2013, Chicago, IL, 2012.

Anderson, E., "Is Women's Labor a Commodity?" *Philosophy & Public Affairs* 19.1, 1990: 71–92.

"Anencephaly: A Devastating Abnormality," *The Durango Herald*, 2/26/2012. Available online at http://durangoherald.com/article/20120227/COLUMNISTS16/702279991.

Applbaum, A. I., J. C. Tilburt, M. T. Collins, and D. Wendler, "A Family's Request for Complementary Medicine after Patient Brain Death," *JAMA* 299.18, 2008: 2188–93.

Aristotle, *Nicomachean Ethics*. Translated by R. Crisp, Cambridge: Cambridge University Press, 2000.

Arras, J. D., "A Case Approach," in Kuhse and Singer 2012, pp. 117–25.

Arras, J. D., E. Fenton, and R. Kukla, *Routledge Companion to Bioethics*. New York: Routledge, 2015.

"ART Success Rates: Latest Data, 2013," Centers for Disease Control and Prevention, 2015. Available online at http://www.cdc.gov/art/artdata/index.html.

Asch, A. and A. Stubblefield, "Growth Attenuation: Good intentions, Bad Decision," *American Journal of Bioethics* 10.1, 2010: 46–8.

Ashcroft, R., "Death Policy in the United Kingdom," in Blank and Merrick 2005, pp.197–219.

Ashcroft, R., A. Lucassen, M. Parker, M. Verkerk, and G. Widdershoven, *Case Analysis in Clinical Ethics*. Cambridge: Cambridge University Press, 2005.

"The Ashley Treatment," *Pillow Angel*. Available online at http://pillowangel.org/Ashley%20Treatment.pdf.

Aulisio, M. P., R. M. Arnold, and S. J. Youngner, eds., *Ethics Consultation: From Theory to Practice*. Baltimore: Johns Hopkins University Press, 2003.

Bakalar, N., "Magnets Fail to Relieve Arthritis Pain," *The New York Times*, 9/24/2013.

Baker, R. B. and L. B. McCullough, *Cambridge World History of Medical Ethics*. Cambridge: Cambridge University Press, 2009.

Barber v Superior Court, 22 Ill.147 Cal.App.3d 1006, 195 Cal. Rptr. 484 (Ct. App. 1983).

Barry, S., "Quality of Life and Myelomeningocele: An Ethical and Evidence-Based Analysis of the Groningen Protocol," *Pediatric Neurosurgery* 46, 2010: 409–14.

Battin, M., R. Rhodes, and A. Silvers, eds., *Physician Assisted Suicide: Expanding the Debate*. New York: Routledge, 1998.

Baumrin, B., "Physician, Stay Thy Hand!" in Battin et al. 1998, pp.177–81.

Beauchamp, T. L., and J. F. Childress, *Principles of Biomedical Ethics*. 6th ed. New York: Oxford University Press, 2009.

Belkin, L., "The Made-to-Order Savior," *The New York Times Magazine*, 1/7/2001.

Berenson, A., "Pinning Down the Money Value of a Person's Life," *The New York Times*, 6/11/2007.

---

1 For other references, see "Suggested Readings" at the end of each chapter.

Berman v Allan, 80 N.J. 421, 404 A2D 8 (1979).

Bernat, J. L., "There Can Be Agreement as to What Constitutes Human Death," in Caplan and Arp 2014, pp. 377–87.

Bernat, J. L., C. M. Culver, and B. Gert, "On the Definition and Criterion of Death," *Annals of Internal Medicine* 94, 1981: 389–94.

Beyene, Y., "Medical Disclosure and Refugees: Telling Bad News to Ethiopian Patients," *The Western Journal of Medicine* 157.3, 1992: 328–33.

Blackmun, H., "Majority Opinion in *Roe v. Wade*," United States Supreme Court, 1973. 410 US 113, 93.

Blank, R. H. and J. C. Merrick, eds., *End-of-Life Decision Making: A Cross-National Study*. Cambridge: MIT Press, 2005.

Boonin, D., *A Defense of Abortion*. Cambridge: Cambridge University Press, 2003.

Bouvia v Superior Court, 225 Cal Rptr297 (Cal App 2 Dist) C7 (1986).

BMA, "Conference Report on Physician Assisted Suicide: A Conference to Promote Consensus," March 3–4 2000. Available at http://www.cmq.org.uk/CMQ/2000/BMA_PAS_conference.htm.

———, "Ethics: A to Z," created 5/8/2012, updated 4/12/2016. Available at https://www.bma.org.uk/advice/employment/ethics/ethics-a-to-z.

Brock, D. W., "The Non-Identity Problem and Genetic Harms: The Case of Wrongful Handicaps," *Bioethics* 9.3/4, 1995: 269–75.

———, "Medical Decisions at the End of Life," in Kuhse and Singer 2012, pp. 263–73.

Brock, D. and A. Buchanan, *Deciding For Others: The Ethics of Surrogate Decisionmaking*. Cambridge: Cambridge University Press, 1989.

Brody, B. A., *Abortion and the Sanctity of Human Life: A Philosophical View*. Cambridge: MIT Press, 1975.

Brody, B. A. and H. T. Engelhardt, *Bioethics: Readings and Cases*. Englewood Cliffs, NJ: Prentice-Hall, 1987.

Bruni, F., "The Cruelest Pregnancy," *The New York Times*, 1/19/2014.

Buchanan, A. and D. Brock, *Deciding for Others: The Ethics of Surrogate Decision Making*. Cambridge: Cambridge University Press, 1989.

Buck v Bell, 274 US 200 (1927).

Calandrillo, S. P. and C. V. Deliganis, "In Vitro Fertilization and the Law: How Legal and Regulatory Neglect Compromised a Medical Breakthrough," *Arizona Law Review* 57.2, 2015: 311–42.

Campbell, A., "A Virtue-ethics Approach," in Ashcroft et al. 2005, pp. 45–56.

Canterbury v Spence, District of Columbia Cir., 464 F2d 772 (1972).

Caplan, A., "Is 'Peter Pan' Treatment a Moral Choice?" *CBS News*, 1/5/2007.

Caplan, A. L. and R. Arp, *Contemporary Debates in Bioethics*. Oxford: Wiley Blackwell, 2014.

Capron, A.M., "Historical Overview: Law and Public Perception," in Lynn 1986, pp. 11–20.

———, "Baby Ryan and Virtual Futility," *Hastings Center Report* 25.2, 1995: 20.

———, "Punishing Mothers," *Hastings Center Report* 28.1, 1998: 31–3.

Carey, B., "Science under Scrutiny," *The New York Times*, 6/16/2015.

Carrese J. and L. Rhodes, "Western Bioethics on the Navajo Reservation: Benefit or Harm?" *JAMA* 274.10, 1995: 826–9.

Carruthers, P., *The Animals Issue: Moral Theory in Practice*. Cambridge: Cambridge University Press, 1992.

Center for Behavioral Health Statistics and Quality, "Results from the 2013 National Survey on Drug Use and Health: Summary of National Findings," *US Department of Health and Human Services*. Available online at http://www.samhsa.gov/data/sites/default/files/NSDUHresultsPDFWHTML2013/Web/NSDUHresults2013.htm.

Center for Disease Control and Prevention, "Abortion Surveillance — United States, 2010." Available online at http://www.cdc.gov/mmwr/preview/mmwrhtml/ss6208a1.htm?s_cid=ss6208a1_w.

Center for the History of Medicine, "Eugenics Legislation," *The Harvard Library*, 2015. Available online at https://collections.countway.harvard.edu/onview/exhibits/show/galtonschildren/eugenics-legislation.

Chiong, W., "Brain Death without Definitions," *Hastings Center Report* 35.6, 2005: 20–30.

———, "There Can Be Agreement as to What Constitutes Human Death," in Caplan and Arp 2014, pp. 388–98.

Cohen, A. I. and C. H. Wellman, *Contemporary Debates in Applied Ethics*. Oxford: Wiley Blackwell, 2005.

Cohen, C., "Give Me Children or I Shall Die!" *Hastings Center Report* 26.2, 1996: 19–27.

Conference of the Medical Royal Colleges, "Diagnosis of Brain Death," *British Medical Journal* 2, 1976: 1187–8.

———, "Diagnosis of death," *British Medical Journal* 1, 1979: 332.

Copp, D., ed., *Oxford Handbook of Ethical Theory*. Oxford: Oxford University Press, 2006.

Court of Appeal Report for 1997. New Zealand. Available online at https://www.courtsofnz.govt.nz/from/judicial-reports/documents/CourtofAppealReport1997.PDF.

Crasnow, S., A.Wylie, W. K. Bauchspies, and E. Potter, "Feminist Perspectives on Science," *The Stanford Encyclopedia of Philosophy*, E. Zalta, ed., 2015. Available online at http://plato.stanford.edu/entries/feminist-science/.

Crobons v Wisconsin National Life Insurance Company and Wyant, 790 F. 2d 475 (1986).

Cruzan v Director, Missouri Department of Health, 497 US 261 (1990).

Culver, C. M. and B. Gert, *Philosophy in Medicine*. New York: Oxford University Press, 1982.

Curlender v Bio-Science Laboratories, 165 Cal. Rptr. at 477 (1980).

Curnutt, J., *Animals and the Law: A Sourcebook*. Santa Barbara: ABC-CLIO, 2001.

Dadlez, E. M. and W. L. Andrews, "Federally Funded Elective Abortion: They Can Run, but They Can't Hyde," *International Journal of Applied Philosophy* 2, 2010: 168–84.

Daniels, N., "Health-Care Needs and Distributive Justice," *Philosophy and Public Affairs* 10.2, 1981: 146–79.

Darwall, S. L., *Philosophical Ethics*. Boulder: Westview, 1997.

Davis, A., "Right to Life of the Handicapped," *Journal of Medical Ethics* 9, 1983: 181.

———, "Permanently Disabled People May Have Curable Depression," *British Medical Journal* 309, 6946, 1994: 53.

———, "Commentary: A Disabled Person's Perspective on Euthanasia," *Disability Studies Quarterly* 24.4, 2004.

Davis, D. S., "Genetic Dilemmas and the Child's Right to an Open Future," *Hastings Center Report* 27.2, 1997: 7–15.

Day, M., "Italy Faces Constitutional Crisis over Coma Woman," *The Guardian*, 2/7/2009.

DeGrazia, D., *Animal Rights: A Very Short Introduction*. Oxford: Oxford University Press, 2002.

———, "Human-Animal Chimeras: Human Dignity, Moral Status, and Species Prejudice," in Gruen, Grabel, and Singer 2007, pp. 168–87.

———, *Creation Ethics: Reproduction, Genetics, and Quality of Life*. Oxford: Oxford University Press, 2012.

Diekema, D. and N. Fost, "Ashley Revisited: A Response to the Critics," *American Journal of Bioethics* 10.1, 2010: 30–44.

Doris, J. M., and the Moral Psychology Research Group, eds., *The Moral Psychology Handbook*. Oxford: Oxford University Press, 2010.

Dowbiggin, I., *A Concise History of Euthanasia: Life, Death, God, and Medicine*. Laham: Rowman and Littlefield, 2005.

Driver, J., *Ethics: The Fundamentals*. Malden: Blackwell, 2007.

Dworkin, G., "Physician-Assisted Death: The State of the Debate," in Steinbock 2007, pp. 375–92.

Dworkin, G., R. G. Frey, and S. Bok, eds., *Euthanasia and Physician-Assisted Suicide*. Cambridge: Cambridge University Press, 1998.

Dwyer, S. and J. Feinberg, *The Problem of Abortion*, 3rd ed. Belmont: Wadsworth, 1997.

Eaton, L., "Ethics Group Rules on Treating Premature Babies," *British Medical Journal* 333.7577, 2006: 1033.

Edwards, S. D., "The Ashley Treatment: A Step Too Far, or Not Far Enough?" *Journal of Medical Ethics* 34.5, 2008: 341–3.

Engelhardt, H. Tristram, Jr., "Rights to Health Care, Social Justice, and Fairness in Health Care Allocations: Frustrations in the Face of Finitude," in *Foundations of Bioethics*, 2nd ed. New York: Oxford University Press, 1996.

Ereshefsky, M., "Species," *The Stanford Encyclopedia of Philosophy*, E. Zalta, ed., 2010. Available online at http://plato.stanford.edu/entries/species/.

European Court of Human Rights, *European Convention on Human Rights*, Sept. 1953. Available online at http://www.echr.coe.int/Documents/Convention_ENG.pdf.

Farzaneh, Z., "The Challenge of Truth Telling across Cultures: A Case Study," *Journal of Medical Ethics and History of Medicine* 3, 2011: 4–11.

Featherstone, K. and J. L. Donovan, "Why Don't They Just Tell Me Straight, Why Allocate It? The Struggle to Make Sense of Participating in a Randomised Controlled Trial," *Social Science and Medicine* 55, 2002: 709–19.

Feinberg, J., *Social Philosophy*. Englewood Cliffs, NJ: Prentice-Hall, 1973.

———, *Harm to Others: The Moral Limits of the Criminal Law*. Oxford: Oxford University Press, 1984.

Fisher, A., *Catholic Ethics for a New Millennium*. Cambridge: Cambridge University Press, 2012.

Florida v Pinzon-Reye, Florida Circuit Court, Highlands County, CF-96-0066ᵃ-XX (1997).

Foley, K. and H. Hendin, "The Oregon Experiment," in *The Case against Assisted Suicide: For the Right to End of Life Care*, pp. 114–74. Baltimore: Johns Hopkins University Press, 2002.

Foot, P., "Euthanasia," *Philosophy and Public Affairs* 2, 1977: 85–112.

Foster, C., *Medical Law: A Very Short Introduction*. Oxford: Oxford University Press, 2013.

Frey, R. G., "Animals and Their Medical Use," in Cohen and Wellman 2005, pp. 91–103.

Frey, R. G. and C. H. Wellman, eds., *A Companion to Applied Ethics*. Oxford: Blackwell, 2003.

Galton, F., "Eugenics: Its Definition, Scope, and Aims," *American Journal of Sociology* 10.1, 1904: 1–25.

Gallup, "Abortion," 2016. Available online at http://www.gallup.com/poll/1576/abortion.aspx.

Ganzini, L., H. D. Nelson, M. A. Lee, D. F. Kraemer, T. A. Schmidt, and M. A. Delorit, "Oregon Physicians' Attitudes about and Experience with End-of-Life Care since Passage of the Oregon Death with Dignity Act," *Journal of the American Medical Association* 285.18, 2001: 2363–9.

Gardiner, D., S. Shemie, A. Manara, and H. Opdam, "International Perspectives on the Diagnosis of Death," *British Journal of Anaesthesia* 108.1, 2012: i13-i28.

Gaylin, W., L. Kass, E. Pellegrino, and M. Siegler, "Doctors Must Not Kill," *Journal of the American Medical Association* 259.14, 1988: 2139–40.

General Medical Council, "End of Life Care Guidance." Available online at http://www.gmc-uk.org/guidance/ethical_guidance/end_of_life_care.asp.

Genetic Science Learning Center, "The History of Cloning," 12/13/2016, http://learn.genetics.utah.edu/content/cloning/clonezone/.

Genomes2People, "The REVEAL Study." Available online at http://www.genomes2people.org/reveal.

"German Doctor Cleared of Transplant Scandal Charges," *Deutsche Welle*, 6/5/2015. Available online at http://www.dw.com/en/german-doctor-cleared-of-transplant-scandal-charges/a-18430971.

Gert, B., C. M. Culver, and K. D. Clouser, *Bioethics: A Return to Fundamentals*. New York: Oxford University Press, 1997.

———, *Bioethics: A Systematic Approach*. New York: Oxford University Press, 2006.

Ghosh, P., "Gene Therapy Stabilises Lungs of Cystic Fibrosis Patient," *BBC*, 3/7/2015. Available online at http://www.bbc.com/news/science-environment-32932922.

Giacino, J. T., J. J. Fins, S. Laureys, and N. D. Schiff, "Disorders of Consciousness after Acquired Brain Injury: The State of the Science," *Nature Reviews Neurology* 10, 2014: 99–114.

Gillon, R. and D. K. Sokol, "Confidentiality," in Khuse and Singer 2012, pp. 513–19.

Glantz, H. L., "The Role of Personhood in Treatment Decisions Made by Courts," *Milbank Mem. Fund. Q. Health Soc.* 61.1, 1983: 76–100.

Glover, J., *Choosing Children: The Ethical Dilemmas of Genetic Intervention*. Oxford: Clarendon Press, 2006.

Goldstein, D. M., *Bioethics: A Guide to Information Sources*. Detroit: Gale Research Company, 1982.

Gonzalez v Carhart, Supreme Court, 550 U.S. 124 (2007).

Gorman, A., "Obamacare Now Pays for Gender Reassignment," *The Daily Beast*, 8/25/2014.

Gorman, J., "The Humanity of Nonhumans," *The New York Times*, 12/10/2013a. Available online at http://www.nytimes.com/2013/12/10/science/considering-the-humanity-of-nonhumans.html?_r=0.

———, "Rights Group Is Seeking Status of 'Legal Person' for Captive Chimpanzee," *The New York Times*, 12/3/2013b.

Gould, S. J., "Nonmoral Nature," *The Unofficial Stephen Jay Gould Archive*, 1982. Available online at http://www.stephenjaygould.org/library/gould_nonmoral.html.

Grady, D., "Signs May Be Evident in Hindsight, but Predicting Violent Behavior Is Tough," *The New York Times*, 9/19/2013.

Greenberg, G., "As Good As Dead," *The New Yorker*, 8/13/2001.

Greenblatt, A., "Fewer Babies Available for Adoption by US Parents," *NPR*, 11/17/2011. Available online at http://www.npr.org/2011/11/17/142344354/fewer-babies-available-for-adoption-by-u-s-parents.

Greif, K. F. and Jon F. Merz, *Current Controversies in the Biological Sciences: Case Studies of Policy Challenges from New Technologies*. Cambridge: MIT Press, 2007.

Gross, M. L., "Avoiding Anomalous Newborns: Preemptive Abortion, Treatment Thresholds and the Case of Baby Messenger," *Journal of Medical Ethics* 26.4, 2000: 242–8.

Gruen, L., "Oocytes for Sale?" *Metaphilosophy* 38, 2–3, 2007: 285–308.

Gruen, L., L. Grabel, and P. Singer, *Stem Cell Research: The Ethical Issues*. Oxford: Blackwell, 2007.

Guttmacher Institute, "Abortion," 2014. Available online at http://www.guttmacher.org/sections/abortion.php.

———, "Induced Abortion in the United States," 2016. Available online at http://www.guttmacher.org/pubs/fb_induced_abortion.html.

Haas, J. M., "Begotten Not Made: A Catholic View of Reproductive Technology," *United States Conference of Catholic Bishops*, 1998. Available online at http://www.usccb.org/issues-and-action/human-life-and-dignity/reproductive-technology/begotten-not-made-a-catholic-view-of-reproductive-technology.cfm.

Hanson, S. S., "Casuistry in a Pluralistic Society," *Philosophy and Medicine* 103, 2009: 101–22.

Hare, R. M., "Abortion and the Golden Rule," in *Essays on Bioethics*, pp. 147–67. Oxford: Clarendon Press, 1993.

Harvard School of Public Health. "The Debate over AZT Clinical Trials," Available online at http://www. hks.harvard.edu/case/azt/ethics/case_2–0.html.

Harris, J., *The Value of Life: An Introduction to Medical Ethics*, New York: Routledge, 1985.

———, "QALYfying the Value of Life," *Journal of Medical Ethics* 13.3, 1987: 117–23.

Hartenstein, M., " 'World's Oldest Mother' Is Dying just 18 Months after Giving Birth at Age 70," *New York Daily News*, 6/14/2010.

Hartocollis, A., "Hard Choice for a Comfortable Death: Sedation," *The New York Times*, 12/26/2009.

Hartocollis, A. and S. Chan, "Albany Judge Blocks Vaccination Rule," *The New York Times*, 10/17/2009.

The Hastings Center, 2010. "Animals Used in Research in the US," Available online at http://animal research.thehastingscenter.org/facts-sheets/animals-used-in-research-in-the-united-states.

Have, H. T., "End-of-Life Decision Making in the Netherlands," in Blank and Merrick 2005, pp. 147–68.

Health and Disability Commissioner, "Report on Opinion, Case 97HDC8872," 6/28/1999. Available online at http://www.hdc.org.nz/media/2402/97HDC8872.pdf.

Held, V., *The Ethics of Care: Personal, Political, Global*, New York: Oxford University Press, 2005.

Hellman, S. and D. S. Hellman, "Of Mice but Not Men: Problems of the Randomized Clinical Trial," *New England Journal of Medicine* 324.22, 1991: 1585–9.

Henshaw, S. and K. Kost, "Trends in the Characteristics of Women Obtaining Abortions, 1974–2004," Guttmacher Institute, 2008. Available online at https://www.guttmacher.org/pubs/2008/09/23/Trends WomenAbortions-wTables.pdf.

Higgs, R., "Truth Telling," in Rhodes et al., 2007, pp. 88–103.

Hope, T., "Rationing and Life-saving Treatments: Should Identifiable Patients Have Higher Priorities?" *Journal of Medical Ethics* 27.3, 2001: 179–85.

House of Lords, *Report of the Select Committee on Medical Ethics*, HL Deb, vol. 554, cc1344–412. Available online at http://hansard.millbanksystems.com/lords/1994/may/09/medical-ethics-select-commit tee-report#column_1346.

———, *Report of the Select Committee on the Assisted Dying for the Terminally Ill Bill*, 2004. Available online at http://www.publications.parliament.uk/pa/ld200405/ldselect/ldasdy/86/8602.htm.

In re A. C. [Angela Carder], 573 A.2d 1235 D.C. App. (1990).

In re Helga Wanglie, Fourth Judicial District (Dist. Ct. Probate Ct. Div.), PX-91–283, Hennepin, Minnesota (1991).

In re Quinlan, 355 A.2d 647 NJ (1976).

In re Requena, 213 NJ Super. 475 517 A 2d 886 (1986).

In the Matter of Baby M, New Jersey Supreme Court, 109 NJ 396, 537 A. 2d 1227 (1988).

Institute of Alcohol Studies, "Socioeconomic groups' relationship with alcohol," 2013. Available online at http://www.ias.org.uk/Alcohol-knowledge-centre/Socioeconomic-groups/Factsheets/Socioeconom ic-groups-relationship-with-alcohol.aspx.

Institute of Medicine, *Non-Heart-Beating Organ Transplantation*. Washington: National Academy Press, 2000. Available online at http://www.nap.edu/openbook.php?record_id=9700&page=114.

"Is the Affordable Care Act Working? – Special Report," *The New York Times*, 10/26/2014.

Jacobson v Massachusetts, 197 U.S. 11, 25 S. Ct. 358, 49 L. Ed. 463 (1905).

Jonas, H., "Philosophical Reflections on Experimenting with Human Subjects," *Daedalus* 98.2, 1969: 219–47.

Jones, R. K., and J. Jerman, "Abortion Incidence and Service Availability in the United States, 2011," Guttmacher Institute, March 2014. Available online at http://www.guttmacher.org/pubs/journals/ psrh.46e0414.pdf.

Jonsen, Albert R., *A Short History of Medical Ethics*. New York: Oxford University Press, 2000.

Jonsen, A. and S. Toulmin, *The Abuse of Casuistry*. Berkeley: University of California Press, 1988.

Kaczor, C., *The Ethics of Abortion: Women's Rights, Human Life, and the Question of Justice*. New York: Rout ledge, 2011.

Kamm, F. M., "Is There a Problem with Enhancement?" *The American Journal of Bioethics* 5.3, 2005: 5–14.

Kant, I., *Groundwork of the Metaphysic of Morals*. H. J. Paton, trans. London: Hutchinson University Library, 1948 [1785].

Kass, L., "I Will Give No Deadly Drug: Why Doctors Must Not Kill," in Foley and Hendin 2002, pp. 17–40.

Katz, J., "Informed Consent—Must It Remain a Fairy Tale?" *Journal of Contemporary Health Law and Policy* 10, 1967: 69–91.

———, *The Silent World of Doctor and Patient*. Baltimore: Johns Hopkins University, 2002.

Kazez, J., "We Should Prohibit the Use of Chimpanzees and Other Great Apes in Biomedical Research," in Caplan and Arp 2014, pp. 271–80.

Keown, J., *Euthanasia, Ethics, and Public Policy: An Argument against Legalisation*. Cambridge: Cambridge University Press, 2002.

Kipnis, K., "Medical Confidentiality," in Rhodes et al. 2007, pp. 104–12.

Kittay, E. and J. Kittay, "Whose Convenience? Whose Truth? A Comment on Peter Singer's 'A Convenient Truth,'" *Bioethics Forum*, 2/28/2007. Available online at http://www.thehastingscenter.org/Bioethics-forum/Post.aspx?id=350.

Kluge, E.-H. W., "Severely Disabled Newborns," in Kuhse and Singer 2012, pp. 274–85.

Koch, W., "USA Faces Critical Adoption Shortage," *USA Today*, 1/10/2013.

Kolata, G., "Parents of Tiny Infants Find Care Choices Are Not Theirs," *The New York Times*, 9/30/1991.

———, "Baby's Painful 2 Years of Life Highlight the High Cost of Futile Medical Care," *The New York Times*, 10/6/1993.

———, "When Morphine Fails to Kill," *The New York Times*, 7/23/1997.

———, "Knotty Challenges in Health Care Costs," *The New York Times*, 3/6/2012.

Kon, A. A., "We Cannot Accurately Predict the Extent of an Infant's Future Suffering: The Groningen Protocol is Too Dangerous," *The American Journal of Bioethics* 8.11, 2008: 23–6.

Kuhse, H. and P. Singer, eds., *Blackwell Companion to Bioethics*, 1st ed. Oxford: Blackwell, 1998.

———, *A Companion to Bioethics*, 2nd ed. Oxford: Blackwell, 2012.

de Las Casas, B., *The Only Way*. Mahwah: Paulist Press, 1992.

Langton, C., "Lawsuit Brewing against Wayne State over 'Painful' Heart Experiments on Dogs," *CBS Detroit*, 11/14/2013. Available online at http://detroit.cbslocal.com/2013/11/14/lawsuit-brewing-against-wayne-state-over-painful-heart-experiments-on-dogs/.

Lee, P. and R. P. George, "The Wrong of Abortion," in Cohen and Wellman 2005, pp. 13–26.

Lehmkuhl, V., "Video Killed the Baboon Lab," *My City Paper*, 9/7/2000.

Lerner, B. A., "When Lobotomy Was Seen as Advanced," *The New York Times*, 12/19/2011.

Letellier, P., "History and Definition of a Word," in *Euthanasia: Ethical and Human Aspects*, vol. 1, pp. 13–26, Council of Europe Publishing, eds., Strasburg: Manhattan Pub., 2003.

Liao, S., J. Savulescu, and M. Sheehan, "The Ashley Treatment: Best Interests, Convenience, and Parental Decision-Making," *Hastings Center Report* 37.2, 2007: 16–20.

Lidz, C. W. et al., "Barriers to Informed Consent," *Annals of Internal Medicine* 99.4, 1983: 539–43.

Lim, J. K. and E. B. Keeffe, "Liver Transplantation for Alcoholic Liver Disease: Current Concepts and Length of Sobriety," *Liver Transplantation* 1.2, 2004: S31–S38.

Lipkin, M., "On Telling Patients the Truth," *Newsweek*, 6/4/1979. Available online at https://philosophy.tamucc.edu/readings/ethics/lipkin-truth-telling?destination=node%2F600.

Little, M. O., "Care: From Theory to Orientation and Back," *Journal of Medicine and Philosophy* 23.2, 1998: 90–209.

———, "The Morality of Abortion," in Frey and Wellman 2003, pp. 319–24.

Locke, J., *Two Treatises of Government*, P. Laslett, ed. Cambridge: Cambridge University Press, 1988 [1689].

Lynn, J., ed., *By No Extraordinary Means: The Choice to Forego Life-Sustaining Food and Water*. Bloomington: Indiana University Press, 1986.

McLaren, A., *A History of Contraception from Antiquity to the Present*. Oxford: Blackwell, 1990.

Maclean, A., *Autonomy, Informed Consent and Medical Law: A Relational Challenge*. Cambridge: Cambridge University Press, 2009.

McMahan, J., *The Ethics of Killing: Problems at the Margins of Life*. Oxford: Oxford University Press, 2002.

———, "Killing Embryos for Stem Cell Research," *Metaphilosophy* 38.2/3, 2007: 170–89.

———, "Death, Brain Death, and Persistent Vegetative State," in Kuhse and Singer 2012, pp. 286–87.

McNeil, D., Jr., "CIA Vaccine Ruse May Have Harmed the War on Polio," *The New York Times*, 7/9/2012.

Mahowald, M. B., *Genes, Women, Equality*. New York: Oxford University Press, 2000.

Malek, M., "Implementing QALYs," *Hayword Medical Communications*, 2001. Available online at http://www.medicine.ox.ac.uk/bandolier/painres/download/whatis/ImplementQALYs.pdf.

Manning, R. C., "The Care Approach," in Khuse and Singer 2012, pp. 105–16.

Marquis, D., "Why Abortion Is Immoral," *Journal of Philosophy* 86.4, 1989: 183–202.

———, "Abortion Revisited," in Steinbock 2007, pp. 395–415.

Matter of Conroy, 98 NJ 321 486 A 2d 1209 (1985).

Matter of Storar and *Matter of Eichner*, 52 NY 2d 363 (1981).

"Max's Story," Polst. Available online at http://www.polst.org/advance-care-planning/polst-experiences/.

May, W. E., "Begetting vs. Making Babies," in *Human Dignity and Reproductive Technology*, pp. 81–92. Lanham, Maryland: University Press of America, 2003.

Mehra, A., "Politics of Participation: Walter Reed's Yellow Fever Experiments," *AMA Journal of Ethics* 11.4, 2009: 326–30.

Mental Capacity Act, Chapter 9, pp. 1–88, *The National Archives*. Available online at http://www.legislation.gov.uk/ukpga/2005/9/pdfs/ukpga_20050009_en.pdf.

Merrick, J. C., "Death and Dying: The American Experience," in Blank and Merrick 2005, pp. 219–42.

Merritt, M. W., J. M. Doris, and G. Harman, "Character," in Doris et al. 2010, pp. 355–401.

Mill, J. S., *On Liberty*. Indianapolis: Bobbs–Merrill, 1956 [1859].

——, *Utilitarianism*, R. Crisp, ed. Oxford: Oxford University Press, 1998 [1861].

Miller, F. D. and R. D. Truog, "Decapitation and the Definition of Death," *Journal of Medical Ethics* 36, 2010: 632–4.

——, *Death, Dying, and Organ Transplantation: Reconstructing Medical Ethics at the End of Life*. Oxford: Oxford University Press, 2011.

Mishra, V., V. Gaigbe-Togbe and J. Ferre, "Abortion Policies and Reproductive Health Around the World," UN Department of Economic and Social Affairs Population Division, 2014. Available online at http://www.un.org/en/development/desa/population/publications/pdf/policy/AbortionPoliciesReproductiveHealth.pdf.

More, T., *Utopia*, D. Baker trans., ed., London: Penguin Books, 2012.

Ms B v NHS Hospital Trust EWHC 429 Fam (2002).

Muellers, B., "New York's Abortion Protest Law Is Praised by Justices, but Few Others," *The New York Times*, 7/30/2014.

Murray, Thomas, "Even if It Worked, Cloning Wouldn't Bring Her Back," *Washington Post*, 4/8/2001.

Muskal, Michael, "Mississippi Man, Kicking in Body Bag, Back from the Dead. Sort Of," *Los Angeles Times*, 2/28/2014.

Nagel, T., "Death," in *Mortal Questions*, pp. 1–10. Cambridge: Cambridge University Press, 1979.

Nancy B v Hôtel-Dieu de Québec et al., 86 DLR 4th 385 (1992).

Natanson v Kline, 186 Kan. 393 350 P.2d 1093 (1960).

Nicklinson v Ministry of Justice, UKSC 38 (2014).

NIH National Human Genome Research Institute, "Cloning," 2015. Available online at https://www.genome.gov/25020028#al-6.

Nisbett, R. E., *The Geography of Thought: How Asians and Westerners Think Differently ... and Why*. New York: The Free Press, 2003.

Noonan, J. T., Jr., "An Almost Absolute Value in History," in *The Morality of Abortion: Legal and Historical Perspectives*, pp. 51–9. Cambridge: Harvard University Press, 1970.

Nozick, R., *Anarchy, State, and Utopia*. New York: Basic Books, 1974.

Nuffield Council on Bioethics, *Critical Care Decisions in Fetal and Neonatal Medicine: Ethical Issues*, 2006. Available at http://nuffieldbioethics.org/wp-content/uploads/2014/07/CCD-web-version-22-June-07-updated.pdf.

Ofri, D., "Doctors Have Feelings, Too," *The New York Times*, 3/28/2012.

Okie, S., "Physician-Assisted Suicide—Oregon and Beyond," *New England Journal of Medicine* 352, 2005: 1627–30.

"Organ Donation Law – Should Dying Babies be Organ Donors?" *Bloomberg Law*, 2007. Available online at http://law.jrank.org/pages/8948/Organ-Donation-Law-Should-Dying-Babies-Be-Organ-Donors.html.

Orlans, F. B., *In the Name of Science: Issues in Responsible Animal Experimentation*. New York: Oxford University Press, 1993.

Ouellette, A., "Putting Law in the Room," *American Journal of Bioethics* 10.1, 2010: 48–50.

Pallis, C., "Whole-brain Death Reconsidered—Physiological Facts and Philosophy," *Journal of Medical Ethics* 9, 1983: 32–7.

Parfit, D., *Reasons and Persons*. Oxford: Clarendon Press, 1987.

Parks, J., "On the Use of IVF by Post-Menopausal Women," *Hypatia* 14.1, 1999: 77–96.

Pazol, K., A. A. Creanga, K. D. Burley, B. Hayes, and D. J. Jamieson, "Abortion Surveillance, United States, 2010." Division of Reproductive Health, National Center for Chronic Disease Prevention and Health Promotion, CDC: *Surveillance Summaries* 62.8, 2013: 1–44. Available online at http://www.cdc.gov/mmwr/preview/mmwrhtml/ss6208a1.htm.

Peikoff, K., "Fearing Punishment for Bad Genes," *The New York Times*, 4/7/2014.

Pellegrino, E. D., "Is Truth Telling to the Patient a Cultural Artifact?" in *JAMA* 268.13, 1992a: 1734–35.

———, "Doctors Must Not Kill," in *Euthanasia: The Good of the Patient*, pp. 27–41. Frederick: University Publishing Group, 1992b.

Pence, G., *Who's Afraid of Human Cloning*. Lanham: Rowman & Littlefield, 1998.

———, *Medical Ethics: Accounts of Ground-Breaking Cases*. New York: McGraw-Hill, 2008.

———, *How to Build a Better Human*. Lanham, MD: Rowman & Littlefield, 2012.

Pentheny O'Kelly, C. de, C. Urch, and E. A. Brown, "The Impact of Culture and Religion on Truth Telling at the End of Life," *Nephrol Dial Transplant* 26, 2011: 3838–42.

Pinker, S., "The Designer Baby Myth," *The Guardian*, 6/4/2003. http://www.theguardian.com/education/2003/jun/05/research.highereducation.

———, "My Genome, My Self," *The New York Times* 1/7/2009. Available online at http://www.nytimes.com/2009/01/11/magazine/11Genome-t.html.

"Polish Rape Victim 'Should have had Abortion Access,'" *BBC*, 10/30/2012.

Pope John Paul II, "The Unspeakable Crime of Abortion," *Evangelium Vitae*, 3/25/1995.

Pope Pius XII, "Address to the Italian Society of Anaesthesiology," 24 February, 1957.

Post, S. G., ed., *Encyclopedia of Bioethics*, 3rd ed. New York: Macmillan, 2004.

President's Commission for the Study of Ethical Problems in Medicine and Biomedical and Behavioral Research, *Deciding to Forego Life-Sustaining Treatment: A Report on the Ethical, Medical, and Legal Issues in Treatment Decisions*, 1983. Available online at http://bioethics.georgetown.edu/pcbe/reports/past_commissions/deciding_to_forego_tx.pdf.

President's Council on Bioethics, *Controversies in the Determination of Death: A White Paper*. Washington DC, 2008. Available online at https://bioethicsarchive.georgetown.edu/pcbe/reports/death/.

Pretty v The United Kingdom, No. 2346/02 ECHR (2002-III).

Purdy, L. M., "Assisted Reproduction, Prenatal Testing, and Sex Selection," in Kuhse and Singer 2012, pp. 178–92.

The Queen on the Application of Mrs Diane Pretty (Appellant) v Director of Public Prosecutions (Respondent) and Secretary of State for the Home Department (Interested Party), UKHL 61 (2001).

R v Cambridge District Health Authority, ex p B (1995).

R v Cox, Crown Court at Winchester, UK 12 BMLR 38 (1992).

R v Latimer, 1 SCR 217 Canada (1997).

R v Latimer, 1 SCR 3 Canada (2001).

R (on the application of Purdy) v Director of Public Prosecutions, UKHL 45 (2009).

Rachels, J., *The End of Life: Euthanasia and Morality*. Oxford: Oxford University Press, 1986.

———, *The Elements of Moral Philosophy*, 2nd ed. New York: McGraw-Hill, 1993.

Rawls, J., *A Theory of Justice*. Cambridge: Harvard University Press, 1971/1999.

Raymond, J., "Reproductive Technologies, Radical Feminism, and Socialist Liberalism," *Journal of Reproductive and Genetic Engineering* 2.2, 1989: 133–42.

Regan, T., *The Case for Animal Rights*. Berkeley and Los Angeles: University of California Press, 1983.

———, "Empty Cages: Animals Rights and Vivisection," in Cohen and Wellman 2005, pp. 77–90.

Reich, W. T., ed., *Encyclopedia of Bioethics*, revised ed. New York: Simon & Schuster, 1995.

Rescher, N., "The Allocation of Exotic Medical Lifesaving Therapy," *Ethics* 79.3, 1969: 173–86.

Rex, A., "Protecting the One Percent: Relevant Women, Undue Burdens, and Unworkable Judicial Bypasses," *Columbia Law Review* 114.1, 2014: 85–128.

Rhodes, R., "Genetic Links, Family Ties, and Social Bonds: Rights and Responsibilities in the Face of Genetic Knowledge," *Journal of Medicine and Philosophy* 23.1, 1998: 10–30.

Rhodes, R., L. P. Francis, and A. Silvers, eds., *Blackwell Guide to Medical Ethics*. Malden: Blackwell, 2007.

Riddle, J., "Birth, Contraception, and Abortion," *Encyclopedia of European Social History*. Detroit: Charles Scribner's Sons, 2001, pp. 181–91.

Rietjens, J. A. C. et al., "Using Drugs to End Life Without an Explicit Request of the Patient," *Death Studies* 31, 2007: 205–21.

Rietjens, J. A. C. et al., "Two Decades of Research on Euthanasia from the Netherlands: What Have We Learnt and What Questions Remain?" *Bioethical Inquiry* 6, 2009: 271–83.

Robertson, J. A., "Involuntary Euthanasia of Defective Newborns: A Legal Analysis," *Stanford Law Review* 27.2, 1975: 213–69.

———, *Children of Choice: Freedom and the New Reproductive Liberties*. Princeton: Princeton University Press, 1994.

Robinson, P., "Prenatal Screening, Sex Selection and Cloning," in Kuhse and Singer 1998, pp. 173–88.

Rodriguez v British Columbia, Attorney General, 3 SCR 519 (1993).

Romesberg, T. L., "Futile Care and the Neonate," *Medscape*, 2003. Available online at http://www.medscape.com/viewarticle/464018_4.

Roy, D. J., J. R. Williams, and F. Baylis, "Medical Ethics, History of the Americas: III. Canada," in Post 2004, pp. 1540–7.

Russell, W.M.S. and R.I. Burch, *The Principles of Humane Experimental Technique*. London: Methuen, 1959.

Saad, L., "US Still Split on Abortion: 47% Pro-Choice, 46% Pro-Life," Gallup, 5/22/2014. Available online at http://www.gallup.com/poll/170249/split-abortion-pro-choice-pro-life.aspx.

Sacred Congregation for the Doctrine of the Faith, "Declaration on Euthanasia," May 5, 1980, http://www.vatican.va/roman_curia/congregations/cfaith/documents/rc_con_cfaith_doc_19800505_euthanasia_en.html.

Sandel, M. J., *Liberalism and the Limits of Justice*, 2nd ed. Cambridge: Cambridge University Press, 1982.

——, "The Case against Perfection: What's Wrong with Designer Children, Bionic Athletes, and Genetic Engineering," *The Atlantic Monthly* 293.3, 2004: 51–62.

Sanghavi, D. M., "Wanting Babies Like Themselves, Some Parents Choose Genetic Defects," *The New York Times*, 12/5/2006.

Savulescu, J., "Procreative Beneficence: Why We Should Select the Best Children," *Bioethics* 15.5/6, 2001: 413–26.

Scalia, A., "Concurring in United States Supreme Court," *Cruzan v Director, Missouri Department of Health*, 1990, in Beauchamp and Veatch 1996, pp. 227–9.

Schabner, D., "Why It Costs More to Adopt a White Baby?" *ABC News*, 3/8/2016.

Schmitz, P. and M. O'Brien, "Observations on Nutrition and Hydration in Dying Cancer Patients," in Lynn 1986, pp. 29–38.

Schneiderman, L. J., N. S. Jecker, and A. R. Jonsen, "Medical Futility: Its Meaning and Ethical Implications," *Annals of Internal Medicine* 112.12, 1990: 949–54.

Schrad, M. L., "Does Down Syndrome Justify Abortion?" *The New York Times*, 9/4/2015.

Seay, G., "Euthanasia and Physicians' Moral Duties," *Journal of Medicine and Philosophy* 30, 2005: 1–17.

Seckler, A.B., D. E. Meier, M. Mulvihill, and B. E. C. Paris, "Substitute Judgment: How Accurate Are Proxy Decisions?" *Annals of Internal Medicine* 115.2, 1991: 92–8.

Sepper, E., "Taking Conscience Seriously," *Virginia Law Review* 98.7, 2012: 1501–75.

Sercu, M., P. Pype, T. Christiaens, M. Grypdonck, A. Derese, and M. Deveugle, "Are General Practitioners Prepared to End Life on Request in a Country Where Euthanasia is Legalized?" *Journal of Medical Ethics* 38.5, 2012: 274–80.

Shaffer-Landau, R., *The Fundamentals of Ethics*. New York: Oxford University Press, 2010.

Shamoo, A. E. and J. L. O'Sullivan, "The Ethics of Research on the Mentally Disabled," in *Health Care Ethics: Critical Issues for the 21st Century*, E. E. Morrison and B. Furlong, eds, 239–50. Sudbury: Jones & Bartlett, 2005.

Shewmon, D. A., "Anencephaly: Selected Medical Aspects," *Hastings Center Report*, 18.5, 1988: 11–19.

——, "'Brain-stem Death,' 'Brain Death,' and Death: A Critical Re-evaluation of the Purported Equivalence," *Issues in Law & Medicine* 14, 1998: 125–45.

Shortland v Northland Health Ltd., 1 NZLR 433 at 444–445 (1998).

Siegler, M., "Confidentiality in Medicine: A Decrepit Concept," *The New England Journal of Medicine* 307.24, 1982: 1518–21.

Singer, P., *Animal Liberation*. New York: Harper Collins, 1975.

——, *Practical Ethics*. Cambridge: Cambridge University Press, 1979.

——, ed., *A Companion to Ethics*, Oxford: Blackwell, 1991.

——, *Rethinking Life and Death: The Collapse of Our Traditional Ethics*. New York: St Martin's, 1994.

——, "Animal Liberation at 30," *New York Review of Books* 50.8, 2003: 23–6.

——, "A Convenient Truth," *The New York Times*, 1/26/2007.

Singer, P. and D. Wells, "In Vitro Fertilisation: The Major Issues," *Journal of Medical Ethics* 9.4, 1983: 192–5.

Sinnott-Armstrong, W., "You Can't Lose What You Ain't Never Had: A Reply to Marquis on Abortion," *Philosophical Studies* 96, 1997: 59–72.

Skorupski, J., *Routledge Companion to Ethics*. Oxford: Routledge, 2010.

Snowdon, C., J. Garcia, and D. Elbourne, "Making Sense of Randomization: Responses of Parents of Critically Ill Babies to Random Allocation of Treatment in a Clinical Trial," *Social Science and Medicine* 45, 1997: 1337–55.

Steinbock, B., *Life Before Birth: The Moral and Legal Status of Embryos and Fetuses*. New York: Oxford University Press, 1992.

——, ed. *Oxford Handbook of Bioethics*. Oxford: Oxford University Press, 2007.

Stenberg v Carhart, 530 U.S. 914 (2000).

Sumner, L. W., *Assisted Death: A Study in Ethics and Law*. Oxford: Oxford University Press, 2011.

Szawarski, P. and V. Kakar, "Classic Cases Revisited: Anthony Bland and Withdrawal of Artificial Nutrition and Hydration in the UK," *Journal of the Intensive Care Society* 13.2, 2012: 126–9.

Takala, T., "The Right to Genetic Ignorance Confirmed," *Bioethics* 13.3/4, 1999: 288–93.

Tanne, J. H., "Emergency Contraception is Under Attack by US Pharmacists," *British Medical Journal* 330, 2005: 983.

Tarasoff v Regents of the University of California, Supreme Court of California, 17 Cal3d 425, 551 P.2d 334 131 (1976).

Teather, D., "Lesbian Couple Have a Deaf Baby by Choice," *The Guardian*, 4/7/2002.

Temkin, O. and C. L. Temkin, eds., *Ancient Medicine*. Baltimore: Johns Hopkins University Press, 1967.

Terry, J., "Agendas for Lesbian Health: Countering the Ills of Homophobia," in *Revisioning Women, Health and Healing: Feminist, Cultural and Technoscience Perspectives*, A. E. Clarke and V. Olesen, pp. 324–40. New York, Routledge: 1999.

Than, N. and I. Brassington, "Agency, Duties, and the 'Ashley Treatment,'" *Journal of Medical Ethics* 35.11, 2009: 658–61.

Thomson, J. J., "A Defense of Abortion," *Philosophy & Public Affairs* 1, 1971: 47–66.

Timmons, M., *Moral Theory: An Introduction*, 2nd ed. Lanham: Rowman & Littlefield, 2013.

Tooley, M., "Abortion and Infanticide," *Philosophy & Public Affairs* 2, 1972: 37–65.

———, "Personhood," in Khuse and Singer 2012: 129–39.

Tran, M., "Assisted Suicide Campaigner Debbie Purdy Dies Aged 51," *The Guardian*, 12/29/2014.

"US Judge Rejects Pharmaceutical Companies' Attempt to Dismiss Thalidomide Cases," Hagens Berman website, 9/27/2013. Available online at https://www.hbsslaw.com/cases/thalidomide/pressrelease/thalidomide-us-judge-rejects-pharmaceutical-companies-attempt-to-dismiss-thalidomide-cases.

US National Library of Medicine, "Myelomeningocele," 11/3/2015. Available online at https://medlineplus.gov/ency/article/001558.htm.

———, "Pregnancy and Substance Abuse," 12/2/2016. Available online at https://medlineplus.gov/pregnancyandsubstanceabuse.html.

Vacco v Quill, United States Supreme Court, 117 Ct. 2293 No. 95–1858 (1997).

Vallely, P., "Better an Abortion than a Mass Grave?" *The Independent*, 6/27/2010. Avilable online at http://www.independent.co.uk/voices/commentators/paul-vallely-better-an-abortion-than-a-mass-grave-2011500.html.

Veatch, R. M., "The Place of Care in Ethical Theory," *Journal of Medicine and Philosophy* 23.2, 1998: 210–24.

Verhagen, E., "The Groningen Protocol for Newborn Euthanasia: Which Way Did the Slippery Slope Tilt?" *Journal of Medical Ethics* 39.5, 2013: 293–5.

Verkerk, M., "A Feminist Care-Ethics Approach to Genetics," in Ashcroft et al. 2005, pp. 133–48.

Warren, M. A., "On the Moral and Legal Status of Abortion," *The Monist* 57, 1973: 43–61.

———, "IVF and Women's Interests: An Analysis of Feminist Concerns," *Bioethics* 2.1, 1988: 37–57.

Washington v Glucksberg, United States Supreme Court, 117 S. Ct. 2258 No. 96–110 (1997).

Wendler, D., "The Ethics of Clinical Research," *The Stanford Encyclopedia of Philosophy*, E. Zalta, ed., 2009/2012. Available online at http://plato.stanford.edu/entries/clinical-research/.

Whitner v State, 492 S.E.2d 777 S.C. (1997).

World Health Organization, "10 Facts About Women's Health," March 2011. Available online at http://www.who.int/features/factfiles/women/en/.

———, "Born too Soon: The Global Action Report on Preterm Birth," New York, May 2012. Available online at http://www.who.int/pmnch/media/news/2012/preterm_birth_report/en/.

World Medical Association, "Declaration of Helsinki: Ethical Principles for Medical Research Involving Human Subjects," 2013 [1964]. Available online at http://www.wma.net/en/30publications/10policies/b3/.

Worthington, R., "Jury to Weigh Father's Guilt in Premature Baby's Death," *Chicago Tribune*, 1/30/1995.